Practical Projects for the Handy Man

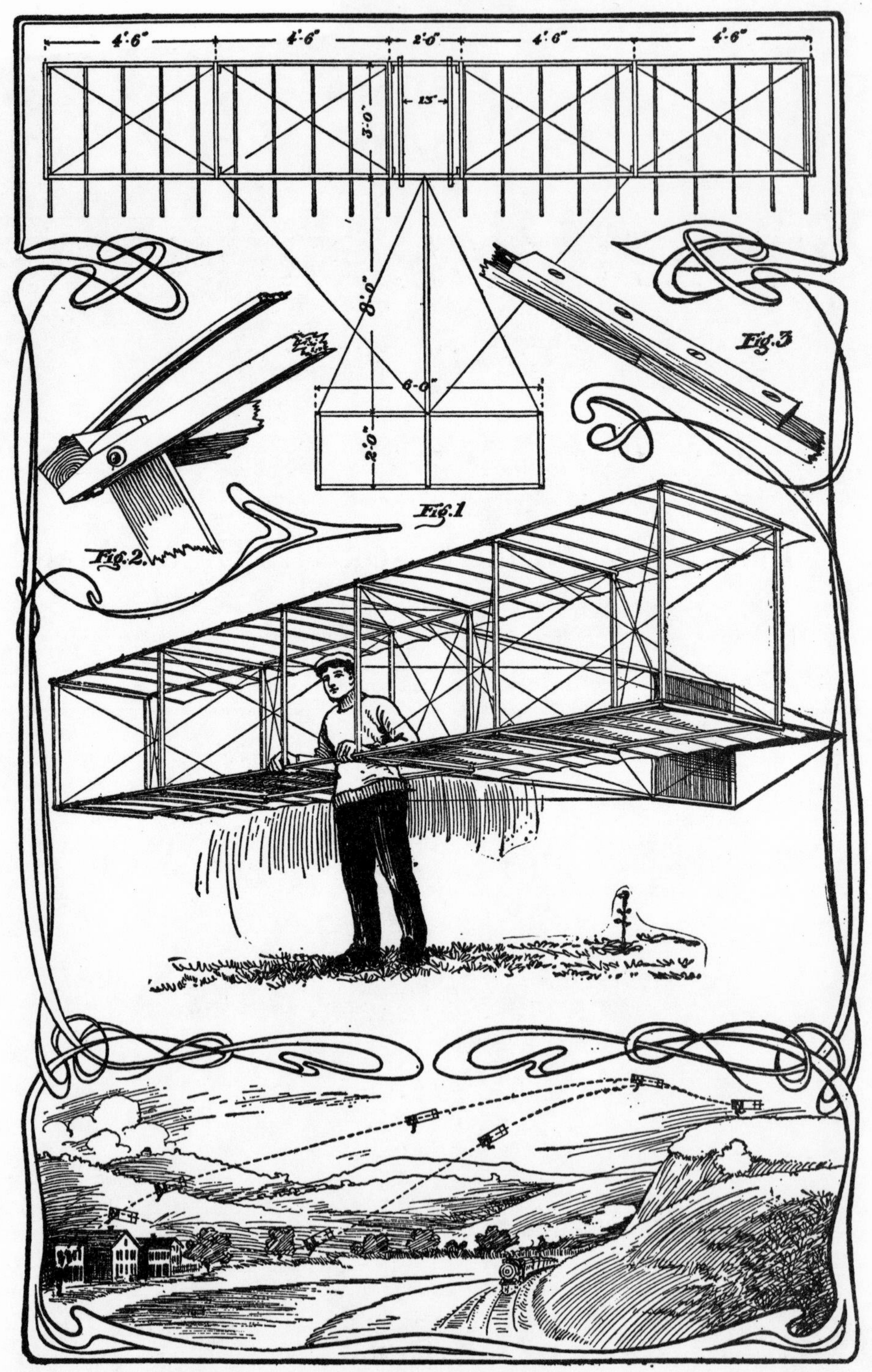

How to Make a Glider

(See page 171)

PRACTICAL PROJECTS FOR THE HANDY MAN

THE EDITORS OF
POPULAR MECHANICS

Foreword by Denis Boyles

THE LYONS PRESS

Originally published in 1913 by Popular Mechanics Press

First Lyons Press edition, April 2001

Printed in Canada

2 4 6 8 10 9 7 5 3 1

Library of Congress Catalog-in-Publication Data is available on file.

FOREWORD

If this book tells you nothing else at all, it will tell you once and for all that they don't build rainy days the way they used to.

Originally published in five volumes as *The Boy Mechanic,* this reprint of the first volume contains sufficient fodder for idle hands that alone can constitute a dream library for a lifer. In solitary.

I found this book one not-very-rainy day browsing through the library looking for information on how to build a flat-bottomed boat. The instructions are in here. Two days later, I was 200 feet offshore and up to my neck in water (I forgot to adequately seal the cracks between the boards), but I'd learned some real important things about boat-building, so the exercise wasn't a wash, even literally. For one thing, I'd learned that even a land-loving lubber such as I could build a craft pond-worthy enough to take me out to look at bass. For another, I discovered in this book how many really cool things there are for a boy mechanic like me to do—and that doing any of them well makes you feel like a man mechanic. Or at least like a handy man, hence the retitling of this book.

Some of the things in these pages are quite ambitious. The lad who learns how to efficiently construct an accelerometer or build a rotary pump or rig the improved mousetrap explained herein isn't just passing time—he's on his way to an IPO. When this book was published, it was assumed that children could understand the ins-and-outs of building a pocket voltammeter. Now we can't make assumptions like that about grown-ups. These days, we print directions on shampoo bottles—even the ones sold at MIT.

Some of the things here are exercises in pure joy. The Chinese kite, which I have built and flown, is a pearl from the Orient. And check out the little bicycle-catamaran or the two-horsepower windmill. It takes time to build it and it needs a little ongoing maintenance, but it's a lot less trouble than parking two horses out front and taking care of them, especially when you consider the wind two horses make. The instructions on how to make a sundial are extraordinarily complete. But my favorite exercise here is on page 376. I took one look at the illustration showing how to measure a tree by using the triangle measure, gave it a shot, and spent the rest of the day sleeping peacefully under a fairly tall, shady oak.

Some of the things in this book are useful always. Need to clean silver or brass, crack a nut, make a hand-vise, ice-fish, or get a button out of a kid's throat? It's all in here.

And of course some of the things in this book are a bit on the dangerous side. This book tells you how to make a scimitar sharp enough to peel the potato on a volunteer's head and a spontoon—a lance with a six-foot-long handle. Nothing in here about lawn darts, though. Check out the trolley-coaster on page 387: the end of the ride is everything. I also do not recommend to your children the dual-winged hang-glider experiment, where you make the wings, slide your arms under them, then jump off a cliff above a racing locomotive, soar over the pretty river and into the nicely drawn town. You might hit a pedestrian.

My practical advice is to buy this book because it is the 21st century, because none of us are handy—even though we all want to be—and because everything in here is just as much fun to read about as it is to build. In fact, just owning this book is a smart way to gain instant confidence. If you also want instant experience, go for the flat-bottomed boat. But wait for warm weather and a smooth sea.

Denis Boyles
Everett, Pennsylvania, 2001

Practical Projects for the Handy Man

A Model Steam Engine

The accompanying sketch illustrates a two-cylinder single-acting, poppet-valve steam engine of home construction.

The entire engine, excepting the flywheel, shaft, valve cams, pistons and bracing rods connecting the upper and lower plates of the frame proper, is of brass, the other parts named being of cast iron and bar steel.

The cylinders, G, are of seamless brass tubing, 1½ in. outside diameter; the pistons, H, are ordinary 1-in. pipe caps turned to a plug fit, and ground into the cylinders with oil and emery. This operation also finishes the inside of the cylinders.

The upright rods binding the top and bottom plates are of steel rod about ⅛-in. in diameter, threaded into the top plate and passing through holes in the bottom plate with hexagonal brass nuts beneath.

The valves, C, and their seats, B, bored with a countersink bit, are plainly shown. The valves were made by threading a copper washer, ⅜ in. in diameter, and screwing it on the end of the valve rod, then wiping on roughly a tapered mass of solder and grinding it into the seats B with emery and oil.

The valve rods operate in guides, D, made of ¼-in. brass tubing, which passes through the top plate and into the heavy brass bar containing the valve seats and steam passages at the top, into which they are plug-fitted and soldered.

The location and arrangement of the valve seats and steam passages are shown in the sketch, the flat bar containing them being soldered to the top plate.

The steam chest, A, over the valve mechanism is constructed of 1-in.

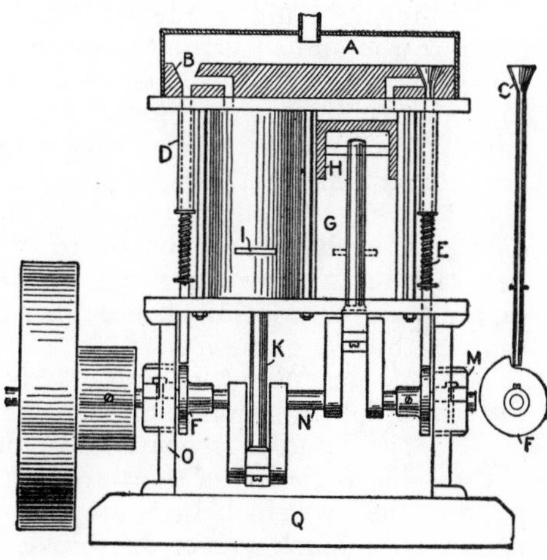

Engine Details

square brass tubing, one side being sawed out and the open ends fitted with pieces of $\frac{1}{16}$-in. sheet brass and soldered in. The steam inlet is a gasoline pipe connection such as used on automobiles.

The valve-operating cams, F, are made of the metal ends of an old typewriter platen, one being finished to shape and then firmly fastened face to face to the other, and used as a pattern in filing the other to shape. Attachment to the shaft, N, is by means of setscrews which pass through the sleeves.

The main bearings, M, on the supports, O, and the crank-end bearings of the connecting rods, K, are split and held in position by machine screws with provision for taking them up when worn.

The exhausting of spent steam is accomplished by means of slots, I, sawed into the fronts of the cylinders at about ⅛ in. above the lowest position of the piston's top at the end of the stroke, at which position of the piston the valve rod drops into the cutout portion of the cam and allows the valve to seat.

All the work on this engine, save turning the pistons, which was done in a machine shop for a small sum, and making the flywheel, this being taken from an old dismantled model, was accomplished with a hacksaw, bench drill, carborundum wheel, files, taps and dies. The base, Q, is made of a heavy piece of brass.

The action is smooth and the speed high. Steam is supplied by a sheet-brass boiler of about 3 pt. capacity, heated with a Bunsen burner.—Contributed by Harry F. Lowe, Washington, D. C.

Magic Spirit Hand

The magic hand made of wax is given to the audience for examination, also a board which is suspended by four pieces of common picture-frame wire. The hand is placed upon the board and answers, by rapping, any question asked by members of the audience. The hand and the board may be examined at any time and yet the rapping can be continued, though surrounded by the audience.

The Magic Wand, London, gives the secret of this spirit hand as follows: The hand is prepared by concealing in the wrist a few soft iron plates, the wrist being afterwards bound with black velvet as shown in Fig. 1. The board is hollow, the top being made of thin veneer (Fig. 2). A small magnet, A, is connected to a small flat pocket lamp battery, B. The board is suspended by four lengths of picture-frame wire one of which, E, is connected to the battery and another, D, to the magnet. The other wires, F and G, are only holding wires. All the wires are fastened to a small ornamental switch, H, which is fitted with a connecting plug at the top. The plug can be taken out or put in as desired.

The top of the board must be made to open or slide off so that when the battery is exhausted a new one can be installed. Everything must be firmly fixed to the board and the hollow space filled in with wax, which will make the board sound solid when tapped.

In presenting the trick, the performer gives the hand and board with wires and switch for examination, keeping the plug concealed in his right hand. When receiving the board back, the plug is secretly pushed into the switch, which is held in the right hand. The hand is then placed on the board over the magnet. When the performer wishes the hand to move he pushes the plug in, which turns on the current and causes the magnet to attract the iron in the wrist, and will, therefore, make the hand rap. The switch can be made similar to an ordinary push button so the rapping may be easily controlled without detection by the audience.

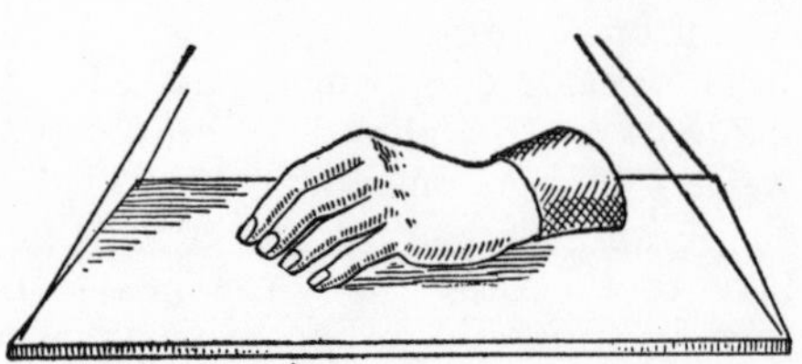

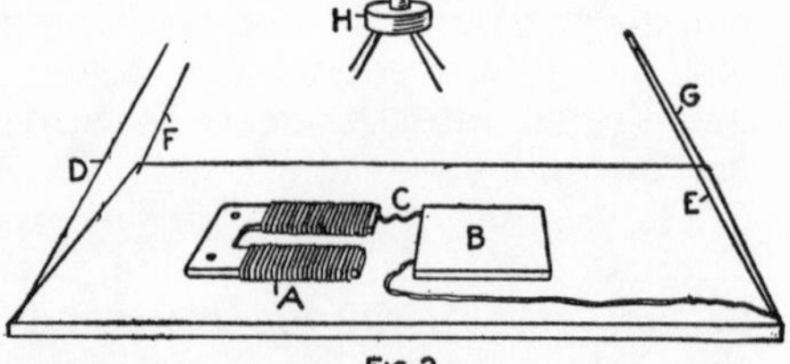

Wax Hand on Board and Electrical Connections

Making Skis and Ski-Toboggans

During the winter months everyone is thinking of skating, coasting or ski-running and jumping. Those too timid to run down a hill standing upright on skis must take their pleasure in coasting or skating.

The ordinary ski can be made into a coasting ski-toboggan by joining two pairs together with bars without injury to their use for running and jumping. The ordinary factory-made skis cost from $2.50 per pair up, but any boy can make an excellent pair for 50 cents.

In making a pair of skis, select two strips of Norway pine free from knots, 1 in. thick, 4 in. wide and 7 or 8 ft. long. Try to procure as fine and straight a grain as possible. The pieces are dressed thin at both ends leaving about 1 ft. in the center the full thickness of 1 in., and gradually thinning to a scant 1/2 in. at the ends. One end of each piece is tapered to a point beginning 12 in. from the end. A groove is cut on the under side, about 1/4 in. wide and 1/8 in. deep, and running almost the full length of the ski. This will make it track straight and tends to prevent side slipping. The shape of each piece for a ski, as it appears before bending, is shown in Fig. 1.

The pointed end of each piece is placed in boiling water for at least 1 hour, after which the pieces are ready for bending. The bend is made on an ordinary stepladder. The pointed ends are stuck under the back of one step and the other end securely tied to the ladder, as shown in Fig. 2. They should remain tied to the ladder 48 hours in a moderate temperature, after which they will hold their shape permanently.

The two straps, Fig. 3, are nailed on a little forward of the center of gravity so that when the foot is lifted, the front

Fig. 1 Fig. 2

Fig. 3—Forming the Skis

of the ski will be raised. Tack on a piece of sheepskin or deer hide where the foot rests, Fig. 4.

The best finish for skis is boiled linseed oil. After two or three applica-

Fig. 4—The Toe Straps

tions the under side will take a polish like glass from the contact with the snow.

The ski-toboggan is made by placing two pairs of skis together side by side

Fig. 5—Ski-Toboggan

and fastening them with two bars across the top. The bars are held with V-shaped metal clips as shown in Fig. 5.—Contributed by Frank Scobie, Sleepy Eye, Minn.

Homemade Life Preserver

Procure an inner tube of a bicycle tire, the closed-end kind, and fold it in four alternate sections, as shown in Fig. 1. Cut or tear a piece of cloth into strips about ½ in. wide, and knot them together. Fasten this long strip of cloth to the folded tube and weave it alternately in and out, having each

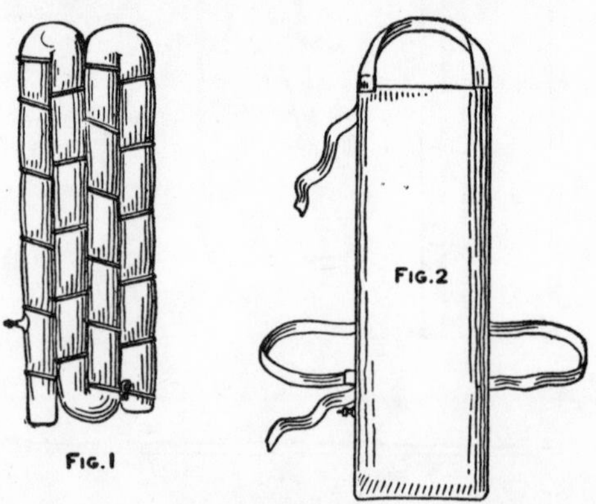

Inner Tube and Cover

run of the cloth about 4 in. apart, until it is bound as shown in Fig. 1.

Make a case of canvas that will snugly fit the folded tube when inflated. The straps that hold the preserver to the body may be made of old suspender straps. They are sewed to the case at one end and fastened at the other with clasps such as used on overall straps. The tube can be easily inflated by blowing into the valve, at the same time holding the valve stem down with the teeth. The finished preserver is shown in Fig. 2.

How to Make Boomerangs

When the ice is too thin for skating and the snow is not right for skis, about the only thing to do is to stay in the house. A boomerang club will help to fill in between and also furnishes good exercise for the muscles of the arm. A boomerang can be made

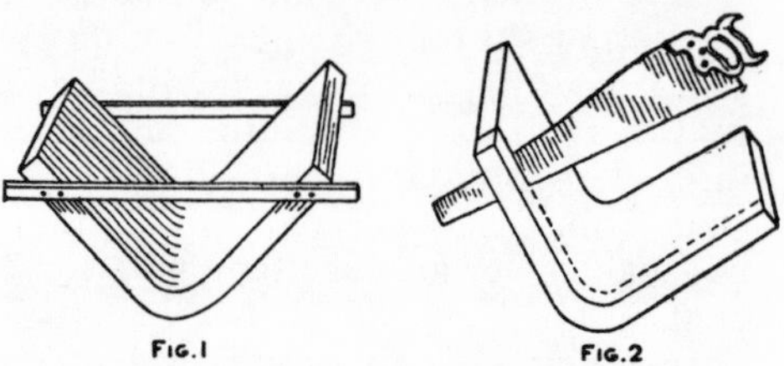

Bending and Cutting the Wood

of a piece of well seasoned hickory plank. The plank is well steamed in a wash boiler or other large kettle and then bent to a nice curve, as shown in Fig. 1. It is held in this curve until dry, with two pieces nailed on the sides as shown.

After the piece is thoroughly dried out, remove the side pieces and cut it into sections with a saw, as shown in Fig. 2. The pieces are then dressed round. A piece of plank 12 in. wide and 2 ft. long will make six boomerangs.

To throw a boomerang, grasp it and hold the same as a club, with the hollow side away from you. Practice first at some object about 25 ft. distant, and in a short time the thrower will be able to hit the mark over 100 ft. away. Any worker in wood can turn out a great number of boomerangs cheaply. —Contributed by J. E. Noble, Toronto, Ontario.

How to Make an Eskimo Snow House

By GEORGE E. WALSH

Playing in the snow can be raised to a fine art if boys and girls will build their creations with some attempt at architectural skill and not content themselves with mere rough work. Working in snow and ice opens a wide field for an expression of taste and invention, but the construction of houses and forts out of this plastic material provides the greatest amount of pleasure to the normally healthy boy or girl.

The snow house of the Eskimo is probably the unhealthiest of buildings made by any savage to live in, but it makes an excellent playhouse in winter, and represents at the same time a most ingenious employment of the arch system in building. The Eskimos build their snow houses without the aid of any scaffolding or interior falsework, and while there is a keystone at the top of the dome, it is not essential to the support of the walls. These are self-supporting from the time the first snow blocks are put down until the last course is laid.

Laying the Snow Bricks

The snow house is of the beehive shape and the ground plan is that of a circle. The circle is first laid out on the ground and a space cleared for it. Then a row of snow blocks is laid on the ground and another course of similar blocks placed on top. The snow blocks are not exactly square in shape, but about 12 in. long, 6 in. high and 4 or 5 in. thick. Larger or smaller blocks can be used, according to size of the house and thickness of the walls.

First, the snow blocks must be packed and pressed firmly into position out of moist snow that will pack. A very light, dry snow will not pack easily, and it may be necessary to use a little water. If the snow is of the right consistency, there will be no trouble in packing and working with it. As most of the blocks are to be of the same size throughout, it will pay to make a mold for them by forming a box of old boards nailed together, minus the top, and with a movable bottom, or rather no bottom at all. Place the four-sided box on a flat board and ram snow in it, forcing it down closely. Then by lifting the box up and tapping the box from above, the block will drop out. In this way blocks of uniform size are formed, which makes the building simpler and easier.

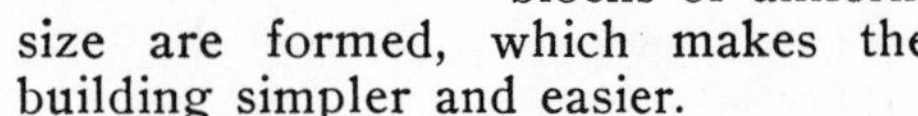

While one boy makes the blocks another can shave them off at the edges and two others can build the house, one inside of the circle and the other outside. The Eskimos build their snow houses in this way, and the man inside stays there until he is completely walled in. Then the door and a window are cut through the wall.

Each layer of snow blocks must have a slight slant at the top toward the center so that the walls will con-

Three-Room Snow House

stantly curve inward. This slant at the top is obtained better by slicing off the lower surfaces of each block before putting it in its course. The top will then have a uniform inward slant.

The first course of the snow house should be thicker than the others, and the thickness of the walls gradually decreases toward the top. A wall, however, made of 6-in. blocks throughout will hold up a snow house perfectly, if its top is no more than 6 or 7 ft. above the ground. If a higher house is needed the walls should be thicker at the base and well up toward the middle.

The builder has no mortar for binding the blocks together, and therefore he must make his joints smooth and even and force in loose snow to fill up the crevices. A little experience will enable one to do this work well, and the construction of the house will proceed rapidly. The Eskimos build additions to their houses by adding various dome-shaped structures to one side, and the young architect can imitate them. Such dome-shaped structures are shown in one of the illustrations.

A fact not well understood and appreciated is that the Eskimo beehive snow house represents true arch building. It requires no scaffolding in building and it exerts no outward thrust. In the ordinary keystone arch used by builders, a temporary structure must be erected to hold the walls up until the keystone is fitted in position, and the base must be buttressed against an outward thrust. The Eskimo does not have to consider these points. There is no outward thrust, and the top keystone is not necessary to hold the structure up. It is doubtful whether such an arch could be built of brick or stone without scaffolding, but with the snow blocks it is a simple matter.

Secret Door Lock

The sketch shows the construction of a lock I have on a door which is quite a mystery to those who do not know how it operates. It also keeps them out. The parts of the lock on the inside of the door are shown in Fig. 1. These parts can be covered so that no one can see them.

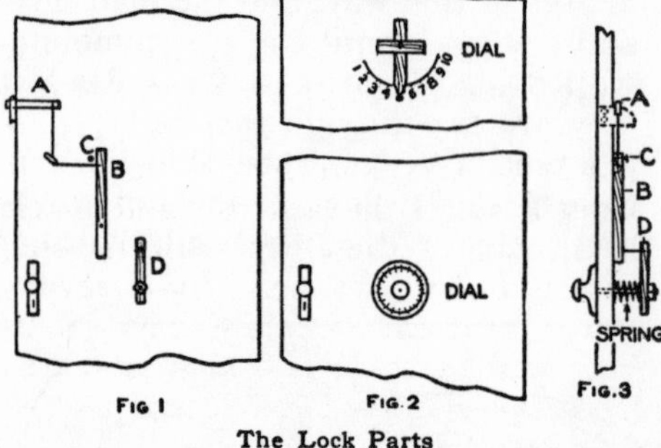

The Lock Parts

The ordinary latch and catch A are attached to the door in the usual manner. The latch is lifted with a stick of wood B, which is about 1 ft. long and 1 in. wide, and pivoted about two-thirds of the way from the top as shown. The latch A is connected to the stick B with a strong cord run through a staple to secure a right-angle pull between the pieces. A nail, C, keeps the stick B from falling over to the left. The piece of wood, D, is 6 or 8 in. long and attached to a bolt that runs through the door, the opposite end being fastened to the combination dial. Two kinds of dials are shown in Fig. 2. The piece D is fastened on the bolt an inch or two from the surface of the door to permit placing a spiral spring of medium strength in between as shown in Fig. 3. The opposite end of the bolt may be screwed into the dial, which can be made of wood, or an old safe dial will do. A nail is driven through the outer end of the piece D and the end cut off so that it will pass over the piece B when the dial is turned. When the dial is pulled out slightly and then turned toward the right, the nail will catch on the piece B and open the latch.—Contributed by Geo. Goodbrod, Union, Ore.

A Convenient Hot-Dish Holder

When taking hot dishes from the stove, it is very convenient to have holders handy for use. For this purpose I screwed two screweyes into the ceiling, one in front of the stove directly above the place where the holder should hang, and the other back of the stove and out of the way. I next ran a strong cord through the two eyes. To one end of the cord I attached a weight made of a clean lump of coal. The cord being just long enough to let the weight hang a few inches above the floor and pass through both screweyes. I fastened a small ring to the other end to keep the cord from slipping back by the pull of the weight. I then fastened two pieces of string to the ring at the end of the cord and attached an iron holder to the end of each string. The strings should be just long enough to keep the holders just over the stove where they are always ready for use, as the weight always draws them back to place.—Contributed by R. S. Merrill, Syracuse, New York.

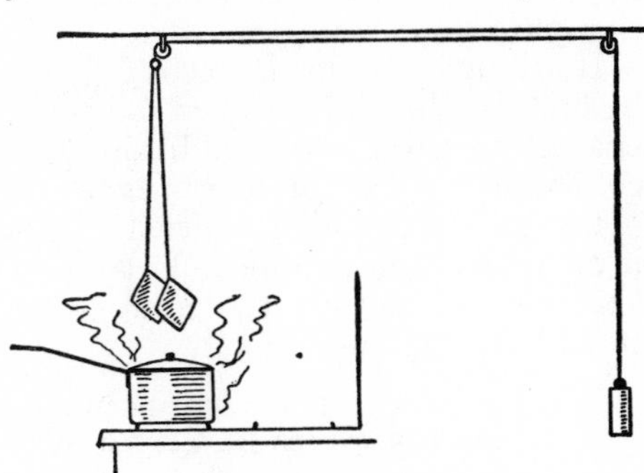

Holders in a Convenient Place

Magic-Box Escape

The things required to make this trick are a heavy packing box with cover, one pair of special hinges, one or two hasps for as many padlocks and a small buttonhook, says the Sphinx. The hinges must be the kind for attaching inside of the box. If ordinary butts are used, the cover of the box must be cut as much short as the thickness of the end board. The hinges should have pins that will slip easily through the parts.

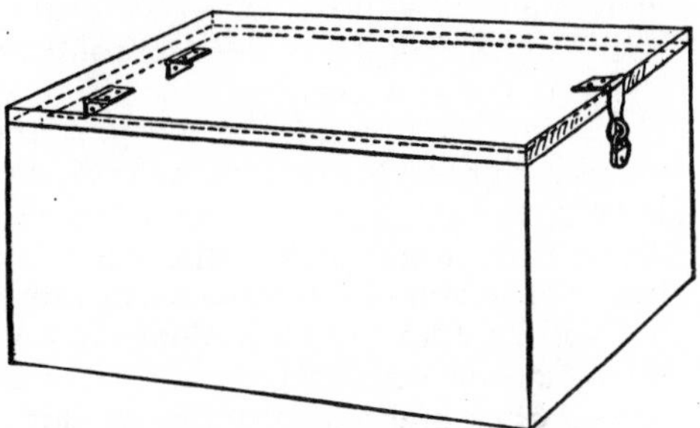

Box with Hinges and Lock

Before entering the box the performer conceals the buttonhook on his person, and as soon as the cover is closed and locked, and the box placed in a cabinet or behind a screen, he pushes the pin or bolt of the hinge out far enough to engage the knob end with the buttonhook which is used to pull the pin from the hinge. Both hinges are treated in this manner and the cover pushed up, allowing the performer to get out and unlock the padlocks with a duplicate key. The bolts are replaced in the hinges, the box relocked and the performer steps out in view.

A Flour Sifter

When sifting flour in an ordinary sieve I hasten the process and avoid the disagreeable necessity of keeping my hands in the flour by taking the top from a small tin lard can and placing it on top of the flour with its sharp edges down. When the sieve is shaken, the can top will round up the flour and press it through quickly.—Contributed by L. Alberta Norrell, Augusta, Ga.

¶An automobile horn with the bulb and reed detached makes a good funnel. It must be thoroughly cleaned and dried after using as a funnel.

How to Make Corner Pieces for a Blotter Pad

To protect the corners of blotting pads such as will be found on almost every writing desk, proceed as follows:

First, make a design of a size proportionate to the size of the pad and make a right-angled triangle, as shown in Fig. 1, on drawing paper. Leave a small margin all around the edge and then place some decorative form therein. Make allowance for flaps on two sides, as shown, which may later be turned back and folded under when the metal is worked. It should be noted that the corners of the design are to be clipped slightly. Also note the slight overrun at the top with the resulting V-shaped indentation.

To make a design similar to the one shown, draw one-half of it, then fold along the center line and rub the back of the paper with a knife handle or some other hard, smooth surface, and the other half of the design will be traced on the second side. With the metal shears, cut out four pieces of copper or brass of No. 22 gauge and with carbon paper trace the shape and decorative design on the metal. Then cut out the outline and file the edges smooth.

Cover the metal over with two coats of black asphaltum varnish, allowing each coat time to dry. Cover the back and all the face except the white background. Immerse in a solution of 3 parts water, 1 part nitric acid and 1 part sulphuric acid. When the metal has been etched to the desired depth, about 1-32 of an inch, remove it and clean off the asphaltum with turpentine. Use a stick with a rag tied on the end for this purpose so as to keep the solution off the hands and clothes. The four pieces should be worked at the same time, one for each corner.

It remains to bend the flaps. Place the piece in a vise, as shown in Fig. 2, and bend the flap sharply to a right angle. Next place a piece of metal of a thickness equal to that of the blotter pad at the bend and with the mallet bring the flap down parallel to the face of the corner piece, Fig. 3. If the measuring has been done properly, the flaps ought to meet snugly at the corner. If they do not, it may be necessary to bend them back and either remove some metal with the shears or to work the metal over farther. All the edges should be left smooth, a metal file and emery paper being used for this purpose.

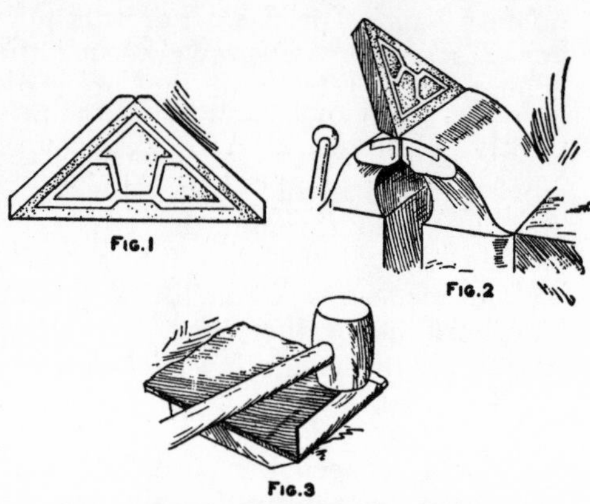

Manner of Forming the Plates

If a touch of color is desired, it may be had by filling the etched parts with enamel tinted by the addition of oil colors, such as are used for enameling b thtubs. After this has dried, smooth it off with pumice stone and water. To keep the metal from tarnishing, cover it with banana-oil lacquer.

Boring Holes in Cork

The following hints will be found useful when boring holes in cork. In boring through rubber corks, a little household ammonia applied to the bit enables one to make a much smoother hole and one that is nearly the same size at both openings. The common cork, if rolled under the shoe sole, can be punctured easily and a hole can be bored straighter. The boring is made easier by boiling the cork, and this operation insures a hole that will be the desired size and remain the size of the punch or bit used.

Self-Lighting Arc Searchlight

A practical and easily constructed self-lighting arc searchlight can be made in the following manner: Procure a large can, about 6 in. in diameter, and cut three holes in its side about 2 in. from the back end, and in the positions shown in the sketch. Two of the holes are cut large enough to hold a short section of a garden hose tightly, as shown at AA. A piece of porcelain tube, B, used for insulation, is fitted tightly in the third hole. The hose insulation A should hold the carbon F rigidly, while the carbon E should rest loosely in its insulation.

The inner end of the carbon E is supported by a piece of No. 25 German-silver wire, C, which is about 6 in. long. This wire runs through the

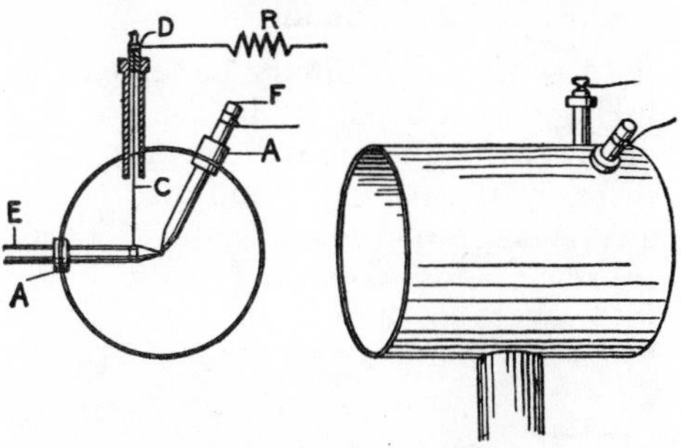

Arc in a Large Tin Can

porcelain tube to the binding post D. The binding post is fastened to a wood plug in the end of the tube. The tube B is adjusted so that the end of the carbon E is pressing against the carbon F. The electric wires are connected to the carbon F and the binding post D. A resistance, R, should be in the line.

The current, in passing through the lamp, heats the strip of German-silver wire, causing it to expand. This expansion lowers the end of the carbon E, separating the points of the two carbons and thus providing a space between them for the formation of an arc. When the current is turned off, the German-silver wire contracts and draws the two carbon ends together ready for lighting again. The feed can be adjusted by sliding the carbon F through its insulation.

A resistance for the arc may be made by running the current through a water rheostat or through 15 ft. of No. 25 gauge German-silver wire.—Contributed by R. H. Galbreath, Denver, Colo.

A Traveler's Shaving Mug

Take an ordinary collapsible drinking cup and place a cake of shaving soap in the bottom ring. This will provide a shaving mug always ready for the traveler and one that will occupy very little space in the grip.

Homemade Snowshoes

Secure four light barrel staves and sandpaper the outside smooth. Take two old shoes that are extra large and cut off the tops and heels so as to leave only the toe covering fastened to the sole. Purchase two long book straps, cut them in two in the middle and fasten the ends on the toe covering, as shown in Fig. 1. The straps are used to attach the snowshoe to the regular shoe. When buckling up the straps be sure to leave them loose enough for the foot to work freely, Fig. 2. Fasten the barrel staves in pairs, leaving a space of 4 in. between them as shown in Fig. 3, with thin strips of wood. Nail the old

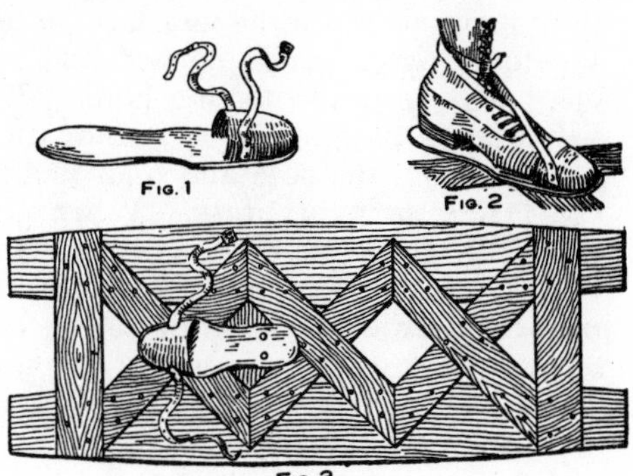

Made from Barrel Staves

shoe soles to crosspieces placed one-third of the way from one end as shown.—Contributed by David Brown, Kansas City, Mo.

Fish Signal for Fishing through Ice

Watching a fishline set in a hole cut in the ice on a cold day is very disagreeable, and the usual method is to

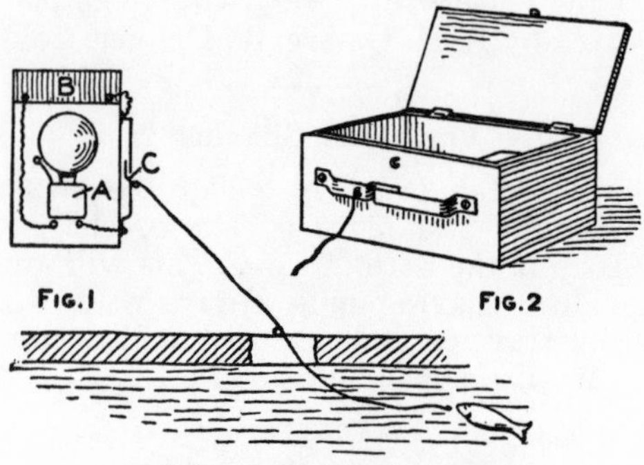

Bell and Battery in a Box

have some kind of a device to signal the fisherman when a fish is hooked. The "tipups" and the "jumping jacks" serve their purpose nicely, but a more elaborate device is the electric signal. A complete electric outfit can be installed in a box and carried as conveniently as tackle.

An ordinary electric bell, A, Fig. 1, having a gong 2½ in. in diameter, and a pocket battery, B, are mounted on the bottom of the box. The electric connection to the bell is plainly shown. Two strips of brass, C, are mounted on the outside of the box. The brass strips are shaped in such a way as to form a circuit when the ends are pulled together. The box is opened and set on the ice near the fishing hole. The fish line is hung over a round stick placed across the hole and then tied to the inside strip of brass. When the fish is hooked the line will pull the brass points into contact and close the electric circuit.

Homemade Floor Polisher

A floor polisher is something that one does not use but two or three times a year. Manufactured polishers come in two sizes, one weighing 15 lb., which is the right weight for family use, and one weighing 25 lb.

A polisher can be made at home that will do the work just as well. Procure a wooden box such as cocoa tins or starch packages are shipped in and stretch several thicknesses of flannel or carpet over the bottom, allowing the edges to extend well up the sides, and tack smoothly. Make a handle of two stout strips of wood, 36 in. long, by joining their upper ends to a shorter crosspiece and nail it to the box. Place three paving bricks inside of the box, and the polisher will weigh about 16 lb., just the right weight for a woman to use. The polisher is used by rubbing with the grain of the wood.—Contributed by Katharine D. Morse, Syracuse, N. Y.

Tying Paper Bag to Make a Carrying Handle

In tying the ordinary paper bag, the string can be placed in the paper in such a way that it will form a handle to carry the package, and also prevent any leakage of the contents. The bag must be long enough for the end to fold over as shown in Fig. 1. The folds are made over the string, as in

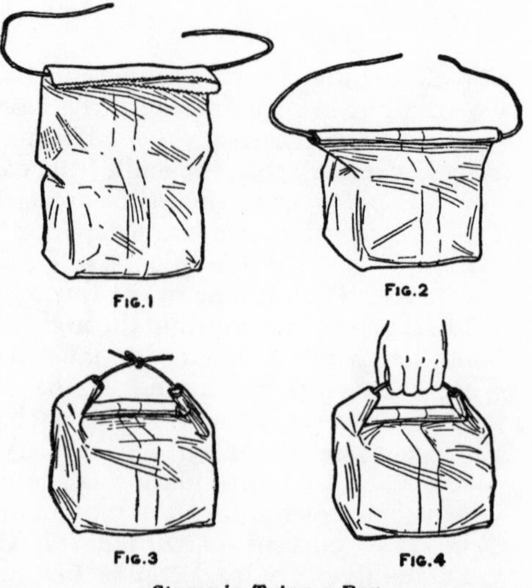

Stages in Tying a Bag

Fig. 2. The string is then tied, Fig. 3, to form a handle, Fig. 4.—Contributed by James M. Kane, Doylestown, Pa.

Equilibrator for Model Aeroplanes

On one of my model aeroplanes I placed an equilibrator to keep it balanced. The device was attached to a crosspiece fastened just below the propeller between the main frame uprights. A stick was made to swing on a bolt in the center of the crosspiece to which was attached a weight at the lower end and two lines connecting the ends of the planes at the upper end. These are shown in Fig. 1. When the aeroplane tips, as shown in Fig. 2, the weight draws the lines to warp the plane so it will right itself automatically.—Contributed by Louis J. Day, Floral Park, N. Y.

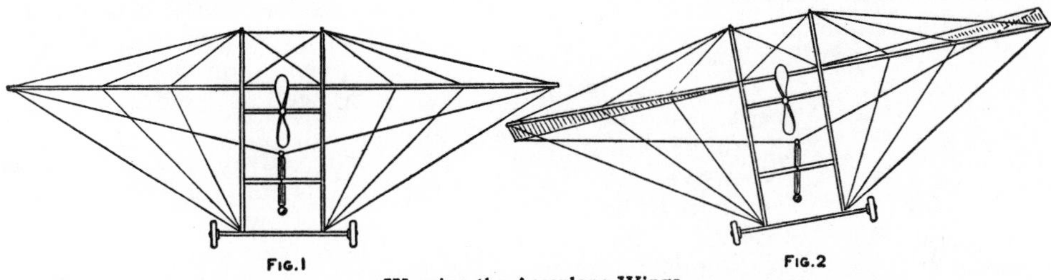

Warping the Aeroplane Wings

Repairing Christmas-Tree Decorations

Small glass ornaments for Christmas-tree decoration are very easily broken on the line shown in the sketch. These can be easily repaired by inserting in the neck a piece of match, toothpick or splinter of wood and tying the hanging string to it.

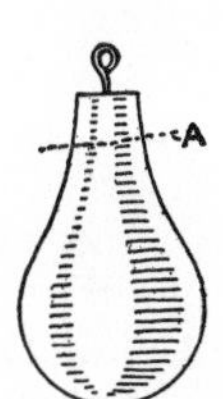

Homemade Scroll Saw

A scroll saw, if once used, becomes indispensable in any home carpenter chest, yet it is safe to say that not one in ten contains it. A scroll saw is much more useful than a keyhole saw for sawing small and irregular holes, and many fancy knick-knacks, such as brackets, bookracks and shelves can be made with one.

A simple yet serviceable scroll saw frame can be made from a piece of cold-rolled steel rod, 3/32 or ¼ in. in diameter, two ⅛-in. machine screws, four washers and four square nuts. The rod should be 36 or 38 in. long, bent as shown in Fig. 1. Place one washer on each screw and put the screws through the eyelets, A A, then place other washers on and fasten in place by screwing one nut on each screw, clamping the washers against the frame as tightly as possible. The saw, which can be purchased at a local hardware store, is fastened between the clamping nut and another nut as shown in Fig. 2.

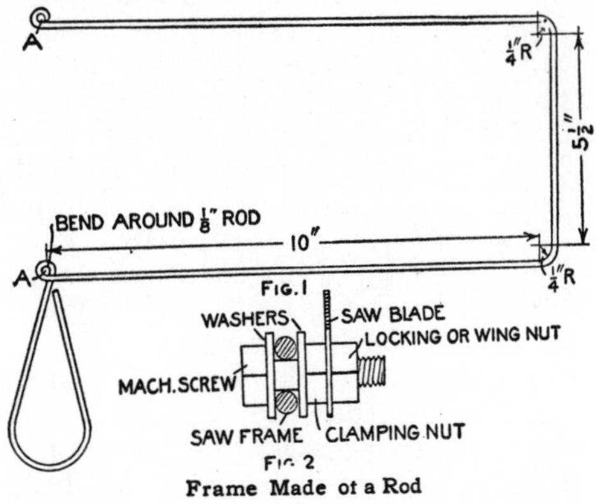

Frame Made of a Rod

If two wing nuts having the same number and size of threads are available, use them in place of the outside nuts. They are easier to turn when inserting a saw blade in a hole or when removing broken blades.—Contributed by W. A. Scranton, Detroit, Michigan.

How to Make a Watch Fob

The fixtures for the watch fob shown —half size—may be made of either brass, copper, or silver. Silver is the most desirable but, of course, the most expensive. The buckle is to be purchased. The connection is to be of leather of a color to harmonize with that of the fixtures. The body of the fob may be of leather of suitable color or of silk. Of the leathers, green and browns are the most popular, though almost any color may be obtained.

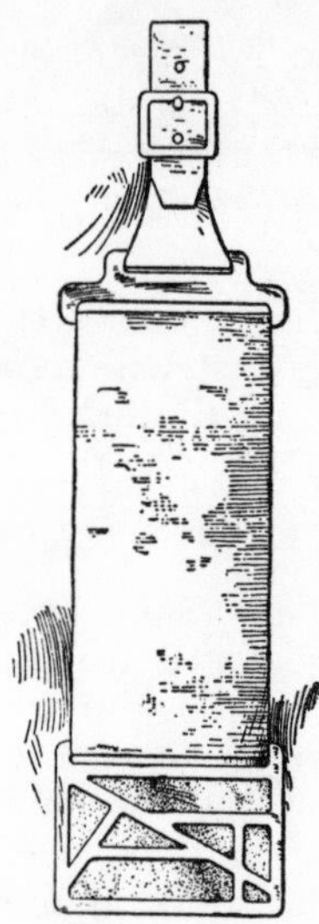

Make full size drawings of the outline and design of the fixtures. With carbon paper trace these on the metal. Pierce the metal of the parts that are to be removed with a small hand drill to make a place for the leather or silk. With a small metal saw cut out these parts and smooth up the edges, rounding them slightly so they will not cut the leather or silk. Next cut out the outlines with the metal shears. File these edges, rounding and smoothing with emery paper. The best way of handling the decorative design is to etch it and, if copper or brass, treat it with color.

For etching, first cover the metal with black asphaltum varnish, on the back and all the parts that are not to be touched with the acid. In the design shown, the unshaded parts should not be etched and should, therefore, be covered the same as the back. Apply two coats, allowing each time to dry, after which immerse the metal in a solution prepared as follows: 3 parts water, 1 part nitric acid, 1 part sulphuric acid. Allow the metal to remain in this until the acid has eaten to a depth of $\frac{1}{32}$ in., then remove it and clean in a turpentine bath, using a swab and an old stiff brush. The amount of time required to do the etching will depend upon the strength of the liquid, as well as the depth of etching desired.

For coloring silver, as well as brass and copper, cover the metal with a solution of the following: ½ pt. of water in which dissolve, after breaking up, five cents' worth of sulphureted potassium. Put a teaspoonful of this into a tin with 2 qt. of water. Polish a piece of scrap metal and dip it in the solution. If it colors the metal red, it has the correct strength. Drying will cause this to change to purple. Rub off the highlights, leaving them the natural color of the metal and apply a coat of banana-oil lacquer.

An Austrian Top

All parts of the top are of wood and they are simple to make. The handle is a piece of pine, 5¼ in. long, 1¼ in. wide and ¾ in. thick. A handle, ¾ in. in diameter, is formed on one end, allowing only 1¼ in. of the other end to remain rectangular in shape. Bore a ¾-in. hole in this end for the top. A 1/16-in. hole is bored in the edge to enter the large hole as shown. The top can be cut from a broom handle or a round stick of hardwood.

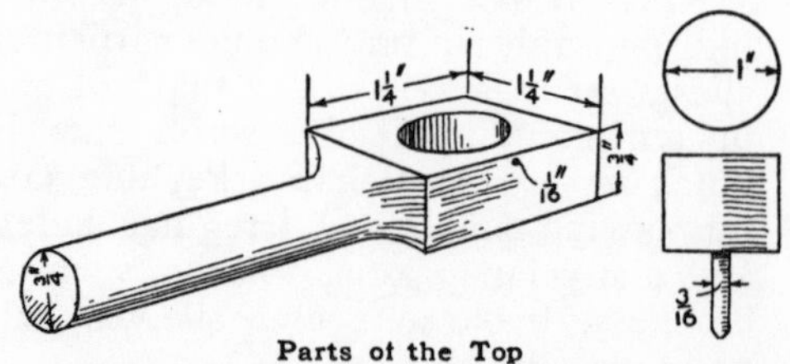

Parts of the Top

To spin the top, take a piece of stout cord about 2 ft. long, pass one end through the 1/16-in. hole and wind it on the small part of the top in the usual way, starting at the bottom and winding upward. When the shank is covered, set the top in the ¾-in. hole. Take hold of the handle with the left hand and the end of the cord with the right hand, give a good quick pull on the cord and the top will jump clear of the handle and spin vigorously.—Contributed by J. F. Tholl, Ypsilanti, Michigan.

Pockets for Spools of Thread

A detachable pocket for holding thread when sewing is shown herewith. The dimensions may be varied to admit any number or size of spools. Each pocket is made to take a certain size spool, the end of the thread being run through the cloth front for obtaining the length for threading a needle. This will keep the thread from becoming tangled and enable it always to be readily drawn out to the required length.—Contributed by Miss L. Alberta Norrell, Augusta, Ga.

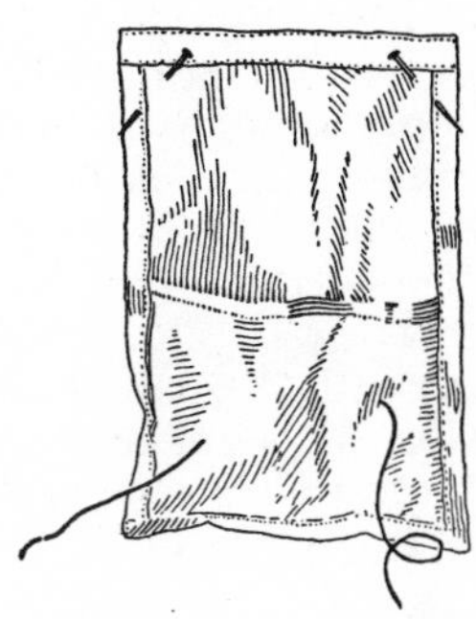

Cleaning Leather on Furniture

Beat up the whites of three eggs carefully and use a piece of flannel to rub it well into the leather which will become clean and lustrous. For black leathers, some lampblack may be added and the mixture applied in the same way.

A Baking Pan

When making cookies, tarts or similar pastry, the housewife often wishes for something by which to lift the baked articles from the pan. The baking tray or pan shown in the sketch not only protects the hands from burns but allows the baked articles easily to slip from its surface. The pan is made from a piece of sheet iron slightly larger than the baking space desired. Each end of the metal is cut so that a part may be turned up and into a roll to make handles for the pan.

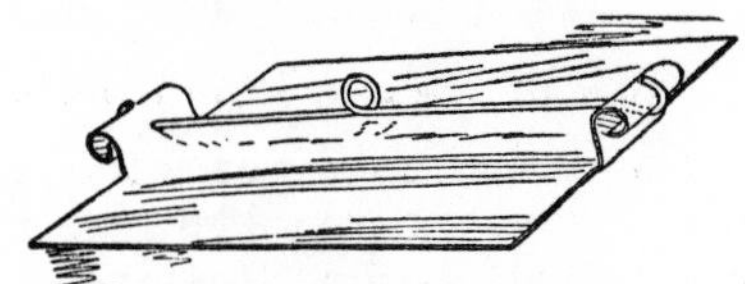

Baking Pan without Sides

A wire or small rod is placed between the handles as shown. This wire is fastened at each end and a loop made in the center. The pan can be removed from the oven by placing a stick through the loop and lifting it out without placing the hands inside the hot oven. The baking surface, having no sides, permits the baked articles to be slid off at each side with a knife or fork.—A. A. Houghton, Northville, Mich.

A Broom Holder

A very simple and effective device for holding a broom when it is not in use is shown in the sketch. It is made of heavy wire and fastened to the wall with two screweyes, the eyes forming bearings for the wire. The small turn on the end of the straight part is to hold the hook out far enough from the wall to make it easy to place the broom in the hook. The weight of the broom keeps it in position.—Contributed by Irl Hicks, Centralia, Mo.

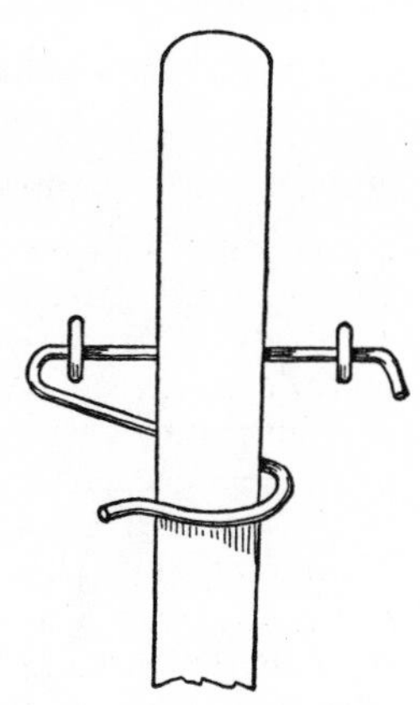

A string for drawing electric wires into bent fixtures can be easily inserted by rolling it into a small ball and blowing it through while holding one end.

A Darkroom Lantern

Procure an ordinary 2-qt. glass fruit jar, break out the porcelain lining in the cover and cut a hole through the metal, just large enough to fit over the socket of an incandescent electric globe, then solder cover and socket together, says Studio Light. Line the inside of the jar with two thicknesses of good orange post-office paper. The best lamp for the purpose is an 8-candlepower showcase lamp, the same as shown in the illustration. Screw the lamp into the socket and screw the cover onto the jar, and you have a safe light of excellent illuminating power.

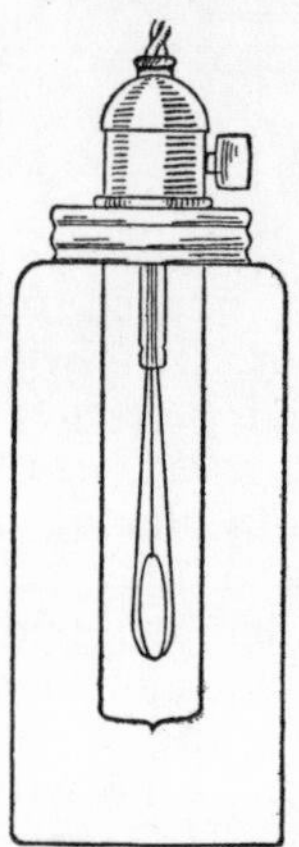

When you desire to work by white light, two turns will remove the jar. If developing papers are being worked, obtain a second jar and line with light orange paper, screw into the cover fastened to the lamp and you have a safe and pleasant light for loading and development. By attaching sufficient cord to the lamp, it can be moved to any part of the darkroom, and you have three lamps at a trifling cost.

Preventing Vegetables from Burning in a Pot

Many housekeepers do not know that there is a simple way to prevent potatoes from burning and sticking to the bottom of the pot. An inverted pie pan placed in the bottom of the pot avoids scorching potatoes. The water and empty space beneath the pan saves the potatoes. This also makes the work of cleaning pots easier as no adhering parts of potatoes are left to be scoured out.

A Clothes Rack

A clothes-drying rack that has many good features can be made as shown in the illustration. When the rack is closed it will fit into a very small space and one or more wings can be used at a time as the occasion or space permits, and not tip over. The rack can be made of any hard wood and the material list is as follows:

1 Center post, 1¼ in. square by 62 in.
4 Braces, 1¼ in. square by 12 in.
16 Horizontal bars, 1 bv 1¼ by 24 in.
4 Vertical pieces, ¼ by 1 by 65 in.

Folding Clothes Rack

Attach the four braces for the feet with finishing nails after applying a good coat of glue.

The horizontal bars are fastened to the vertical pieces with rivets using washers on both sides. The holes are bored a little large so as to make a slightly loose joint. The other ends of the bars are fastened to the center post with roundhead screws. They are fastened, as shown in the cross-section sketch, so it can be folded up.—Contributed by Herman Fosel, Janesville, Wis.

Homemade Shower Bath

A Shower Bath That Costs Less Than One Dollar to Make

While in the country during vacation time, I missed my daily bath and devised a shower bath that gave complete satisfaction. The back porch was inclosed with sheeting for the room, and the apparatus consisted of a galvanized-iron pail with a short nipple soldered in the center of the bottom and fitted with a valve and sprinkler. The whole, after filling the pail with water, was raised above one's head with a rope run over a pulley fastened to the roof of the porch, and a tub was used on the floor to catch the water. A knot should be tied in the rope at the right place, to keep it from running out of the pulley while the pail is lowered to be filled with water, and a loop made in the end, which is placed over a screwhook turned into the wall. If the loop is tied at the proper place, the pail will be raised to the right height for the person taking the shower bath.

The water will run from 10 to 15 minutes. The addition of some hot water will make a splendid shower bath.—Contributed by Dr. C. H. Rosenthal, Cincinnati, O.

How to Make Small Sprocket Wheels

As I needed several small sprocket wheels and had none on hand, I made them quickly without other expense than the time required, from scrap material. Several old hubs with the proper size bore were secured. These were put on an arbor and turned to the size of the bottom of the teeth. Holes were drilled and tapped to correspond to the number of teeth required and old stud bolts turned into them. The wheels were again placed on the arbor and the studs turned to the required size. After rounding the ends of the studs, the sprockets were ready for use and gave perfect satisfaction.—Contributed by Charles Stem, Phillipsburg, New York.

Pot-Cover Closet

The sides of the cover closet are cut as shown in Fig. 1 and shelves are nailed between them at a slight angle.

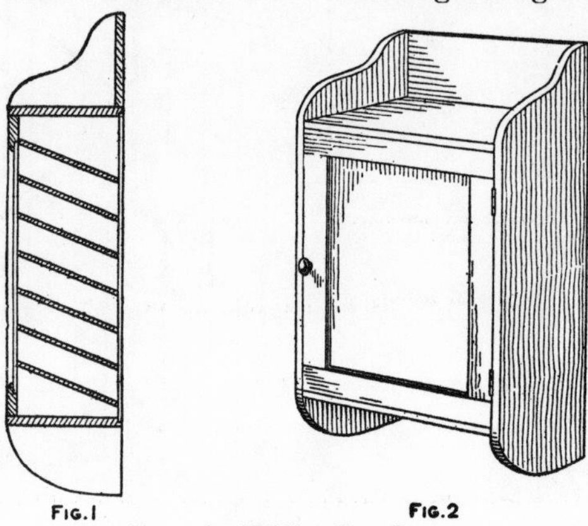

Closet for Holding Pot Covers

No dimensions are given as the space and the sizes of the covers are not always the same. The back is covered with thin boards placed vertically. The front can be covered with a curtain or a paneled door as shown.—Contributed by Gilbert A. Wehr, Baltimore, Md.

Aid in Mixing Salad Dressing

Some cooks find it a very difficult matter to prepare salad dressing, principally mayonnaise dressing, as the constant stirring and pouring of oil and liquids are required in the operation. The simple homemade device shown in the accompanying sketch greatly as-

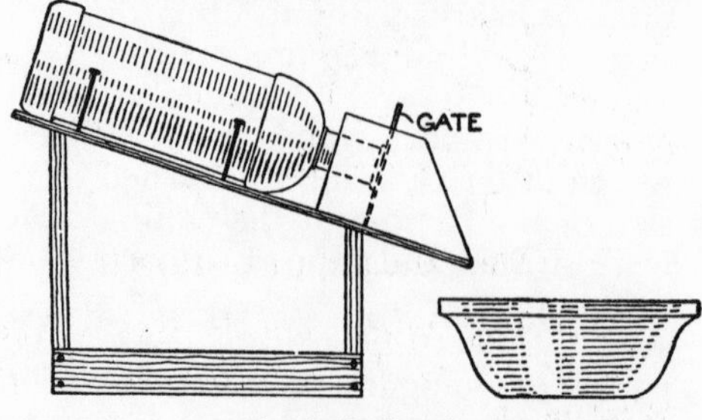

Bottle in Stand

sists in this work. It consists of a stand to hold a bottle, the mouth of which rests against a small gate directly in the rear of the attached tin trough. The weight of the bottle and the contents against the gate serves as a check or stopper. If the gate is raised slightly, it will permit a continuous flow of liquid of the desired amount.

Saving Overexposed Developing Prints

In using developing papers, either for contact printing or enlargements, you are, by all rules of the game, entitled to a certain number of overexposed prints, says a correspondent of Camera Craft. But there is no reason why you should lose either the paper or the time and trouble expended in making these prints. By using the following method, you can turn these very dark prints into good ones.

First: these overexposed prints must be fully developed. Do not try to save them by rushing them out of the developer into the short-stop or fixing bath. The results will be poor, and, if you try to tone them afterward, the color will be an undesirable, sickly one. Develop them into strong prints, thoroughly fix, and wash until you are sure all hypo is removed. In my own practice, I carry out this part of the work thoroughly, then dry the prints and lay aside these dark ones until there is an accumulation of a dozen or more, doing this to avoid too frequent use of the very poisonous bleaching solution. The bleacher is made up as follows and should be plainly marked "Poison."

Cyanide of potassium	2 oz.
Iodide of potassium	20 gr.
Water	16 oz.

Place the dry print, without previous wetting, in this solution. It will bleach slowly and evenly, but, when it starts to bleach, transfer it to a tray of water, where it will continue to bleach. When the desired reduction has taken place, stop the action at once by immersing the print in a 10-per-cent solution of borax. The prints may be allowed to remain in this last solution until they are finished. A good final washing completes the process. This washing must be thorough and a sponge or a tuft of cotton used to clean the surface of the print.

With a little practice, this method of saving prints that are too dark becomes easy and certain. The prints are lightened and at the same time improved in tone, being made blue-black with a delicate and pleasing quality that will tempt you to purposely overexpose some of your prints in order to tone them by this method for certain effects. The process is particularly valuable to the worker in large sizes, as it provides a means of making quite a saving of paper that would otherwise be thrown away.

An Ironing-Board Stand

An ordinary ironing board is cut square on the large end and a slot cut 1½ in. wide and 4 in. long to admit the angle support. The support is placed against the table and the board

Stand Attached to Table

is pressed down against the outer notch which jams against the table, thus holding the board rigid and in such a position as to give free access for ironing dresses, etc.—Contributed by T. L. Gray, San Francisco, Cal.

A Desk Blotting Pad

Procure four sheets of blotting paper, preferably the colored kind, as it will appear clean much longer than the white. The size of the pad depends on the size of the blotting paper.

Fold four pieces of ordinary wrapping paper, 5 by 15 in. in size, three times, to make it 5 by 5 in. Fold each one from corner to corner as shown in Fig. 1 and again as in Fig. 2. Paste the last fold together and the corner holders are complete. Put one on each corner of the blotting paper. They can be fastened with a small brass paper fastener put through the top of the holder. The blotting paper can

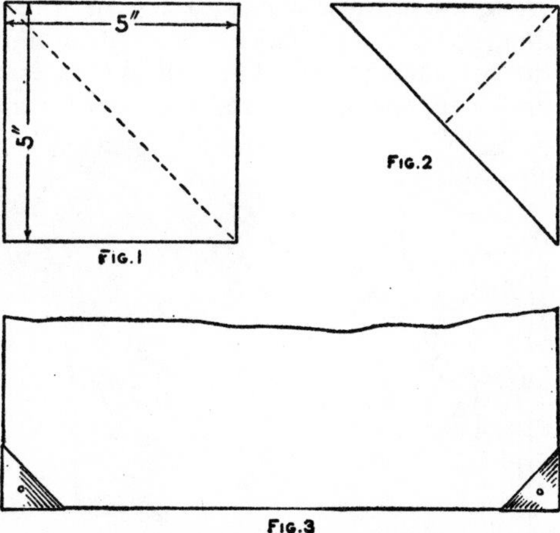

Paper Corners for Blotter Pads

be easily changed by removing the holders and fasteners. Corners complete are shown in Fig. 3.—Contributed by J. Wilson Aldred Toronto, Canada.

Sleeve Holders for Lavatories

A very handy article is an attachment on wash basins or lavatories for holding the sleeves back while washing the hands. It is very annoying to have the sleeves continually slip down and become wet or soiled. The simple device shown herewith can be made with bent wires or hooks and attached in such a way that it can be dropped out

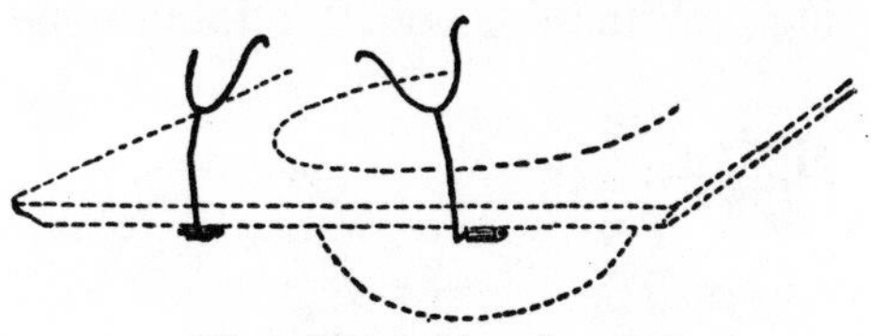

Wires Attached to a Lavatory

of the way when not in use.—Contributed by L. J. Monahan, Oshkosh, Wisconsin.

¶A pencil eraser will remove the tarnish from nickel plate, and the ink eraser will remove the rust from drawing instruments.

How to Make a Brass Bookmark

Secure a piece of brass of No. 20 gauge, having a width of $2\frac{1}{4}$ in. and a length of 5 in. Make a design similar to that shown, the head of which is 2 in. wide, the shaft 1 in. wide below the

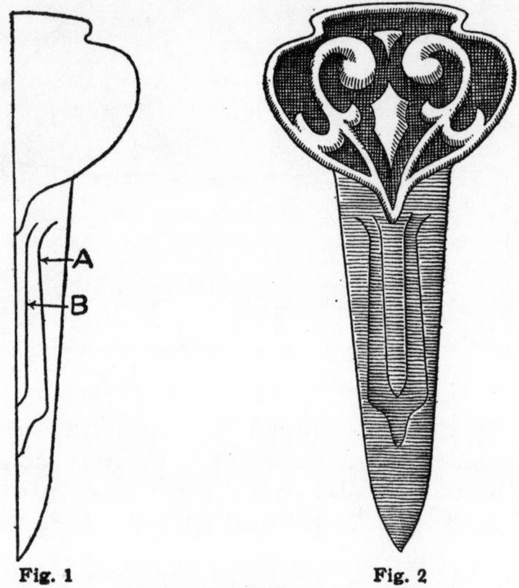

Fig. 1 Fig. 2

The Pattern and the Finished Bookmark

head and the extreme length $4\frac{1}{2}$ in. Make one-half of the design, as shown in Fig. 1, freehand, then trace the other half in the usual way, after folding along the center line. Trace the design on the metal, using carbon paper, which gives the outline of the design Fig. 2.

With the metal shears, cut out the outline as indicated by the drawing. With files, smooth off any rough-

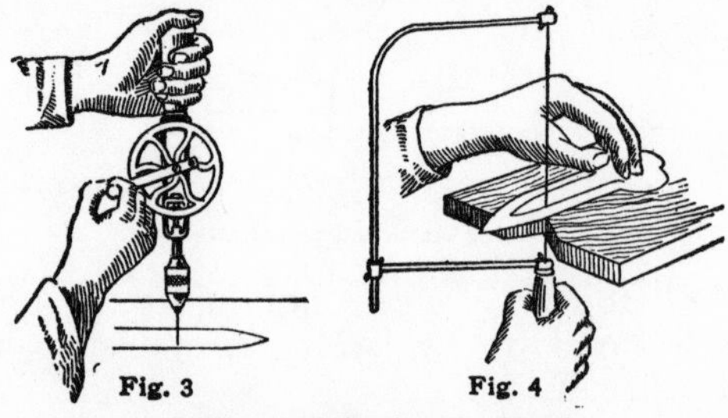

Fig. 3 Fig. 4

Drilling and Sawing the Metal

ness and form the edge so that it shall be nicely rounded.

The parts of the design in heavy color may be treated in several ways. A very satisfactory treatment is obtained by etching, then coloring. Clean the metal thoroughly with pumice stone and water or with alcohol before the design is applied. Cover all the metal that is not to be lowered with a thick coating of asphaltum. Allow this to dry, then put on a second coat. After this has dried, thoroughly immerse the metal in a solution composed as follows: 3 parts water, 1 part sulphuric acid, 1 part nitric acid.

Allow the metal to remain in this solution until the exposed part has been eaten about $\frac{1}{32}$ in. deep, then remove it and clean off the asphaltum, using turpentine. Do not put the hands in the solution, but use a swab on a stick.

For coloring olive green, use 2 parts water to 1 part permuriate of iron. Apply with a small brush.

The lines at A and B will need to be cut, using a small metal saw. Pierce a hole with a small drill, Fig. 3, large enough to receive the saw and cut along the lines as in Fig. 4. A piece of wood with a V-shaped notch which is fastened firmly to the bench forms the best place in which to do such sawing. The teeth of the saw should be so placed that the sawing will be done on the downward stroke. The metal must be held firmly, and the saw allowed time to make its cut, being held perpendicular to the work.

After the sawing, smooth the edges of the metal with a small file and emery paper. The metal clip may be bent outward to do this part of the work.

Cheesebox-Cover Tea Tray

The cover from a cheesebox can be converted into a tea tray that is very dainty for the piazza, or for serving an invalid's breakfast.

First sandpaper the wood until it is smooth, then stain it a mahogany color. The mahogany stain can be obtained ready prepared. After the stain has dried, attach brass handles, which can be obtained for a small sum at an upholsterer's shop. A round embroidered doily in the bottom adds to the appearance of the tray.—Contributed by Katharine D. Morse, Syracuse, New York.

Piercing-Punch for Brass

Drill a ½-in. hole through a block of pine or other soft wood 2 in. thick. Tack over one end of the hole a piece of pasteboard in which seven coarse sewing-machine needles have been inserted. The needles should be close together and pushed through the pasteboard until the points show. The hole is then filled with melted babbitt metal. When this is cold, the block is split and the pasteboard removed. This tool makes neat pierced work and in making brass shades, it does the work rapidly.—Contributed by H. Carl Cramer, East Hartford, Conn.

Kitchen Chopping Board

Cooks can slice, chop or mince vegetables and various other food rapidly by placing the little device, as shown, on a chopping board. It is an ordinary staple, driven in just far enough to allow a space for the end of an ordinary pointed kitchen knife to fit in it. The staple is driven in the edge of the chopping board. The knife can be raised and lowered with one hand, as

Knife Attached to the Board

the material is passed under the blade with the other. Great pressure can be applied and the knife will not slip.—Contributed by M. M. Burnett, Richmond, Cal.

Sew straps to the sides of mattresses and they can be handled much easier.

A Carpenter's Gauge

The home workshop can be supplied with a carpenter's gauge without any expense by the use of a large spool and

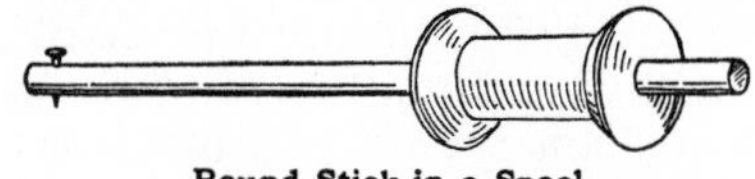

Round Stick in a Spool

a round stick of wood. The stick should be dressed to fit the hole in the spool snugly and a small brad driven through one end so that the point will protrude about $\frac{1}{16}$ in.

The adjustment of the gauge is secured by driving the stick in the hole in the direction desired. A better way and one that will make the adjusting easy is to file the point end of a screw-eye flat and use it as a set screw through a hole in the side of the spool.

A Flatiron Rest

The iron rest and wall hanger shown in the sketch is made of sheet iron. The upturned edges of the metal are

Board or Wall Iron Rest

bent to fit the sloping sides of the iron. The holder and iron can be moved at the same time.—Contributed by W. A. Jaquythe, Richmond, Cal.

Use for Paper Bags

When groceries are delivered, save the paper bags and use them for storing bread and cakes. Tie the neck of the bag with a string and it will keep the contents fresh and clean.—Contributed by Mrs. L. H. Atwell, Kissimmee, Florida.

If a little chalk is rubbed on a file before filing steel, it will keep the chips from sticking in the cuts on the file and scratching the work.

A Homemade Steam Turbine

By WILLIAM H. WARNECKE

Procure some brass, about $\frac{3}{16}$ in. thick and 4 in. square; 53 steel pens, not over ¼ in. in width at the shank; two enameled, or tin, saucers or pans, having a diameter on the inside part of about 4½ in.; two stopcocks with ⅛-in. holes; one shaft; some pieces of brass, ¼ in. thick, and several ⅛-in. machine screws.

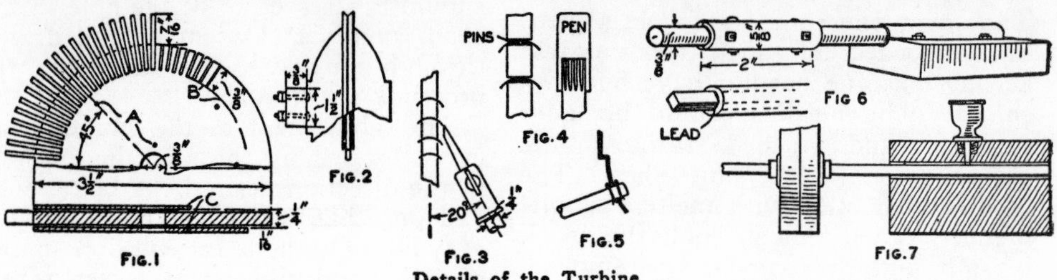

Details of the Turbine

Lay out two circles on the $\frac{3}{16}$-in. brass, one having a diameter of 3½ in. and the other with a diameter of 2¾ in. The outside circle is the size of the finished brass wheel, while the inside circle indicates the depth to which the slots are to be cut. Mark the point where a hole is to be drilled for the shaft, also locate the drill holes, as shown at A, Fig. 1. After the shaft hole and the holes A are drilled in the disk, it can be used as a template for drilling the side plates C.

The rim of the disk is divided into 53 equal parts and radial lines drawn from rim to line B, indicating the depth of the slots. Slots are cut in the disk with a hacksaw on the radial lines. A small vise is convenient for holding the disk while cutting the slots.

When cutting the disk out of the rough brass, sufficient margin should be left for filing to the true line. The slots should be left in their rough state as they have a better hold on the pens which are used for the blades. The pens are inserted in the slots and made quite secure by forcing ordinary pins on the inside of the pens and breaking them off at the rim, as shown in Fig. 4.

When the pens are all fastened two pieces of metal are provided, each about 1 in. in diameter and $\frac{1}{32}$ in. thick, with a ⅜-in. hole in the center, for filling pieces which are first placed around the shaft hole between the disk and side plates C, Fig. 1. The side plates are then secured with some of the ⅛-in. machine screws, using two nuts on each screw. The nuts should be on the side opposite the inlet valves. The shaft hole may also be filed square, a square shaft used, and the ends filed round for the bearings.

The casing for the disk is made of two enameled-iron saucers, Fig. 2, bolted together with a thin piece of asbestos between them to make a tight joint. A ¾-in. hole is cut near the edge of one of the saucers for the exhaust. If it is desired to carry the exhaust beyond the casing, a thin pipe can be inserted ¼ in. into the hole. Holes are drilled through the pipe on both inside and outside of the casing, and pins inserted, as shown in Fig. 5. Solder is run around the outside pin to keep the steam from escaping. At the lowest point of the saucer or casing a ⅛-in. hole is drilled to run off the water. A wood plug will answer for a stopcock.

If metal dishes, shaped from thick material with a good coating of tin, can be procured, it will be much easier to construct the casing than if enameled ware is used. The holes can be easily drilled and the parts fitted together closely. All seams and surfaces around fittings can be soldered.

Nozzles are made of two stopcocks having a ⅛-in. hole. These are connected to a ⅜-in. supply pipe. The nozzles should be set at an angle of 20 deg. with the face of the disk. The nozzle or stopcock will give better results if the discharge end is filed parallel to the face of the disk when at an angle of 20 deg. There should be a space of $\frac{1}{16}$ in. between the nozzle and the blades to allow for sufficient play, Fig. 3.

The bearings are made of ¼-in. brass and bolted to the casing, as shown, with ⅛-in. machine screws and nuts. Two nuts should be placed on each screw. The pulley is made by sliding a piece of steel pipe on the engine shaft and fastening it with machine screws and nuts as shown in Fig. 6. If the shaft is square, lead should be run into the segments.

The driven shaft should have a long bearing. The pulley on this shaft is made of pieces of wood nailed together, and its circumference cut out with a scroll saw. Flanges are screwed to the pulley and fastened to the shaft as shown in Fig. 7.

The bearings are made of oak blocks lined with heavy tin or sheet iron for the running surface. Motion is transmitted from the engine to the large pulley by a thin but very good leather belt.

Homemade Telegraph Key

A simple and easily constructed telegraph key may be made in the following manner: Procure a piece of sheet brass, about $\frac{1}{32}$ in. thick, and cut out a strip 3½ in. long by ¾ in. wide. Bend as shown in Fig. 1 and drill a hole for the knob in one end and a hole for a screw in the other. Procure a small wood knob and fasten it in place with a small screw. Cut a strip of the same brass 2¾ in. long and $\frac{5}{16}$ in. wide and bend as shown in Fig. 2. Drill two holes in the feet for screws to fasten it to the base, and one hole in the top part for a machine screw, and solder a small nut on the under side of the metal over the hole.

Mount both pieces on a base 4¼ by 2¾ by ¼ in., as in Fig. 3, and where

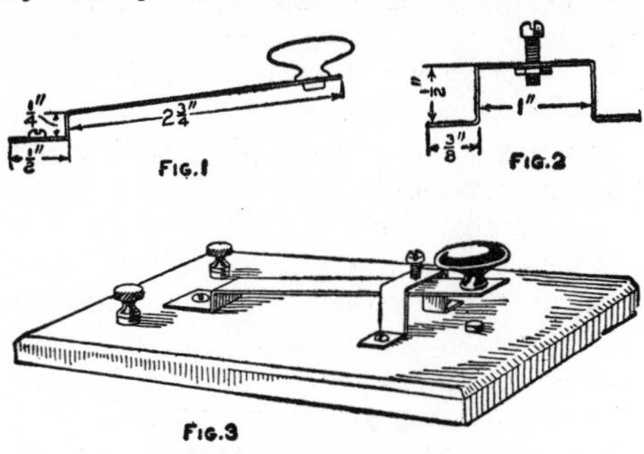

Brass Key on a Wood Base

the screw of the knob strikes the base when pressed down, put in a screw or brass-headed tack for a contact. Fasten the parts down with small brass wood-screws and solder the connections beneath the base. Binding-posts from an old battery cell are used on the end of the base. The screw on top of the arch is used to adjust the key for a long or short stroke.—Contributed by S. V. Cooke, Hamilton, Canada.

Keeping Food Cool in Camps

Camps and suburban homes located where ice is hard to get can be provided with a cooling arrangement herein described that will make a good substitute for the icebox. A barrel is sunk in the ground in a shady place, allowing plenty of space about the outside to fill in with gravel. A quantity of small stones and sand is first put in wet. A box is placed in the hole over the top of the barrel and filled in with clay or earth well tamped. The porous condition of the gravel drains the surplus water after a rain.

The end of the barrel is fitted with a light cover and a heavy door hinged to the box. A small portion of damp sand is sprinkled on the bottom of the barrel. The covers should be left open occasionally to prevent mold and to remove any bad air that may have collected from the contents.—Contributed by F. Smith, La Salle, Ill.

Homemade Work Basket

Secure a cheese box about 12 in. high and 15 in. or more in diameter. It will pay you to be careful in selecting this box. Be sure to have the cover. Score the wood deeply with a carpenter's gauge inside and out 3½ in. from the top of the box. With repeated scoring the wood will be almost cut through or in shape to finish the cut with a knife. Now you will have the box in two pieces. The lower part, 8½ in. deep over all, we will call the basket, and the smaller part will be known as the tray.

Remove the band from the cover and cut the boards to fit in the tray flush with the lower edge, to make the bottom. Fasten with ¾-in brads. The kind of wood used in making these boxes cracks easily and leaves a rough surface which should be well sandpapered.

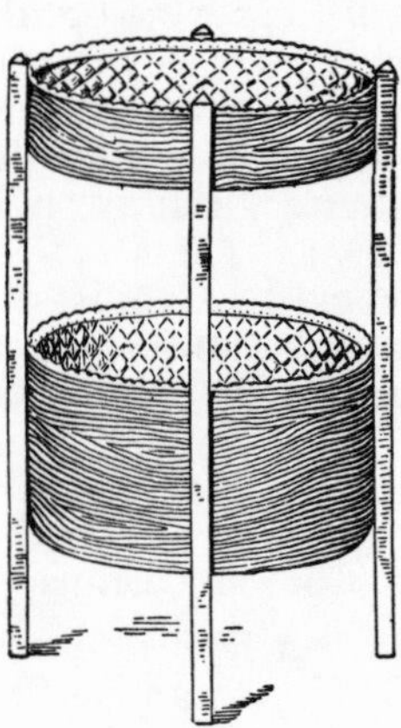

The four legs are each ¾ in. square and 30½ in. long. The tops should be beveled to keep them from splintering at the edges. With a string or tape measure, find the circumference of the tray or basket and divide this into four equal parts, arranging the lap seam on both to come midway between two of the marks. When assembling, make these seams come between the two back legs.

The tray is placed 1¼ in. from the top end and the basket 6¾ in. from the bottom end of the legs. Notch the legs at the lower point about ⅛ in. deep and 1¼ in. wide to receive the band at the lower end of the basket. Fasten with ¾-in. screws, using four to each leg, three of which are in the basket. Insert the screws from the inside of the box into the legs.

Stain the wood before putting in the lining. If all the parts are well sandpapered, the wood will take the stain nicely. Three yards of cretonne will make a very attractive lining. Cut two sheets of cardboard to fit in the bottom of the tray and basket. Cover them with the cretonne, sewing on the back side. Cut four strips for the sides from the width of the goods 5½ in. wide and four strips 10 in. wide. Sew them end to end and turn down one edge to a depth of 1 in. and gather it at that point,—also the lower edge when necessary. Sew on to the covered cardboards. Fasten them to the sides of the tray and basket with the smallest upholsterers' tacks. The product of your labor will be a very neat and useful piece of furniture.—Contributed by Stanley H. Packard, Boston, Mass.

A Window Display

A novel and attractive aeroplane window display can be easily made in the following manner: Each aeroplane is cut from folded paper, as shown in the sketch, and the wings bent out on the dotted lines. The folded part in the center is pasted together. Each aeroplane is fastened with a small thread from the point A as shown. A figure of an airman can be pasted to each aeroplane. One or more of the aeroplanes can be fastened in the blast of an electric fan and kept in flight the same as a kite. The fan can be concealed to make the display more real. When making the display, have the background of such

Paper Aeroplanes in Draft

a color as to conceal the small threads holding the aeroplanes.—Contributed by Frederick Hennighausen, Baltimore, Md.

How to Make a Flint Arrowhead

If you live where flints abound, possess the requisite patience and the knack of making things, you can, with the crudest of tools and a little practice, chip out as good arrowheads as any painted savage that ever drew a bow.

Select a piece of straight-grained flint as near the desired shape as possible. It may be both longer and wider than the finished arrow but it should not be any thicker. The side, edge and end views of a suitable fragment are shown in Fig. 1. Hold the piece with one edge or end resting on a block of wood and strike the upper edge lightly with a hammer, a small boulder or anything that comes handy until the piece assumes the shape shown in Fig. 2.

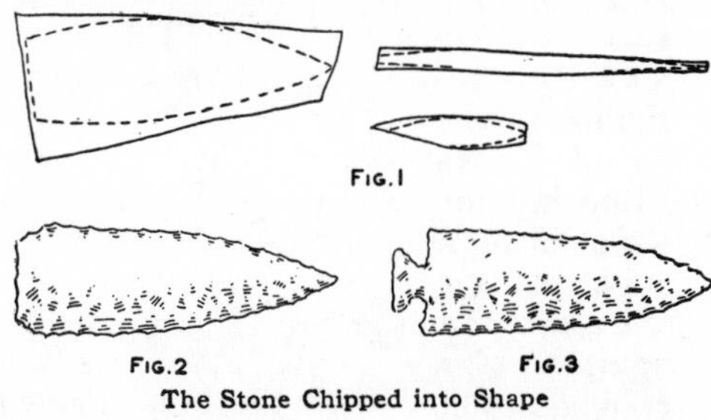

The Stone Chipped into Shape

The characteristic notches shown in the completed arrow, Fig. 3, are chipped out by striking the piece lightly at the required points with the edge of an old hatchet or a heavy flint held at right angles to the edge of the arrow. These heads can be made so that they cannot be distinguished from the real Indian arrowheads.—Contributed by B. Orlando Taylor, Cross Timbers, Mo.

An Opening Handle for a Stamp Pad

A stamp pad is a desk necessity and the cleanliness of one depends on keeping it closed when it is not in use. The opening and closing of a pad requires both hands and consequently the closing of a pad is often neglected in order to avoid soiling the fingers. This trouble can be avoided if the pad is fitted with a small handle as shown in the sketch. Take the ordinary pad and work the hinge until it opens freely.

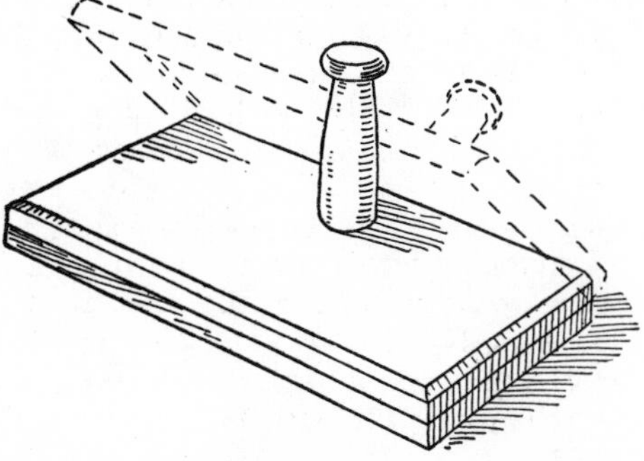

Handle on Cover

If necessary apply a little oil and spread the flanges of the cover slightly.

Saw off the top of a common wood clothespin just above the slot, saving all the solid part. Fasten this to the cover near the back side in an upright position with a screw. A tap on the front side of the pin will turn it over backward until the head rests on the desk thus bringing the cover up in the upright position. When through using the pad, a slight tap on the back side of the cover will turn it down in place—Contributed by H. L. Crockett, Gloversville, N. Y.

Concrete Kennel

The kennel shown in the illustration is large enough for the usual size of dog. It is cleanly, healthful and more ornamental than the average kennel. This mission style would be in keeping with the now popular mission and semi-mission style home, and, with

Finished Kennel

slight modifications, it could be made to conform with the ever beautiful colonial home. It is not difficult to build and will keep in good shape for many years.

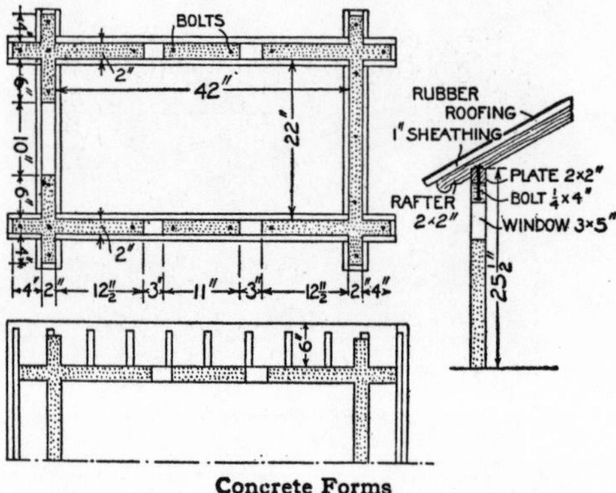

Concrete Forms

The dimensions and the manner of making the forms for the concrete, and the location for the bolts to hold the plate and rafters, are shown in the diagram.—Contributed by Edith E. Lane, El Paso, Texas.

Nutshell Photograph Novelty

Split an English walnut in the center, remove the contents, and scrape out the rough parts. Make an oval opening by filing or grinding. If a file is used, it should be new and sharp. After this is done, take a small half-round file and smooth the edges into shape and good form.

Photograph in the Shell

The photograph print should be quite small—less than ½ in. across the face. Trim the print to a size a little larger than the opening in the shell, and secure it in place with glue or paste. It may be well to fill the shell with cotton. Mount the shell on a small card with glue, or if desired, a mount of different shape can be made of burnt woodwork.—Contributed by C. S. Bourne, Lowell, Mass.

Spoonholder on a Kettle

In making marmalade and jellies the ingredients must be stirred from time to time as the cooking proceeds. After stirring, some of the mixture always remains on the spoon. Cooks often lay the spoon on a plate or stand it against the cooking utensil with the handle down. Both of these methods are wasteful. The accompanying illustration shows a device made of sheet copper to hold the spoon so that the drippings will return to the cooking utensil. The copper is not hard to bend and it can be shaped so that the device can be used on any pot or kettle.—Contributed by Edwin Marshall, Oak Park, Ill.

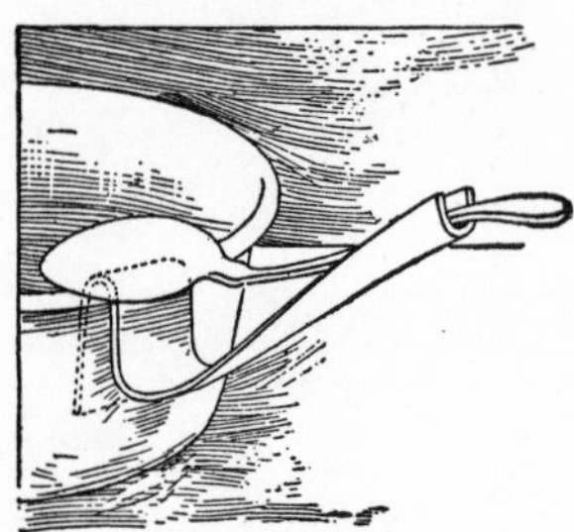

Repairing Cracked Gramophone Records

Some time ago I received two gramophone records that were cracked in shipment but the parts were held together with the paper label. As these were single-faced disk records, I used the following method to stick them together: I covered the back of one with shellac and laid the two back to back centering the holes with the crack in one running at right angles to the crack in the other. These were placed on a flat surface and a weight set on them. After several hours' drying, I cleaned the surplus shellac out of the holes and played them.

As the needle passed over the cracks the noise was hardly audible. These records have been played for a year and they sound almost as good as new.—Contributed by Marion P. Wheeler, Greenleaf, Oregon.

New Use for a Vacuum Cleaner

An amateur mechanic who had been much annoyed by the insects which were attracted to his electric lights found a solution in the pneumatic moth-trap described in a recent issue of Popular Mechanics. He fixed a funnel to the end of the intake tube of a vacuum cleaner and hung it under a globe. The insects came to the light, circled over the funnel and disappeared. He captured several pounds in a few hours.—Contributed by Geo. F. Turl, Canton, Ill.

Filtering with a Small Funnel

In filtering a large amount of solution one usually desires some means other than a large funnel and something to make the watching of the process unnecessary. If a considerable quantity of a solution be placed in a large bottle or flask, and a cork with a small hole in it inserted in the mouth, and the apparatus suspended in an inverted position over a small funnel so that the opening of the cork is just below the water level in the funnel, the filtering process goes on continuously with no overflow of the funnel.

As soon as the solution in the funnel is below the cork, air is let into the flask and a small quantity of new solution is let down into the funnel. The process works well and needs no watching, and instead of the filtrate being in a large filter paper, it is on one small piece and can be handled with ease.—Contributed by Loren Ward, Des Moines, Iowa.

A Postcard Rack

The illustration shows a neat rack for postcards. Those having homes

Finished Rack

with mission-style furniture can make such a rack of the same material as the desk, table or room furnishings and finish it in the same manner.

The dimensions are given in the detail sketch. The two ends are cut from 1/4-in. material, the bottom being 3/8 in. thick. Only three pieces are required, and as they are simple in design, anyone can cut them out with a

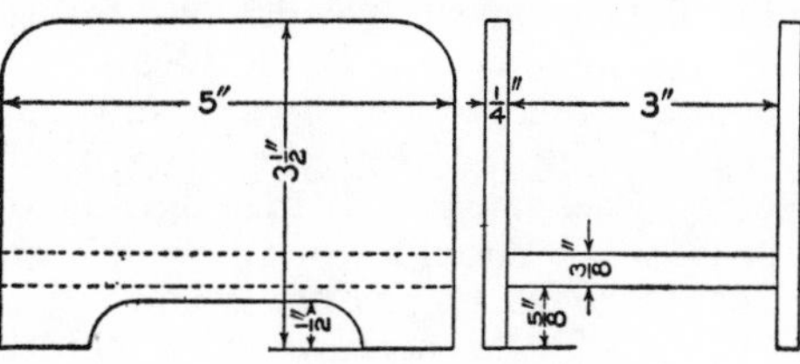

Details of the Rack

saw, plane and pocket knife.—Contributed by Wm. Rosenberg, Worcester, Mass.

Substitute Shoe Horn

A good substitute for a shoe horn is a handkerchief or any piece of cloth used in the following way: Allow part of the handkerchief or cloth to enter the shoe, place the toe of the foot in the shoe so as to hold down the cloth, and by pulling up on the cloth so as to keep it taut around the heel the foot will slide into the shoe just as easily as if a shoe horn were used.—Contributed by Thomas E. Dobbins, Glenbrook, Conn.

Building a Small Photographic Dark Room

In building a photographic dark room, it is necessary to make it perfectly light-tight, the best material to use being matched boards. These boards are tongued and grooved and when put together effectually prevent the entrance of light.

The next important thing to be considered is to make it weather-tight, and as far as the sides are concerned the matched boards will do this also, but it is necessary to cover the roof with felt or water-proof paper.

The best thickness for the boards is 1 in., but for cheapness ¾ in. will do as well, yet the saving is so little that the 1-in. boards are preferable.

The dark room shown in the accompanying sketch measures 3 ft. 6 in. by 2 ft. 6 in., the height to the eaves being 6 ft. Form the two sides shown in Fig 1, fixing the crosspieces which hold the boards together in such positions that the bottom one will act as a bearer for the floor, and the second one for the developing bench. Both sides can be put together in this way, and both exactly alike. Keep the ends of the crosspieces back from the edges of the boards far enough to allow the end boards to fit in against them.

One of the narrow sides can be formed in the same way, fixing the crosspieces on to correspond, and then these three pieces can be fastened together by screwing the two wide sides on the narrow one.

Lay the floor next, screwing or nailing the boards to the crosspieces, and making the last board come even with the ends of the crosspieces, not even with the boards themselves. The single boards can then be fixed, one on each side of what will be the doorway, by screwing to the floor, and to the outside board of the sides. At the top of the doorway, fix a narrow piece between the side boards, thus leaving a rectangular opening for the door.

The roof boards may next be put on, nailing the to each other at the ridge, and to the sides of the room at the outsides and eaves. They should overhang at the sides and eaves about 2 in., as shown in Figs. 3 and 4.

One of the sides with the crosspieces in place will be as shown in Fig. 2 in section, all the crosspieces and bearers intersecting around the room.

The door is made of the same kind of boards held together with crosspieces, one of which is fastened so as to fit closely to the floor when the door is hinged, and act as a trap for the light. The top crosspiece is also fastened within 1 in. of the top of the door for the same reason.

Light traps are necessary at the sides and top of the door. That at the hinged side can be as shown at A, Fig. 5, the closing side as at B, and the top as at C in the same drawing. These are all in section and are self-explanatory. In hinging the door, three butt hinges should be used so as to keep the joint close.

The fittings of the room are as shown sectionally in Fig. 6, but before fixing these it is best to line the room with heavy, brown wrapping paper, as an additional safeguard against the entrance of light.

The developing bench is 18 in. wide, and in the middle an opening, 9 by 11 in., is cut, below which is fixed the sink. It is shown in detail in Fig. 7, and should be zinc lined.

The zinc should not be cut but folded as shown in Fig. 8, so that it will fit inside the sink. The bench at each side of the sink should be fluted (Fig. 9), so that the water will drain off into the sink. A strip should be fixed along the back of the bench as shown in Figs. 6 and 9, and an arrangement of slats (Fig. 10), hinged to it, so as to drop on the sink as in Fig. 6, and shown to a larger scale in Fig. 11.

A shelf for bottles and another for plates, etc., can be fixed above the developing bench as at D and E (Fig. 6) and another as F in the same drawing. This latter forms the bottom of the tray rack, which is fixed on as shown

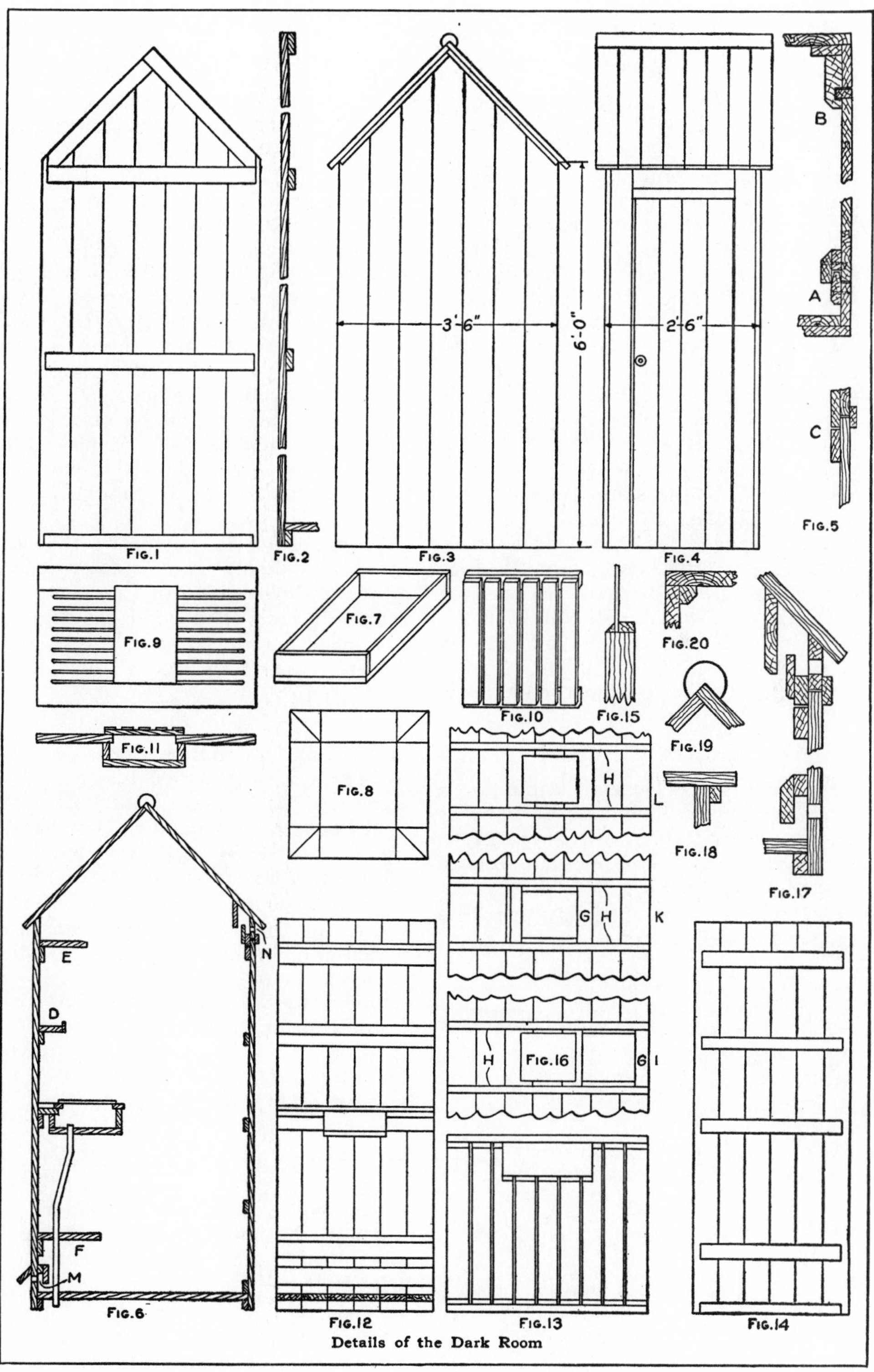

Details of the Dark Room

in Fig. 13. The divisions of the tray rack are best fitted loosely in grooves formed by fixing strips to the shelves and under the bench and sink as in Fig. 13.

Extra bearing pieces will be wanted for the shelves mentioned above, these being shown in Fig. 14. The window is formed by cutting an opening in the side opposite the door, and fixing in it a square of white glass with strips of wood on the inside and putty on the outside, as in Fig. 15. A ruby glass is framed as shown at G, Fig. 16, and arranged to slide to and fro in the grooved runners H, which makes it possible to have white light, as at I, or red light as at K, Fig. 16. The white glass with runners in position is shown at L in the same drawing, but not the red glass and frame. Ventilation is arranged for by boring a series of holes near the floor, as at M, Fig. 6, and near the roof as at N in the same drawing, and trapping the light without stopping the passage of air, as shown in the sections, Fig. 17.

The finish of the roof at the gables is shown in Fig. 18, the strip under the boards holding the felt in position when folded under, and the same is true of the roll at the top of the roof in Fig. 19.

The house will be much strengthened if strips, as shown in Fig. 20, are fastened in the corners inside, after lining with brown paper, screwing them each way into the boards.

The door may have a latch or lock with a knob, but should in addition have two buttons on the inside, fixed so as to pull it shut tightly at top and bottom. A waste pipe should be attached to the sink and arranged to discharge through the floor. A cistern with pipe and tap can be fastened in the top of the dark room, if desired, or the room may be made with a flat roof, and a tank stand on it, though this is hardly advisable.

It is absolutely necessary that the room be well painted, four coats at first is not too many, and one coat twice a year will keep it in good condition.

A brick foundation should be laid so that no part of the room touches the ground.

The Versatile Querl

"Querl" is the German name for a kitchen utensil which may be used as an egg-beater, potato-masher or a lemon-squeezer. For beating up an egg in a glass, mixing flour and water, or stirring cocoa or chocolate, it is better than anything on the market.

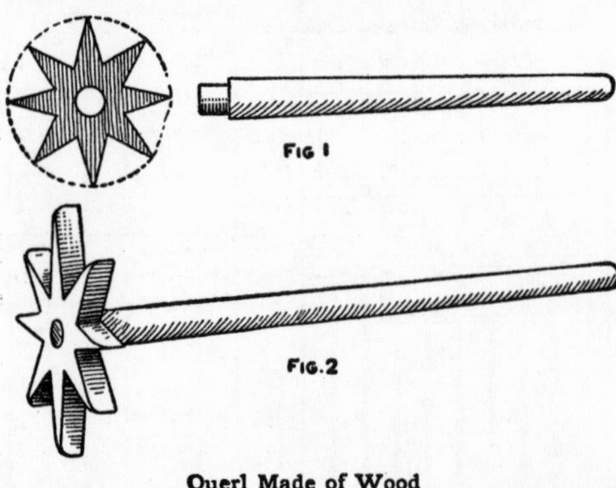

Querl Made of Wood

This utensil is made of hardwood, preferably maple or ash. A circular piece about 2 in. in diameter is cut from ½-in. stock and shaped like a star as shown in Fig. 1, and a ⅜-in. hole bored in the center for a handle. The handle should be at least 12 in. in length and fastened in the star as shown in Fig. 2.

In use, the star is placed in the dish containing the material to be beaten or mixed and the handle is rapidly rolled between the palms of the hands.—Contributed by W. Karl Hilbrich, Erie, Pennsylvania.

An Emergency Soldering Tool

Occasionally one finds a piece of soldering to do which is impossible to reach with even the smallest of the ordinary soldering irons or coppers. If a length of copper wire, as large as the job will permit and sufficiently long to admit being bent at one end to form a rough handle, and filed or dressed to a point on the other, is heated and tinned exactly as a regular copper should be, the work will cause no trouble on account of inaccessibility.—Contributed by E. G. Smith, Eureka Springs, Ark.

Smoothing Paper after Erasing

When an ink line is erased the roughened surface of the paper should be smoothed or polished so as to prevent the succeeding lines of ink from spreading. A convenient desk accessory for this purpose can be made of a short

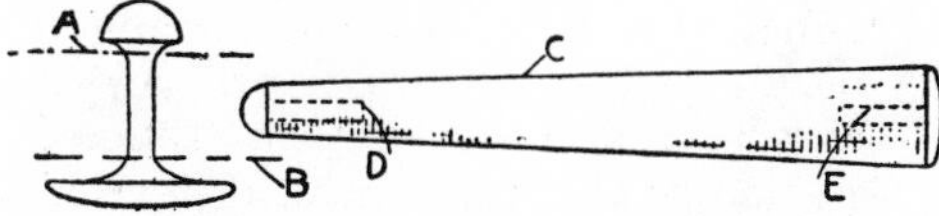

Collar Button Ends in Wood Stick

piece of hardwood and two bone collar buttons.

File off the head of one button at A and the base from another at B. Bore a small hole D and E in each end of the wood handle C and fasten the button parts in the holes with glue or sealing wax. The handle can be left the shape shown or tapered as desired. The small end is used for smoothing small erasures and the other end for larger surfaces.

A Cherry Seeder

An ordinary hairpin is driven part way into a small round piece of wood, about 3/8 in. in diameter and 2 or 2½ in. long, for a handle, as shown in the sketch. The hairpin should be a very

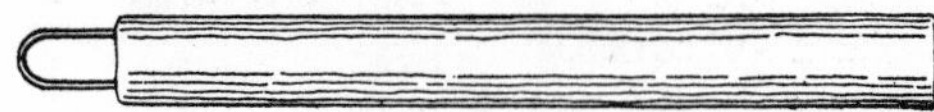

Hairpin in Stick

small size. To operate, simply insert the wire loop into the cherry where the stem has been pulled off and lift out the seed.—Contributed by L. L. Schweiger, Kansas City, Mo.

A Dovetail Joint

The illustration shows an unusual dovetail joint, which, when put together properly is a puzzle. The tenon or tongue of the joint is sloping on three surfaces and the mortise is cut sloping to match. The bottom surface of the mortise is the same width at

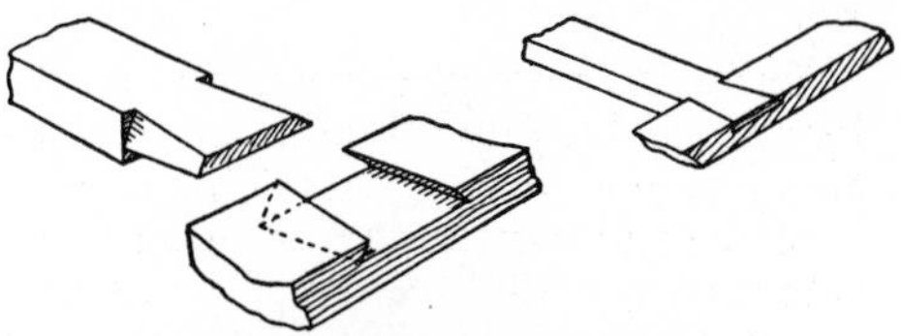

Shape of Tenon and Mortise

both ends, the top being tapering toward the base of the tongue.—Contributed by Wm. D. Mitchell, Yonkers, New York.

Base for Round-End Bottles

The many forms of round-bottomed glass bottles used in chemical laboratories require some special kind of support on which they can be safely placed from time to time when the chemist

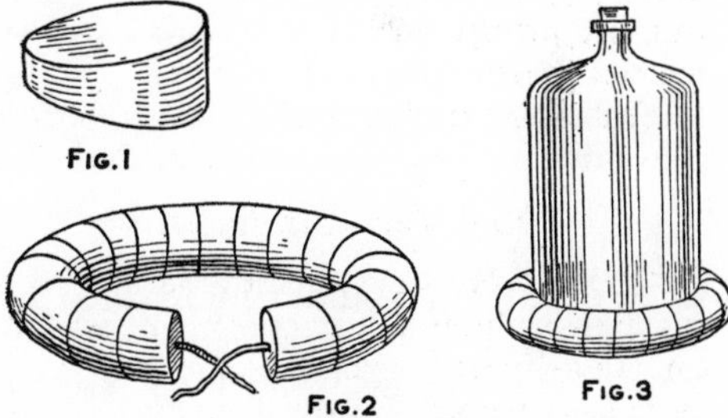

Base Made of Corks

does not, for the moment, need them. These supports should not be made of any hard material nor should they be good conductors of heat, as such qualities would result in frequent breakage.

A French magazine suggests making the supports from the large corks of glass jars in which crystal chemicals are usually supplied from the dealers. The manner of making them is clearly shown in the sketch. Each cork is cut as in Fig. 1 and placed on a wire ring (Fig. 2) whose ends are twisted together and the last section of cork is cut through from the inner side to the center and thus fitted over the wire covering the twisted ends, which binds them together. The corks in use are shown in Fig. 3.

Rustic Window Boxes

Instead of using an ordinary green-painted window box, why not make an artistic one in which the color does not clash with the plants contained in it but rather harmonizes with them.

Such a window box can be made by anyone having usual mechanical ability, and will furnish more opportunities for artistic and original design than many other articles of more complicated construction.

The box proper should be made a little shorter than the length of the window to allow for the extra space taken up in trimming and should be nearly equal in width to the sill, as shown in Fig. 1. If the sill is inclined, as is usually the case, the box will require a greater height in front, to make it set level, as shown in Fig. 2.

The box should be well nailed or screwed together and should then be painted all over to make it more durable. A number of ½-in. holes should be drilled in the bottom, to allow the excess water to run out and thus prevent rotting of the plants and box.

Having completed the bare box, it may be trimmed to suit the fancy of the maker. The design shown in Fig. 1 is very simple and easy to construct, but may be replaced with a panel or other design. One form of panel design is shown in Fig. 3.

Trimming having too rough a surface will be found unsuitable for this work as it is difficult to fasten and cannot be split as well as smooth trimming. It should be cut the proper length before being split and should be fastened with brads. The half-round hoops of barrels will be found very useful in trimming, especially for filling-in purposes, and by using them the operation of splitting is avoided. After the box is trimmed, the rustic work should be varnished, in order to thoroughly preserve it, as well as improve its appearance.

Artistic Flower Boxes

Antidote for Squirrel Pest

To the owner of a garden in a town where squirrels are protected by law, life in the summer time is a vexation. First the squirrels dig up the sweet corn and two or three replantings are necessary. When the corn is within two or three days of being suitable for cooking, the squirrels come in droves from far and near. They eat all they can and carry away the rest. When the corn is gone cucumbers, cabbages, etc., share the same fate, being partly eaten into. At the risk of being arrested for killing the squirrels I have used a small target rifle morning and night, but during my absence the devastation went on steadily. Last year they destroyed my entire corn crop. Traps do no good; can't use poison, too dangerous. But I have solved the difficulty; it's easy.

Shake cayenne pepper over the various vegetables which are being ruined, and observe results.

Homemade Electric Stove

By J. F. THOLL

The construction of an electric stove is very simple, and it can be made by any home mechanic having a vise and hand drill. The body is made of sheet or galvanized iron, cut out and drilled as shown in Fig. 1.

Each long projection represents a leg, which is bent at right angles on the center line by placing the metal in the jaws of a vise and hammering the metal over flat. If just the rim is gripped in the vise, it will give a rounding form to the lower part of the legs. The small projections are bent in to form a support for the bottom.

The bottom consists of a square piece of metal, as shown in Fig. 2. Holes are drilled near the edges for stove bolts to fasten it to the bottom projections. Two of the larger holes are used for the ends of the coiled rod and the other two for the heating-wire terminals. The latter holes should be well insulated with porcelain or mica. The top consists of a square piece of metal drilled as shown in Fig. 3. Four small ears are turned down to hold the top in place.

One end of the coiled rod is shown in Fig. 4. This illustrates how two pins are inserted in holes, drilled at right angles, to hold the coil on the bottom plate. The coiled rod is $\frac{3}{16}$ in. in diameter and 27 in. long. The rod is wrapped with sheet asbestos, cut in ½-in. strips.

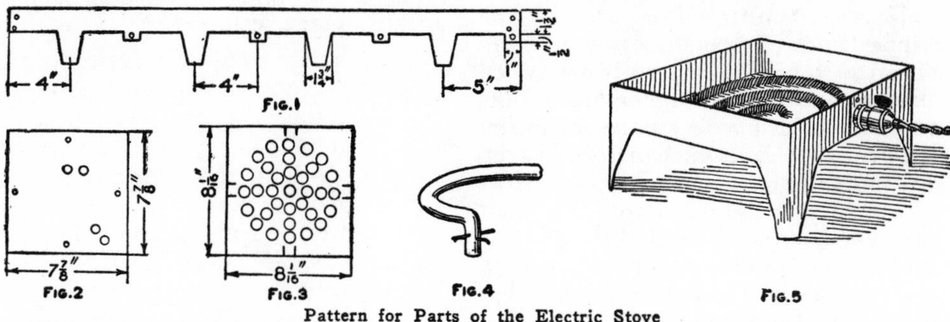

Pattern for Parts of the Electric Stove

The length of the heating wire must be determined by a test. This wire can be purchased from electrical stores. Stovepipe wire will answer the purpose when regular heating wire cannot be obtained. The wire is coiled around the asbestos-covered rod, so that no coil will be in contact with another coil. If, by trial, the coil does not heat sufficiently, cut some of it off and try again. About 9½ ft. of No. 26 gauge heating wire will be about right. The connection to an electric-lamp socket is made with ordinary flexible cord, to which is attached a screw plug for making connections.

Glass-Cleaning Solution

Glass tumblers, tubing and fancy bottles are hard to clean by washing them in the ordinary way, as the parts are hard to reach with the fingers or a brush. The following solution makes an excellent cleaner that will remove dirt and grease from crevices and sharp corners. To 9 parts of water add 1 part of strong sulphuric acid. The acid should be added to the water slowly and not the water to the acid. Add as much bichromate of potash as the solution will dissolve. More bichromate of potash should be added as the precipitate is used in cleaning. The chemicals can be purchased cheaply from a local drug store, and made up and kept in large bottles. The solution can be used over and over again.—Contributed by Loren Ward, Des Moines, Iowa.

Automatic-Closing Kennel Door

When the neighborhood cats are retired for the night and there is nothing more to chase, my fox terrier seems to realize that his usefulness

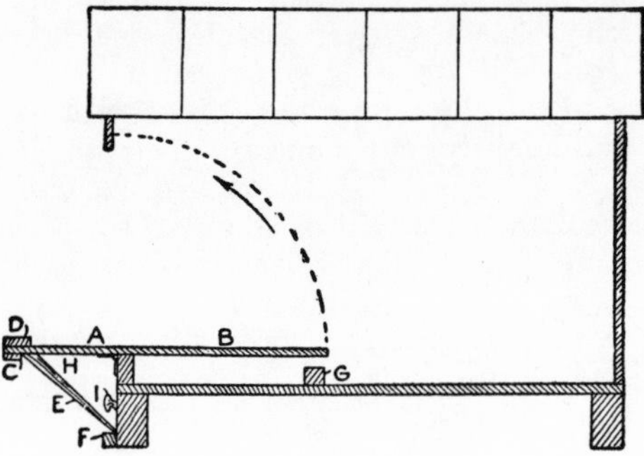

Diagram of Closing Door

for the day is over and begs to be put in his kennel that he may not bark at the moon as some dogs are apt to do. This necessitates my putting him out at a time when it may not be convenient. Frequently in stormy weather this is a disagreeable duty and I found a way to obviate it by making a trapdoor device for his kennel as shown in the sketch whereby he may lock himself in when he crosses the threshold.

The outer half A of the hinged trapdoor is made heavier than the inner half B by a cleat, C, and a strip, D, to cause the door to swing shut. The tripper stick E is set between cleats C and F to hold the door open. When the dog steps on the inner half of the trapdoor B, it falls to stop G, releasing tripper stick E (which is heavier on the top end H) to cause it to fall clear of the path of the trapdoor. The door then swings shut in the direction of the arrow, the latch I engaging a slot in the door as it closes, and the dog has locked himself in for the night. The latch I is made of an old-fashioned gate latch which is mortised in the bottom joist of the kennel. When releasing the dog in the morning the door is set for the evening.—Contributed by Victor Labadie, Dallas, Texas.

Polishing Cloths for Silver

Mix 2 lb. of whiting and ½ oz. of oleic acid with 1 gal. of gasoline. Stir and mix thoroughly. Soak pieces of gray outing flannel of the desired size —15 by 12 in. is a good size—in this compound. Wring the surplus fluid out and hang them up to dry, being careful to keep them away from the fire or an open flame. These cloths will speedily clean silver or plated ware and will not soil the hands.

In cleaning silver, it is best to wash it first in hot water and white soap and then use the polishing cloths. The cloths can be used until they are worn to shreds. Do not wash them. Knives, forks, spoons and other small pieces of silver will keep bright and free from tarnish if they are slipped into cases made from the gray outing flannel and treated with the compound.

Separate bags for such pieces as the teapot, coffee pot, hot-water pot, cake basket and other large pieces of silverware will keep them bright and shining.—Contributed by Katharine D. Morse, Syracuse, N. Y.

A Book-Holder

Books having a flexible back are difficult to hold in an upright position when copying from them. A makeshift combination of paperweights and other books is often used, but with unsatisfactory results.

Box Corner Makes a Book Holder

The book-holder shown in the sketch will hold such books securely, allow the pages to be turned easily and conceal the smallest possible portion of each page.

The holder can be cut out of a box corner and fitted with two screweyes, which have the part shown by the dotted lines at A (Fig. 1) removed. The length of the back board determines the slope for the book rest.—Contributed by James M. Kane, Doylestown, Pa.

Clamping a Cork

It is aggravating to continually break the cork of the stock mucilage bottle because of its sticking to the neck of the bottle after a supply has been poured out. If a stove bolt is inserted lengthwise through the cork with a washer on each end and the nut screwed up tightly, as shown in the sketch, the cork may be made to last longer than the supply of mucilage and can be placed in a new bottle and used over and over again.

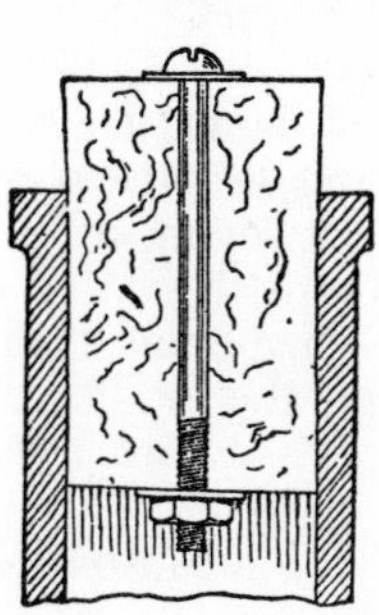

Withdrawing Paper from under an Inverted Bottle

Invert a bottle on a piece of paper near the edge of a table top and ask any one to remove the paper without overturning the bottle. They will at once jerk the paper with the result that the bottle will turn over. To remove the paper just strike the table top with your right fist while pulling the paper slowly with your left hand. As you strike the table the bottle will jump and release the paper.—Contributed by Maurice Baudier, New Orleans, La.

ℭA bone collar button makes a good substitute for a plug in repairing a puncture in a single-tube bicycle tire.

Broom Holder Made of a Hinge

The broom holder shown in the sketch is made of an ordinary hinge with one wing screwed to the wall. The loose wing has a large hole drilled in it to receive the handle of the broom. The manner of holding the broom is plainly shown in the sketch. — Contributed by Theodore L. Fisher, Waverly, Ill.

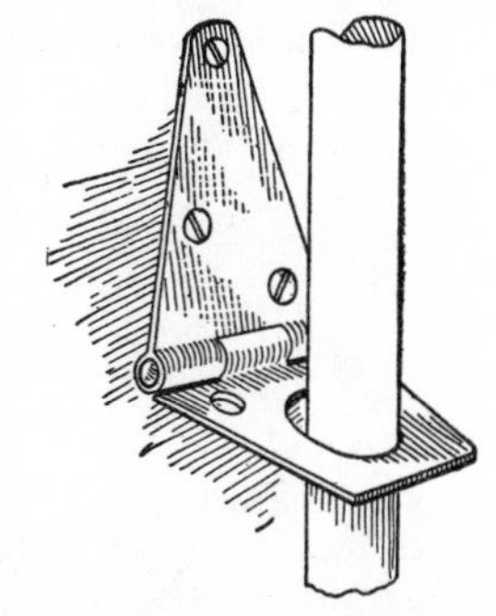

Making Proofs before the Negative Dries

A correspondent of Camera Craft makes proofs from his developed, but unfixed, negatives, by squeezing a sheet of wet bromide paper into contact with the wet film and giving an exposure several times longer than would be required under ordinary conditions, using the paper dry. If the developer is well rinsed out of the film, the exposure to artificial light necessary to make a print will have no injurious effect upon the negative, which is, of course, later fixed and washed as usual.

Flower-Pot Stand

A very useful stand for flower pots can be made of a piece of board supported by four clothes hooks. The top may be of any size suitable for the flower pot. The hooks which serve as legs are fastened to the under side of the board in the same manner as fastening the hook to a wall.—Contributed by Oliver S. Sprout, Harrisburg, Pa.

A Line Harmonograph

As an apparatus capable of exciting interest, probably nothing so easily constructed surpasses the harmonograph. Your attention will be completely absorbed in the ever changing, graceful sweep of the long pendulum, the gyrations of which are faithfully recorded in the resulting harmonogram.

A careless impetus given to the pendulum may result in a very beautiful harmonogram, but you may try innumerable times to duplicate this chance record without success. No two harmonograms are exactly alike. The harmonograph, while its pendulum swings in accordance with well known natural laws, is exceedingly erratic when it comes to obeying any preconceived calculations of its operator. In this uncertainty lies the charm. If time hangs heavily or a person is slightly nervous or uneasy, a harmonograph is a good prescription.

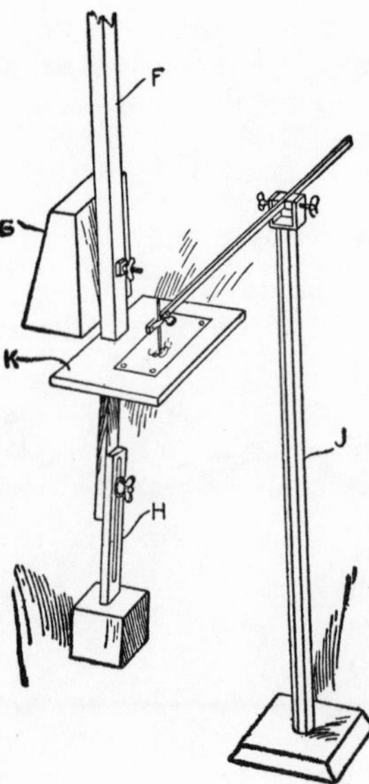

Fig. 1

The prime essential in a well working harmonograph is a properly constructed universal joint. Where such a joint is made with pivots for its bearings, one pair of pivots are very liable to have more friction than the other, which retards the movement and causes the harmonograph to undergo a continuous change of axis. To obviate this difficulty, the joint should be made similar to those used on scales. The general appearance of such a joint is shown in the first illustration, Fig. 1. Stirrups A and B are made of 7/8 by 1/4-in. metal. Holes are drilled in each end of these stirrups and filed out as shown at C. The two holes shown in the center of the stirrup A are drilled to fasten the apparatus to the ceiling. Two corresponding holes are drilled in B to fasten the long pendulum F to the joint. The cross of the joint D has the ends shaped as shown at E. The rounded shoulder on E is to prevent the cross from becoming displaced by a jar or accident. The ends of the cross are inserted through the holes C of the stirrups, then slipped back so the knife edges engage in the V-shaped holes of the stirrups. The cross must be so made that the knife edges will be in the same plane. This can be determined by placing two of the knife edges on the jaws of a vise and then laying two rules across the other two edges. The rules should just touch the jaws of the vise and the two knife edges of the cross. This makes a universal joint almost free from friction and, what is most important, prevents the pendulum from twisting on its own axis.

The pendulum F should be made of ash or oak, 1 3/4 by 2 in., with a length depending on the height of the ceiling. A length of 7 ft. is about right for a 10-ft. ceiling.

A small table or platform, K, as shown in the lower part of Fig. 1, is fastened to the lower end of the pendulum as a support for the cards on which harmonograms are made. A weight, G, of about 30 or 40 lb.—a box filled with small weights will do—is attached to the pendulum just above the table. Another weight of about 10 lb. is attached as shown at H. A pedestal, J, provides a means of support for the stylus. The stylus arm should have pin-point bearings, to prevent any side motion.

The length of the short pendulum H, which can be regulated, as shown in Fig. 1, should bear a certain and exactly fixed relation to the length of the main pendulum, for the swinging times of pendulums are inversely proportionate to their lengths, and unless the shorter pendulum is, for instance, exactly one-third, one-fourth, one-fifth, etc., as long as the other, that is, makes respectively 3, 4 or 5 swings to one swing of the long pendulum, they will not harmonize and a perfect harmonogram is not obtained.

A good stylus to contain the ink is easily made from a glass tube 1/4 in. in diameter. Heat the tube in an alcohol or Bunsen flame and then, by drawing the two portions apart and twisting at the same time, the tube may be drawn to a sharp point. An opening of any desired size is made in the point by rubbing it on a whetstone. Owing to the fact that the style of universal joint described has so little friction, the stylus point must be very fine, or the lines will overlap and blur. A small weight, such as a shoe buttoner, placed on the arm near the stylus will cause enough friction to make the pendulum "die" faster and thus remedy the trouble.—Contributed by Wm. R. Ingham, Rosemont, Arizona.

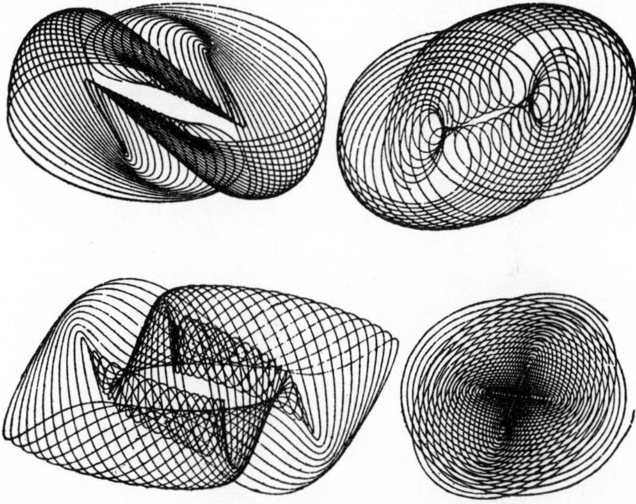

Lines Made with the Harmonograph

Cutting Circular Holes in Thin Sheet Metal

In arts and crafts work, occasion often arises to cut a perfectly circular hole in sheet copper or brass. To saw and file it out takes time and skill. Holes up to 3 in. in diameter can be cut quickly and accurately with an ordinary expansive bit.

Fasten the sheet metal to a block of wood with handscrews or a vise. Punch a hole, with a nail set or punch, in the center of the circle to be cut, large enough to receive the spur of the expansive bit. A few turns of the brace will cut out the circle and leave a smooth edge.—Contributed by James T. Gaffney, Chicago.

Key Card for Writing Unreadable Post Cards

A key card for use in correspondence on postals that makes the matter unreadable unless the recipient has a duplicate key card is made as follows: Rule two cards the size of postal, one for the sender and one for the receiver, dividing them into quarters. These quarters are subsequently divided into any convenient number of rectangular parts—six in this case.

These parts are numbered from one to six in each quarter beginning at the outside corners and following in the same order in each quarter. Cut out one rectangle of each number with a sharp knife, distributing them over the whole card. Then put a prominent figure 1 at the top of one side, 2 at the bottom and 3 and 4 on the other side. The numbering and the cutouts are shown in Fig. 1. The two key cards are made alike.

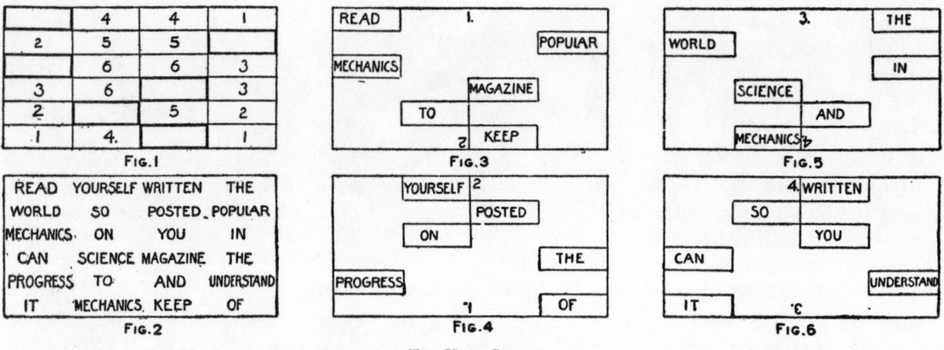

The Key Cara

The key card is used by placing it over a postal with the figure 1 at the top and writing in the spaces from left to right as usual, Fig. 3, then put 2 at the top, Fig. 4, and proceed as before, then 3 as in Fig. 5, and 4 as in Fig. 6. The result will be a jumble of words as shown in Fig. 2, which cannot be read to make any sense except by use of a key card.—Contributed by W. J. Morey, Chicago.

Homemade Carpenter's Vise

The sketch shows an easily made, quick-working wood vise that has proved very satisfactory. The usual screw is replaced by an open bar held on one end by a wedge-shaped block,

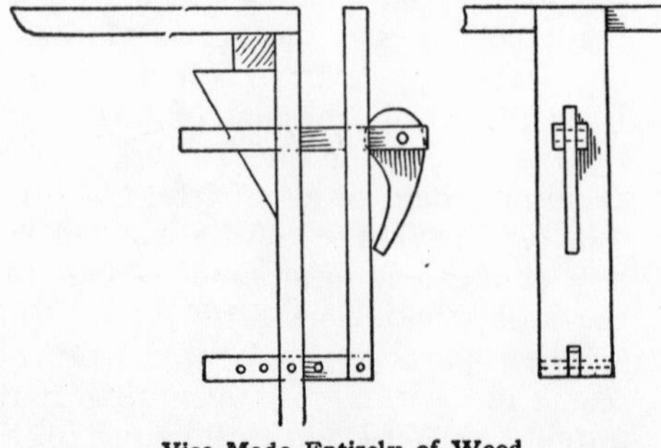
Vise Made Entirely of Wood

and the excess taken up on the other end by an eccentric lever. The wedge is worked by a string passing through the top of the bench and should be weighted on the other end to facilitate the automatic downward movement. The capacity of the vise, of course, depends on the size and shape of the wedge-shaped block.—Contributed by J. H. Cruger, Cape May City, N. J.

Toning Blue on Bromide and Platinum

After some experimenting to secure a blue tone on bromide prints, a correspondent of the Photographic Times produced a very pleasing bluish green tint by immersing the prints in a solution composed of 30 gr. of ferricyanide of potash, 30 gr. citrate of iron and ammonia, ½ oz. acetic acid and 4 oz. of water. After securing the tint desired, remove the prints, rinse them in clean water for a few minutes, and then place them in a dilute solution of hydrochloric acid. Wash the prints thoroughly and hang them up with clips to dry.

Cutting Loaf Bread

When cutting a loaf of bread do not slice it from the outer crusted end. Cut through the center, then cut slices from the center toward the ends. The two cut surfaces can be placed together, thus excluding the air and keeping the bread fresh as long as there is any left to slice.—Contributed by L. Alberta Norrell, Augusta, Ga.

How to Make an Electric Toaster

The electric toaster shown in the sketch is not hard to make. The framework comprising the base and the two uprights may be made either of hardwood or asbestos board, says Popular Electricity. If constructed of the former, the portion of the base under the coil, and the inside surfaces of the two uprights should be covered with a 1/8-in. sheet of well made asbestos paper, or thin asbestos board may be substituted for this lining. Asbestos board is to be preferred, and this material in almost any degree of hardness may be purchased. It can be worked into shape and will hold woodscrews. The detail drawing gives all dimensions necessary to shape the wood or asbestos board.

After preparing the base and uprights, drill 15 holes, 1/4 in. deep, into the inside face of each upright to support the No. 6 gauge wires shown. The wires at the top and bottom for holding the resistance wire are covered with asbestos paper and the holes for these wires are 3/4 in. from the top and bottom, respectively, of the uprights. The wires that form the cage about the heater coil and are used for a support for the toast are 15 pieces of No. 6 gauge iron wire each 8 in. long. The screws that hold the uprights in position should have the heads countersunk on the under side of the base. The binding-posts should now be set in position and their protecting covering containing the reinforced cord left until the other parts are finished.

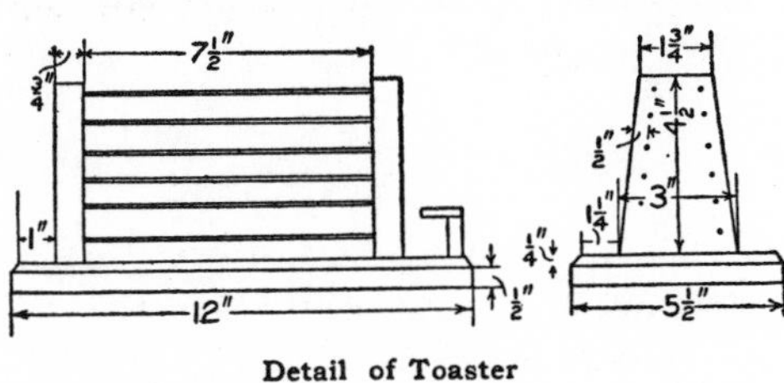

Detail of Toaster

To assemble, secure one upright in position using 1½-in. wood-screws. Place the other upright where it belongs without fastening it and put the stretcher wires for holding the resistance wire in place. Put the asbestos paper on these and with the assistance of a helper begin winding on the heater coil. Use 80 ft. of 18-per-cent No. 22 gauge German-silver wire. Wind the successive turns of wire so they will not touch each other and fasten at each end with a turn or two of No. 16 gauge copper wire. When this is complete have the helper hold the stretcher wires while you tip the unfastened upright out and insert the wires of the cage, then fasten the upright in place.

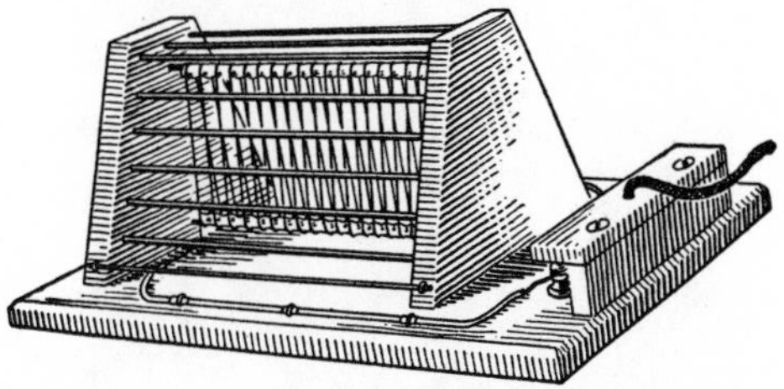

Toaster Complete

The wire from the binding-posts to the coil may be what is known as underwriters' wire or asbestos-covered wire No. 14 gauge, which is held in place by double-headed tacks containing an insulation at the head. These may be procured from electrical supply houses. Connect the reinforced cord and terminals to the binding screws and fasten the cover in place. This toaster will take four amperes on 110-volt circuit.

Cabinet for the Amateur's Workshop

One of the most convenient adjuncts to an amateur's workbench is a cabinet of some sort in which to keep nails, rivets, screws, etc., instead of leaving them scattered all about the bench. A very easily made cabinet for this purpose is shown in the accompanying illustration. The case may be made of ½-in. white pine or white wood of a suitable size to hold the required number of drawers which slide on strips of the same material, cut and dressed ½ in. square. The drawers are made of empty cigar boxes of uniform size,

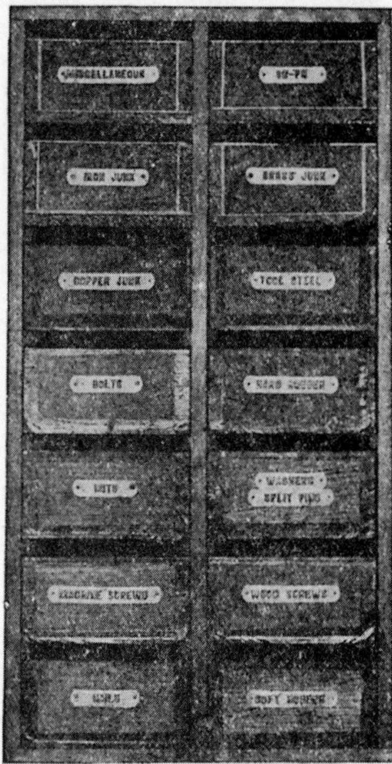

Empty Cigar Boxes Used for Drawers

which, if one is not a smoker, may be readily obtained from any cigar dealer, as they are usually thrown away when empty.

Small knobs may be added if desired, but these are not necessary, as the spaces shown between the drawers give ample room to grasp them with the fingers. Labels of some kind are needed, and one of the neatest things for this purpose is the embossed aluminum label, such as is stamped by the well known penny-in-the-slot machines to be found in many railroad stations and amusement places.—Contributed by Frederick E. Ward, Ampere, N. Y.

¶Photograph prints can be kept from curling when dry, by giving them the same treatment as was once used on films. Immerse for 5 minutes in a bath made by adding ¼ oz. of glycerine to 16 oz. of water.

Soldering for the Amateur

Successful soldering will present no serious difficulties to anyone who will follow a few simple directions. Certain metals are easier to join with solder than others and some cannot be soldered at all. Copper, brass, zinc, tin, lead, galvanized iron, gold and silver or any combination of these metals can be easily soldered, while iron and aluminum are common metals that cannot be soldered.

It is necessary to possess a soldering copper, a piece of solder, tinner's acid, sandpaper or steel wool, a small file and a piece of sal ammoniac. If the soldering copper is an old one, or has become corroded, it must be ground or filed to a point. Heat it until hot (not red hot), melt a little solder on the sal ammoniac, and rub the point of the copper on it, turning the copper over to thoroughly tin the point on each face. This process is known as tinning the iron and is very necessary to successful work.

After the copper is tinned you may place it in the fire again, being careful about the heat, as too hot an iron will burn off the tinning.

The parts to be soldered must be thoroughly cleaned by sandpapering or the use of steel wool until the metal shows up bright. Then apply the acid only to the parts to be soldered with a small stiff brush or a small piece of cloth fastened to a stick, or in a bent piece of tin to form a swab.

Tinner's acid is made by putting as much zinc in commercial muriatic acid as will dissolve. This process is best accomplished in an open earthenware dish. After the acid has ceased to boil and becomes cool it may be poured into a wide-mouthed bottle which has a good top or stopper, and labeled "Poison."

Place the parts to be soldered in their correct position and apply the hot copper to the solder, then to the joint to be soldered, following around with the copper and applying solder as is necessary.

In joining large pieces, it is best to

"stick" them together in several places to hold the work before trying to get all around them. A little practice will soon teach the requisite amount of solder and the smoothness required for a good job.

In soldering galvanized iron, the pure muriatic acid should be used, particularly so when the iron has once been used.—C. G. S., Eureka Springs, Ark.

Washboard Holder

When using a washboard it will continually slip down in the tub. This is considerable annoyance, especially if a large tub is used. The washboard can be kept in place with small metal hooks, as shown in the sketch. Two of these are fastened to the back of

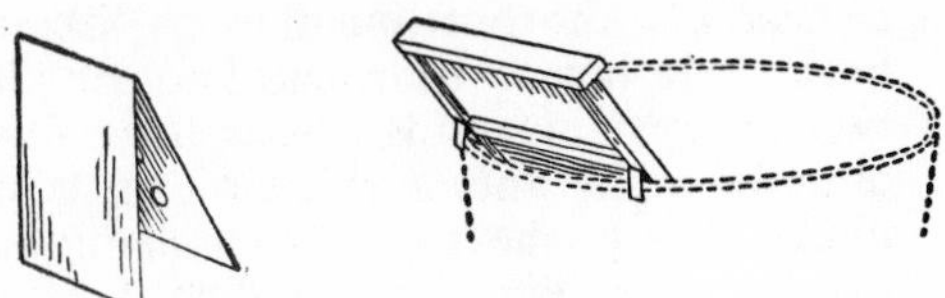

Clip on the Washboard

the washboard in the right place to keep it at the proper slant.—Contributed by W. A. Jaquythe, Richmond, California.

A Mission Bracket Shelf

The shelf consists of six pieces of wood A, B, C, D, E and F. The material can be of any wood. I have one made of mahogany finished in natural color, and one made of poplar finished black. The dimensions given in the detail drawings are sufficient for anyone to make this bracket. The amount of material required is very small and can be made from scrap, or purchased from a mill surfaced and sanded. The parts are put together with dowel pins.—Contributed by A. Larson, Kenosha, Wis.

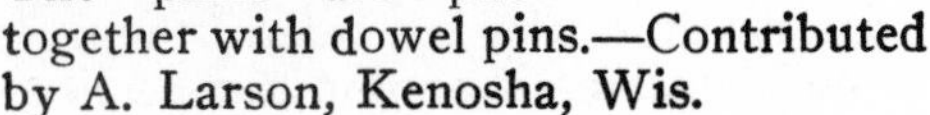

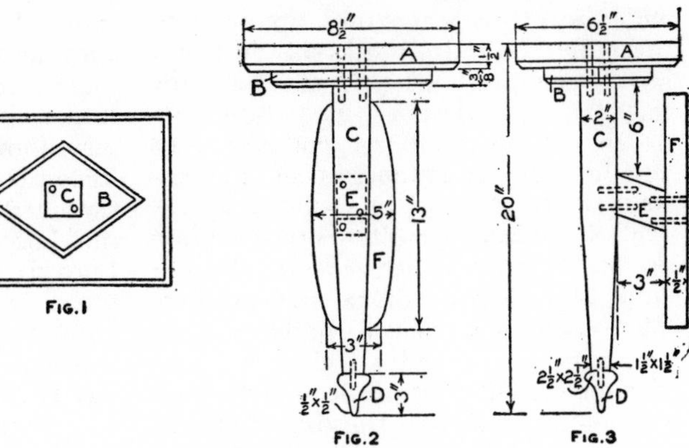

Details of the Wall Bracket

How to Make a Finger Ring

While the wearing of copper rings for rheumatism may be a foolish notion, yet there is a certain galvanic action

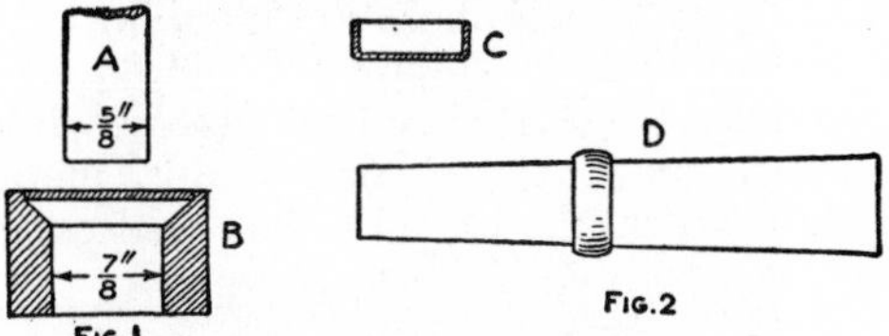

Tools for Forming the Ring

set up by the contact of the acid in the system of the afflicted person with the metal of the ring. Apart from this, however, a ring may be made from any metal, such as copper, brass and silver, if such metals are in plate or sheet form, by the following method:

All the tools necessary are a die and punch which are simple to make and will form a ring that will fit the average finger. Take a ¾-in. nut, B, Fig. 1, and drill out the threads. This will leave a clear hole, ⅞ in. in diameter, or a hole drilled the desired size in a piece of iron plate will do as well. Countersink the top of the hole so that the full diameter of the countersink will be 1¼ in. This completes the die. The punch A, is made of a piece of ⅝-in. round iron, slightly rounded on the end so that it will not cut through the metal disk. The dimensions shown in Fig. 1 can be changed to suit the size of the finger to be fitted.

The metal used should be about $\frac{1}{16}$ in. thick and 1¼ in. in diameter. Anneal it properly by heating and plunging in water. Lay it on the die so that it will fit nicely in the countersink and drive it through the hole by striking the punch with a hammer. Hold the punch as nearly central as possible when starting to drive the metal through the hole. The disk will come out pan shaped, C, and it is only necessary to remove the bottom of the pan to have a band which will leave a hole ⅝ in. in diameter and 1¼ in. wide. Place the band, D, Fig. 2, on a stick so that the edges can be filed and rounded to shape. Finish with fine emery cloth and polish. Brass rings can be plated when finished.—Contributed by H. W. Hankin, Troy, N. Y.

How to Bind Magazines

A great many readers of Popular Mechanics Magazine save their copies and have them bound in book form and some keep them without binding. The bound volumes make an attractive library and will always be valuable works of reference along mechanical lines. I bind my magazines at home evenings, with good results. Six issues make a well proportioned book, which gives two bound volumes each year.

The covers of the magazines are removed, the wire binders pulled out with a pair of pliers and the advertising pages removed from both sides, after which it will be found that the remainder is in sections, each section containing four double leaves or sixteen pages. These sections are each removed in turn from the others, using a pocket knife to separate them if they stick, and each section is placed as they were in the magazine upon each preceding one until all six numbers have been prepared. If started with the January or the July issue, the pages will be numbered consecutively through the entire pages of the six issues.

The sections are then prepared for sewing. They are evened up on the edges by jarring on a flat surface. They are then placed between two pieces of board and all clamped in a vise. Five cuts, ⅛ in. deep, are made with a saw across the back of the sections, as shown in Fig. 1. Heavy plain paper is used for the flyleaves. The paper is cut double the same as the leaves comprising the sections, making either one or two double sections for each side as desired.

A frame for sewing will have to be made as shown in Fig. 2 before the work can be continued on the book. The frame is easily made of four pieces of wood. The bottom piece A should be a little larger than the book. The two upright pieces B are nailed to the outside edge, and a third piece, C, is nailed across the top. Small nails are driven part way into the base C to correspond to the saw cuts in the sections. A piece of soft fiber string is stretched from each nail to the crosspiece C and tied.

Coarse white thread, size 16 or larger, is used for the sewing material. Start with the front of the book. Be sure that all sections are in their right places and that the flyleaves are provided in the front and back. Take the sections of the flyleaves on top, which should be notched the same as the saw cuts in the book sections, and place them against the strings in the frame. Place the left hand on the inside of the leaves where they are folded and start a blunt needle, threaded double, through the notch on the left side of the string No. 1 in Fig. 2. Take hold of the needle with the right hand and pass it to the left around the string No. 1, then back through the notch on the right side. Fasten the thread by tying or making a knot in the end and passing the needle through it. After drawing the thread tightly, pass the needle through the notch on the left side of the string No. 2, passing it around the string and tying in the same manner as for No. 1. Each section is fastened to the five strings in the same manner, the thread being carried across from each tie from No. 1 to 2 then to 3 and so on

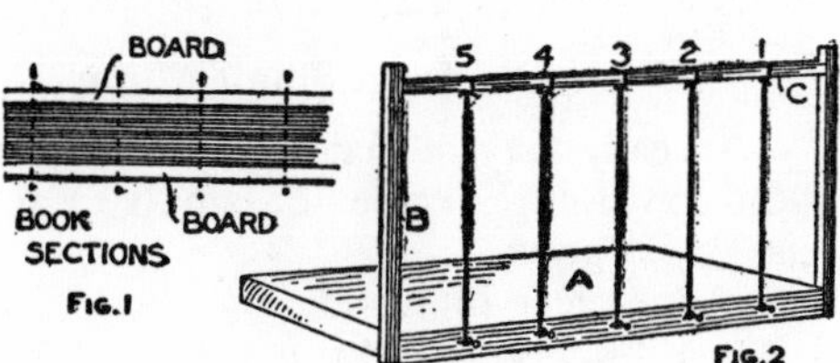

Frame for Sewing Sections

until all strings are tied. The string No. 5 is treated in the same manner only that the needle is run through on the left side of the string a second time, leaving the needle on the outside in position for the next section, which is fastened the same as the first, the needle being passed through the notch on the right side of the string No. 5, and then to string No. 4, passing around on the right side and back on the left and so on. Keep the thread drawn up tightly all the time.

After the sewing is completed cut the strings, allowing about 2 in. of the ends extending on each side. The fibers of these ends are separated and combed out so that they can be glued to the covers to serve as a hinge. A piece of cheesecloth is cut to the size of the back and glued to it. Ordinary liquid glue is the best adhesive to use.

Procure heavy cardboard for the covers and cut two pieces ½ in. longer and just the same width as the magazine pages. The covering can be of cloth, leather or paper according to the taste and resources of the maker. The covering should be cut out 1 in. larger on all edges than both covers and space on the back. Place the cardboard covers on the book, allowing a margin of ¼ in. on all edges except the back, and measure the distance between the back edges of the covers across the back of the book.

Place the cardboard covers on the back of the covering the proper distance apart as measured for the back, and mark around each one. Spread a thin coat of glue on the surface of each and lay them on by the marks made. Cut a notch out of the covering so it will fold in, and, after gluing

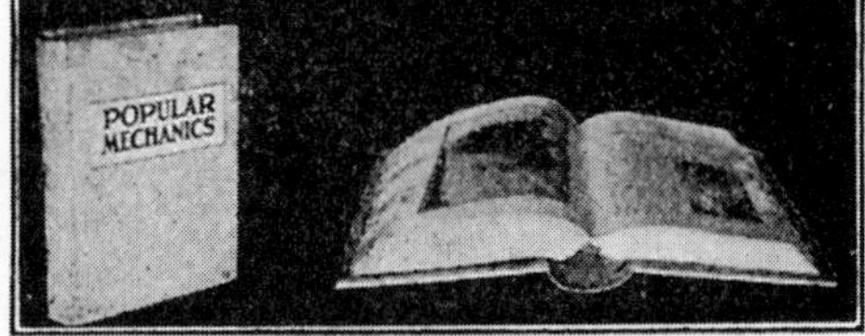

The Bound Book

a strip of paper to the covering between the covers to strengthen the back, fold over the outside edges of the covering and glue it down all around.

Place the cover on the book in the right position, glue the hinges fast to the inside of the covers, then glue the first flyleaf to the inside of the cover on both front and back and place the whole under a weight until dry.—Contributed by Clyde E. Divine, College View, Nebr.

Metal Coverings for Leather Hinges

A method of making a leather hinge work as well as an ordinary steel butt is to cover the wings with sheet metal. The metal can be fastened with nails or screws over the parts of the leather attached to the wood. Tinplate, iron

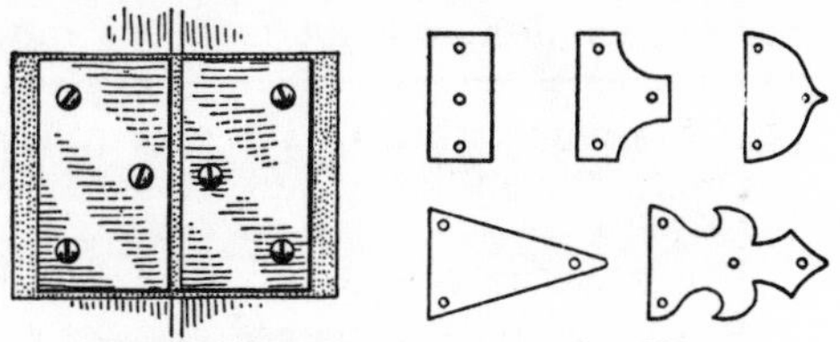

Metal Parts Screwed on Leather Hinge

hoops, zinc or thin brass cut in neat designs will make a leather hinge appear as well as a metal hinge.—Contributed by Tom Hutchinson, Encanto, Cal.

¶A hot-water bottle held against a porous plaster will assist in quickly removing it from the skin.

How to Make a Cheap Bracket Saw

For the frame use 3/8-in. round iron, bending it as shown in the diagram and filing a knob on each end, at opposite sides to each other, on which to hook the blade.

For the blade an old talking-machine

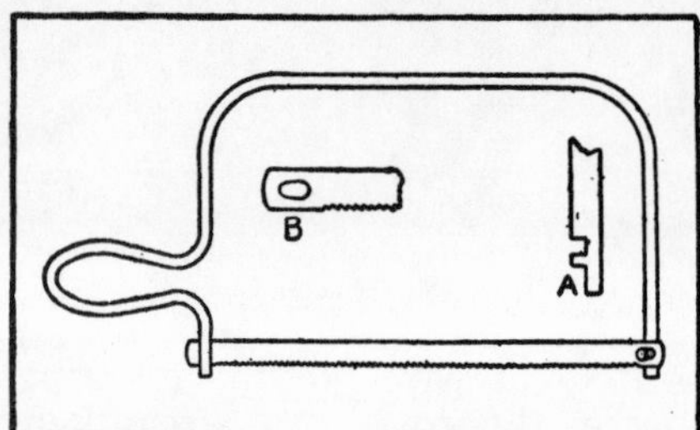

Hacksaw Frame and Blade

spring or a clock spring will do nicely. Heat the spring enough to take some of the temper out of it, in order to drill the holes in the ends, as shown, and file in the teeth. Make the blade 12 in. long, with 10 teeth to the inch. A and B show how the blade fits on the frame. —Contributed by Willard J. Hays, Summitville, Ohio.

How to Make a Cannon

A cannon like the one in the cut may be made from a piece of 1-in. hydraulic pipe, A, with a steel sleeve, B, and a long thread plug, C. Be sure to get hydraulic pipe, or double extra heavy, as it is sometimes called, as common gas pipe is entirely too light for this purpose. Don't have the pipe too long or the cannon will not make as much

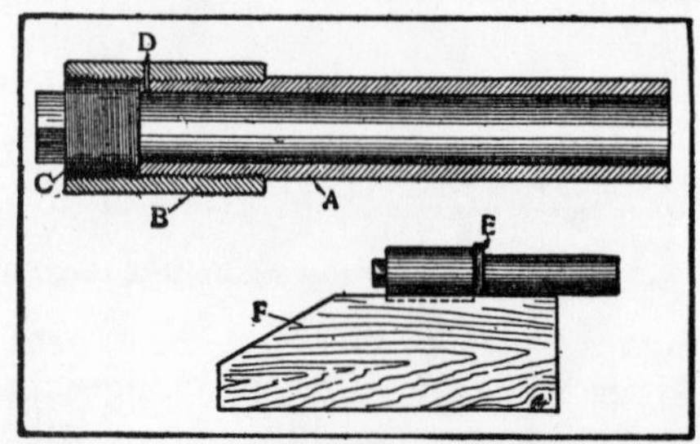

Toy Cannon

noise. Seven or eight inches is about the right length for a 1-in. bore. Screw the plug and pipe up tightly and then drill a 1/16-in. fuse hole at D.

If desired the cannon may be mounted on a block of wood, F, by means of a U-bolt or large staple, E. —Contributed by Carson Birkhead, Moorhead, Miss.

Controller for a Small Motor

An easy way of making a controlling and reversing device for small motors is as follows:

Cut a piece of wood (A) about 6 in. by 4½ in., and ¼ in. thick, and another piece (B) 6 in. by 1 in., and ¼ in. thick. Drive a nail through this near the center for a pivot (C). To the under side of one end nail a copper brush (D) to extend out about an inch. On the upper side, at the same end, nail another brush (E) so that it projects at both sides and is bent down to the level of the end brush. Then on the board put

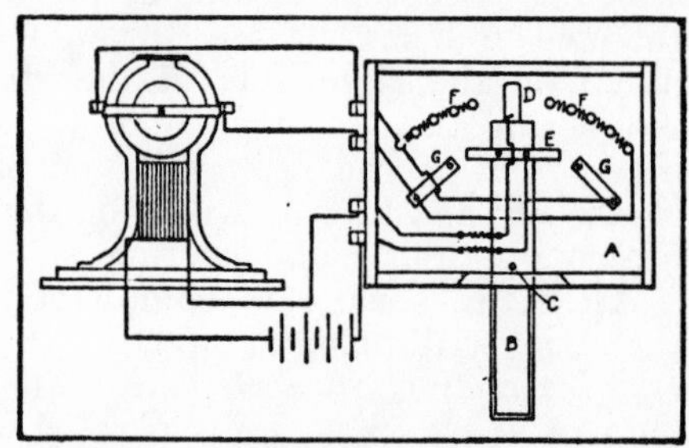

Reverse for Motor

a semi-circle of brass-headed tacks as shown at F, leaving a small space at the middle and placing five tacks on either side, so that the end brush will come in contact with each one. Connect these tacks on the under side of the board with coils of German-silver wire, using about 8 in. of wire to each coil. Fix these by soldering or bending over the ends of the tacks. Then nail two strips of copper (G) in such position that the side brush will remain on the one as long as the end brush remains on the tacks on that side.

Put sides about 1½ in. high around this apparatus, raising the board a little from the bottom to allow room for the coil. A lid may be added if desired. Connect up as shown.—Contributed by Chas. H. Boyd. Philadelphia.

How to Make a Simple Water Rheostat

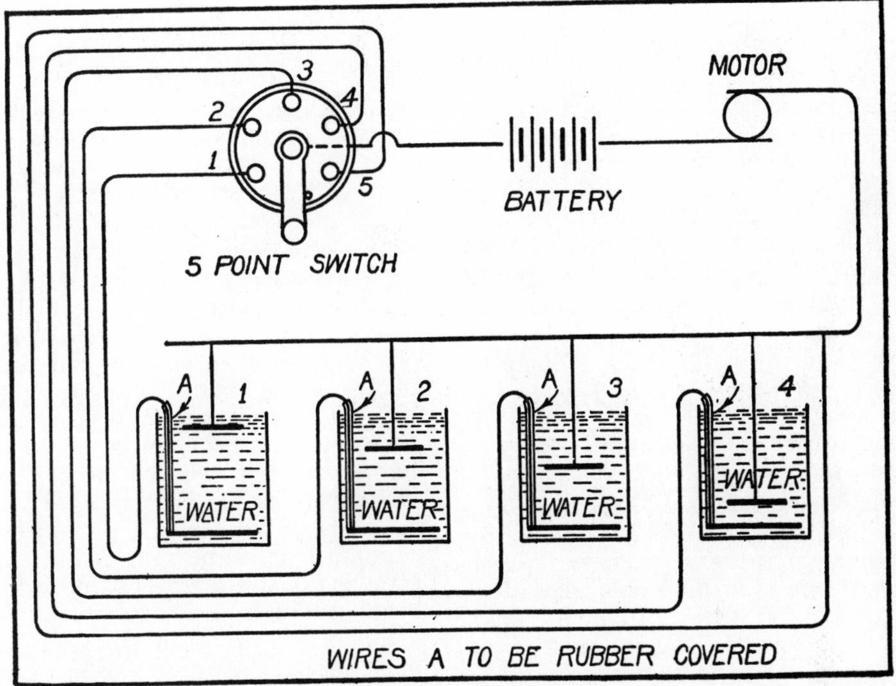

Wiring Plan for Water Rheostat

The materials necessary are: One 5-point wood-base switch, 4 jars, some sheet copper or brass for plates, about 5 ft. of rubber-covered wire, and some No. 18 gauge wire for the wiring.

The size of the jars depends on the voltage. If you are going to use a current of low tension, as from batteries, the jars need not be very large, but if you intend to use the electric-light current of 110 voltage it will be necessary to use large jars or wooden boxes made watertight, which will hold about 6 or 7 gal. Each jar to be filled with 20 parts water to 1 part sulphuric acid. Jars are set in a row in some convenient place out of the way.

Next cut out eight copper or brass disks, two for each jar. Their size also depends on the voltage. The disks that are placed in the lower part of the jars are connected with a rubber-covered wire extending a little above the top of the jar.

To wire the apparatus, refer to the sketch and you will see that jar No. 1 is connected to point No. 1 on switch; No. 2, on No. 2, and so on until all is complete and we have one remaining point on switch. Above the jars place a wire to suspend the other or top disks in the solution. This wire is also connected to one terminal on the motor and to remaining point on switch. The arm of the switch is connected to one terminal of battery, or source of current, and the other terminal connected direct to remaining terminal of motor.

Put arm of switch on point No. 1 and lower one of the top disks in jar No. 1 and make contact with wire above jars. The current then will flow through the motor. The speed for each point can be determined by lowering top disks in jars. The top disk in jar No. 2 is lower down than in No. 1 and so on for No. 3 and No. 4. The connection between point No. 5 on switch, direct to wire across jars, gives full current and full speed.

How to Build a Toboggan Sled

By A. BOETTE

The first object of the builder of a sled should be to have a "winner," both in speed and appearance. The accompanying instructions for building a sled are designed to produce these results.

The sled completed should be 15 ft. 2 in. long by 22 in. wide, with the cushion about 15 in. above the ground. For the baseboard select a pine board 15 ft. long, 11 in. wide and 2 in. thick, and plane it on all edges. Fit up the baseboard with ten oak foot-rests, 22 in. long, 3 in. wide and 3/4 in. thick. Fasten them on the under side of the baseboard at right angles to its length and 16 in. apart, beginning at the rear. At the front 24 or 26 in. will be left without cross bars for fitting on the auto front. On the upper side of the cross bars at their ends on each side screw a piece of oak 1 in. square by 14 ft. long. On the upper side of the baseboard at its edge on each side screw an oak strip 3 in. wide by 3/4 in. thick and the length of the sled from the back to the auto front. These are to keep the cushion from falling out. See Fig. 1. For the back of the sled use the upper part of a child's high chair, taking out the spindles and resetting them in the rear end of the baseboard. Cover up the outside of the spindles with a piece of galvanized iron.

The construction of the runners is shown by Figs. 2 and 3. The stock required for them is oak, two pieces 30 in. by 5 in. by 1 1/4 in., two pieces 34 in. by 5 in. by 1 1/4 in., two pieces 14 in. by 6 in. by 2 in., and four pieces 14 in. by 2 in. by 1 in. They should be put together with large screws about 3 in. long. Use no nails, as they are not substantial enough. In proportioning them the points A, B and C, Fig. 2, are important. For the front runners these measurements are: A, 30 in.; B, 4 in.; C, 15 1/2 in., and for the rear runners: A, 34 in.; B, 7 in.; C, 16 1/2 in. The screweyes indicated must be placed in a straight line and the holes for them carefully centered. A variation of 1/16 in. one way or another would cause a great deal of trouble. For the steel runners use 3/8-in. cold-rolled steel flattened at the ends for screw holes. Use no screws on the running surface, however, as they "snatch" the ice.

The mechanism of the front steering gear is shown at Fig. 3 A 3/4-in. steel rod makes a good steering rod. Flatten the steering rod at one end and sink it into the wood. Hold it in place by means of an iron plate drilled to receive the rod and screwed to block X. An iron washer, Z, is used to reduce friction; bevel block K to give a rocker motion. Equip block X with screweyes, making them clear those in the front runner, and bolt through. For the rear runner put a block with screweyes on the baseboard and run a bolt through.

Construct the auto front (Fig. 4) of 3/4-in. oak boards. The illustration shows how to shape it. Bevel it toward all sides and keep the edges sharp, as sharp edges are best suited for the brass trimmings which are to be added. When the auto front is in place enamel the sled either a dark maroon or a creamy white. First sandpaper all the wood, then apply a coat of thin enamel. Let stand for three days and apply another coat. Three coats of enamel and one of thin varnish will make a fine-looking sled. For the brass trimmings use No. 27 B. & S. sheet brass 1 in. wide on all the front edges and pieces 3 in. square on the cross bars to rest the feet against. On the door of the auto front put the monogram of the owner or owners of the sled, cutting it out of sheet brass.

For the steering-wheel procure an old freight-car "brake" wheel, brass-plated. Fasten a horn, such as used on automobiles, to the wheel.

Make the cushion of leather and stuff it with hair. The best way is to get some strong, cheap material, such as burlap, sew up one end and make in

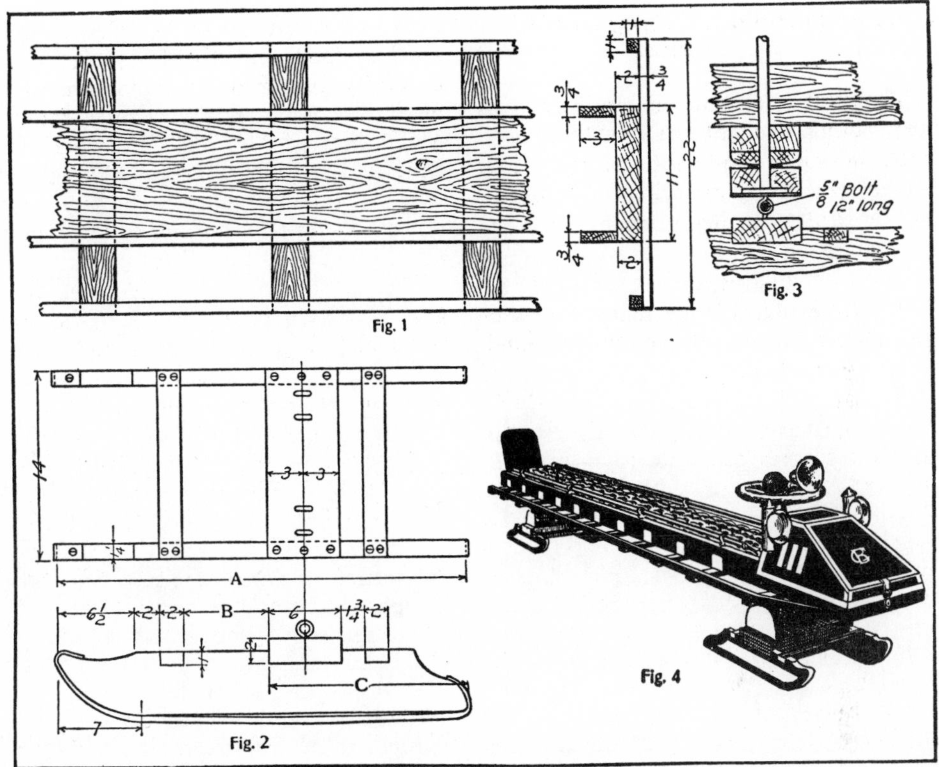

Constructing a "Winner" Toboggan Sled

the form of an oblong bag. Stuff this as tightly as possible with hair. Then get some upholstery buttons, fasten a cord through the loop, bring the cord through to the underside of the cushion, and fasten the button by slipping a nail through the knot. Then put a leather covering over the burlap, sewing it to the burlap on the under side. Make the cushion for the back in the same way. On top of the cushion supports run a brass tube to serve the double purpose of holding the cushion down and affording something to hold on to.

If desired, bicycle lamps may be fastened to the front end, to improve the appearance, and it is well to have a light of some kind at the back to avoid the danger of rear-end collisions.

The door of the auto front should be hinged and provided with a lock so that skates, parcels, overshoes, lunch, etc., may be stowed within. A silk pennant with a monogram adds to the appearance.

If desired, a brake may be added to the sled. This can be a wrought-iron lever 1½ in. by ½ in. by 30 in. long, so pivoted that moving the handle will cause the end to scrape the ice. This sled can be made without lamps and horn at a cost of about $15, or with these for $25, and the pleasure derived from it well repays the builder. If the expense is greater than one can afford, a number of boys may share in the ownership.

Burning Inscriptions on Trees

Scrape off the bark just enough to come to the first light under coating, which is somewhat moist. With a lead pencil make an outline of the inscription to be burnt on the tree and bring the rays of a large magnifying glass not quite to a fine focus on the same. The tree will be burnt along the pencil marks, and if the glass is not held in one spot too long, the inscription will be burnt in as evenly as if it had been written.—Contributed by Stewart H. Leland, Lexington, Ill.

How to Make Small Gearwheels Without a Lathe

To make small models sundry small gears and racks are required, either cut for the place or by using the parts from an old clock. With no other tools than a hacksaw, some files, a compass,

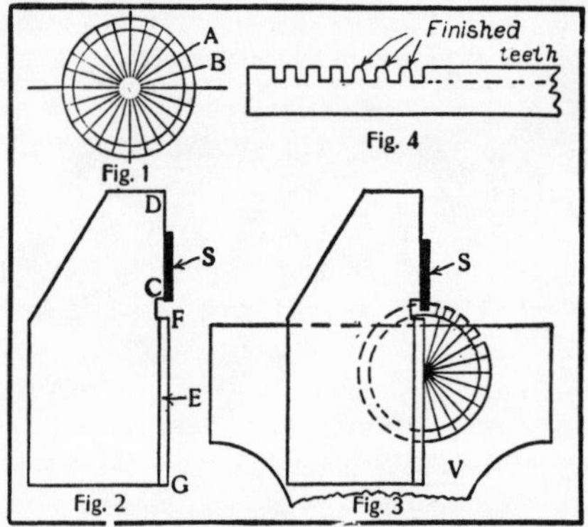

Making Model Wheels

and with the exercise of a little patience and moderate skill, very good teeth may be cut on blank wheels.

First take the case of a small gearwheel, say 1 in. outside diameter and $\frac{1}{16}$ in. thick, with twenty-four teeth. Draw a circle on paper, the same diameter as the wheel. Divide the circumference into the number of parts desired, by drawing diameters, Fig. 1. The distance AB will be approximately the pitch. Now describe a smaller circle for the base of the teeth and halfway between these circles may be taken as the pitch circle.

Now describe a circle the same size as the largest circle on a piece of $\frac{1}{16}$-in. sheet metal, and having cut it out and filed it up to this circle, fasten the marked-out paper circle accurately over it with glue. Saw-cuts can now be made down the diameters to the smaller circle with the aid of a saw guide, Fig. 2, made from $\frac{1}{16}$-in. mild steel or iron. This guide should have a beveled edge, E, from F to G, to lay along the line on which the saw-cut is to be made. The straight-edge, CD, should be set back one-half the thickness of the saw-blades, so that the center of the blade, when flat against it, will be over the line FG. A small clearance space, FC, must be made to allow the teeth of the saw to pass.

The guide should then be placed along one of the diameters and held in position until gripped in the vise, Fig. 3. The first tooth may now be cut, care being taken to keep the blade of the saw flat up to the guiding edge. The Model Engineer, London, says if this is done and the saw-guide well made, the cut will be central on the line, and if the marking-out is correct the teeth will be quite uniform all the way round. A small ward file will be needed to finish off the teeth to their proper shape and thickness.

In making a worm wheel the cuts must be taken in a sloping direction, the slope and pitch depending on the slope and pitch of the worm thread, which, though more difficult, may also be cut with a hacksaw and file.

A bevel wheel should be cut in the same manner as the spur wheel, but the cut should be deeper on the side which has the larger diameter. To cut a rack the pitch should be marked along the side, and the guide and saw used as before (Fig. 4).

How to Make Four Pictures on One Plate

Secure two extra slides for the plateholders and cut one corner out on one

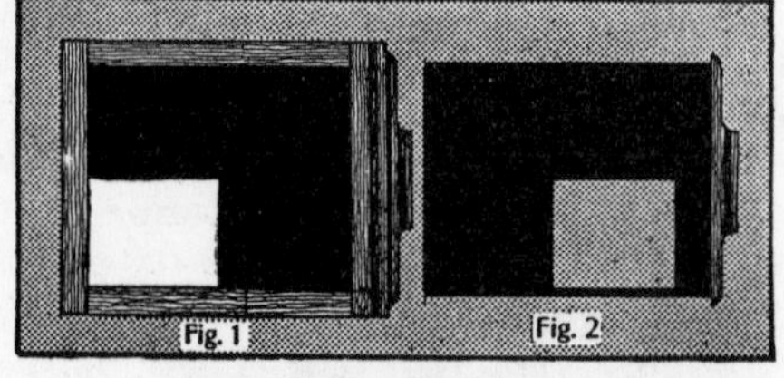

Four Photos on One Plate

of them, as shown in Fig. 1. Make a hole in the other, as shown in Fig. 2. With a lead pencil draw on the ground glass one line vertical and one horizontal, each in the center. This will divide the ground glass into four equal parts.

Focus the camera in the usual manner, but get the picture desired to fill only one of the parts on the ground glass. Place the plate-holder in position and draw the regular slide; substitute one of the slides prepared and expose in the usual way.

If a small picture is to be made in the lower left-hand corner of the plate, place the prepared slide with the corner cut, as shown in Fig. 1. The slide may be turned over for the upper left-hand corner and then changed for slide shown in Fig. 2 for the upper and lower right-hand corners.

Electric Blue-Light Experiment

Take a jump-spark coil and connect it up with a battery and start the vibrator. Then take one outlet wire, R, and connect to one side of a 2-cp. electric lamp, and the other outlet wire, B, hold in one hand, and press all fingers of the other hand on globe at point A. A bright, blue light will come from the wires in the lamp to the surface of the globe where the fingers touch. No shock will be perceptible.

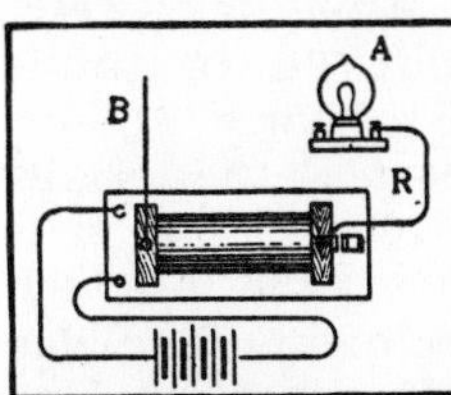

Interesting Electrical Experiment

The materials necessary for performing this experiment are: Telephone receiver, transmitter, some wire and some carbons, either the pencils for arc lamps, or ones taken from old dry batteries will do.

Run a line from the inside of the house to the inside of some other building and fasten it to one terminal of the receiver. To the other terminal fasten another piece of wire and ground it on the water faucet in the house. If there is no faucet in the house, ground it with a large piece of zinc.

Fasten the other end to one terminal of the transmitter and from the other terminal of the same run a wire into the ground. The ground here should consist either of a large piece of carbon,

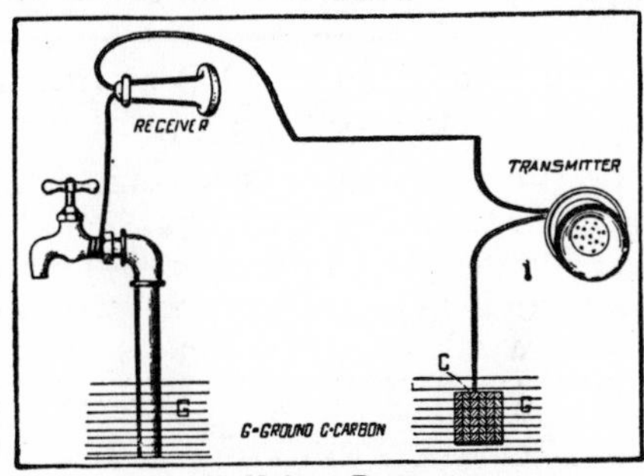

A Unique Battery

or several pieces bound tightly together.

If a person speak into the transmitter, one at the receiver can hear what is said, even though there are no batteries in the circuit. It is a well-known fact that two telephone receivers connected up in this way will transmit words between two persons, for the voice vibrating the diaphragm causes an inductive current to flow and the other receiver copies these vibrations. But in this experiment, a transmitter which induces no current is used. Do the carbon and the zinc and the moist earth form a battery?—Contributed by Wm. J. Slattery, Emsworth, Pa.

A Cheap Fire Alarm

An electrical device for the barn that will give an alarm in case of fire is shown in the accompanying diagram. A is a wooden block, which is fastened under the loft at a gable end of the barn; B is an iron weight attached to the string C, and this string passes up through the barn to the roof, then over a hook or pulley and across the barn, under the gable, and is fastened to the opposite end of the barn.

D D are binding posts for electric wires. They have screw ends, as shown, by which means they are fastened to the wooden block A. They also hold the brass piece E and the strip of spring brass F in place against the wooden block. G is a leather strap fastened to the weight B and the spring F connected to the latter by a small sink bolt.

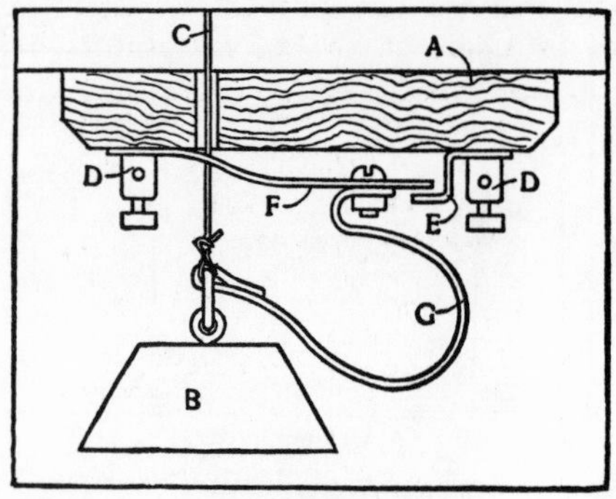

Electric Fire Alarm

At the house an electric bell is placed wherever convenient. Several battery cells, of course, are also needed. Dry batteries are most convenient. The battery cells and bell are connected in the usual manner, and one wire from the bell and one from the battery are strung to the barn and connected to the binding posts D D.

If a fire occurs in the hay-mow the blaze will generally shoot toward the gable soon after it starts, and will then burn the string C, which allows the weight B to fall and pull the brass spring against the iron piece E, which closes the circuit and rings the bell in the house.

If desired, the string may be stretched back and forth under the roof several times or drawn through any place that is in danger of fire.—Contributed by Geo. B. Wrenn, Ashland, Ohio.

How to Make a Small Electric Furnace

Take a block of wood and shape into a core. One like a loaf of bread, and about that size, serves admirably. Wrap a layer of asbestos around it and cover this with a thin layer of plaster-of-paris. When the plaster is nearly dry wind a coil of No. 36 wire around it, taking care that the wire does not touch itself anywhere. Put another course of plaster-of-paris on this, and again wind the wire around it. Continue the process of alternate layers of plaster and wire until 500 ft. or more of the latter has been used, leaving about 10 in. at each end for terminals. Then set the whole core away to dry.

For a base use a pine board 10 in. by 12 in. by 1 in. Bore four holes at one end for binding-posts, as indicated by E E. Connect the holes in pairs by ordinary house fuse wire. At one side secure two receptacles, B B, and one single post switch, C. Place another switch at I and another binding-post at F. The oven is now ready to be connected.

Withdraw the wooden core from the coils of wire and secure the latter by bands of tin to the board. Connect the ends of the wire to binding-posts E and F, as shown. From the other set of binding-posts, E, run a No. 12 or No. 14 wire, connecting lamp receptacles, B B, and switch, C, in parallel. Connect these three to switch, D, in series with binding-post, F, the terminal of the coil. Place 16-cp. lights in the receptacles and connect the fuses with a 110-volt lighting circuit. The apparatus is now ready for operation. Turn on switch, D, and the lamps, while C is open. The coil will commence to become warm, soon drying out the plaster-of-paris. To obtain more heat open one lamp, and to obtain still more open the other and close switch C.—Contributed by Eugene Tuttles, Jr., Newark, Ohio.

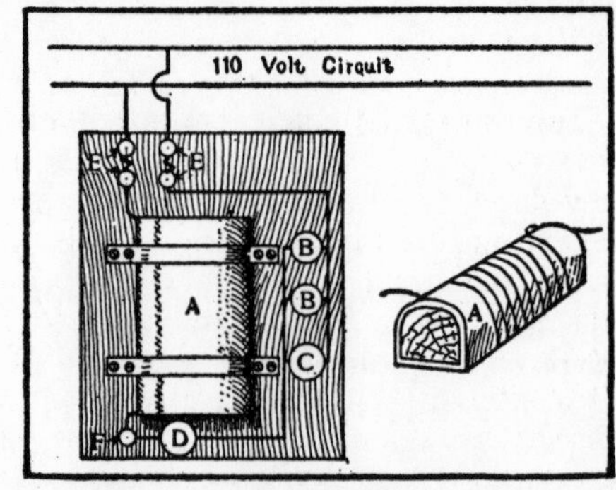

Electric Furnace

How to Make an Ammeter

Every amateur mechanic who performs electrical experiments will find use for an ammeter, and for the benefit of those who wish to construct such an instrument the following description is given: The operative principle of this instrument is the same as that of a galvanometer, except that its working position is not confined to the magnetic meridian. This is accomplished by making the needle revolve in a vertical instead of a horizontal plane. The only adjustment necessary is that of leveling, which is accomplished by turning the thumbscrew shown at A, Fig. 1, until the hand points to zero on the scale.

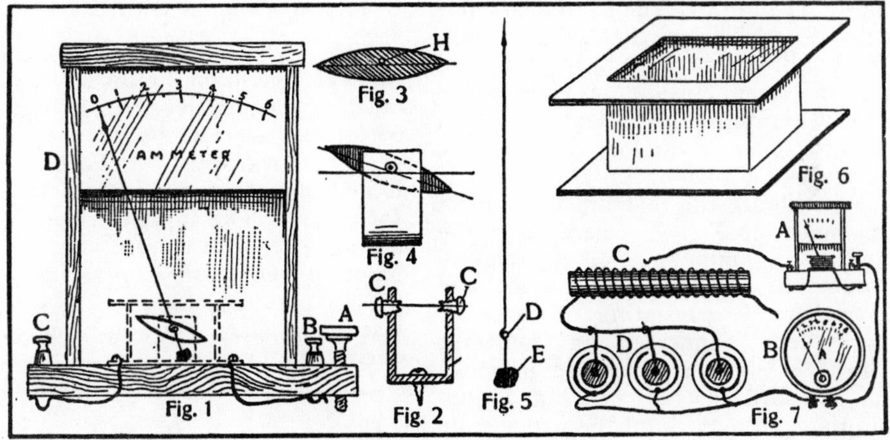

Complete Ammeter and Details

First make a support, Fig. 2, by bending a piece of sheet brass to the shape indicated and tapping for the screws CC. These should have hollow ends, as shown, for the purpose of receiving the pivoted axle which supports the hand. The core, Fig. 3, is made of iron. It is 1 in. long, 1/4 in. wide and 1/8 in. thick. At a point a little above the center, drill a hole as shown at H, and through this hole drive a piece of knitting-needle about 1/2 in. long, or long enough to reach between the two screws shown in Fig. 2. The ends of this small axle should be ground pointed and should turn easily in the cavities, as the sensitiveness of the instrument depends on the ease with which this axle turns.

After assembling the core as shown in Fig. 4, it should be filed a little at one end until it assumes the position indicated. The pointer or hand, Fig. 5, is made of wire, aluminum being preferable for this purpose, although copper or steel will do. Make the wire 4 1/2 in. long and make a loop, D, 1/2 in. from the lower end. Solder to the short end a piece of brass, E, of such weight that it will exactly balance the weight of the hand. This is slipped on the pivot, and the whole thing is again placed in position in the support. If the pointer is correctly balanced it should take the position shown in Fig. 1, but if it is not exactly right a little filing will bring it near enough so that it may be corrected by the adjusting-screw.

Next make a brass frame as shown in Fig. 6. This may be made of wood, although brass is better, as the eddy currents set up in a conductor surrounding a magnet tend to stop oscillation of the magnet. (The core is magnetized when a current flows through the instrument.) The brass frame is wound with magnet wire, the size depending on the number of amperes to be measured. Mine is wound with two layers of No. 14 wire, 10 turns to each layer, and is about right for ordinary experimental purposes. The ends of the wire are fastened to the binding posts B and C, Fig. 1.

A wooden box, D, is then made and provided with a glass front. A piece of paper is pasted on a piece of wood, which is then fastened in the box in such a position that the hand or pointer will lie close to the paper scale. The box is 5½ in. high, 4 in. wide and 1¾ in. deep, inside measurements. After everything is assembled put a drop of solder on the loop at D, Fig. 5, to prevent it turning on the axle.

To calibrate the instrument connect as shown in Fig. 7, where A is the homemade ammeter; B, a standard ammeter; C, a variable resistance, and D, a battery, consisting of three or more cells connected in multiple. Throw in enough resistance to make the standard instrument read 1 ohm and then put a mark on the paper scale of the instrument to be calibrated. Continue in this way with 2 amperes, 3 amperes, 4 amperes, etc., until the scale is full. To make a voltmeter out of this instrument, wind with plenty of No. 36 magnet wire instead of No. 14, or if it is desired to make an instrument for measuring both volts and amperes, use both windings and connect to two pairs of binding posts.—Contributed by J. E. Dussault, Montreal.

How to Make a Three-Way Cock for Small Model-Work

In making models of machines it is often necessary to contrive some method for a 3- or 4-way valve or cock. To make one, secure a pet cock and drill and tap hole through, as shown in the cut. If for 3-way, drill in only to the opening already through, but if for a 4-way, drill through the entire case and valve. Be sure to have valve B turned so as to drill at right angles to the opening through it. After drilling, remove the valve, take off the burr with a piece of emery paper and replace ready for work.

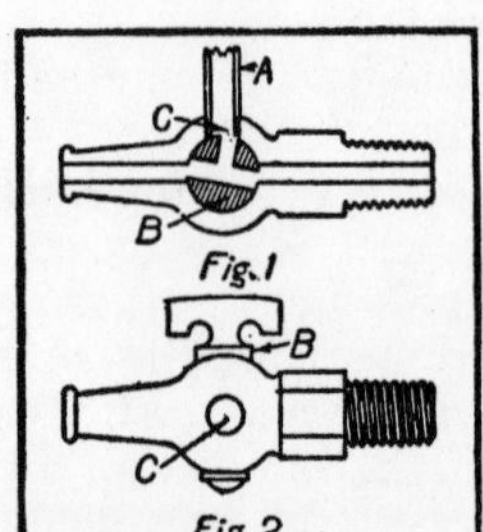

Easy Experiments with Electric-Light Circuit

An electric-light circuit will be found much less expensive than batteries for performing electrical experiments. The sketch shows how a small arc light and motor may be connected to the light socket, A. The light is removed and a plug with wire connections is put in its place. One wire runs to the switch, B, and the other connects with the water rheostat, which is used for reducing the current.

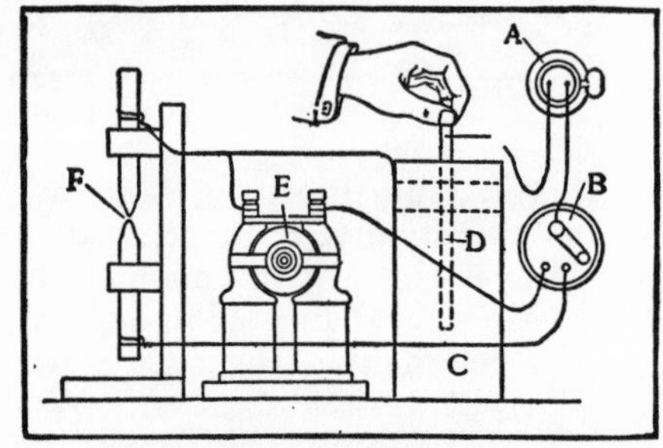

Arc-Light Motor and Water Rheostat

A tin can, C, is filled nearly to the top with salt water, and a metal rod, D, is passed through a piece of wood fastened at the top of the can. When the metal rod is lowered the current increases, and as it is withdrawn the current grows weaker. In this way the desired amount of current can be obtained.

By connecting the motor, E, and the arc light, F, as shown, either one may be operated by turning switch B to the corresponding point. The arc light is easily made by fastening two electric-light carbons in a wooden frame like that shown. To start the light, turn the current on strong and bring the points of the carbons together; then separate slightly by twisting the upper carbon and at the same time drawing it through the hole.

How to Make an Interrupter

The Wenult interrupter is an instrument much used on large coils and is far more efficient than the usual form of vibrators. It can also be used with success on small coils as well as large. Although it is a costly instrument to purchase, it can be made with practically no expense and the construction is very simple.

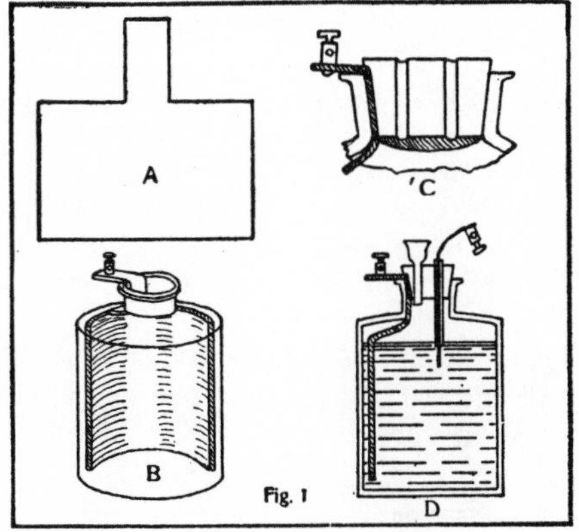

Details of Interrupter

First procure a wide-mouthed bottle about 4 in. high, provided with a rubber stopper. This stopper should be pierced, making two holes about ¼ in. in diameter.

From a sheet of lead $\frac{1}{16}$ in. in thickness cut a piece shaped like A, Fig. 1. Common tea lead folded several times will serve the purpose. When in the bottle this lead should be of such a size that it will only reach half way around, as shown in B. To insert the lead plate, roll it up so it will pass through the neck of the bottle, then smooth it out with a small stick until it fits against the side, leaving the small strip at the top projecting through the neck of the bottle. Bend this strip to one side and fit in the stopper, as shown in C. A small binding-post is fastened at the end of the strip.

Having fixed the lead plate in position, next get a piece of glass tube having a bore of about 1/32 of an inch in diameter. A piece of an old thermometer tube will serve this purpose. Insert this tube in the hole in the stopper farthest from the lead plate. Get a piece of wire that will fit the tube and about 6 in. long, and fasten a small binding-post on one end and stick the other into the tube. This wire should fit the hole in the tube so it can be easily moved. In the hole nearest the lead plate insert a small glass funnel.

The interrupter as it is when complete is shown at D, Fig. 1. Having finished the interrupter, connect it with the electric-light circuit as shown in Fig. 2. Fill the bottle with water to about the line as shown in D, Fig. 1. Adjust the wire in the small glass tube so that it projects about ⅛ in. Add sulphuric acid until the water level rises about $\frac{1}{16}$ in. Turn on the current and press the button, B. If all adjustments are correct, there will be a loud crackling noise from the interrupter, a violet flame will appear at the end of the wire and a hot spark will pass between the secondary terminals. If the interrupter does not work at first, add more sulphuric acid through the funnel and press the wire down a

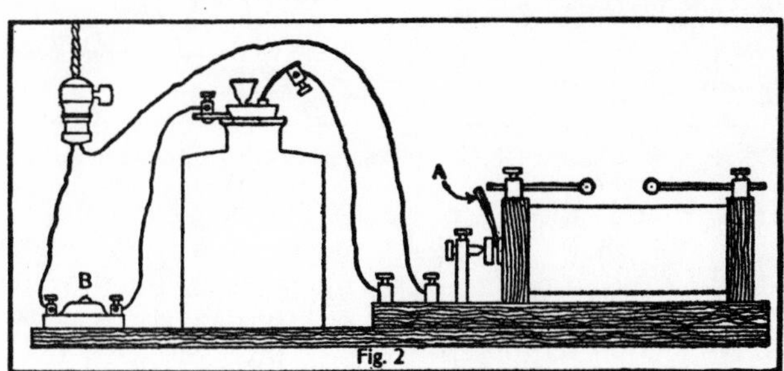

The Completed Instrument

little more into the liquid. A piece of wood, A, Fig. 2, should be inserted in vibrator to prevent it from working.—Contributed by Harold L. Jones, Carthage, N. Y.

A Miniature "Pepper's Ghost" Illusion

Probably many readers have seen a "Pepper's Ghost" illusion at some amusement place. As there shown, the audience is generally seated in a dark room at the end of which there is a stage with black hangings. One of the audience is invited onto the stage, where he is placed in an upright open coffin. A white shroud is thrown over his body, and his clothes and flesh gradually fade away till nothing but his skeleton remains, which immediately begins to dance a horrible rattling jig. The skeleton then fades away and the man is restored again.

A simple explanation is given in the Model Engineer. Between the audience and the coffin is a sheet of transparent glass, inclined at an angle so as to reflect objects located behind the scenes, but so clear as to be invisible to the audience and the man in the coffin. At the beginning the stage is lighted only from behind the glass. Hence the coffin and its occupant are seen through the glass very plainly. The lights in front of the glass (behind the scenes) are now raised very gradually as those behind the glass are turned down, until it is dark there. The perfectly black surface behind the glass now acts like the silver backing for a mirror, and the object upon which the light is now turned—in this case the skeleton—is reflected in the glass, appearing to the audience as if really occupying the stage.

The model, which requires no special skill except that of carpentry, is constructed as shown in the drawings.

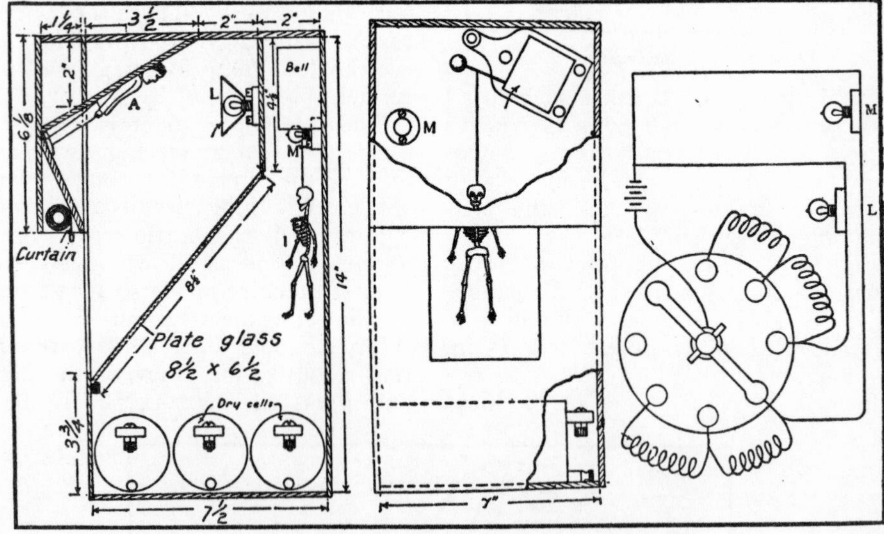

Construction of the "Pepper's Ghost" Illusion

The box containing the stage should be 14 in. by 7 in. by 7½ in., inside dimensions. The box need not be made of particularly good wood, as the entire interior, with the exception of the glass, figures and lights, should be colored a dull black. This can well be done by painting with a solution of lampblack in turpentine. If everything is not black, especially the joints and background near A, the illusion will be spoiled.

The glass should be the clearest possible, and must be thoroughly cleansed. Its edges should nowhere be visible, and it should be free from scratches and imperfections. The figure A should be a doll about 4 in. high, dressed in brilliant, light-colored garments. The skeleton is made of papier maché, and can be bought at Japanese stores. It should preferably be one with arms suspended by small spiral springs, giving a limp, loose-jointed effect. The method of causing the skeleton to dance is shown in the front view. The figure is hung from the neck by a blackened stiff wire attached to the hammer wire of an electric bell, from which the gong has been removed. When the bell works he will kick against the rear wall, and wave his arms up and down, thus giving as realistic a dance as anyone could expect from a skeleton.

The lights, L and M, should be miniature electric lamps, which can be run by three dry cells. They need to give a fairly strong light, especially L, which should have a conical tin reflector to increase its brilliancy and prevent its being reflected in the glass.

Since the stage should be some distance from the audience, to aid the illusion, the angle of the glass and the inclination of the doll, A, has been so designed that if the stage is placed on a mantle or other high shelf, the image of A will appear upright to an observer sitting in a chair some distance away, within the limits of an ordinary room. If it is desired to place the box lower down, other angles for the image and glass may be found necessary, but the proper tilt can be found readily by experiment.

The electric connections are so simple that they are not shown in the drawings. All that is necessary is a two-point switch, by which either L or M can be placed in circuit with the battery, and a press button in circuit with the bell and its cell.

If a gradual transformation is desired, a double-pointed rheostat could be used, so that as one light dims the other increases in brilliancy, by the insertion and removal of resistance coils.

With a clear glass and a dark room this model has proved to be fully as bewildering as its prototype.

Experiment with Colored Electric Lamps

To many the following experiment may be much more easily performed than explained: Place the hand or other object in the light coming from two incandescent lamps, one red and

Two-Colored Hand

one white, placed about a foot apart, and allow the shadow to fall on a white screen such as a table-cloth. Portions of the shadow will then appear to be a bright green. A similar experiment consists in first turning on the red light for about a minute and then turning it off at the same time that the white one is turned on. The entire screen will then appear to be a vivid green for about one second, after which it assumes its normal color.

To Explode Powder with Electricity

A 1-in. hole was bored in the center of a 2-in. square block. Two finishing-nails were driven in, as shown in the sketch. These were connected to terminals of an induction coil. After everything was ready the powder was poured in the hole and a board weighted with rocks placed over the block. When the button is pressed

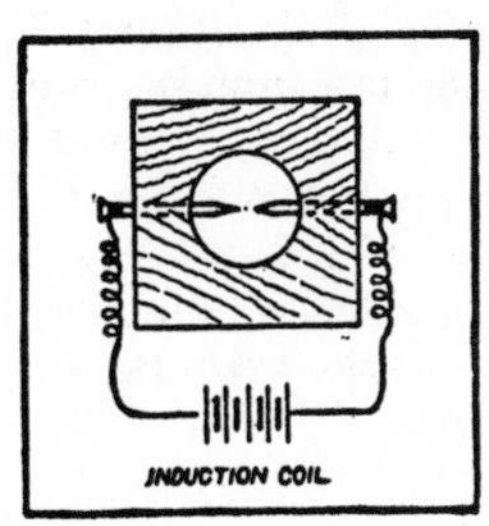

or the circuit closed in some other way the discharge occurs. The distance between the nail points—which must be bright and clean—should be just enough to give a good, fat spark.—Contributed by Geo. W. Fry, San Jose, Cal.

Simple Wireless System

The illustrations will make plain a simple and inexpensive apparatus for wireless telegraphy by which I have had no difficulty in sending messages across 1½ miles of water surface. It is so simple that the cuts scarcely need explanation. In Fig. 1 is seen the sending apparatus, consisting of a 40-cell battery connected with two copper plates 36 by 36 by ⅛ in. The plates are separated 6 in. by a piece of hard rubber at each end.

In Fig. 2 are seen duplicates of these insulated plates, connected with an ordinary telephone receiver. With this receiver I can hear distinctly the electric signals made by closing and opening the Morse key in Fig. 1, and I believe that in a short time I shall be able to perfect this system so as to send wireless messages over long distances.—Contributed by Dudley H. Cohen, New York.

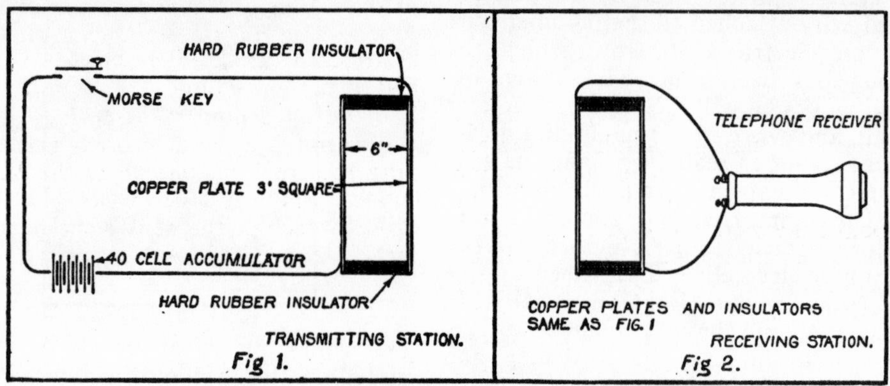

Simple Wireless System

ℭTo prevent water colors from crawling, add a few drops of ammonia or lime water, or a solution of sal soda.

Small Electrical Hydrogen Generator

A small hydrogen generator may be made from a fruit jar, A (see sketch), with two tubes, B and C, soldered in the top. The plates E can be made of tin or galvanized iron, and should be separated about ⅛ in. by small pieces of wood. One of these plates is connected to metal top, and the wire from the other passes through the tube B, which is filled with melted rosin or wax, to make it airtight. This wire connects to one side of a battery of two cells, the other wire being soldered to the metal top of the jar, as shown. The jar is partly filled with a very dilute solution of sulphuric acid, about 1 part of acid to 20 of water.

When the current of electricity passes between the plates E, hydrogen gas is generated, which rises and passes through the rubber hose D, into the receiver G. This is a wide-mouth bottle, which is filled with water and inverted over a pan of water, F. The gas

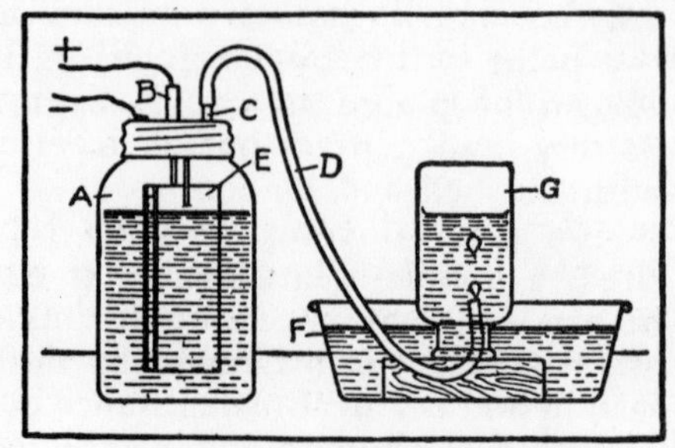

Hydrogen Generator

bubbling up displaces the water and fills the bottle.

If the receiver is removed when half full of gas, the remaining space will be filled with air, which will mix with the gas and form an explosive mixture. If a lighted match is then held near the mouth of the bottle a sharp report will be heard.

If the bottle is fitted with a cork containing two wires nearly touching, and the apparatus connected with an induction coil, in such a manner that a spark will be produced inside the bottle, the explosion will blow out the cork or possibly break the bottle. Caution should be used to avoid being struck by pieces of flying glass if this experiment is tried, and under no condition should a lighted match or spark be brought near the end of the rubber hose D, as the presence of a little air in the generator will make an explosive mixture which would probably break the jar.

Gasoline Burner for Model Work

When making a small model traction engine or a locomotive the question arises, "What shall the fuel be?" If you have decided to use gasoline, then a suitable burner is necessary. A piece of brass tubing about 3 in. in diameter and 6 in. long with caps screwed on both ends and fitted with a filling plug and a bicycle valve makes a good gasoline supply tank, says the Model Engineer, London. The bicycle valve is used to give the tank an air pressure which forces the gasoline to the burner.

The burner is made from a piece of brass tube, A, as is shown in the illustration, ½ in. in diameter and 2½ in. long, which is plugged up at both ends, one end being drilled and reamed out to $\frac{5}{16}$ in. Three rows of holes $\frac{1}{16}$ in. in diameter are drilled in the brass tube. One row is drilled to come directly on top, and the other two at about 45° from the vertical. It is then fitted to a sheet-steel base, B, by means of the clips, C C, Fig. 1. A piece of ⅛-in. copper pipe, P, is then coiled around the brass tube, A, which forms the vaporizing coil. This coil should have a diameter

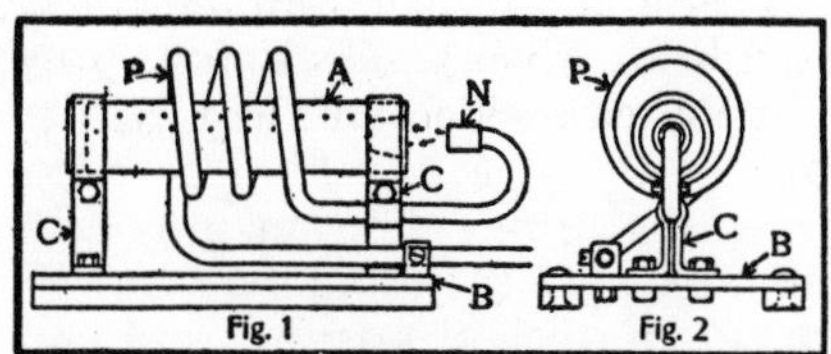

Gasoline Burner

of only 1 in. One end of the copper tube is bent around so it will point directly into the reamed-out hole in the end of the brass tube, A. A nipple, N, is made by drilling a ⅛-in. hole halfway through a piece of brass and tapping to screw on the end of the ⅛-in. copper pipe. A 1/64-in. hole is then drilled through the remaining part of the nipple. The other end of the copper tube is connected to the supply tank. The distance between the nipple, N, and the ends of the tube, A, should be only $\frac{5}{16}$ of an inch. Fig. 2 shows the end view.

A Homemade Telephone Receiver

A telephone receiver that will do good work may be built very cheaply as follows: For the case use an ordinary ½-lb. baking-powder box with a

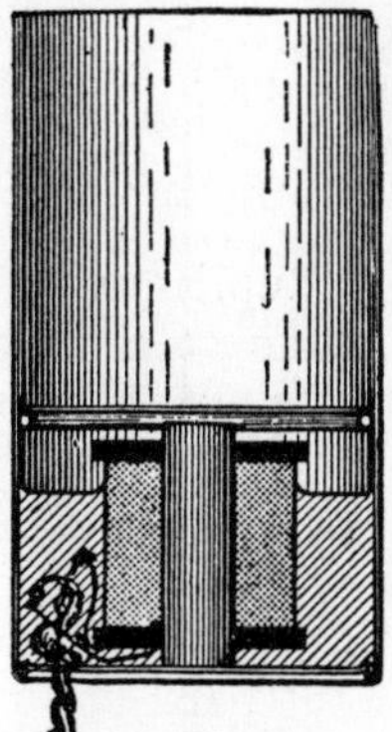

piece of heavy wire soldered on the inside, $1\frac{5}{16}$ in. from the bottom. For the magnet use a piece of round hardened steel about ⅜ in. in diameter and 1¼ in. long. If desired, a piece of an old round file may be used for the magnet core, which should be magnetized previous to assembling, either by passing a current of electricity around it, or by direct contact with another magnet. The steel core should be wound with about 250 ft. of No. 36 insulated wire, the ends of which should be soldered to a piece of lamp cord, passed through a hole in the bottom of the can and knotted inside to prevent pulling out.

A disk of thin sheet-iron, such as is used by photographers for tintypes (Ferrotype), should be cut to the diameter of the can, taking care not to bend the iron. The magnet should then be placed in the bottom of the can in an upright position and enough of a melted mixture of beeswax and resin poured in to hold it in position.

While the wax is still in a plastic condition the magnet should be located centrally and adjusted so that the end will be $\frac{1}{16}$ in. or less below the level of the top of the copper ring.

After the wax has hardened the disk is slipped in and fastened tightly by a ring of solder when the instrument is ready for use.

How to Bind Magazines

An easy way to bind Popular Mechanics in volumes of six months each is to arrange the magazines in order and tie them securely both ways with a strong cord. It is well to put two or three sheets of tough white paper, cut to the size of the pages, at the front and back for fly leaves.

Clamp the whole in a vise or clamp with two strips of wood even with the back edges of the magazines. With a sharp saw cut a slit in the magazines and wood strips about ½ in. deep and slanting as shown at A and B, Fig. 1. Take two strips of stout cloth, about 8 or 10 in. long and as wide as the distance between the bottoms of the sawed slits. Lay these over the back edge of the pack and tie securely through the slits with a string thread—wrapping and tying several times (C, Fig. 2).

If you have access to a printer's paper knife, trim both ends and the front edge; this makes a much nicer book, but if the paper knife cannot be used, clamp the whole between two boards and saw off the edges, boards and all, smoothly, with a fine saw.

Cut four pieces of cardboard, ¼ in. longer and ¼ in. narrower than the magazines after they have been trimmed. Lay one piece of the board on the book and under the cloth strips. Use ordinary flour paste and paste the strips to the cardboard and then rub paste all over the top of the strips and the board. Rub paste over one side of another piece of board and put it on top of the first board and strips, pressing down firmly so that the strips are held securely between the two boards. Turn the book over and do the same with the other two boards.

After the paste has dried a few minutes take a piece of strong cloth, duck or linen, fold and cut it 1 in. larger all around than the book, leaving the folded edge uncut. Rub paste over one of the board backs and lay one end of the cloth on it, smoothing and creasing as shown at A, Fig. 3. Turn the book over and paste the other side. The back edges should have a good coat of paste and a strip of paper

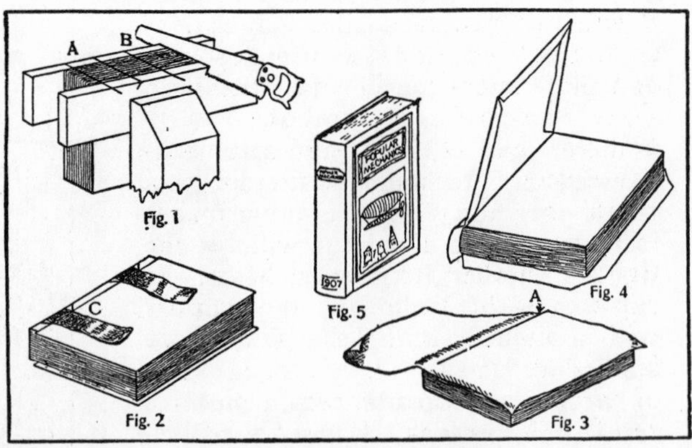

Process of Homemade Binding

the width of the thickness of the pack pasted on before pasting the cloth to the second board back.

Cut off the corners and fold over the edges of the cloth, pasting them down (Fig. 4). Rub paste on one side of a fly leaf and press the back down on it. Turn the book over and paste a fly leaf to the other back after the edges of the cloth have been folded down. The backs must not be opened until the fly leaves are thoroughly dry. Trim and tuck in the ends of the strip at the back edge.

When fixed this way your magazines make one of the most valuable volumes you can possibly add to your library of mechanical books.—Contributed by Joseph N. Parker, Bedford City, Va.

A Homemade Acetylene-Gas Generator

A simple acetylene-gas generator used by myself for several years when out on camping trips was made of a galvanized-iron tank, without a head, 18 in. in diameter and 30 in. deep, B, as shown in the sketch. Another tank, A, is made the same depth as B, but its diameter is a little smaller, so that inverted it will just slip easily into the tank B. In the bottom, or rather the top now, of tank A is cut a hole, and a little can, D, is fitted in it and soldered. On top and over can D is soldered a large tin can screw. A rubber washer is fitted on this so that when the screw top, E, is turned on it, the joint will be gas-tight. Another can, C, which will just slip inside the little can, is perforated with a number of holes. This can C is filled about half full of broken pieces of carbide and then placed in the little can D. A gas cock, H, is soldered onto tank A, as shown, from which the gas may be taken through a rubber tube. Fill tank B with water and set tank A into it. This will cause some air to be inclosed, which can be released by leaving the cock open until tank A settles down to the point where the water will begin to run in the perforations of the little tank. The water then comes in contact with the carbide and forms gas, which expands and stops the lowering of tank A. Then the cock must be closed and tubing attached. It is dangerous to attempt to strike a match to light a jet or the end of the cock while air is escaping and just as the first gas is being made. Wait until the tank is well raised up before doing this.—Contributed by James E. Noble, Toronto, Ont.

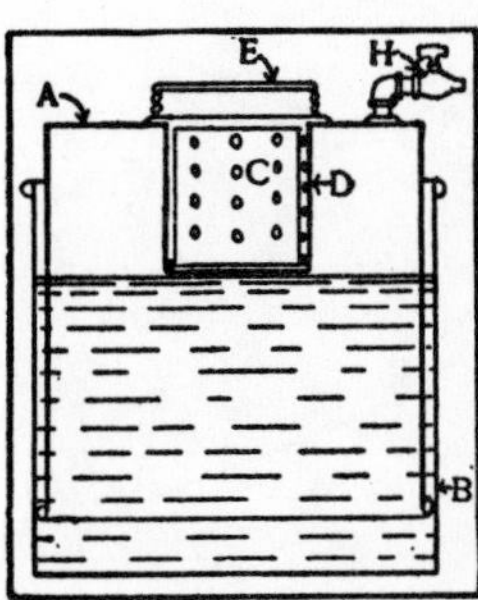

Homemade Annunciator

When one electric bell is operated from two push-buttons it is impossible to tell which of the two push-buttons is being operated unless an annunciator or similar device is used. A very simple annunciator for indicating two numbers can be made from a small box, Fig. 1, with an electric-bell magnet, A, fastened in the bottom. The armature, B, is pivoted in the center by means of a small piece of wire and has an indicator or hand, C, which moves to either right or left, depending on which half of the magnet is magnetized. If the back armature, D, of the magnet is removed the moving armature will work better, as this will prevent the magnetism from acting on both ends of the armature.

The wiring diagram, Fig. 2, shows how the connections are to be made. If the push-button A is closed, the bell will ring and the pointer will point at 1, while the closing of the push-button B will ring the bell and move the pointer to 2.—Contributed by H. S. Bott, Beverly, N. J.

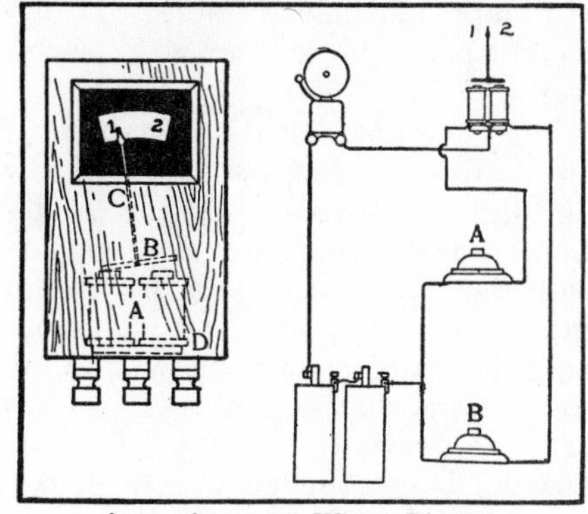

Annunciator and Wiring Diagram

How to Make a Box Kite

As some of the readers of Amateur Mechanics may desire to build a box kite, a simple method of constructing one of the modern type is given in detail as follows: The sticks should be made of straight-grained wood, which may be either spruce, basswood or white pine. The longitudinal corner spines, A A, should be 3/8 in. square by 42 in. long, and the four diagonal struts, B, should be 1/4 in. by 1/2 in., and about 26 in. long. Two cloth bands should be made to the exact dimensions given in the sketch and fastened to the four longitudinal sticks with 1-oz. tacks. It is well to mark the positions of the sticks on the cloth bands, either with a soft lead-pencil or crayon, in order to have the four sides of each band exactly equal. The ends of the bands should be lapped over at least 1/2 in. and sewed double to give extra strength, and the edges should be carefully hemmed, making the width, when finished, exactly 12 in. Probably the best cloth for this purpose is nainsook, although lonsdale cambric or light-weight percaline will answer nearly as well.

The diagonal struts, B, should be cut a little too long, so that they will be slightly bowed when put in position, thus holding the cloth out taut and flat. They should be tied together at the points of intersection and the ends should be wound with coarse harnessmaker's thread, as shown at C, to prevent splitting. The small guards, D, are nailed or glued to the longitudinal sticks to prevent the struts slipping out of position. Of course the ends of the struts could be fastened to the longitudinal strips if desired, but if made as described the kite may be readily taken apart and rolled up for convenience in carrying.

The bridle knots, E, are shown in detail at H and J. H is a square knot, which may be easily loosened and

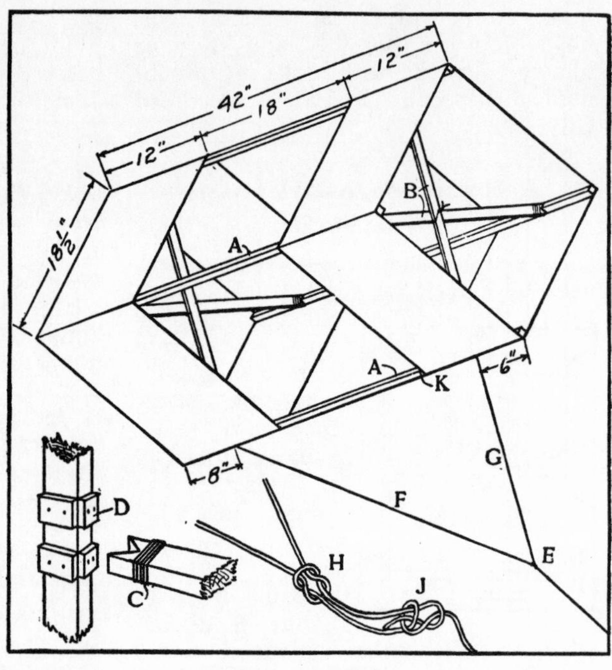

Detail of Box Kite

shifted to a different position on the bridle, thus adjusting the lengths of F and G. A bowline knot should be tied at J, as shown, to prevent slipping. If the kite is used in a light wind, loosen the square knot and shift nearer to G, thus shortening G and lengthening F, and if a strong wind is blowing, shift toward F, thereby lengthening G and making F shorter. In a very strong wind do not use the bridle, but fasten a string securely to the stick at K.—Contributed by Edw. E. Harbert, Chicago.

¶An experienced photographer uses blacklead for grooves about a camera or holder. A small quantity is rubbed well into the grooves and on the edges of shutters, that refuse to slide easily, with gratifying results. Care must be taken to allow no dust to settle in the holders, however.

Simple Open-Circuit Telegraph Line

By using the circuit shown in the sketch for short-distance telegraph lines, the extra switches and wiring found in many circuits are done away with. Closing either key will operate both sounders, and, as the resistance of

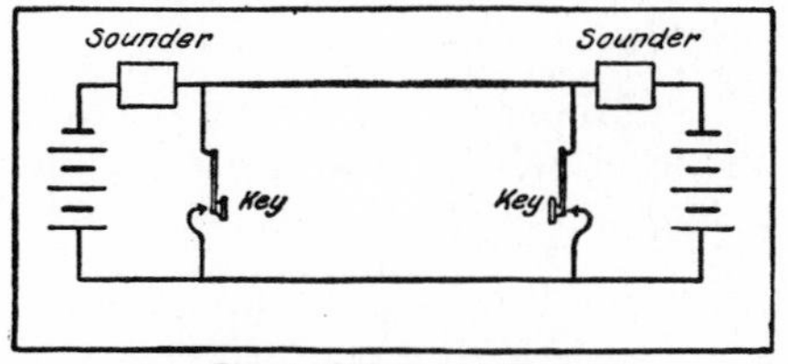

Simple Telegraph Line

the sounders is very high, the batteries do not run down for a long time.—Contributed by A. D. Stoddard, Clay Center, Kan.

How to Make a Thermo Battery

A thermo battery, for producing electricity direct from heat, can be made of a wooden frame, A, with a number of nails, B, driven in the vertical piece and connected in series with heavy copper wires, C. The connections should all be soldered to give good results, as the voltage is

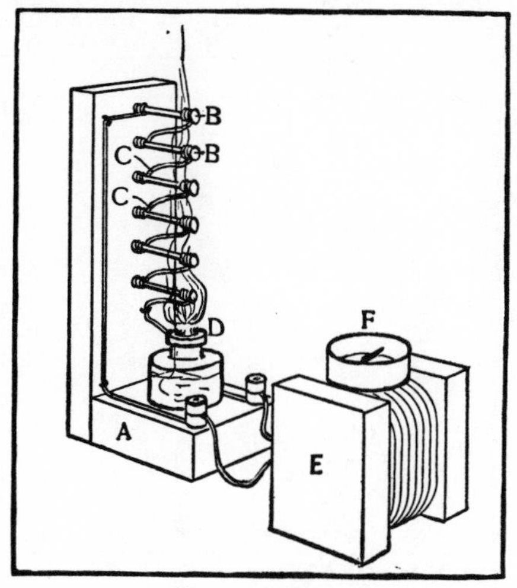

Thermo Battery

very low and the resistance of an unsoldered joint would stop the current.

The heat may be supplied by an alcohol lamp or other device, and the current may then be detected by means of a simple galvanometer consisting of a square spool of No. 14 or No. 16 single-covered wire, E, with a pocket compass, F, placed on top. Turn the spool in a north and south direction, or parallel with the compass needle. Then, when the nail heads are heated and the circuit completed, the needle will swing around it at right angles to the coils of wire. Applying ice or cold water to the nail heads will reverse the current.—Contributed by A. C. A., Chicago.

How to Discharge a Toy Cannon by Electricity

A device for discharging a toy cannon by electricity can be easily made by using three or four dry batteries, a switch and a small induction coil

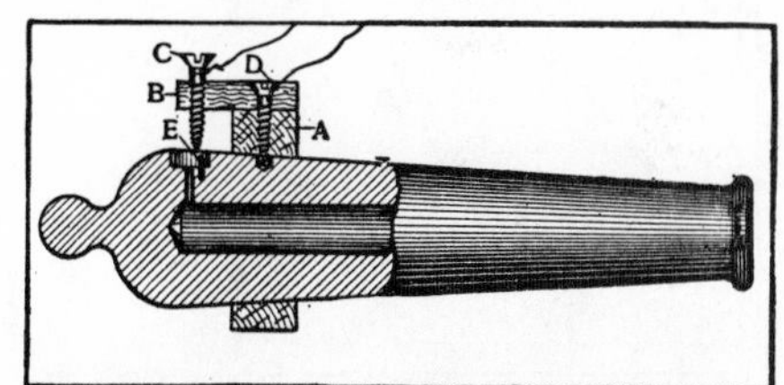

Electrical Attachment for Discharging Toy Cannon

capable of giving a ⅛-in. spark. Fasten a piece of wood, A, to the cannon, by means of machine screws or, if there are no trunnions on the cannon, the wood may be made in the shape of a ring and slipped on over the muzzle. The fuse hole of the cannon is counterbored as shown and a small hole is drilled at one side to receive a small piece of copper wire, E. The wood screw, C, nearly touches E and is connected to one binding post of the induction coil. The other binding post is connected with the wood screw, D, which conducts the current into the cannon, and also holds the pieces of wood, A and B, in position.

When the cannon is loaded, a small quantity of powder is placed in the counterbore, and the spark between C and E ignites this and discharges the cannon. A cannon may be fired from a distance in this way, and as there is no danger of any spark remaining after the current is shut off, it is safer than the ordinary cannon which is fired by means of a fuse.—Contributed by Henry Peck, Big Rapids, Mich.

Simple Electric Lock

The illustration shows an automatic lock operated by electricity, requiring a strong magnet, but no weights or strings, which greatly simplifies the device over many others of the kind.

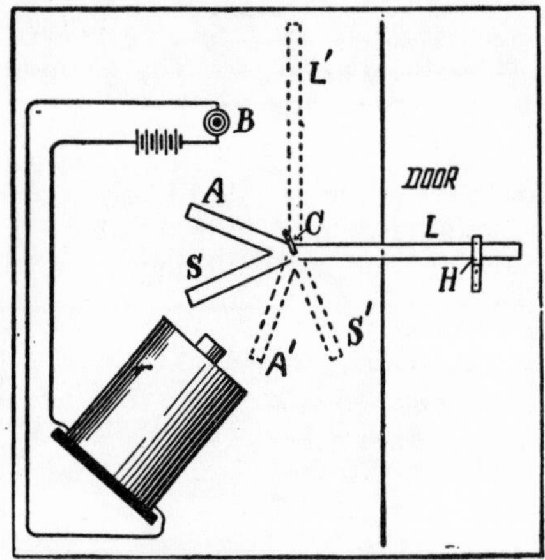

Lock Operated by a Magnet

The weight of the long arm, L, is just a trifle greater than the combined weights of the short arms, A and S. The fulcrum of the lever is at C, where there is a staple. The lever swings on one arm of the staple and the other arm is so placed that when the lever is in an upright position, with the long arm at L′, it will not fall because of its greater weight but stays in the position shown. The purpose of this is to leave the short arm, A, when in position at A′, within the reach of the magnet. Arm L rests on an L-shaped hook, H; in this position the door is locked.

To unlock the door, press the button, B. The momentum acquired from the magnet by the short arms, A and S, is sufficient to move the long arm up to the position of L′. To lock the door, press the button and the momentum acquired from the magnet by the short arms, now at A′ and S′, is sufficient to move the long arm down from L′ to the position at L.—Contributed by Benjamin Kubelsky, Chicago.

Direct-Connected Reverse for Small Motors

A simple reverse for small motors can be attached directly to the motor as shown in Fig. 1. Fig. 2 shows the construction of the reverse block: A is a strip of walnut 5/8 in. square and 3/8 in. thick with strips of brass or copper (BB) attached as shown. Holes (CC) are drilled for the wire connections and they must be flush with the surface of the block. A hole for a 1/2-in. screw is bored in the block. In Fig. 1, D is a thin strip of walnut or other dense, hard wood fitted to the binding posts of the brush holders, to receive the screw in the center.

Before putting the reverse block on the motor, remove all the connections between the lower binding posts and the brush holders and connect both ends of the field coil to the lower posts. Bend the strips BB (Fig. 2) to the proper position to make a wiping contact with the nuts holding the strip of wood D, Fig. 1. Put the screw in tight

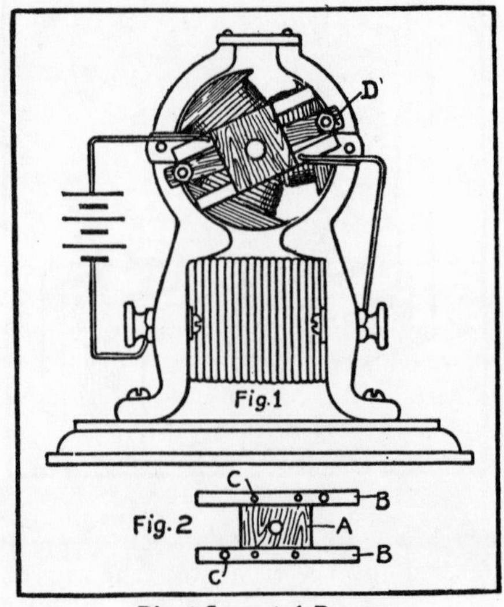

Direct-Connected Reverse

enough to make the block turn a little hard. Connect as shown in the illustration. To reverse, turn the block so the strips change connections and the motor will do the rest.—Contributed by Joseph B. Keil, Marion, Ohio.

A Handy Ice Chisel

Fishing through the ice is great sport, but cutting the first holes preparatory to setting the lines is not always an easy task. The ice chisel here described will be found very handy, and may be made at very slight expense.

In the top of an old ax-head drill a $\frac{9}{16}$-in. hole, and then tap it for a $\frac{3}{8}$-in. gas-pipe, about 18 in. long. Thread the other end of the pipe, and screw on

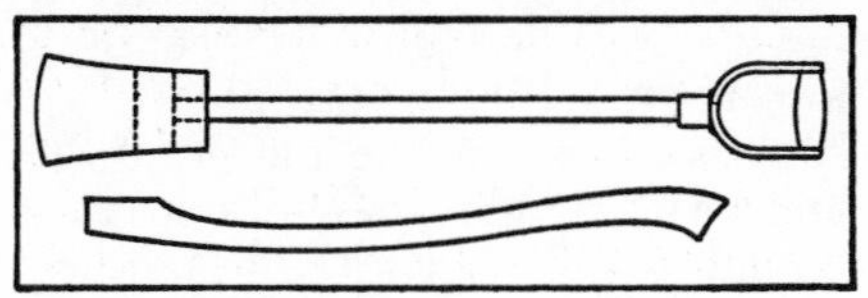

Combination Ax and Ice Chisel

an old snow-shovel handle. When ready for use, screw the two pieces together and you have your chisel complete.

A short ax-handle may be included in the outfit. When the holes are finished and your lines set, unscrew the pipe from the head of the ax, put in the handle, and your ax is ready to cut the wood to keep your fire going.—Contributed by C. J. Rand, West Somerville, Mass.

More Uses for Pipe Fittings

It would seem that the number of useful articles that can be made from pipes and fittings is unlimited. The sketch shows two more that may be added to the list. A and B are front and side views of a lamp-screen, and C is a dumbbell. The lamp-shade is particularly useful for shading the eyes when reading or writing and, if enameled white on the concave side, makes an excellent reflector for drawing at night, or for microscopic work.

The standard and base, consisting of an ordinary pipe flange bushed down to receive the upright nipple, are enameled a jet black, and if the device is to be used on a polished table, a piece of

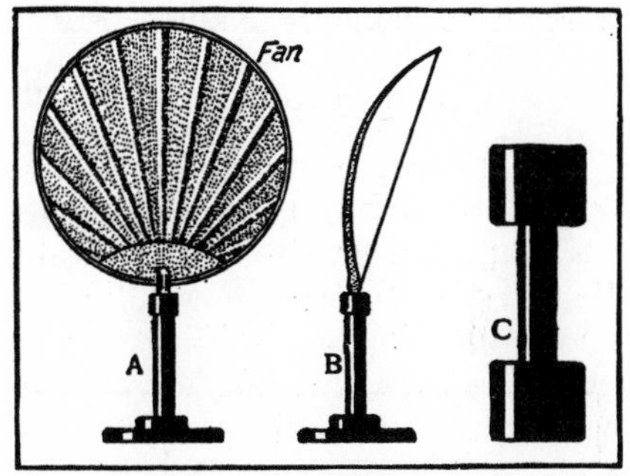

Lamp Shade and Dumbbell

felt should be glued to the bottom. A good way to hold the fan in the nipple is to use a small wedge.

The dumbbells are made of short pieces of $\frac{3}{4}$-in. pipe with $1\frac{1}{2}$-in. couplings fastened to each end by pouring melted lead in the space between the pipes and the couplings. The appearance is greatly improved by enameling black, and if desired the handles may be covered with leather.—Contributed by C. E. Warren, M. D., North Easton, Mass.

Sealing-Wax Bent While Cold

If a piece of sealing-wax is supported in a horizontal position by one end, as shown at A in the sketch, it will gradually bend to the shape indicated by the dotted lines B. To attempt bending it with the hands would result in breaking it unless a steady pressure were applied for a long time. This peculiar property is also found in ice.

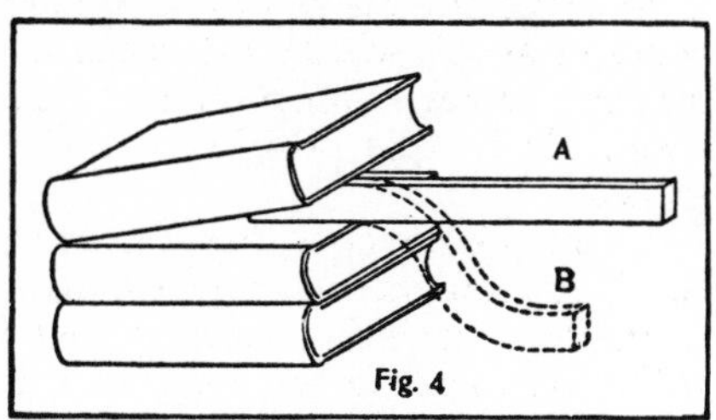

Bending Cold Sealing-Wax

Homemade Pottery Kiln

A small kiln for baking clay figures may be built at a cost of $1. The following shows the general plan of such a kiln which has stood the test of 200 firings, and which is good for any work requiring less than 1400° C.

Get an iron pail about 1 ft. high by 1 ft. across, with a cover. Any old pail which is thick enough will do, while a new one will cost about 80 cents. In the bottom of this cut a 2-in. round hole and close it with a cork or wood plug, A, Fig. 1, which shall project at least 2 in. inside the pail. Make a cylindrical core of wood, B, Fig. 1, 8 in. long and 8 in. across. Make a

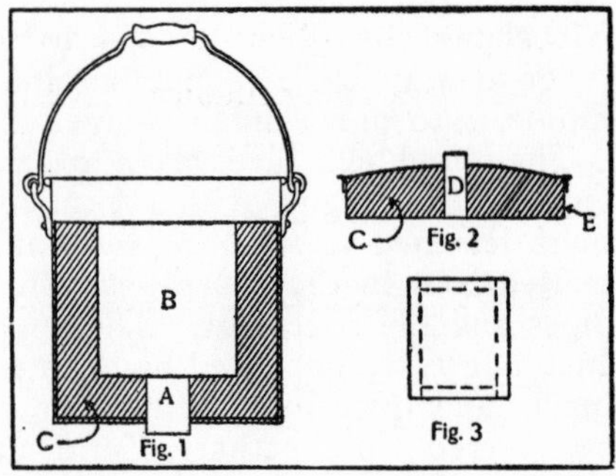

Homemade Pottery Kiln

mixture of clay, 60%; sand, 15%; and graphite, 25%, kneading thoroughly in water to a good molding consistency. Line the pail, bottom and sides, with heavy paper and cover the core with same. Now pack the bottom of the pail thoroughly with a 2-in. layer of the clay mixture, and on it set the paper-wrapped core, carefully centering it. The 2 in. of space between the core and the sides of the pail all around is to be filled with clay, C, as is shown in the sketch, using a little at a time and packing it very tight. In like manner make the cover of the kiln, cutting the hole a little smaller, about 1 in. At the edge or rim of the cover encircle a 2-in. strip of sheet iron, E, Fig. 2, to hold the clay mixture, C. Set aside for a few days until well dried.

While these are drying you may be making a muffle, if there is to be any glazing done. This is a clay cylinder (Fig. 3) with false top and bottom, in which the pottery to be glazed is protected from any smoke or dust. It is placed inside the kiln, setting on any convenient blocks which will place it midway. The walls of the muffle should be about 1/2 in. thick, and the dimensions should allow at least 1 in. of space all around for the passage of heat between it and the walls of the kiln. By the time the clay of the kiln is well dried, it will be found that it has all shrunk away from the iron about 3/8 in. After removing all the paper, pack this space—top, bottom and sides—with moist ground asbestos. If the cover of the pail has no rim, it may be fastened to the asbestos and clay lining by punching a few holes, passing wire nails through and clinching them. Fit all the parts together snugly, take out the plugs in the top and bottom, and your kiln is ready for business. The handle of the pail will be convenient for moving it about, and it can be set on three bricks or some more elaborate support, as dictated by fancy and expense.

The temperature required for baking earthenware is 1250°-1310°, C.; hotel china, 1330°; hard porcelain, 1390°-1410°. These temperatures can not be obtained in the above kiln by means of the ordinary Bunsen burner. It will be necessary either to buy the largest size Bunsen, or make one yourself, if you have the materials. If you can get a cone which can be screwed into an inch pipe, file the opening of the cone to 1/16 in. diameter, and jacket the whole with a 2 1/2-in. pipe. The flame end of this burner tube should be about 4 1/2 in. above the cone opening and should be covered with gauze to prevent flame from snapping back. When lighted, the point of the blue flame, which is the hottest part, should be just in the hole in the bottom of the kiln. Such a burner will be cheaply made and will furnish a kiln temperature of 1400°, but it will burn a great deal of gas.

A plumber's torch of medium size will cost more in the beginning, but will be cheaper in operation. Whatever burner is used, the firing should be gradual, and with especial caution the first time. By experiment you will find that a higher temperature is obtained by placing a 1-in. pipe 2 ft. long over the lid hole as a chimney. It would be still more effective to get another iron pail, 2 in. wider than the kiln, and get a down draft by inverting it over the kiln at whatever height proves most suitable.—G. L. W.

How to Make a Small Medical Induction Coil

The coil to be described is 3½ in., full length of iron core, and ¾ in. in diameter.

Procure a bundle of small iron wire, say ¼ in. in diameter, and cut it 3½ in. long; bind neatly with coarse thread and file the ends smooth (Fig. 1). This done, make two wood ends, 1¼ by 1¼ in. and ⅜ in. thick, and varnish. Bore holes in the center of each so the core will fit in snugly and leave about ¼ in. projecting from each end (Fig. 1).

After finishing the core, shellac two layers of thick paper over it between the ends; let this dry thoroughly. Wind two layers of bell magnet wire over this, allowing several inches of free wire to come through a hole in the end. Cover with paper and shellac as before.

Wind about ⅛ in. of fine wire, such as used on telephone generators, around the coil, leaving long terminals. Soak the whole in melted paraffin and let cool; bind tightly with black silk.

The vibrator is made of a piece of thin tin to which is soldered the head of an iron screw and on the other side a small piece of platinum, which can be taken from an old electric bell (Fig. 2).

Of course, a regulator must be had for the vibrator; this can be accomplished by bending a stout piece of copper wire as shown. The connections and the base for setting up are shown in the figures.—Contributed by J. T. R., Washington, D. C.

Mechanical Trick With Cards

The following mechanical card trick is easy to prepare and simple to perform:

First, procure a new deck, and divide it into two piles, one containing the red cards and the other the black ones, all cards facing the same way. Take the red cards, square them up and place in a vise. Then, with a plane, plane off the upper right hand corner and lower left hand corner, as in Fig. 1, about $\frac{1}{16}$ in.

Then take the black cards, square them up, and plane off about $\frac{1}{16}$ in. on the upper left hand corner and lower right hand corner, as in Fig. 2.

Next restore all the cards to one pack, taking care to have the first card red, the next black, and so on, every alternate card being the same color.

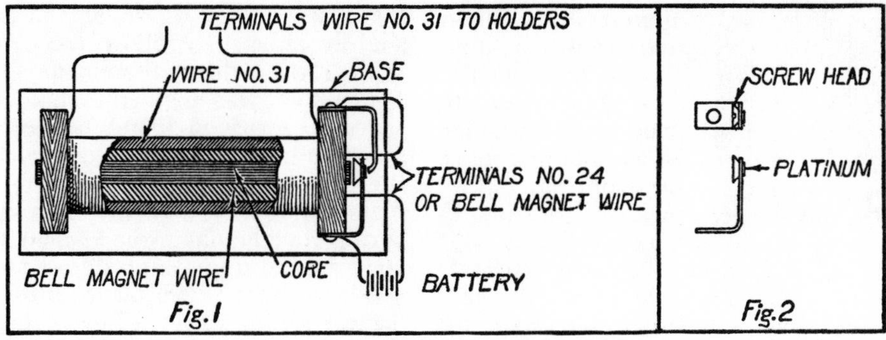

Medical Induction Coil

Bend the pack so as to give some spring to the cards, and by holding one thumb on the upper left-hand corner

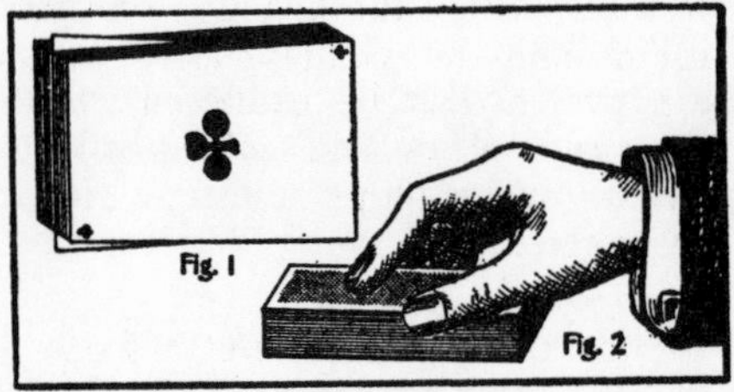

Card Trick

all the cards will appear red to the audience; place thumb in the center at top of pack and they will appear mixed, red and black; with thumb on upper right-hand corner all cards appear black. You can display either color called for.—Contributed by Ralph Gingrich, Chicago.

How to Make a Rain Gauge

An accurate rain gauge may be easily constructed from galvanized iron, as shown in the sketch herewith. The funnel, A, overlaps and rests on the body, B, and discharges into the tube, C, the area of which is one-tenth that of the top of the funnel. The depth of the water in C is thus ten times the actual rainfall, so that by measuring it with a stick marked off in tenths of an inch, we obtain the result in hundredths of an inch.

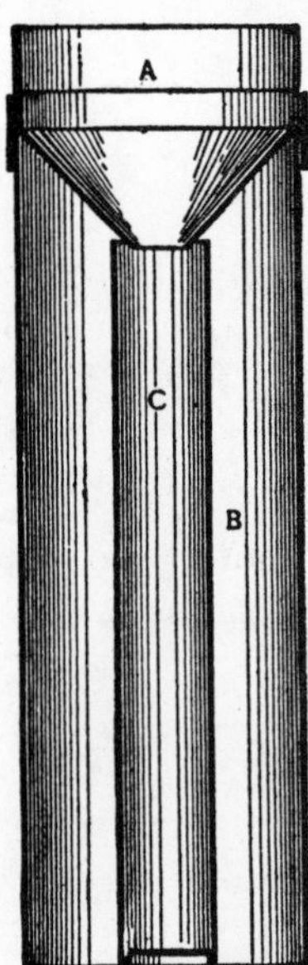

A good size to make the rain gauge is as follows: A, 8 in. diameter; C, 2.53 in.; length of C, about 20 in. It should be placed in an exposed location, so that no inaccuracy will occur from wind currents. To find the fall of snow, pour a known quantity of warm water on the snow contained in the funnel and deduct the quantity poured in from the total amount in the tube.—Contributed by Thurston Hendrickson, Long Branch, N. J.

How to Make an Aquarium

In making an aquarium, the first thing to decide on is the size. It is well not to attempt building a very large one, as the difficulties increase with the size. A good size is 12 by 12 by 20 in., and this is inexpensive to build.

First buy one length of 3/4 by 1/8-in. angle iron for the frame, F, Fig. 1. This can be obtained at any steel shop and should cost about 20 cents. All the horizontal pieces, B, should be beveled 45° at the ends and drilled for 3/16-in. stove bolts. The beveling may be done by roughing out with a hacksaw and finishing with a file. After all the pieces are cut and beveled they should be drilled at the ends for the 3/16-in. stove bolts, C. Drill all the horizontal pieces, B, first and then mark the holes on the upright pieces, A, through the holes already drilled, thus making all the holes coincide. Mark the ends of each piece with a figure or letter, so that when they are assembled, the same ends will come together again. The upright pieces, A, should be countersunk as shown in the detail, and then the frame is ready to assemble.

After the frame has been assembled take it to glazier and have a bottom made of skylight glass, and sides and ends of double-thick window glass. The bottom glass should be a good fit, but the sides and ends should be made slightly shorter to allow the cement, E, to form a dovetail joint as shown. When the glass is put in the frame a space, D, will be found between the glass and the horizontal pieces, B, of the frame. If this were allowed to remain the pressure of the water would spring the glass and cause a leak at E; so it is filled up with plaster of paris.

The cement, E, is made as follows: Take 1 gill of plaster of paris, 1 gill of litharge, 1 gill of fine white sand, and

⅓ of a gill of finely powdered rosin. Mix well and add boiled linseed oil and turpentine until as thick as putty. Let

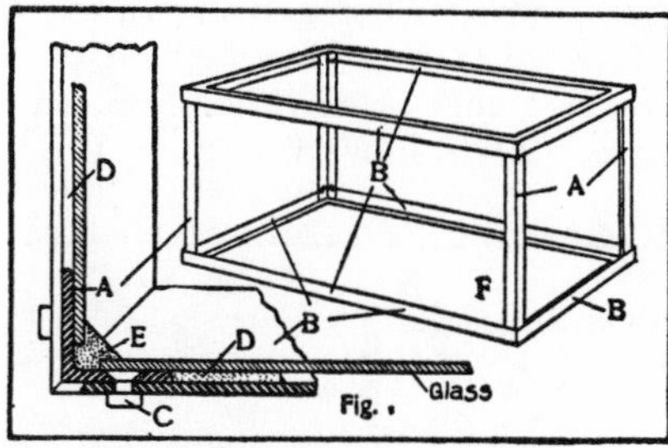

Detail of Aquarium Frame

the cement dry three or four days before putting any water in the aquarium.

In choosing stock for the aquarium it should be remembered that a sufficient quantity of vegetable life is required to furnish oxygen for the fish. In a well balanced aquarium the water requires renewal only two or three times a year. It is well to have an excess of plants and a number of snails, as the snails will devour all the decaying vegetable matter which would otherwise poison the water and kill the fish.

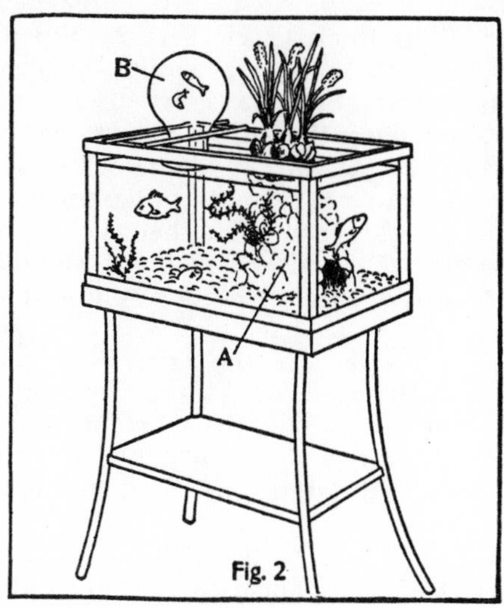

Aquarium Finished

If desired, a centerpiece (A, Fig. 2) can be made of colored stones held together by cement, and an inverted jar can be supported in the position shown at B. If the mouth of the jar is below the surface of the water it will stay filled and allow the fish to swim up inside as shown. Some washed pebbles or gravel should be placed on the bottom, and, if desired, a few Chinese lilies or other plants may be placed on the centerpiece.

Homemade Pneumatic Lock

Mount an old bicycle hand-pump, A, on the door by means of a metal plate, B, having a swinging connection at C. Fasten the lever, D, to the door knob, and make a hinge connection with the pump by means of a piece of sheet

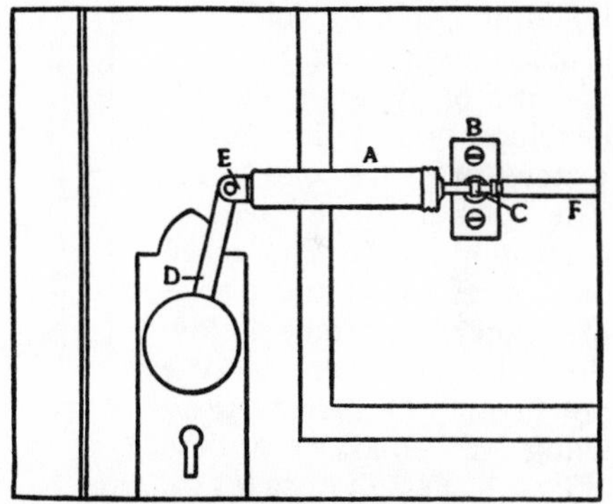

Pneumatic Door-Opener

brass, E, soldered to the end of the cylinder. All this apparatus is on the inside of the door and is connected by a small rubber tube, F, to a secret mouthpiece placed at some convenient location. A small piece of spring brass, screwed to the door frame, will open the door about ½ in. when the operator blows in the mouthpiece, or if the door is within reach of the mouthpiece, the operator may push the door at the same time that he blows, thus doing away with the spring, which is only used to keep the door from relocking.

One way of making the air connection with the outside is to bend the tube F around and stick it through the keyhole. Few burglars would ever think to blow in the keyhole.—Contributed by Orton E. White, Buffalo, N. Y.

A Homemade Water Motor

By MRS. PAUL S. WINTER

In these days of modern improvements, most houses are equipped with a washing-machine, and the question that arises in the mind of the householder is how to furnish the power to run it economically. I referred this question to my husband, with the result that he built a motor which proved so very satisfactory that I prevailed upon him to give the readers of Amateur Mechanics a description of it, hoping it may solve the same question for them.

A motor of this type will develop about ½ hp. with a water pressure of 70 lb. The power developed is correspondingly increased or decreased as the pressure exceeds or falls below this. In the latter case the power may be increased by using a smaller pulley. Fig. 1 is the motor with one side removed, showing the paddle-wheel in position; Fig. 2 is an end view; Fig. 3 shows one of the paddles, and Fig. 4 shows the method of shaping the paddles. To make the frame, several lengths of scantling 3 in. wide by 1 in. thick (preferably of hard wood) are required. Cut two of them 4 ft. long, to form the main supports of the frame, AA, Fig. 1; another, 2 ft. 6 in. long, for the top, B, Fig. 1; another, 26 in. long, to form the slanting part, C, Fig. 1; and another, D, approximately 1 ft., according to the slant given C. After nailing these together as shown in the illustration, nail two short strips on each side of the outlet, as at E, to keep the frame from spreading.

Cut two pieces 30 in. long. Lay these on the sides of the frame with their center lines along the line FF, which is 15 in. from the outside top of the frame. They are shown in Fig. 2 at GG. Do not fasten these boards now, but mark their position on the frame. Two short boards 1 in. wide

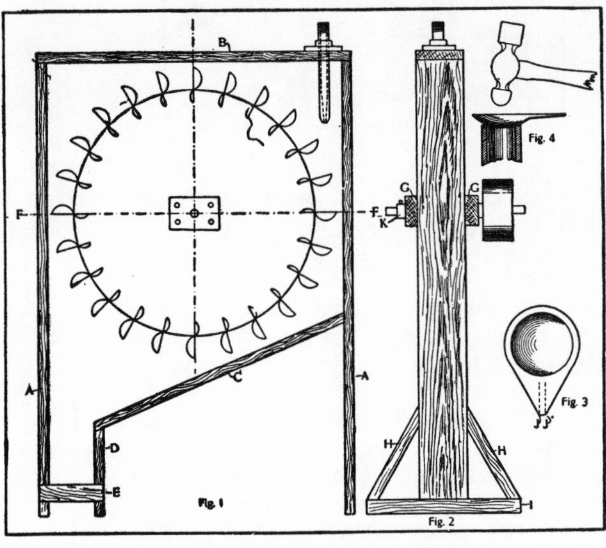

Detail of Homemade Waterwheel

by 1 in. thick (HH, Fig. 2) and another 1 in. by 1½ in. (I, Fig. 2) form a substantial base.

Cut the wheel from sheet iron $\frac{1}{16}$ in. thick, 24 in. in diameter. This can be done roughly with hammer and chisel and then smoothed up on an emery wheel, after which cut 24 radial slots ¾ in. deep on its circumference by means of a hacksaw. On each side of the wheel at the center fasten a rectangular piece of ¼-in. iron 3 by 4 in. and secure it to the wheel by means of four rivets; after which drill a ⅝-in. hole through the exact center of the wheel.

Cut 24 pieces of 1/32-in. iron, 1½ by 2½ in. These are the paddles. Shape them by placing one end over a section of 1-in. pipe, and hammer bowl-shaped with the peen of a hammer, as shown in Fig. 4. Then cut them into the shape shown in Fig. 3 and bend the tapered end in along the lines JJ, after which place them in the slots of the wheel and bend the sides over to clamp the wheel. Drill 1/8-in. holes through the wheel and sides of the paddles and rivet paddles in place. Next secure a 5/8-in. steel shaft 12 in. long to the wheel about 8 in. from one end by means of a key. This is done by cutting a groove in the shaft and a corresponding groove in the wheel and fitting in a piece of metal in order to secure the wheel from turning independently of the shaft. Procure two collars or round pieces of brass (KK, Fig. 2) with a 5/8-in. hole through them, and fasten these to the shaft by means of set screws to prevent it from moving lengthwise.

Make the nozzle by taking a piece of 1/2-in. galvanized pipe 3 1/2 in. long and filling it with babbitt metal; then drill a 3/16-in. hole through its center. Make this hole conical, tapering from 3/16 in. to a full 1/2 in. This is best done by using a square taper reamer. Then place the nozzle in the position shown in Fig. 1, which allows the stream of water to strike the buckets full in the center when they reach the position farthest to the right.

Take the side pieces, GG, and drill a 1-in. hole through their sides centrally, and a 1/4-in. hole from the tops to the 1-in. holes. Fasten them in their proper position, with the wheel and shaft in place, the shaft projecting through the holes just mentioned. Now block the wheel; that is, fasten it by means of wedges or blocks of wood until the shaft is exactly in the center of the inch holes in the side pieces. Cut four disks of cardboard to slip over the shaft and large enough to cover the inch holes. Two of these are to be inside and two outside of the frames (one to bear against each side of each crosspiece). Fasten these to the crosspieces by means of tacks to hold them securely. Pour melted babbitt metal into the 1/4-in. hole to form the bearings. When it has cooled, remove the cardboard, take down the crosspieces, and drill a 1/8-in. hole from the top of the crosspieces through the babbitt for an oil-hole.

Secure sufficient sheet zinc to cover the sides of the frame. Cut the zinc to the same shape as the frame and let it extend down to the crosspieces EE. Tack one side on. (It is well to tack strips of heavy cloth—burlap will do—along the edges under the zinc to form a water-tight joint.) Fasten the crosspiece over the zinc in its proper position. Drill a hole through the zinc, using the hole in the crosspiece as a guide. Then put the wheel in a central position in the frame, tack the other side piece of zinc in place and put the other crosspiece in place. Place the two collars mentioned before on the shaft, and fasten so as to bear against the crosspieces, in order to prevent the wheel and shaft from moving sidewise. If the bearings are now oiled, the shaft should turn easily and smoothly. Fasten a pulley 4 or 6 in. in diameter to the longest arm of the shaft.

Connect the nozzle to a water faucet by means of a piece of hose; place the outlet over a drain, and belt the motor direct to the washing-machine, sewing-machine, ice-cream freezer, drill press, dynamo or any other machinery requiring not more than 1/2 hp.

This motor has been in use in our house for two years in all of the above ways, and has never once failed to give perfect satisfaction. It is obvious that, had the wheel and paddles been made of brass, it would be more durable, but as it would have cost several times as much, it is a question whether it would be more economical in the end. If sheet-iron is used, a coat of heavy paint would prevent rust and therefore prolong the life of the motor. The motor will soon pay for itself in the saving of laundry bills. We used to spend $1 a month to have just my husband's overalls done at the laundry, but now I put them in the machine, start the motor, and leave them for an hour or so. At the end of this time they are perfectly clean, and I have noticed that they wear twice as long as when I sent them to the laundry.

How to Make Silhouettes

Photography in all branches is truly a most absorbing occupation. Each of us who has a camera is constantly experimenting, and every one of us is delighted when something new is suggested for such experiments.

To use a camera in making silhouettes select a window facing north if possible, or if used only at times when the sun is not on it, any window will do, says the Photographic Times. Raise the window shade half way, remove any white curtains there may be, and in the center of the lower pane of glass paste by the four corners a sheet of tissue paper that is perfectly smooth and quite thick, as shown in the sketch at B. Darken the rest of the window, shutting out all light from above and the sides. Place a chair so that after being seated the head of the subject will come before the center of the tissue paper, and as near to it as possible, and when looking straight before him his face will be in clear profile to the camera.

Draw the shades of all other windows in the room. Focus the camera carefully, getting a sharp outline of the profile on the screen. Do not stop down the lens, as this makes long exposure necessary, and the subject may move.

Correct exposure depends, of course, on the lens, light and the plate. But remember that a black and white negative is wanted with as little detail in the features as possible. The best plate to use is a very slow one, or what is called a process plate.

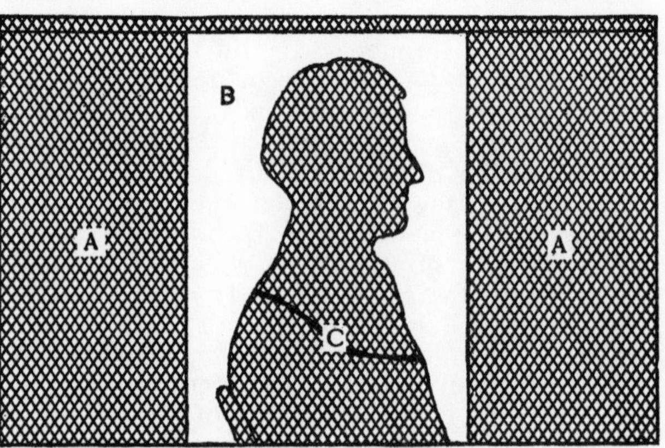

Making a Silhouette with the Camera

In developing get all possible density in the high lights, without detail in the face, and without fog. Printing is best done on contrasty development paper with developer not too strong.

The ideal silhouette print is a perfectly black profile on a white ground. With a piece of black paper, any shape in stopping off print may be made as shown at C in the sketch.

How to Make a Galvanoscope

A galvanoscope for detecting small currents of electricity can be made from a coil of wire, A; a glass tube, B, full of water; a core, C; and a base, D, with binding posts as shown. The core C, which is made of iron and cork, is a trifle lighter than the water it displaces and will therefore normally remain in the top of the tube; but as soon as a current of electricity passes through the coil, the core is drawn down out of sight. The current required is very small, as the core is so nearly balanced that the least attraction will cause it to sink.

The glass tube may be a test tube, as shown in Fig. 2, or an empty developer tube. If one has neither a test tube nor developer tube, an empty pill bottle may be used. The washers at the ends of the coil can be made of fiber, hard rubber, or wood; or can be taken from an old magnet. The base may be made of wood or any other insulating material and should have four short legs on the bottom. Make the coil of single-covered wire about No. 18 and connect ends to binding posts as shown in Fig. 2.

The core is made by pushing a small nail through a piece of cork. It should be made so that it will rise slowly when placed under water. Some filing may be necessary to get the weight just right, but it should be remembered that the buoyancy of the core can be adjusted after the parts are assembled, by pressing the cork in the bottom of the test tube. This causes compression in the water so that some is forced into the upper cork, reducing its displacement and causing it to sink. The lower cork is then slowly withdrawn, by twisting, until the core slowly rises.

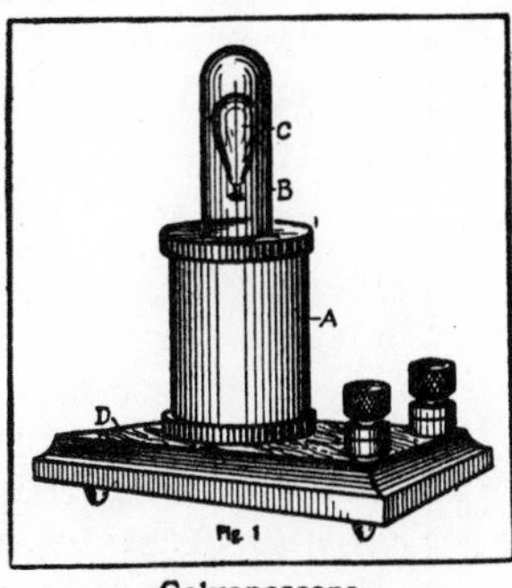

Galvanoscope

The instrument will then be adjusted ready for use.

Connect the binding posts to a single cell of battery—any kind will do, as a slight current will answer. On com-

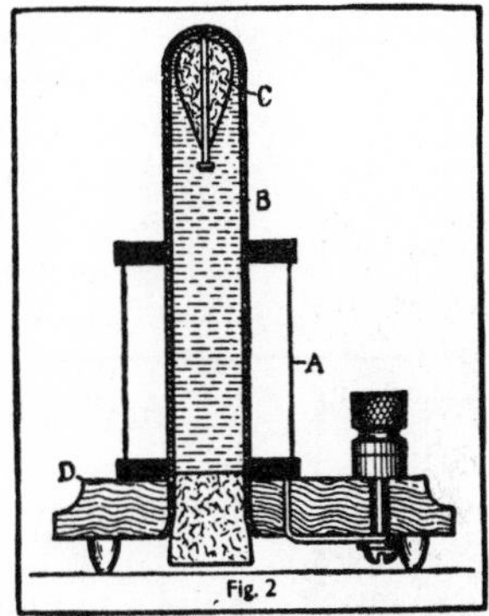

Interior View

pleting the circuit the core will descend; or put in a switch or push button on one of the battery wires. If the button be concealed where the operator can reach it, the core will obey his command to rise or fall, according to his control of the current. This is a mysterious looking instrument, the core being moved without visible connection to any other part.

¶To lubricate sheet metal mix 1 qt. whale oil, 1 lb. white lead, 1 pt. water and 3 oz. finest graphite. Apply with a brush before the metal enters the dies.

An Optical Top

One of the latest optical delusions, and one not easy to explain, is Benham's color top. Cut out the black and white disk shown in the figure, and paste on a piece of stiff cardboard. Trim the edges of the cardboard to match the shape of the disk, and make a pinhole in the center. Cut the pin in half and push it through from the under side until the head of the pin touches the cardboard. Spin slowly in a strong light and some of the lines will appear colored. The colors appear different to different people, and are changed by reversing the rotation.

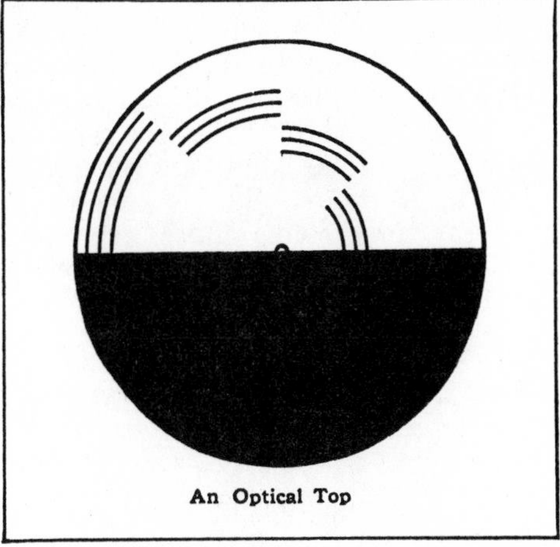
An Optical Top

Card Trick with a Tapered Deck

Another simple trick to perform but one not easily detected, is executed by using a tapered deck of cards as shown in Fig. 1. A cheap deck of cards is evened up square, fastened in a vise and planed along the edge in such a manner that all the pack will be tapered about $\frac{1}{16}$ in. This taper is exaggerated in the illustration which shows

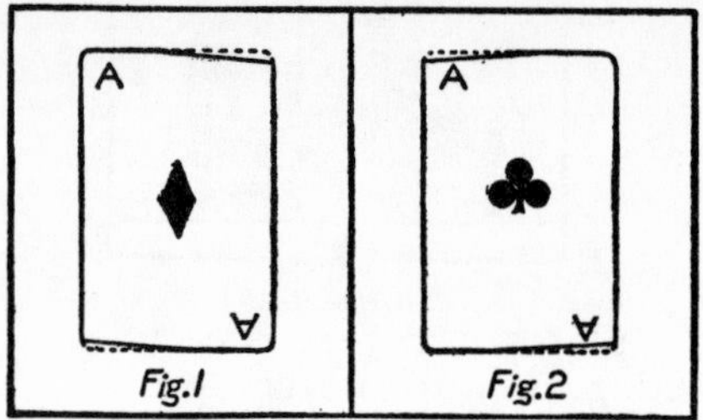

Cards from a Tapered Deck

one card that has been turned end for end.

It is evident that any card reversed in this way can be easily separated from the other cards in the pack, which makes it possible to perform the following trick: The performer spreads the cards out, fan-like, and asks an observer to withdraw a card, which is then replaced in any part of the pack. After thoroughly shuffling the cards the performer then holds the deck in both hands behind his back and pronouncing a few magic words, produces the card selected in one hand and the rest of the pack in the other. This is accomplished by simply turning the deck end for end while the observer is looking at his card, thus bringing the wide end of the selected card at the narrow end of the pack when it is replaced. The hands are placed behind the back for a double purpose, as the feat then seems more marvelous and the observers are not allowed to see how it is done.

In prize games, players having the same score are frequently called upon to cut for low to determine which shall be the winner, but a fairer way is to cut for high as a person familiar with the trick shown in Fig. 2 can cut the cards at the ace, deuce, or three spot, nearly every time, especially if the deck is a new one. This is done by simply pressing on the top of the deck as shown, before cutting, thus causing the increased ink surface of the high cards to adhere to the adjacent ones. A little practice will soon enable one to cut low nearly every time, but the cards must be grasped lightly and the experiment should be performed with a new deck to obtain successful results. —Contributed by D. B. J., Chicago.

A Constant-Pressure Hydrogen Generator

By fitting three bottles, A, B, C, with rubber stoppers and connecting with glass tubes as shown in the sketch, hydrogen or other gases produced in a similar manner may be generated under constant pressure. In making hydrogen, bottle B is partly filled with zinc nodules formed by slowly pouring melted zinc into water. Hydrochloric acid is then poured in the small funnel, thus partly filling bottles A and C. When the acid rising from C comes in contact with the zinc, hydrogen gas is generated and fills bottle B. The gas continues to generate until the pressure is sufficient to force the acid back down the tube into bottle C, when the action ceases. As fast as the gas is used the acid rises in the tube and generates more, thus keeping the pressure nearly constant, the pressure depending on the difference between the levels of the acid in bottle A and bottle B. As this device is easily upset, a ring-stand should be used to prevent its being broken, or if it is to be a permanent apparatus it may be mounted on a substantial wooden base. This apparatus may also be used for preparing acetylene gas or almost any gas which

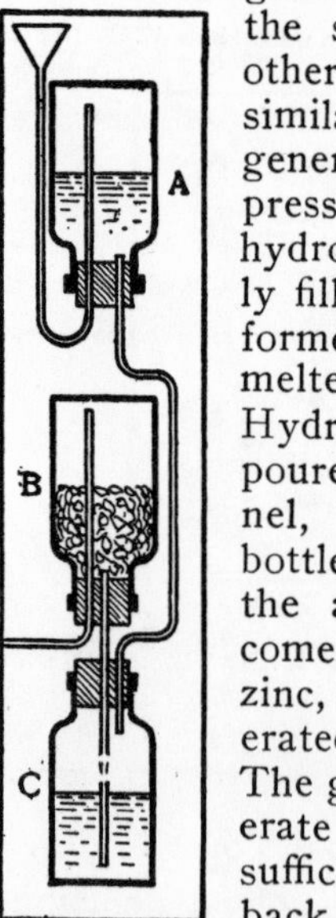

requires a mixture of a solid and liquid in its preparation.—Contributed by C. S. J., Detroit.

Restoring Tone to a Cracked Bell

Many a bell with a deadened tone due to a cracked rim, can be given its original clear ringing sound by sawing out the crack with a common hacksaw. Make the saw cut along the line of the crack. The opening caused by the saw will allow the free vibration of the metal.—Contributed by F. W. Bently, Jr., Huron, S. Dak.

How to Make a Paper Phonograph Horn

Secure a piece of tubing about 1¾ in. long that will fit the connection to the reproducer, and wrap a quantity of heavy thread around one end as shown in the enlarged sketch A, Fig. 1. Form a cone of heavy paper, 9 in. long and 3 in. in diameter, at the larger end with the smaller end to fit the diameter of the tube A, making it three-ply thick and gluing the layers together. Attach this cone on the tube A where the thread has been wrapped with glue, as shown in Fig. 2. Fig. 2 is also an enlarged sketch. Make ten pieces about 1 ft. 10 in. in length and 3 in. wide from the thin boards of a biscuit or cracker box. Cut an arc of a circle in them on a radius of 2 ft. (Fig. 3). Make a 10-sided stick, 12 in. long, that will fit loosely in the tube A, to which nail the 10 pieces as shown in Fig. 4, connecting the bottom by cross pieces, using care to keep them at equal distances apart and in a circle whose diameter is about 2 ft.

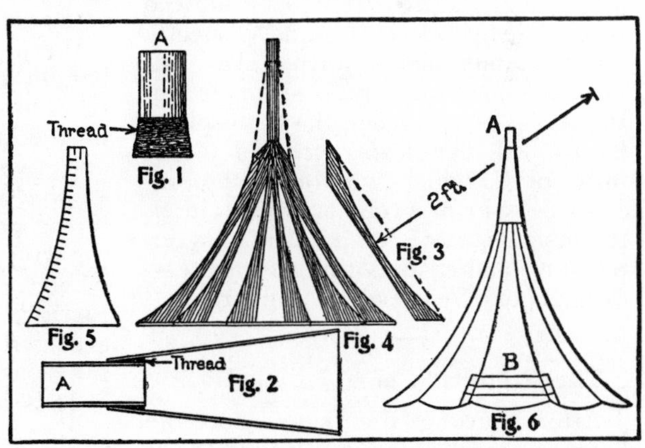

Detail of Phonograph Horn

The cone is placed over the stick as shown by the dotted lines in Fig. 4 and temporarily fastened in position. Cut out paper sections (Fig. 5) that will cover each space between the 10 pieces, allowing 1 in. on one side and the top, in which to cut slits that will form pieces to overlap the next section and to attach with glue. Fasten the sections all around in like manner. The next course is put on in strips overlapping as shown at B, Fig. 6. Finish by putting on sections in the same way as the first course, making it three-ply thick. Remove the form, trim to suit and glue a piece of paper over the edge. When the glue is thoroughly hardened, put on two coats of white and one of blue paint, shading it to suit and striping it with gold bronze.

How to Make a Hygrometer

A homemade hygrometer, for determining the degree of moisture in the atmosphere, is shown in the accompanying sketch and consists of a board, A, with a nail at each end to hold the silk thread B. A second piece of silk thread, C, is tied to the center of B and connects with an indicating hand or pointer supported by the bracket D. The axle on which the pointer revolves consists of a piece of round wood, about the size of a lead-pencil, with a pin driven in each end. A piece of tin, E, is cut V-shaped at each end and bent up at the ends to form bearings for the pins. The silk thread C is fastened to the wooden axle and is wrapped one or two turns around it, so that when

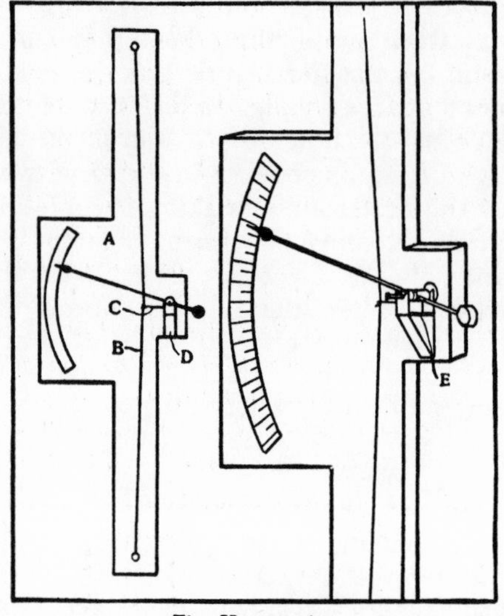

The Hygrometer

the thread is pulled the pointer will move on the scale. It will be noticed that the thread B is not perfectly straight, but bends toward D. For this reason a very small shrinkage of B, such as occurs when the atmosphere is dry, will cause an increased movement of C, which will be further increased in the movement of the pointer. An instrument of this kind is very interesting and costs nothing to make.—Contributed by Reader, Denver.

The Protection of a Spring Lock

After shutting the front door and hearing the spring lock snap into its socket, most people go off with a child-like faith in the safety of their goods and chattels. But the cold fact is that there is scarcely any locking device which affords less protection than the ordinary spring lock. It is the simplest thing in the world for a sneak-thief to slip a thin knife between the door-casing and the strip, push back the bolt, and walk in.

Fortunately, it is equally easy to block that trick. Take a narrow piece of tin 3 or 4 in. long, bend it at right angles throughout its length, and tack it firmly in the angle between the casing and strip, so as to make it impossible to reach the bolt without tearing off the strip.

Another way is to drive nails through the strip at intervals of half an inch, enough to protect the bolt from being meddled with.

A Controller and Reverse for a Battery Motor

Secure a cigar or starch box and use to make the base, B. Two wood-base switches, S S, are cut off a little past the center and fastened to the base with a piece of wood between them. The upper switch, S, is connected to different equal points on a coil of wire, W, while the lower switch, S, is connected each point to a battery, as shown. The reverse switch, R, is made from two brass or copper strips fastened at the top to the base with screws and joined together by a piece of hard rubber or wood with a small handle attached. Connect wires A to the armature and wires F to the field of the motor. By this arrangement one, two or three and so on up until all the battery cells are used and different points of resistance secured on the coil of wire. The reverse lever when moved from right to left, or left to right, changes the direction of the armature in the motor from one way to the other.—Contributed by J. Fremont Hilscher, Jr., West St. Paul, Minn.

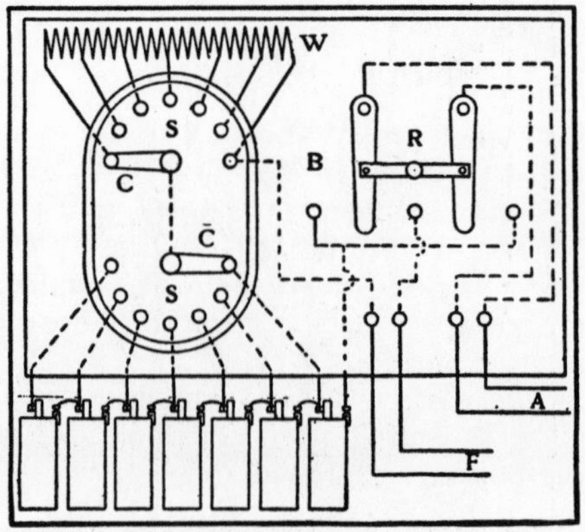

Motor Reverse and Controller

How to Build a Grape Arbor

A grape arbor made of white pine, put together as shown in the sketch, will last for several years. The 2 by 4-in. posts, A, are 7 ft. long. The feet, B, are made 2 by 4 in., 4 ft. long, and rest on a brick placed under each end.

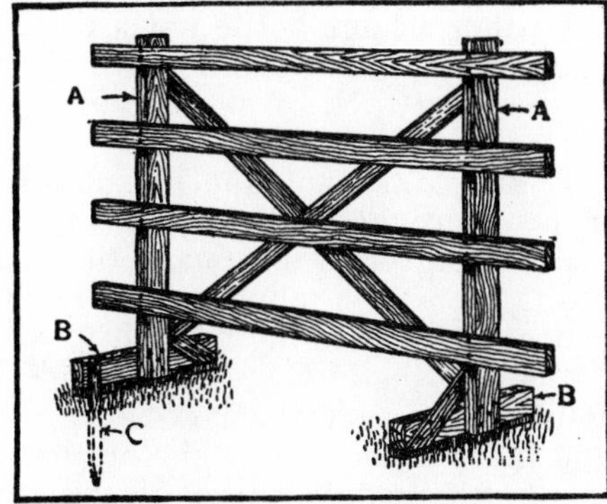

Grape-Arbor Trellis

How to Make a Toy Steam Engine

A toy engine can be easily made from old implements which can be found in nearly every house.

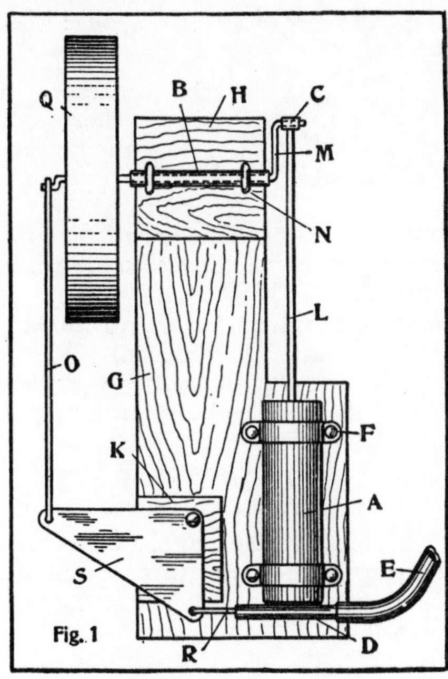

Toy Steam Engine Assembled

The cylinder A, Fig. 1, is an old bicycle pump, cut in half. The steam chest D, is part of the piston tube of the same pump, the other parts being used for the bearing B, and the crank bearing C. The flywheel Q can be any small-sized iron wheel; either an old sewing-machine wheel, pulley wheel, or anything available. We used a wheel from an old high chair for our engine. If the bore in the wheel is too large for the shaft, it may be bushed with a piece of hard wood. The shaft is made of heavy steel wire, the size of the hole in the bearing B.

The base is made of wood, and has two wood blocks, H and K, 3/8 in. thick, to support bearing B, and valve crank S, which is made of tin. The hose E connects to the boiler, which will be described later. The clips F F are soldered to the cylinder and nailed to the base, and the bearing B is fastened by staples.

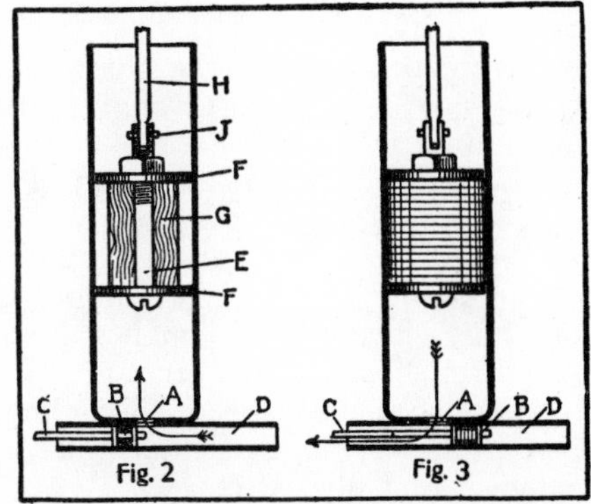

Valve Motion and Construction of Piston

The valve motion is shown in Figs. 2 and 3. In Fig. 2 the steam is entering the cylinder, and in Fig. 3 the valve B has closed the steam inlet and opened the exhaust, thus allowing the steam in the cylinder to escape.

The piston is made of a stove bolt, E, Fig. 2, with two washers, F F, and a cylindrical piece of hard wood, G. This is wound with soft string, as shown in Fig. 3, and saturated with thick oil. A slot is cut in the end of the bolt E, to receive the connecting rod H. The valve B is made of an old bicycle spoke, C, with the nut cut in half and filed down as shown, the space between the two halves being filled with string and oiled.

The valve crank S, Fig. 1, is cut out of tin, or galvanized iron, and is moved

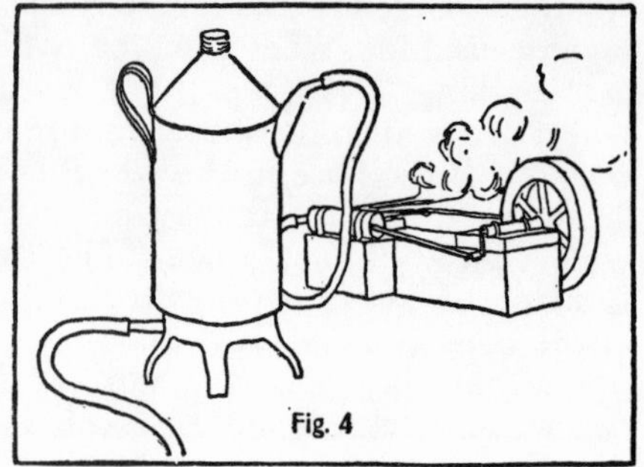

Engine in Operation

by a small crank on the shaft. This crank should be at right angles to the main crank.

The boiler, Fig. 4, can be an old oil can, powder can, or a syrup can with a tube soldered to it, and is connected to the engine by a piece of rubber tubing. The heat from a small gas stove will furnish steam fast enough to run the engine at high speed. This engine was built by W. G. Schuh and A. J. Eustice, of Cuba, Wis.

Writing with Electricity

Soak a piece of white paper in a solution of potassium iodide and water for about a minute and then lay it on a piece of sheet metal. Connect the sheet metal with the negative or zinc side of a battery and then, using the positive wire as a pen, write your name or other inscription on the wet paper.

Electrolytic Writing

The result will be brown lines on a white background.—Contributed by Geo. W. Fry, San Jose, Cal.

To Photograph a Man in a Bottle

Neither a huge bottle nor a dwarfed man is necessary for this process, as it is merely a trick of photography, and a very amusing trick, at that.

First, photograph the person to be inclosed in the bottle against a dark plain background and mark the exact position on the ground glass. Let the exposure be just long enough to show the figure distinctly. Then place an empty bottle against a dark background and focus so as to have the outlines of the bottle inclose those of the man. Let this exposure be about twice the length of the first, and the desired result is obtained.

A Musical Windmill

Make two wheels out of tin. They may be of any size, but wheel A must be larger than wheel B. On wheel A fasten two pieces of wood, C, to cross in the center, and place a bell on the four ends, as shown. The smaller wheel, B, must be separated from the other with a round piece of wood or an old spool. Tie four buttons with split rings to the smaller wheel, B. The blades on the wheels should be bent opposite on one wheel from the others so as to make the wheels turn in different directions. When turning, the buttons will strike the bells and make them ring constantly.

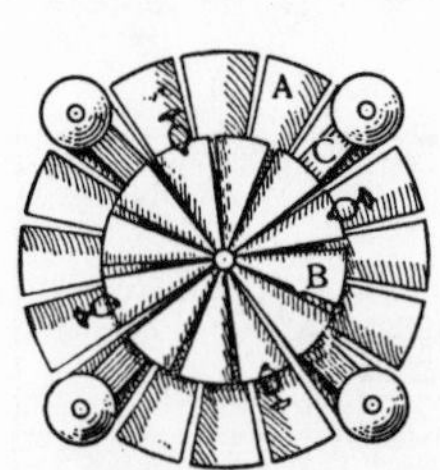

Optical Illusions

By giving the page a revolving or rinsing motion the three circular figures printed on the next page appear to rotate. The best effect will be produced by laying the book down flat on the desk or table and revolving, first

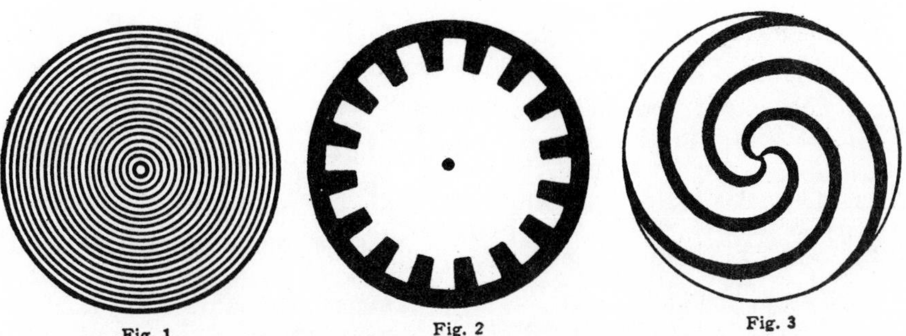
Fig. 1 Fig. 2 Fig. 3

Move These Figures Rapidly with a Rinsing Motion

in one direction and then in the opposite direction, in such a way that any given point on the page will describe a circle of about ½ in. diameter. Fig. 1 then appears to rotate in the same direction as the revolution; Fig. 2 appears to revolve in the opposite direction, and Fig. 3 appears to revolve sometimes in the same direction and at other times in the opposite direction.

A curious effect can be produced with Fig. 1 by covering up Figs. 2 and 3 with a piece of plain paper and laying a coin or other small object on the paper. If the vision is then concentrated on the coin or other object while same is being revolved, Fig. 1 will be seen to rotate.

Barrel-Stave Hammock

A hammock made of barrel staves is more comfortable than one would think, considering the nature of the material employed in making it. Good smooth staves should be selected for this purpose, and if one cares to go to a little trouble a thorough sandpapering will make a great improvement. Cut half circles out of each stave, as shown at AA, and pass ropes around

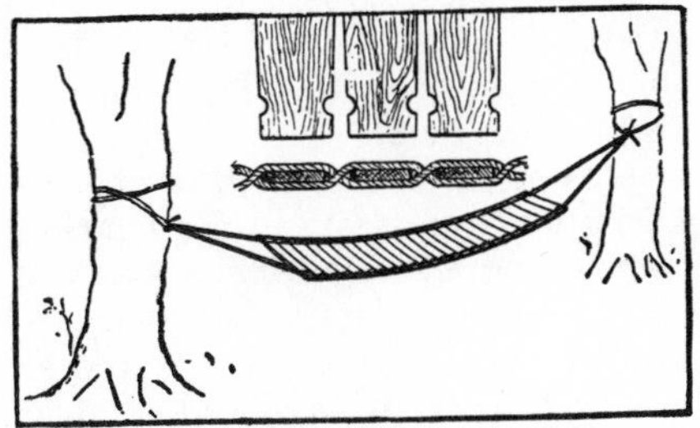
Cheap and Comfortable

the ends as shown at B. When finished the weight will then be supported by four ropes at each end, which allows the use of small-sized ropes, such as clothes lines. A hammock of this kind may be left out in the rain without injury.—Contributed by H. G. M., St. Louis, Mo.

A Singing Telephone

Those who have not already tried the experiment may be interested to know that a telephone may be made to sing by holding the receiver about $\frac{1}{16}$ in. from the transmitter, as shown in the illustration. The experiment will

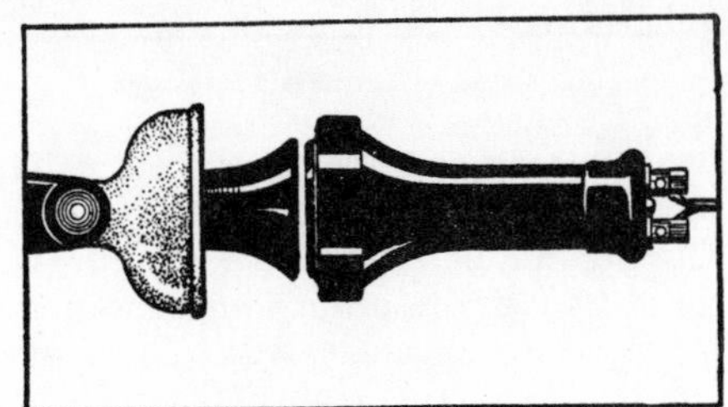
To Make a Telephone Sing

work well on most telephones, but not on all.

When the receiver is placed in the position shown it acts like an ordinary buzzer, and the function of the transmitter will then be that of an interrupter. The slightest movement of the transmitter diaphragm will cause an increased movement of the receiver diaphragm. This in turn will act on the transmitter, thus setting up sympathetic vibrations between the two, which accounts for the sound.

A Microscope Without a Lens

By E. W. DAVIS

Nearly everyone has heard of the pin-hole camera, but the fact that the same principle can be used to make a microscope, having a magnifying power of 8 diameters (64 times) will perhaps be new to some readers.

To make this lensless microscope, procure a wooden spool, A (a short spool, say ½ or ¾ in. long, produces a higher magnifying power), and enlarge the bore a little at one end. Then blacken the inside with india ink and allow it to dry. From a piece of thin transparent celluloid or mica, cut out a small disk, B, and fasten to the end having the enlarged bore, by means of brads. On the other end glue a piece of thin black cardboard, C, and at the center, D, make a small hole with the point of a fine needle. It is very important that the hole D should be very small, otherwise the image will be blurred.

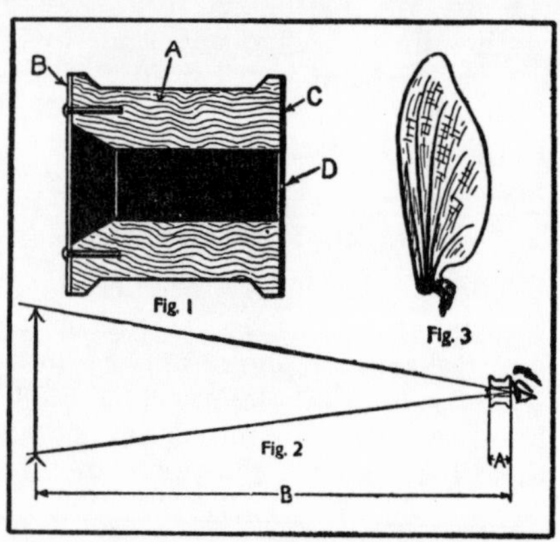

Detail of Lensless Microscope

To use this microscope, place a small object on the transparent disk, which may be moistened to make the object adhere, and look through the hole D. It is necessary to have a strong light to get good results, and, as in all microscopes of any power, the object should be of a transparent nature.

The principle on which this instrument works is illustrated in Fig. 2. The apparent diameter of an object is inversely proportional to its distance from the eye, i. e., if the distance is reduced to one-half, the diameter will appear twice as large; if the distance is reduced to one-third, the diameter will appear three times as large, and so on. As the nearest distance at which the average person can see an object clearly is about 6 in., it follows that the diameter of an object ¾ in. from the eye would appear 8 times the normal size. The object would then be magnified 8 diameters, or 64 times. (The area would appear 64 times as large.) But an object ¾ in. from the eye appears so blurred that none of the details are discernible, and it is for this reason that the pin-hole is employed.

Viewed through this microscope, a fly's wing appears as large as a person's hand, held at arm's length, and has the general appearance shown in Fig. 3. The mother of vinegar examined in the same way is seen to be swarming with a mass of wriggling little worms, and may possibly cause the observer to abstain from all salads forever after. An innocent-looking drop of water, in which hay has been soaking for several days, reveals hundreds of little infusoria, darting across the field in every direction. These and hundreds of other interesting objects may be observed in this little instrument, which costs little or nothing to make.

How to Make a Telegraph Key and Sounder

The sounder, Fig. 1, is made from an old electric-bell magnet, D, fastened to a wooden base. The lever, A, can be made of brass and the armature, C, is made of iron. The pivot, E, is made from a wire nail and is soldered to A. It should be filed to a point at each end so as to move freely in the bearings, B, which are pieces of hard wood.

The spring, H, is fastened at each end by pins, bent as shown, and should not be too strong or the magnet will be unable to move the armature. The

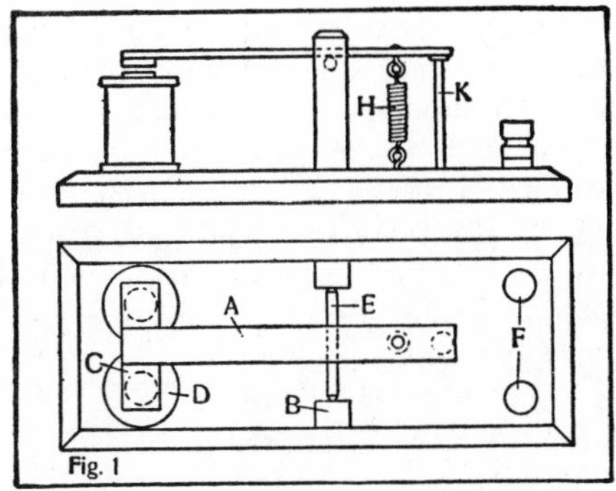

SOUNDER—A, brass; B, wood; C, soft iron; DD, coils wound with No. 26 wire; E, nail soldered on A; FF, binding posts; H spring

stop, K, is a wire nail driven deep enough in the base to leave about 1/8 in. between the armature and the magnet. The binding posts, F, may be taken from old dry batteries and are connected to the two wires from the magnet by wires run in grooves cut in the base.

The base of the key, Fig. 2, is also made of wood and has two wooden bearings, E, which are made to receive a pivot, similar to the one used in the sounder. The lever of the key is made of brass and has a hardwood knob, A, fastened near the end. A switch, D, connects with the pivot at F and can be either made from sheet brass, or taken from a small one-point switch. The binding posts are like those of the sounder, and are connected to the contacts, K, by wires run in grooves cut in the wood

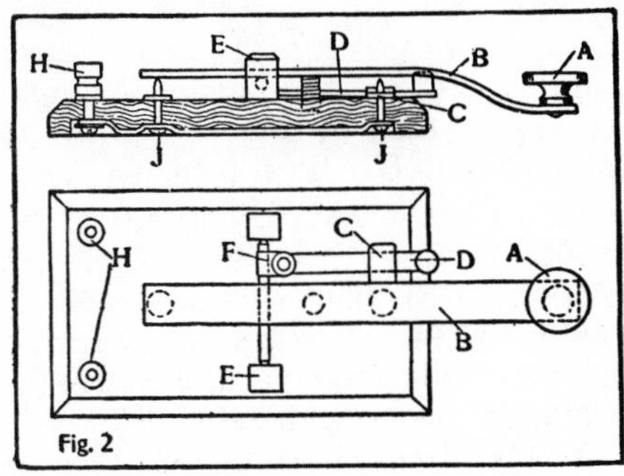

KEY—A, wood; B, brass or iron soldered to nail; C, brass; D, brass; E, wood; F, connection of D to nail; HH, binding posts

How to Make a Music Cabinet

A neat music cabinet can be made as shown in the accompanying sketch. Each side, A A, Fig. 1, is cut from a board about 36 in. in length and 16 in. wide. Both are alike and can be cut from the same pattern. As the front legs curve out a little the main body of the boards A A should be 15 in. wide. The back, B, should be about 22 in. long by 16 in. wide and set in between sides A A. Cut the top, C, 16 in. long and 14 1/4 in. wide. The bottom must be the same length as the top and 13 1/2 in. wide.

The door, D, can be made panel as shown, or a single piece, 16 in. wide and about 20 in. long. All material used is to be made from boards that will dress to 3/4 in. thick.

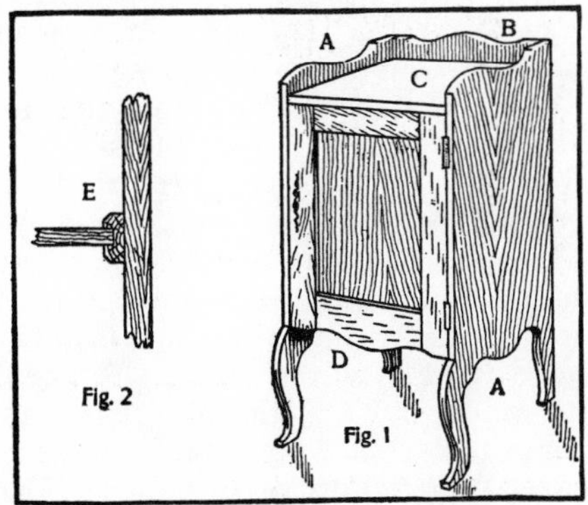

How to Make a Music Cabinet

Shelving may be put in as shown in Fig. 2 and made from 1/4-in. material. Make 12 cleats, E, 13 1/2 in. long, from a strip of wood 1/2 by 3/4 in., with a groove 1/4 by 1/4 in. cut in them. Fasten 6 cleats evenly spaced on the inside of each of the sides, A A, with 3/4-in. brads. This will give seven spaces for music and as the shelves are removable two places can be made into one.

Easily Made Wireless Coherer

A good wireless coherer may be made with very little expense, the only materials necessary being a glass tube, two corks, a magnetized needle and a quantity of iron and silver filings. Push a piece of wire through one cork and place in the bottom of the tube, as shown in the sketch.

Pour in the filings and insert the top cork with the needle pushed through from above. The point of the needle should barely touch the filings and by slightly agitating the tube the iron filings will separate from the silver and cling to the magnetized needle, as shown.

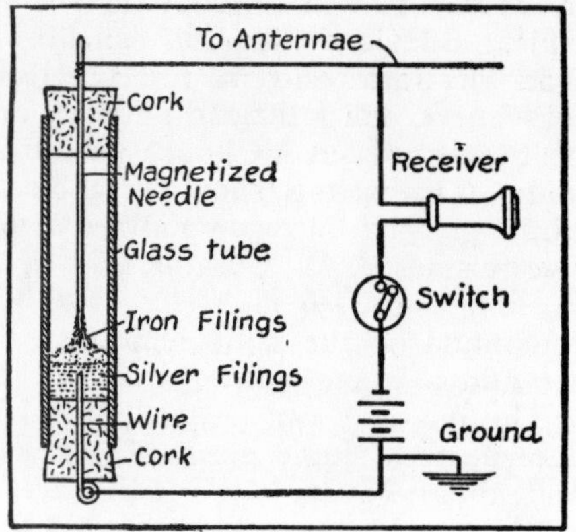

Detail of Coherer

In operation, the device must stand on end and should be connected in the circuit as shown in the sketch. When the electrical waves strike the needle, the conductivity of the filings is established and a click is heard in the receiver.—Contributed by Carl Formhals, Garfield, Ill.

One-Wire Telegraph Line

The accompanying wiring diagram shows a telegraph system that requires no switches and may be operated with open-circuit batteries on a one-wire line with ground connections at each end. Any telegraph set in which the key makes double contact can be connected up in this way.—Contributed by R. A. Brown, Fairport, N. Y.

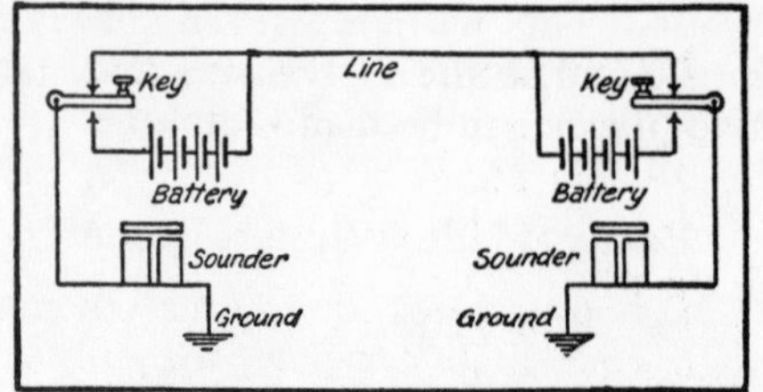

Diagram of One-Wire Line

How to Make a Water Rheostat

A water rheostat may be made by fitting a brass tube with a cork, through which a piece of wire is passed. The brass tube may be an old bicycle hand pump, A (see sketch), filled with water. Pushing the wire, B, down into the water increases the surface in contact, and thus decreases the resistance. An apparatus of this kind is suitable for regulating the current from an induction coil, when the coil is not provided with a regulator, and by using a piece of pipe instead of the tube, it can be used to regulate the speed of a motor.

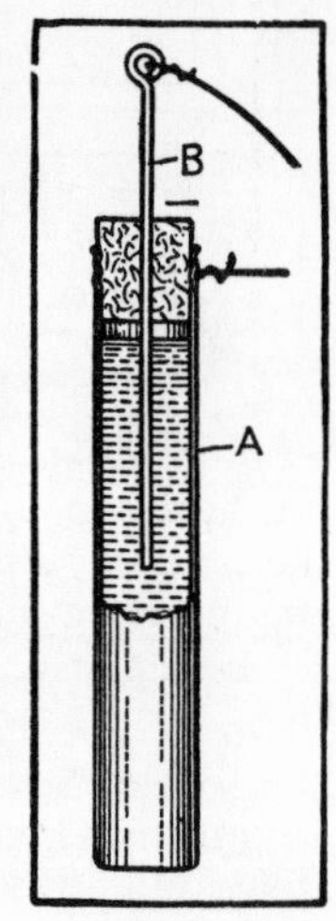

Water Rheostat

When the pipe is used, a piece of brass or copper rod should be substituted for the wire, in order to increase the surface. Adding salt to the water will decrease the resistance, and, when used with a motor, will give a greater speed.—Contributed by John Koehler, Ridgewood, N. J.

Electric Door-Opener

A very convenient and efficient device for unlocking any door fitted with a spring lock is shown in the accompanying sketches. A fairly stiff spring, A, is connected by a flexible wire cord to the knob B. The cord is also fastened to a lever, C, which is pivoted at D and is released by a magnetic trigger, E, made from the armature and magnet of an old electric bell.

When the circuit is completed by means of a secret contact device outside the door, the magnet, F, pulls down the armature, which releases the trigger and allows the spring to open the lock. If there are metal numbers on the outside of the door they may be used for the secret contact, if desired,

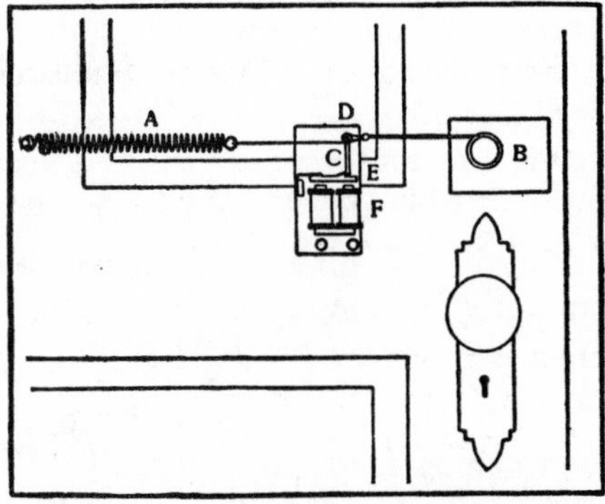

Apparatus Placed on Inside of Door

but if there are no numbers on the door, a small contact-board may be constructed by driving about 12 brass-headed tacks into a thin piece of wood and making connections at the back as shown in the wiring diagram.

In this particular diagram the tacks numbered 1 and 7 are used for unlocking the door, the others being connected with the electric-bell circuit as indicated, for the purpose of giving an alarm should anybody try to experiment with the secret contacts. By means of a pocket knife or other metal article the operator can let himself in at any time by connecting the tacks numbered 1 and 7, while a person not knowing the combination would be liable to sound the alarm. Of course, the builder of this device may choose a combination of his own and may thus prevent anybody else from entering the door, even those who read this description.—Contributed by Perry A. Borden, Gachville, N. B.

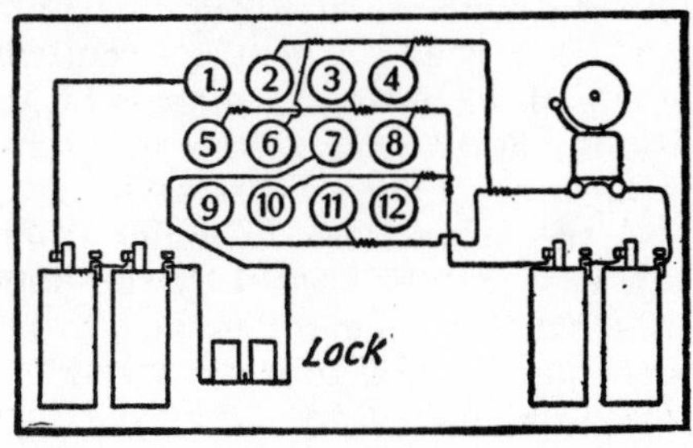

Wiring Diagram

How to Tighten a Curtain-Roller Spring

A common table fork can be used to hold the little projection on the end of a curtain roller for tightening the spring. Hold the fork firmly with one hand while turning the roller with the other. Do not let go of the fork until the little catches are set in position to prevent the spring from turning, or else the fork may be thrown off with dangerous force.

Alarm Clock Chicken Feeder

An automatic poultry feeder, which will discharge the necessary amount of corn or other feed at any desired time, may be made by using an alarm clock as shown in the sketch. A small wire trigger rests on the winding key and supports the swinging bottom of the food hopper by means of a piece of string which connects the two. When the alarm goes off the trigger drops and allows the door to open, thus discharging the contents of the hopper.

After the device has been in operation for some time the hens will run to the feeder whenever the bell rings.—Contributed by Dr. H. A. Dobson, Washington, D. C.

Homemade Disk-Record Cabinet

Select some boards that have a nice grain and about 1 in. thick and 12 in. wide. Cut the end pieces each 36 in. long and trim down the edges so as to make them 11⅜ in. wide. The top board is made 28 in. long and full 12 in. wide. The three shelves are cut 25 in. long and the edges trimmed so they will be 11⅜ in. wide. The distance between the bottom of the top board and the top of the first shelf should be 3 in. Two drawers are fitted in this space, as shown in Fig. 1. A series of grooves are cut ¼ in. wide, ¼ in. deep and ¾ in. apart on one side of the top and bottom shelves, as shown in Fig. 2, and on both sides of the middle shelf. The shelves should be spaced 9⅝ in. for 10-in. records and 5⅝ in. for 6-in. records. A neat scroll design is cut from a board 25 in. long to fill up and finish the space below the bottom shelf.—Contributed by H. E. Mangold, Compton, Cal.

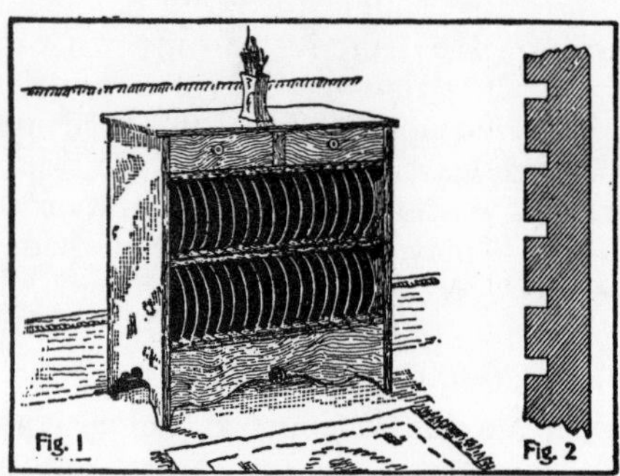

Cabinet Holding 32 Records

A Battery Rheostat

In a board 7 in. long and 5 in. wide bore holes about ¼ in. apart, in a semicircle 2 in. from the bottom, and cut notches in top end to correspond with the holes. From a piece of brass a switch, C, is cut with a knob soldered on at the end. Nails for stops are placed at DD. Two binding-posts are placed in board at A and B. With about 9 ft. of fine iron wire attach one end to the bottom of post A and run through first hole and over in first notch to back of board and then through second hole and over second notch and so on until E is reached, where the other end of wire is fastened. Connect switch to post B.—Contributed by Edmund Kuhn, Jr., East Orange, N. J.

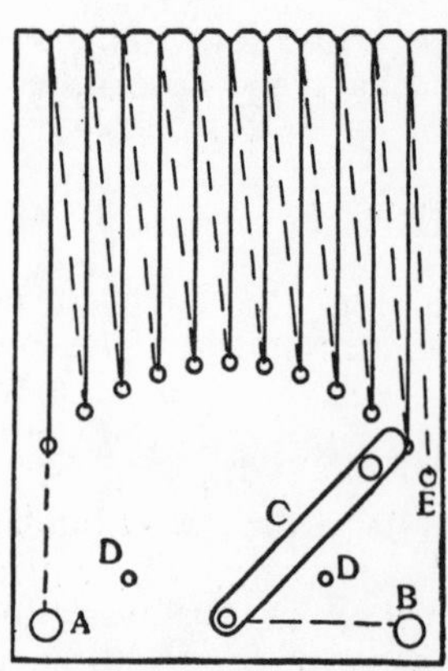

Automatic Time Switch

This device may be used to either open or close the circuit at any desired time. An alarm clock is firmly fastened to a wooden bracket and provided with a small wood or metal drum, A, to which is fastened a cord, B. The other end of the cord is tied to the switch handle so that when the alarm goes off the switch is either opened or closed, depending on whether the cord is passed over pulley C or pulley D.

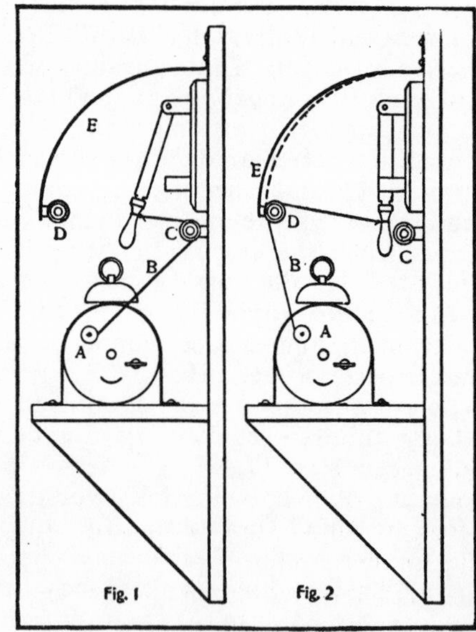

Will Open or Close Circuit as Desired

When the cord is passed over pulley C, as shown in Fig. 1, the circuit will be closed when the alarm goes off, but if it is passed over D the circuit will be opened. Pulley D is fastened to a piece of spring steel, E, which in operation is bent, as shown by the dotted lines, thus causing the switch to snap open quickly and prevent forming an arc.—Contributed by Douglas Royer, Roanoke, Va.

How to Make a Rotary Pump

A simple rotary pump is constructed on the principle of creating a vacuum in a rubber tube and so causing water to rise to fill the vacuum. Figs. 3, 4 and 5 show all the parts needed, excepting the crank and tubing. The dimensions and description given are for a minimum pump, but a larger one could be built in proportion.

Through the center of a block of wood 4 in. square and 7/8 in. thick (A, Figs. 1, 2 and 3) saw a circular opening 2 7/8 in. in diameter. On each side of this block cut a larger circle 3 1/4 in. in diameter, having the same center as the first circle (Fig. 3). Cut the last circles only 1/4 in. deep, leaving the first circle in the form of a ridge or track 3/8 in. wide, against which the rubber tubing, E, is compressed by wheels. Bore two 1/4-in. holes (HH, Fig. 1) from the outside of the block to the edge of the inner circle. Put the rubber tube, E, through one of these holes, pass it around the track and out through the other hole. Notice the break (S) in the track; this is necessary in order to place in position the piece holding the wheels.

Fig. 4 shows the wheel-holder, B. Make it of hard wood 3 1/8 in. long, 1 in. wide and a little less than 7/8 in. thick, so that it will run freely between the sides (Fig. 5) when they are placed. Cut two grooves, one in each end, 1 in. deep and 1/2 in. wide. In these grooves place wheels, CC, to turn on pins of stout wire. These wheels should be 3/4 in. in diameter. When placed in the holder their centers must be exactly 2 in. apart, or so arranged that the distance between the edge of the wheels

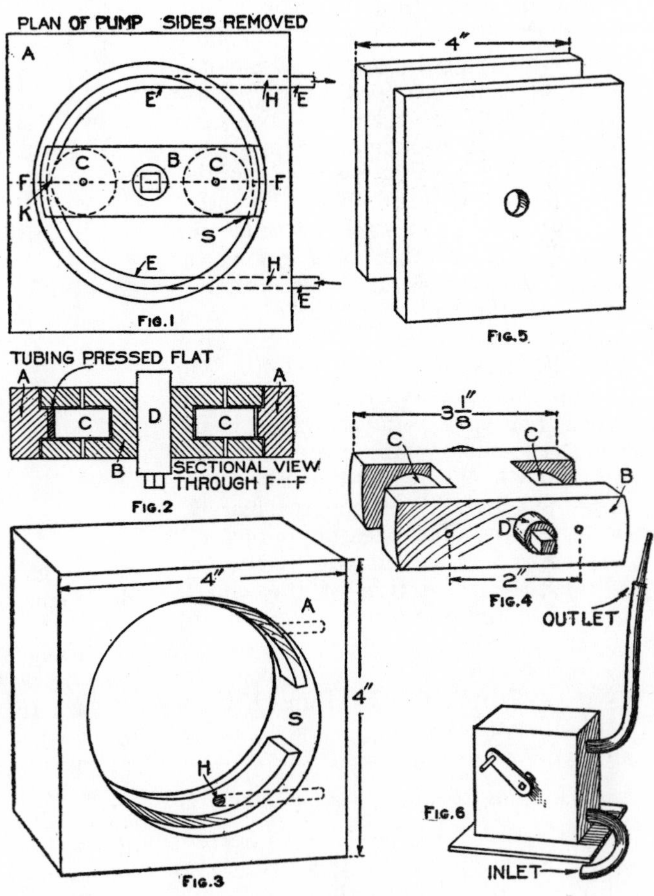

Details of Rotary Pump

and the track (K, Fig. 1) is equal to the thickness of the tubing when pressed flat. If the wheels fit too tightly, they will bind; if too loose, they will let the air through. Bore a hole through the middle of the wheel-holder and insert the crankpin, D, which should be about 1/2 in. in diameter. The crankpin should fit tightly; if necessary drive a brad through to keep it from slipping.

In the sides (Fig. 5) bore a hole in the center of the crankpin to run in loosely. Now put all these parts together, as shown in the illustration. Do not fasten the sides too securely until you have tried the device and are sure it will run smoothly. For the crank a bent piece of stout wire or a nail will serve, though a small iron wheel is better, as it gives steadiness to the motion. In this case a handle must be attached to the rim of the wheel to serve as a crank. The drive wheel from a broken-down eggbeater will do nicely. For ease in handling the pump, a platform should be added.

To use the pump, fill the tube with water and place the lower end of the tube in a reservoir of water. Make a nozzle of the end of a clay pipe stem for the other end of the tube. Then turn the crank from left to right. The first wheel presses the air out of the tube, creating a vacuum which is immediately filled with water. Before the first wheel releases the tube at the top, the other wheel has reached the bottom, this time pressing along the water that was brought up by the first wheel. If the motion of the wheels is regular, the pump will give a steady stream. Two feet of ¼-in. tubing, costing 10 cents, is all the expense necessary.—Contributed by Dan H. Hubbard, Idana, Kan.

How to Make a Fire Screen

A screen which will not interfere with the radiation of the heat from the fire, and will keep skirts and children safe can be made at little expense out of some strap iron. The screen which is shown in Fig. 1, stands 20 in. high from the base to the top cross-piece and is made of ¾ by ¼-in. and ½ by ¼-in. iron. The top and bottom pieces marked AA, Fig. 1, are ¾ by ¼ in. and are 30 in. long, bent at an angle to fit the fireplace 7 in. from each end, as shown in Fig. 2. The three legs marked BBB, Fig. 1, are of the same size iron and each leg will take 34 in. of material. In shaping the feet of these three pieces give them a slight tendency to lean toward the fire or inside of screen, says a correspondent in the Blacksmith and Wheelwright. In the two cross bars 1 in. from each end, A in Fig. 2, mark for hole and 3 in. from that mark the

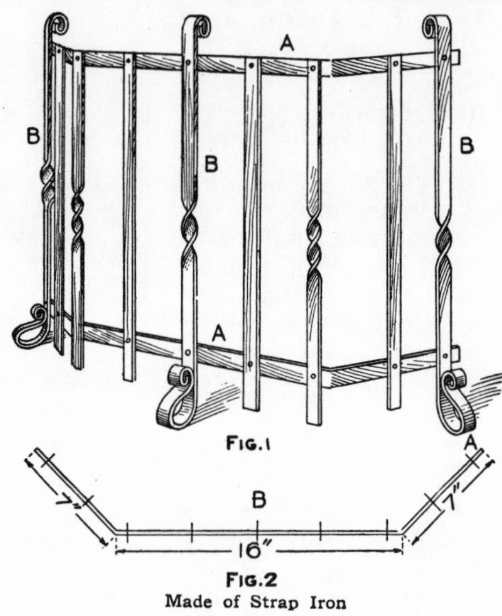

Fig. 2
Made of Strap Iron

next hole. Take the center of the bar, B, 15 in. from each end, and mark for a hole, and 3½ in. on each side mark again and 3½ in. beyond each of these two, mark again.

Mark the legs 2¾ in. from the bottom and 2 in. from the top and after making rivet-holes rivet them to the cross bars, AA, Fig. 1.

Cut six pieces, 17½ in. long and punch holes to fit and rivet onto the remaining holes in cross bars, AA, Fig. 1. Clean it up and give it a coat of black Japan or dead black.

Trap for Small Animals

This is a box trap with glass sides and back, the panes of glass being held in place by brads placed on both sides. The animal does not fear to enter the box, because he can see through it; when he enters, however, and touches the bait the lid is released and, dropping, shuts him in. This is one of the easiest traps to build and is usually successful.

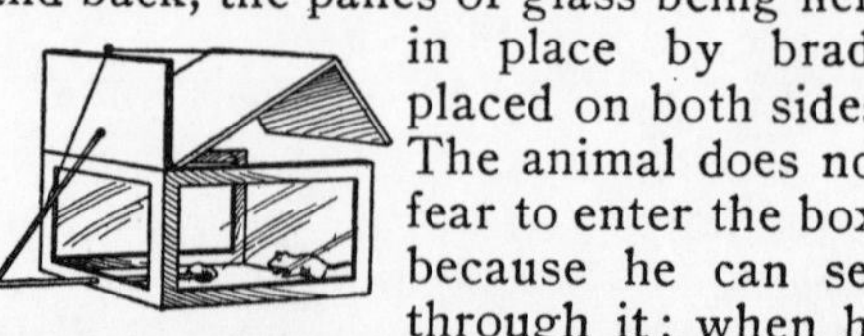

Homemade Grenet Battery

Procure an ordinary carbon-zinc, sal-ammoniac battery and remove the zinc rod. If the battery has been used before, it is better to soak the carbon cylinder for a few hours to remove any remaining crystals of sal ammoniac from its pores.

The truncated, conical zinc required is known as a fuller's zinc and can be bought at any electrical supply dealer's, or, it may be cast in a sand mold from scrap zinc or the worn-out zinc rods from sal-ammoniac batteries. It should be cast on the end of a piece of No. 14 copper wire. Amalgamation is not necessary for the zinc one buys, but if one casts his own zinc, it is necessary to amalgamate it or coat it with mercury. This may be done as follows:

Dip a piece of rag in a diluted solution of sulphuric acid (water 16 parts, acid 1 part); rub the zinc well, at the same time allowing a few drops of mercury to fall on a spot attacked by the acid. The mercury will adhere, and if the rubbing is continued so as to spread the mercury, it will cover the entire surface of the zinc, giving it a bright, silvery appearance.

Next procure what is known as a wire connector. This is a piece of copper tube about 1½ in. long having two thumb screws, one on each end on opposite sides (Fig. 2). The upper screw is to connect the battery wire, the lower one to raise and lower the zinc. The battery is now complete, and the solution (Fig. 1) must be prepared. Proceed as follows:

In 32 oz. of water dissolve 4 oz. potassium bichromate. When the bichromate has all dissolved, add slowly, stirring constantly, 4 oz. sulphuric acid. Do not add the acid too quickly or the heat generated may break the vessel containing the solution. Then pour the solution into the battery jar, until it is within 3 in. of the top. Thread the wire holding the zinc through the porcelain insulator of the carbon cylinder and also through the wire connector. Pull the zinc up as far as it will go and tighten the lower thumb screw so that it holds the wire secure. Place the carbon in the jar. If the solution touches the zinc, some of it should be poured out. To determine whether or not the zinc is touched by the solution, take out the carbon and lower the zinc. If it is wet, there is too much liquid in the jar. The battery is now ready for use.

To cause a flow of electricity, lower the zinc until it almost touches the bottom of the jar and connect an electric bell or other electrical apparatus by means of wires to the two binding posts.

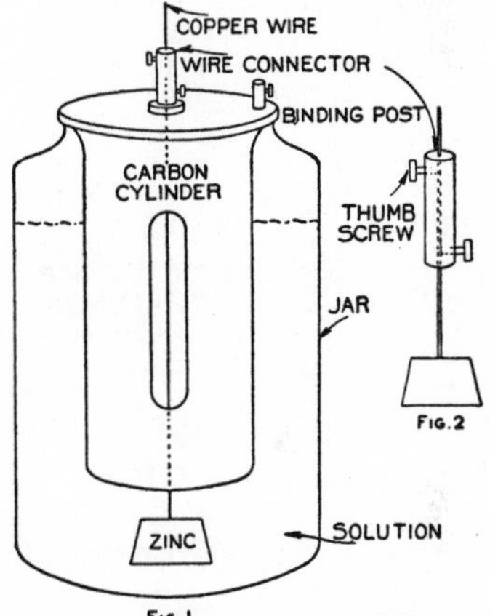

Details of Homemade Battery

This battery when first set up gives a current of about two volts. It is useful for running induction coils, or small electric motors. When through using the battery, raise the zinc and tighten the lower thumb screw. This prevents the zinc wasting away when no current is being used.—Contributed by H. C. Meyer, Philadelphia.

Door-Opener for Furnace

The accompanying diagram shows an arrangement to open the coal door of a furnace. When approaching the furnace with a shovelful of coal it is usually necessary to rest the shovel on the top of the ash door, while the coal door is being opened. With my device it is only necessary to press the foot pedal, which opens the door. After putting in the coal, pressing the pedal closes the door. The pulley in the ceiling must be placed a little in front of the door, in order to throw

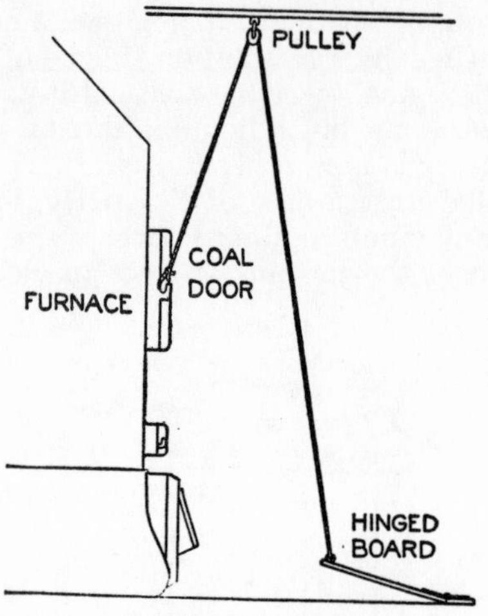

Furnace Door Opener

the door open after lifting it from the catch. A large gate hinge is used to hold the pedal to the floor.—Contributed by Edward Whitney, Madison, Wis.

How to Make an Efficient Wireless Telegraph

By GEORGE W. RICHARDSON

A simple but very efficient wireless telegraph may be constructed at slight cost from the following description:

The sending apparatus consists of nothing but an induction coil with a telegraph key inserted in the primary circuit, i. e., the battery circuit. This apparatus may be purchased from any electrical-supply house. The price of the coil depends upon its size, and upon the size depends the distance signals can be transmitted. If, however, one wishes to construct his own coil he can make and use, with slight changes, the jump-spark coil described elsewhere in this book. This coil, being a 1-in. coil, will transmit nicely up to a distance of one mile; while a 12-in. coil made on the same plan will transmit 20 miles or even more under favorable conditions.

Change the coil described, as follows: Insert an ordinary telegraph key in the battery circuit, and attach two small pieces of wire with a brass ball on each, by inserting them in the binding-posts of the coil as shown at B B″. Of these two terminal wires one is grounded to earth, while the other wire is sent aloft and is called the aerial line. This constitutes all there is to the sending apparatus.

Now for the receiving apparatus. In the earlier receiving instruments a coherer was used, consisting of a glass tube about ⅛-in. diameter, in which were two silver pistons separated by nickel and silver filings, in a partial vacuum. This receiver was difficult of adjustment and slow in transmission. An instrument much less complicated and inexpensive and which will work well can be made thus:

Take a 5-cp. incandescent lamp and break off the tip at the dotted line, as shown in Fig. 5. This can be done by giving the glass tip or point a quick blow with a file or other thin edged piece of metal. Then with a blow-torch heat the broken edges until red hot and turn the edges in as seen in Fig. 6. Remove the carbon filament in the lamp and bend the two small platinum wires so they will point at each other as in Fig. 6, W W. Screw the lamp into an ordinary wall socket which will serve as a base as in Fig. 7. Make a solution of 1 part sulphuric acid to 4 parts of water, and fill the lamp about two-thirds full (Fig. 7). This will make an excellent receiver. It will be necessary to adjust the platinum points, W W, to suit the distance the message is to be worked. For a mile or less the points should be about $\frac{1}{16}$ in. apart, and closer for longer distances.

The tuning coil is simply a variable choking coil, made of No. 14 insulated copper wire wound on an iron core, as shown in Fig. 7. After winding, carefully scrape the insulation from one side of the coil, in a straight line from top to bottom, the full length of the coil, uncovering just enough to allow a good contact for the sliding piece. The tuning is done by sliding the contact piece, which is made of light copper wire, along the convolutions of the tuning coil until you can hear the signals. The signals are heard in a telephone receiver, which is shown connected in shunt across the binding-posts of the lamp holder with one or two cells of dry battery in circuit, Fig. 7.

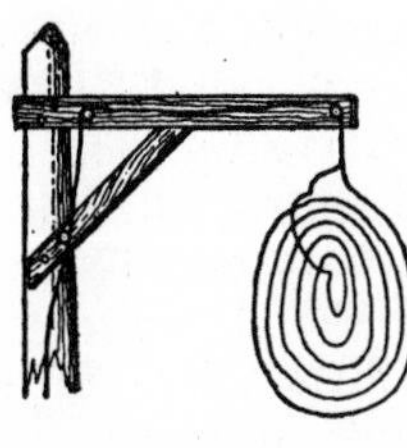

The aerial line, No. 6 stranded, is run from binding-post B through the choking or tuning coil, and for best results should extend up 50 ft. in the air. To work a 20-mile distance the line should be 100 or 150 ft. above the ground. A good way is to erect a wooden pole on a house or barn and carry the aerial wire to the top and out to the end of a gaff or arm.

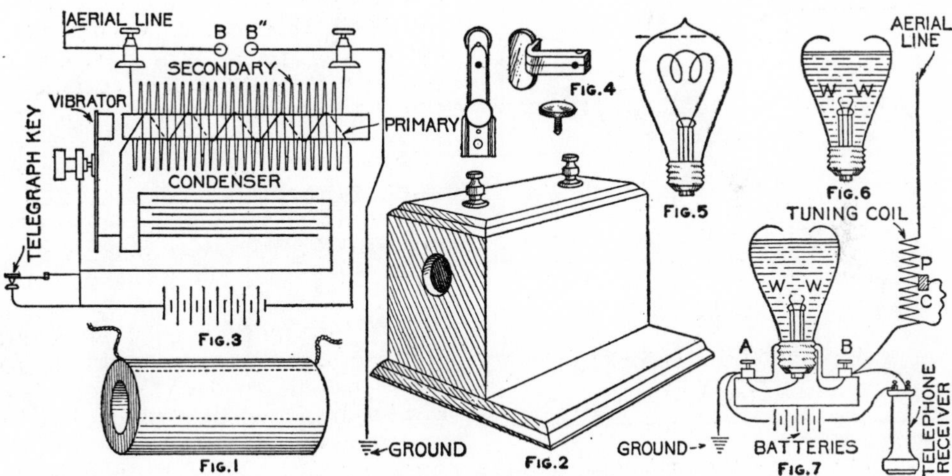

To the end of the aerial wire fasten a bunch of endless loops made of about No. 14 magnet wire (bare or insulated), attaching both ends tó the leading or aerial wire. The aerial wire should not come nearer than 1 ft. at any point to any metal which is grounded.

Run a wire from the other binding-post, A, to the ground and be sure to make a good ground connection.

For simple experimental work on distances of 100 ft. only, an ordinary automobile spark coil can be used in place of the more elaborate coil, Figs. 1 to 4.

The above-mentioned instruments have no patents on them, and any one is at liberty to build and use them. The writer does not claim to be the originator, but simply illustrates the above to show that, after all, wireless is very simple when it is once understood. The fundamental principles are that induction travels at right angles, 90°, to the direction of the current. For an illustration, if a person standing on a bridge should drop a pebble into the water below, after contact he would note circles radiating out over the surface of the water. These circles, being at right angles, 90°, to the direction of the force that caused the circles, are analogous to the flow of induction, and hence the aerial line, being vertical, transmits signals horizontally over the earth's surface.

¶When filling nail holes in yellow pine use beeswax instead of putty, as it matches the color well.

How to Make a Lathe

A small speed-lathe, suitable for turning wood or small metal articles, may be easily made at very little expense. A lathe of this kind is shown in the cut (Fig. 1), where A is the headstock, B the bed and C the tailstock. I run my lathe by power, using an electric motor and countershaft, but it could be run by footpower if desired. A large cone pulley would then be required, but this may be made in the same manner as the small one, which will be described later.

The bed of the machine is made of wood as shown in Figs. 2 and 3, hardwood being preferable for this purpose. Fig. 2 shows an end view of the assembled bed, and Fig. 3 shows how the ends are cut out to receive the side pieces.

The headstock, Fig. 6, is fastened to the bed by means of carriage bolts, A, which pass through a piece of wood, B, on the under side of the bed. The shaft is made of ¾-in. steel tubing about ⅛ in. thick, and runs in babbitt bearings, one of which is shown in Fig. 5.

To make these bearings, cut a square hole in the wood as shown, making half of the square in each half of the bearing. Separate the two halves of the bearing slightly by placing a piece of cardboard on each side, just touching the shaft. The edges which touch the shaft should be notched like the teeth of a saw, so as to allow the babbitt to run into the lower half of the bearing. The notches for this purpose may be about ⅛ in. pitch and ⅛ in. deep. Place pieces of wood against the ends of the bearing as shown at A and B, Fig. 4, and drill a hole in the top of the bearing as shown in Fig. 4.

The bearing is then ready to be poured. Heat the babbitt well, but not hot enough to burn it, and it is well to have the shaft hot, too, so that the babbitt will not be chilled when it strikes the shaft. If the shaft is thoroughly chalked or smoked the babbitt will not stick to it. After pouring, remove the shaft and split the bearing with a round, tapered wooden pin. If the bearing has been properly made, it will split along the line of the notched cardboard where the section of the metal is smallest. Then drill a hole in the top as shown at A, Fig. 5, drilling just deep enough to have the point of the drill appear at the lower side. This cavity acts as an oil cup and prevents the bearing from running dry.

The bolts B (Fig. 5) are passed

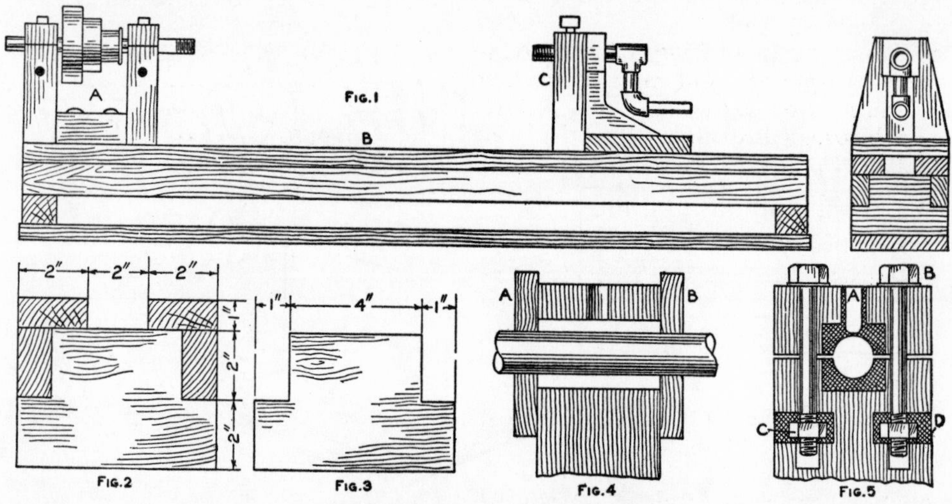

Assembled Lathe Bed and Bearing Details

through holes in the wood and screwed into nuts C, which are let into holes

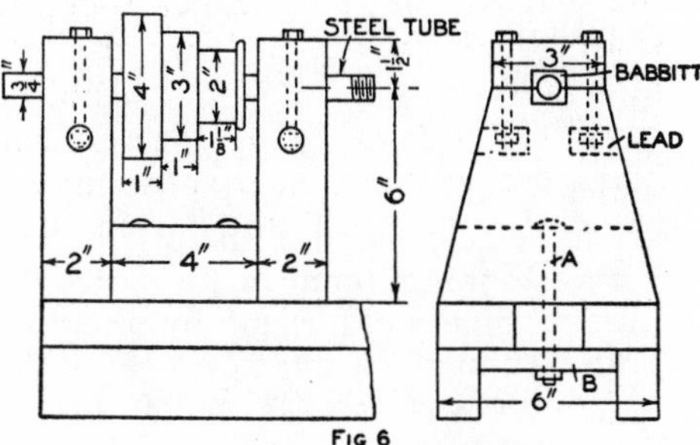

Headstock Details

D, the holes afterward being filled with melted lead.

This type of bearing will be found very satisfactory and may be used to advantage on other machines. After the bearings are completed the cone pulley can be placed on the shaft. To make this pulley cut three circular pieces of wood to the dimensions given in Fig. 6 and fasten these together with nails and glue. If not perfectly true, they may be turned up after assembling, by rigging up a temporary toolrest in front of the headstock.

The tailstock (Fig. 7) is fastened to the bed in the same manner as the headstock, except that thumb nuts are used on the carriage bolts, thus allowing the tailstock to be shifted when necessary. The mechanism of the center holder is obtained by using a ½-in.

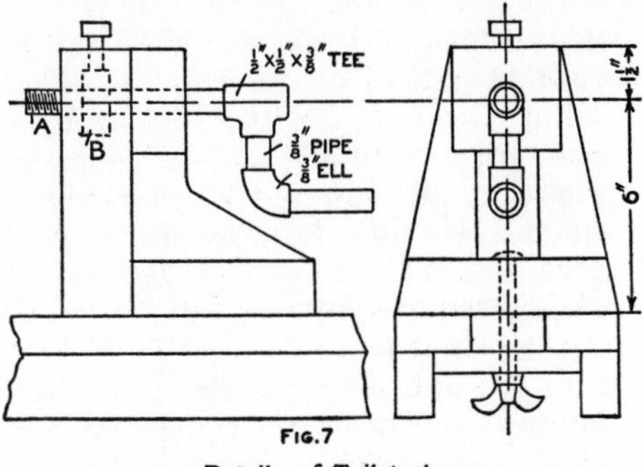

Details of Tailstock

pipe, A, and a ½-in. lock nut, B, embedded in the wood.

I found that a wooden tool-rest was not satisfactory, so I had to buy one, but they are inexpensive and much handier than homemade tool rest.—Contributed by Donald Reeves, Oak Park, Ill.

To Use Old Battery Zincs

When the lower half of a battery zinc becomes eaten away the remaining part can be used again by suspending it from a wire as shown in the cut. Be sure and have a good connection at the zinc binding post and cover that with melted paraffin. This prevents corrosion, which would otherwise occur from the action of the sal ammoniac or other chemical. The wire may be held at the top by twisting it around a piece

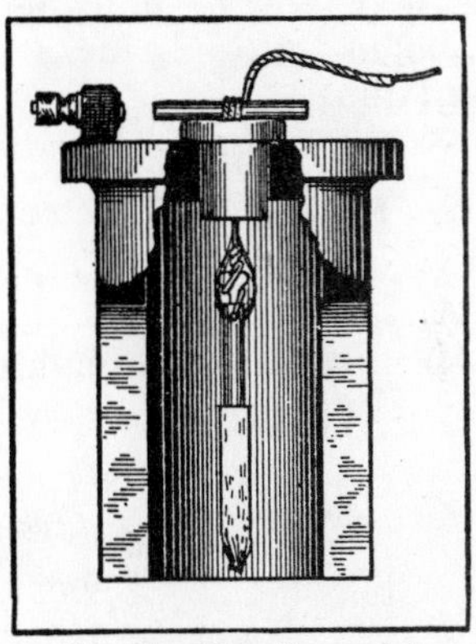

Showing Zinc Suspended

of wood or by driving a peg through the hole in the porcelain insulator.—Contributed by Louis Lauderbach, Newark, N. J.

Callers' Approach Alarm

This alarm rings so that callers approaching the door may be seen before they ring the bell and one can exercise his pleasure about admitting them.

If one has a wooden walk, the alarm is easy to fix up. Take up about 5 ft. of the walk and nail it together so as to make a trapdoor that will work easily. Place a small spring under one end to hold it up about ¼ in. (A, Fig. 2). Nail a strip of tin along the under side of the trap near the spring and fasten another strip on the baseboard, so that they will not touch, save when a weight is on the trap. Connect up an electric bell, putting the batteries and bell anywhere desired, and using rubber-covered wire outside the house, and the alarm is complete.

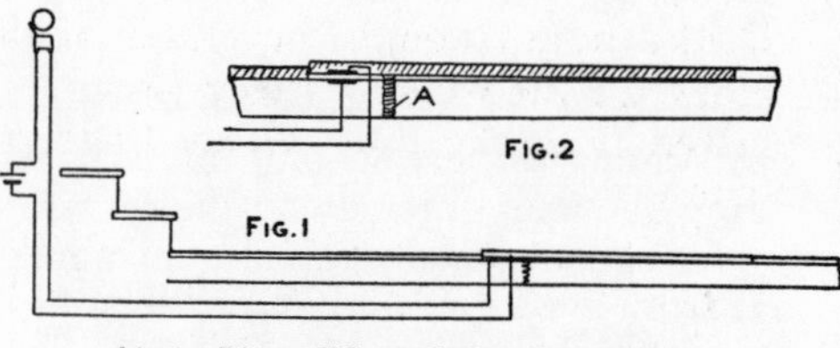

Alarm Rings When Caller Approaches

When a person approaching the house steps on the trap, the bell will ring and those in the house can see who it is before the door bell rings.—Contributed by R. S. Jackson, Minneapolis, Minn.

Easy Method of Electroplating

Before proceeding to electroplate with copper, silver or other metal, clean the articles thoroughly, as the least spot of grease or dirt will prevent the deposit from adhering. Then polish the articles and rub them over with a cloth and fine pumice powder, to roughen the surface slightly. Finally, to remove all traces of grease, dip the articles to be plated in a boiling potash solution made by dissolving 4 oz. American ash in 1½ pt. of water. Do not touch the work with the hands again. To avoid touching it, hang the articles on the wires, by which they are to be suspended in the plating bath, before dipping them in the potash solution; then hold them by the wires under running water for ten minutes to completely remove every trace of the potash.

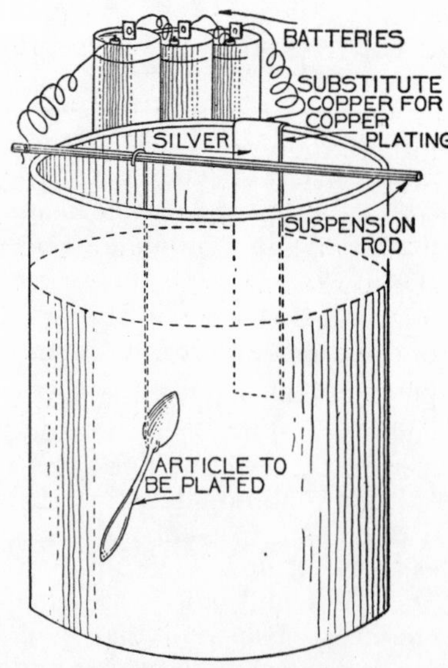

Electroplating Apparatus

For plating with copper prepare the following solution: 4 oz. copper sulphate dissolved in 12 oz. water; add strong ammonia solution until no more green crystals are precipitated. Then add more ammonia and stir until the green crystals are re-dissolved giving an intense blue solution. Add slowly a strong solution of potassium cyanide until the blue color disappears, leaving a clear solution; add potassium cyanide again, about one-fourth as much in bulk as used in the decolorizing process. Then make the solution up to 2 qt. with water. With an electric pressure of 3.5 to 4 volts, this will give an even deposit of copper on the article being plated.

A solution for silverplating may be prepared as follows: Dissolve ¾ oz. of commercial silver nitrate in 8 oz. of water, and slowly add a strong solution of potassium cyanide until no more white precipitate is thrown down. Then pour the liquid off and wash the precipitate carefully. This is best done by filling the bottle with water, shaking, allowing precipitate to settle and then pouring off the water. Repeat six times. Having finished washing the precipitate, slowly add to it a solution of potassium cyanide until all the precipitate is dissolved. Then add an excess of potassium cyanide—about as much as was used in dissolving the precipitate—and make the solution up to 1 qt. with water. This solution, with an electric pressure of 2 to 4 volts, will give a good white coat of silver in twenty minutes to half-an-hour; use

2 volts for large articles, and 4 volts for very small ones. If more solution is required, it is only necessary to double all given quantities.

Before silverplating, such metals as iron, lead, pewter, zinc, must be coated with copper in the alkaline copper bath described, and then treated as copper. On brass, copper, German silver, nickel and such metals, silver can be plated direct. The deposit of silver will be dull and must be polished. The best method is to use a revolving scratch brush; if one does not possess a buffing machine, a hand scratch brush is good. Take quick, light strokes. Polish the articles finally with ordinary plate powder.

The sketch shows how to suspend the articles in the plating-bath. If accumulators are used, which is advised, be sure to connect the positive (or red) terminal to the piece of silver hanging in the bath, and the negative (or black) terminal to the article to be plated. Where Bunsen cells are used, the carbon terminal takes the place of the positive terminal of the accumulator.—Model Engineer.

An Ingenious Electric Lock for a Sliding Door

The apparatus shown in Fig. 1 not only unlocks, but opens the door, also, by simply pressing the key in the keyhole.

In rigging it to a sliding door, the materials required are: Three flat pulleys, an old electric bell or buzzer, about 25 ft. of clothesline rope and some No. 18 wire. The wooden catch, A (Fig. 1), must be about 1 in. thick and 8 in. long; B should be of the same wood, 10 in. long, with the pivot 2 in. from the lower end. The wooden block C, which is held by catch B, can be made of a 2-in. piece of broomstick. Drill a hole through the center of this block for the rope to pass through, and fasten it to the rope with a little tire tape.

When all this is set up, as shown in Fig. 1, make a key and keyhole. A ¼-in. bolt or a large nail sharpened to a point, as at F, Fig. 3, will serve for the key. To provide the keyhole, saw a piece of wood, I, 1 in. thick by 3 in. square, and bore a hole to fit the key in the center. Make a somewhat larger block (E, Fig. 3) of thin wood with a ⅛-in. hole in its center. On one side of this block tack a piece of tin (K, Fig. 3) directly over the hole. Screw the two blocks together, being careful to bring the holes opposite each other. Then, when the point of the key touches the tin, and the larger part (F, Fig. 3) strikes the bent wire L, a circuit is completed; the buzzer knocks catch A (Fig. 1), which rises at the opposite end and allows catch B to fly forward and release the piece of broomstick C. The weight D then falls and jerks up the hook-lock M, which unlocks the door, and the heavier weight N immediately opens it.

Thus, with a switch as in Fig. 3, the door can only be opened by the person who has the key, for the circuit cannot be closed with an ordinary nail or wire. B, Fig. 2, shows catch B, Fig. 1, enlarged; O, Fig. 2, is the cut through which the rope runs; H, Fig. 1, is an elastic that snaps the catch back into

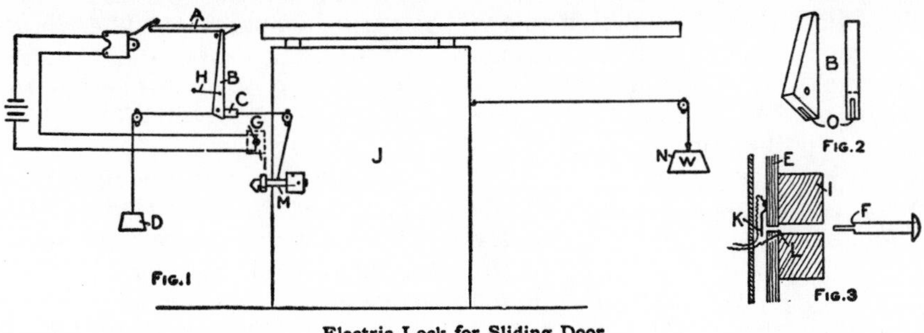

Electric Lock for Sliding Door

place, and at G the wires run outside to the keyhole.

This arrangement is very convenient when one is carrying something in one hand and can only use the other. Closing the door winds up the apparatus again.—Contributed by E. H. Klipstein, 116 Prospect St., East Orange, New Jersey.

Parlor Magic for Winter Evenings

By C. H. CLAUDY

You are seated in a parlor at night, with the lights turned low. In front of you, between the parlor and the room back of it, is an upright square of brightly burning lights, surrounding a perfectly black space. The magician stands in front of this, in his shirt sleeves, and after a few words of introduction proceeds to show the wonders of his magic cave. Showing you plainly that both hands are empty, he points with one finger to the box, where immediately appears a small white china bowl. Holding his empty hand over this bowl, some oranges and apples drop from his empty hand into the bowl. He removes the bowl from the black box, or cave, and hands its contents round to the audience. Receiving the bowl again, he tosses it into the cave, but it never reaches the floor—it disappears in mid-air.

The illusions he shows you are too many to retail at length. Objects appear and disappear. Heavy metal objects, such as forks, spoons and jack-knives, which have been shown to the audience and which can have no strings attached to them, fly about in the box at the will of the operator. One thing changes to another and back again, and black art reigns supreme.

Now all this "magic" is very simple and requires no more skill to prepare or execute than any clever boy or girl of fourteen may possess. It is based on the performance of the famous Hermann, and relies on a principle of optics for its success. To prepare such a magic cave, the requisites are a large soap box, a few simple tools, some black paint, some black cloth, and plenty of candles.

The box must be altered first. One end is removed, and a slit, one-third of the length from the remaining end, cut in one side. This slit should be as long as the width of the box and about five inches wide. On either side of the box, half way from open end to closed end, should be cut a hole, just large enough to comfortably admit a hand and arm.

Next, the box should be painted black both inside and out, and finally lined inside with black cloth. This lining must be done neatly—no folds must show and no heads of tacks. The interior must be a dead black. The box is painted black first so that the cloth used need not be very heavy; but if the cloth be sufficiently thick, no painting inside is required. The whole inside is to be cloth-lined, floor, top, sides and end.

Next, the illumination in front must be arranged. If you can have a plumber make you a square frame of gas-piping, with tiny holes all along it for the gas to escape and be lit, and connect this by means of a rubber tube to the gas in the house, so much the better; but a plentiful supply of short candles will do just as well, although a little more trouble. The candles must be close together and arranged on little brackets around the whole front of the "cave" (see small cut), and should have little pieces of bright tin behind them, to throw the light toward the audience. The whole function of these candles is to dazzle the eyes of the spectators, heighten the illusion, and prevent them seeing very far into the black box.

Finally, you must have an assistant, who must be provided with either black gloves or black bags to go over his hands and arms, and several black drop curtains, attached to sticks greater in length than the width of the box, which are let down through the slit in the top.

The audience room should have only low lights; the room where the cave is should be dark, and if you can drape portieres between two rooms around the box (which, of course, is on a table) so much the better.

The whole secret of the trick lies in the fact that if light be turned away from anything black, into the eyes of him who looks, the much fainter light reflected from the black surface will not affect the observer's eye. Consequently, if, when the exhibitor puts his hand in the cave, his confederate behind inserts his hand, covered with a black glove and holding a small bag of black cloth, in which are oranges and apples, and pours them from the bag into a dish, the audience sees the oranges and apples appear, but does not see the black arm and bag against the black background.

The dish appears by having been placed in position behind a black curtain, which is snatched swiftly away at the proper moment by the assistant. Any article thrown into the cave and caught by the black hand and concealed by a black cloth seems to disappear. Any object not too large can be made to "levitate" by the same means. A picture of any one present may be made to change into a grinning skeleton by suddenly screening it with a dropped curtain, while another curtain is swiftly removed from over a pasteboard skeleton, which can be made to dance either by strings, or by the black veiled hand holding on to it from behind, and the skeleton can change to a white cat.

But illusions suggest themselves. There is no end to the effects which can be had from this simple apparatus, and if the operators are sufficiently well drilled the result is truly remarkable to the uninitiated. The illusion, as presented by Hermann, was identical with this, only he, of course, had a big stage, and people clothed in black to creep about and do his bidding, while here the power behind the throne is but a black-veiled hand and arm. It can be made even more complicated by having two assistants, one on each side of the box, and this is the reason why it was advised that two holes be cut. This enables an absolutely instantaneous change as one uncovers the object at the moment the second assistant covers and removes the other.

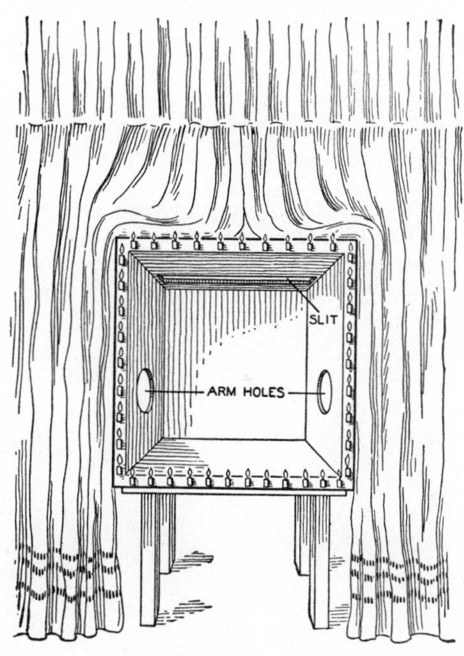

The Magic Cave

It is important that the assistants remain invisible throughout, and if portieres are impossible, a screen must be used. But any boy ingenious enough to follow these simple instructions will not need to be told that the whole success of the exhibition depends upon the absolute failure of the audience to understand that there is more than one concerned in bringing about the curious effects which are seen. The exhibitor should be a boy who can talk; a good "patter"—as the magicians call it—is often of more value than a whole host of mechanical effects and helpers. It is essential that the exhibitor and his confederate be well drilled, so that the latter can produce the proper effects at the proper cue from the former. Finally, never give an exhibition with the "cave" until you have watched the illusions from the front yourself; so that you can determine whether everything connected with the draping is right, or whether some stray bit of light reveals what you wish to conceal.

Reversing-Switch for Electrical Experiments

A homemade reversing-switch, suitable for use by students of electrical and engineering courses in performing experiments, is shown in the diagram.

Referring to Fig. 1, A represents a pine board 4 in. by 4 in. and a is a circular piece of wood about ¼ in. square, with three brass strips, b^1, b^2, b^3, held down on it by two terminals, or binding posts, c^1, c^2, and a common screw,

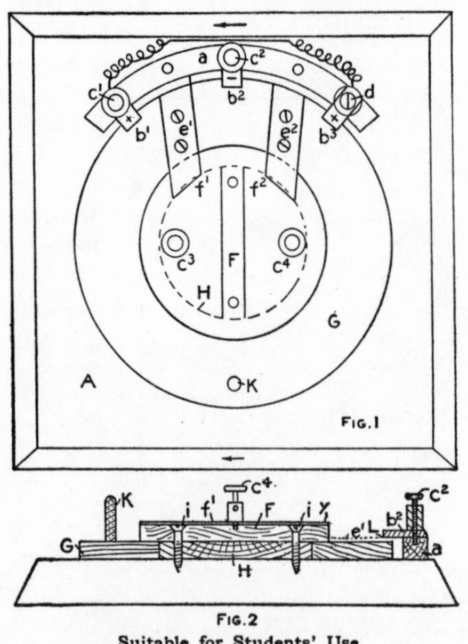

Fig. 2
Suitable for Students' Use

d. Post c^1 is connected to d by means of an insulated wire, making them carry the same kind of current (+ in the sketch).

About the center piece H moves a disk, held down by another disk F (Fig. 2), which is fastened through the center piece to the wooden base, A, by means of two wood screws. On the disk G are two brass strips, e^1 and e^2, so arranged that, when handle K is turned to one side, their one end just slips under the strips b^1, b^2, or b^2, b^3, respectively, making contact with them, as shown in Fig. 2, at L, while their other ends slide in two half-circular brass plates f^1, f^2, held down on disk F by two other terminals, c^3, c^4, making contact with them as shown at y, Fig. 2.

The action of the switch is shown in Fig. 1. Connect terminal c^1 to the carbon of a battery, and c^2 to the zinc. Then, if you turn handle K to the right, so that the strips e^1 and e^2 touch b^1 and b^2, respectively, terminal c^3 will show +, and c^1 — electricity; vice versa, if you turn the handle to the left so that e^1 and e^2 touch b^2 and b^3, respectively, terminal c^3 will show —, and c^4 + electricity.

The switch is easy to make and of very neat appearance.

How to Receive Wireless Telegraph Messages with a Telephone

Any telephone having carbon in the transmitter (all ordinary telephones have carbon transmitters) can be used to receive wireless messages by simply making a few changes in the connections and providing a suitable antenna. Connect the transmitter and receiver in series with three dry cells and run one wire from the transmitter to the antenna. Connect the other transmitter wire to a water or gas pipe in order to ground it, and then hold the receiver to your ear. Any wireless telegraph message within a radius of one mile will cause the transmitter to act as a coherer, thus making the message audible in the receiver.

By using an ordinary telephone transmitter and receiver and a ½-in. jump spark coil, a complete wireless telegraph station may be made, which will send or receive messages for a radius of one mile. The accompanying wiring diagram shows how to make the connections. By putting in an extra switch three of the sending batteries may be switched in when receiving,

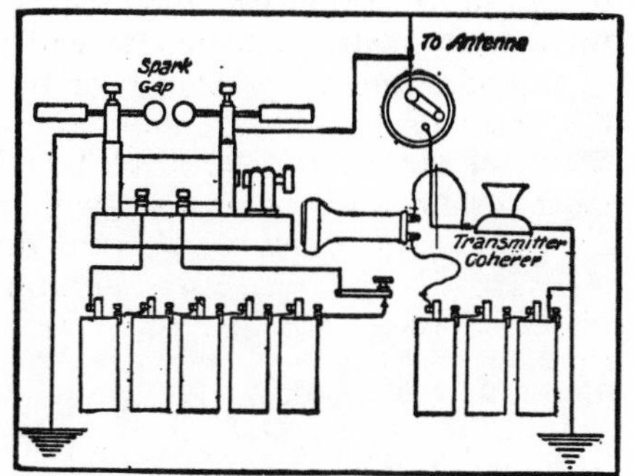

Wiring Diagram for Wireless Telegraph

thus obviating the necessity of an extra set of batteries.—Contributed by A. E. Joerin.

Connecting Up Batteries to Give Any Voltage

Referring to the illustration: A is a five-point switch (may be homemade); B is a one-point switch, and C and C¹ are binding posts. When switch B is closed and A is on No. 1,

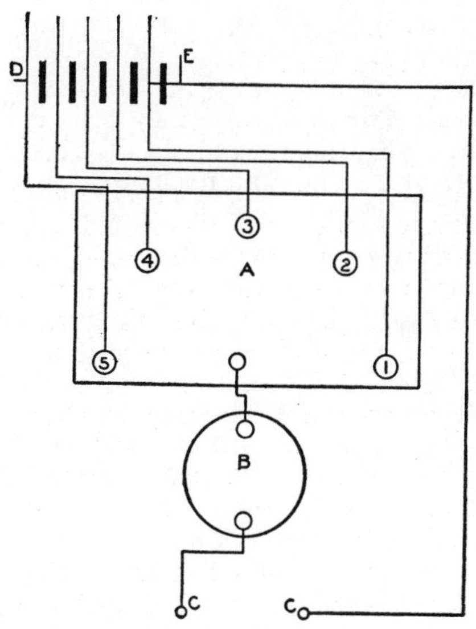

you have the current of one battery; when A is on No. 2 you receive the current from two batteries; when on No. 3, from three batteries; when on No. 4, from four batteries, and when on No. 5, from five batteries. More batteries may be connected to each point of switch B.

I have been using the same method for my water rheostat (homemade). I have the jars of water where the batteries are and the current coming in at a and b.—Contributed by Eugene F. Tuttle, Jr., Newark, Ohio.

A Simple Accelerometer

A simple accelerometer for indicating the increase in speed of a train was described by Mr. A. P. Trotter in a paper read before the Junior Institution of Engineers of Great Britain. The device consists of an ordinary 2-ft. rule, A, with a piece of thread tied to the 22-in. mark, as shown in the sketch, and supporting the small weight, B, which may be a button or other small object.

The device thus arranged, and placed on the window-sill of the car, will indicate the acceleration and retardation as follows: Every ½ in. traveled by the thread, over the bent portion of the rule, indicates an increase of or decrease of velocity to the extent of 1 ft. per second for each second. Thus, if the thread moved 2¼ in. in a direction opposite to the movement of the train, then the train would be increasing its speed at the rate of 4½ ft. per second.

If the thread is tied at the 17-in. mark, then each half inch will represent the mile per hour increase for each second. Thus if the thread moves 1 in., it shows that the train is gaining 2 miles an hour each second.

An Egg-Shell Funnel

Bottles having small necks are hard to fill without spilling the liquid. A funnel cannot be used in a small opening, and pouring with a graduate glass requires a steady hand. When you do not have a graduate at hand, a half egg-shell with a small hole pricked in the end will serve better than a funnel. Place the shell in an oven to brown the surface slightly and it will be less brittle and last much longer.—Contributed by Maurice Baudier, New Orleans, La.

Handy Electric Alarm

An electric alarm which one may turn off from the bed without arising combined with a light which may be turned on and off from a lying position, so one can see the time, is the device of H. E. Redmond, of Burlington, Wis.

The alarm clock rests on a shelf, A,

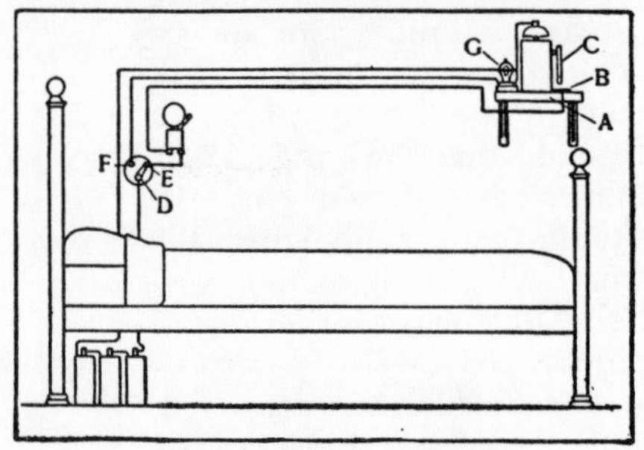

Handy Electric Alarm

which has a piece of metal, B, fastened in such a position that the metal rod C, soldered to the alarm winder, will complete the circuit and ring the bell. The two-point switch D is closed normally at E, but may be closed at F any time desired, thus turning on the small incandescent light G, which illuminates the face of the clock. When the alarm goes off, the bell will continue to ring until the switch is opened.

To Keep Dogs and Cats Away from the Garbage-Can

Last summer I was annoyed a great deal by dogs upsetting our garbage-can on the lawn, but finally executed a plan that rid the yard of them in one afternoon.

I first secured a magneto out of an old telephone, then drove a spike in a damp place under the porch, attached a wire to the spike and ran the wire to one of the poles of the magneto. Then I set the garbage-can on some blocks of wood, being careful not to have it touch the ground at any point. I next ran a wire from the other pole of the

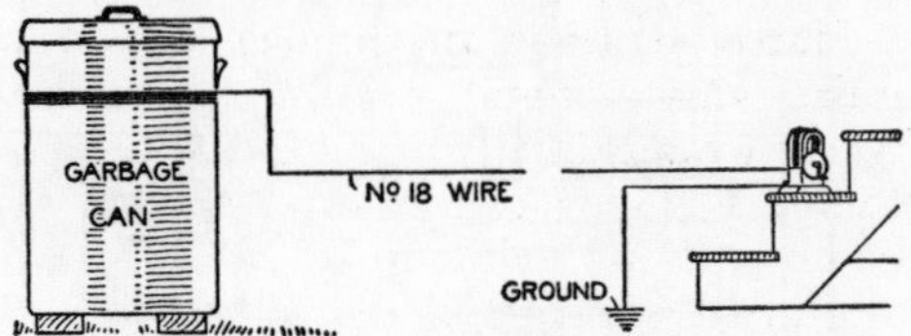

magneto to the can, wrapping the wire around the can several times. Then I sat down on the porch to wait.

It was not long before a big greyhound came along, putting his fore-paws on the top of the can to upset it. At the same instant I gave the magneto a quick turn, which sent the dog away a very surprised animal. This was repeated several times during the afternoon with other dogs, and with the same result.—Contributed by Gordon T. Lane, Crafton, Pa.

How to Cross a Stream on a Log

When crossing a water course on a fence rail or small log, do not face up or down the stream and walk sideways, for a wetting is the inevitable result. Instead, fix the eye on the opposite shore and walk steadily forward. Then if a mishap comes, you will fall with one leg and arm encircling the bridge.—C. C. S.

Relay Made from Electric Bell

It is not necessary to remove the adjusting-screw when changing an electric bell into a relay.

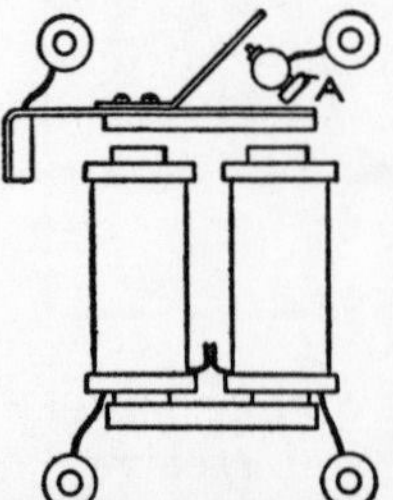

Simply twist it around as at A and bend the circuit-breaking contact back as shown. It may be necessary to remove the head of the screw, A, to prevent short-circuiting with the armature.—Contributed by A. L. Macey, New York City.

Foundry Work at Home

I. The Equipment

Many amateur mechanics who require small metal castings in their work would like to make their own castings. This can easily be done at home without going to any great expense, and the variety and usefulness of the articles produced will make the equipment a good investment.

With the easily made devices about to be described, the young mechanic can make his own telegraph keys and sounders, battery zincs, binding posts, engines, cannons, bearings, small machinery parts, models and miniature objects, ornaments of various kinds, and duplicates of all these, and many other interesting and useful articles.

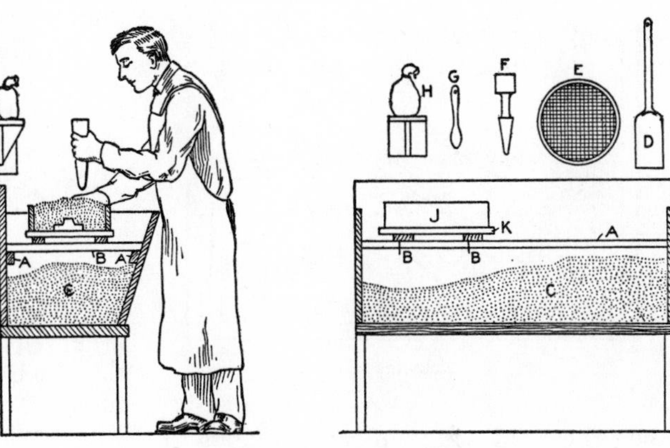

Fig. 1—Convenient Arrangement of Bench and Tools

The first thing to make is a molding-bench, as shown in Fig. 1. It is possible to make molds without a bench, but it is a mistake to try to do this, as the sand is sure to get on the floor, whence it is soon tracked into the house. The bench will also make the operation of molding much easier and will prove to be a great convenience.

The bench should be made of lumber about 1 in. thick and should be constructed in the form of a trough, as shown. Two cleats, A A, should be nailed to the front and back to support the cross-boards, BB, which in turn support the mold while it is being made. The object of using the cleats and removable cross-boards instead of a stationary shelf is to give access to the sand, C, when it is being prepared.

About one or two cubic feet of fine molding-sand will be required, which may be purchased at the nearest foundry for a small sum. Yellow sand will be found a little better for the amateur's work than the black sand generally used in most foundries, but if no yellow sand can be obtained the black kind will do. If there is no foundry near at hand, try using sand from other sources, giving preference to the finest sand and that which clings together in a cake when compressed between the hands. Common lake or river sand is not suitable for the purpose, as it is too coarse and will not make a good mold.

For mixing and preparing the sand a small shovel, D, and a sieve, E, will be required. If desired the sieve may be homemade. Ordinary wire netting such as is used in screen doors, is about the right mesh, and this, nailed to replace the bottom of a box, makes a very good sieve.

The rammer, F, is made of wood, and is wedge-shaped at one end and flat at the other, as shown. In foundries each molder generally uses two rammers, but for the small work which will be described one will be sufficient. An old teaspoon, G, will be found useful in the molding operations and may be hung on the wall or other convenient place when not in use.

The cloth bag, H, which can be made

of a knitted stocking, is filled with coal-dust, which is used for a parting medium in making the molds. Take a small lump of soft coal and reduce to powder by pounding. Screen out all the coarse pieces and put the remainder in the bag. A slight shake of the bag

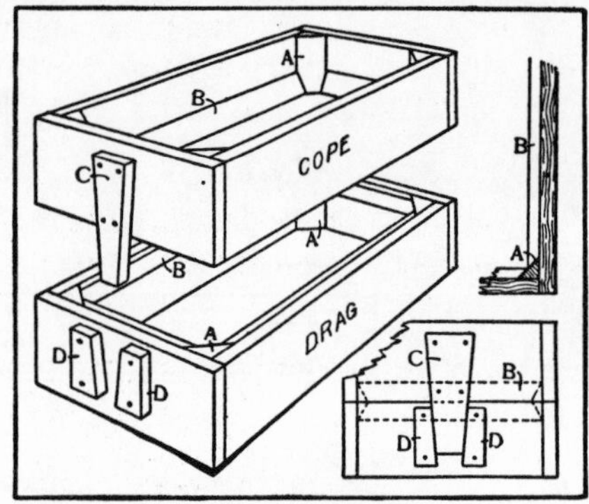

Fig. 2—Homemade Flask

over the mold will then cause a cloud of coal-dust to fall on it, thus preventing the two layers of sand from sticking, but this operation will be described more fully later on.

The flask, J, Fig. 1, is shown more clearly in Fig. 2. It is made of wood and is in two halves, the "cope," or upper half, and the "drag," or lower part. A good way to make the flask is to take a box, say 12 in. by 8 in. by 6 in. high, and saw it in half longitudinally, as shown. If the box is not very strong, the corners should be braced with triangular wooden strips, A A, which should be nailed in, previous to sawing. The wooden strips B B are used to hold the sand, which would otherwise slide out of the flask when the two halves of the mold are separated.

The dowels, CC, are a very important part of the flask as upon them depends the matching of the two halves of the mold. A wedge-shaped piece, CC, is nailed to each end of the cope, and the lower pieces, DD, are then nailed on the drag so that they just touch C when the flask is closed. The two halves of the flask will then occupy exactly the same relative position whenever they are put together.

After the flask is done make two boards as shown at K, Fig. 1, a little larger than the outside of the flask. A couple of cleats nailed to each board will make it easier to pick up the mold when it is on the floor.

A cast-iron glue-pot makes a very good crucible for melting the metal, which can be either aluminum, white metal, zinc or any other metal having a low melting-point. This completes the equipment with the exception of one or two simple devices which will now be described.

II—How to Make a Mold

Having finished making the flask and other equipment, as described, everything will be ready for the operation of molding. It would be well for those who have never had any experience in this line to visit a small brass foundry, where they can watch the molders at work, as it is much easier to learn by observation; but they must not expect to make a good mold at the first trial. The first attempt usually results in the sand dropping out of the cope when it is being lifted from the drag, either because of insufficient ramming around the edges or because the sand is too dry.

A good way to tell when the sand is moist enough is to squeeze it in the hand. If it forms into a cake and shows all the finger-marks, it has a sufficient amount of moisture, but if it crumbles or fails to cake it is too dry. An ordinary watering-pot will be found useful in moistening the sand, but care should be taken not to get it too wet, or the hot metal coming in contact with it when the mold is poured will cause such rapid evaporation that the mold will "boil" and make a poor casting. A little practice in this operation will soon enable the molder to determine the correct amount of moisture.

When molding with sand for the first time it will be necessary to screen it all before using it, in order to remove the lumps, and if water is added, the sand should be thoroughly shoveled until the moisture is evenly distributed. The sand is then ready for molding.

The operation of making a mold is as follows: The lower half of the flask, or "drag," and the pattern to be molded are both placed on the cover board as shown at A. A quantity of sand sufficient to completely cover the pattern is then sifted into the drag, which is then filled level with the top with unscreened sand. This is rammed down slightly with the rammer, and then more sand is added until it becomes heaped up as shown at B. It is then rammed again as before.

It is impossible to describe just how hard a mold should be rammed, but by observing the results the beginner can tell when a mold is too hard or too soft, and thus judge for himself. If the sand falls out of the flask when lifting the cope, or if it opens up or spreads after it is poured, it shows that the mold has been rammed too little, and if the surface of the sand next to the pattern is cracked it shows that the mold has been rammed too hard. It will be found that the edges of the mold can stand a little more ramming than the middle. In finishing the ramming, pound evenly all over the surface with the blunt end of the rammer.

After ramming, scrape off the surplus sand with a straight-edged stick, as shown at C, and scatter about $\frac{1}{16}$ in. of loose sand over the surface for a good bearing. Place another cover board on top, as shown at D, and by grasping with both hands, as shown, turn the drag other side up. Remove the upper cover board and place the upper half of the flask, or "cope," in position, as shown at E.

In order to prevent the two layers of sand sticking together, the surface of the sand at E should be covered with coal-dust. This is done by shaking the coal-dust bag over the flask, after which the dust on the pattern may be removed by blowing. The cope is then filled with sand and rammed in exactly the same manner as in the case of the drag.

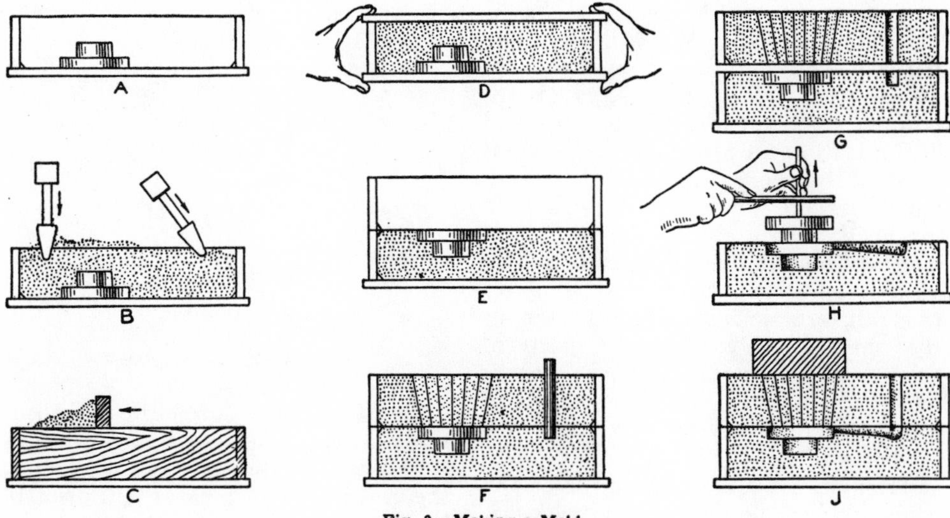

Fig. 3—Making a Mold

After the ramming is done a number of vent holes are made, as shown at F, from the surface of the mold to the pattern, in order to allow the escape of air and steam when the mold is being poured. These vent holes may be made by pushing a wire about the size of a knitting-needle down through the sand until it touches the pattern. The "sprue," or pouring-hole, is next cut, by means of the sprue-cutter shown at the right, which consists of a piece of thin brass or steel tubing about ¾ in. in diameter.

Now comes the critical part of the molding operation—that of lifting the cope from the drag. It is here that the amateur often becomes discouraged, as the sand is liable to fall out of the cope and spoil the mold; but with a little practice and patience the molder can lift the cope every time without breaking it, as shown at G.

The next operation is that of cutting the gate, which carries the molten metal from the sprue to the opening left by the pattern. This is done with a spoon, a channel being cut about ¾ in. wide and about ¼ in. deep. The pattern is then drawn from the mold, as shown at H, by driving a sharp-pointed steel rod into the pattern and lifting it from the sand. When a metal pattern is used a thread rod is used, which is screwed into a tapped hole in the pattern. Before drawing it is well to tap the drawing-rod lightly with another and larger rod, striking it in all directions and thus loosening the sand slightly from the pattern. Some molders tap the pattern gently when withdrawing, as shown at H, in order to loosen any sand which has a tendency to stick.

After drawing the pattern, place the cope back on the drag, as shown at J. Place a brick or other flat, heavy object on top of the mold above the pattern, to prevent the pressure of the melted metal separating the two halves of the mold, and then pour.

III—Melting and Pouring

Having prepared one or more molds, the next operation is that of melting and pouring. An ordinary cast-iron glue-pot makes a good crucible and can be easily handled by a pair of tongs, made out of steel rod, as shown in the sketch. In order to hold the tongs together a small link can be slipped on over the handle, thus holding the crucible securely.

A second piece of steel rod bent in the form of a hook at the end is very useful for supporting the weight of the crucible and prevents spilling the molten metal should the tongs slip off the crucible. The hook is also useful for removing the crucible from the fire, which should be done soon after the metal is entirely melted, in order to prevent overheating. The metal should be poured into the mold in a small stream, to give the air a chance to escape, and should not be poured directly into the center of the opening, as the metal will then strike the bottom hard enough to loosen the sand, thus making a dirty casting.

Fig. 4—Pouring the Metal

If, after being poured, the mold sputters and emits large volumes of steam, it shows that the sand is too wet, and the castings in such cases will probably be imperfect and full of holes.

A mold made in the manner previously described may be poured with any desired metal, but a metal which is easily melted will give the least trouble. One of the easiest metals to melt and one which makes very attractive castings is pure tin. Tin melts at a temperature slightly above the melting point of solder, and, although somewhat expensive, the permanent brightness and silverlike appearance of the castings is very desirable. A good "white metal" may be made by mixing 75% tin, 15% lead, 5% zinc and 5% antimony. The object of adding antimony to an alloy is to prevent shrinkage when cooling.

A very economical alloy is made by melting up all the old type-metal, babbitt, battery zincs, white metal and other scrap available, and adding a little antimony if the metal shrinks too much in cooling. If a good furnace is available, aluminum can be melted without any difficulty, although this metal melts at a higher temperature than any of the metals previously mentioned.

In casting zincs for batteries a separate crucible, used only for zinc, is very desirable, as the presence of a very small amount of lead or other impurity will cause the batteries to polarize. A very good way to make the binding posts is to remove the binding posts from worn-out dry batteries and place them in the molds in such a way that the melted zinc will flow around them.

The time required for a casting to solidify varies with the size and shape of the casting, but unless the pattern is a very large one about five minutes will be ample time for it to set. The casting is then dumped out of the mold and the sand brushed off. The gate can be removed with either a cold chisel or a hacksaw, and the casting is then ready for finishing.

Battery Switch

In cases where batteries are used in series and it is desirable to change the strength and direction of the current frequently, the following device will be found most convenient. In my own case I used four batteries, but any reasonable number may be used. Referring to the figure, it will be seen that by moving the switch A toward the left the current can be reduced from four batteries to none, and then by moving the switch B toward the right the current can be turned on in the opposite direction to the desired strength. In the various positions of these two switches the current from each individual cell, or from any adjacent pair of cells, may be used in either direction.—Contributed by Harold S. Morton, Minneapolis.

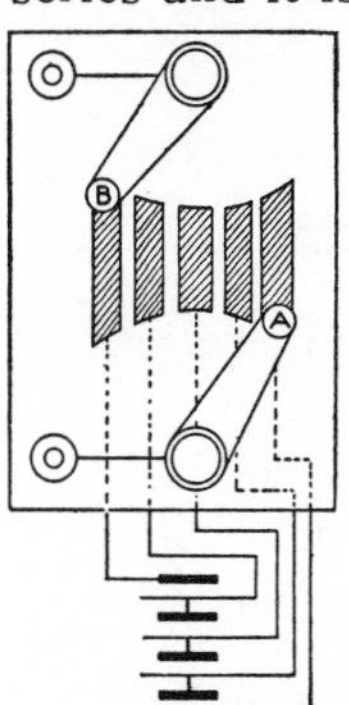

An Optical Illusion

The engraving shows a perfectly straight boxwood rule laid over a number of turned brass rings of various sizes. Although the effect in the illustration is less pronounced than it was in reality, it will be noticed that the rule appears to be bent, but sighting along the rule from one end will show that it is perfectly straight.

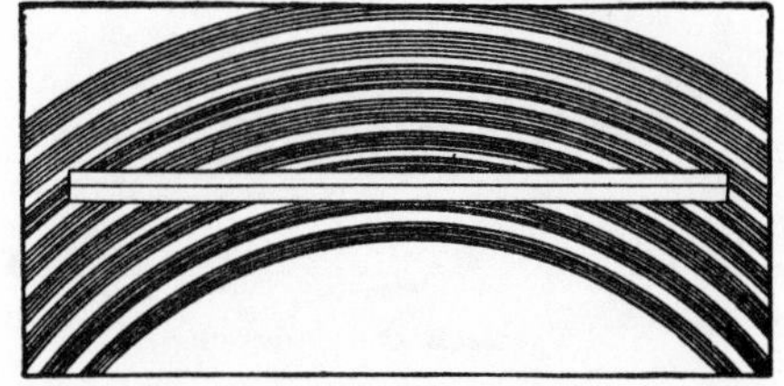

An Optical Illusion

The brass rings also appear distorted. The portions on one side of the rule do not appear to be a continuation of those on the other, but that they really are can be proved by sighting in the same manner as before.—Contributed by Draughtsman, Chicago.

New Method of Lifting a Table

To perform this feat effectively the little device illustrated will be required. To make it take a sheet-iron band, A, 3/4 in. wide and attach a strap to fasten on the forearm between the wrist and elbow. Put a sharp needle point, B, through the sheet-iron so that it extends 3/4 in. outward. Make one of these pieces for each arm.

In lifting the table first show the hands unprepared to the audience and also a light table, removing the cover to show that the surface of the table is not prepared in any way. Then replace the table, rest the hands upon it and at the same time press the needle points in the arm pieces into the wood of the table, which will be sufficient to hold it, says a correspondent of the Sphinx. Then walk down among the audience.

How to Make a Paddle Boat

A rowboat has several disadvantages. The operation of the oars is both tiresome and uninteresting, and the oarsman is obliged to travel backward.

Paddle Boat in Operation

By replacing the oars with paddles, as shown in the illustration, the operator can see where he is going and enjoy the exercise much better than with oars. He can easily steer the boat with his feet, by means of a pivoted stick in the bottom of the boat, connected by cords to the rudder.

At the blacksmith shop have a 5/8-in. shaft made, as shown at A, Fig. 2. It will be necessary to furnish a sketch giving all the dimensions of the shaft, which should be designed to suit the dimensions of the boat, taking care that sufficient clearance is allowed, so that the cranks in revolving will not strike the operator's knees. If desired, split-wood handles may be placed on the cranks, to prevent them from rubbing the hands.

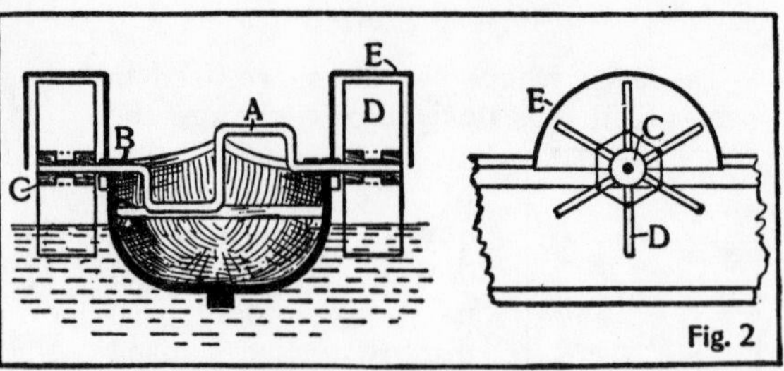

Detail of Paddle Boat

The bearings, B, may be made of hardwood, but preferably of iron pipe filled with melted babbitt. If babbitt is used, either thoroughly smoke or chalk the shaft or wrap paper around it to prevent the babbitt sticking. The pieces of pipe may be then fastened to the boat by means of small pipe straps, such as may be obtained at any plumber's at a very small cost.

The hubs, C, should be made of wood, drilled to fit the shaft and mortised out to hold the paddles, D. The covers, E, may be constructed of thin wood or galvanized iron and should be braced by triangular boards, as shown in Fig. 1. If galvanized iron is used, it should be exposed to the weather two or three months before painting, or the paint will come off, spoiling its appearance.

Peculiar Properties of Ice

Of all the boys who make snowballs probably few know what occurs during the process. Under ordinary conditions water turns to ice when the temperature falls to 32°, but when in motion, or under pressure, much lower temperatures are required to make it a solid. In the same way, ice which is somewhat below the freezing point can be made liquid by applying pressure, and will remain liquid until the pressure is removed, when it will again return to its original state. Snow, being simply finely divided ice, becomes liquid in places when compressed by the hands, and when the pressure is removed the liquid portions solidify and unite all the particles in one mass. In extremely cold weather it is almost impossible to make a snowball, because a greater amount of pressure is then required to make the snow liquid.

This process of melting and freezing under different pressures and a constant temperature is well illustrated by the experiment shown in Figs. 1, 2 and 3. A block of ice, A, Fig. 1, is sup-

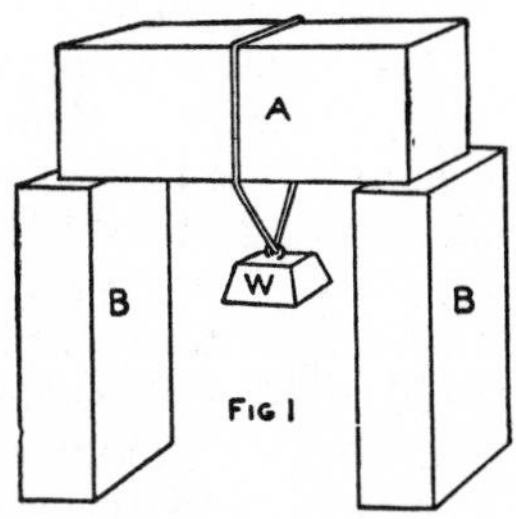

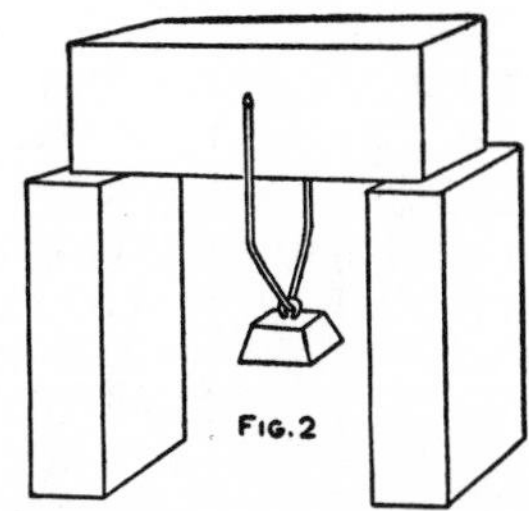

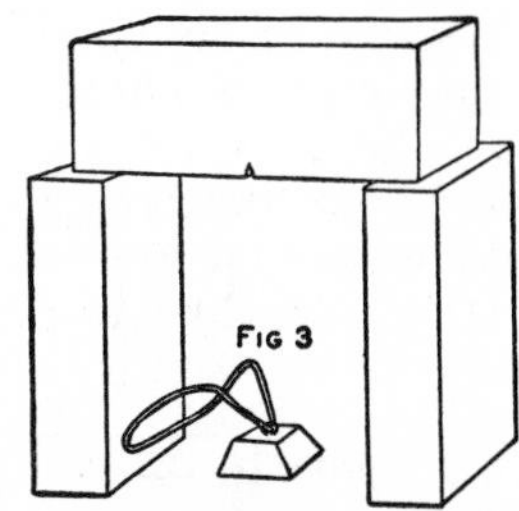

Experiment with a Block of Ice

ported at each end by boxes BB, and a weight, W, is hung on a wire loop which passes around the ice as shown. The pressure of the wire will then melt the ice and allow the wire to sink down through the ice as shown in Fig. 2. The wire will continue to cut its way through the ice until it passes all the way through the piece, as shown in Fig. 3. This experiment not only illustrates how ice melts under pressure, but also how it solidifies when the pressure is removed, for the block will still be left in one piece after the wire has passed through.

Another peculiar property of ice is its tendency to flow. It may seem strange that ice should flow like water, but the glaciers of Switzerland and other countries are literally rivers of ice. The snow which accumulates on the mountains in vast quantities is turned to ice as a result of the enormous pressure caused by its own weight, and flows through the natural channels it has made in the rock until it reaches the valley below. In flowing through these channels it frequently passes around bends, and when two branches come together the bodies of ice unite the same as water would under the same conditions. The rate of flow is often very slow; sometimes only one or two feet a day, but, no matter how slow the motion may be, the large body of ice has to bend in moving.

This property of ice is hard to illustrate with the substance itself, but may be clearly shown by sealing-wax, which resembles ice in this respect. Any attempt to bend a piece of cold sealing-wax with the hands results in breaking it, but by placing it between books, as shown on page 65, or supporting it in some similar way, it will gradually change from the original shape A, and assume the shape shown at B.

Return-Call Bell With One Wire

To use only one wire for a return-call bell connect up as shown in the diagram, using a closed circuit or gravity battery, B. The current is flowing through both bells all the time, the same as the coils of a telegraph sounder, but is not strong enough to ring both connected in series. Pressing

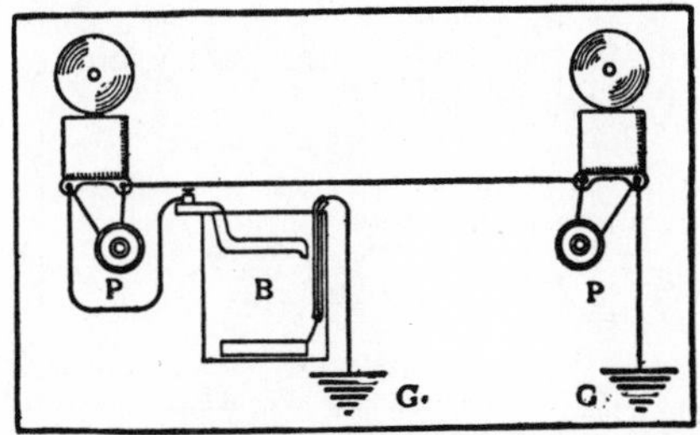

Wiring Diagram

either push button, P, makes a short circuit of that bell and rings the one at the other end of the line.—Contributed by Gordon T. Lane, Crafton, Pa.

Circuit Breaker for Induction Coils

Amateurs building induction coils are generally bothered by the vibrator contacts blackening, thus giving a high resistance contact, whenever there is any connection made at all. This trouble may be done away with by departing from the old single-contact vibrator and using one with self-cleaning contacts as shown. An old bell magnet is rewound full of No. 26 double cotton-covered wire and is mounted

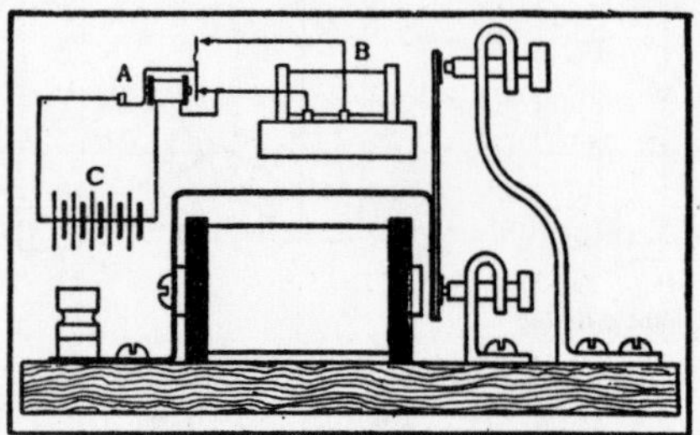

Interrupter for Induction Coil

upon one end of a piece of thin sheet iron 1 in. by 5 in. as per sketch. To the other end of the strip of iron is soldered a piece of brass 1/64 in. by 1/4 in. by 2 in., on each end of which has been soldered a patch of platinum foil 1/4 in. square.

The whole is connected up and mounted on a baseboard as per sketch, the contact posts being of 1/16 in. by 1/2 in. brass, bent into shape and provided with platinum tipped thumb screws. The advantage of this style of an interrupter is that at each stroke there is a wiping effect at the heavy current contact which automatically cleans off any carbon deposit.

In the wiring diagram, A is the circuit breaker; B, the induction coil, and C, the battery.—Contributed by A. G. Ward, Wilkinsburg, Pa.

Spit Turned by Water Power

Many of the Bulgarian peasants do their cooking in the open air over bonfires. The illustration shows a labor-saving machine in use which enables the cook to go away and leave meat roasting for an hour at a time. The

For a Summer Camp

illustration shows how the spit to which the meat is fastened is constantly turned by means of a slowly moving water wheel. Some of our readers may wish to try the scheme when camping out. The success depends upon a slow current, for a fast-turning wheel will burn the meat.

A Short-Distance Wireless Telegraph

The accompanying diagrams show a wireless-telegraph system that I have used successfully for signaling a distance of 3,000 ft. The transmitter consists of an induction coil, about the size used for automobiles, a key or push-button for completing the circuit, and five dry batteries. The small single-point switch is left open as shown when sending a message, but when receiving it should be closed in order that the electric waves from the antenna may pass through the coherer. The coherer in this case is simply two electric-light carbons sharpened to a wedge at one end with a needle con-

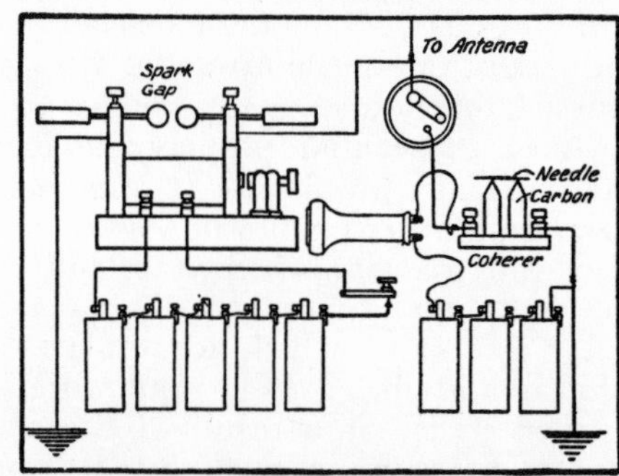

Wiring Diagram for Wireless Telegraph

necting the two, as shown. An ordinary telephone receiver is connected in series with the coherer, as shown. To receive messages hold the receiver to the ear and close the switch, and answer by opening the switch and operating the key.—Contributed by Coulson Glick, Indianapolis.

Automatic Draft-Opener

A simple apparatus that will open the draft of the furnace at any hour desired is illustrated. The parts are: A, furnace; B, draft; C, draft chain; D, pulleys; E, wooden supports; F, vertical lever; G, horizontal lever; H, cord; I, alarm clock; J, weight. K shows where and how the draft is regulated during the day, the automatic

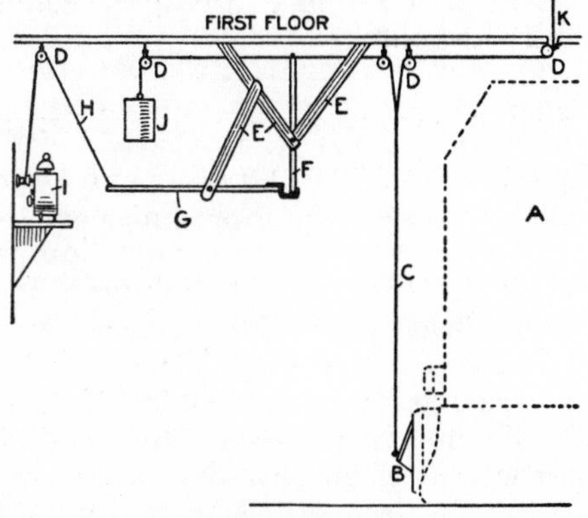

Draft Regulator

device being used to open it early in the morning. The spool on the alarm clock is fastened to the alarm key by sawing a slit across the top of the spool and gluing it on. When the alarm goes off a cord is wound up on the spool and pulls the horizontal lever up, which releases the vertical lever and allows the weight to pull the draft open.—Contributed by Gordon Davis, Kalamazoo, Mich.

A Window Conservatory

During the winter months, where house plants are kept in the home, it is always a question how to arrange them so they can get the necessary light without occupying too much room.

The sketch shows how a neat window conservatory may be made at small cost that can be fastened on the house just covering a window, which will provide a fine place for the plants. The frame (Fig. 2) is made of about 2 by 2-in. material framed together as shown in Fig. 3. This frame should be made with the three openings of such a size that a four-paned sash, such as used for a storm window, will fit nicely in them. If the four vertical pieces that are shown in Fig. 2 are dressed to the right angle, then it will be easy to put on the finishing corner boards that hold the sash.

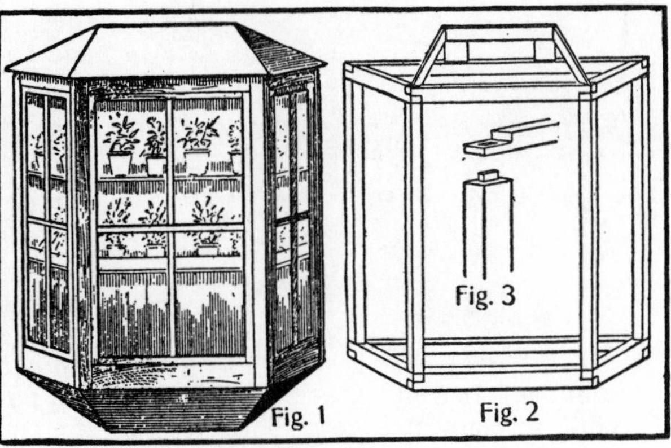

Artistic Window Boxes

The top, as well as the bottom, is constructed with two small pieces like the rafters, on which is nailed the sheathing boards and then the shingles on top and the finishing boards on the bottom.

How to Make an Electroscope

An electroscope for detecting electrified•bodies may be made out of a piece of note paper, a cork and a needle. Push the needle into the cork, and cut the paper in the shape of a small arrow. Balance the arrow on the needle

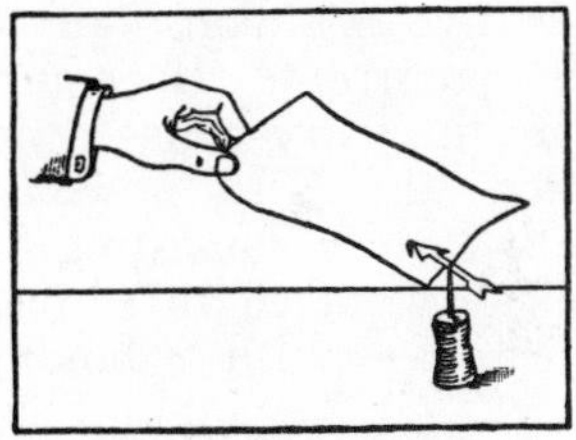

Simple Electroscope

as shown in the sketch, and the instrument will then be complete. If a piece of paper is then heated over a lamp or stove and rubbed with a piece of cloth or a small broom, the arrow will turn when the paper is brought near it.—Contributed by Wm. W. Grant, Halifax, N. S., Canada.

Miniature Electric Lighting

Producing electric light by means of small bulbs that give from one-half to six candle power, and a suitable source of power, is something that will interest the average American boy.

These circular bulbs range from 1/4 to 2 in. in diameter, and cost 27 cents

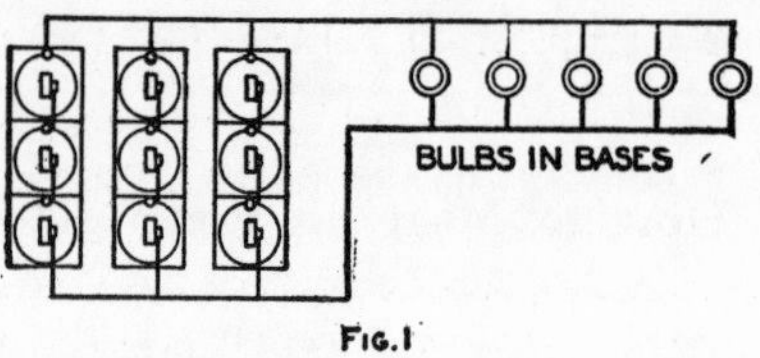

Fig. 1

each complete with base. They are commonly known as miniature battery bulbs, since a battery is the most popular source of power. The 1/2-cp. bulbs are usually 2 1/2 volts and take 1/4 ampere of current. It requires about three medium dry cells to operate it. However, there is now upon the market a battery consisting of 3 small dry cells connected in series, put up in a neat case with 2 binding posts, which sells for 25 cents. This is more economical than dry cells, as it gives about 4 volts and 3 amperes. It will run as large a lamp as 3 1/2 volts, 1 cp., for some time very satisfactorily. More than one lamp can be run by connecting the bulbs in parallel, as indicated by Fig. 1, which shows the special battery with 3 dry cells in the case, and the 2 binding posts for connection with

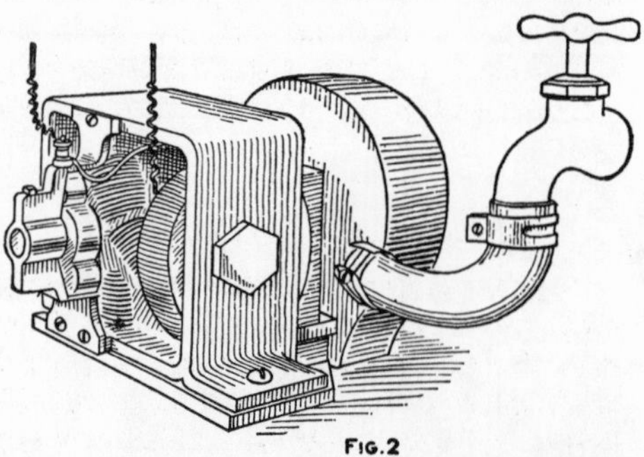

Fig. 2

the bulbs. In this case it is also advisable to connect several batteries in parallel also, so as to increase the current, but maintain the voltage constant. Thus, the individual cells are in multiple series, i. e., multiples of series of three. By keeping in mind the ampere output of the battery and rating of the lamp, one can regulate the batteries as required. It must be remembered, in this connection, that any battery which is drawn upon for half of its output will last approximately three times as long, as if drawn upon for its total output. Thus, in any system of lamps, it is economical to provide twice as many batteries as necessary. This also supplies a means of still maintaining the candle power when the batteries are partially exhausted, by connecting them in series. However, this must be done with very great caution, as the lights will be burnt out if the voltage is too high.

Persons living in the city will find an economical means of lighting lamps by securing exhausted batteries from any garage, where they are glad to have them taken away. A certain number of these, after a rest, can be connected up in series, and will give the proper voltage.

In conclusion, for battery power: Connecting batteries in series increases the voltage, and slightly cuts down the current or amperage, which is the same as that of one battery; while connecting batteries in parallel increases the amperage, but holds the voltage the same as that of one cell. Thus, if the voltage and amperage of any cell be known, by the proper combination of these, we can secure the required voltage and amperage to light any miniature lamp. And it might be said that dry cells are the best for this purpose, especially those of low internal resistance.

For those having a good water supply there is a more economical means of maintenance, although the first cost is greater. Fig. 2 shows the scheme. A small dynamo driven by a water motor attached to a faucet, generates the power for the lights. The cost of the smallest outfit of the kind is about $3 for the water motor and $4 for the dynamo. This dynamo has an output of 12 watts, and will produce from 18 to 25 cp., according to the water pressure obtainable. It is advisable to install the outfit in the basement, where the water pressure is the greatest, and then lead No. 18 B & S. double-insulated wire wherever needed. The dynamo can also be used as a motor,

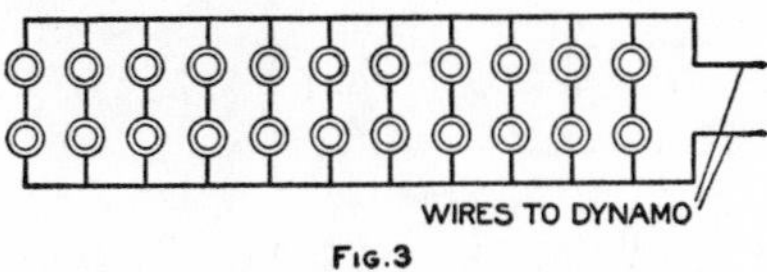

Fig. 3

and is wound for any voltage up to ten. The winding should correspond to the voltage of the lamps which you desire to run. However, if wound for 6 volts, one could run parallel series of two 3-volt, 1-cp. lamps; making, as in Fig. 3, 11 series, or 22 lights. If wound for 10 volts, it would give 1¼ amperes and run four 6-cp. lamps. Thus, it will be seen that any candle power lamp can be operated by putting the proper number of lights in each series, and running the series in parallel. So, to secure light by this method, we simply turn on the water, and the water consumption is not so great as might be imagined.

For the party who has electric light in his house there is still an easier solution for the problem of power. If the lighting circuit gives 110 volts he can connect eleven 10-volt lamps in series. These will give 3 cp. each, and the whole set of 11 will take one ampere of current, and cost about the same as a 32-cp. lamp, or 1¼ cents per hour. Simply connect the miniature circuit to an Edison plug, and insert in the nearest lamp socket. Any number of different candle power lamps can be used providing each lamp takes the same amount of current, and the sum of their voltages equals the voltage of the circuit used. This arrangement of small lights is used to produce a widely distributed, and diffused light in a room, for display of show cases, and for Christmas trees. Of all these sources of power the two last are the most economical, and the latter of these two has in its favor the small initial cost. These lamps are by no means playthings or experiments, but are as serviceable and practical as the larger lamps.—Contributed by Lindsay Eldridge, Chicago.

How to Make a New Language

Anyone possessing a phonograph can try a very interesting and amusing experiment without going to any expense. Remove the belt and replace with a longer one, which can be made of narrow braid or a number of strands of yarn. The new belt should be long enough to allow crossing it, thus reversing the machine. This reverses every sound on the record and changes it to such an extent that very few words can be recognized.

How to Make a Cup-and-Saucer Rack

The rack is made of any suitable kind of wood, and the sides, A, are cut just alike, or from one pattern. The shelves are made in various widths to fit the sides at the places where they are wanted. The number of shelves can be varied and to suit the size of the dishes. Cup hooks are placed on top and bottom shelves. It is hung on the wall the same as a picture from the molding. —Contributed by F. B. Emig, Santa Clara, Cal.

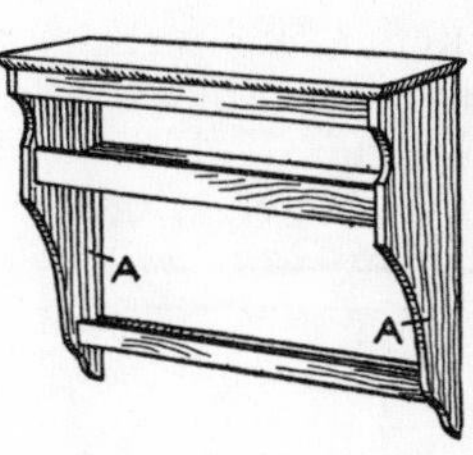

Reversing a Small Motor

All that is necessary for reversing the motor is a pole-changing switch. Connect the two middle posts of the switch with each other and the two outside posts with each other. Then connect one of the outside posts of the switch to one brush of the motor and one middle post to the other brush.

Connect one bar of the switch to one

end of the field coil and the other bar to one pole of the battery, and connect the other pole of the battery to the other field coil. To reverse the motor, simply change the switch.

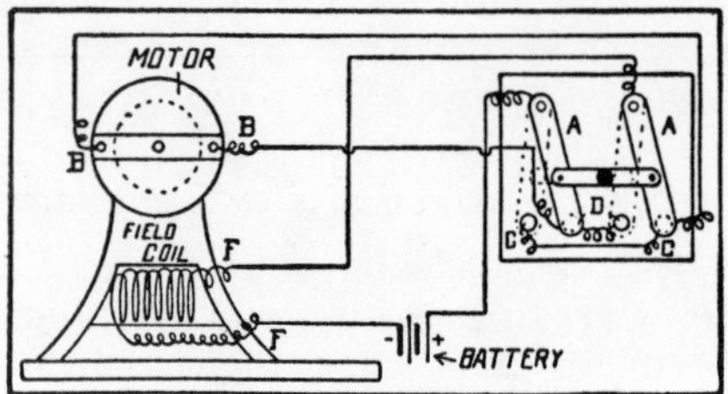

Reverse for a Small Motor

Referring to the illustration, the letters indicate as follows: FF, field of motor; BB, brushes of motor; AA, bars of pole-changing switch; DD, center points of switch; CC, outside points of switch.—Contributed by Leonard E. Parker, Plymouth, Ind.

To Drive Away Dogs

The dogs in my neighborhood used to come around picking up scraps. After I connected up my induction coil, as shown in the sketch, we were not bothered with them. A indicates the ground; B, switch; and C, a bait of meat, or a tempting bone.—Contributed by Geo. W. Fry, 903 Vine St., San Jose, Cal.

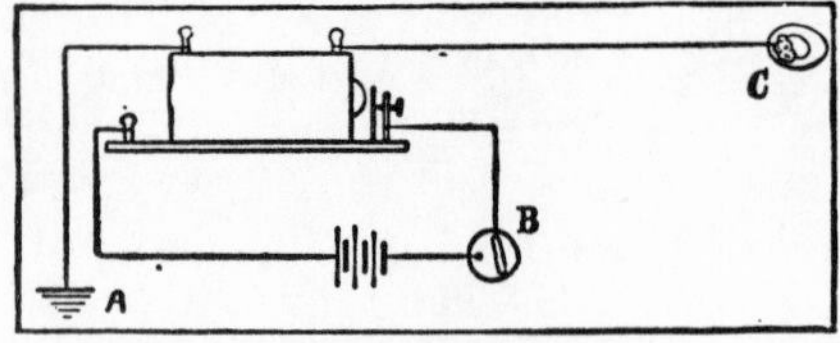

Shocking-Machine

An Automatic Lock

The illustration shows an automatic lock operated by electricity, one cell being sufficient. When the circuit is broken a weight, A, attached to the end of the armature B, tends to push the other end of the armature into the screw eye or hook C, which is in the door, thus locking the door.

To unlock the door, merely push the button E. The magnet then draws the armature out of the screw eye and the door is unlocked. The dotted line at D shows the position of the armature when the circuit is complete and the door unlocked. The weight must be in proportion to the strength of the magnet. If it is not, the door will not lock, or would remain locked. The button can be hidden, as it is the key to the lock.—Contributed by Claude B. Melchior, Hutchinson, Minn.

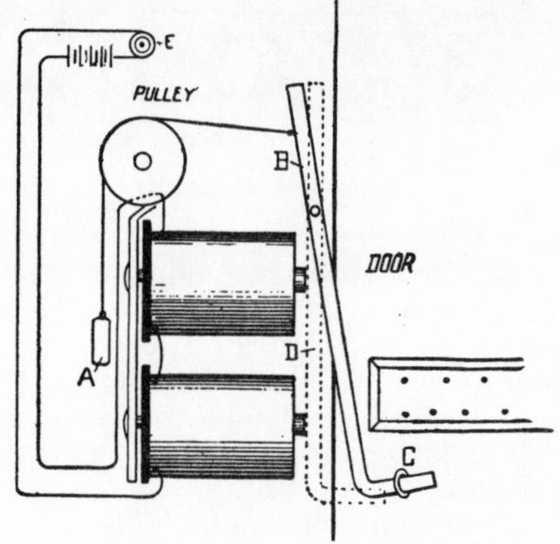

Automatic Electric Lock for Doors

Experiment with Two-Foot Rule and Hammer

An example of unstable equilibrium is shown in the accompanying sketch. All that is needed is a 2-foot rule, a hammer, a piece of string, and a table or bench. The experiment works best

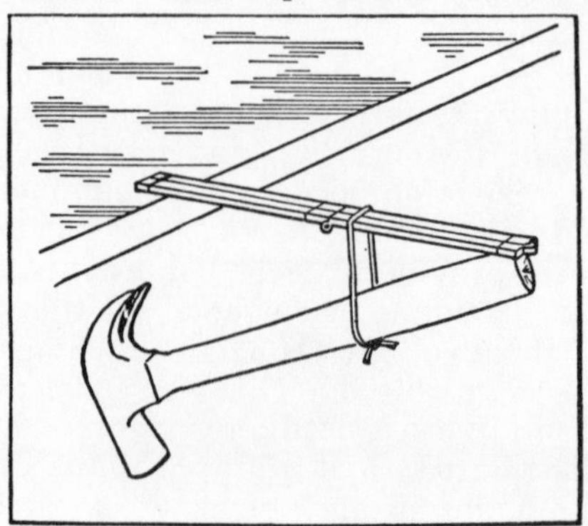

An Experiment in Equilibrium

with a hammer having a light handle and a very heavy head.

Tie the ends of the string together, forming a loop, and pass this around the hammer handle and rule. Then place the apparatus on the edge of the table, where it will remain suspended as shown.—Contributed by Geo. P. Schmidt, Culebra, Porto Rico, W. I.

Simple Current Reverser

On a block of hardwood draw a square (Fig. 1) and drill a hole in each corner of the square. Fill these holes with mercury and connect them to four binding posts (Fig. 1).

On another block of wood fasten two wires, as shown in Fig. 2, so that their ends can be placed in the holes in the first block. Then connect up with the

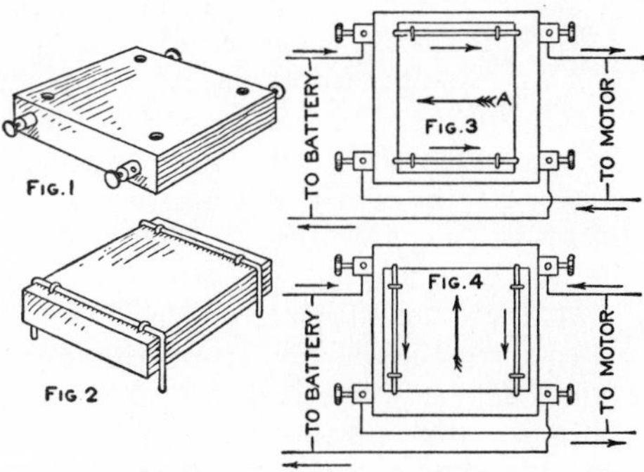

Details of Reverser

motor and battery as in Fig. 3. When the block is placed on with the big arrow A pointing in the direction indicated in Fig. 3, the current flows with the small arrows. To reverse turn through an angle of 90 degrees (Fig. 4). — Contributed by F. Crawford Curry, Brockville, Ontario, Canada.

Alarm Clock to Pull up Furnace Draft

A stout cord, A, is attached to the draft B of the furnace, run through a pulley, C, in the ceiling and has a window weight, D, attached at the other end. A small stick is put through a loop in the cord at about the level of the table top on which the alarm clock F stands. The other end of stick E is placed under the key G of the alarm clock. When the alarm rings in the early morning, the key turns, the stick

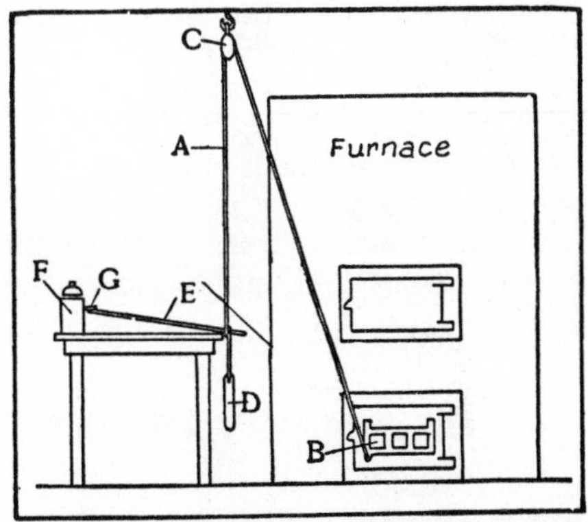

Automatic Time Draft-Opener

falls away, releasing the weight, which pulls the draft open.—Contributed by Edward Whitney, 18 Gorham St., Madison, Wis.

How to Transmit Phonograph Music to a Distance

An interesting experiment, and one calculated to mystify any one not in the secret, is to transmit the music or speech from a phonograph to another part of the house or even a greater distance. For an outdoor summer party the music can be made to come from a bush, or tree, or from a bed of flowers. The apparatus is not difficult to construct.

The cut shows the arrangement. Procure a long-distance telephone transmitter, D, including the mouthpiece, and fasten it to the reproducer of the phonograph. Also a watch case re-

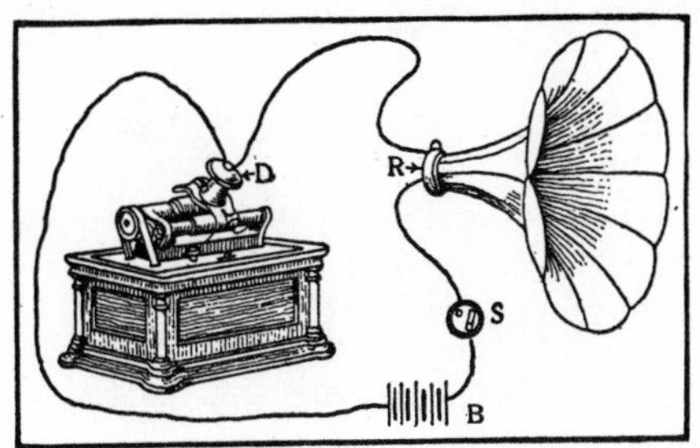

The Long-Distance Phonograph

ceiver, R, which fasten to the horn. These parts may be purchased from any electrical-supply house. Connect two wires to the transmitter, running one direct to the receiver, and the other to the battery, thence to a switch, S, and then to the receiver. The more batteries used the louder will be the sound produced by the horn, but avoid using too much battery or the receiver is apt to heat.—Contributed by Wm. J. Farley, Jr., Camden, N. J.

How to Make a Telescope

With a telescope like the one here described, made with his own hands, a farmer boy not many years ago discovered a comet which had escaped the watchful eyes of many astronomers.

First, get two pieces of plate glass, 6 in. square and 1 in. thick, and break the corners off to make them round, grinding the rough edges on a grindstone. Use a barrel to work on, and

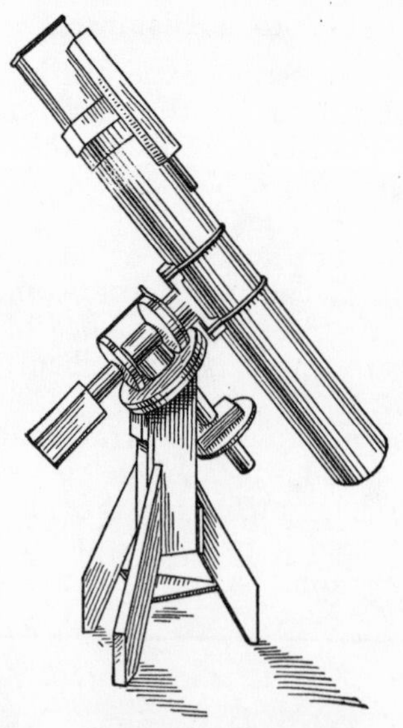

Homemade Telescope

fasten one glass on the top of it in the center by driving three small nails at the sides to hold it in place. Fasten, with pitch, a round 4-in. block of wood in the center on one side of the other glass to serve as a handle.

Use wet grain emery for coarse grinding. Take a pinch and spread it evenly on the glass which is on the barrel, then take the glass with the handle and move it back and forth across the lower glass, while walking around the barrel; also rotate the glass, which is necessary to make it grind evenly. The upper glass or speculum always becomes concave, and the under glass or tool convex.

Work with straight strokes 5 or 6 in. in length; after working 5 hours hold the speculum in the sunshine and throw the rays of the sun onto a paper; where the rays come to a point gives the focal length. If the glass is not ground enough to bring the rays to a point within 5 ft., the coarse grinding must be continued, unless a longer focal length is wanted.

Have ready six large dishes, then take 2 lb. flour emery and mix in 12 qt. of water; immediately turn the water into a clean dish and let settle 30 seconds; then turn it into another dish and let settle 2 minutes, then 8 minutes, 30 minutes and 90 minutes, being careful not to turn off the coarser emery which has settled. When dry, turn the emery from the 5 jars into 5 separate bottles, and label. Then take a little of the coarsest powder, wetting it to the consistency of cream, and spread on the glass, work as before (using short straight strokes 1½ or 2 in.) until the holes in the glass left by the grain emery are ground out; next use the finer grades until the pits left by each coarser grade are ground out. When the two last grades are used shorten the strokes to less than 2 in. When done the glass should be semi-transparent, and is ready for polishing.

When polishing the speculum, paste a strip of paper 1⅓ in. wide around the convex glass or tool, melt 1 lb. of pitch and turn on to it and press with the wet speculum. Mold the pitch while hot into squares of 1 in., with ¼-in. spaces, as in Fig. 1. Then warm and press again with the speculum, being careful to have all the squares touch the speculum, or it will not polish evenly. Trim the paper from the edge with a sharp knife, and paint the squares separately with jeweler's rouge, wet till soft like paint. Use a binger to spread it on with. Work the speculum over the tool the same as when grinding, using straight strokes 2 in. or less.

When the glass is polished enough to reflect some light, it should be tested with the knife-edge test. In a dark room, set the speculum against the wall, and a large lamp, L, Fig. 2, twice the focal length away. Place a large sheet of pasteboard, A, Fig. 2, with a small needle hole opposite the blaze, by the side of the lamp, so the light

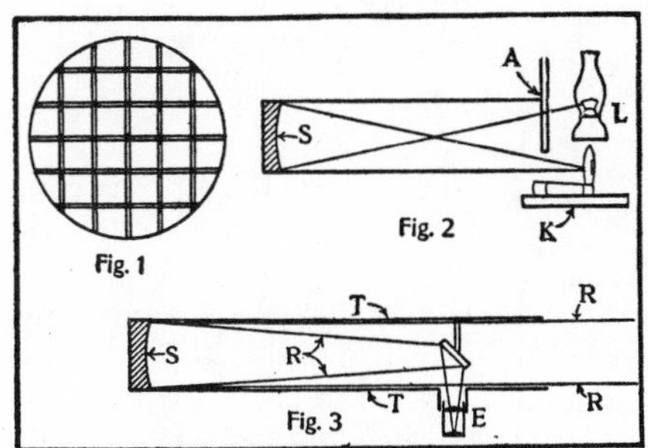

Detail of Telescope Construction

from the blaze will shine onto the glass. Place the speculum S, Fig. 2, so the rays from the needle hole will be thrown to the left side of the lamp (facing the speculum), with the knife mounted in a block of wood and edgeways to the lamp, as in K, Fig. 2. The knife should not be more than 6 in. from the lamp. Now move the knife across the rays from left to right, and look at the speculum with the eye on the right side of the blade. When the focus is found, if the speculum is ground and polished evenly it will darken evenly over the surface as the knife shuts off the light from the needle hole. If not, the speculum will show some dark rings, or hills. If the glass seems to have a deep hollow in the center, shorter strokes should be used in polishing; if a hill in the center, longer strokes. The polishing and testing done, the speculum is ready to be silvered. Two glass or earthenware dishes, large enough to hold the speculum and 2 in. deep, must be procured. With pitch, cement a strip of board 8 in. long to the back of the speculum, and lay the speculum face down in one of the dishes; fill the dish with distilled water, and clean the face of the speculum with nitric acid, until the water will stick to it in an unbroken film.

The recipe for silvering the speculum is:

Solution A:	
Distilled water	4 oz.
Silver nitrate	100 gr.
Solution B:	
Distilled water	4 oz.
Caustic stick potash (pure by alcohol)	100 gr.
Solution C:	
Aqua Ammonia.	
Solution D:	
Sugar loaf	840 gr.
Nitric acid	39 gr.
Alcohol (pure)	25 gr.

Mix solution D and make up to 25 fluid oz. with distilled water, pour into a bottle and carefully put away in a safe place for future use, as it works better when old.

Now take solution A and set aside in a small bottle one-tenth of it, and pour the rest into the empty dish; add the ammonia solution drop by drop; a dark brown precipitate will form and subside; stop adding ammonia solution as soon as the bath clears. Then add solution B, then ammonia until bath is clear. Now add enough of the solution A, that was set aside, to bring the bath to a warm saffron color without destroying its transparency. Then add 1 oz. of solution D and stir until bath grows dark. Place the speculum, face down, in the bath and leave until the silver rises, then raise the speculum and rinse with distilled water. The small flat mirror may be silvered the same way. When dry, the silver film may be polished with a piece of chamois skin, touched with rouge, the polishing being accomplished by means of a light spiral stroke.

Fig. 3 shows the position of the glasses in the tube, also how the rays R from a star are thrown to the eyepiece E in the side of the tube. Make the tube I of sheet iron, cover with paper and cloth, then paint to make a non-conductor of heat or cold. Make the mounting of good seasoned lumber.

Thus an excellent 6-in. telescope can be made at home, with an outlay of only a few dollars. My telescope is 64 in. long and cost me just $15, but I used all my spare time in one winter in making it. I first began studying the heavens through a spyglass, but an instrument such as I desired would cost $200—more than I could afford. Then I made the one described, with which I discovered a new comet not before observed by astronomers.—John E. Mellish.

How to Make "Freak" Photographs

The "freak" pictures of well-known people which were used by some daily newspapers recently made everybody wonder how the distorted photographs were made. A writer in Camera Craft gives the secret, which proves to be easy of execution. The distortion is accomplished by the use of prisms, as follows: Secure from an optician or leaded-glass establishment, two glass prisms, slightly wider than the lens mount. The flatter they are the less they will distort. About 20 deg. is a satisfactory angle. Secure them as shown by the sectional sketch, using strawboard and black paper. Then make a ring to fit over the lens mount and connect it with the prisms in such a way as to exclude all light from the camera except that which passes through the face of the prisms. The inner surface of this hood must be dull black. The paper which comes around plates answers nicely. If the ring which slips over the lens mount is lined with black velvet, it will exclude all light and hold firmly to the mount. Place over lens, stop down well after focusing, and proceed as for any picture.

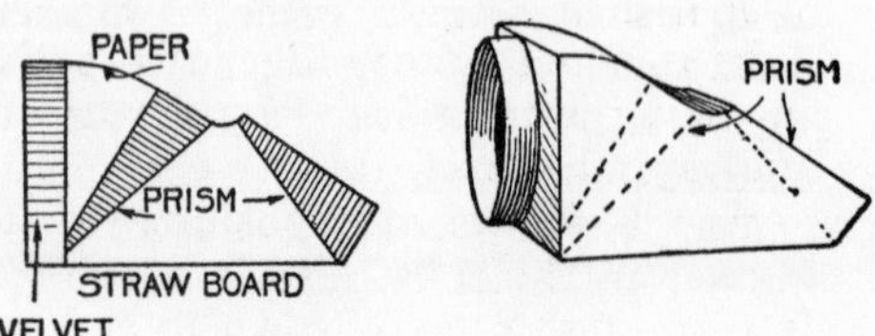

Arrangement of Prisms

Another Electric Lock

The details of the construction of an electrically operated lock are shown in the illustration. When the door is closed and the bolt A pushed into position, it automatically locks. To unlock, push the button D, which act will cause the electromagnet to raise the latch C, when the bolt may be drawn and the door opened.—Contributed by A. D. Zimmerman, Boody, Ill.

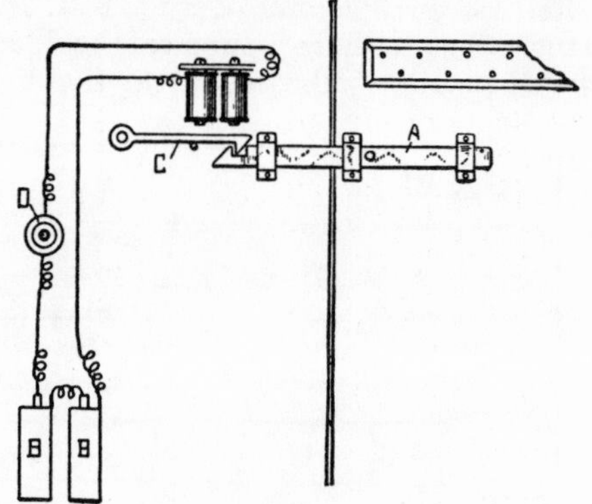

Simple Electric Lock

How to Mix Plaster of Paris

For the mixing of plaster of Paris for any purpose, add the plaster gradually to the water, instead of the contrary, says the Master Painter. Do not stir it, just sprinkle it in until you have a creamy mass without lumps. Equal parts of plaster and water is approximately the correct proportion. The addition of a little vinegar or glue water will retard the setting of the plaster, but will not preserve its hardening. Marshmallow powder also retards the setting. In this way the plaster may be handled a long time without getting hard. If you wish the plaster to set extra hard, then add a little sulphate of potash, or powdered alum.

Enlarging with a Hand Camera

Everyone who owns a hand camera has some pictures he would like enlarged. It is not necessary to have a large camera to do this, as the process is exceedingly simple to make large pictures from small negatives with the same hand camera.

A room from which all light may be excluded and a window through which the light can enter without obstruction from trees or nearby buildings, with a shelf to hold the camera and a table with an upright drawing-board attached, complete the arrangement. The back is taken out of the camera and fitted close against the back of the shelf, which must be provided with a hole the same size and shape as the opening in the back of the camera. The negative used to make the enlarged print is placed in the shelf at A, Fig. 1. The rays of the clear, unobstructed light strike the mirror, B, and reflect through the negative, A, through the lens of the camera and on the board, as shown in Fig. 2. The window must be darkened all around the shelf.

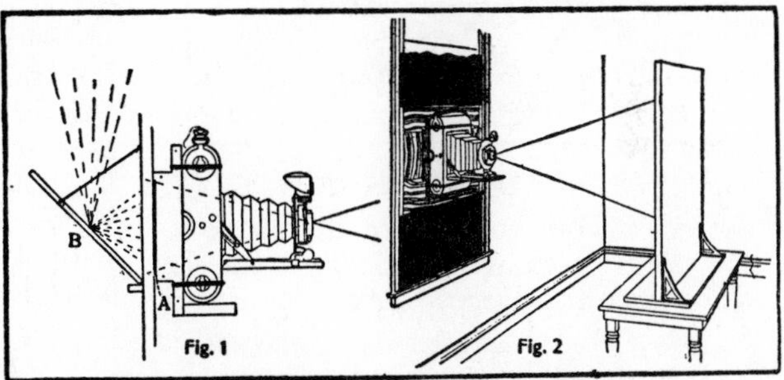

Making Large Pictures with a Small Camera

After placing the negative and focusing the lens for a clear image on the board, the shutter is set and a bromide paper is placed on the board. The paper is exposed, developed and fixed by the directions that are inclosed in the package of bromide papers.

¶Don't pull a lamp hung by flexible cord to one side with a wire and then fasten to a gas pipe. I have seen a wire become red hot in this manner. If the lamp hung by a cord must be pulled over, use a string.

A Curious Compressed-Air Phenomenon

Push a pin through an ordinary business card and place the card against one end of a spool with the pin inside the bore, as shown in the sketch. Then blow through the spool, and it will be found that the card will not be blown away, but will remain suspended without any visible support. This phenomenon is explained by the fact that the air radiates from the center at a velocity which is nearly constant, thereby producing a partial vacuum between the spool and the card. Can the reader devise a practical application of this contrivance?

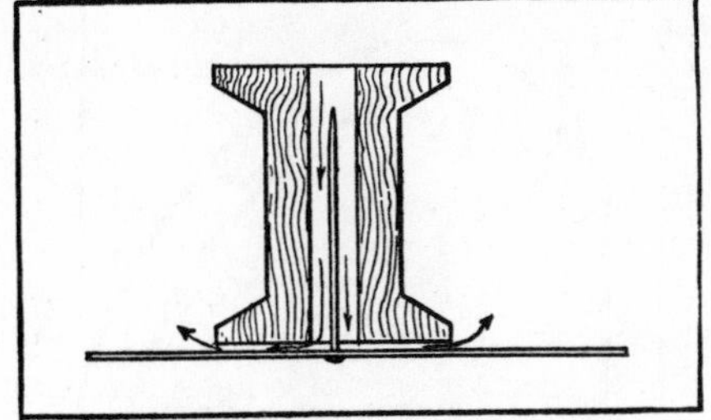
Experiment with Spool and Card

Simple Switch for Reversing a Current

Take two strips of copper or brass and fasten them together by means of gutta-percha (Fig. 1); also provide them with a handle. Saw out a rectangular block about one and one-half times as long as the brass strips and fasten to it at each end two forked pieces of copper or brass, as in Fig. 2. Fasten on the switch lever, as at A and

B, Fig. 2, so that it can rotate about these points. Connect the wires as shown in Fig. 3. To reverse, throw

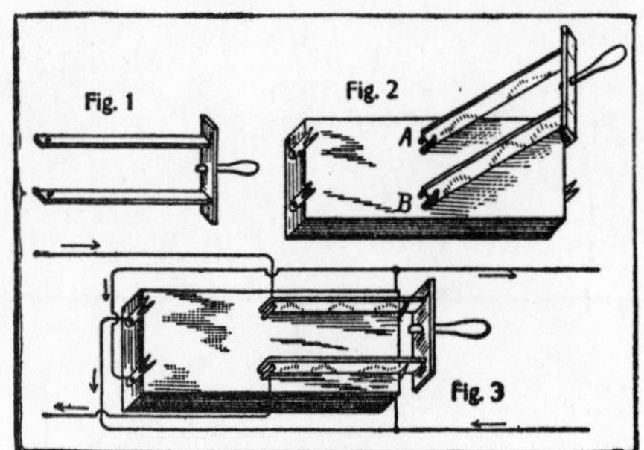

Simple Current-Reversing Switch

the lever from one end of the block to the other.—Contributed by R. L. Thomas, San Marcos, Tex.

Novel Mousetrap

A piece of an old bicycle tire and a glass fruit jar are the only materials required for making this trap. Push one end of the tire into the hole, making sure that there is a space left at the end so that the mice can get in. Then

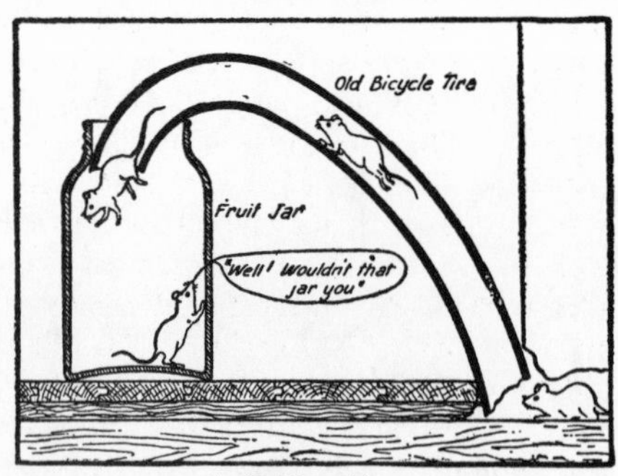

A Baitless Trap

bend the other end down into a fruit jar or other glass jar. Bait may be placed in the jar if desired, although this is not necessary.—Contributed by Geo. G. McVicker, North Bend, Neb.

ℭA brilliant polish may be given to tarnished nickel by immersing in alcohol and 2 per cent of sulphuric acid from 5 to 15 seconds. Take out, wash in running water, rinse in alcohol, and rub dry with linen cloth.

Homemade Arc Light

By rewinding an electric-bell magnet with No. 16 wire and connecting it in series with two electric-light carbons, as shown in the sketch, a small arc will be formed between the carbon points when the current is applied. In the sketch, A is the electric-bell magnet; B, the armature; C C, carbon sockets; D, carbons, and E E, binding posts. When connected with 10 or 12 dry batteries this lamp gives a fairly good light.—Contributed by Morris L. Levy, San Antonio, Tex.

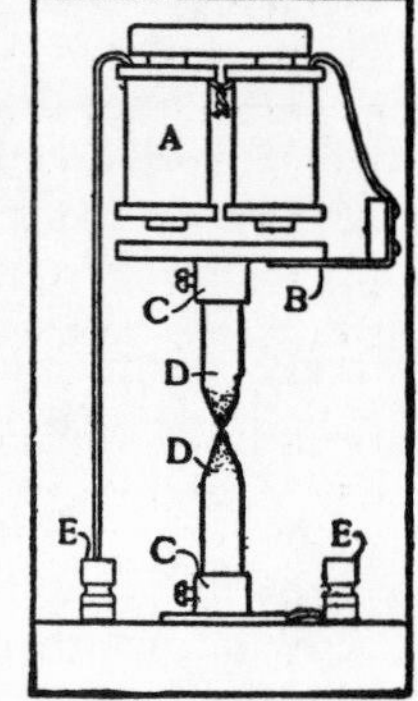

Arc Light

Lighting an Incandescent Lamp with an Induction Coil

An incandescent lamp of low candlepower may be illuminated by connecting to an induction coil in the manner shown in the sketch. One wire is connected to the metal cap of the lamp and the other wire is fastened to the glass tip. If the apparatus is then placed in the dark and the current turned on, a peculiar phosphorescent glow will fill the whole interior of the lamp. The induction coil used for this purpose should give a spark about ½ in. long or more.—Contributed by Joseph B. Bell, Brooklyn.

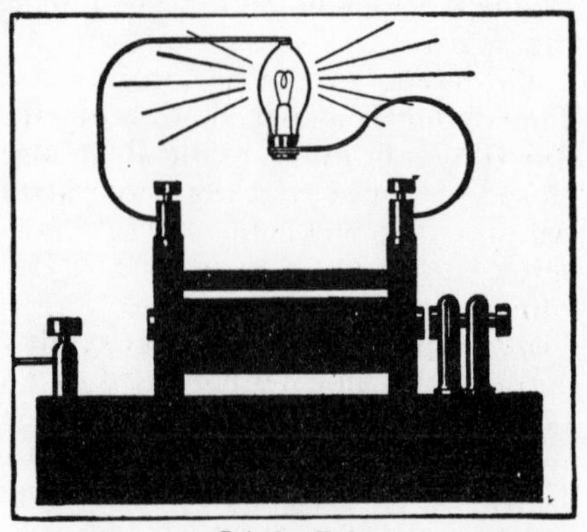
Geissler Tube

How to Make a Jump-Spark Coil

The induction coil is probably the most popular piece of apparatus in the electrical laboratory, and particularly is it popular because of its use in experimental wireless telegraphy. Ten years ago wireless telegraphy was a dream of scientists; today it is the plaything of school-boys and thousands of grown-up boys as well.

Divested of nearly all technical phrases, an induction coil may be briefly described as a step-up transformer of small capacity. It comprises a core consisting of a cylindrical bundle of soft-iron wires cut to proper length. By means of two or more layers of No. 14 or No. 16 magnet wire, wound evenly about this core, the bundle becomes magnetized when the wire terminals are connected to a source of electricity.

Should we now slip over this electromagnet a paper tube upon which has been wound with regularity a great and continuous length of No. 36 magnet wire, it will be found that the lines of force emanating from the energized core penetrate the new coil-winding almost as though it were but a part of the surrounding air itself, and when the battery current is broken rapidly a second electrical current is said to be induced into the second coil or secondary.

All or any of the parts of an induction coil may be purchased ready-made, and the first thing to do is to decide which of the parts the amateur mechanic can make and which would be better to buy ready-made. If the builder has had no experience in coil-winding it would probably pay to purchase the secondary coil ready-wound, as the operation of winding a mile or more of fine wire is very difficult and tedious, and the results are often unsatisfactory. In ordering the secondary it is always necessary to specify the length of spark desired.

The following method of completing a 1-in. coil illustrates the general details of the work. The same methods and circuits apply to small and larger coils. The ready-made secondary is in solid cylindrical form, about 6 in. long and 2⅝ in. diameter, with a hole through the winding 1¼ in. in diameter, as shown in Fig. 1. The secondary will stand considerable handling without fear of injury, and need not be set into a case until the primary is completed. The primary is made of fine annealed No. 24 iron wire cut 7 in. or 8 in. in length, as the maker prefers, and bundled to a diameter of ⅞ in. The wires may be straightened by rolling two or three at a time between two pieces of hard wood. If the amateur has difficulty in procuring this wire, the entire core may be purchased ready-made.

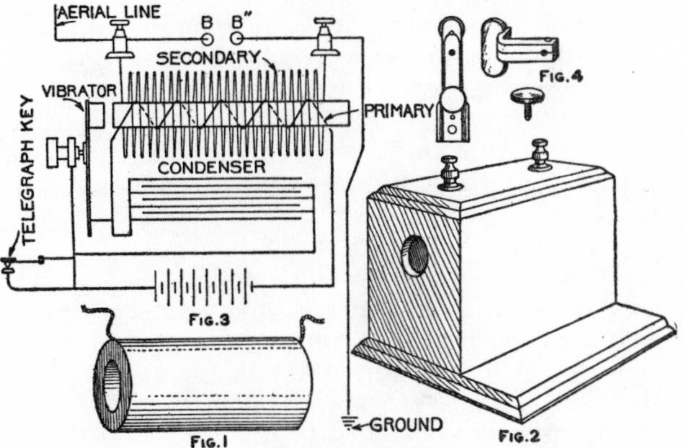

Jump-Spark Coil

After the core wires are bundled, the core is wrapped with one or two layers of manila paper. The straighter the wire the more iron will enter into the construction of the core, which is desirable. Beginning half an inch from one end, No. 16 cotton-covered magnet wire is wound from one end to the other evenly and then returned, making two layers, and the terminals tied down to the core with twine. Core and primary are then immersed in boiling paraffine wax to which a small quantity of resin and beeswax has been added. This same wax may be used later in sealing the completed coil into a box. Over this primary is now wrapped one layer of okonite tape, or same thickness of heavily shellacked muslin. This completed primary will now allow of slipping into the hole in the secondary.

Should the secondary have been purchased without a case, a wooden box of mahogany or oak is made, large enough to contain the secondary and with an inch to spare all around, with room also for a small condenser; but if it is not convenient to do this work, a box like that shown in Fig. 2 may be purchased at a small cost. A 7/8-in. hole is bored in the center of one end, through which the primary core projects 1/8 in. This core is to be used to attract magnetically the iron head of a vibrating interrupter, which is an important factor of the coil. This interrupter is shaped as in Fig. 4, and is fastened to the box in such a way that the vibrator hammer plays in front of the core and also that soldered connections may be made inside the box with the screws used in affixing the vibrator parts to the box. The condenser is made of four strips of thin paper, 2 yd. long and 5 in. wide, and a sufficient quantity of tin-foil. When cut and laid in one continuous length, each piece of tin-foil must overlap the adjoining piece a half inch, so as to form a continuous electrical circuit. In shaping the condenser, one piece of the paper is laid down, then the strip of tin-foil, then two strips of paper and another layer of foil, and finally the fourth strip of paper. This makes a condenser which may be folded, beginning at one end and bending about 6 in. at a time. The condenser is next wrapped securely with bands of paper or tape, and boiled in pure paraffine wax for one hour, after which it is pressed under considerable weight until firm and hard. One of the sheets of tin-foil is to form one pole of the condenser, and the other sheet, which is insulated from the first, forms the other pole or terminal. (This condenser material is purchasable in long strips, ready for assembling.)

The wiring diagram, Fig. 3, shows how the connections are made. This method of connecting is suitable for all coils up to 1½-in. spark, but for larger coil better results will be obtained by using an independent type of interrupter, in which a separate magnet is used to interrupt the circuit. Besides the magnetic vibrators there are several other types, such as the mercury dash-pot and rotary-commutator types, but these will become better known to the amateur as he proceeds in his work and becomes more experienced in coil operation.

Combined Door Bell and Electric Alarm

This device consists of a battery and bell connection to an alarm clock which also acts as a door bell, the whole being mounted on a board 18 in. long and 12 in. wide.

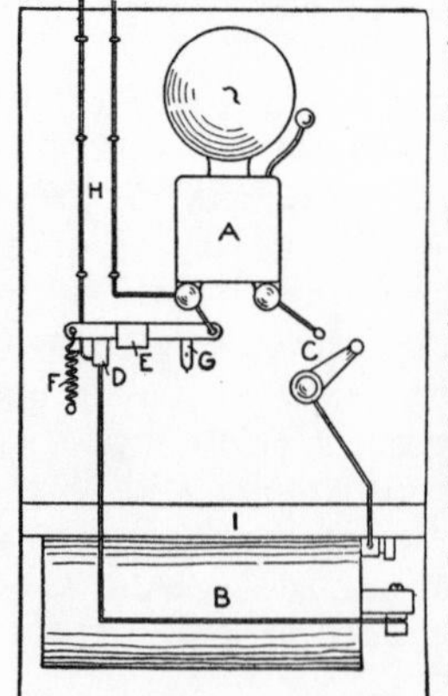

Referring to the sketch accompanying this article, the letters indicate as follows: A, bell; B, battery; C, switch; D, V-shaped copper strip; E, copper lever with 1-in. flange turned on one side, whole length, 4 in.; F, spring to throw lever E down in V-shaped piece to make connection; G, lever to hold out E when device is used as a door bell; lines H, go, one from bell, A, and one from battery, B, to the door; I, shelf for clock.

See that the ring in the alarm key of the clock works easily, so that when it is square across the clock it will drop down. Fasten a piece of copper about

1 in. long to key, then wind the alarm just enough so that the key stands straight up and down. Place the clock on the shelf and the key under the flange of lever E. Pull lever G down out of the way and close the lever on the switch. The alarm key will turn and drop down, letting lever E drop into the V-shaped piece D and make connection.

For the door-bell connection close lever on switch C, and put G up so that D and E do not come in contact. If any one is ill and you do not want the bell to ring, open switch C.

The wiring for this device may all be on the back of the board. The switch and levers are fastened with small screw bolts, which allows wiring at the back. Saw two spools in half and fasten the halves to the four corners of the board at the back, and the apparatus may be put up where one likes.

To Build a Small Brass Furnace

Bend a piece of stout sheet iron 23 in. by 12 in. round so that the inside diameter is 7 in., and then rivet the seam. Fit in a round piece of sheet iron for the bottom. Make a hole about the size of a shilling in the side, 2 in. from the bottom. This is for blowing.

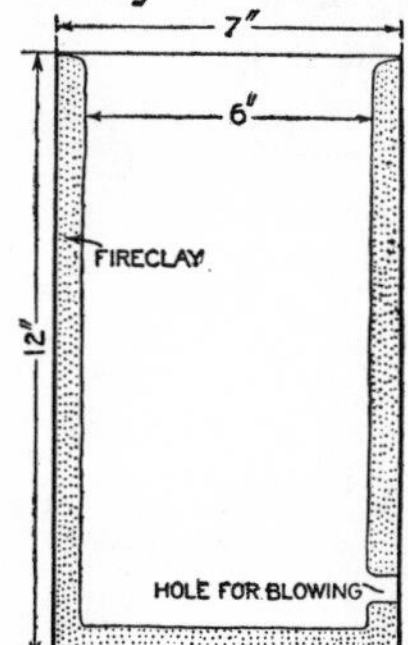

Line the furnace, bottom and sides with fire-clay to a depth of ½ in. Use charcoal to burn and an ordinary bellows for blowing, says the Model Engineer, London. The best blast is obtained by holding the nozzle of the bellows about an inch from the hole, instead of close to it.

¶Don't wrap paper around a lamp for a shade. You might go away and forget it and a fire might be started from the heat. Use a glass or metal shade. That is what they are for.

Why Gravity Batteries Fail to Work

Many amateur electricians and some professionals have had considerable trouble with gravity batteries. They

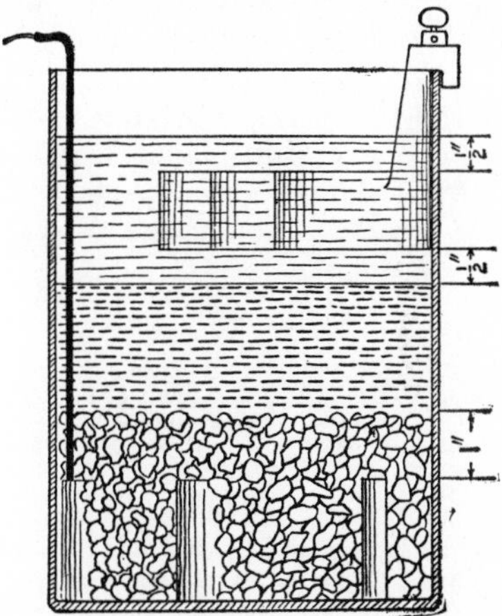

Setting Up a Gravity Battery

follow directions carefully and then fail to get good results. The usual trouble is not with the battery itself, but with the circuit. A gravity battery is suitable only for a circuit which is normally closed. It is therefore undesirable for electric bells, induction coils and all other open-circuit apparatus. The circuit should also have a high resistance. This makes it impractical for running fan motors, as the motor would have to be wound with fine wire and it would then require a large number of batteries to give a sufficiently high voltage.

To set up a gravity battery: Use about 3½ lb. of blue stone, or enough to cover the copper element 1 in. Pour in water sufficient to cover the zinc ½ in. Short-circuit for three hours, and the battery is ready for use. If desired for use immediately, do not short-circuit, but add 5 or 6 oz. of zinc sulphate.

Keep the dividing line between the blue and white liquids about ½ in. below the bottom of the zinc. If too low, siphon off some of the white liquid and add the same amount of water, but do not agitate or mix the two solutions. This type of battery will give about 0.9 of a volt, and should be used on a circuit of about 100 milli-amperes.

A Skidoo-Skidee Trick

In a recent issue of Popular Mechanics an article on "The Turning Card Puzzle" was described and illustrated. Outside of the scientific side involved, herein I describe a much better trick. About the time when the expression "skidoo" first began to be used I invented the following trick and

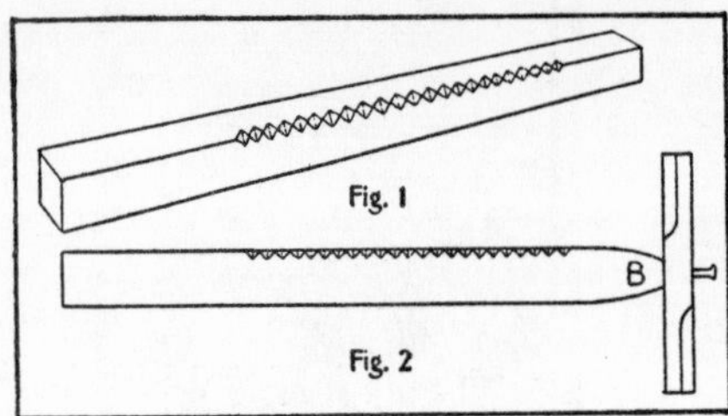

How to Cut the Notches

called it "Skidoo" and "Skidee," which created much merriment. Unless the trick is thoroughly understood, for some it will turn one way, for others the opposite way, while for others it will not revolve at all. One person whom I now recall became red in the face by shouting skidoo and skidee at it, but the thing would not move at all, and he finally from vexation threw the trick into the fire and a new one had to be made. Very few can make it turn both ways at will, and therein is the trick.

Take a piece of hardwood $\frac{3}{8}$ in. square and about 9 in. long. On one of the edges cut a series of notches as indicated in Fig. 1. Then slightly taper the end marked B until it is nicely rounded as shown in Fig. 2. Next make an arm of a two-arm windmill such as boys make. Make a hole through the center of this one arm. Enlarge the hole slightly, enough to allow a common pin to hold the arm to the end B and not interfere with the revolving arm. Two or three of these arms may have to be made before one is secured that is of the exact proportions to catch the vibrations right.

To operate the trick, grip the stick firmly in one hand, and with the forward and backward motion of the other allow the first finger to slide along the top edge, the second finger along the side, and the thumb nail will then vibrate along the notches, thus making the arm revolve in one direction. To make the arm revolve in the opposite direction—keep the hand moving all the time, so the observer will not detect the change which the hand makes—allow the first finger to slide along the top, as in the other movement, the thumb and second finger changing places: e. g., in the first movement you scratch the notches with the thumb nail while the hand is going from the body, and in the second movement you scratch the notches with the nail of the second finger when the hand is coming toward the body, thus producing two different vibrations. In order to make it work perfectly (?) you must of course say "skidoo" when you begin the first movement, and then, no matter how fast the little arm is revolving when changed to the second movement, you must say "skidee" and the arm will immediately stop and begin revolving in the opposite direction. By using the magic words the little arm will obey your commands instantly and your audience will be mystified. If any of your audience presume to dispute, or think they can do the same, let them try it. You will no doubt be accused of blowing or drawing in your breath, and many other things in order to make the arm operate. At least it is amusing. Try it and see.—Contributed by Charles Clement Bradley, Toledo, Ohio.

Radium acts upon the chemical constituents of glass, porcelain and paper, imparting to them a violet tinge; changes white phosphorus to yellow, oxygen to ozone, affects photograph plates and produces many other curious chemical changes.

On its official trial trip the British torpedo boat destroyer "Mohawk" attained the record speed of a little over 39 miles an hour.

How to Enlarge from Life in the Camera

Usually the amateur photographer gets to a point in his work where the miscellaneous taking of everything in sight is somewhat unsatisfying. There are many special fields he may enter, and one of them is photomicrography. It is usually understood that this branch of photography means an expensive apparatus. If the worker is not after too high a magnification, however, there is a very simple and effective means of making photomicrographs which requires no additional apparatus that cannot be easily and quickly constructed at home.

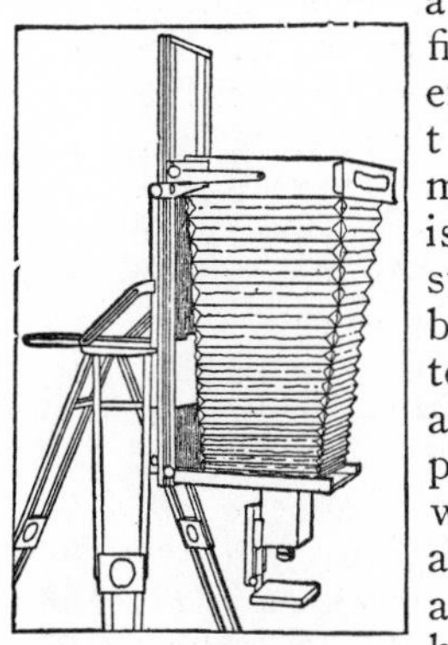

Reproduced with this article is a photograph of dandelion seeds—a magnification of nine diameters or eighty-one times. The apparatus which produced this photograph consisted of a camera of fairly long draw, a means for holding it vertical, a short-focus lens, and, if possible, but not essential, a means for focusing that lens in a minute manner. On top of the tripod is the folding arrangement, which is easily constructed at home with two hinged boards, an old tripod screw, an old bedplate from a camera for the screw to fit in, and two sliding brass pieces with setscrews that may be purchased from any hardware store under the name of desk sliding braces. To the front board is attached a box, carrying the lens and the bed of the sliding object carrier, which can be moved forward and back by the rack and pinion, that also can be obtained from hardware stores. If the bed for the object carrier be attached to the bed of the camera instead of to the front board, the object carrier need have no independent movement of its own, focusing being done by the front and back focus of the camera; but this is less satisfactory, particularly when accurate dimensions are to be determined, says the Photographic Times. This out need not be confined to seeds alone, but small flowers, earth, chemicals, insects, and the thousand and one little things of daily life—all make beautiful subjects for enlarged photographs. These cannot be made by taking an ordinary photograph and enlarging through a lantern. When a gelatine dry plate is magnified nine diameters, the grains of silver in the negative will be magnified also and produce a result that will not stand close examination. Photographs made by photomicrography can be examined like any other photographs and show no more texture than will any print.

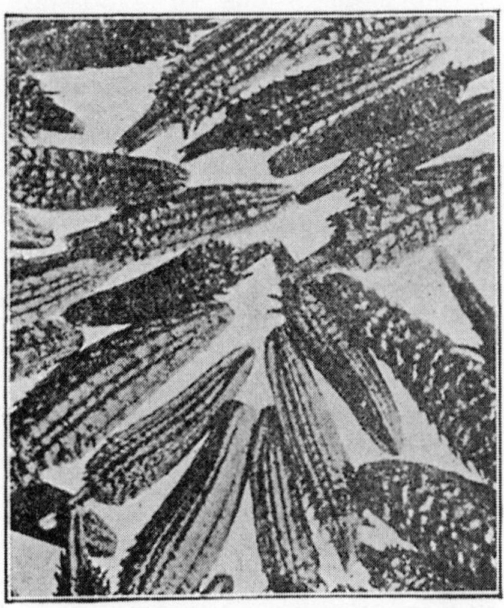

Magnified Nine Diameters

Steel Pen Used in Draftsman's Ink-Bottle Cork

A steel pen makes an ideal substitute for a quill in the stopper of the draftsman's ink bottle. The advantage of this substitute is that there is always one handy to replace a broken or lost pen, while it is not so with the quill.—Contributed by George C. Madison, Boston, Mass.

How to Make a Pilot Balloon

By E. Goddard Jorgensen

Unusual interest is being displayed in ballooning, and as it is fast becoming the favorite sport many persons would like to know how to construct a miniature balloon for making experiments. The following table will give the size, as well as the capacity and lifting power of pilot balloons:

Diameter.	Cap. in Cu. Ft.	Lifting Power.
5 ft.	65	4 lb.
6 ft.	113	7 lb.
7 ft.	179	11 lb.
8 ft.	268	17 lb.
9 ft.	381	24 lb.
10 ft.	523	33 lb.
11 ft.	697	44 lb.
12 ft.	905	57 lb.

The material must be cut in suitable shaped gores or segments. In this article we shall confine ourselves to a 10-ft. balloon. If the balloon is 10 ft. in diameter, then the circumference will be approximately 3 1/7 times the diameter, or 31 ft. 5 in. We now take one-half this length to make the length of the gore, which is 15 ft. 7½ in. Get a piece of paper 15 ft. 7½ in. long and 3 ft. wide from which to cut a patterr, Fig. 1. A line, AB, is drawn lengthwise and exactly in the middle of the paper, and a line, CD, is drawn at right angles to AB and in the middle of the paper lengthways. The intersecting point of AB and CD is used for a center to ascribe a circle whose diameter is the same as the width of the paper, or 3 ft. Divide one-quarter of the circle into 10 equal parts and also divide one-half of the line AB in 10 equal parts. Perpendicular lines are drawn parallel with the line CD intersecting the division points made on the one-half line AB. Horizontal and parallel lines with AB are drawn intersecting the division points made on the one-quarter circle and intersecting the perpendicular line drawn parallel with CD. A line is now drawn from B to E and from E to F, and so on, until all the intersecting lines are touched and the point C is reached. This will form the proper curve to cut the pattern. The paper is now folded on the line AB and then on the line CD, keeping the marked part on the outside. The pattern is now cut, cutting all four quarters at the same time, on the curved line from B to C. When the paper is unfolded you will have a pattern as shown in Fig. 2. This pattern is used to mark the cloth, and after marked is cut the same shape and size.

The cloth segments are sewed together, using a fine needle and No. 70 thread, making a double seam as shown in Fig. 3. When all seams are completed you will have a bag the shape shown in Fig. 4. A small portion of one end or a seam must be left open for inflating. A small tube made from the cloth and sewed into one end will make a better place for inflating and to tie up tightly.

It is now necessary to varnish the bag in order to make it retain the gas.

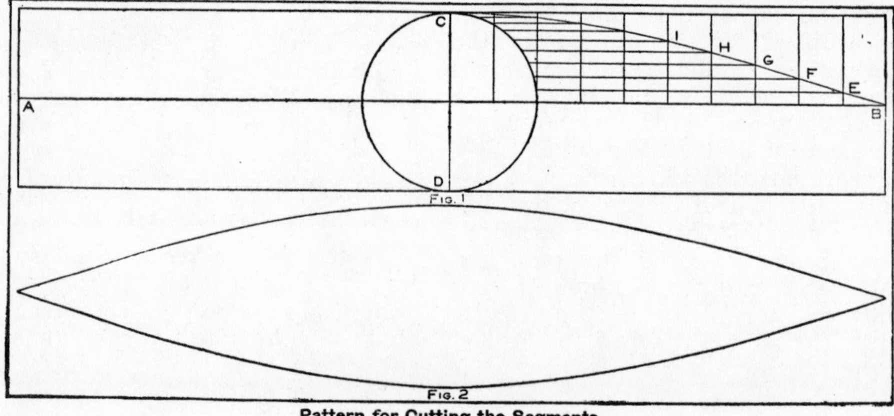

Pattern for Cutting the Segments

Procure 1 gal. of the very best heavy body, boiled linseed oil and immerse the bag in it. The surplus oil is squeezed out by running the bag through an ordinary clothes wringer several times. The bag is now placed in the sun for a thorough drying. Put the remaining oil in a kettle with $\frac{1}{8}$ lb. of beeswax and boil well together. This solution is afterward diluted with turpentine so it will work well. When the bag is dry apply this mixture by rubbing it on the bag with a piece of flannel. Repeat this operation four times,

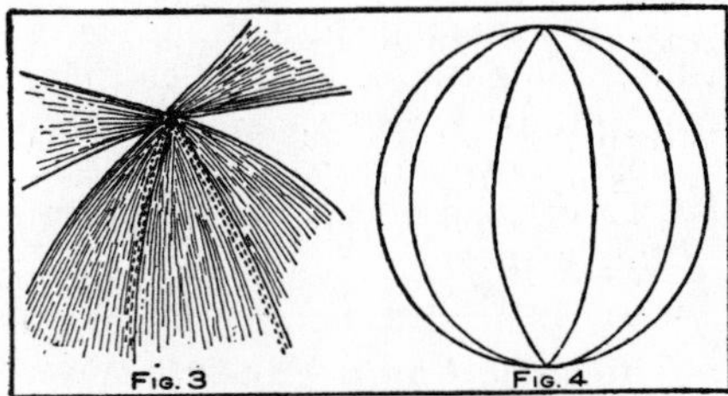

Sewing Segments Together

being sure of a thorough drying in the sun each time. For indoor coating and drying use a small amount of plumbic oxide. This will dry rapidly in the shade and will not make the oil hard.

Fill the bag with air by using a pair of bellows and leave it over night. This test will show if the bag is airtight. If it is not tight then the bag needs another rubbing. The next operation is to fill the bag with gas.

Hydrogen gas is made from iron and sulphuric acid. The amounts necessary for a 10-ft. balloon are 125 lb. of iron borings and 125 lb. of sulphuric acid. 1 lb. of iron, 1 lb. of sulphuric acid and 4 lb. of water will make 4 cu. ft. of gas in one hour. Secure two empty barrels of about 52 gal. capacity and connect them, as shown in Fig. 5, with $\frac{3}{4}$-in. pipe. In the barrel, A, place the iron borings and fill one-half full of clear water. Fill the other barrel, B, with water 2 in. above the level of the water in barrel A. This is to give a water pressure head against foaming when the generator is in action. About 15 lb. of lime should be well mixed with the water in the barrel B. All

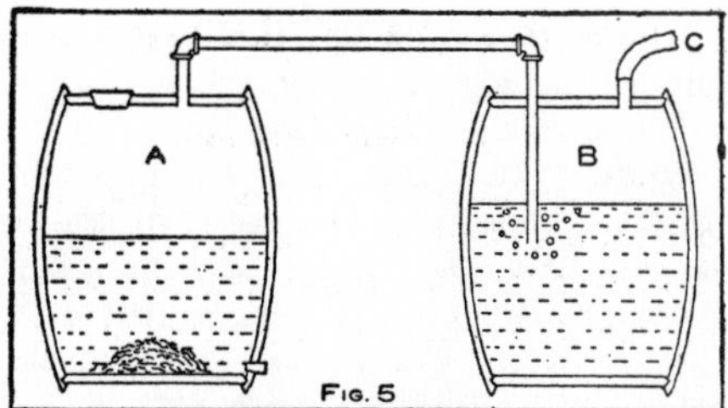

The Hydrogen Generator

joints must be sealed with plaster of Paris. Pour in one-half of the acid into the barrel, A, with the iron borings. The barrels are kept tight while the generation is going on with the exception of the outlet, C, to the bag. When the action is stopped in the generator barrel, A, let the solution run out and fill again as before with water and acid on the iron borings. The outlet, C, should be always connected with the bag while the generator is in action. The $\frac{3}{4}$-in. pipe extending down into the cooling tank, B, should not enter into the water over 8 in. When filled with gas the balloon is ready for a flight at the will of the operator.

How to Clean a Clock

It is very simple to clean a clock, which may sound rather absurd. For an amateur it is not always necessary to take the clock to pieces. With a little care and patience and using some benzine, a clean white rag, a sable brush and some oil a clock can be cleaned and put into first-class running order. The benzine should be clean and free from oil. You can test benzine by putting a little on the back of the hand; if it is good it will dry off, leaving the hand quite clean, but if any grease remains on the hand, it is not fit to use.

The oil should be of the very best that can be procured. Vegetable oils should never be used. Clock oil can be procured from your druggist or jeweler.

All loose dirt should be removed from the works by blowing with bellows, or a fan, or dusting with a dry brush; in the latter case great care should be exercised not to injure any of the parts. Dip the brush in the benzine and clean the spindles and spindle holes, and the teeth of the escapement wheel. After washing a part, wipe the brush on the rag and rinse in the benzine; this should be repeated frequently, until no more dirt is seen.

When the clock has dried, oil the spindle holes carefully; this may be done with a toothpick or a sliver of wood cut to a fine point. Oil the tooth of the escapement wheel slightly, using a fine brush.

How to Make Blueprint Lantern Slides

Lantern slides of a blue tone that is a pleasing variety from the usual black may be made from spoiled or old plates which have not been developed, by fixing, washing well and then dipping five minutes in the following solution:

A.	Green iron ammonium citrate..	150 gr.
	Water	1 oz.
B.	Potassium ferrocyanide	50 gr.
	Water	1 oz.

Prepare the solutions separately and mix equal parts for use, at the time of employment. Dry the plates in the dark, and keep in the dark until used. Printing is done in the sun, and a vigorous negative must be used, says the Moving Picture World. Exposure, 20 to 30 minutes. Wash 10 minutes in running water and dry. Brown or purple tones may be had by sensitizing with the following solution instead of the above:

Distilled water	1 oz.
Silver nitrate	50 gr.
Tartaric or citric acid...........	½ oz.

Bathe the plates 5 minutes, keeping the fingers out of the solution, to avoid blackened skin. Dry in the dark. Print to bronzing under a strong negative; fix in hypo, toning first if desired.

A Substitute for a Ray Filter

Not many amateur photographers possess a ray filter. A good substitute is to use the orange glass from the ruby lamp. This can be held in position in front of the lens with a rubber band. A longer exposure will be necessary, but good cloud effects can be procured in this manner.

Electric Lamp Experiments

Incandescent electric lamps can be made to glow so that they may be seen in a dark room by rubbing the globe on clothing or with a paper, leather or tinfoil and immediately holding near a ½-in. Ruhmkorff coil which is in action but not sparking. The miniature 16-cp., 20 and 22-volt lamps will show quite brilliantly, but the 110-volt globes will not glow. When experimenting with these globes everything should be dry. A cold, dry atmosphere will give best results.

Annual Regatta, Port Melbourne, Australia

How to Make a Simple Wireless Telegraph

By ARTHUR E. JOERIN

An efficient wireless-telegraph receiving apparatus for distances up to 1,000 ft. may be constructed in the following manner: Attach a watchcase telephone receiver to a dry cell, or battery, of any make. The negative pole, or zinc, of the cell is connected to a ground wire. This is done by attaching to a gas or water pipe. The positive pole, or carbon, of the cell is connected to the aerial line. This aerial collector can be made in various ways, either by using a screen wire or numerous wires made in an open coil and hung in the air. File a V-shaped groove in the upper end of the carbon of the cell. Attach a small bent copper wire in the binding post that is attached to the zinc of the cell. In the bend of this wire and the V-shaped groove filed into the carbon, lay a needle. This will complete the receiving station. Use a spark coil in connection with a telegraph key for the sending station, making a ground with one wire, and have the other connected with another aerial line.

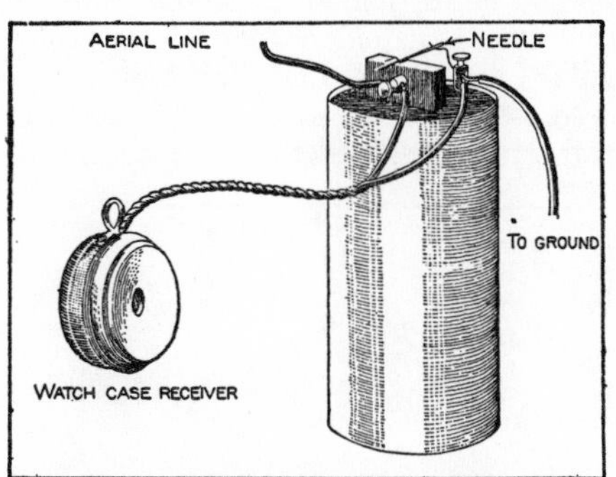

For Distances up to 1000 Feet

By connecting the telephone receiver to the cell and at the same time having a short circuit a receiving station is made. As the telephone offers a high resistance, part of the current will try to take the shorter high resistance through the needle. If the waves strike across the needle, the resistance is less, and thus less current travels through the telephone receiver. If the wave ceases, the resistance between the needle and the carbon is increased, and as less current will flow the short way, it is compelled to take the longer metallic way through the windings of the receiver, which will cause the clickings that can be heard.

To Preserve Putty

Putty, when left exposed to the air, will soon become dry and useless. I have kept putty in good condition for more than a year by placing it in a glass jar and keeping it entirely covered with water.

How to Make a Small Storage Battery

The cell of a storage battery consists of two plates, a positive and a negative, made of lead and placed in a dilute solution of sulphuric acid. Large batteries made of large cells have a great number of plates, both positive and negative, of which all positive plates are connected to one terminal and the negative plates to the other terminal. The storage cell, as described below, is the right size to be charged by a few gravity cells and is easily made.

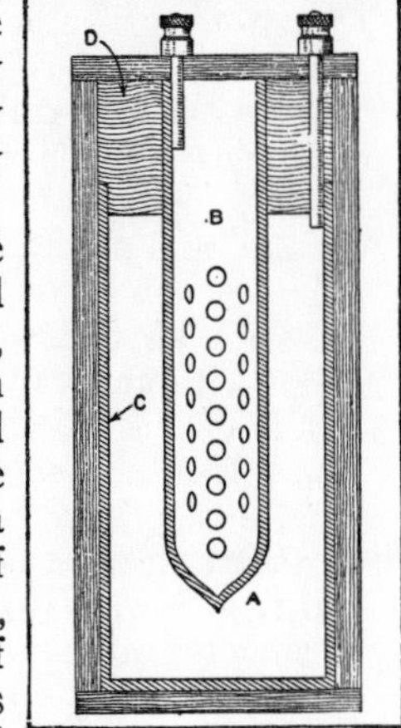

Secure a piece of 1¾-in. lead pipe, 5 in. long, and cut both ends smooth and square with the pipe. Solder a circular disk of lead to one end, forming a cup of the pipe. As this cup must hold the sulphuric acid it must be perfectly liquid-tight.

It is also necessary to get another lead pipe of the same length but only ¾ in. in diameter. In this pipe should be bored as many ⅛-in. holes as possible, except for about 1 in. on each end. One end of this tube is hammered together as shown at A in the sketch to make a pocket to hold the paste. This, of course, does not need to be watertight.

A box of wood is made to hold the larger tube or cup. This box can be square, and the corners left open around the cup can be filled with sawdust. A support is now made from a block of wood to hold the tube, B, in place and to keep it from touching the cup C. This support or block, D, is cut circular with the same diameter as the lead cup C. The lower portion of the block is cut away so it will just fit inside of the cup to form a stopper. The center of this block is now bored to make a hole the same size as the smaller lead pipe. Place the lead pipe in the hole and immerse it in smoking hot paraffine wax, and leave it until the wood has become thoroughly saturated with the hot wax. Use care to keep the wax from running on the lead at any place other than the end within the wood block. Two binding-posts should be attached, one to the positive, or tube B, and the other to the negative, or tube C, by soldering the joint.

A paste for the positive plate is made from 1 part sulphuric acid and 1 part water with a sufficient amount of red lead added to make of thick dry consistency. When mixing the acid and water, be sure to add the acid to the water and not the water to the acid. Also remember that sulphuric acid will destroy anything that it comes in contact with and will make a painful burn if it touches the hands. Stir the mixture with a stick and when a good dry paste is formed, put it into the smaller tube and ram it down until the tube is almost filled. The paste that may have come through the holes is scraped off and the tube set aside to dry. The large tube or cup is filled with a diluted solution of sulphuric acid. This solution should be about one-twelfth acid. The cell is now complete and ready for storing the current.

The cell may be charged with three gravity cells. These are connected in series and the positive terminal binding-post on the storage cell is connected to the wire leading from the copper plate in the gravity cell. The other plate is connected to the zinc. The first charge should be run into the cell for about one week and all subsequent charges should only take from 10 to 12 hours.

Fitting a Plug in Different Shaped Holes

A certain king offered to give the prince his liberty if he could whittle a plug that would fit four different-shaped holes, namely: a square hole, a round one, an oblong one and a triangular one, says the Pathfinder. A broomstick was used to make the plug and it was whittled in the shape shown

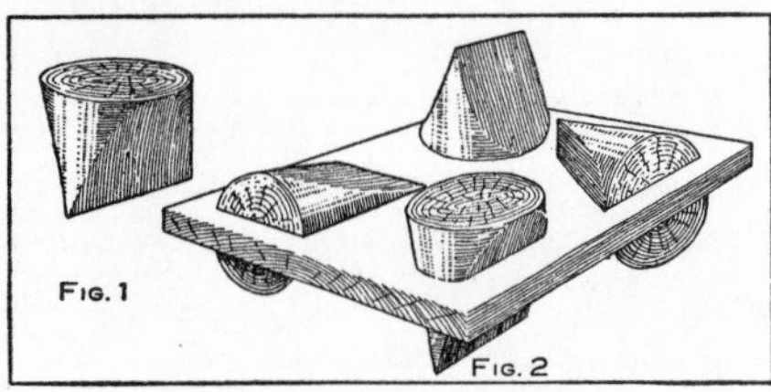

Fits Four Different Shaped Holes

in Fig. 1. The holes in the different places as shown in Fig. 2, were fitted by this one plug.

How to Make a Lightning Arrester

Secure a piece of wood about 3½ in. square that will furnish a nice finish and round the corners and make a small rounding edge as shown in the sketch.

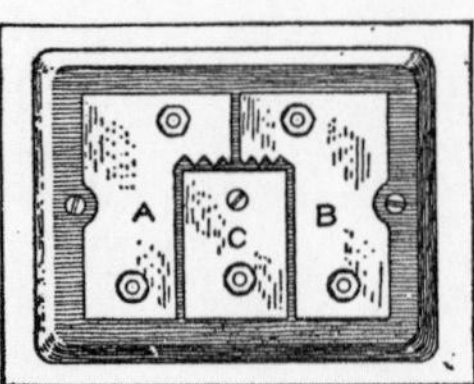

From a piece of brass $\frac{1}{16}$ in. thick cut two pieces alike, A and B, and match them together, leaving about $\frac{1}{16}$ in. between their upper edges and fasten them to the wood with binding-posts. The third piece of brass, C, is fitted between the pieces A and B allowing a space of $\frac{1}{16}$-in. all around the edge. One binding-post and a small screw will hold the piece of brass, C, in place on the wood. The connections are made from the line wires to the two upper binding-posts and parallel from the lower binding-posts to the instrument. The third binding-post on C is connected to the ground wire. Any heavy charge from lightning will jump the saw teeth part of the brass and is grounded without doing harm to the instruments used.—Contributed by Edwin Walker, Chicago, Ill.

A Home-Made Punt

A flat bottom boat is easy to make and is one of the safest boats, as it is not readily overturned. It has the advantage of being rowed from either end, and has plenty of good seating capacity.

This punt, as shown in Fig. 1, is built 15 ft. long, about 20 in. deep and 4 ft. wide. The ends are cut sloping for about 20 in. back and under. The sides are each made up from boards held together with battens on the inside of the boat near the ends and in the middle. One wide board should be used for the bottom piece. Two pins are driven in the top board of each side to serve as oarlocks.

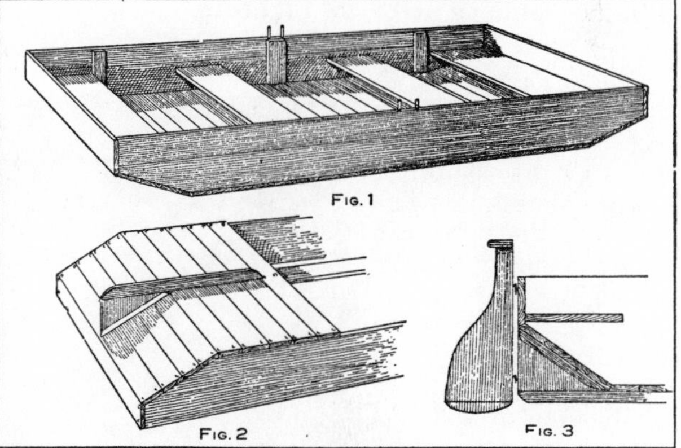

Easy to Build and Safe to Use

The bottom is covered with matched boards not over 5 in. wide. These pieces are placed together as closely as possible, using white lead between the joints and nailing them to the edges of the side boards and to a keel strip that runs the length of the punt, as shown in Fig. 2. Before nailing the boards place lamp wicking between them and the edges of the side boards. Only galvanized nails should be used. In order to make the punt perfectly watertight it is best to use the dryest lumber obtainable. At one end of the punt a skag and a rudder can be attached as shown in Fig. 3.

Photographers' Printing Frame Stand

When using developing papers it is always bothersome to build up books or small boxes to make a place to set the printing frame in front of the light. Details for making a small stand that

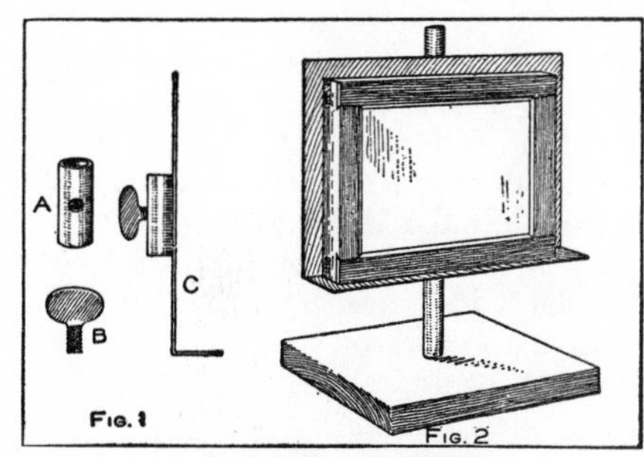

Adjustable to Any Height

is adjustable to any desired height are shown in the sketch. In Fig. 1 is shown the construction of the sliding holder. A piece of $\frac{1}{4}$-in. gas pipe, A, is cut 1 in. long and fitted with a thumbscrew, B. The piece of pipe is soldered to the middle on the back side of a piece of metal that is about 4 by $4\frac{1}{2}$ in. with its lower edge turned up to form a small shelf as shown at C. The main part of the stand is made by inserting a $\frac{5}{16}$-in. rod tightly into a block of hard maple wood that is 1 in. thick and 3½-in. square (Fig 2). The pipe that is soldered to the metal support will slide up and down the rod and the thumbscrew can be set to hold it at the desired point.

Heat and Expansion

Take an electric light bulb from which the air has not been exhausted and immerse it in water and then break off the point. As there is a vacuum in the bulb it will quickly fill with water. Shake the bulb gently until a part of the water is out and then screw the bulb into a socket with the point always downward. Apply the current and the heated air inside will soon expand and force the water out with great rapidity. Sometimes this experiment can be done several times by using the same bulb.—Contributed by Curtiss Hill, Tacoma, Wash.

Photographing a Streak of Lightning

The accompanying illustration is a remarkable photograph of a streak of lightning. Many interesting pictures of this kind can be made during a storm at night. The camera is set in a place where it will not get wet and left standing with the shutter open and the plate ready for the exposure. Should a lightning streak appear within the range of the lens it will be made on the plate, which can be developed in the usual manner. It will require some attention to that part of the sky within the range of the lens so as to not make a double exposure by letting a second flash enter the open lens.—Contributed by Charles H. Wagner.

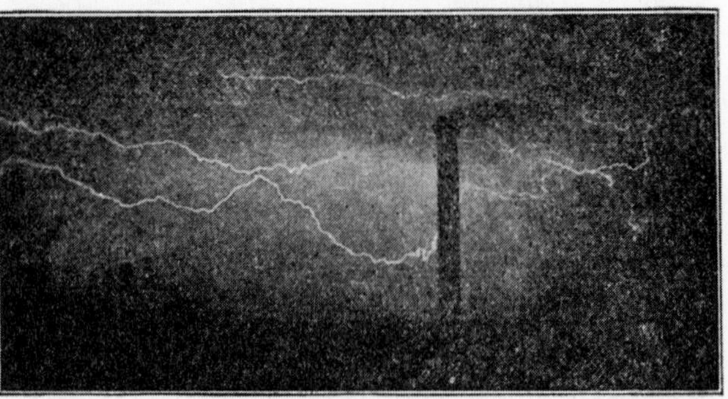

Borax may be used as a solvent for shellac gum.

How to Make a Small Single-Phase Induction Motor

By C. H. Bell

The following notes on a small single-phase induction motor, without auxiliary phase, which the writer has made, may be of interest to some of our readers, says the Model Engineer. The problem to be solved was the construction of a motor large enough to drive a sewing machine or very light lathe, to be supplied with 110-volt alternating current from a lighting circuit, and to consume, if possible, no more current than a 16-cp. lamp. In designing, it had to be borne in mind that, with the exception of insulated wire, no special materials could be obtained.

The principle of an induction motor is quite different from that of the commutator motor. The winding of the armature, or "rotor," has no connection with the outside circuit, but the current is induced in it by the action of the alternating current supplied to the winding of the field-magnet, or "stator." Neither commutator nor slip rings are required, and all sparking is avoided. Unfortunately, this little machine is not self-starting, but a slight pull on the belt just as the current is turned on is all that is needed, and the motor rapidly gathers speed provided no load is put on until it is in step with the alternations of the supply. It then runs at constant speed whether given much or little current, but stops if overloaded for more than a few seconds.

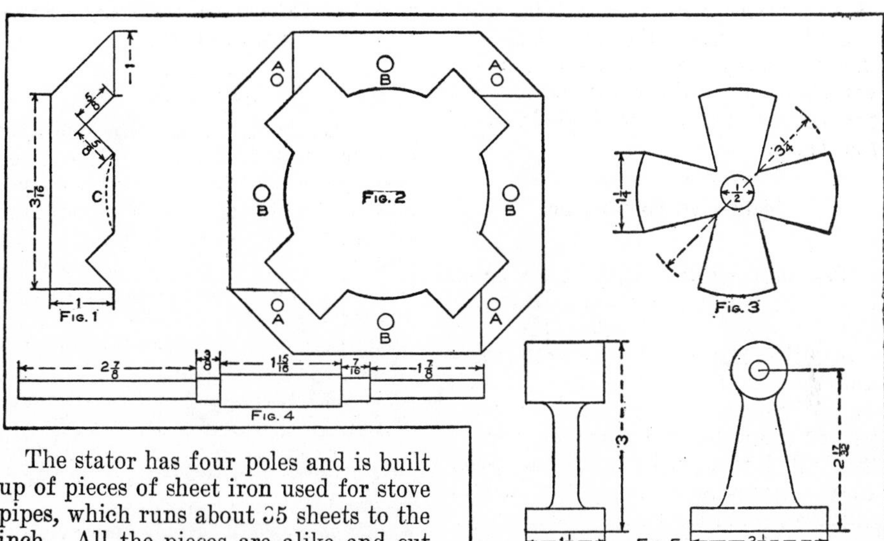

Fig. 1 Fig. 2 Fig. 3 Fig. 4 Fig. 5

The stator has four poles and is built up of pieces of sheet iron used for stove pipes, which runs about 35 sheets to the inch. All the pieces are alike and cut on the lines with the dimensions as shown in Fig. 1, with the dotted line, C, to be filed out after they are placed together. Each layer of four is placed with the pointed ends of the pieces alternately to the right and left so as to break joints as shown in Fig. 2. The laminations were carefully built up on a board into which heavy wires had been driven to keep them in place until all were in position and the whole could be clamped down. In the middle of the pieces $\frac{1}{4}$-in. holes, B, were then drilled and $\frac{1}{4}$-in. bolts put in and tightened up, large holes being cut through the wood to enable this to be done. The armature tunnel was then carefully filed out and all taken apart again so that the rough edges could be scraped off and the laminations given a thin coat of shellac varnish on one side. After assembling a second time, the bolts were coated with shellac and put into place for good. Holes 5-32 in. in diameter were drilled in the corners, A, and filled with rivets, also varnished before they were put in. When put together they should make a piece 2 in. thick.

This peculiar construction was adopted because proper stampings were not available, and as every bit of sheet iron had to be cut with a small pair of tinners' snips, it was important to have a very simple outline for the pieces. They are not particularly accurate as it is, and when some of them got out of their proper order while being varnished, an awkward job occurred in the magnet which was never entirely corrected. No doubt some energy is lost through the large number of joints, all representing breaks in the magnetic circuit, but as the laminations are tightly held together and the circuit is about as compact as it could possibly be, probably the loss is not as great as it would appear at first sight.

The rotor is made of laminations cut from sheet iron, as shown in Fig. 3, which were varnished lightly on one side and clamped on the shaft between two nuts in the usual way. A very slight cut was taken in the lathe afterwards to true the circumference. The shaft was turned from $\frac{1}{2}$-in. wrought iron, no steel being obtainable, and is shown with dimensions in Fig. 4. The bearings were cast of babbitt metal, as shown in Fig. 5, in a wooden mold and bored to size with a twist drill in the lathe. They are fitted with ordinary wick lubricators. Figures 6 and 7 are sections showing the general arrangement of the machine.

The stator is wound full with No. 22 double cotton-covered copper wire,

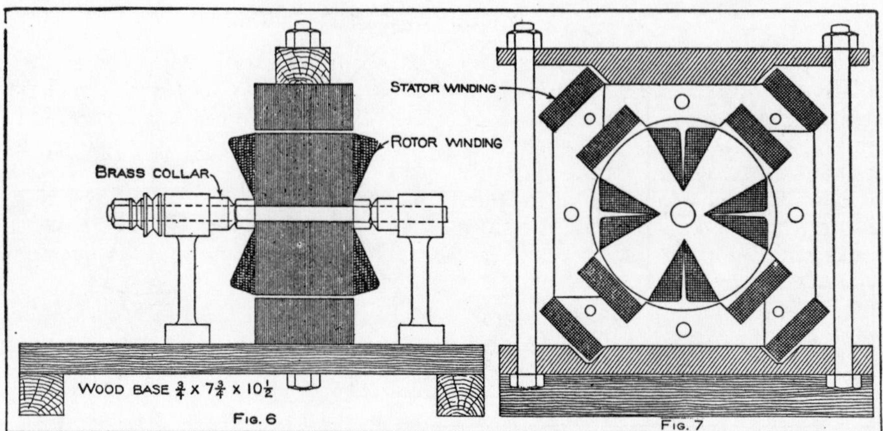

about $2\frac{1}{2}$ lb. being used, and the connections are such as to produce alternate poles—that is, the end of the first coil is joined to the end of the second, the beginning of the second to the beginning of the third, and the end of the third to the end of the fourth, while the beginnings of the first and fourth coils connect to the supply.

The rotor is wound with No. 24 double cotton-covered copper wire, each limb being filled with about 200 turns, and all wound in the same direction. The four commencing ends are connected together on one side of the rotor, and the four finishing ends are soldered together on the other. All winding spaces are carefully covered with two layers of cambric soaked in shellac, and as each layer of wire was wound, it was well saturated with varnish before the next was put on.

This type of motor has drawbacks, as before stated, but if regular stampings are used for the laminations, it would be very simple to build, having no commutator or brushes, and would not easily get out of order. No starting resistance is needed, and as the motor runs at constant speed, depending upon the number of alterations of the supply, a regulating resistance is not needed.

The pain of carbolic acid burns can be relieved promptly by washing with alcohol, if applied immediately. If too late for alcohol to be of use, brush with water containing saturated solution of picric acid.

How to Make a Paper Book Cover

Book covers become soiled in handling and especially school books. Various methods are applied for making a temporary cover that will protect the book cover. A paper cover can be quickly made by using a piece of paper larger than both covers on the book when they are open. Fold the paper on the long dotted line, as shown in Fig. 1. When the folds are made the paper should then be just as wide as the book cover is high. The ends are then folded on the short dotted lines, which will make it appear as shown in Fig. 2. The paper thus folded is placed on the book cover as shown in Fig. 3—Contributed by C. E. McKinney, Jr., Newark, N. J.

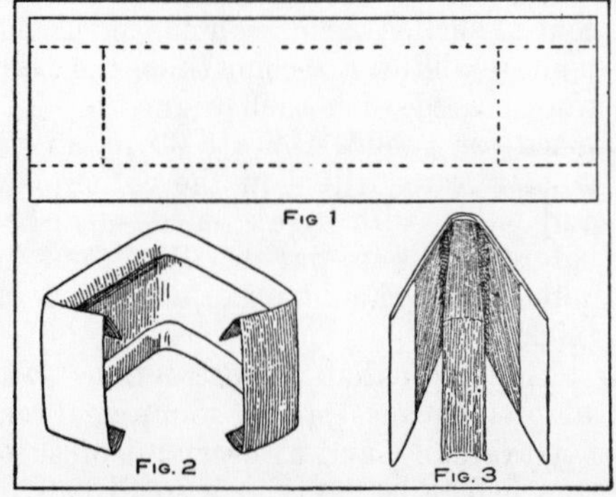

To Protect Book Covers

How to Make Lantern Slides

The popularity of lantern slides, and especially of colored ones, as a means of illustrating songs, has caused so large a demand for this class of work that almost any amateur may take up slide making at a good profit. The lantern slide is a glass plate, coated with slow and extremely fine-grained emulsion. The size is $3\frac{1}{4}$ by 4 in. A lantern slide is merely a print on a glass plate instead of on paper. Lantern slides can be made in two different ways. One is by contact, exactly the same as a print is made on paper, and the other by reduction in the camera. In making slides by contact, select the negative and place it in the printing frame and put the lantern plate upon it, film to film. Clamp down the back and expose just as in making a print. A good method of exposing is to hold a lighted match about 3 in. from the frame for three or more seconds according to the density.

Development is carried on in the same manner as with a negative. The image should appear in about a minute, and development should be over in three or four minutes. If the exposure has been correct, the high lights will stay white throughout the development and will come out as clear glass after fixing. It is best to use the developers recommended by the manufacturer of the plates used, the formulas being found in each package of plates. It is best, also, to use a plain fixing bath, which must be fresh and kept as cool as possible in hot weather.

The lantern-slide film that is new on the market can be handled in the same manner as the glass-plate slide, except that the binding is different. The results are the same and the slides are not so bulky to handle. Being unbreakable, they are much used by travelers. The manner of binding them for use in a lantern is described on the circular inclosed with the film.

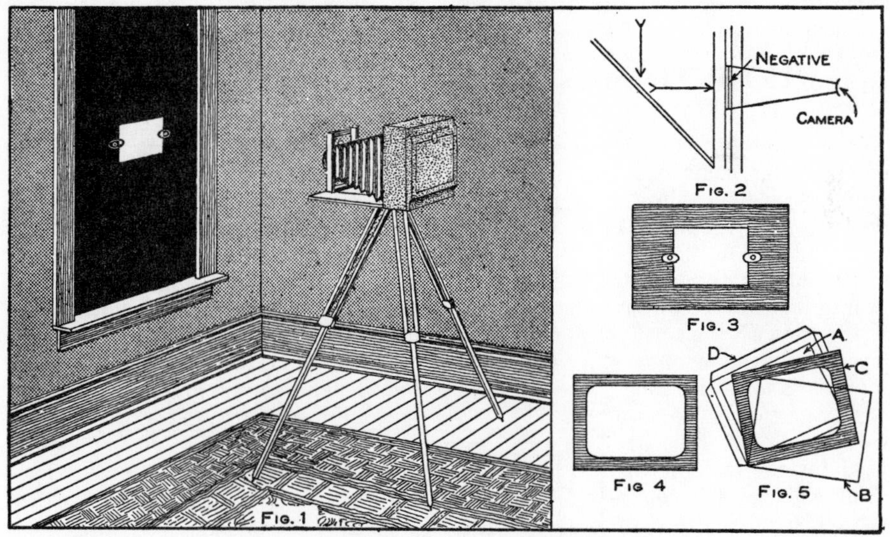

The Camera as It is Arranged in Front of the Window for Reducing the Size of a Picture, and the Method of Binding the Slides

When the negative is larger than the lantern-slide plate, and it is desirable to reduce the entire view upon the slide, a little extra work will be necessary. Select a room with one window, if possible, and fit a light-proof frame into it to keep out all light with the exception of a hole in which to place the negative, as shown in Fig. 1. Unless this hole is on a line with the sky it will be necessary to place a sheet of white cardboard at an angle of 45 deg. on the outside of the frame to reflect the light through the negative as shown in Fig. 2. Make or secure an inside kit to place in the plate holder of your camera to hold the lantern slide plate as shown in Fig. 3. Draw lines with a pencil, outlining on the ground glass of the camera the size of the lantern slide plate, and in the place where the plate will be in the plate holder when placed in position in the camera. This will enable you to focus to the proper size. Place the camera in front of the hole in the frame, place the negative in the hole and focus the camera for the lantern slide size. Expose with a medium stop for about 20 seconds and treat the plate the same as with the contact exposure.

When dry the lantern slide plate may be tinted any color by means of liquid colors. These can be purchased from any photo material store. In coloring the slide plate it is only necessary to moisten the gelatine film from time to time with a piece of cloth dampened in water. The colors may then be spread evenly with a soft brush, which should be kept in motion to prevent spots.

The slide is put together by placing a mat made of black paper, as shown in Fig. 4, on the gelatine side of the lantern slide, A, Fig. 5, and then a plain glass, B, over the mat, C, and the three bound together with passepartout tape, D. Contrasty negatives make the best slides, but the lantern slide plate should be made without any attempt to gain density.

HOW TO MAKE A PORCH SWING CHAIR

The material needed for making this porch swing chair are two pieces of round wood $2\frac{1}{2}$ in. in diameter and 20 in. long, and two pieces $1\frac{1}{4}$ in. in diameter and 40 in. long. These longer pieces can be made square, but for appearance it is best to have them round or square with the corners rounded. A piece of canvas, or other stout cloth, 16 in. wide and 50 in. long, is to be used for the seat. The two short pieces of wood are used for the ends of the chair and two 1-in. holes are bored in each end of them $1\frac{1}{2}$ in. from the ends, and between the holes and the ends grooves are cut around them to make a place to fasten ropes, as shown at B, Fig. 1. The two longer pieces are used for the sides and a tenon is cut on each end of them to fit in the 1-in. holes bored in the end pieces, as shown at A, Fig. 1. The canvas is now tacked on the end pieces and the pieces given one turn before placing the mortising together.

The chair is now hung up to the porch ceiling with ropes attached to a large screw eye or hook. The end of the chair to be used for the lower part is held about 16 in. from the floor with ropes direct from the grooves in the end pieces to the hook. The upper end is supported by using a rope in the form of a loop or bail, as shown in Fig. 2. The middle of the loop or bail

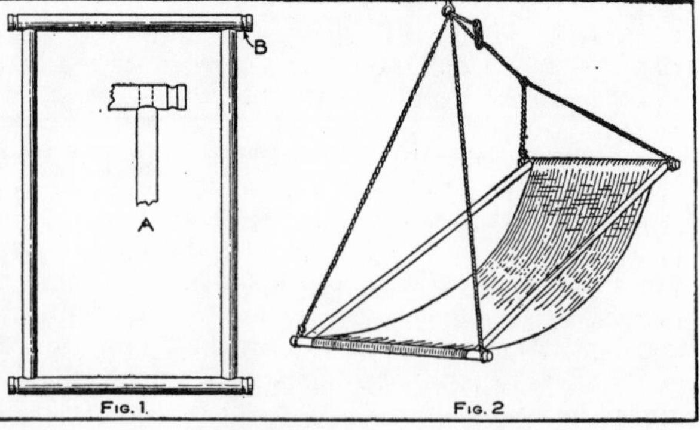

Fig. 1. Fig. 2

should be about 15 in. from the end piece of the chair. Another rope is attached to the loop and through the hook and to a slide as shown. This will allow for adjustment to make the device into a chair or a hammock.—Contributed by Earl R. Hastings, Corinth, Vt.

How to Find the Blind Spot in the Eye

Make a small black circular dot $\frac{1}{2}$ in. in diameter on a piece of cardboard and about 3 in. from the center of this dot draw a star. Hold the cardboard so that the star will be directly in front of one eye, while the dot will be in front of the other. If the star is in front of the left eye, close the right eye and look steadily at the star while you move the cardboard until the point is reached where the dot disappears. This will prove the presence of a blind spot in a person's eye. The other eye can be given the same experiment by turning the cardboard end for end. The blind spot does not indicate diseased eyes, but it simply marks the point where the optic nerve enters the eyeball, which point is not provided with the necessary visual end organs of the sight, known as rods and cones.

A wax from the rafie palm of Madagascar is being used as a substitute for beeswax.

Home-Made Water Wheel Does Family Washing

The accompanying sketch illustrates a very ingenious device which does the family washing, as well as to operate other household machines. A disk 1 in. in thickness and 10 in. in diameter was cut from a piece of rough board, and on its circumference were nailed a number of cup-shaped pieces cut from old tin cans. A hole was then bored through the center of the disk and an old piece of iron rod was driven through to form a shaft. Two holes were then bored opposite each other through the sides of a wooden box in which the disk was placed, allowing the shaft to project through the holes. A small grooved wooden pulley was driven tightly on one of the projecting ends of the shaft. The top of the box was then tightly closed and a hole, large enough to admit the nozzle of a garden hose, was bored so that the jet of water would flow upon the tin buckets that were nailed to the circumference of the wheel or disk. Another hole was bored in the bottom of the box large enough to allow the waste water to run away freely. A belt, made from an ordinary sash cord, was run from the small pulley on the waterwheel to a large pulley, as shown in Fig. 1. A pitman was attached to the large pulley, which operates the washing machine by its reciprocating motion, and the length of the stroke is adjusted by moving the position of the hinge joint on the arm of the washing machine, as shown in Fig. 2. The pressure at the nozzle is about 20 lb. per square inch, and is sufficient to drive the waterwheel under all ordinary circumstances.—Contributed by P. J. O'Gara, Auburn, Cal.

An Optical Illusion

When looking at the accompanying sketch you will say that the letters are alternately inclined to the right and left. They are not so and can be proved by measuring the distance of the top and bottom of any vertical strokes from the edge of the entire block. They will be found to be exactly the same distance. Or take any of the horizontal strokes of the four letters and see how far their extremities are from the top and bottom of the entire block. It will be found that a line joining the extremities of the strokes are strictly parallel to the top or bottom and that they are not on a slant at all. It is the slant of the numerous short lines that go to make up the letter as a whole that deceives the eye.

Home-Made Micrometer

It often becomes necessary to find the thickness of material so thin, or inconvenient to measure, that a rule or other measuring device will not serve the purpose. A simple, fairly accurate, and easily made apparatus of the micrometer form may be constructed as shown by the accompanying sketch. Secure a common iron or brass bolt about ¼-in. in diameter and about 2½ in. long, with as fine a thread as possible, and the thread cut to within a short distance of the head of the bolt. The head of the bolts should have a slot cut for the use of a screwdriver. Clamp together two blocks of wood with square corners which are about 1 in. wide, ¾ in. thick and 2½ in. long and fasten them together with small pieces nailed across the ends. The width of the blocks will then be about 2 in. Bore a ¼-in. hole through the center of the blocks in the 2 in. direction. Remove the clamp and set the nut into one of the blocks, so that the hole will be continuous with the hole in the wood. Cut out a piece from the block combination, leaving it shaped like a bench, and glue the bottoms of the legs to a piece of thin board about 2½ in. square for a support.

Solder one end of a stiff wire that is about 2 in. long to the head of the bolt at right angles to the shaft, and fix a disc of heavy pasteboard with a radius equal to the length of the wire, and with its circumference graduated into equal spaces, to serve in measuring revolutions of the end of the wire, to the top of the bench. Put the bolt in the hole, screwing it through the nut,

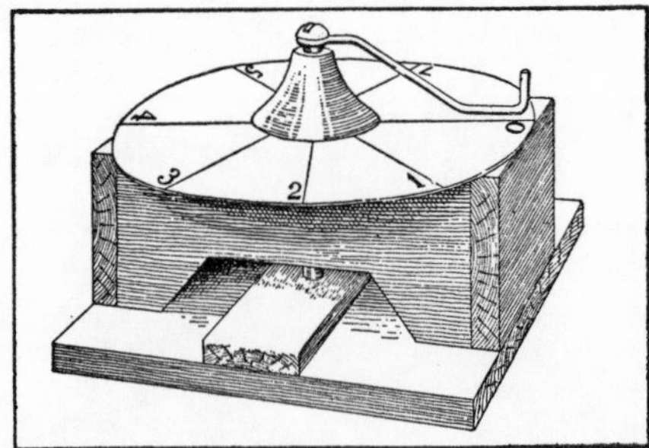

and the construction is complete. The base is improved for the measuring work by fastening a small piece of wood on the board between the legs of the bench. A small piece of metal is glued on this piece of wood at the point where the bolt meets it.

Find the number of threads of the screw to the inch by placing the bolt on a measuring rule, and counting the threads in an inch of its length. The bolt in making one revolution will descend a distance equal to the distance between the threads.

The device is used by placing the object whose thickness is to be measured on the base under the bolt, and screwing the bolt down until its end just touches the object, then removing the object, and screwing the bolt down until its end just touches the base, carefully noting while doing so the distance that the end of the wire moves over the scale. The part of a rotation of the bolt, or the number of rotations with any additional parts of a rotation added, divided by the number of threads to the inch, will be the thickness of the object. Quite accurate measurements may be made with this instrument, says the Scientific American, and in the absence of the expensive micrometer, it serves a very useful purpose.

Another Electric Lamp Experiment

Break a portion of the end off from a 16-cp. globe that has been thrown away as useless. Shake the globe until all the filament is broken away, leaving only the ends of the platinum wire exposed. Screw the globe into a socket that sets upright and fill it with salt water. Make one connection to the socket from the positive wire of a 110-volt circuit and the other to a ground. When the current is turned on small stars will be seen in the globe, which show up fine at night.—Contributed by Lindsay McMillan, Santa Maria, Cal.

Two or three applications of milk which are wiped up with a dry cloth will remove india ink spots on carpets.

Feat of Balancing on Chairs

Among the numerous physical exercises is the feat of balancing on the two rear legs of a chair while one foot rests on the front part of the seat and the other on the back of the chair. This may appear to be a hard thing to do, yet with a little practice it may be accomplished. This exercise is one of many practiced by the boys of a boys' home for an annual display given by them. A dozen of the boys will mount chairs at the same time and keep them in balance at the word of a commanding officer.

How to Make a Merry-Go-Round Swing

A 6 by 6-in. piece of wood 12 ft. long is used for the center pole. Bore a $\frac{3}{4}$-in. hole in each end to a depth of 6 in. Place a $\frac{3}{4}$-in. bolt in each hole, the bolt being long enough to protrude 2 in. beyond the end of the wood. Short pieces of wood are nailed on the center pole about 2 ft. from the end that is to be used for the bottom. This should form a hub on which to place the inner ends of the extending spokes that hold the platform. The spokes are made from twelve pieces of 2 by 4-in. material 12 ft. long.

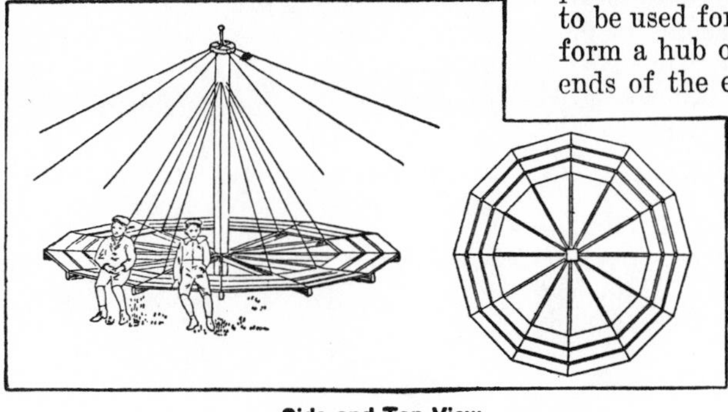

Side and Top View

Usually a wheel can be found in a scrap pile suitable to place on the pin that is in the top end of the center pole. The wheel should be open or have spokes. This wheel is used to attach wires for guying. The bottom pin in the center pole is placed in a hole that is bored into a block of wood about 12 in. square and 3 or 4 in. thick. A piece of sheet metal should be drilled and placed on the pin between the block and end of the pole to make a smooth bearing. The center pole is now placed in position and guyed with six wires that are about 35 ft. long. Stakes are driven into the ground and the wires fastened to them and to the wheel at the top end of the pole. Care should be taken when attaching the wires to get the center pole to stand perpendicular. Twelve hooks should be placed at equal distances around the center pole about 1 ft. from the top end. Wires are fastened to these hooks and to the twelve 2 by 4-in. pieces used for the spokes. The wires should be tied around each spoke about 2 ft. from the ends. Space the spokes with equal divisions and cover the outer 2 ft. of the ends with boards, as shown in the plan sketch on the right hand end of the drawing. The boards may be nailed or bolted. If bolted and the wires made in a loop at the hooks, the swing can easily be taken apart and changed from one place to another.—Contributed by A. O. Graham, Fort Worth, Tex.

Home-Made Arc Lamp

The frame of the lamp is made from bar metal $\frac{3}{4}$ in. wide and $\frac{1}{8}$ in. thick, bent and welded to make a continuous loop in the shape as shown at G in the sketch. This frame should be about $10\frac{1}{2}$ in. long with the upper or wider part 4 in. long, and the lower part $6\frac{1}{2}$ in. long. The width should be about $5\frac{1}{4}$ in. at the top and 4 in. at the bottom. A cross bar, L, made of the same material, is fitted into the off-set in the frame and riveted. Holes are drilled through the frame and brass bushings, H and J, are fitted for bearings to receive the adjusting brass rod, B, which should be $\frac{1}{4}$ in. in diameter. A brass curtain rod can be used for the rod B, and on its lower end a socket, P, is soldered.

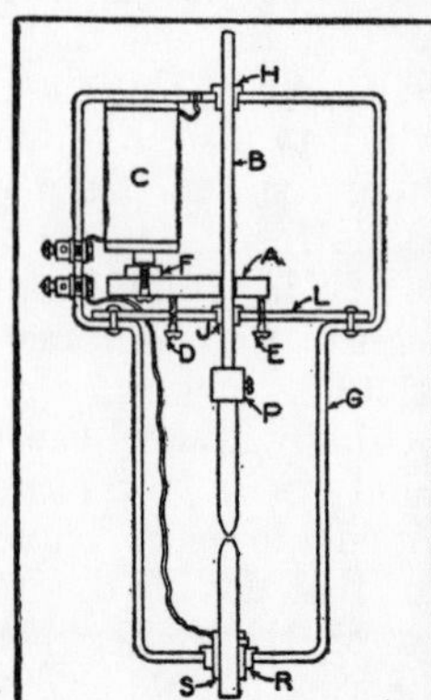

A piece of brass 2 in. long, $\frac{1}{2}$ in. wide and $\frac{1}{8}$ in. thick is used for the armature, A, to be operated by the magnet coil, C. The coil, C, is made in the usual manner by wrapping No. 14 cotton-covered magnet wire on a wooden spool that has a soft iron core. The spool is about $2\frac{1}{2}$ in. long. The armature, A, is drilled, making a hole just a little larger than the rod, B, and is adjusted in place by two set screws, D and E. A soft piece of iron, F, is fastened to the opposite end of the armature with a screw, which should be placed directly under the end of the coil's core. This end of the armature may be kept from swinging around by placing it between a U-shaped piece of brass fastened to the cross piece L. At the bottom end of the frame, and directly centering the holes H and J, a hole is drilled to receive a hard rubber bushing, R, for insulating the brass ferrule, S, that holds the lower carbon.

One connection is made from the main to the upper binding-post, which is in turn connected to one terminal of the coil, C, the other coil terminal being attached to the frame. The other main connection is made to the lower binding-post, which is also connected to the brass ferrule, S, by soldering. The two binding-posts are insulated from the frame the same as the ferrule S. When using on a 110-volt circuit there must be some resistance in connection, which may be had by using german silver wire, or a water rheostat heretofore described.—Contributed by Arthur D. Bradley, Randolph, Mass.

The Mexican government has appropriated $25,000,000 for irrigation work.

How to Hang Your Hat on a Lead Pencil

Take a smooth hexagon lead pencil, one without either rubber or metal end, and place it against a door or window casing; then with a firm, heavy pressure slide the pencil some 3 or 4 in. and it will stay as if glued to the casing. You may now hang your hat on the end of the pencil.

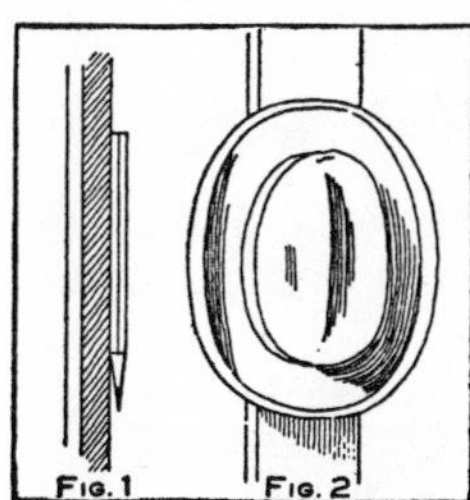

When you slide the pencil along the casing, do it without any apparent effort, and it will appear to your audience as though you had hypnotized it. This is a very neat trick if performed right. Figure 1 shows the pencil on the casing and Fig. 2 the hat hanging on it.

Tying a Knot for Footballs

One of the most prominent English football clubs kept the tying of this knot on the rubber hose of their football a secret and never allowed all of its members to know how it was tied. This tie can be used on grain sacks, and in numerous other like instances. Make one loop in the cord and then another exactly the same way, as

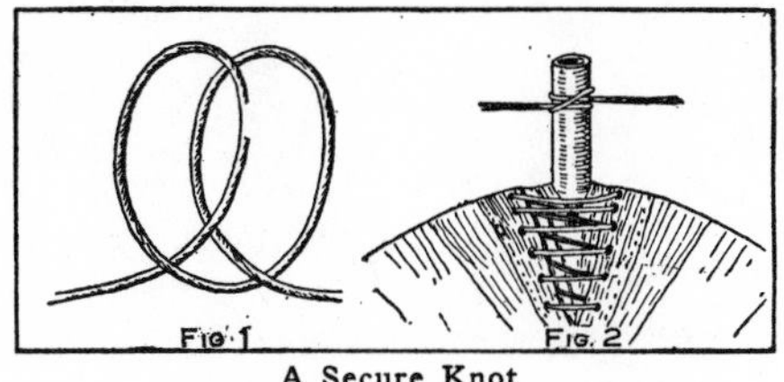

A Secure Knot

shown in Fig. 1, placing the end of the cord under the first loop, then pulling at each end of the cord as in Fig. 2.—A. E. J.

¶Stove polish consists of 2 parts graphite, 4 parts copperas and 2 parts boneblack, mixed with water to form a paste.

How to Give an Electric Shock While Shaking Hands

There is nothing quite so startling as to receive an electric shock unexpectedly and such a shock may be given to a friend while shaking hands upon meeting. The shock produced is not harmful and the apparatus can be carried in the pocket. It consists of a small induction coil that can be constructed at home.

The core of the coil, A, Fig. 1, is constructed in the usual manner, of small soft-iron wire to make a bundle about $\frac{3}{16}$ in. in diameter and 2 in. long. The coil ends are made from cardboard, about 1 in. in diameter, with a $\frac{3}{16}$-in. hole in the center. The hole

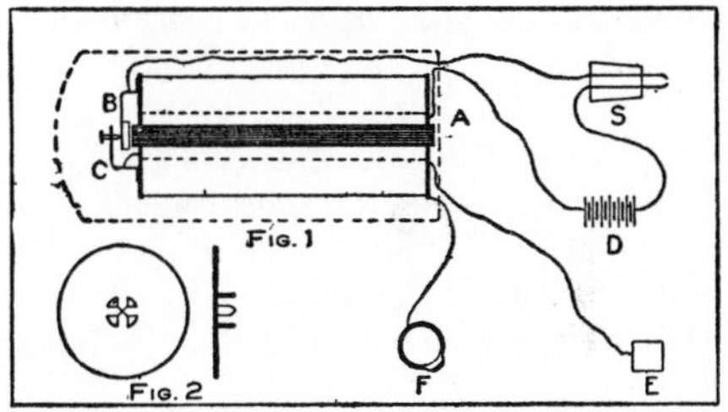

Details of Induction Coil

should be cut as shown in Fig. 2, so as to have four small pieces that can be bent out, leaving the projections as shown. After wrapping three or four turns of paper around the bundle of wires the cardboard ends are put on with the projections inside, so the coils of wire will hold them in place. About 70 turns of No. 24 gauge double-covered magnet wire is first placed on the core, for the primary, and then 1,500 turns of No. 32 or 34 gauge double-covered wire is wrapped on top of the primary, for the secondary. Sufficient length of wire must be left outside at each end of both windings to make connections. The vibrator B, Fig. 1, and the support C are made from thin spring steel, about ⅛ in. wide, bent as shown and securely fastened to the cardboard end of the coil. The armature is made from a soft piece of iron, about $\frac{3}{16}$ in. in diameter and $\frac{1}{16}$ in. thick, which is soldered to the end of the vibrator directly opposite the end of the core. A small screw is fitted in the end of the support, C, for adjustment, which should be tipped with platinum and also a small piece of platinum placed where the screw will touch the vibrator, B.

One of the primary wires is connected to the screw support. The vibrator is connected to a flash lamp battery, D. The other primary wire is connected to a switch, S, which in turn is connected to the other terminal of the battery. The switch, S, may be made from a $\frac{3}{8}$-in. cork with the wires put through about $\frac{3}{16}$ in. apart and allow them to project about $\frac{1}{2}$ in. The plate E is cut about $\frac{1}{2}$ in. square from a piece of copper and is fastened to the heel of one shoe and connected with a wire from the secondary coil which must be concealed inside of the trouser leg. The other secondary wire is connected through the coat sleeve to a finger ring, F. The vibrator screw must be properly adjusted. When the vibrator is not working the armature should be about $\frac{1}{16}$ in. from the core and directly opposite.

The coil when complete will be about $2\frac{1}{2}$ in. long and 1 in. in diameter. The coil can be placed in an old box that has been used for talcum powder or shaving stick. The space around the coil in the box can be filled with paper to keep it tight.

The coil and battery are carried in the pockets and the cork button put in the outside coat pocket, where it can be pressed without attracting attention.

Experiment with Heat

Place a small piece of paper, lighted, in an ordinary water glass. While the paper is burning turn the glass over and set into a saucer previously filled with water. The water will rapidly rise in the glass, as shown in the sketch.

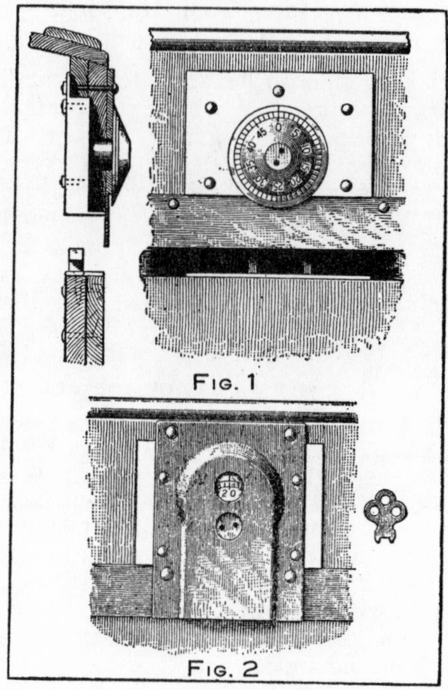

Fig. 1

Fig. 2

How to Attach a Combination Trunk Lock

A small combination lock for chests can be purchased for a small sum of money and attached to a trunk cover after first removing the old lock as shown in Fig. 1. It is necessary to add $\frac{1}{2}$ in. to the thickness of the trunk lid or cover. This may be done by placing a brass plate $\frac{1}{8}$ in. thick on the outside and a board $\frac{3}{8}$ in. thick on the inside. The lock, brass plate, board and trunk cover are all securely riveted together. The support for the dial is soldered to the brass plate.

The hasp, if that be the name for the double toothed arrangement that catches into the lock, was to be secured by only three brass screws, which seemed to be insufficient, says a correspondent of the Metal Worker; therefore a piece of heavy tin was formed over the front of the trunk, which is only $\frac{3}{8}$-in. board, the hasp tinned and soldered to the back of the now U-shaped tin, and the tin placed over the board and all fastened in position. The tin is 4 in. wide, 16 in. long and when placed over the board, it laps down about 8 in. between the boards, and the same distance inside of the new board, as shown by the heavy line in the cross section, Fig. 1. Wrought nails are used which pass twice through the tin and both boards, and then well clinched. The three screws were then put in the hasp.

The knob on the dial extends out too far, which may be filed off and two holes substituted, as shown, with which to operate the dial. An old key is filed down in the shape shown in Fig. 2 to fit the two holes.

As the dial is convex it will need protection to prevent injury by rough handling. A leather shield may be used for this purpose, which is cut with two holes, one for the key and the other to permit the operator to observe the numbers on the dial. The shield answers a further purpose of preventing any bystander from noting the numbers on the dial.

AN ELECTRIC ILLUSION BOX

The accompanying engravings show a most interesting form of electrically operated illusion consisting of a box divided diagonally and each division alternately lighted with an electric lamp. By means of an automatic thermostat arranged in the lamp circuit causing the lamps to light successively, an aquarium apparently without fish one moment is in the next instant swarming with live gold fish; an empty vase viewed through the opening in the box suddenly is filled with flowers, or an empty cigar box is seen and immediately is filled with cigars.

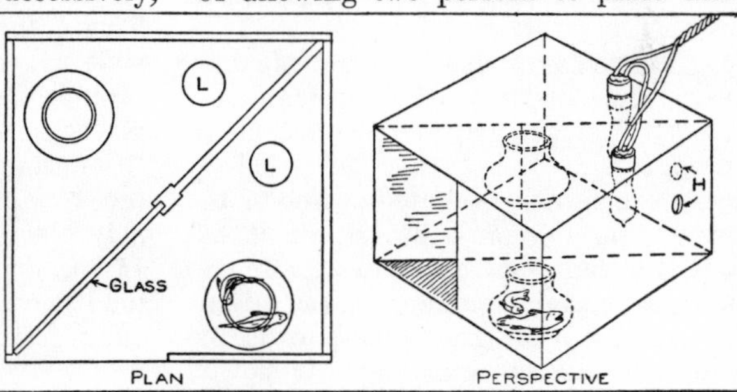

Construction of Magic Boxes

These electric magic boxes as shown are made of metal and oxidized copper finished, but for ordinary use they can be made of wood in the same shape and size. The upper magic boxes as are shown in the engraving are about 12 in. square and 8½ in. high for parlor use and the lower boxes are 18 in. square and 10½ in. high for use in window displays. There is a partition arranged diagonally in the box as shown in the plan view, which completely divides the box into two parts. One-half the partition is fitted with a plain, clear glass as shown. The partition and interior of the box are rendered non-reflecting by painting with a dull, not shiny, black color. When making of wood, a door must be provided on the side or rear to make changes of exhibits. If the box is made large enough, or in the larger size mentioned, openings may be made in the bottom for this purpose, and also used in case of performing the magic trick of allowing two persons to place their heads in the box and change from one to the other.

The electric globes are inserted as shown at LL through the top of the box, one in each division. When the rear part is illuminated, any article arranged within that part will be visible to the spectator looking into the box through the front opening, but when the front part is illuminated, and the back left dark, any article placed therein will be reflected in the glass, which takes the same position to the observer as the one in the rear. Thus a plain aquarium is set in the rear part and one with swimming fish placed in

Four Electric Magic Boxes Complete for Use

the front, and with the proper illumination one is changed, as it appears, into the other. When using as a window display, place the goods in one part and the price in the other. Many other changes can be made at the will of the operator.

Electric lamps may be controlled by various means to produce different effects. Lamps may be connected in parallel and each turned on or off by means of a hand-operated switch or the button on the lamp socket, or if desired a hand-operated adjustable resistance may be included in the circuit of each lamp for gradually causing the object to fade away or reappear slowly.

Instead of changing the current operated by hand, this may be done automatically by connecting the lamps in parallel on the lighting circuit and each connected in series with a thermostatic switch plug provided with a heating coil which operates to automatically open and close the circuit through the respective lamp.

When there is no electric current available, matches or candles may be used and inserted through the holes H, as shown in the sketch, alternately.

Painting over putty that has not become dry will cause scaling or cracking around the edges of the putty.

Photo Print Washing Tank

The accompanying sketch shows a simple form of a print washing tank that tips from side to side by the weight of the water. For prints 4 by 5 and 5 by 7 in. a tank 2 ft. long and 1 ft. wide will be about the right size. This tank is then divided with a partition placed exactly in the center. This partition should extend 3 or 4 in. above the top of the tank. The partition may also extend below the tank about $1\frac{1}{2}$ in., or a piece of this width put on the bottom, as shown at A in the sketch.

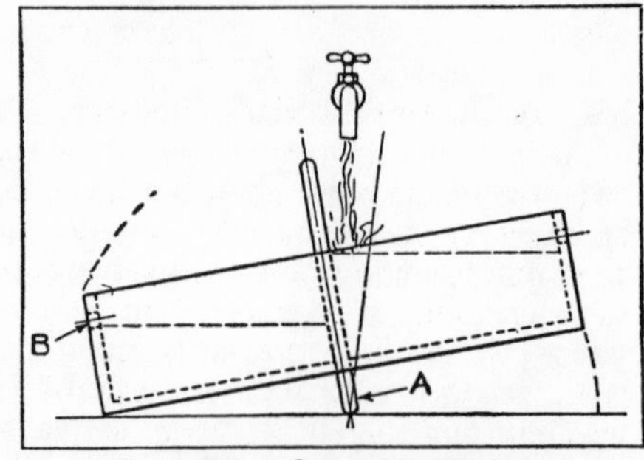

Keeps Prints Constantly Moving

A row of holes about $\frac{1}{2}$ in. in diameter is bored through each end of the tank, as shown at B. These holes will allow the water to spill out while the opposite side is filling. The tank may be made from $\frac{1}{2}$-in. material and when completed as shown, lined with oil cloth to make it watertight. The tank is placed with the partition directly under a water tap and the flow of water will cause it to tip from time to time, keeping the prints constantly moving about in the water.

Home-Made Soldering Clamps

Take a cotter pin and bend it over a small rod to bring the points together, as shown in the sketch. This will make a spring clamp that is opened to slip over the articles to be clamped together by inserting a scratch awl or scriber between the legs at the bowed portion. To make a more positive clamp before bending the legs to a bow, slip a short coil of wire over the pin, passing it down to the ring end. Wire $^1/_{32}$ in. in diameter wound over a wire slightly larger in diameter than that of the cotter will do. In soldering, smoke the legs well to avoid solder adhering to them. The clamp is tightened by pushing up the coil ring toward the bow of the legs and then twisting it like a nut, the coil being wound right-handed, so that it will have a screw effect.

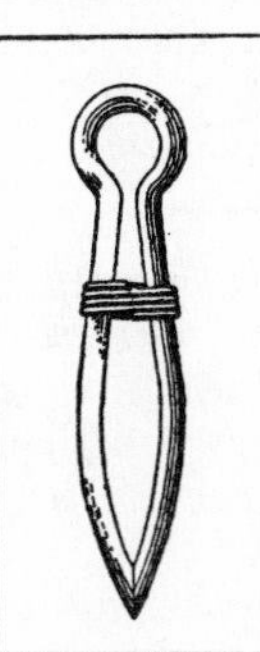

A Telephone Experiment

If the small apparatus, as shown in the accompanying sketch, is attached to the under side of an ordinary dining table, it will, if connected to a telephone circuit, set the table in vibration, so that any number of people who put their ears flat upon the table will hear the voice of a person speaking from a distance, apparently coming out of the table, says the Model Engineer.

A small piece of wood, A, Fig. 1, is cut about 5 in. square, to the center of which is attached a small piece of soft iron wire, such as used for cores of induction coils, about 4 in. long and bent in the form of a hook at the lower end, as shown at B. This wire is attached to the block of wood, A, as shown in Fig. 2. The end of the wire is soldered to a small brass plate which is set in the block so it will be level or flush with the top of the block and then fastened with two screws. The block A is fastened to the under side of the table with two screws. A small coil, C, is made by winding No. 24 silk or cotton covered wire around a small tube, either a piece of glass, a short straw or a quill. The coil is made tapering as shown without using wood ends. This coil is slipped over the wire B previous to soldering it to the small brass plate. The ends of the coil are connected to two binding-posts which are fastened to the block A. A small lead weight weighing 2 or 3 oz. is hung on the hook made in the lower end of the wire B.

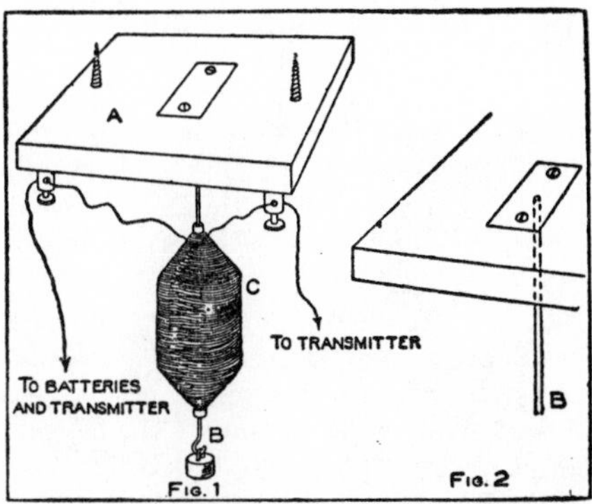

Mechanical Table Talk

When all connections are made, as shown in Fig. 1, and the block fastened to the under side of the table, the apparatus is ready for use, and has only to be connected to an ordinary telephone transmitter and batteries as shown. The apparatus will work to a certain extent even if the weight is removed, though not so clear.

Some workmen use tallow on lag or wood screws. Try beeswax for this purpose. It is much cleaner to use and is just as good if not better.

How to Make an Induction Coil

A small shocking coil, suitable for medical purposes, may be constructed of materials found in nearly every amateur mechanic's collection of odds and ends. The core, A, Fig. 1, is a piece of round soft iron rod about $\frac{1}{4}$ in. in diameter and about 4 in. long. A strip of stiff paper about $\frac{3}{4}$ in. wide is covered with glue and wrapped around one end of the core, as shown at B, until the diameter is about $\frac{3}{8}$ in. The portion of the core remaining uncovered is then wrapped with a piece of paper about 4 in. wide. No glue is used on this piece, as it is removed later to form the space, C, after the paper shell, D, has been wound upon it. This paper shell is made of stiff paper and glue the same as B and is made about 3/64 in. thick. Two pieces of hardwood, EE, $1\frac{3}{4}$ in. square and about $\frac{5}{16}$ in. thick, are drilled in the center and glued on the ends of the paper shell as shown.

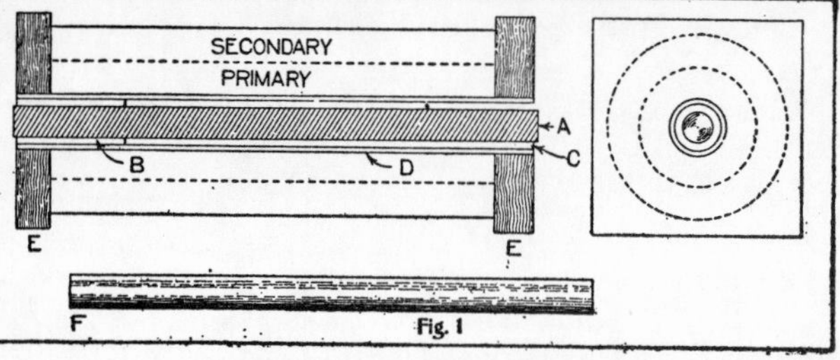

Fig. 1

The primary winding consists of 4 or 5 layers of No. 18 or 20 single cotton-covered magnet wire, the ends of which may be passed through small holes in the wooden ends. If a drill small enough is not available, the holes may be made with a hot knitting needle or a piece of wire heated to redness. After the primary coil is wound it should be thoroughly insulated before winding the secondary. This may be done by wrapping with 4 or 5 thicknesses of paper.

The secondary coil should be wound with single covered wire, preferably silk-covered, although cotton will do. The more turns there are on the secondary the higher the voltage will be, so the wire used must be fine. Number 32 to 36 will give good results, the latter giving more voltage but less amperage. Each layer of the secondary winding should be insulated from the others by a piece of thin paraffined paper wrapped over each layer as it is finished. It is well not to wind to the extreme ends of the paper insulations, but to leave a space of about $\frac{1}{8}$ in. at each end of the winding to prevent the wires of one layer slipping over the ends of the paraffin paper and coming in contact with the layer beneath, thus causing a short circuit. The secondary winding should have at least a dozen layers and should be carefully wound to prevent short circuiting.

In order to reduce the strength of the current a piece of brass tubing, F, is pushed into the space, C, surrounding the core, or if no brass tubing of the required size is on hand, roll a paper tube, cover with 4 or 5 thicknesses of tinfoil and then wrap with more paper, using glue to hold the tinfoil in place and to keep the tube from unwinding. When the tube is pushed all the way in, the current produced

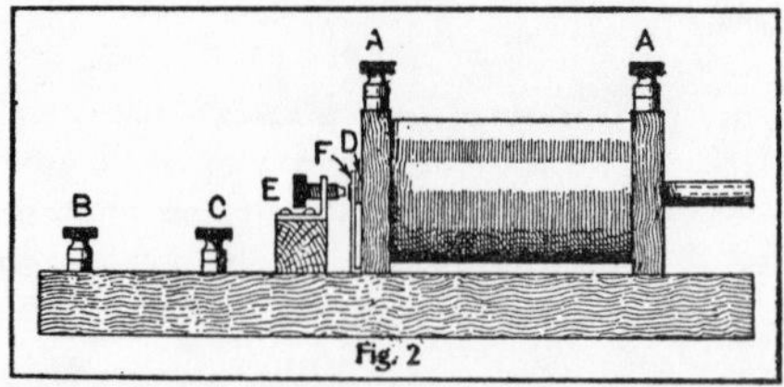

Fig. 2

will be almost unnoticeable, but when it is withdrawn the current will be so strong that a person cannot let go the handles until the coil is shut off. After the secondary coil is wound it should be covered with stiff paper, and the whole coil, including the wood ends, should then be enameled black.

It is then ready to be mounted on a wooden base as shown in Fig. 2. The secondary terminals are connected to the binding-posts, AA, which may be fastened on the base if desired. One wire from the primary is connected with the binding-post, B, and the other is connected with the armature, D, which may be taken from an old electric bell. The contact screw, E, also from an electric bell, is connected to the binding-post, C. The contact spring, F, should be bent against and soldered to the armature in order to make the vibrations more rapid.

If a false bottom is used on the base, all the wiring may be concealed, which adds greatly to the appearance, and if desired a small switch may be added. The handles, which may be old bicycle pumps or electric light carbons, are connected to the binding-posts, AA, by means of wires about 3 or 4 ft. long. This coil when operating with the tube pulled all the way out and connected to a single dry cell will give a current stronger than most persons can stand.

Home-Made Toaster

Each outside frame of the toaster is made from one piece of wire 30 in. long. These are bent in a perfect square making each side 7 in. long. This will allow 1 in. on each end for tying by twisting the ends together. The first two wires inside and on each side of each frame are 8 in. long. Eight wires will be required for this purpose and as they are 8 in. long ½ in. is allowed on each end for a bend around the outside frame, as shown in the sketch. The two middle wires are extensions of the handles. Each of these wires are made from a piece about 26 in. long and bent in the shape of a U. The ends of the wire are bent around the frame in the same manner

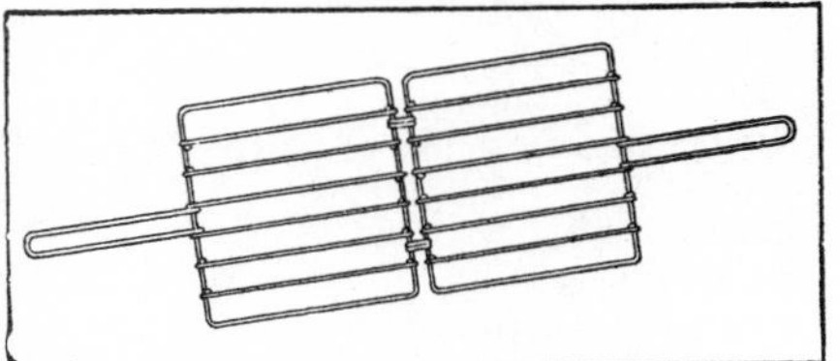

as the other wires. This will leave the handle laying across the other side of the frame. The frame is fastened to the handle on this side by giving the handle one turn around the frame. The inside edges of the frame are now tied together with a small ring of wire which is loose enough to allow each half to swing freely.—C. D. M.

Home-Made Shocking Machine

An ordinary electric bell may be connected up in such a way as to produce the same results as an expensive

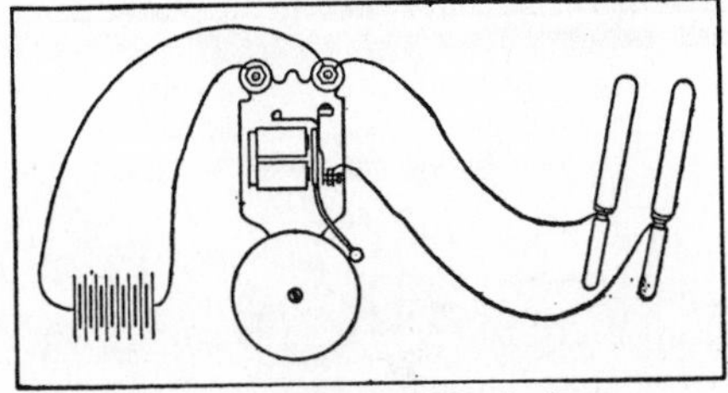

Inexpensive and Effectual

shocking machine. The connections are made from the batteries to the bell in the usual manner. Two other wires are then connected, one to the binding-post of the bell that is not insulated from the frame and the other to the adjusting screw on the make and break contact of the bell as shown in the sketch. The other ends of the wires are connected each to a common table knife. This will give quite a good shock and a much larger one can be had by placing one knife in a basin of water and while holding the other knife in one hand, dipping the fingers of the other hand in the water.—Contributed by D. Foster Hall.

Mix venetian red with quite thick arabic muscilage, making it into a putty, and press this well into the cracks of mahogany before finishing. The putty should be colored to suit the finish of the wood, says the Master Painter, by adding such dry color to the gum as will give the best result.

How to Make a Thermoelectric Battery

By ARTHUR E. JOERIN

A novel way of producing an electric current by means of hot and cold water, heat from a match or alcohol lamp, is obtained from a device constructed as shown in the sketch. Take two hardwood boards, marble, or slate plates, about 8 or 10 in. long, place them together, as in Fig. 1, and mark and drill about 500 holes. These two pieces should be separated about 8 in. and fastened with boards across the ends, as shown in Fig. 2.

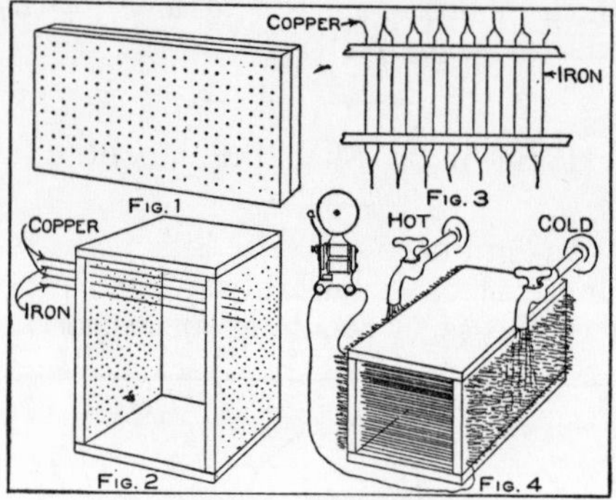

Details of Battery

Take soft copper wire, not smaller than No. 18 gauge, and cut in lengths to pass through the holes in the two boards, leaving sufficient end to make a tie. It will require about 70 ft. of wire to fill one-half the number of holes. Also, cut the same number of lengths from the same gauge galvanized-iron wire to fill the remaining holes. The wires are put through the holes in the boards alternately, that is: begin with copper, the next hole with iron, the next copper, the next iron, and so on, twisting the ends together as shown in Fig. 3. The connections, when complete, should be copper for the first and iron for the last wire.

When the whole apparatus is thus strung, the connections, which must be twisted, can be soldered. Connect one copper wire to the bell and the other terminal, which must be an iron wire, to the other post of the bell. The apparatus is then short-circuited, yet there is no current in the instrument until a lighted match, or, better still, the flame of an alcohol lamp is placed at one end only.

Best results are obtained by putting ice or cold water on one side and a flame on the other. The experimenter may also place the whole apparatus under sink faucets with the hot water turned on at one terminal and the cold water at the other. The greater the difference of temperature in the two terminals, the more current will be obtained.

Very interesting experiments may thus be performed, and these may lead to the solving of the great thermoelectric problem.

How to Make a Hygrometer

Mount a wire on a board which is used for a base and should be 3/8 by 4 by 8 in., as shown in the sketch. A piece of catgut—a string used on a violin will do—is suspended from the bent end of the wire. A hand or pointer is cut from a piece of tin and secured to the catgut string about 1/2 in. from the base. A small piece of wood and some glue will fasten the pointer to the string. The scale is marked on a piece of cardboard, which is fastened to the base and protected with a piece of glass.—Contributed by J. Thos. Rhamstine.

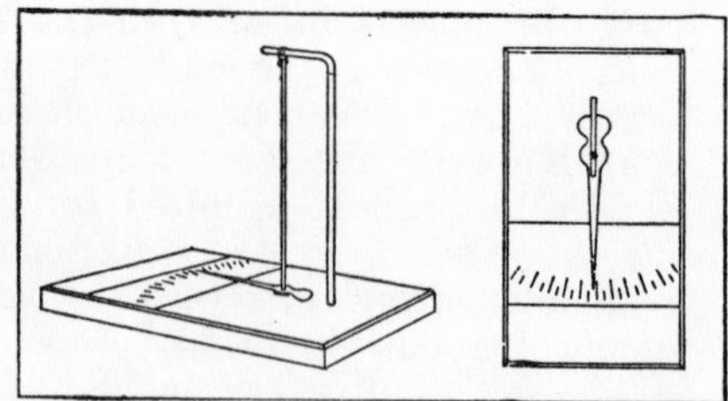
Simple Hygrometer

Softening Leather in Gloves and Boots

The leather in high-top boots and gauntlet gloves may be softened and made waterproof by the use of plain mutton tallow. Apply hot and rub in well with the fingers

How to Make a Mission Library Table

The mission library table, the drawings for which are here given, has been found well proportioned and of pleasing appearance. It can be made of any of the several furniture woods in common use, such as selected, quarter-sawed white oak which will be found exceptionally pleasing in the effect produced.

If a planing mill is at hand the stock can be ordered in such a way as to avoid the hard work of planing and sandpapering. Of course if mill-planed stock cannot be had, the following dimensions must be enlarged slightly to allow for "squaring up the rough."

This Picture is from a Photograph of the Mission Table Described in This Article

For the top, order 1 piece $1\frac{1}{8}$ in. thick, 34 in. wide and 46 in. long. Have it S-4-S (surface on four sides) and "squared" to length. Also, specify that it be sandpapered on the top surface, the edges and ends.

For the shelf, order 1 piece $\frac{7}{8}$ in. thick, 22 in. wide and 42 in. long, with the four sides surfaced, squared and sandpapered the same as for the top.

For the side rails, order 2 pieces $\frac{7}{8}$ in. thick, 6 in. wide and 37 in. long, S-4-S and sanded on one side. For the end rails, 2 pieces $\frac{7}{8}$ in. thick, 6 in. wide and 25 in. long. Other specifications as for the side rails.

For the stretchers, into which the shelf tenons enter, 2 pieces $1\frac{1}{8}$ in. thick, $3\frac{3}{4}$ in. wide and 25 in. long, surfaced and sanded on four sides. For the slats, 10 pieces $\frac{5}{8}$ in. thick, $1\frac{1}{2}$ in. wide and 17 in. long, surfaced and sanded on four sides. For the keys, 4 pieces $\frac{3}{4}$ in. thick, $1\frac{1}{4}$ in. wide and $2\frac{7}{8}$ in. long, S-4-S. This width is a little wide; it will allow the key to be shaped as desired.

The drawings obviate any necessity for going into detail in the descrip-

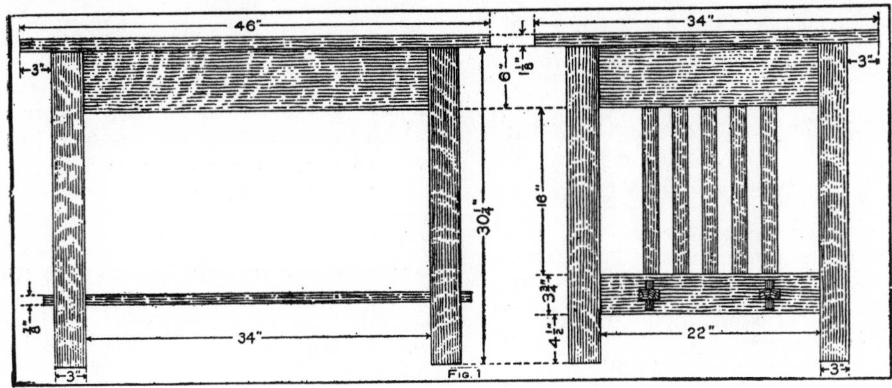

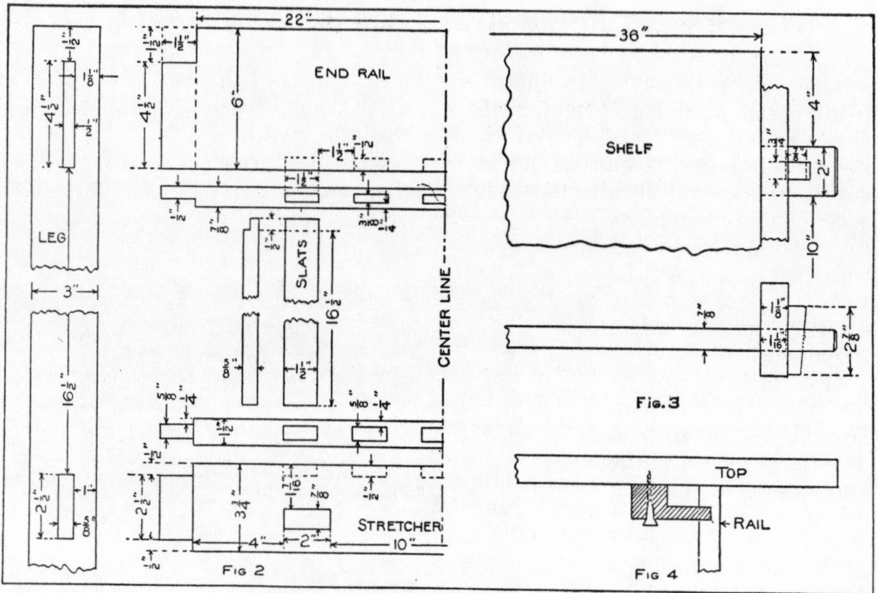

Fig 2 Fig. 3 Fig 4

tion. Fig. 1 gives an assembly drawing showing the relation of the parts. Fig. 2 gives the detail of an end. The tenons for the side rails are laid off and the mortises placed in the post as are those on the end. Care must be taken, however, not to cut any mortises on the post, below, as was done in cutting the stretcher mortises on the ends of the table. A good plan is to set the posts upright in the positions they are to occupy relative to one another and mark with pencil the approximate positions of the mortises. The legs can then be laid flat and the mortises accurately marked out with a fair degree of assurance that they will not be cut where they are not wanted and that the legs shall "pair" properly when effort is made to assemble the parts of the table.

The table ends should be glued up first and the glue allowed to harden, after which the tenons of the shelf may be inserted and the side rails placed.

There is a reason for the shape, size and location of each tenon or mortise. For illustration, the shape of the tenon on the top rails permits the surface of the rail to extend almost flush with the surface of the post at the same time permitting the mortise in the post to be kept away from that surface. Again, the shape of the ends of the slats is such that, though they may vary slightly in length, the fitting of the joints will not be affected. Care must be taken in cutting the mortises to keep their sides clean and sharp and to size.

In making the mortises for the keyed tenons, the length of mortise must be slightly in excess of the width of the tenon—about $\frac{1}{8}$ in. of play to each side of each tenon. With a shelf of the width specified for this table, if such allowance is not made so that the tenons may move sideways, the shrinkage would split the shelf.

In cutting across the ends of the shelf, between the tenons, leave a hole in the waste so that the turning saw or compass saw can be inserted. Saw within one-sixteenth of the line, after which this margin may be removed with chisel and mallet.

In Fig. 3 is shown two views of the keyed tenon and the key. The mortise for the key is to be placed in the middle of the tenon. It will be noted that this mortise is laid out $1\frac{1}{16}$ in. from the shoulder of the tenon while the stretcher is $1\frac{1}{8}$ in. thick. This is to insure the key's pulling the shelf tightly against the side of the stretcher.

Keys may be made in a variety of shapes. The one shown is simple and structurally good. Whatever shape is used, the important thing to keep in mind is that the size of the key and the slant of its forward surface where it passes through the tenon must be kept the same as the mortise made for it in the tenon.

The top is to be fastened to the rails by means either of wooden buttons, Fig. 4, or small angle irons.

There are a bewildering number of mission finishes upon the market. A very satisfactory one is obtained by applying a coat of brown Flemish water stain, diluted by the addition of water in the proportion of 2 parts water to 1 part stain. When this has dried, sand with number 00 paper, being careful not to "cut through." Next, apply a coat of dark brown filler; the directions for doing this will be found upon the can in which the filler is bought. One coat usually suffices. However, if an especially smooth surface is desired a second coat may be applied in a similar manner.

After the filler has hardened, a very thin coat of shellac is to be put on. When this has dried it should be sanded lightly and then one or two coats of wax should be properly applied and polished. Directions for waxing are upon the cans in which the wax is bought. A beautiful dull gloss so much sought by finishers of modern furniture will be the result of carefully following these directions.

A Hanger for Trousers

Secure two clothes pins of the metal spring kind for the clamps of the hanger. The pins are fastened one to each end of a looped galvanized wire. This wire should be about 6 in. long after a coil is bent in the center as shown in the sketch. The diameter of the wire should be about $\frac{1}{8}$ in.

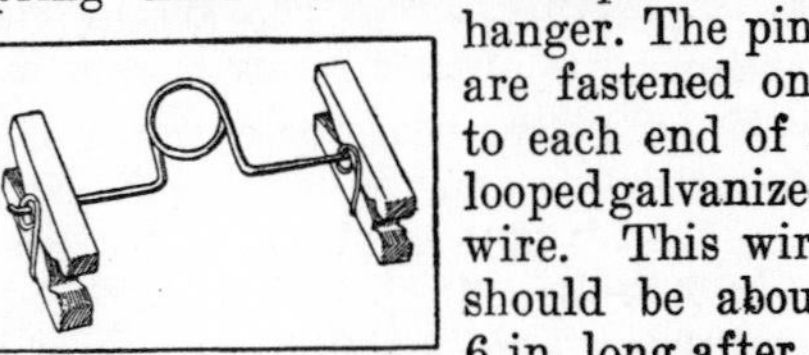

How to Make an Adjustable Negative Washer

The sketch herewith shows a washing box for negatives made from an ordinary wooden box. As can be seen, the grooved partition, A, is removable, and as several places are provided for its insertion, the tank can be made to accommodate any one of several sizes of plates, says Camera Craft. The other stationary partition, B, which does not reach quite to the bottom of the tank, is placed immediately next to the end of the tank, leaving a channel between the two for the inflow of the wash water. A narrow, thin strip, C, is fastened to the bottom of the tank to keep the plates slightly raised, at the same time allowing a clearer flow of the water from the bottom upwards to the discharge.

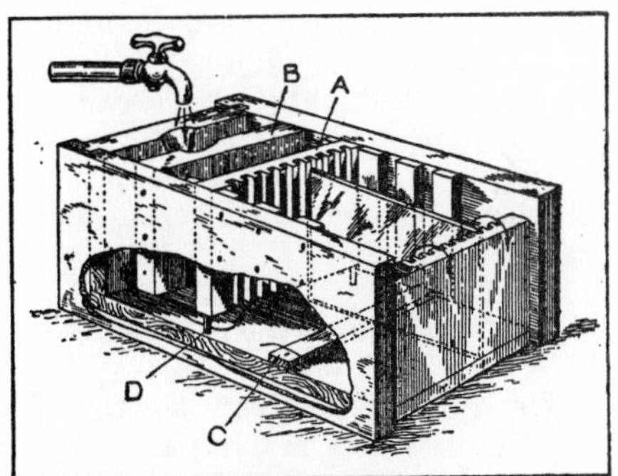

Washing Box

The water enters the narrow partition at the end, flows under the partitions B and A, then upward between and parallel to the surface of the plates, escaping at the opposite end over the top of the tank end, in which the upper part has been cut away for that purpose. The depth of this cut, in the upper part of the tank end, should allow the overflow to be a trifle higher than the width of the largest size plate for which the tank is fitted. Partition B being stationary, can be nailed in position permanently, allowing the bottom edge to clear the bottom of the tank the desired distance. Partition A being movable should have attached to its bottom edge a couple of nails, D, or better still, wooden pegs, which will keep it also above the bottom of the tank at the desired height.

A coat of paraffin paint should be applied, and, just before it sets perfectly hard, any rough spots trimmed down with a knife or chisel and a second lighter coat applied. If the wood is very dry and porous a preliminary coat of the paint should be applied and allowed to soak into the pores. It is also well to apply a coat of the paint to the joints at the corners and around the edge of the bottom before nailing together.

Turn-Down Shelf for a Small Space

The average amateur photographer does not have very much space in which to do his work. The kitchen is the room used ordinarily for finishing the photographs. In many instances there will not be space enough for any extra tables, and so a temporary place is prepared from boxes or a chair on which to place the trays and chemicals. Should there be space enough on one of the walls a shelf can be made to hang down out of the way when not in use. A shelf constructed on this order may be of any length to suit the space or of such a length for the purpose intended. A heavy piece of wood, about

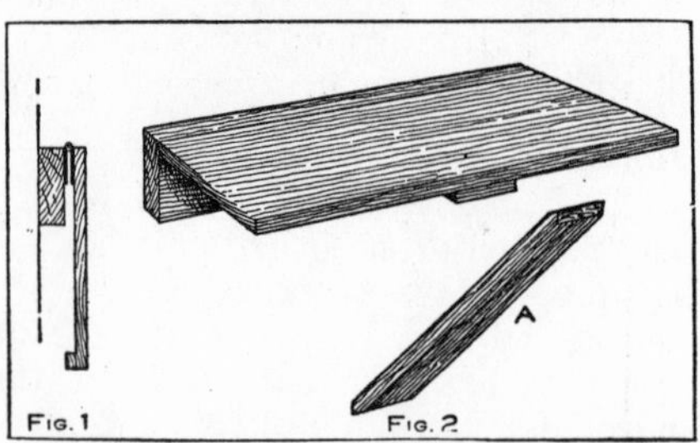

Turn-Down Shelf

1½ in. thick, and 4 to 6 in. wide, is first fastened to the wall at the proper height with nails, or, much better, large screws.

The shelf is cut and planed smooth from a board 12 in. wide and about 1 in. thick. This board is fastened to the piece on the wall with two hinges as shown in Fig. 1. A small cleat is nailed to the outer and under edge of the board and in the middle as shown. This is used to place a support under the outer edge of the shelf. The support, A, Fig. 2, should be long enough to extend diagonally to the floor or top of the baseboard from the inner edge of the cleat when the shelf is up in its proper place.—L. L.

Home-Made Electric Battery Massage

A simple and cheap electric massage device can be made by using three or

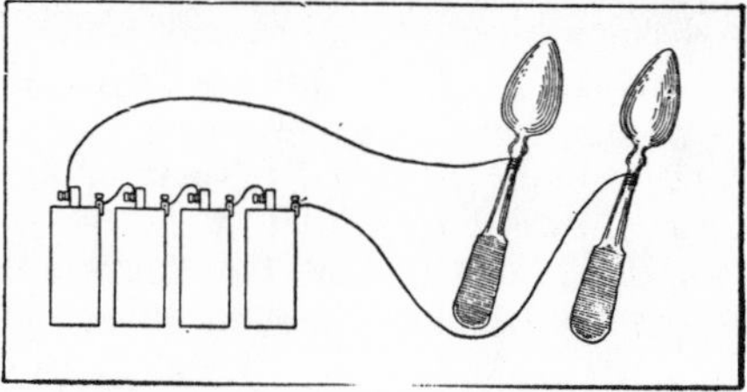

Turn-Down Shelf

four cells of dry battery connected to two ordinary silver tablespoons, as shown in the sketch. The handles of the spoons should be insulated or the operator can wear either kid or rubber gloves.

How to Make Tint Lantern Slides

Purchase some lantern slide plates and fix them in hypo without exposing, in the usual manner, same as you would an exposed plate, says the Moving Picture World. This leaves a thin, perfectly transparent emulsion film on the glass, which will readily take color. Mix a rather weak solution of clear aniline dye of the desired color and dip the plate in it, wiping the plate side clean. If not dark enough, dip again and again until desired tint is attained, letting it dry between each dipping. A very light blue tint slide will brighten a yellow film considerably, but the tint must be very light, just a bare tint.

A Bicycle Catamaran

The accompanying photographs show a bicycle boat made to carry two persons. This boat is constructed by using two galvanized iron tubes 18 ft. long and 12 in. in diameter, tapered at the front end down to cast-iron points, and the rear end shaped to attach rudders. These tubes are placed 26 in. apart, giving the boat an extreme width of 50 in.

This Catamaran Carries Two People

The cylinders support a platform and on the rear end of this platform is constructed a paddle wheel 52 in. in diameter with 16 spokes. On the end of each spoke is fastened a galvanized sheet metal blade 6 in. wide and 8 in. long. A large guard placed over the paddle wheel forms a seat for one person and a chair in front on the platform provides a place for a second person.

The person in front helps to propel the boat with hand levers which are connected with rods to sprocket wheels on each side of the platform. The occupant of the rear seat contributes his part of the power with his feet on pedals of the shaft that carries the sprocket wheels. This shaft and sprocket wheels drive the paddle wheel by side chains of the bicycle kind. The boat is steered from the rear seat by ropes attached to double rudders. This boat will run at considerable speed and is very steady in rough water as it goes directly through large waves instead of going over them.—Contributed by Ernest Schoedsack, Council Bluffs, Iowa.

How to Make a Lead Pencil Rheostat

Take an ordinary lead pencil and cut seven notches at equal intervals on the pencil down to and around the lead, leaving it bare. A seven-point switch is constructed on a board of suitable size making the points by using screws that will go through the board. A small piece of tin or brass will do for a switch and is fastened as shown. The connections are made on the back side of the board as shown by the dotted lines. This will reduce 40 to 50 volts down to 5 or 10 volts for short lengths of time.—Contributed by Roy Newby, San Jose, Cal.

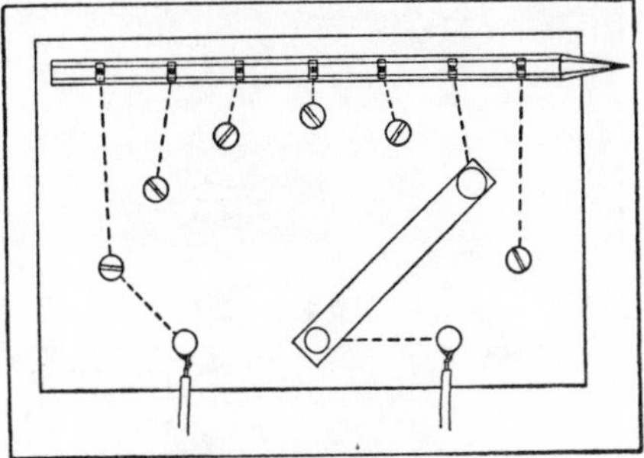

Simple Rheostat

Homemade Shoe Rack

The accompanying sketch explains how a boy can make his own shoe rack that can be placed on the wall in

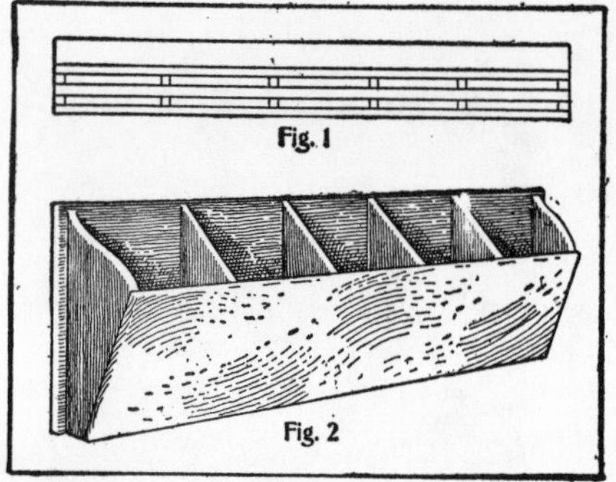

the clothes closet. Figure 1 shows the construction of the bottom to permit the dirt to fall through. Two boards, 9 in. wide and about 3 ft. long, with six partitions between, as shown, will make pockets about 6 in. long. The width of the pockets at the bottom is 2 in. and at the top 5 in.—Contributed by Guy H. Harvey, Mill Valley, Cal.

How to Waterproof Canvas

The method used by the British navy yards for waterproofing and painting canvas so it will not become stiff and cracked is as follows: One ounce of yellow soap and ½ pt. of hot water are mixed with every 7 lb. of paint to be used. The mixture is applied to the canvas with a brush. This is allowed to dry for two days and then a coat of the same paint, without the soap, is laid on. When this last coat is dry the canvas may be painted any color desired. After three days of drying the canvas may be folded up without sticking together, and is, of course, waterproof. Canvas waterproofed in this manner makes an excellent covering for portable canoes and canvas boats. The color mixture for the soap and second application is made from 1 lb. of lampblack and 6 lb. of yellow ocher, both in oil; the finish coat may be any color desired. When no paint is to be used on the canvas it may be waterproofed with a mixture made from soft soap dissolved in hot water, and a solution of iron sulphate added. Iron sulphate, or ferrous sulphate, is the green vitriol. The vitriol combines with the potash of the soap, and the iron oxide is precipitated with the fatty acid as insoluble iron soap. This precipitate is then washed, dried and mixed with linseed oil.

Building a House in a Tree Top

The accompanying photograph shows a small house built in a tree top 20 ft. from the ground. The house is 5 ft. wide, 5 ft. 1 in. long, and 6 ft. 6 in. high. A small platform, 2 ft. wide, is built on the front. Three windows are

Lofty Sentry Box for Guarding Watermelon Patch

provided, one for each side, and a door in front. The entrance is made through a trap door in the floor of the house. This house was constructed by a boy 14 years old and made for the purpose of watching over a melon patch.—Contributed by Mack Wilson, Columbus, O.

How to Make a Lamp Stand and Shade

A library light stand of pleasing design and easy construction is made as follows: Square up a piece of white oak so that it shall have a width and thickness of 1¾ in. with a length of 13 in. Square up two pieces of the same kind of material to the same width and thickness, but with a length of 12 in. each. Square up two pieces to a width and length of 3 in. each with a thickness of 1⅛ in.

If a planing mill is near, time and patience will be saved by ordering one piece 1¾ in. square and 40 in. long, two pieces 1⅛ in. thick and 3 in. square, all planed and sandpapered on all surfaces. The long piece can then be cut at home to the lengths specified above.

The 13-in. piece is for the upright and should have a ½-in. hole bored the full length through the center. If the bit is not long enough to reach entirely through, bore from each end, then use a red-hot iron to finish. This hole is for the electric wire or gas pipe if gas is used.

The two pieces for the base are alike except the groove of one is cut from the top and of the other from the under side, as shown. Shape the under sides first. This can best be done by placing the two pieces in a vise, under sides together, and boring two holes with a 1-in. bit. The center of each hole will be 2½ in. from either end and in the crack between the pieces. The pieces can then be taken out, lines gauged on each side of each, and the wood between the holes removed with turning saw and scraper steel.

The width of the grooves must be determined by laying one piece upon the other; a trysquare should be used to square the lines across the pieces, however, gauge for depth, gauging both pieces from their top surfaces. Chisel out the grooves and round off the corners as shown in the sketch, using a ¾-in. radius.

These parts may be put together and fastened to the upright by means of two long screws from the under side, placed to either side of the ½-in. hole. This hole must be continued through the pieces forming the base.

The braces are easiest made by taking the two pieces which were planed to 1⅛ in. thick and 3 in. square and drawing a diagonal on each. Find the middle of this diagonal by drawing the central portion of the other diagonal; at this point place the spur of the bit and bore a 1-in. hole in each block.

Saw the two blocks apart, sawing

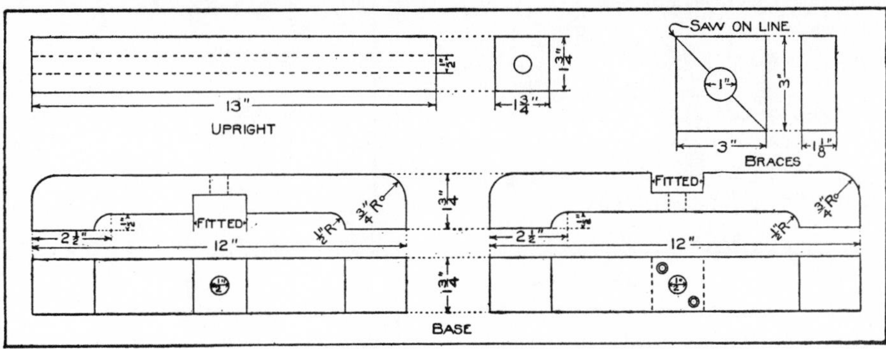

Details of Construction of Library Lamp Stand

along a diagonal of each. Plane the surfaces on the saw cut smooth and sandpaper the curve made by the bit. Fasten the braces in place by means of roundhead blued screws.

To make a shade such as is shown in the illustration is rather difficult. The shade is made of wood glued up and has art glass fitted in rabbets cut on the inner edges. Such shades can be purchased ready to attach. The sketch shows one method of attaching. Four small pieces of strap iron are bent to the shape shown and fastened to the four sides of the upright. Electric globes—two, three or four may be attached as shown.

The kind of wood finish for the stand will depend upon the finish on the wooden shade, if shade is purchased. Brown Flemish is obtained by first staining the wood with Flemish water stain diluted by the addition of two parts water to one part stain. When this is dry, sandpaper the "whiskers" which were raised by the water and fill with a medium dark filler. Directions will be found on the filler cans. When the filler has hardened, apply two coats of wax.

The metal shade as shown in the sketch is a "layout" for a copper or brass shade of a size suitable for this particular lamp. Such shades are frequently made from one piece of sheet metal and designs are pierced in them as suggested in the "layout." This piercing is done by driving the point of a nail through the metal from the under side before the parts are soldered or riveted together. If the parts are to be riveted, enough additional metal must be left on the last panel to allow for a lap. No lap is needed when joints are soldered.

A better way, and one which will permit the use of heavier metal, is to cut each side of the shade separately and fasten them together by riveting a piece of metal over each joint. The shape of this piece can be made so as to accentuate the rivet heads and thus give a pleasing effect.

For art-glass the metal panels are cut out, the glass is inserted from the under side and held in place by small clips soldered to the frame of the shade.

Pleasing effects are obtained by using one kind of metal, as brass, and reinforcing and riveting with another metal, such as copper.

The Completed Lamp

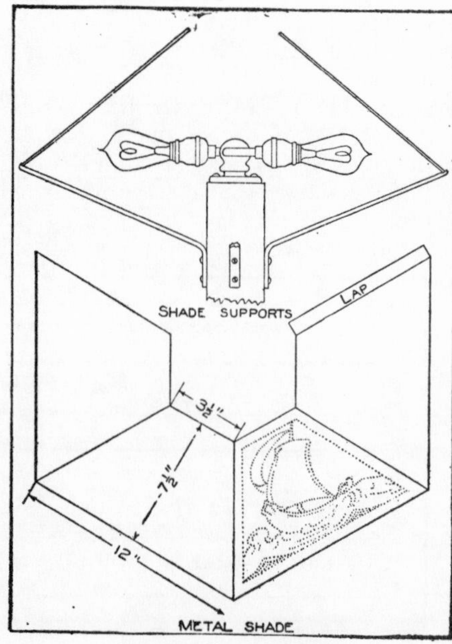

Construction of Shade

Illuminating a Watch Dial at Night

This picture shows a watch holder, with a device to receive an ordinary electric pocket lamp and battery. The battery is set in a bracket under which a reflector extends downward to throw the light on the dial of the watch and to protect the eyes from the direct light. The entire stand and bracket are made from sheet metal. The base is formed to make a tray to hold pins and collar buttons. It is not necessary to seek in the darkness for a push button or switch, as in ordinary devices, but a light pressure with the palm of the hand will make the lamp glow.

Home-Made Photographic Copying Stand

The difficulties of bad lighting on small articles can be entirely avoided by the use of a suitable support for the camera, the object and the background.

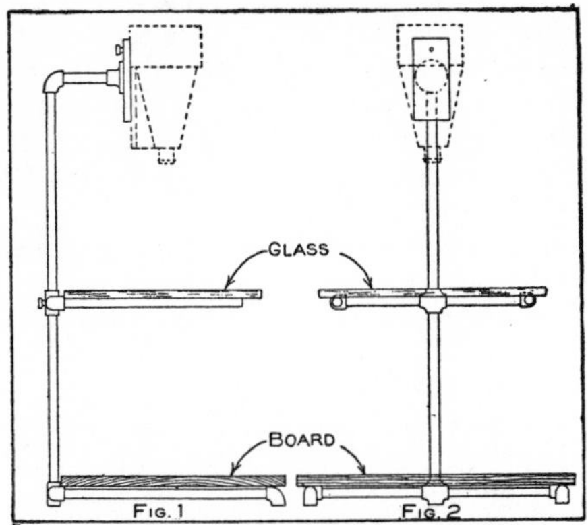

Secures Good Light on Small Objects

For illustrations it is often an advantage to show an object with a perfectly plain background and no deep shadows. When using the stand as illustrated this is a very simple matter. Figure 1 shows the side, and Fig. 2 the front view of this stand. The stand is very easily constructed from pipe and pipe fittings. The main pipe of the stand will need to be of proper length to suit the focus of your camera. This can be determined by finding the length from the lens to the object after the bellows are extended to their full length. The arms holding the glass, as shown in the sketch, should be set at a point about the middle of the main tube. The cross that holds the middle arms should be $\frac{3}{4}$ in. one way and $\frac{1}{2}$ in. the other. This will allow for adjustment of the glass table. A small set screw provided in the back of this cross will hold the table in any position desired. The pipes and other connections are all $\frac{1}{2}$ in. and the lengths of the pipes are made suitable for the size of the camera. When a small object is to be photographed it is placed upon the glass table and the background fastened to the board. In this manner small objects can be photographed without any deep shadow on one side. The bottom cross and ells should be corked so as to prevent any slipping and damage to the floor.

Home-Made Pocket Lamp

A simple and safe pocket lamp that will last for about 6 months without extra expense can be made at home for a few cents.

Have your druggist take a strong vial of clear glass, or a pill bottle with screw or cork top and put into it a piece of phosphorus about the size of a pea and fill the bottle one-third full of pure olive oil that has been heated for 15 minutes—but not boiled. Cork tightly and the result will be a luminous light in the upper portion of the bottle. If the light becomes dim, uncork and recork again. The lamp will retain its brilliancy for about 6 months. This makes a perfectly safe lamp to carry. These lamps are used by watchmen of powder magazines. Care should be exercised in handling the phosphorus, as it is very poisonous.

How to Make a Tangent Galvanometer

Secure a piece of wood ½ in. thick and cut out a ring with an outside diameter of 10½ in. and an inside diameter of 9 in. and glue to each side two other rings ¼ in. thick with the same inside diameter as the first ring and 11 in. outside diameter, thus forming a ¼-in. channel in the circumference of the ring. If a lathe is at hand, this ring can be made from a solid piece and the channel turned out. Cut another circular piece 11 in. in diameter for a base. Make a hole in the center of this piece 1 in. wide and 6 5/16 in. long, into which the ring first made should fit so that its inner surface is just even with the upper surface of the baseboard. The ring is held upright in the hole by a small strip screwed to the base as shown. All screws and brads that are used must be of brass. The cutting of these circular pieces is not so difficult if a band saw driven by power is used. They can be cut by means of a key-hole saw if a band saw is not accessible.

Before mounting the ring on the base, the groove should be wound with 8 turns of No. 16 double cotton-covered magnet wire. The two ends may be tied together with a string to hold them temporarily.

Fasten two strips of wood ¼ in. thick, ⅝ in. wide and 11 in. long across the sides of the ring with their upper edges passing exactly through the center of the ring. An ordinary pocket compass, about 1¼ in. in diameter, is fitted in these strips so that the center of the needle or pointer will be exactly in the center of the ring and its zero point mark at the half-way point between the two strips. Put the ring in place on the base, as shown in the sketch, and connect the two ends of the wire to two binding-posts that are previously attached to the base. Coat the entire surface with brown shellac. Any deviation from the dimensions will cause errors in the results obtained by its use.

Remove all pieces of iron or steel and especially magnets in the near vicinity of the instrument when in use. Place the galvanometer on a level table and turn it until the needle, pointing north and south, and swinging freely, lies exactly in the plane of the coil, as shown in the cut. The needle then will point to zero if the directions have been followed closely. Connect one

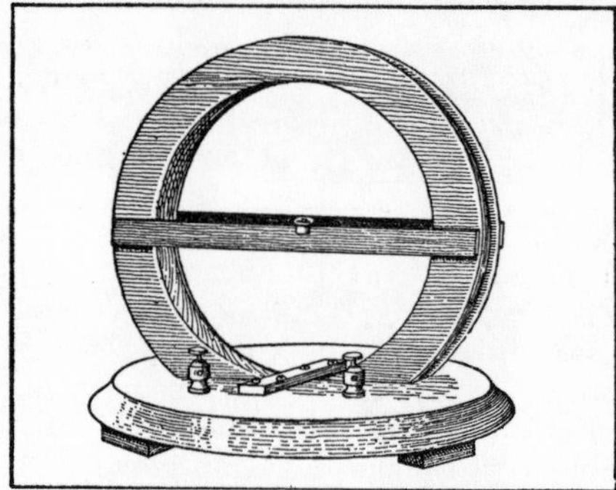

Tangent Galvanometer

cell of battery to the instrument and allow the current to flow through the coils. The needle of the compass will be deflected to one side or the other, and will finally come to rest at a certain angle—let us say 45 deg. The dimensions of the instrument are such that when the deflection is 45 deg. the current flowing through the coils upon the ring is ½ ampere. The ampere is the unit chosen to designate the strength of the electric current. For other angles the value of the current may be found from the following table:

Angles.	Current.
10 deg.	.088 amp.
20 "	.182 "
30 "	.289 "
40 "	.420 "
45 "	.500 "
50 "	.600 "
55 "	.715 "
60 "	.865 "
70 "	1.375 "

As the magnetic force that acts upon a magnet needle varies in different places the values given for the current will not be true in all parts of the country. The table gives correct values for the immediate vicinity of Chicago and that part of the United States lying east of Chicago, and north of the Ohio river. The results given should be multiplied by 1.3 for places south of the Ohio river and east of the Mississippi.

Home-Made X-Ray Instrument

Two cylinders, AA, are mounted on a base, B, and mirrors, CC, are fitted at an angle of 45 deg. into these cylinders. Corresponding mirrors, EE, are put in the base parallel with those in the cylinders. An opening extends downward from D of each cylinder so that light entering at one end of the

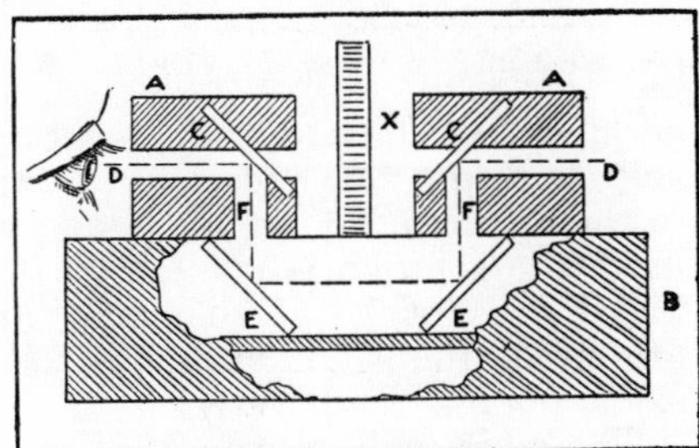

Details of X-Ray Machine

cylinder is reflected down at right angles by the first mirror to the second, from the second to the third, from the third to the fourth which reflects the light to the eye. Thus the light never passes through the cylinders and the observer does not see through, but around any object inserted at X between the cylinders.

How to Make a Non-Polarizing Battery

Bichromate batteries are very expensive to maintain and dry cells do not furnish enough amperage for some kinds of experimental work. A cell of battery that will run 10 hours with an output of over 1 ampere can be made as follows: Secure a jar about 4 in. in diameter and 8 in. high and place in the bottom of this jar the lower half of a tin baking powder can, to which a wire has been soldered for connections. Place in the can a mixture of 2 oz. black oxide of copper, 1 oz. black oxide of manganese and some iron filings.

Purchase a small crowfoot zinc and hang it about 1 in. above the half can. Prepare a 10 per cent solution of caustic soda and fill the jar within 1 in. of the top. Place on top the solution a thin layer of kerosene or paraffin. The cell will only cost about 50 cents to make and 25 cents for each renewal. When renewing, always remove the oil with a siphon.—Contributed by Robert Canfield, University Park, Colo.

A Home-Made Barometer

Take $\frac{1}{4}$ oz. of pulverized campnor, 62 gr. of pulverized nitrate of potassium, 31 gr. nitrate of ammonia and dissolve in 2 oz. alcohol. Put the solution in a long, slender bottle, closed at the top with a piece of bladder containing a pinhole to admit air, says Metal Worker. When rain is coming the solid particles will tend gradually to mount, little crystals forming in the liquid, which otherwise remains clear; if high winds are approaching the liquid will become as if fermenting, while a film of solid particles forms on the surface; during fair weather the liquid will remain clear and the solid particles will rest at the bottom.

A door lock may be lubricated by using some lead scraped from the lead in a pencil and put in the lock. This may be done by putting the scrapings on a piece of paper and blowing them into the lock through the keyhole.

Where bolts are subject to rust, the threads should be painted with pure white lead; then they will not rust fast.

When painting yellow pine exposed to the weather add a little pine tar with the priming coat.

Revolving a Wheel with Boat Sails

A novel windmill or revolving wheel can be made by placing a light wheel so it will turn freely on the end of a post, and placing four small sailing boats at equal points on the rim of the wheel. It makes no difference which way the wind blows, the wheel will revolve in one direction. In Fig. 1 the direction of the wind is shown by the arrows, and how the sails catch the wind and cause the wheel to revolve. Figure 2 shows how the wheel will appear when complete. This device makes an attractive advertising sign.

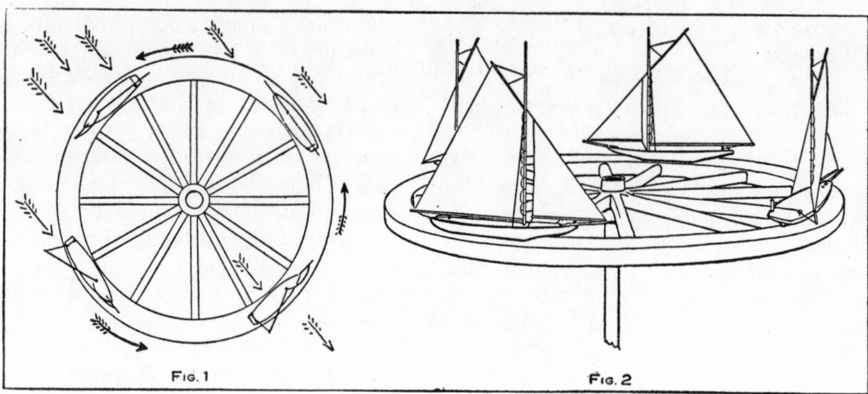

An Unusual Type of Windmill

A Floating Electromagnet

A piece of iron placed in a coil of wire carrying a current of electricity becomes an electromagnet. If such a coil and iron core be made small enough they can be attached to a cork and the cork, floating on a solution, will allow the magnet to point north and south. The sketch shows how to make such an instrument. A coil of insulated wire is wrapped around a small iron core, leaving a few inches of each end free for connections. The insulation is removed from these ends and they are run through a piece of cork. Attach to the wires, on the under side of the cork, a piece of zinc to one end and a piece of copper to the other. The cork is then floated on a solution of acid, with the zinc and copper hanging in the solution. If zinc and copper are used, the solution is made from water and blue vitriol. If zinc and carbon are used, the solution is made from sal ammoniac and water.

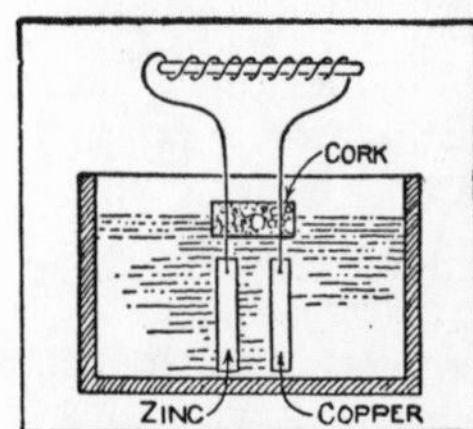

The float will move about on the solution until the magnet iron will point north and south. If two of them are floating on the same solution, they will move about and finally arrange themselves end to end with the coils and magnet cores pointing north and south.—Contributed by C. Lloyd Enos.

A Fish Bait

A very effective fish bait is made by inclosing a live minnow in a short section of glass tube, which is filled with water and both ends closed with corks. This is used in place of the spoon.

Homemade Air Thermometer

The illustration shows the complete thermometer. The water in the glass tube is caused to rise and fall by the expansion and contraction of the air in the tin box.

A paper-fastener box, about 1¼ in.

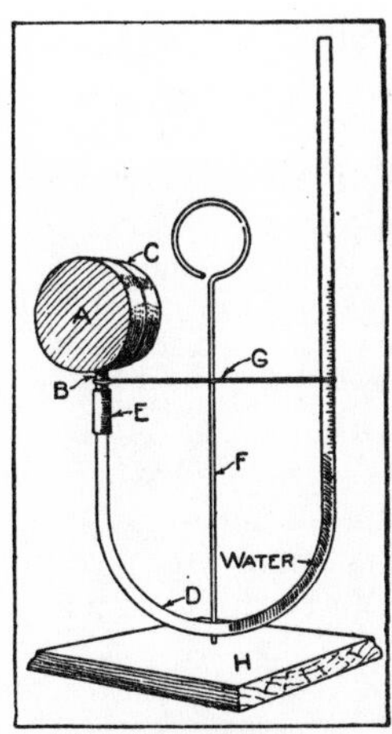

Air Thermometer

deep and 2 in. in diameter will serve very well for the box A. Solder in the side of the box a 1-in. piece of ¼-in. brass tubing, B, and then solder on the cover, C, so that the only escape for the air is through the brass tube. Secure a piece of ¼-in. glass tubing—not shorter than 18 in.—and bend it as shown at D in the sketch. Hold the part of the tube to be bent in the broad side of a gas jet, and in a minute or two the tube will bend with its own weight. Any angle can be given glass tubing in this way. Connect the glass tube to B with a short piece of rubber hose, E. If the hose is not a tight fit, bind with a short piece of fine copper wire. The standard, F, is made from a piece of No. 10 wire about 10 in. long. To this standard solder the supporting wire, G—No. 14 wire will do. On one side bend the wire around the tube B, and on the other around the glass tube, D.

The base, H, can be made of oak, stained and varnished. The bottom of the box, A, is covered with lampblack so as to readily absorb all heat that strikes the surface. The black should not be put on until just before you paint the supports, cover and rim of the box with gold or silver paint. Hold the bottom of the box to be blackened over a little burning cotton saturated with turpentine.

The scale on the glass can be etched with hydrofluoric acid, or made with a little black paint. The water can be put in with a medicine dropper. This instrument will measure the amount of heat given by a candle some 20 or 30 ft. away.—Contributed by J. Thos. Rhamstine.

Home-Made Battery Voltmeter

Secure a piece of brass tube 3 in. long that has about ¼-in. hole. Put ends, A, 1¼ in. square and cut from heavy cardboard on this tube. Make a hole in the center of each cardboard just large enough to allow the brass tube to fit tight. Put on two or three layers of stout paper around the brass tube and between the cardboard ends. Wind evenly about 2 oz. of No. 26 cotton-covered magnet wire on the paper between the ends and leave about 2 in. of wire on each end extending from the coil. Use a board ½ in. thick, 3 in. wide and 6 in. long for the base and fasten the coil to it, as shown in Fig. 1. Bore holes for binding-posts, B, one on each side of the board, and connect the two wires from the coil to them. At the other end of the board and in the center drive a wire nail and attach a small spring, C, to it. The spring should be about 1 in. long. Take a small piece of soft iron, D, ½ in. long and just large enough to slip freely through the brass

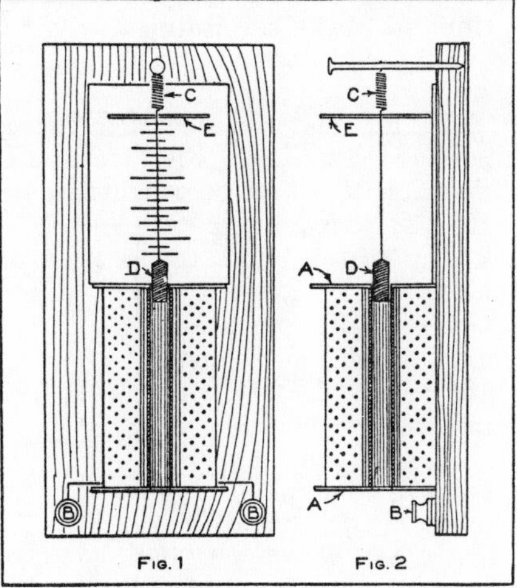

Battery Voltmeter Construction

tube and solder a piece of copper wire to it; the other end of the copper wire being hooked to the spring, C. The copper wire must be just long enough to allow the piece of iron, D, to hang part way in the end of the coil and still hold the spring in place. A circular piece of cardboard, E, is slipped over the spring to where the spring joins the wire. This cardboard is to serve as the pointer. A piece of paper 1½ in. wide and 2½ in. long is glued to the board so that it will be directly under the cardboard pointer and fit snugly up against the top of the coil.

The paper can be calibrated by connecting one cell of battery to the binding-posts. The iron plunger, D, is drawn into the tube and consequently the pointer, E, is drawn nearer to the coil. Make a mark directly under the place where the pointer comes to rest. At the place mark the number of volts the cell reads when connected with a voltmeter. Do the same with two or three cells and mark down the result on the scale. By dividing off the space between these marks you may be able to obtain a surprisingly correct reading when connected with the battery cells to be tested.—Contributed by Edward M. Teasdale, Cuba, N. Y.

How to Make a Folding Canvas Cot

All the material required to make the cot as shown in Fig. 1 consists of wood 1½ in. square of which two pieces are 6 ft. long; two pieces 2 ft. 3 in. long; two pieces 2½ ft. long; four pieces 1½ ft. long; four hinges; some sheet metal and 2¼ yd. of 8-oz. canvas.

Make a rectangle of the two long pieces and the two 2-ft. 3-in. pieces of wood as shown in Fig. 2, nailing well the corners together and reinforcing with a strip of sheet metal as shown in Fig. 3. The four pieces 1½ ft. long are used for the legs, and two of them are nailed to one of the pieces 2½ ft. long, making a support as shown in Fig. 5.

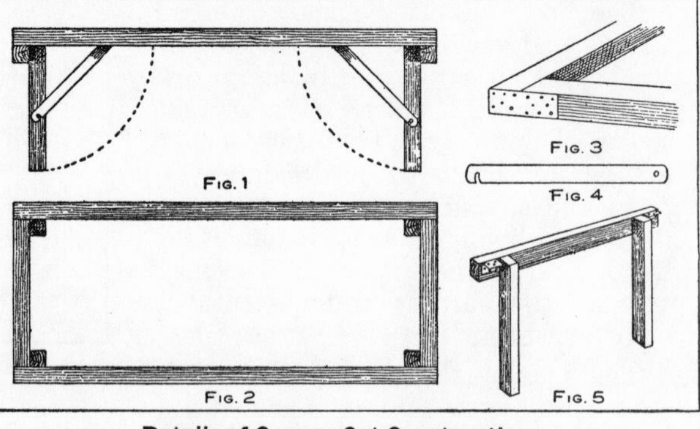

Details of Canvas Cot Construction

Make two of these—one for each end. The hinges are attached as shown in Fig. 5 and the whole support is fastened just under the end pieces of the frame by hinges. Four pieces of sheet metal are cut as shown in Fig. 4 and fastened to the body of the frame with their lower ends hooking over pins driven in each leg at the proper place. The canvas is stretched as tight as possible over the two long side pieces and fastened on the outside edge of each piece with large headed tacks. The legs will fold up as shown by the dotted line and the cot can be stored in a small space.—Contributed by R. J. Smith, Milwaukee, Wis.

How to Make a Small Geissler Tube

At first this would seem to be a difficult piece of work, yet a good and beautiful Geissler tube can be made at home in the following manner:

Procure a glass tube about 3½ ft. long having a hole through its center about ⅛ or ¼ in. in diameter, about 1 in. of No. 30 platinum wire and enough mercury to fill the tube and a small bowl. About 1½ lb. of mercury will be sufficient. The first thing to do is to seal ½ in. of platinum wire in one end of the tube. This is done by holding the end of the tube with the right hand and taking hold of the tube with the left hand about 4 in. from the right hand. Hold the tube in a flame of a bunsen burner in such manner that the flame will strike the tube midway between the hands, as shown in Fig. 1, and keep turning the tube so as to get an even heat. When the glass becomes soft, re-

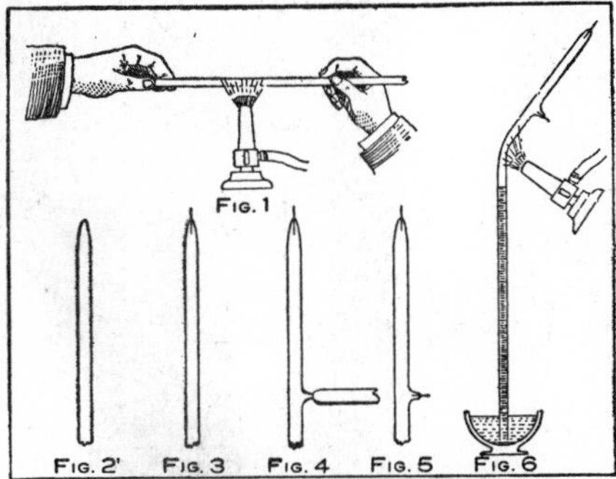

Construction of Geissler Tube

move the tube from the flame and quickly draw it out into a fine thread. Break this thread off about $\frac{1}{8}$ in. from the long part of the tube and the end will appear as shown in Fig. 2. Take $\frac{1}{2}$ in. of the platinum wire and slip it through the fine hole made by breaking the glass thread so that one-half of the wire will be inside of the long tube. If the end of the tube is now placed in the flame of the burner, the glass will adhere to the platinum wire and the wire will thus be sealed in the tube. The finished end will appear as shown in Fig. 3. This tube as described will be 8 in. long, although nearly any size could be made in the same way.

Measure 8 in. from the sealed end and place the tube at that point in the flame, holding in the left hand. At the same time take the piece of glass that was broken off at the end in the first operation and hold it in the flame with the right hand. When both the tube and piece of glass are soft, touch the soft part of the tube with the end of the glass and draw the tube out into a point like that shown in Fig. 4. Break off the piece of glass, thus leaving a small aperture in the long tube. Seal the remaining $\frac{1}{2}$ in. of platinum in this aperture in the same manner as before, being careful not to heat the tube too suddenly. The tube is now ready for filling and the upper part will appear as shown in Fig. 5.

The air is expelled from the tube by filling with mercury. This may be done by making a paper funnel and pouring the mercury slowly into the tube through the funnel. When the tube is filled to within $\frac{1}{2}$ in. of the funnel remove the funnel and tap the side of the tube gently in order to remove any small air bubbles that may be clinging to the sides of the tube. The air bubbles will rise and come to the top. The tube now must be filled completely, expelling all the air. Place a finger over the end of the tube to keep the mercury in and invert the tube and set the end in the bowl of mercury. The mercury in the tube will sink until the level will be at about 30 in., leaving 8 in. of vacuum at the top. The next operation is to seal the tube at the half-way point between the lower platinum wire and the mercury level.

As the lower end of the tube must be kept at all times in the bowl of mercury until the tube is sealed, an assistant will be necessary for this last operation. Have the assistant hold the tube in the mercury at a slight angle, using care to always keep the lower end in the mercury, while you hold the burner in the left hand and allow the flame to strike the tube at the stated point. The part of the tube above this point will gradually bend over of its own weight as the glass softens. When it reaches the angle of about 60 deg., Fig. 6, take hold of the tube with the right hand, still keeping the flame on the tube, and gradually draw the softened portion out until it separates from the main tube.

The tube is now finished and when the platinum wires are attached to the terminals of a spark coil a beautiful blue light will appear in the tube with a dark space at the negative end or cathode.—Contributed by David A. Keys, Toronto, Can.

Nuts that are rusted fast can often be loosened by giving a hard turn in the tightening direction.

Greasy stoves may be cleaned with a strong solution of lye or soda.

How to Make a Take-Down Background Frame

Many amateur photographers who desire to do portrait work at home have left the subject alone for the want of a suitable background. A frame such as is used by the professional is entirely out of the question in most homes, says a correspondent of Camera Craft. The frame as shown in the sketch was devised and its chief advantage lies in the fact that when not in use it can be compactly tied together and stored away in a closet.

Almost any wood may be used in constructing this frame, but yellow pine is the best, as it is easily obtained and at the same time very well suited for such work. All pieces are to be dressed on all sides.

Two upright pieces are cut from ¾-in. material 2 in. wide and 5 ft. 9 in. long and two blocks are fastened on the ends of each that are to be used for the bottom, as shown in Fig. 1. These blocks are each 2 by 6 in. and ¼ in. thick. The base is made from a piece ¾ in. thick, 3 in. wide and 5 ft. 4 in. long. A crosspiece ¾ in. thick, 3 in. wide and 12 in. long, cut in the shape shown in Fig. 2, is screwed on each end of the base with 3-in. wood screws, as shown in Fig. 3. Four blocks ¼ in. thick, 1 in. wide and 3 in. long are nailed to the sides of the base piece parallel with and at a distance of 2 in. from the end of same. This forms a slot, Fig. 4, to receive the pieces nailed to the ends of the uprights. To secure a rigid frame it is essential that this joint be accurately put together.

Procure a piece of thick tin or brass and make two pieces like the pattern shown in Fig. 5, with each projection 3 in. long. The width of the crosspiece is 1 in. and the single projection ¾ in. These are bent and nailed, one on each end of a piece of wood that is ¼ in. thick, 1 in. wide and 5 ft. long, as in Fig. 6. These will form two pockets that will fit over the tops of the uprights. The frame is put together as shown in Fig. 7. Any background that will hang straight without need of being stretched can be hung on this frame.

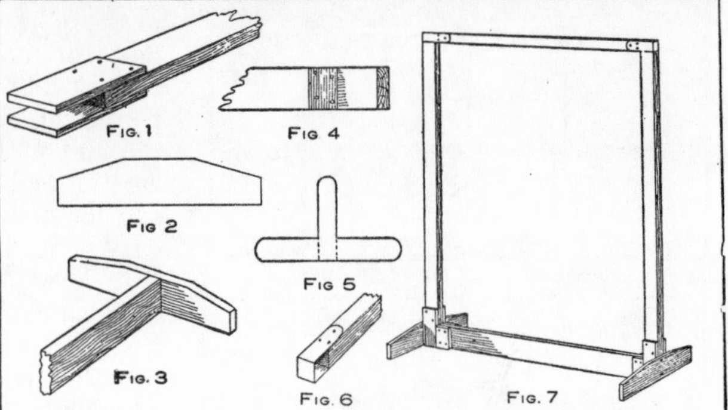

Details of Background Frame

Home-Made Kite Reel

This kite reel is constructed from two old pulleys and a few pipe fittings. The large pulley is about 14 in. in diameter, on the face of which are riveted flat strips of iron with extending arms. These arms are reinforced by riveting smaller pieces from one to the

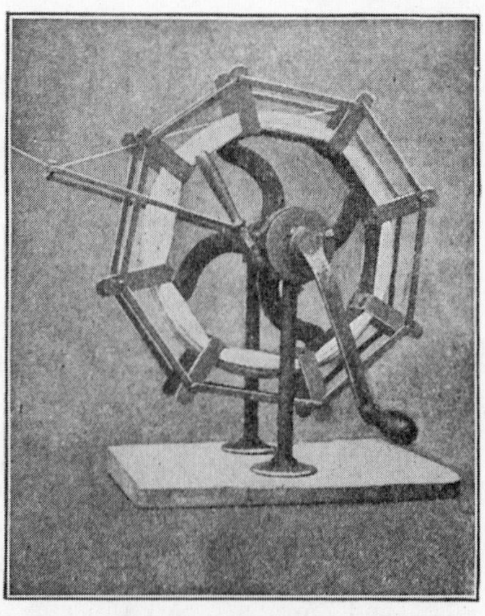
Old Pulleys and Pipe Fittings

other, which connects all arms together on both sides of the wheel. Mounted on the shaft with the pulleys is a guide for the kite wire or string. The photograph shows that this guide permits of being moved entirely over the top of the reel. The smaller pulley is attached to the shaft and used as a brake. The brake is used only when running out the wire or string, first removing the crank.

Attaching Runners to a Bicycle for Winter Use

Instead of storing away your bicycle

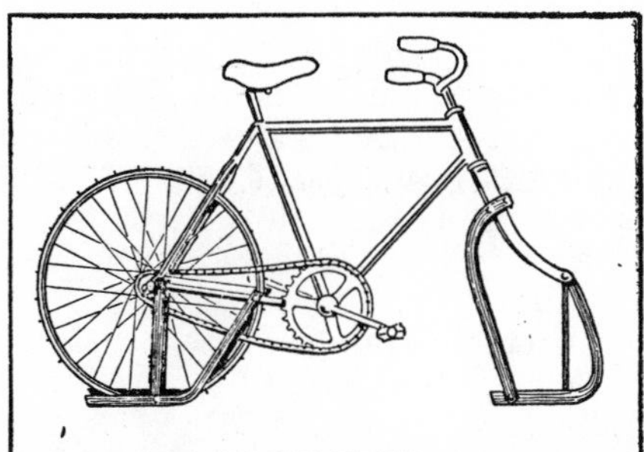

Bicycle Fitted with Runners for Snow

for the winter, attach runners and use it on the ice. The runners can be made from ¼-in. by 1-in. iron and fastened to the bicycle frame as shown in the sketch. The tire is removed from the rim of the rear wheel and large screws turned into the rim, leaving the greater part of the screw extending. Cut off the heads of the screws and file them to a point. The rear runners should be set so the rim of the wheel will be about ½ in. above the runner level.—Contributed by C. R. Welsh, Manhattan, Kan.

A Paper That Makes Green Prints

A coating for ordinary paper that is said to give green prints is made with a two per cent solution of gelatine, says Photography, and sensitized with the following solution:

Potassium Bichromate	15 gr.
Magnesium Sulphate	25 gr.
Water	1 oz.

This mixture is spread over the paper in the usual way and the paper dried in the dark. Printing is carried rather far. The print is washed, then surface dried or blotted off on a pad and laid film upwards on a sheet of glass, and the following developer is applied with a wad of cotton wool wrung out:

Pyrocatechin	5 gr.
Water	1 oz.

The picture assumes a rich green color when developed, and is then washed for five or ten minutes and dried quickly by heat.

Copies Made from Wax Molds by Electro-Deposition

Fine copies of wax impressions can be made in the following manner: Procure an ordinary tumbler and fill it with a strong solution of sulphate of copper, which is made by dissolving two cents' worth of blue vitriol in ½ pt. of water. After this is done make a porous cell by rolling a piece of brown paper around a stick and fastening the edge with sealing wax; also, fix a bottom to the cell in the same way. Make a solution of one part of oil of vitriol and 5 parts of water and pour this mixture into the porous cell. Wind the end of a copper wire around the end of a piece of zinc and place the zinc in the porous cell. Attach the other end of the wire to the wax impression.

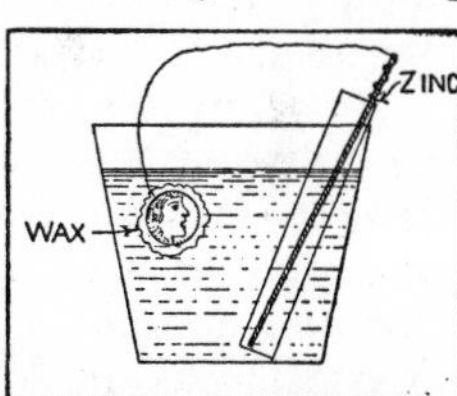

The wax impression is made by pouring melted beeswax on the article you wish to reproduce and removing after the wax gets cold. The wax mold then should be coated with black lead and polished. This is done with a camel's hair brush. A fine copy can be made on the wax impression after the battery has been running about 12 hr.—Contributed by Edward M. Teasdale.

How to Make Skating Shoes

Remove the clamp part, as shown in Fig. 1, from an ordinary clamp skate. Drill holes in the top part of the skate

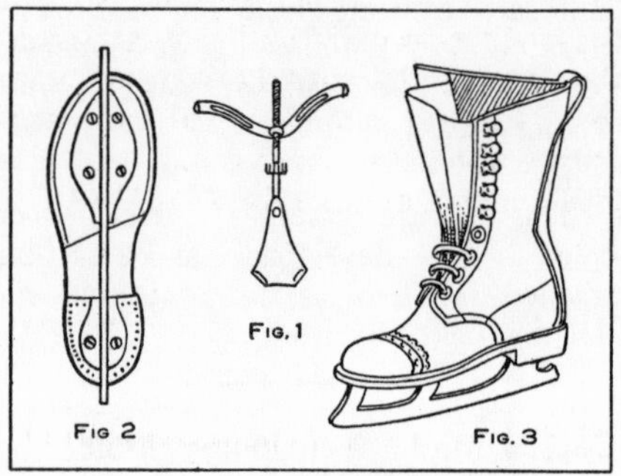

Skating Shoes

for screws. Purchase a pair of high shoes with heavy soles and fasten the skates to the soles with screws, as shown in Fig. 2. When completed the skating shoes will have the appearance shown on Fig. 3. These will make as good skating shoes as can be purchased, and very much cheaper.—Contributed by Wallace C. Newton, Leominster, Mass.

How to Make a Self-Setting Rabbit Trap

Secure a good-sized box, say, 1 ft. high, 1½ ft. wide, and 3 ft. long; and to the bottom, about 10 in. from one end, fasten a 2-in. square piece, A, Fig. 1, extending the width of the box. Place a 10-in. board sloping from the end of the box to the cleat A. The swing door B, Fig. 1, is made as shown

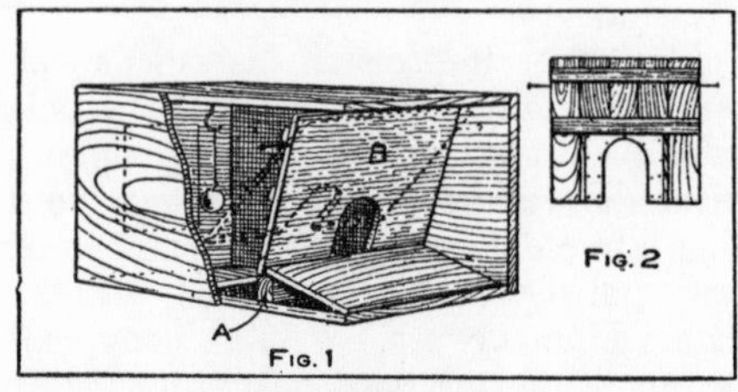

Self-Setting Trap

in Fig. 2, which represents the back side of the door. Sheet metal or tin is cut to the proper size and tacked around the edge of the hole. This prevents the animal from gnawing its way out, also provides a way to make the hole of different sizes for squirrels or other animals. The hole in the door should be about 2 in. wide and 4 in. high for rabbits. The door is made to swing freely on two large nails driven through the sides of the box. The hole in the door being only large enough to admit a small portion of the rabbit's head, the rabbit will push its way through to the bait, causing the door to swing back and up, and it will close by its own weight when the animal is inside. A small door is provided in the other end to remove the animals caught.

The advantage of this trap is that where one animal is caught others are liable to follow, and several rabbits will be trapped at a time. Then, too, the rabbits are not harmed in any way as they would be if caught in an ordinary trap.—Contributed by H. F. Church, Alexandria, Va.

How to Make an Atomizer

Secure a good-sized test tube and fit it with a cork. Take two glass tubes, with about ⅛-in. hole, and bend them as shown in the sketch. This is done by heating them at the proper point over a gas flame until they are soft. Two holes are bored through the cork and the bent tubes inserted in them, as shown in the sketch, so that one of the tubes will extend nearly to the bottom of the test tube and the other just projecting through the cork. The spray tube may be made with a fine hole by first securing a tube longer than necessary and heating it at the proper point

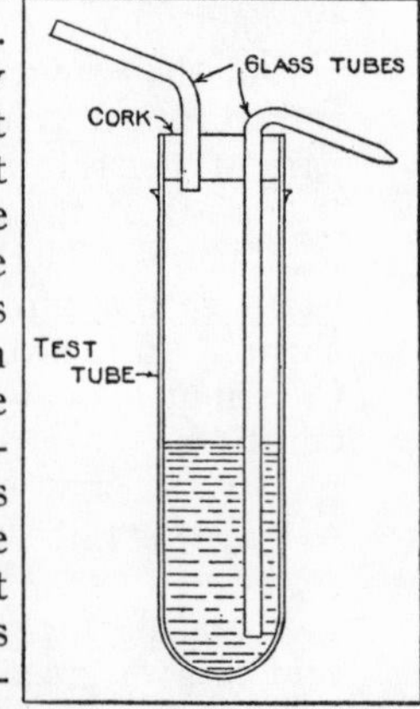

and drawing the tube out into a fine thread. The thread is broken off at the proper place to make a small hole.

Home-Made Kits for the Camera

If you have a 5- by 7-in. camera and wish to use some 4- by 5-in. plates, make a few simple kits to hold the smaller plates and fit the larger holders, says Camera Craft. Take two pieces of pasteboard, A and B, black surfaced if possible, and exactly 5 by 7 in. in size. The piece A will form the back of the kit and should have an opening cut in the center 4 by 5 in. in size. Paste a piece of strong black paper, C, over the under side of it to keep the plate from falling through. Cut an opening in the other piece, B, but cut it ¼ in. shorter. This opening, being ⅛ in. shorter at each end, will retain the plate in position and cut off only that small amount of plate surface when the plate is exposed in the camera. Cut a piece of thin black cloth, D, 1 in. wide and 5 in. long. Lay it down on a piece of newspaper and coat one side with gum or mucilage. Stand the two pieces of 5- by 7-in. black cards on end together so that they will be square and true and bind the other ends with the strip of cloth so as to form a hinge. The two cards form a thickness about equal to a thick glass plate, and go in the holder in the same way. Lay one of these kits down against the ground side of the focusing screen and draw a line around, inside of the opening. This will be a guide as to just what will be secured upon the smaller plate when the kits are used.

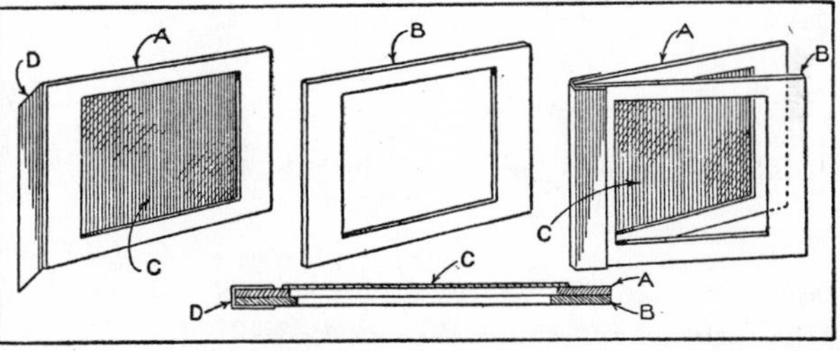

How to Make a Miniature Stage

A good smooth box, say 8 in. wide, 10 in. high and 12 in. long, will serve the purpose for the main part of this small theater. Cut two rectangular holes, Fig. 1, one in each end and exactly opposite each other. Place a screw eye about ½ in. from the edge on each side of these openings. Fit an axle in the screw eyes and fasten a spool to the middle of the axle. On one of the two spools attach another smaller spool, Fig. 2, to be used as a driving pulley. Cut out the front part of the box down to a level with the top of the spools.

Details of the Miniature Mechanical Stage

Connect the spools with a belt made from tape about ¾ in. wide. On this belt fasten figures cut from heavy paper and made in the form of people, automobiles, trolley cars, horses and dogs. A painted scenery can be made in behind the movable tape. The front part of the box may be draped with curtains, making the appearance of the ordinary stage, as shown in Fig. 3. A small motor will run the spools and drive the tape on which the figures are attached.—Contributed by William M. Crilly, Jr., Chicago.

A Floating Compass Needle

When a thoroughly dry and clean sewing needle is carefully placed on the surface of water the needle will float even if the density of steel is 7 or 8 times that of water. A sewing needle thus floating upon water may be used as a compass, if it has previously been magnetized. The needle will then point north and south, and will maintain this position if the containing vessel is moved about; if the needle is displaced by force it will return to its position along the magnetic meridian as soon as the restraint is removed.

Home-Made Dog Cart

The accompanying photograph shows a boy with his "dogmobile." The photograph was taken when they were on a new pavement which had 2 in. of sand left by the pavers and a grade of 6 per cent. The machine is nothing more than a boy's rubber-tired wagon on which are mounted a box for a seat and a wheel steering device extending above and below the board of the wagon. The front wheels are guided by ropes attached from each end of the axle and a few turns around the lower end of the steering rod. A pair of shafts are attached to the rear, into which the dog is harnessed.

Dog-Power Cart

How to Make a Dry Battery Cell

Dry battery cells are composed of the same materials for the poles, but instead of the liquid commonly used a paste is formed by mixing sal ammoniac and other salts with water and packed in the cell so it cannot spill.

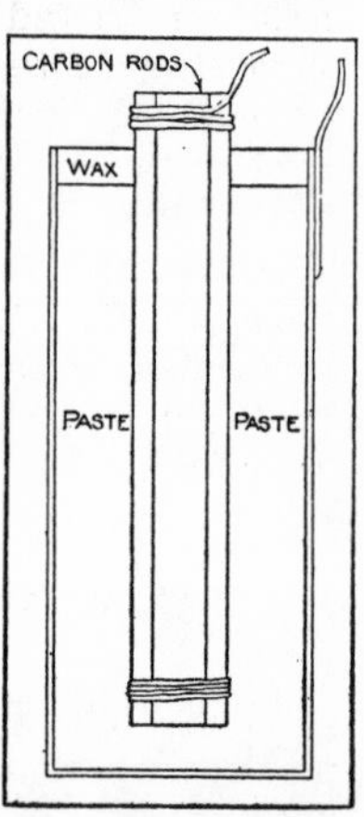

A cell of this kind can easily be made, and to make it the proper size a sheet of zinc 8½ in. long and 6 in. wide will be required. This zinc is rolled into a cylinder 2½ in. in diameter. This will allow for a lap of ⅝ in., which is tightly soldered only on the outside of the seam. Close one end of the cylinder by soldering a disk of zinc over it, making a watertight receptacle. All soldering should be done on the outside and none of the solder allowed to run on the inside of the seam. All seams on the inside should be painted with asphaltum in order to cover any particles of solder. Do not paint any surface, only the joints. Secure three carbon rods ½ in. in diameter and 6 in. long which are copper plated. Carbons used in arc lamps will do. File the rods to remove the copper plate, leaving about ½ in. of the plate at one end. Tie the three rods in a close bundle with the copper-plated ends together and make a contact with each rod by soldering a wire to the plated ends, allowing one end of the wire to project about 2 in. for a connection. The plated ends of the carbons should be covered with paraffin for about 1 in. This is done by immersing them in a dish of smoking hot melted paraffin until the pores are thoroughly saturated.

The salts for filling are ¼ lb. zinc oxide, ¼ lb. sal ammoniac, ¾ lb. plaster of paris, ¼ lb. chloride of zinc mixed into a paste by adding ½ pt. of water. Form a ½-in. layer of paste in the bottom of the cylinder and place the ends of the carbon rods on this with their plated ends up. Hold the rods in the center of the cylinder and put the paste in around the rods with a stick. Pack the paste in, closely filling the cylinder to within ¾ in. of the top. This space at the top is filled with a mixture of ½ lb. of rosin and 2 oz. beeswax melted together. This wax seals the cell and prevents any evaporation. Connection is made to the zinc by soldering a wire to the outside of the cylinder.

How to Paraffin Wire

The following description of how to make an apparatus with which to paraffin wire as needed makes clear a method of construction that is simple and easy to put together in a short time.

Secure a pan to be used for this purpose only; one that will hold about 1 qt. The details of the construction are given in the diagram, in which P is the pan; B is a base of 1-in. pine; S is the spool of wire supported near one end of the base by nailing on standards H and H; F is a spool, with narrow flanges, supported near the bottom of the pan by the standards T and T. These may be made of two short pieces of a roller fitted into the holes bored in the base; A is a block of 1-in. pine with a piece of leather tacked on one side. Four nails should be driven in the base just outside of the edge of the pan to keep it from sliding off the pan.

Bore a hole in the base between the two spools and pass the wire through this hole, under the spool in the paraffin, then through a small hole in the leather and a notch in the block A, and a notch between the base and the pan. Tie a string around the wire between the leather and the paraffin, making the knots so they will not pull through the hole in the leather. This makes the wire smooth, and by making the string tighter or looser you can regulate the thickness of the paraffin, says Electrician and Mechanic. Place the pan on the stove; when the paraffin is melted, pull out the wire as needed. To keep the pan from sliding place a flatiron or some other weight on it.

Peat is used in Germany for bedding, fodder, filter, fuel and packing purposes.

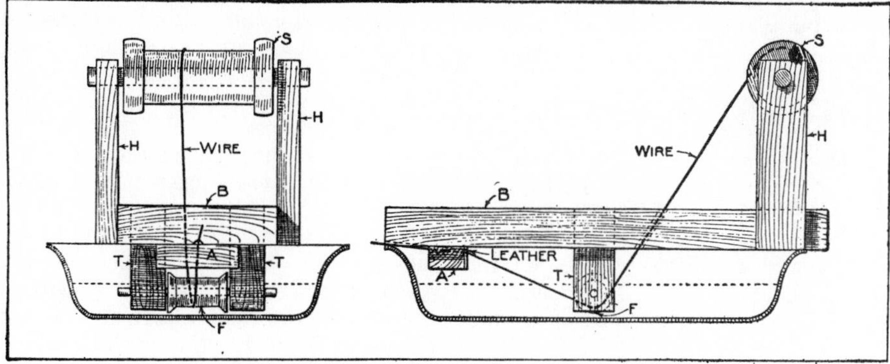

Home-Made Apparatus for Paraffining Wire

Scientific Explanation of a Toy

In a recent issue of Popular Mechanics an article on "The Turning Card Puzzle" was described and illustrated. Outside of the scientific side involved, herein I describe a much better trick. About the time when the expression "skidoo" first began to be used I invented the following trick and called it "Skidoo" and "Skidee," which created much merriment. Unless the trick is thoroughly understood, for some it will turn one way, for others the opposite way, while for others it will not revolve at all. One person whom I now recall became red in the face by shouting skidoo and skidee at it, but the thing would not move at all, and he finally, from vexation, threw the trick into the fire and a new one had to be made. Very few can make it turn both ways at will, and therein is the trick.

Take a piece of hardwood ⅜ in. square and about 9 in. long. On one of the edges cut a series of notches as indicated in Fig 1. Then slightly taper the end marked B until it is nicely rounded as shown in Fig. 2. Next make an arm of a two-arm windmill such as boys make. Make a hole through the center of this one arm. Enlarge the hole slightly, enough to allow a common pin to hold the arm to the end B and not interfere with the revolving arm. Two or three of these arms may have to be made before one is secured that is of the exact proportions to catch the vibrations right.

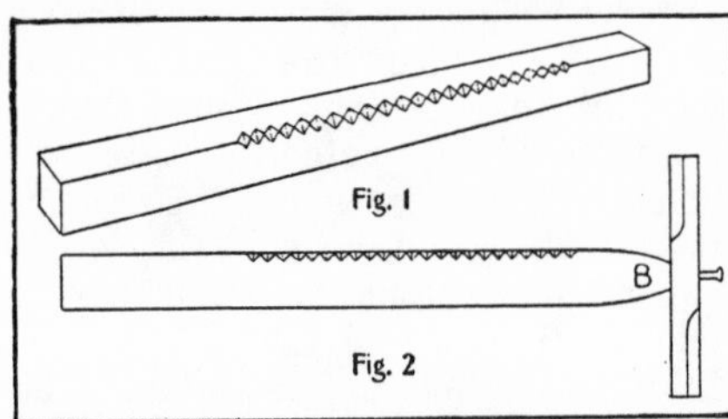

How to Cut the Notches

To operate the trick, grip the stick firmly in one hand, and with the forward and backward motion of the other allow the first finger to slide along the top edge, the second finger along the side, and the thumb nail will then vibrate along the notches, thus making the arm revolve in one direction. To make the arm revolve in the opposite direction—keep the hand moving all the time, so the observer will not detect the change which the hand makes—allow the first finger to slide along the top, as in the other movement, the thumb and second finger changing places: e. g., in the first movement you scratch the notches with the thumb nail while the hand is going from the body, and in the second movement you scratch the notches with the nail of the second finger when the hand is coming toward the body, thus producing two different vibrations. In order to make it work perfectly (?) you must of course say "skidoo" when you begin the first movement, and then, no matter how fast the little arm is revolving when changed to the second movement, you must say "skidee" and the arm will immediately stop and begin revolving in the opposite direction. By using the magic words the little arm will obey your commands instantly and your audience will be mystified. If any of your audience presume to dispute, or think they can do the same, let them try it. You will no doubt be accused of blowing or drawing in your breath, and many other things in order to make the arm operate. At least it is amusing. Try it and see.—Contributed by Charles Clement Bradley, Toledo, Ohio.

The foregoing article describing the "Skidoo-Skidee Trick" appeared in a recent issue of Popular Mechanics. I have been told that a similar arrangement is used by a tribe of Indians in the state of Washington, by the Hindoos in India, and one friend tells me that they were sold on the streets of our large cities many years ago.

This toy interested me so much that I have made an investigation into the causes of its action, and I think the results may be of interest.

To operate, one end of the notched stick is held firmly in the left hand, while with the right hand a nail or match stick is rubbed along the notched edge, at the same time pressing with the thumb or finger of the moving hand against the oblique face of the stick. The direction of rotation depends upon which face is pressed. A square stick with notches on edge is best, but the section may be circular or even irregular in shape.

The experiments were as follows:

1. A rectangular stick had notches cut on one face. When the pressure was applied upon a face normal to the first, no rotation resulted. If the pressure was upon an edge, rotation was obtained.

2. Irregular spacing of the notches did not interfere with the action. The depth of the notches was also unimportant, although it should be suited to the size of the nail for best results.

3. The hole in the revolving piece must be larger than the pin; if there is a close fit no rotation is obtained.

4. The center of gravity of the revolving piece must lie within the hole. If the hole is not well centered the trick cannot be performed.

5. If the stick be clamped in a vise no results are obtained; with this exception: if the stick has enough spring, and the end clamped is far enough away from the notched portion, the rotation may be obtained.

The above experiments led me to the conclusion that the operation of the device is dependent upon a circular motion of the pin, and this was confirmed by the following experiments. The action is somewhat similar to swinging the toy known as a locust around with a slight circular motion of the hand. It is necessary to show here that a slight circular motion is sufficient to produce the result and, secondly, that such motion can be produced by the given movements of the hands.

6. A piece of brass rod was clamped in the chuck of a lathe, and a depression made in the end slightly eccentric, by means of a center punch. If the end of the pin is inserted in this depression,

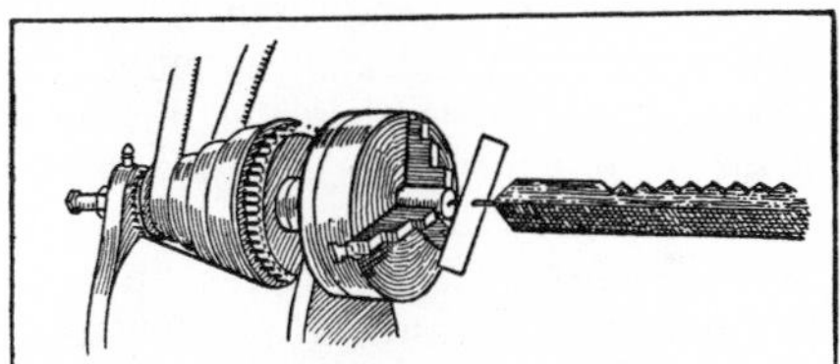

The Lathe Experiment

while the hand holding the other end of the stick is kept as nearly as possible in the axis of the lathe, rotation of the lathe will produce rotation of the revolving piece. Speeds between 700 and 1,100 r. p. m. gave the best results.

7. A tiny mirror was attached to the end of the pin, and the hand held in the sunlight so that a spot of sunlight was reflected upon the wall. The notches were then rubbed in the usual way. The spot of light upon the wall moved in a way which disclosed two components of motion, one circular and one due to the irregular movements of the hand holding the stick. Usually the orbit was too irregular to show a continuous and closed circular path, but at times the circular motion became very pronounced. It was observed and the direction of rotation correctly stated by a man who was unaware of the source of the motion.

The production of the circular motion can be explained in this way: When the rubbing nail comes to a notch the release of pressure sends the stick upward; this upward motion against the oblique pressure upon the (say) right hand side gives also a lateral component of motion towards the left. As the nail strikes the opposite side of the notch the stick is knocked down again, this motion relieves somewhat the oblique pressure from the right hand side, and the reaction from the holding (left) hand moves the stick to the right slightly, so that it is back in the old position for the next upward motion. Thus a circular or elliptic motion is repeated for each notch, and the direction of this motion is the same whether the nail be rubbed forward or back. For oblique side pressure from the right (notches assumed upward), the motion of the stick and hence of the revolving piece will be counter-clockwise; if the pressure is from the left, it will be clockwise.

That the motion of the revolving piece is due to a swinging action, and not to friction of the pin in the hole, is proved by experiments 3 and 4.—Contributed by M. G. Lloyd, Ph.D., Washington, D. C.

Home-Made Lantern

The accompanying picture shows a lantern which can be made almost anywhere for immediate use. All that is needed is an empty tomato or coffee can, a piece of wire and a candle. Make a hole a little smaller than the diameter of a candle and about one-third of the way from the closed end of the can, as shown. A wire is tied around the can, forming a handle for carrying. This kind of lantern can be carried against almost any wind and the light will not be blown out.—Contributed by G. A. Sloan, Duluth, Minn.

Tin Can Lantern

A Study of Splashes

When a rough, or greasy, or dusty sphere falls into a liquid, the liquid is forced away from the sphere. If the sphere is quite smooth the liquid rises up around and enclosing it in a sheath, says Knowledge and Scientific News.

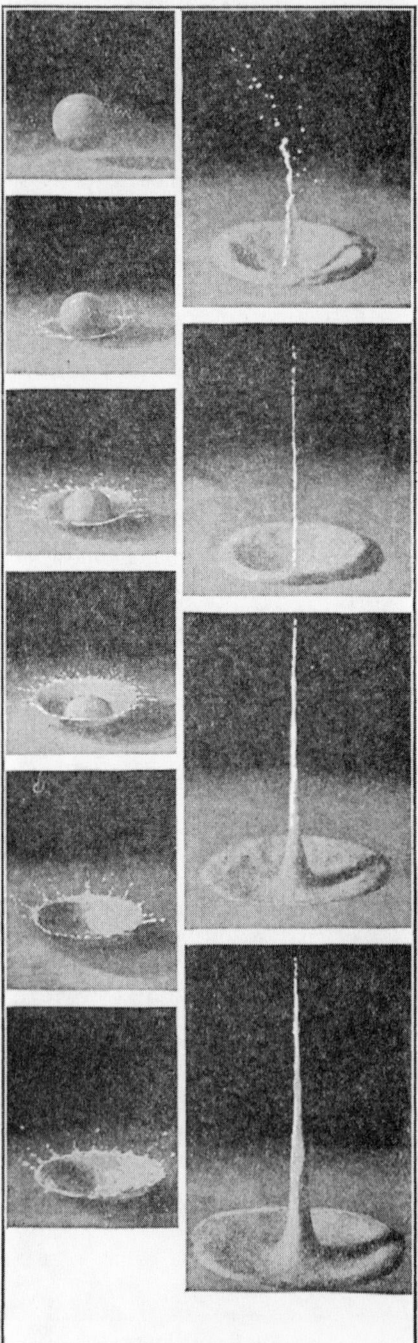

Splashes from a Sphere in Milk and Water

Reproduced herewith are a series of photographs showing successive stages in the entry of a rough sphere into milk and water, and the resultant "basket splash." The diameter of this sphere was about 3/5 in., and the height of the fall about 6 in. Examination of the photographs shows that the liquid, instead of flowing over and wetting the surface of the sphere, is driven violently away, so far as can be seen from the photographs, the upper portion is, at first, unwetted by the liquid. The gradual thickening of the crater wall and the corresponding reduction in the number of its lobes as the subsidence proceeds is beautifully shown. Thereafter there rises from the depth of the crater an exquisite jet which in obedience to the law of segmentation at once splits up in its upper portion into little drops, while at the same time it gathers volume from below and rises ultimately as a tall, graceful column to a height which may be even greater than that from which the sphere fell.

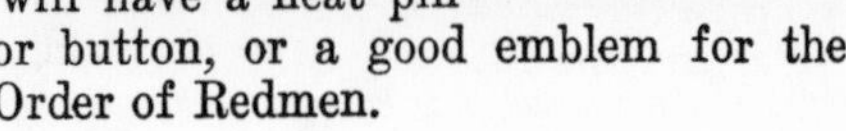

How to Make a Stick Pin

A fine stick pin or button can be made from a new one-cent piece. Carefully file out all the metal around the Indian head and slightly round the edges. Solder a pin to the back of the head when it is to be used for a stick pin. If a collar button base is soldered to the back of the head instead of the pin it can be used for a button. These can be gold plated by a jeweler and then you will have a neat pin or button, or a good emblem for the Order of Redmen.

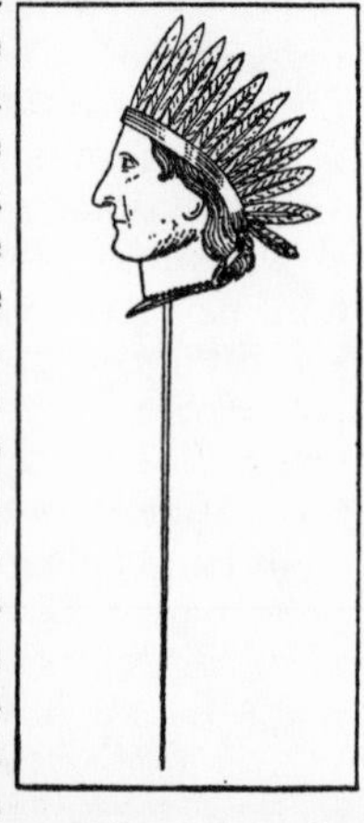

How to Make a Miniature Electric Locomotive

A miniature electric railway is a thing that attracts the attention of almost any person. The cost of a toy electric locomotive is beyond the reach of many boys who could just as well make such a toy without much expense and be proud to say they "built it themselves." The electric locomotive described herewith uses for its power a small battery motor costing about $1. The first thing to do is to make the wheels and axles. If one has no lathe, the wheels can be turned at some machine shop. Four wheels are made from a round bar of metal, as shown in Fig. 1. Each wheel is $\frac{1}{4}$ in. thick and 1 in. in diameter, with a $\frac{1}{16}$-in. flange and a $\frac{1}{4}$-in. hole drilled in the center. Each pair of wheels is fitted on a $\frac{1}{4}$-in. axle, about $2\frac{5}{8}$ in. long. One of the axles should be fitted with a grooved belt wheel, as shown. Make the frame from three pieces of heavy brass, as shown in Fig. 2.

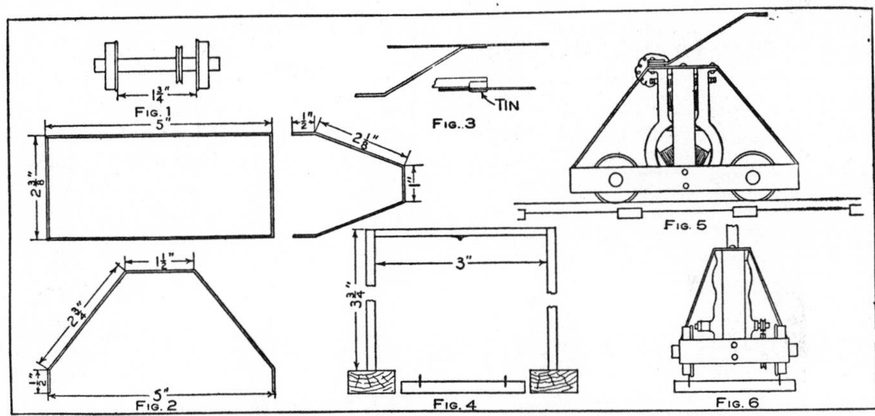

The Different Parts for Making the Electric Locomotive

The first piece, or main part of the frame, is made from brass, $\frac{3}{4}$ in. wide and 16 in. long, bent into an oblong shape and the ends soldered or bolted together. If the ends are to be soldered, before doing so drill four $\frac{1}{4}$-in. holes 1 in. from the ends and insert the ends of the axles. The other two pieces are $\frac{1}{2}$ in. wide and of the dimensions shown in the sketch. These pieces are riveted in the middle of the oblong frame, each in its proper place. The motor is now bolted, bottom side up, to the top of the piece fastened to the frame lengthwise. A trolley, Fig. 3, is made from a piece of clock spring, bent as shown, and a small piece of tin soldered to the top end for a brush connection. A groove is made in the tin to keep the trolley wire in place.

The trolley wire is fastened to supports made of wood and of the dimensions given in Fig. 4. The trolley should be well insulated from the frame. The parts, put together complete, are shown in Fig. 5. Run a belt from the pulley on the motor to the grooved wheel on the axle, as shown in Fig. 6, and the locomotive is ready for running.

In making the connections the travel of the locomotive may be made more complicated by placing a rheostat and controlling switches in the line, so that the engine can be started and stopped at will from a distance and the speed regulated. Automatic switches can be attached at the ends of the line to break the circuit when the locomotive passes a certain point.

One connection from the batteries is made to the trolley wire and the other to a rail. The connection for the motor runs from one binding post to the trolley and this connection must be well insulated to avoid a short-circuit. The other binding-post is connected to the frame.

The cost of making the wheels and purchasing the track will not be over $1.50. The track can be made from strips of tin put in a saw cut made in pieces of wood used for ties. This will save buying a track.—Contributed by Maurice E. Fuller, San Antonio, Texas.

Demagnetizing a Watch

A test can be made to know if your watch is magnetized by placing a small compass on the side of the watch nearest the escapement wheel. If the compass pointer moves with the escapement wheel the watch is magnetized. A magnetized watch must be placed in a

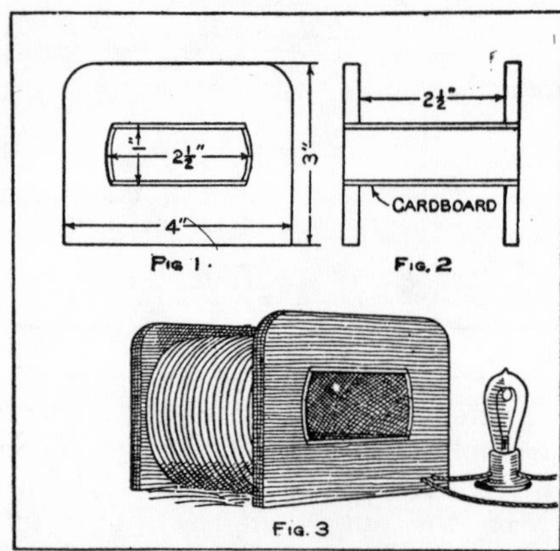

Watch Demagnetizer

coil that has an alternating current of electricity flowing through it to remove the magnetism. A demagnetizer can be made as shown in the illustration. Two end pieces for the coil are made as shown in Fig. 1 from ¼-in. wood. These ends are fastened together, Fig. 2, with cardboard 3 in. long glued to the inside edges of the holes cut in them. Wind upon the spool thus formed about 2 lb. of No. 16 cotton-covered copper wire. As it will be necessary to place a 16-cp. lamp in series with the coil, both the coil and lamp can be mounted on a suitable base and connected as shown in Fig. 3. The current, which must be 110-volt alternating current, is turned on the lamp and coil and the magnetized watch slowly drawn through the opening in the center of the coil.—Contributed by Arthur Liebenberg, Cincinnati, O.

How to Make a Pocket Skate Sharpener

Secure a square file and break off a piece, Fig 1, the length of a paper clip, Fig. 2. Draw the temper in the ends of this piece of file, but do not heat the center. This can be done by wrapping a wet piece of cloth or asbestos around the middle and holding it in the jaws of a pair of tongs which will only leave the end uncovered and projecting from the tongs about ½ in. Hold this projecting end in a flame of a plumber's torch until it is a dull red. Allow this to cool slowly while in the tongs. When cold treat the other end in the same way. This will draw the temper in only the ends which are filed, as shown in Fig. 1, and holes drilled in them. Also drill a hole in each end of the spring on the paper clip to match those drilled in the piece of file. Fasten the file in the clip with small bolts, as shown in Fig. 3. When the file gets filled with filings it can be removed and cleaned. Place the runner of the skate in the clip and hold flat on the surface of the runner. If the piece of file is fitted to the same width as the skate runner the sides of the paper clip will hold the file level with the surface of the runner without any trouble. Push the clip back and forth until the skate is sharpened.

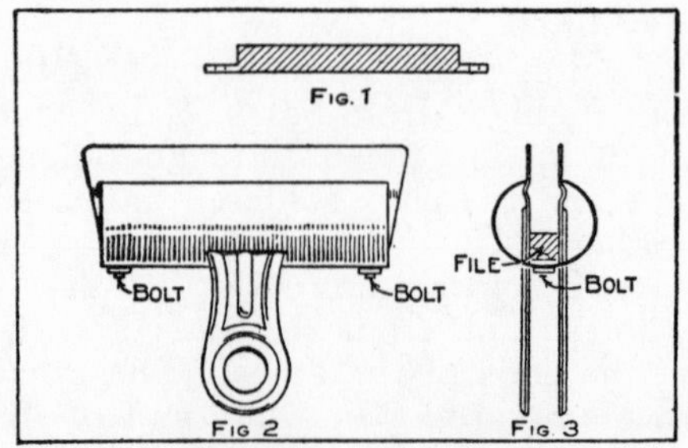

Sharpener for Skates

Old-Time Magic

Trick with a Coin in a Wine Glass

The accompanying sketch shows a trick of removing a dime from the bottom of an old-fashioned wine glass without touching the coin. The dime is first placed in the bottom of the glass and then a silver quarter dropped in on top. The quarter will not go all the way down. Blow hard into the glass in the position shown and the dime will fly out and strike the blower on the nose.

Untying-a-Knot Trick

Tie a double knot in a silk handkerchief, as shown in the accompanying sketch and tighten the last tie a little by slightly drawing the two upper ends; then continue to tighten much more, pulling vigorously at the first corner of the handkerchief, and as this end belongs to the same corner it cannot be pulled much without loosening the twisted line of the knot to become a straight line. The other corner forms a slip knot on the end, which can be drawn out without disturbing the form, or apparent security of the knot, at the moment when you cover the knot with the unused part of the handkerchief.

When the trick is to be performed, tie two or three very hard knots that are tightly drawn and show your audience that they are not easy to untie. The slip knot as described then must be made in apparently the same way and untied with the thumb while the knot is in the folds of the handkerchief.

Gear-Cutting Attachment for Small Lathes

When in need of small gears for experimental or model machines the amateur usually purchases them, never thinking that he could make them on his own lathe. A small attachment can be made to fasten in the tool post of a lathe and the attachment made to take a mandrel on which to place the blank for cutting a gear. The frame is made from a $\frac{1}{2}$-in. square iron bent as shown in the sketch with the projecting end filed to fit the tool post of the lathe. A pair of centers are fitted, one of which should have a screw thread and lock nut for adjustment in putting in and removing the mandrel.

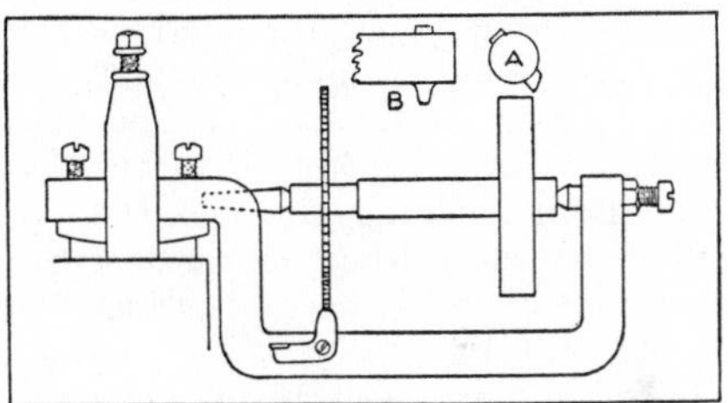

Gear-Cutting Attachment for Lathes

All the old clock wheels that can be found should be saved and used for index wheels. All of these wheels should be fitted to one end of the mandrel. The blank wheel is put on the outer end of the mandrel and a clock wheel having the number of teeth desired placed on the other end. When the mandrel is put in between the centers a small pawl is fastened with a screw to the frame with its upper end engaging in a tooth of the clock wheel. One clock wheel will index more than one number of teeth on a blank wheel. For instance: if the clock wheel has 18 teeth it can be made to index 6, 9 or 18 teeth to the blank by moving the number of teeth each time 3, 2 and 1 respectively.

In the sketch, A shows the end of

the cutter and B the side and the shape of the cutting tool. When the cutter A, which is in a mandrel placed in the centers of the lathe, has finished a cut for a tooth, the pawl is disengaged and the mandrel turned to another tooth in the clock wheel.

In order to get the desired height it is sometimes necessary to block up the lathe head and the final depth of the tooth adjusted by the two screws in the projecting end of the frame which rests on the rocker in the tool post. Should too much spring occur when cutting iron gears the frame can be made rigid by blocking up the space between it and the lathe bed.

The cutter mandrel is placed in the centers of the lathe, or should the lathe head be raised, a short mandrel with the cutter near the end can be placed in a chuck, and adjusted to run true. The frame holding the mandrel, gear blank and clock wheel is inserted in the tool post of the lathe and adjusted for depth of the cutter. The lathe is started and the gear blank fed on the cutter slowly until the tooth is cut. The pawl is released and the mandrel turned to the proper number of teeth and the operation repeated. In this manner gears 3 in. in diameter can be made on a 6-in. swing lathe.—Contributed by Samuel C. Bunker, Brooklyn, N. Y.

Wire Terminals for Battery Connections

Good connections on the end of wires for batteries can be made from cotter pins, Fig. 1, about $1\frac{1}{2}$ in. long. Each end of the wire is put through the eye of a cotter pin, twisted around itself and soldered. The connection and eye are then covered with tape as shown in Fig. 2. When connecting to batteries, spread the pin and push the parts under the nut with one part on each side of the binding-post. When the nuts are tightened the connection will be better than with the bare wire.—Contributed by Howard S. Bott.

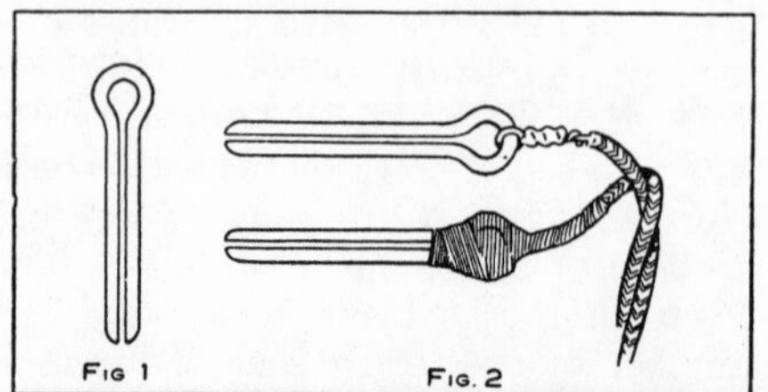

Cotter Pin Wire Terminals

Simple Arts and Crafts Leather Work

Very interesting and useful pieces of leather work can be done with nothing more for equipment than a cup-pointed nail set such as carpenters use, and a nut pick.

The accompanying illustrations show some of the things that can be made. Beginning at the left and reading to the right they are:—Case for court-plaster, coin purse, lady's card case, eye glass cleaner or pen wiper (has chamois skin within). Second row:—Two book marks, note book, blotter back, book mark. Third row:—Pin ball (has saddler's felt between the two leather disks), tea cosey, gentleman's card case or bill book. Fourth row:—Needle or pin case, tea cosey, lady's belt bag, watch fob ready for fastenings.

Procure a piece of Russian calf modeling leather. (1.) Make on paper the design wanted. (2.) Moisten the back side of the leather with sponge or cloth with as much water as it will take yet not show through on the face side. (3.) Place the leather on some hard non-absorbent material, such as brass or marble. (4.) Place the paper design on the leather and, holding it in place with the left hand, trace the outline of the object and the decorative design with the nut pick so as to make a V-shaped groove in the leather. (5.) Take the paper off and working on the leather directly make the grooves deeper. (6.) With the cup-pointed nail set stamp the background promiscuously. This is done by making an effort to hold the point of the set about $\frac{1}{4}$ in. above the surface, at the same time striking light, rapid blows on the top with a hammer or mallet.

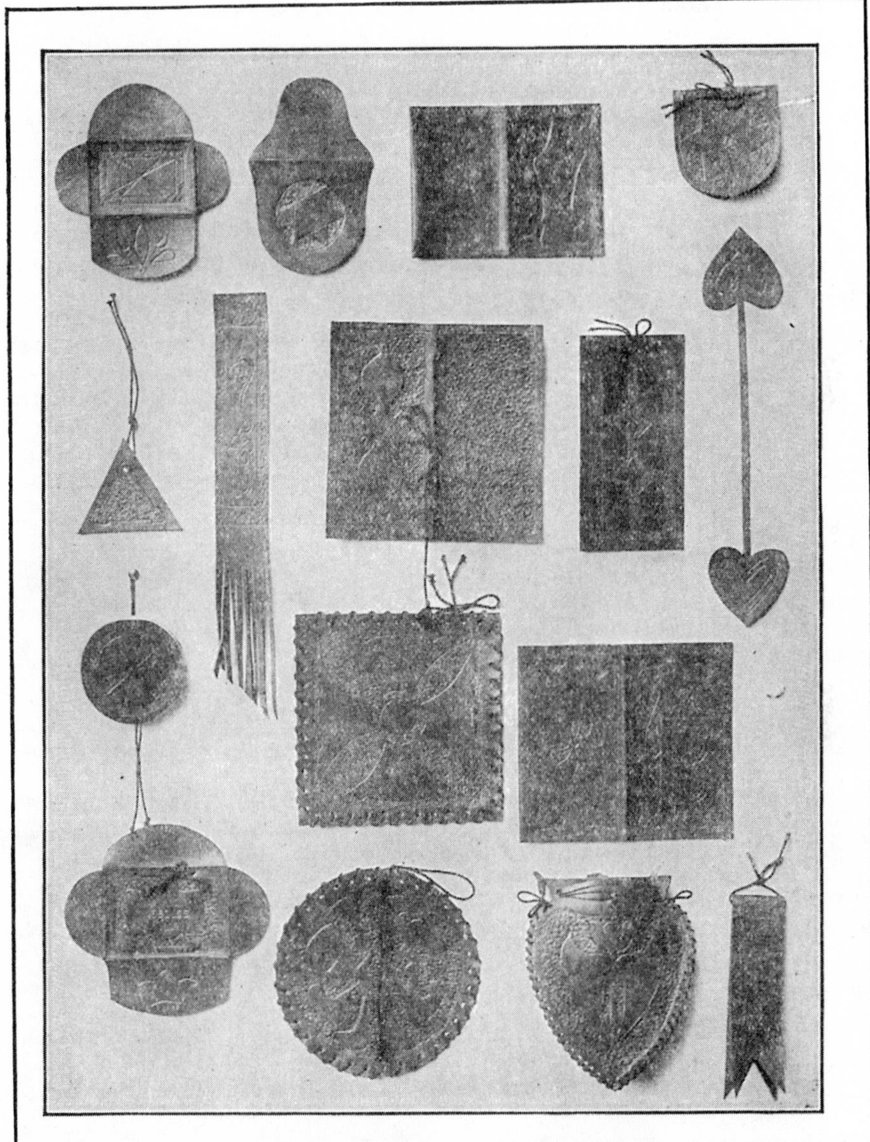

This Work Is Done with a Nail Set and Nut Pick

With such objects as coin purses and card cases, a sewing machine will be needed to fasten the parts together. An ordinary machine will do. Frequently the parts are fastened by punching holes and lacing through these with leather thongs or silk cord.

In making symmetrical designs such as are here shown, draw center lines across the required space, dividing it into as many parts as desired. Make free-hand one quarter of the design, if four parts are to be alike, or one-half of the design, if but two parts. Fold over along these center lines. Put a piece of double-surfaced carbon paper between the parts and trace over the design already drawn.

How to Make a Simple Still

A still to distill water can be made from a test tube, some heavy rubber hose, and an ordinary bottle. Secure

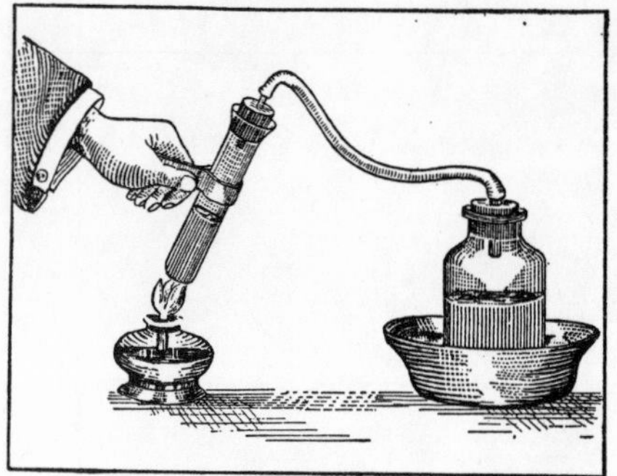

Distilling Water

a stopper for the test tube, and bore a hole through the center, into which fit a small piece of tube. The bottle is also fitted with a stopper containing a piece of tube, and both bottle and test tube connected with a rubber tube.

The test tube is partly filled with water and supported or held over an alcohol lamp. The bottle should stand in a basin of cold water. When the water in the test tube begins to boil the steam passes over to the bottle, where it condenses. The basin should be supplied with cold water as fast as it begins to get warm. The rubber tube will not stand the heat very long and if the still is to be used several times, a metal tube should be supplied to connect the test tube and bottle.

Homemade Mariner's Compass

Magnetize an ordinary knitting needle, A, and push it through a cork, B, and place the cork exactly in the middle of the needle. Thrust a pin, C, through the cork at right angles to the needle and stick two sharpened matches in the sides of the cork so that they will project downward as shown. The whole arrangement is balanced on a thimble with balls of wax stuck on the heads of the matches. If the needle is not horizontal, pull it through the cork to one side or the other, or change

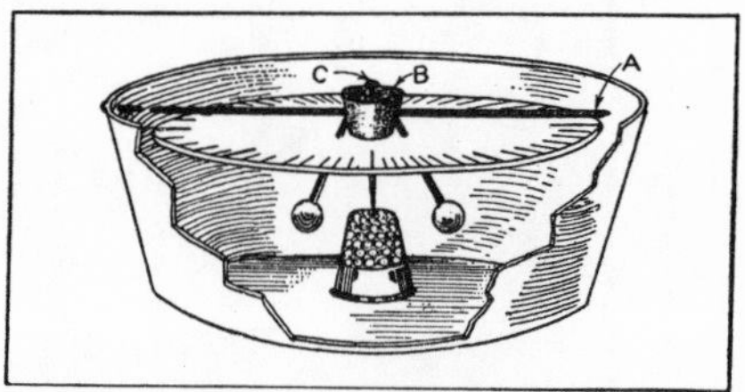

Magnetized Needle Revolving on a Pin

the wax balls. The whole device is placed in a glass berry dish and covered with a pane of glass.

ℭAdd aluminum bronze to a white or light paint that is to be used for lettering on a dark ground.

Quartz Electrodes Used in Receiving Wireless Messages

Wireless messages have been received at Washington, D. C., from Key West, Florida, a distance of 900 miles, through a receiving instrument in which two pieces of quartz of different composition were used on the electrodes. In making an instrument of this kind the quartz can be purchased from a dealer in minerals. One piece must contain copper pyrites and the other zincites. The electrodes are made cupping to hold the minerals and each should have a screw adjustment to press the pieces of quartz in contact with each other. Connect as

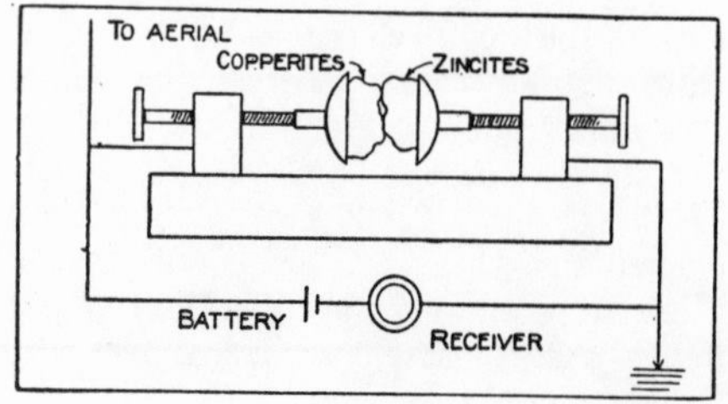

Details of the Receiving Instrument

shown in the illustration, using a high resistance receiver.—Contributed by Edwin L. Powell, Washington, D. C.

How to Make a Glider

By Carl Bates

A gliding machine is a motorless aeroplane, or flying-machine, propelled by gravity and designed to carry a passenger through the air from a high point to a lower point some distance away. Flying in a glider is simply coasting down hill on the air, and is the most interesting and exciting sport imaginable. The style of glider described in this article is known as the "two-surface" or "double-decked" aeroplane, and is composed of two arched cloth surfaces placed one above the other.

In building a glider the wood material used should be straight-grained spruce, free from knots. First prepare from spruce planks the following strips of wood. Four long beams $\frac{3}{4}$ in. thick, $1\frac{1}{4}$ in. wide and 20 ft. long; 12 crosspieces $\frac{3}{4}$ in. thick, $\frac{3}{4}$ in. wide and 3 ft. long; 12 uprights $\frac{1}{2}$ in. thick, $1\frac{1}{2}$ in. wide and 4 ft long; 41 strips for the bent ribs $\frac{3}{16}$ in. thick, $\frac{1}{2}$ in. wide and 4 ft. long; 2 arm sticks 1 in. thick, 2 in. wide and 3 ft. long; the rudder sticks $\frac{3}{4}$ in. square and 8 ft long; several strips $\frac{1}{2}$ in. by $\frac{3}{4}$ in. for building the vertical and horizontal rudders. The frames for the two main surfaces should be constructed first, by bolting the crosspieces to the long beams at the places shown by the dimensions in Fig. 1. If 20-ft. lumber cannot be procured, use 10-ft. lengths and splice them, as shown in Fig. 3. All bolts used should be $\frac{1}{8}$ in. in diameter and fitted with washers on both ends. These frames formed by the crosspieces should be braced by diagonal wires as shown. All wiring is done with No. 16 piano wire.

The 41 ribs may be nailed to the main frames on the upper side by using fine flat-headed brads $\frac{7}{8}$ in. long. These ribs are spaced 1 ft. apart and extend 1 ft. beyond the rear edges of the main frames, as shown in Fig. 1. After nailing one end of a rib to the front long beam, the rib is arched by springing down the loose end and nailing to the rear beam. The ribs should have a curve as shown in Fig. 2, the amount of curvature being the same in all the ribs.

The frames of the main surfaces are now ready to be covered with cloth. Cambric or bleached muslin should be used for the covering, which is tacked to the front edge, stretched tightly over the bent ribs and fastened securely with tacks to the rear ends of the ribs. The cloth should also be glued to the ribs for safety. In the center of the lower plane surface there should be an opening 2 ft. wide and 4 ft. long for the body of the operator. Place the two main surfaces 4 ft. apart and connect with the 12 uprights, placed in the corner of each crosspiece and beam. The uprights are fastened by bolting to the crosspieces, as shown in Fig. 2. The whole structure is made strong and rigid by bracing with diagonal wires, both laterally and longitudinally.

The vertical rudder is to keep the machine headed into the wind and is not movable. This rudder is made of cloth stretched over a light wooden frame, which is nailed to the rudder sticks connecting to the main frame. The horizontal rudder is also made of cloth stretched over a light wooden frame, and arranged to intersect the vertical rudder at its center. This rudder is held in position and strengthened by diagonal wires and guy wires. The horizontal rudder is also immovable, and its function is to prevent the machine from diving, and also to keep it steady in its flight. The rudders are fastened to the glider by the two rudder sticks, and these sticks are held rigid by diagonal wires and also by guy wires leading to the sides of the main frames as shown in Fig. 1. The two arm sticks should be spaced about 13 in. apart and bolted to the long beams in the center of the opening in the lower plane where the operator is to take his position.

The glider should be examined to see

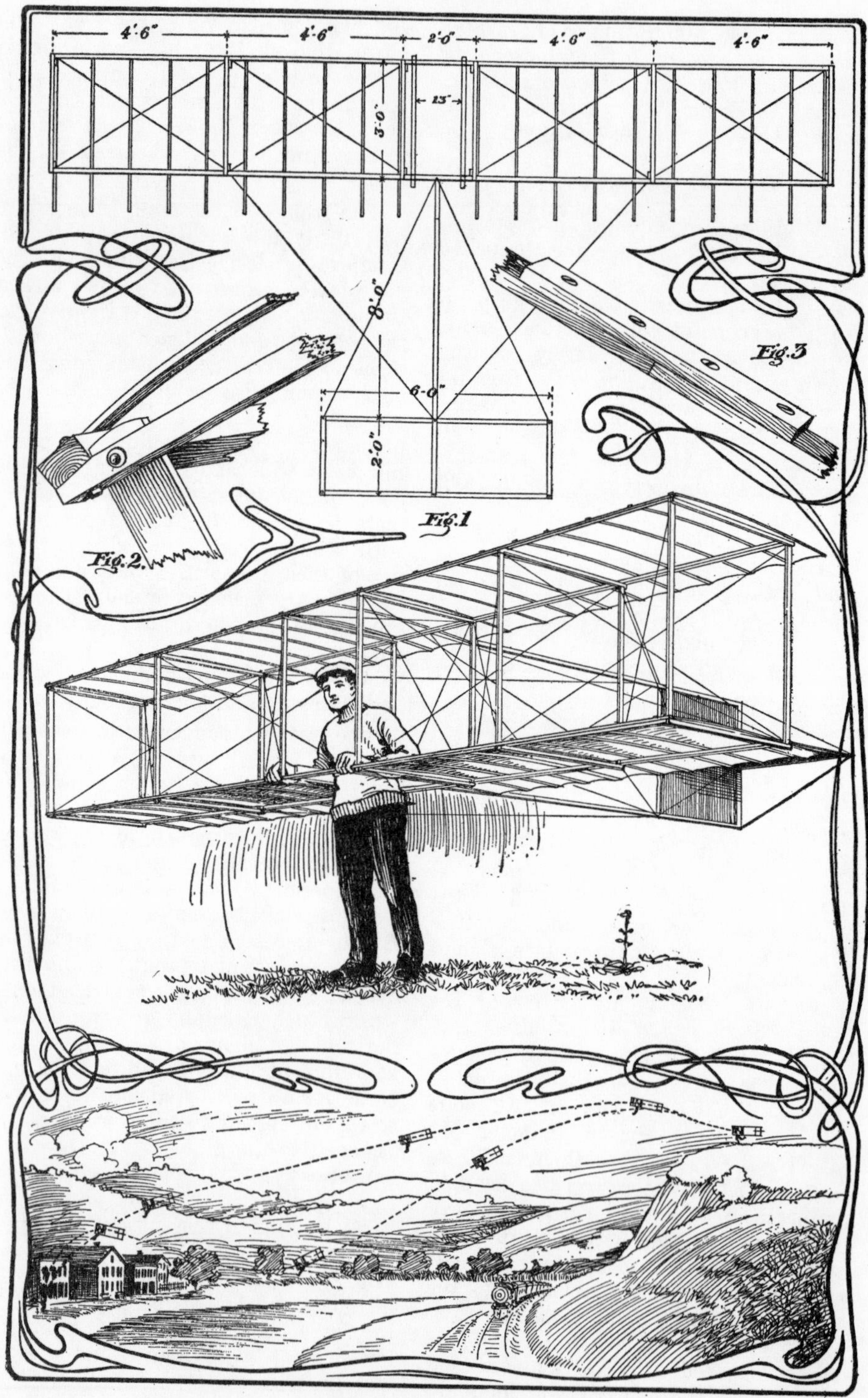

Details of the Glider

that the frame is not warped or twisted. The surfaces must be true or the machine will be hard to balance when in flight. To make a glide, take the glider to the top of a hill, get in between the arm sticks and lift the machine up until the arm sticks are under the arms as shown, run a few steps against the wind and leap from the ground. You will find that the machine has a surprising amount of lift, and if the weight of the body is in the right place you will go shooting down the hillside in free flight. The landing is made by pushing the weight of the body backwards. This will cause the glider to tip up in front, slacken speed and settle. The operator can then land safely and gently on his feet. Of course, the beginner should learn by taking short jumps, gradually increasing the distance as he gains skill and experience in balancing and landing.

The proper position of the body is slightly ahead of the center of the planes, but this must be found by experience. The machine should not be used in winds blowing faster than 15 miles an hour. Glides are always made against the wind, and the balancing is done by moving the legs. The higher the starting point the farther one may fly. Great care should be exercised in making landings, otherwise the operator might suffer a sprained ankle or perhaps a broken limb. The illustration shows two lines of flight from a hilltop, the glider travels on the upper line caused by the body of the operator taking a position a little back of the proper place, and on the lower line he changes his position from front to back while flying, which causes the dip in the line.

Boys Representing the Centaur

This is a diversion in which two boys personate a Centaur, a creature of Greek mythology, half man and half horse. One of the players stands erect and the other behind him in a stooping position with his hands upon the first player's hips, as shown in Fig. 1. The second player is covered over with a shawl or table cover which is pinned around the waist of the first player. A tail made of strips of cloth or paper is pinned to the rear end of the cover. The first player should hold a bow and arrow and have a cloak thrown loosely over his shoulder as shown in Fig. 2. Imitation hoofs of pasteboard may be made and fastened over the shoes.

Making Up the Centaur

Home-Made Ladle for Melting Babbitt

Secure a large sized old bicycle bell and rivet a heavy wire or strap iron on one side for a handle. When heated a little, hammer out the edge on one side for a lip to pour from. This makes a good ladle for melting small amounts of babbitt or lead.—Contributed by L. M. Olson, Bellingham, Wash.

How to Make a Flash Lamp

Indoor photographs are made much better with the use of a flashlight than by depending on light from windows. The lighting can be made from any direction to suit the operator. If lighting flash powder when not in a regular flash lamp the flash cannot be depended upon and in some instances is dangerous. To make a simple and inexpensive flash lamp, first secure from your druggist an empty salve box about 3 in. in diameter. While at the drug store get 3 ft. of small rubber tubing; this will cost about 15 cents. Now visit the tin shop and get a small piece of scrap tin 3 or 4 in. square; a piece of brass or steel wire, about the size of stove pipe wire, 14 in. long. These with a strip of light asbestos paper and some small iron wire, about the size of door screen wire, will complete the material list.

Carefully punch a hole through the salve box on one side near the bottom with a 10-penny nail. Cut a strip of tin 2 in. long and about $\frac{3}{8}$ in. wide and roll this around an 8-penny nail so as to form a small tube which will just fit the hole made in the salve box. Next roll up a strip of tin $\frac{1}{2}$ in. wide into a small cup about $\frac{3}{8}$ in. in diameter at one end and $\frac{1}{4}$ in. at the other.

Place the tube in the nail hole so that one end comes almost to the center of the box inside and the other end projects about $\frac{1}{2}$ in. outside the box. Cut out a little place for the tube to enter the cup at the small end and then solder the tube and cup to the bottom of the box as shown in the illustration. The tube and cup should be well soldered on the seams to make them airtight. Bend a ring on one end of the larger piece of wire, making it $2\frac{1}{2}$ in. in diameter and form the remaining portion of the wire into a spiral, soldering the end in the bottom of the box near the cup. Wrap the ring at the top of the spiral piece of wire all the way around with the strip of asbestos paper, wrapping them together over and over until the entire ring is covered. Slip the end of the rubber tube over the tin tube on the side of the box and the flash lamp is complete.

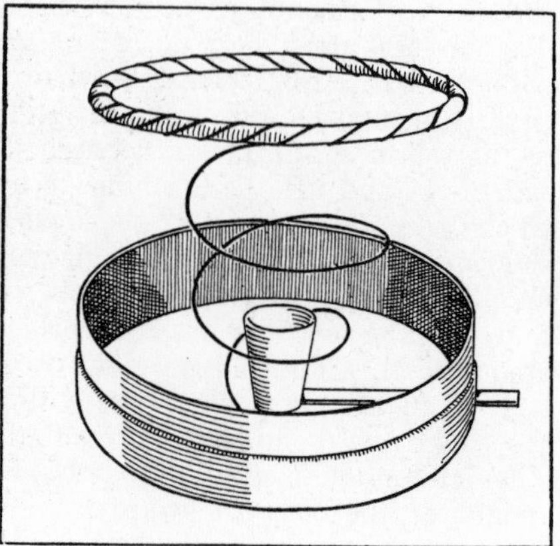

Made from a Tin Salve Box

To make a flash with this lamp fill the little cup in the center with flash powder and moisten the asbestos ring with alcohol. When all is ready for the picture the alcohol is lighted and a quick blow of the breath through the rubber tube will force the flash powder upward into the flame and cause the flash.

When through with the lamp place the cover over it, pushing the asbestos ring down inside the box. Wind the rubber tubing around the box and you have a neat outfit that can be carried in the pocket.

Photographing the New Moon

To make a photograph of the moon is quite difficult and no good picture can be made without an expensive apparatus. At home and with your own hand camera you can make a good picture of the new moon by the use of a flash light on a tennis ball, the tennis ball taking the part of the moon. The ball is suspended in front of a black cloth screen, the camera focused by holding a burning match near the ball and the exposure made by burning a

Tennis Ball Photographed

small quantity of flash powder at one side and a little below the ball. The light from the flash only striking one side of the ball gives the effect of the new moon.—Photo by M. M. Hunting, Dayton, O.

Old-Time Magic—Part II

Removing Scissors from a Cord

A piece of strong cord is doubled and fastened to a pair of scissors with a slip knot, as shown in Fig. 1. After passing the ends of the cord through the thumb hole of the scissors they are tied fast to a chair, door knob or any other object that may be of sufficient size to make the ends secure. The trick is to release the scissors without cutting the cord.

Take hold of the loop end of the cord in the lower handle and drawing it first through the upper handle and then completely over the blades of the scissors, as shown in Fig. 2. This is very simple when you know how, but puzzling when the trick is first seen.

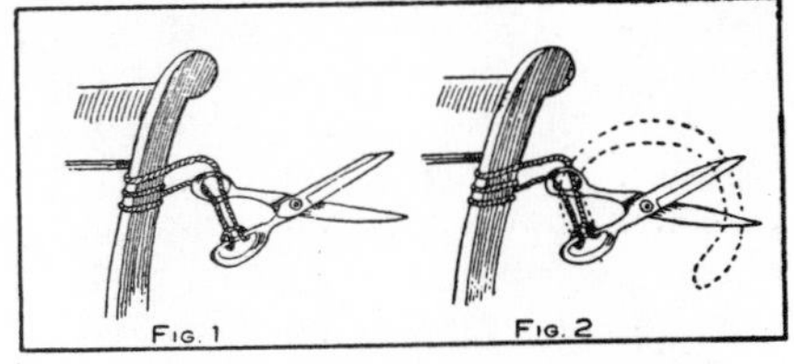

How the Scissors Are Removed

Coin and Card on the First Finger

This is a simple trick that many can do at the first attempt, while others will fail time after time. It is a good trick to spring upon a company casually if you have practiced it beforehand. A playing card is balanced on the tip of the forefinger and a penny placed on top immediately over the finger end, as shown in the sketch. With the right-hand forefinger and thumb strike the edge of the card sharply. If done properly the card will fly away, leaving the penny poised on the finger end.

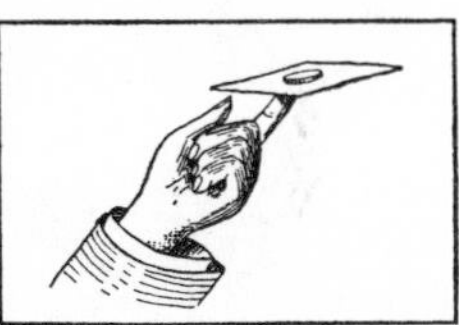

How to Make Sealing Wax Hat Pins

Select a stick of sealing wax of the desired color for the foundation of the hat pin. Hold the end of the stick over a flame until the wax is soft enough to drop; then put it on the hat-pin head. When sufficient wax has adhered to the pin, hold the lump over the flame, revolving the pin at the same time so the wax will not drop and the head will form a round ball. The head can be made in any shape desired while warm. When the desired shape has been obtained, cool thoroughly in cold water and dry carefully.

Stripes and designs may be put on the foundation by applying drops of other brilliant colored wax, and by careful manipulation the wax when warm can be made to flow around the pin head and form pretty stripes and designs. If a certain color is to be more prominent, the wax to make this color must be applied last and the pin put through the flame again. Cool in water and dry, as before, and pass once more through the flame to obtain the lustre.

Old-Time Magic—Part III

Disappearing Coin

While this is purely a sleight-of-hand trick, it will take very little practice to cause the coin to disappear instantly. Take a quarter of a dollar between the thumb and finger, as shown, and by a rapid twist of the fingers whirl the coin and at the same time close the hand, and the coin will disappear up your coat sleeve. On opening the hand the coin will not be seen. Take three quarters and hold one in the palm of the left hand, place the other two, one between the thumb and finger of each hand, then give the coin in the right hand a whirl, as described, closing both hands quickly. The coin in the right hand will disappear up your sleeve, and the left hand on being unclosed will contain two quarters, while the one in the right shall have disappeared.

Sticking a Coin Against the Wall

Cut a small notch in a coin—ten-cent piece or quarter will do—so a small point will project. When this is pressed firmly against a wood casing or partition the coin will stick tightly.

A Chinese Outdoor Game

The accompanying illustration shows the "grand whirl," or the Chinese students' favorite game. This game is played by five persons, four of them turning around the fifth or central figure with their arms locked about each other and the two outside persons swinging in midair with their bodies almost horizontal.

Chinese Doing the Grand Whirl

Home-Made Photograph of a Lightning Flash

How many times has each amateur photographer tried to photograph the lightning's flash? Some good pictures have been obtained by a ceaseless effort on the part of the operator. Here is a method by which you can make a picture of a streak of lightning on a clear night in your own house. Paste two strips of black paper on a piece of glass that is 10 in. square so as to leave a clear space through the center 2 in. or more in width. Smoke this uncovered space over a candle's flame until the soot is thick enough to prevent light passing through. Take a sharp lead pencil and outline a flash of lightning upon the smoked surface, using a fine needle to make the smaller lines, and then set the glass up against the back of two boxes which are set to have a space between them of 4 or 5 in.

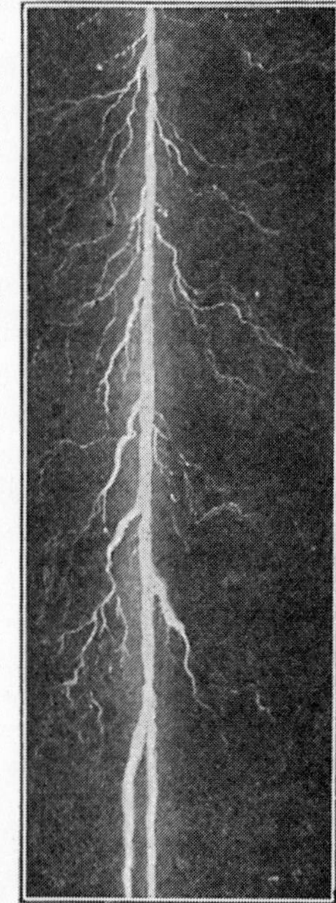

A lighted candle is held behind the glass so the light will shine through for focusing the camera. After darkening the room set your camera ready for the exposure and burn a small quantity of flash light powder in the same place in which the candle was held. This will make an impression upon the plate of the flash drawn on the smoked glass.

How to Make a Static Machine

Static electricity is produced by revolving glass plates upon which a number of sectors are cemented; these sectors, passing through neutralizing brushes, distribute electric charges to collecting combs attached to discharging rods. The glass selected for the plates must be clear white glass, free from wrinkles, and of a uniform thickness. Two plates are necessary to make this machine, and the glass should be of sufficient size to cut a circular plate 16 in. in diameter. A hole must be made exactly in the center of each plate, and this should be done before cutting the circle. One of the best ways to make the hole is to drill the glass with a very hard-tempered drill, the cutting edge of which should be kept moistened with 2 parts turpentine and 1 part sweet oil while drilling. The hole is to be made ¾ in. in diameter. The circle is then marked on each plate and cut with a glass cutter. The plates are trued up, after they are mounted, by holding a piece of emery wheel to the edges while they are turning. Water should be applied to the edges while doing the work.

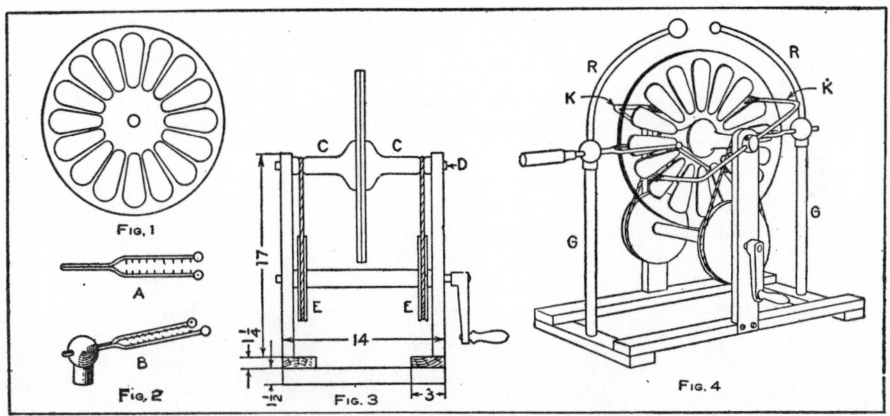

Details of a Homemade Static Machine

The sectors are cut from tinfoil, 1½ in. wide at one end, ¾ in. at the other, and 4 in. long. A thin coat of shellac varnish is applied to both sides of the plates, and 16 sectors put on one side of each plate, as shown in Fig. 1. The divisions can be marked on the opposite side of the plate and a circle drawn as a guide to place the sectors at proper intervals.

The sectors should lie flat on the glass with all parts smoothed out so that they will not be torn from their places as the plates revolve. The shellac should be tacky when the pieces of tinfoil are put in place.

The collectors are made, as shown in Fig. 2, from about ¼-in. copper wire with two brass balls soldered to the ends. The fork part is 6 in. long and the shank 4 in. Holes are drilled on the inside of the forks, and pins inserted and soldered. These pins, or teeth, should be long enough to be very close to the sectors and yet not scratch them when the plates are turning.

The frame of the machine is made from any kind of finished wood with dimensions shown in Fig. 3, the side pieces being 24 in. long and the standards 3 in. wide. The two pieces, C C, Fig. 3, are made from solid, close-grained wood turned in the shape shown, with the face that rests against the plate 4 in. in diameter, and the outer end 1½ in. in diameter, the smaller end being turned with a groove for a round belt. Before turning the pieces a hole is bored through each piece for the center, and this hole must be of such a size as to take a brass tube that has an internal diameter of $\frac{3}{4}$ in. The turned pieces are glued to the glass plates over the center holes and on the same side on which the sectors are fastened. Several hours' time will be required for the glue to set. A fiber washer is then put between the plates and a brass tube axle placed through the hole. The plates, turned wood pieces, and brass axle turn on a stationary axle, D.

The drive wheels, EE, are made from $\frac{7}{8}$-in. material 7 in. in diameter, and are fastened on a round axle cut from a broom handle. This wood axle is centrally bored to admit a metal rod tightly, and extends through the standards with a crank attached to one end.

Two solid glass rods, GG, Fig. 4, 1 in. in diameter and 15 in. long, are fitted in holes bored into the end pieces of the frame. Two pieces of 1-in. brass tubing and the discharging rods, RR, are soldered into two hollow brass balls 2 or $2\frac{1}{2}$ in. in diameter. The shanks of the collectors are fitted in these brass balls with the ends extending, to which insulating handles are attached. Brass balls are soldered to the upper ends of the discharging rods, one having a 2-in. ball and the other one $\frac{3}{4}$ in. in diameter.

Caps made from brass are fitted tightly on the ends of the stationary shaft, D, and drilled through their diameter to admit heavy copper rods, KK, which are bent as shown. Tinsel or fine wire such as contained in flexible electric wire are soldered to the ends of these rods, and the brushes thus made must be adjusted so they will just touch the plates. The caps are fitted with screws for adjusting the brushes. These rods and brushes are called the neutralizers. A little experimenting will enable one to properly locate the position of the neutralizers for best results.—Contributed by C. Lloyd Enos, Colorado City, Colo.

A Concrete Swimming Pool

Several boys from a neighborhood in the suburbs of a large city concluded to make for themselves a swimming tank of concrete. The money was raised by various means to purchase the cement, and the work was done by themselves. The ground was selected in a secluded spot in a neighbor's back yard and a hole dug to a depth of 4 ft., 12 ft. wide and 22 ft. long. The concrete was made by mixing 1 part cement, 4 parts sand and 10 parts gravel together and the bulk moistened with water. The bottom was made the same as laying a sidewalk, and forms were only used for the inside of the surrounding wall. The tank may be hidden with shrubbery or vines planted to grow over a poultry wire fence.

Home-Made Swimming Pool

Old-Time Magic—Part IV

Cutting a Thread Inside of a Glass Bottle

This is a trick which can only be performed when the sun shines, but it

The Glass Directs the Sun's Rays

is a good one. Procure a clear glass bottle and stick a pin in the lower end of the cork. Attach a thread to the pin and tie a small weight to the end of the thread so it will hang inside the bottle when the cork is in place. Inform your audience that you will sever the thread and cause the weight to drop without removing the cork.

All that is required to perform the feat is to hold a magnifying glass so as to direct the sun's rays on the thread. The thread will quickly burn and the weight fall.

Removing a Key from a Double String

Tie the ends of a 5-ft. string together, making a double line on which a key is placed and the string held as shown by the dotted lines in the sketch. Turn the palms of the hands toward you and reach over with the little finger of the right hand and take hold of the inside line near the left-hand thumb. Reverse the operation and take hold of the inside line near right-hand thumb with the little finger of the left hand. You will then have the string as it appears in the sketch. Quickly let loose of the string with a little finger on one hand and a thumb on the other and pull the string taut. The key will drop from the string.

How to Bore a Square Hole

You would not consider it possible to bore a square hole in a piece of cardboard, yet such a thing can be done. Take a cardboard or a thin piece of wood, fold and place it between two pieces of board with the fold up; the boards are then put in a vise as shown. Start the bit with the screw point in the fold, using a 1-in. bit, and bore a

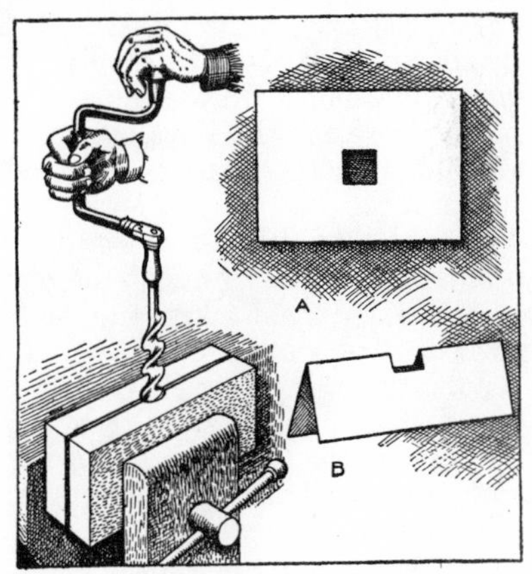

Boring a Square Hole

hole $\frac{1}{2}$ in. deep. When the cardboard is taken from the vise it will appear as shown at B and when unfolded, as at A.

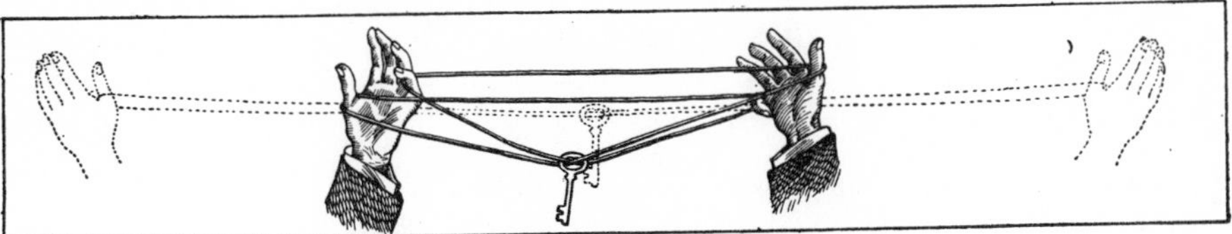

"The Key Will Drop from the String"

HOW TO MAKE COPPER TRAYS

Copper trays such as are shown in the accompanying illustration are very useful as well as ornamental about the house. They can be used to keep pins and needles, pens and pencils, or cigar ashes, etc. They are easily made, require no equipment in the way of tools except what are usually found about the house, unless it would be the metal shears, and when the decorations are well designed and the metal nicely colored, they make attractive little pieces to have about.

The first thing to do in preparation for making them is to prepare the design. Simple designs work out better than fussy ones and are more likely to be within the ability of the amateur. Having determined the size of the tray, draw on paper an oblong to represent it. Inside this oblong draw another one to represent the lines along which the metal is to be bent up to form the sides. Inside this there should be drawn still another oblong to represent the margin up to which the background is to be worked. The trays shown are $5\frac{3}{4}$ by $6\frac{3}{4}$ in., the small ash tray 4 by 4 in., the long pen and pencil tray $4\frac{3}{4}$ by $9\frac{1}{2}$ in. The second oblong was $\frac{3}{4}$ in. inside the first on all, and the third one $\frac{1}{4}$ in. inside the second on all.

If the decoration is to have two parts alike—symmetrical—divide the space with a line down the middle. Draw one-half the design free hand, then fold along this line and trace the second half from this one. If the lines have been drawn with soft pencil, rubbing the back of the paper with a knife handle will force enough of the lead to the second side so that the outline can be determined. Four-part symmetry will require two lines and two foldings, etc.

For the metal working there will be needed a pair of tin shears, two spikes, file, flat and round-nosed pliers, screwdriver and sheet copper of No. 23 gauge. Proceed as follows: 1. Cut off a piece of copper so that it shall have $\frac{1}{2}$ in. extra metal on each of the four sides. 2. With a piece of carbon paper trace upon the copper lines that

Articles Made from Copper

shall represent the margin of the tray proper and the lines along which the upturned sides of the tray are to be bent; also trace the decorative design. 3. With a nail make a series of holes in the extra margin, about $\frac{3}{4}$ in. apart and large enough to take in a $\frac{3}{4}$-in. slim screw. 4. Fasten the metal to a thick board by inserting screws in these holes. 5. With a 20-penny wire nail that has the sharpness of its point filed off, stamp the background promiscuously. By holding the nail about $\frac{1}{4}$ in. above the work and striking it with the hammer, at the same time striving to keep it at $\frac{1}{4}$ in. above the metal, very rapid progress can be made. This stamping lowers the background and at the same time raises the design. 6. Chase or stamp along the border of the design and background, using a nail filed to chisel edge. This is to make a clean, sharp division between background and design. 7. When the stamping is completed, remove the screws and the metal from the board and cut off the extra margin with the metal shears. File the edges until they are smooth to the touch. 8. With the flat pliers "raise" one side of the tray, then the other side. 9. Raise the ends, adjusting the corners as shown in the illustration. Use the round-nosed pliers for this purpose.

Copper is frequently treated chemically to give it color. Very pretty effects may be obtained by covering the tray with turpentine, then moving it about over a flame such as a bunsen burner until the turpentine burns off. The copper will "take on" almost all the colors of a rainbow, and the effect will be most pleasing.

Photograph of a Clown Face

At first glance the accompanying photograph will appear as if the person photographed is wearing a false face or has his face painted like a clown. On close observation you will notice that the face is made on the bald head of the person sitting behind the table. The eyes, nose and mouth are cut from black paper and pasted on the bald spot. The subject's face is horizontal and resting upon his hands.

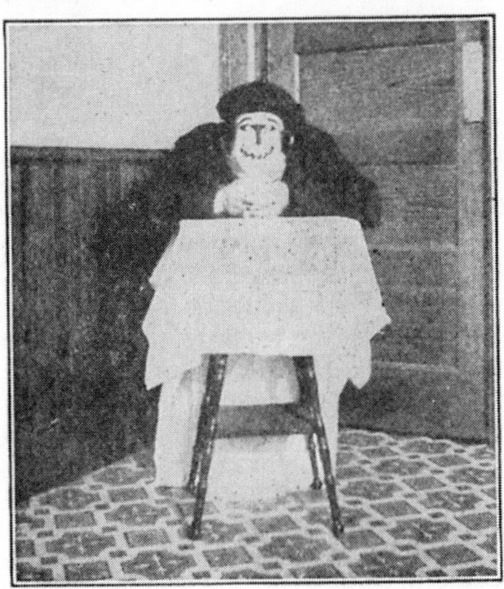

A Bald Head Photographed

Finger Mathematics

By Charles C. Bradley

All machinists use mathematics. Ask a machinist what would be the product of 9 times 8 and his ready reply would be 72, but change the figures a little and say 49 times 48 and the chances are that instead of replying at once he will have to figure it out with a pencil. By using the following method it is just as easy to tell at a glance what 99 times 99 are as 9 times 9. You will be able to multiply far beyond your most sanguine expectations.

In the first numbering, begin by holding your hands with the palms toward the body and make imaginary numbers on the thumbs and fingers as follows: Thumbs, 6; first fingers, 7; second fingers, 8; third fingers, 9, and fourth fingers, 10. Suppose you desire to multiply 8 by 9, put the eighth finger on one hand against the ninth finger of the other hand as shown.

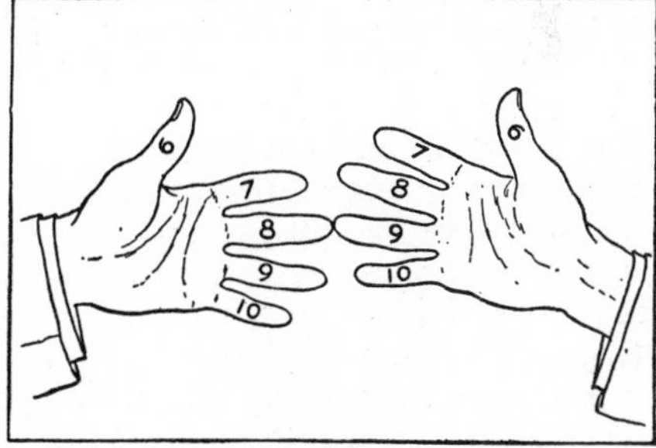

"8 Times 9"

The two joined fingers and all the fingers above them (calling the thumbs fingers) are called the upper fingers and each has a value of ten, which tens are added. All the fingers below the joined fingers are termed the lower fingers, and each of the lower fingers represents a unit value of one. The sum of the units on one hand should be multiplied by the sum of the units on the other hand. The total tens added to this last named sum will give the product desired. Thus: Referring to above picture or to your hands we find three tens on the left hand and four tens on the right, which would be 70. We also find two units on the left hand and one on the right. Two times one are two, and 70 plus 2 equals 72, or the product of 8 times 9.

Supposing 6 times 6 were the figures. Put your thumbs together; there are no fingers above, so the two thumbs represent two tens or 20; below the thumbs are four units on each hand, which would be 16, and 20 plus 16 equals 36, or the product of 6 times 6.

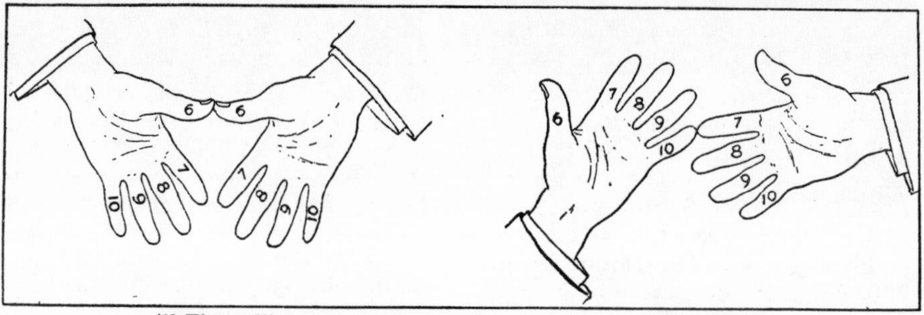

"6 Times 6" "10 Times 7"

Supposing 10 times 7 is desired. Put the little finger of the left hand against the first finger of the right hand. At a glance you see seven tens or 70. On the right hand you have three units and on the left nothing. Three times nothing gives you nothing and 70 plus nothing is 70.

In the second numbering, or numbers above 10, renumber your fingers; thumbs, 11; first fingers, 12, etc. Let us multiply 12 by 12.

Put together the tips of the fingers labeled 12. At a glance you see four tens or 40. At this point we leave the method explained in Case 1 and ignore the units (lower fingers) altogether. We go back to the upper fingers again

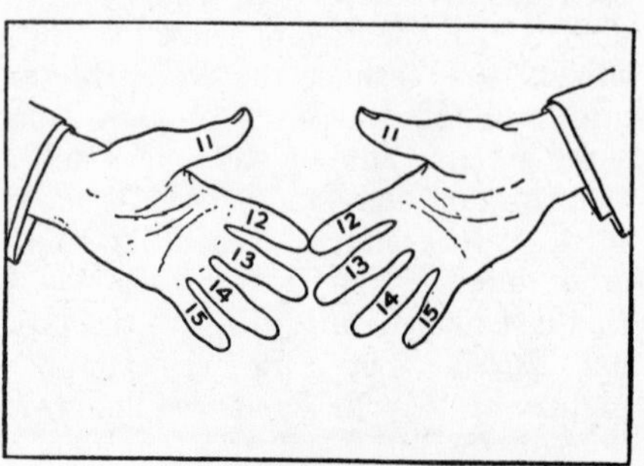

"12 Times 12"

and multiply the number of upper fingers used on the one hand by the number of upper fingers used on the other hand, viz., 2 times 2 equals 4. Adding 4 to 40 gives us 44. We now add 100 (because anything over 10 times 10 would make over 100) and we have 144, the product of 12 times 12.

The addition of 100 is arbitrary, but being simple it saves time and trouble. Still, if we wish, we might regard the four upper fingers in the above example as four twenties, or 80, and the six lower fingers as six tens, or 60; then returning to the upper fingers and multiplying the two on the right hand by the two on the left we would have 4; hence 80 plus 60 plus 4 equals 144; therefore the rule of adding the lump sum is much the quicker and easier method.

Above 10 times 10 the lump sum to add is 100; above 15 times 15 it is 200; above 20 times 20, 400; 25 times 25, 600, etc., etc., as high as you want to go.

In the third numbering to multiply above 15 renumber your fingers, beginning the thumbs with 16, first finger 17, and so on. Oppose the proper finger tips as before, the upper fingers representing a value of 20. Proceed as in the first numbering and add 200. Take for example 18 times 18.

At a glance we see six twenties plus 2 units on left hand times 2 units on right hand plus 200 equals 324.

In the fourth numbering the fingers are marked, thumbs, 21, first fingers 22, etc., the value of the upper fingers being 20. Proceed as in the second numbering, adding 400 instead of 100.

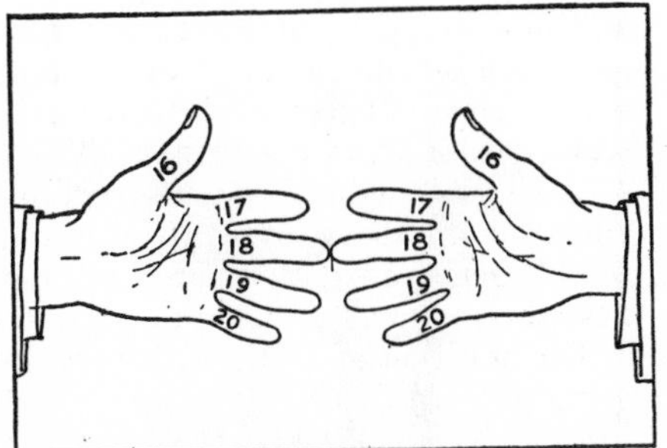

"18 Times 18"

Above 25 times 25 the upper fingers represent a value of 30 each and after proceeding as in the third numbering you add 600 instead of 200.

This system can be carried as high as you want to go, but you must remember that for figures ending in 1, 2, 3, 4 and 5 proceed as in the second numbering. For figures ending in 6, 7, 8, 9 and 10 the third numbering applies.

Determine the value of the upper fingers whether they represent tens, twenties, thirties, forties, or what. For example, any two figures between 45 and 55, the value of the upper fingers would be 50, which is the half-way point between the two fives. In 82 times 84 the value of the upper fingers would be 80 (the half-way point between the two fives, 75 and 85, being 80). And the lump sum to add.

Just three things to remember: Which numbering is to follow, whether the one described in second or third numbering; the value which the upper fingers have; and, lastly, the lump sum to add, and you will be able to multiply faster and more accurately than you ever dreamed of before.

Optical Illusions

If a person observes fixedly for some time two balls hanging on the end of cords which are in rapid revolution, not rotation, about a vertical axis, the direction of revolution will seem to reverse. In some experiments two incandescent "pills" of platinum sponge, such as are used for lighting gas-burners, were hung in tiny aluminum bells from a mica vane wheel which was turned constantly and rapidly in one direction by hot air from a gas flame to keep the platinum in a glow. The inversion and reversion did not take place, as one might suppose, at the will of the observer, but was compulsory and followed regular rules. If the observer watches the rotating objects from the side, or from above or from below, the inversion takes place against his will; the condition being that the image on the retina shall be eccentric. It takes place also, however, with a change in the convergence of the optical axes, whether they are parallel to each other or more convergent. Also when the image on the retina is made less distinct by the use of a convex or concave lens, the revolution seems to reverse; further, in the case of a nearsighted person, when he removes his spectacles, inver-

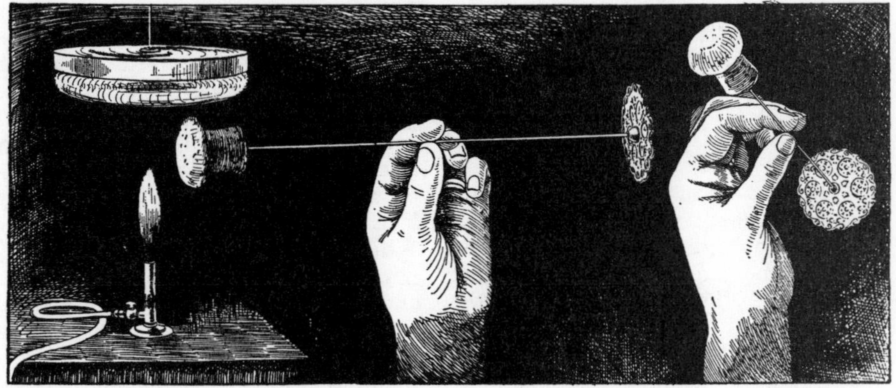

Illusions Shown by Revolving Platinum Sponge "Pills" and Hat Pins

sion results every time that the image on the retina is not sharp. But even a change in the degree of indistinctness causes inversion.

The cause of this optical illusion is the same where the wings of windmills are observed in the twilight as a silhouette. It is then not a question of which is the front or the back of the wheel, but whether one of the wings or the other comes towards the observer. The experiment is made more simple by taking a hat pin with a conspicuous head, holding it firmly in a horizontal position, and putting a cork on the point. Looking at it in semi-darkness, one seems to see sometimes the head of the pin, sometimes the point towards him, when he knows which direction is right. The inversion will be continued as soon as one observes fixedly a point at the side. Here it is a question of the perception of depth or distance; and this is the same in the case of the rotating balls; the direction of seeming revolution depends on which one of them one considers to be the front one and which the rear one.

From the foregoing the following conclusion may be reached: When, in the case of a perception remitting two appearances, one fixedly observes one of these and then permits or causes change in the sharpness of the image on the retina, the other appearance asserts itself.

Steam Engine Made from Gas Pipe and Fittings

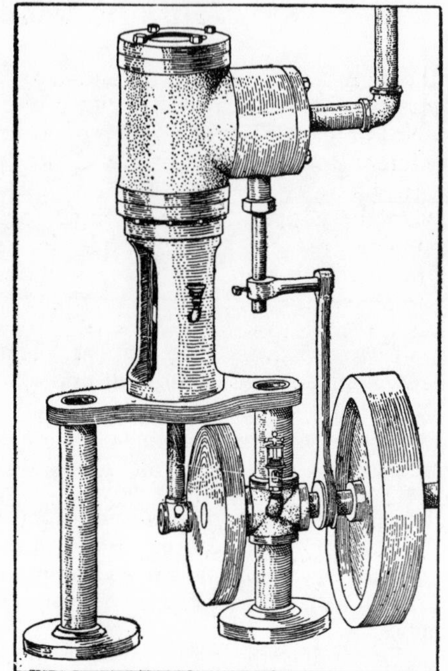

The Engine Is About 20 Inches High

Almost all the material used in the construction of the parts for the small steam engine illustrated herewith was made from gas pipe and fittings. The cylinder consists of a 3-in. tee, the third opening being threaded and filled with a cast-iron plug turned to such a depth that when the interior was bored out on a lathe the bottom of the plug bored to the same radius as the other part of the tee. The outside end of the plug extended about $\frac{1}{4}$-in. and the surface was made smooth for the valve seat. A flat slide valve was used.

The ports were not easy to make, as they had to be drilled and chipped out. The steam chest is round, as it had to be made to fit the round tee connection. The crosshead runs in guides made from a piece of gas pipe with the sides cut out and threads cut on both ends. One end is screwed into a rim turned on the cylinder head and the other is fitted into an oblong plate. Both ends of this plate were drilled and tapped to receive $1\frac{1}{2}$-in. pipe.

The main frame consists of one $1\frac{1}{2}$-in. pipe 10 in. long and one made up from two pieces of pipe and a cross to make the whole length 10 in. These pipes were then screwed into pipe flanges that served as a base. The open part of the cross was babbitted to receive the main shaft. The end of the shaft has a pillow block to take a part of the strain from the main bearing. The eccentric is constructed of washers. While this engine does not give much power, it is easily built, inexpensive, and any one with a little mechanical ability can make one by closely following out the construction as shown in the illustration.—Contributed by W. H. Kutscher, Springfield, Ill.

How to Make a Copper Bowl

To make a copper bowl, such as is shown in the illustration, secure a piece of No. 21 gauge sheet copper of a size sufficient to make a circular disk 6½ in. in diameter.

Cut the copper to the circular form and size just mentioned, and file the edge so that it will be smooth and free from sharp places. With a pencil compass put on a series of concentric rings about ½ in. apart. These are to aid the eye in beating the bowl to form.

The tools are simple and can be made easily. First make a round-nosed mallet of some hard wood, which should have a diameter of about 1¼ in. across the head. If nothing better is at hand, saw off a section of a broom handle, round one end and insert a handle into a hole bored in its middle. Next take a block of wood, about 3 by 3 by 6 in., and make in one end a hollow, about 2 in. across and ½ in. deep. Fasten the block solidly, as in a vise, and while holding the copper on the hollowed end of the block, beat with the mallet along the concentric rings.

Begin at the center and work along the rings—giving the copper a circular movement as the beating proceeds—out toward the rim. Continue the circular movement and work from the rim back toward the center. This operation is to be continued until the bowl has the shape desired, when the bottom is flattened by placing the bowl, bottom side up, on a flat surface and beating the raised part flat.

Beating copper tends to harden it and, if continued too long without proper treatment, will cause the metal to break. To overcome this hardness, heat the copper over a bed of coals or a Bunsen burner to a good heat. This process is called annealing, as it softens the metal.

The appearance of a bowl is greatly enhanced by the addition of a border. In the illustration the border design shown was laid out in pencil, a small hole was drilled with a band drill in each space and a small-bladed metal saw inserted and the part sawed out.

To produce color effects on copper, cover the copper with turpentine and

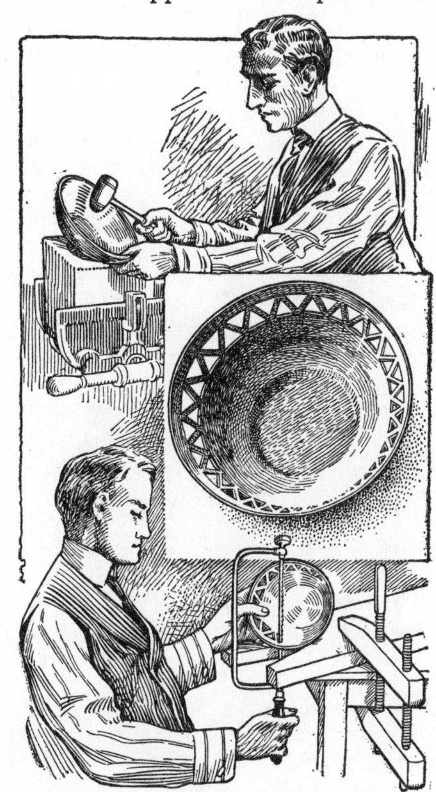

Shaping the Bowl and Sawing the Lace

hold over a Bunsen burner until all parts are well heated.

Cleaning Furniture

After cleaning furniture, the greasy appearance may be removed by adding some good, sharp vinegar to the furniture polish. Vinegar, which is nothing else than diluted acetic acid, is one of the best cleansers of dirty furniture.

Melting Lead in Tissue Paper

Take a buckshot, wrap it tightly in one thickness of tissue paper, and, holding the ends of the paper in the fingers of each hand, place the part that holds the shot over the flame of a match just far enough away from the flame not to burn the paper. In a few seconds unfold the paper and you will find that the shot has melted without even scorching the paper.—Contributed by W. O. Hay, Camden, S. C.

The Principles of the Stereograph

Each of our eyes sees a different picture of any object; the one sees a trifle more to the right-hand side, the other to the left, especially when the object is near to the observer. The stereoscope is the instrument which effects this result by bringing the two pictures together in the senses. The stereograph produces this result in another way than by prisms as in the stereoscope. In the first place there is

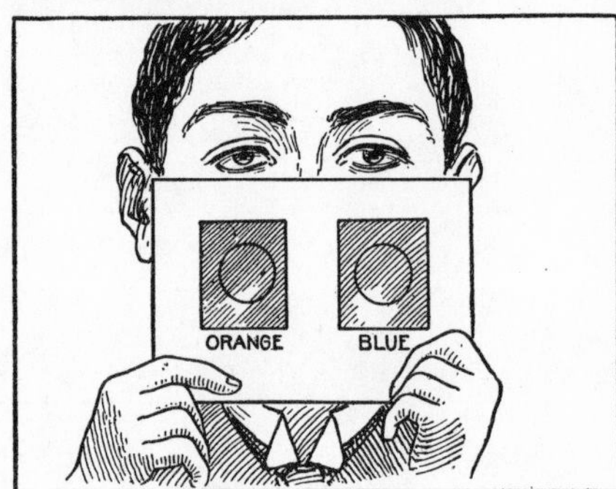

Looking Through the Colored Gelatine

only one picture, not two mounted side by side. The stereograph consists of a piece of card, having therein two circular openings about 1¼ in. diameter, at a distance apart corresponding to the distance between the centers of the pupils. The openings are covered with transparent gelatine, the one for the left eye being blue, that for the right, orange. The picture is viewed at a distance of about 7 in. from the stereograph. As a result of looking at it through the stereograph, one sees a colorless black and white picture which stands out from the background. Try looking at the front cover of Popular Mechanics through these colored gelatine openings and the effect will be produced.

If one looks at the picture first with the right eye alone through the orange glass, and then with the left eye through the blue glass, one will understand the principle on which the little instrument works. Looking through the blue glass with the left eye, one sees only those portions which are red on the picture. But they seem black. The reason is that the red rays are absorbed by the blue filter. Through the orange gelatine all the white portions of the picture seem orange, because of the rays coming from them, and which contain all the colors of the spectrum; only the orange rays may pass through. The red portions of the picture are not seen, because, although they pass through the screen, they are not seen against the red ground of the picture. It is just as though they were not there. The left eye therefore sees a black picture on a red background.

In the same way the right eye sees through the orange screen only a black picture on a red background; this black image consisting only of the blue portions of the picture.

Any other part of complementary colors than blue and orange, as for instance red and green, would serve the same purpose.

The principle on which the stereograph works may be demonstrated by a very simple experiment. On white paper one makes a picture or mark with a red pencil. Looking at this through a green glass it appears black on a green ground; looking at it through a red glass of exactly the same color as the picture, it, however, disappears fully.

Through the glass one will see only a regular surface of the color of the glass itself, and without any picture. Through a red glass a green picture will appear black.

So with the stereograph; each eye sees a black picture representing one of the pictures given by the stereoscope; the only difference being that in the case of the stereograph the background for each eye is colored; while both eyes together see a white background.

In the pictures the red and the green lines and dots must not coincide; neither can they be very far apart in order to produce the desired result. In order that the picture shall be "plastic," which increases the sense of depth and shows the effect of distance in the picture, they must be a very trifle apart. The arrangement of the two pictures can be so that one sees the pictures either in front of or on the back of the card on which they are printed. In order to make them appear before the card, the left eye sees through a blue screen, but the red picture which is seen by it is a black one, and lies to the right on the picture; and the right eye sees the left-hand picture. The further apart the pictures are, the further from the card will the composite image appear.

In the manufacture of a stereoscope the difficulty is in the proper arrangement of the prisms; with the stereograph, in the proper choice of colors.

Mercury Make-and-Break Connections for Induction Coils

Induction coils operating on low voltage have a make-and-break connection called the "buzzer" to increase the secondary discharge. Two types of make-and-break connection are used, the common "buzzer" operated by the magnetism of the core in the coil and the mercury break operated by a small motor. The sketch herewith shows how to make the motor-operated break. Two blocks of wood are nailed together in the shape of an L and a small motor fastened to the top of the vertical piece. The shaft of the motor is bent about $\frac{1}{8}$ in. in the shape of a crank, so that in turning it will describe a circle $\frac{1}{4}$ in. in diameter. A small connecting bar is cut from a piece of brass $\frac{1}{8}$ in. thick, $\frac{1}{4}$ in. wide and 1 in. long and a hole drilled in each end; one hole to fit the motor shaft and the other to slip on a No. 12 gauge wire. Two L-shaped pieces of brass are fastened to the side of the block and drilled with holes of such a size that a No. 12 gauge wire will slip through snugly. Place a No. 12 gauge wire in these holes and bend the top end at right angles.

Motor-Driven Make-and-Break

Put the connecting brass bar on the motor shaft with washers fitted tight on each side and slip the other end over the bent end of the wire. Have the wire plenty long so it can be cut to the proper length when the parts are all in place. A small round bottle about $\frac{1}{2}$ in. in diameter is now fitted in a hole that has been previously bored into the middle of the bottom block and close up to the vertical piece. This should only be bored about half way through the block. The wire is now cut so at the length of the stroke the end will come to about one-half the depth, or the middle of the bottle.

Fill the bottle with mercury to a point so that when the motor is running, the end of the wire will be in the mercury for about one-half of the stroke. Cover the mercury over with a little alcohol. A No. 14 gauge iron wire is bent and put into the side of the bottle with the end extending to the bottom. The other end of this wire is attached to one binding-post placed at the end of the bottom block. The other binding-post is connected to a small brass brush attached to the side of the vertical piece, which is placed with some pressure on the moving wire. The motor can be run with a current from a separate course or connected as shown on the same batteries with the coil. The proper height of the mercury can be regulated for best results. The motor must run continuous if the coil is used for writing code signals, wireless, etc.—Contributed by Haraden Pratt, San Francisco, Cal.

How to Make a Barometer

Atmospheric pressure is measured by the barometer. The weight of the air in round numbers is 15 lb. to the square inch and will support a column of water 1 in. square, 34 ft. high, or a column of mercury (density 13.6) 1 in. square, 30 in. high.

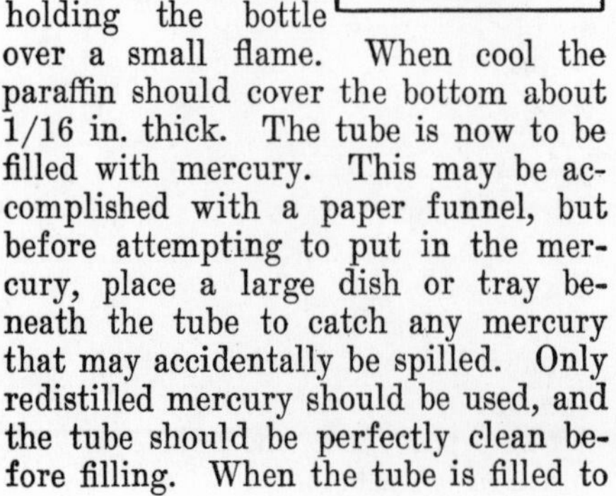

The parts necessary to make a simple barometer are, a glass tube $\frac{1}{8}$ in. internal diameter and about 34 in. long, a bottle 1 in. inside diameter and 2 in. high. Seal one end of the tube by holding it in the flame of a gas burner, which will soon soften the glass so it can be pinched together with pliers. Put a little paraffin in the bottle and melt it by holding the bottle over a small flame. When cool the paraffin should cover the bottom about 1/16 in. thick. The tube is now to be filled with mercury. This may be accomplished with a paper funnel, but before attempting to put in the mercury, place a large dish or tray beneath the tube to catch any mercury that may accidentally be spilled. Only redistilled mercury should be used, and the tube should be perfectly clean before filling. When the tube is filled to within 1 in. of the open end place the forefinger over the hole and tilt the tube up and down so all the air will gather at the finger end. The filling is continued until the tube is full of mercury. The glass bottle containing the wax covered bottom is now placed over the end of the tube and pressed firmly to insure an airtight fit with the tube. The bottle and tube are inverted and after a few ounces of mercury are put in the bottle the tube may be raised out of the wax, but be careful not to bring its edge above the surface of the mercury.

The instrument is put aside while the base is being made, or, if you choose, have the base ready to receive the parts just described when they are completed. Cut a base from a piece of $\frac{7}{8}$-in. pine 3 in. wide and 40 in. long. In this base cut a groove to fit the tube and the space to be occupied by the bottle is hollowed out with a chisel to a depth of $\frac{3}{4}$ in., so the bottle rests on one-half of its diameter above the surface of the board and one-half below. The instrument is made secure to the base with brass strips tacked on as shown in the sketch. After the instrument is in place put enough mercury in the bottle so the depth of the mercury above the bottom end of the tube will be about $\frac{1}{2}$ in.

The scale is made on a piece of cardboard 2 in. wide and 4 in. long. The 4 in. are marked off and divided into sixteenths, and the inches numbered 27 up to 31. The scale is fastened to the base with glue or tacks and in the position behind the tube as shown in the sketch. Before fastening the scale, the instrument should be compared with a standard barometer and the scale adjusted so both readings are the same. But if a standard barometer is not available, the instrument, if accurately constructed, will calibrate itself.

In general, a drop in the mercury indicates a storm and bad weather, while a rise indicates fair weather and in winter a frost. Sudden changes in the barometer are followed by like changes in weather. The slow rise of the mercury predicts fair weather, and a slow fall, the contrary. During the frosty days the drop of the mercury is followed by a thaw and a rise indicates snow.

Home-Made Post or Swinging Light

Remove the bottom from a round bottle of sufficient size to admit a wax or tallow candle. This can be done with a glass cutter or a hot ring the size of the outside of the bottle, which is slipped quickly over the end. Procure a metal can cover, a cover from a baking powder can will do, and fit it on the end where the bottom was removed. The cover is punched full of holes to admit the air and a cross cut in the center with the four wings thus made by the cutting turned up to form a place to insert the candle. The metal cover is fastened to the bottle with wires as shown in the sketch. This light can be used on a post or hung from a metal support.

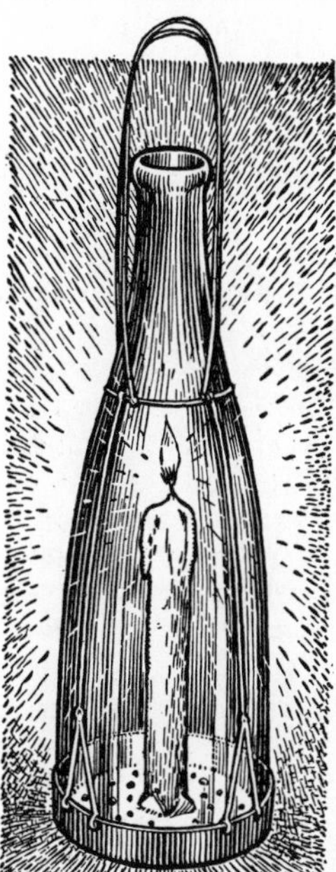

A Checker Puzzle

Cut a block from a board about 3 in. wide and 10 in. long. Sandpaper all the surfaces and round the edges slightly. Mark out seven 1-in. squares on the surface to be used for the top and color the squares alternately white and black. Make six men by sawing a curtain roller into pieces about $\frac{3}{8}$ in. thick. Number the pieces 1, 2, 3, 5, 6 and 7, and place them as shown in Fig. 1. The puzzle is to make the first three change places with the last three and

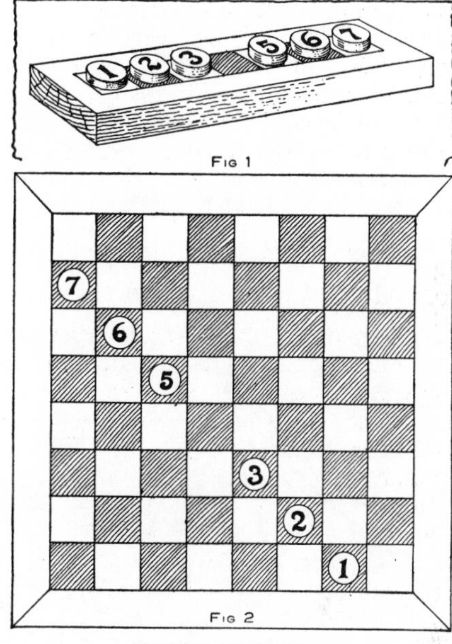

Position of the Men

move only one at a time. This may be done as follows:

Move 1—Move No. 3 to the center.
Move 2—Jump No. 5 over No. 3.
Move 3—Move No. 6 to No. 5's place.
Move 4—Jump No. 3 over No. 6.
Move 5—Jump No. 2 over No. 5.
Move 6—Move No. 1 to No. 2's place.
Move 7—Jump No. 5 over No. 1.
Move 8—Jump No. 6 over No. 2.
Move 9—Jump No. 7 over No. 3.
Move 10—Move No. 3 into No. 7's place.
Move 11—Jump No. 2 over No. 7.
Move 12—Jump No. 1 over No. 6.
Move 13—Move No. 6 into No. 2's place.
Move 14—Jump No. 7 over No. 1.
Move 15—Move No. 1 into No. 5's place.

After the 15 moves are made the men will have changed places. This can be done on a checker board, as shown in Fig. 2, using checkers for men, but be sure you so situate the men that they will occupy a row containing only 7 spaces.—Contributed by W. L. Woolson, Cape May Point, N. J.

Covering railroad signals with gold leaf has taken the place of painting on some roads. Gold leaf will stand the wear of the weather for 15 or 20 years, while paint requires recovering three or four times a year.

How to Make a Bell Tent

A bell tent is easily made and is nice for lawns, as well as for a boy's camping outfit. The illustrations show a plan of a tent 14 ft. in diameter. To make such a tent, procure unbleached tent duck, which is the very best material for the purpose, says the Cleveland Plain Dealer. Make 22 sections, shaped like Fig. 3, each 10 ft. 6 in. long and 2 ft. 2 in. wide at the bottom, tapering in a straight line to a point at the top. These dimensions allow for the laid or lapped seams, which should be double-stitched on a machine. The last seam sew only for a distance of 4 ft. from the top, leaving the rest for an opening. At the end of this seam stitch on an extra gusset piece so that it will not rip. Fold back the edges of the opening and the bottom edge of the bell-shaped cover and bind it with wide webbing, 3 in. across and having eyelets at the seams for attaching the stay ropes. Near the apex of the cover cut three triangular holes 8 in. long and 4 in. wide at the bottom and hem the edges. These are ventilators. Make the tent wall of the same kind of cloth 2 ft. 2 in. high. Bind it at the upper edge with webbing and at the bottom with canvas. Also stitch on coarse canvas 6 in. wide at the bottom, and the space between the ground and the wall when the tent is raised, fill with canvas edging. Stitch the upper edge of the wall firmly to the bell cover the point indicated by the dotted line Fig. 2.

For the top of the tent have the blacksmith make a hoop of $\frac{1}{4}$-in. round galvanized iron, 6 in. diameter. Stitch the canvas at the apex around the hoop and along the sides. Make the apex into a hood and line it with stiff canvas. Have the tent pole 3 in. in diameter, made in two sections, with a socket joint and rounded at the top to fit into the apex of the tent.

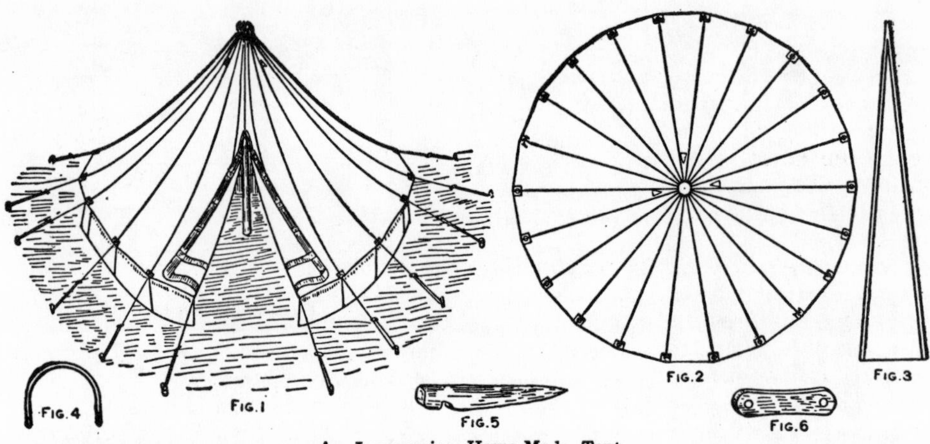

An Inexpensive Home-Made Tent

In raising the tent, fasten down the wall by means of loops of stout line fastened to its lower edge and small pegs driven through them into the ground, Fig. 5. Run the stay ropes from the eyelets in the circular cover to stakes (Fig. 5) stuck in the ground. Use blocks, as in Fig. 6, on the stay ropes for holding the ends and adjusting the length of the ropes.

Simple X-Ray Experiment

The outlines of the bones of the hand may be seen by holding a piece of rice paper before the eyes and placing the spare hand about 12 in. back of the rice paper and before a bright light. The bony structure will be clearly distinguishable.—Contributed by G. J. Tress, Emsworth, Pa.

How to Make a Candle Shade

Lay out the pattern for the shade on a thin piece of paper, 9 by 12 in., making the arcs of the circle with a pencil compass. As shown in the sketch, the pattern for this particular shade covers a half circle with 2¾ in. added. Allowance must be made for the lap and as ¼ in. will do, a line is drawn parallel ¼ in. from the one drawn through the center to the outside circle that terminates the design.

Nail a thin sheet of brass, about 9 in. wide by 12 in. long, to a smooth board of soft wood, then trace the design on the brass by laying a piece of carbon paper between the pattern and the brass. After transferring the design to the brass, use a small awl to punch the holes in the brass along the outlines of the figures traced. Punch holes in the brass in the spaces around the outlined figures, excepting the ¼ in. around the outside of the pattern. When all the holes are punched, remove the brass sheet from the board and cut it along the outer lines as traced from the pattern, then bend the brass carefully so as not to crease the figures appearing in relief. When the edges are brought together by bending, fasten them with brass-headed nails or brads.

If a wood-turning lathe is at hand, the shade can be made better by turning a cone from soft wood that will fit the sheet-brass shade after it is shaped and the edges fastened together. The pattern is traced as before, but before punching the holes, cut out the brass on the outside lines, bend into shape, fasten the ends together and place on the wood cone. The holes are now punched on the outlines traced from the pattern and the open spaces made full of holes. The holes being punched after the shade is shaped, the metal will stay and hold the perfect shape of a cone much better.

The glass-beaded fringe is attached on the inside of the bottom part with small brass rivets or brads placed about ¾ in. apart. The thin sheet brass may be procured from the local hardware dealer and sometimes can be purchased from general merchandise stores.—Contributed by Miss Kathryn E. Corr, Chicago.

Punching the Holes

Completed Shade Pattern

A Putty Grinder

Having a large number of windows to putty each week, I found it quite a task to prepare the putty. I facilitated the work by using an ordinary meat cutter or sausage grinder. The grinder will soften set putty and will quickly prepare cold putty. It will not, however, grind old putty or make putty from whiting and oil. —Contributed by H. G. Stevens, Dunham, Que.

Home-Made Small Churn

Many people living in a small town or in the suburbs of a city own one

Making Butter

cow that supplies the family table with milk and cream. Sometimes the cream will accumulate, but not in sufficient quantities to be made into butter in a large churn. A fruit jar usually takes the place of a churn and the work is exceedingly hard, the jar being shaken so the cream will beat against the ends in the process of butter-making. The accompanying sketch shows clearly how one boy rigged up a device having a driving wheel which is turned with a crank, and a driven wheel attached to an axle having a crank on the inner end. This crank is connected to a swinging cradle with a wire pitman of such a size as to slightly bend or spring at each end of the stroke. The cradle is made with a cleat fastened to each end, between which is placed the fruit jar, partially filled with cream. The jar is wedged in between the cleats and the churning effected by turning the crank.—Contributed by Geo. E. Badger, Mayger, Oregon.

Home-Made Round Swing

Gas pipe and fittings were used wherever possible in the making of the swing as shown in the photograph. The diagram drawing shows the construction. A 6-in. square cedar post is set in the ground about 3 ft., allowing 2 ft. to remain above the ground and a 7/8-in. piece of shafting is driven into the top part of this post for an axle. A cast-iron ring, or, better still, a heavy wheel with four spokes of such a size as to be drilled and tapped for 1/2-in. pipe is used for the hub, or center on which the frame swings. If a wheel is selected, the rim must be removed and only the spokes and hub used. The hole in the hub must be 7/8 in. or less, so the hub can be fitted to the shafting that is driven in the post. A large washer is placed on top of the post and the hub or cast-iron ring set on the washer.

The drilled and tapped holes in the four spokes are each fitted with a 4 1/2-ft. length of 1/2-in. pipe. These pipes are each fitted with a tee on the end and into this tee uprights of 1/2-in. pipe in suitable lengths are screwed, and also

The Merry-Go-Round Complete

short lengths with a tee and axle for the 6-in. wheel are fitted in the under side of the tee. The uprights at their upper ends are also fitted with tees and each joined to the center pipe with 1/2-in. pipe flattened on the inner end and fastened with bolts to a flange.

The bottom part of the cloth covering is held in place by a ½-in. pipe, bent to the desired circle. Four braces made from ½-in. pipe connect each spoke and seat to the flange on the center pipe. An extra wheel 18 in. in diameter is fitted in between two seats and used as the propelling wheel. This wheel has bicycle cranks and pedals and carries a seat or a hobby horse. The four seats are fastened to the four pipes with ½-in. pipe clamps.

Small miniature electric lights are fastened to the overhead braces and supplied with electric current carried through wires to the swing by an ingenious device attached to the under side of the cast-iron ring or hub of the wheel. A ring of fiber on which two brass rings are attached is fastened to the hub and connections are made to the two rings through two brushes fastened to the post with a bracket. The wires run under the surface of the ground outside and connected to the source of electricity. The wires from the brass rings run through the center pipe to the top and are connected to the lamp sockets.

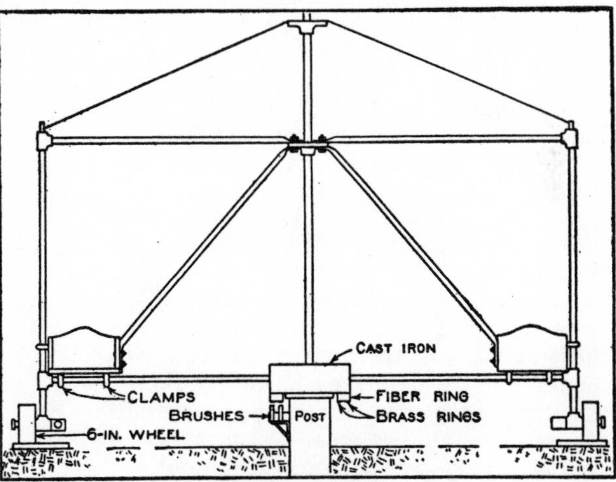

Details of the Swing

Old-Time Magic—Part V

The Disappearing Coin

This is an uncommon trick, entirely home-made and yet the results are as startling as in many of the professional tricks. A small baking-powder can is employed to vanish the coin, which should be marked by one of the audience for identification. Cut a slot in the bottom on the side of the can, as shown in Fig. 1. This slot should be just large enough for the coin that is used to pass through freely, and to have its lower edge on a level with the bottom of the can.

The nest or series of boxes in which the coin is afterwards found should consist of four small sized flat pasteboard boxes square or rectangular shaped and furnished with hinged covers. The smallest need be no larger than necessary to hold the coin and each succeeding box should be just large enough to hold the next smaller one which in turn contains the others.

A strip of tin about 1 by 1¾ in. is bent in the shape as shown in Fig. 2 to serve as a guide for the coin through the various boxes. This guide is inserted about ⅛ in. in the smallest box between the cover and the box and three rubber bands wrapped around the box as indicated. This box is then enclosed in the next larger box, the guide being allowed to project between the box and the cover, and the necessary tension is secured by three rubber bands around the box as before. In like manner the remaining boxes are adjusted so that finally the prepared nest of boxes appears as in Fig. 3.

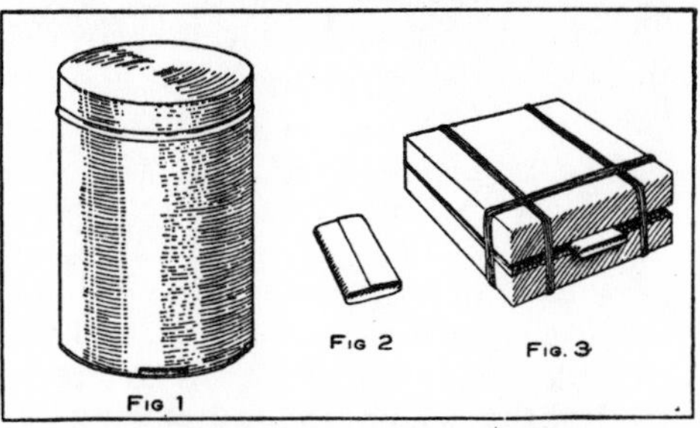

Appliances for the Disappearing Coin

The coin can easily be passed into the inner box through the tin guide, then the guide can be withdrawn which permits the respective boxes to close and the rubber bands hold each one in a closed position.

The performer comes forward with the tin can in his right hand, the bottom of the can in his palm with the slot at the right side. He removes the cover with the left hand and passes his wand around the inner part of the can which is then turned upside down to prove that it contains nothing. The marked coin is dropped into the can by some one in the audience. The cover is replaced and the can shaken so the coin will rattle within. The shaking of the can is continued until the coin has slipped through the slot into his palm. The can is then placed on the table with his left hand. Then apparently he looks for something to cover the can. This is found to be a handkerchief which was previously prepared on another table concealing the nest of boxes. The coin in the right hand is quickly slipped into the guide of the nest of boxes, which was placed in an upright position, and the guide withdrawn, and dropped on the table. The performer, while doing this, is explaining that he is looking for a suitable cover for the can, but as he cannot find one he takes the handkerchief instead. The handkerchief is spread over the can and then he brings the nest of boxes. He explains how he will transfer the coin and passes his wand from the can to the boxes. The can is then shown to be empty and the boxes given to one in the audience to be opened. They will be greatly surprised to find the marked coin within the innermost box.

How to Keep Film Negatives

There are many devices for taking care of film negatives to keep them from curling and in a place easily accessible. Herewith is illustrated a method by which anyone can make a place for the negatives produced by his or her special film camera. The device is made up similar to a post card album with places cut through each leaf to admit each corner of the negatives. The leaves are made from white paper and when the negatives are in place the pictures made on them can

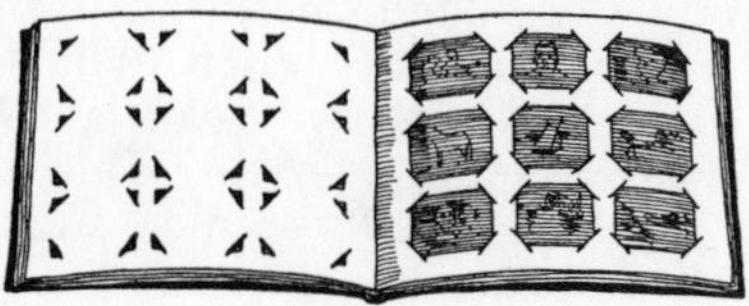

Negatives on White Paper Background

easily be seen through to the white paper background. These leaves can be made up in regular book form, or tied together similar to a loose-leaf book, thus adding only such pages as the negatives on hand will require.—Contributed by H. D. Harkins, St. Louis, Mo.

Home-Made Match Safe

Cut a piece of tin in the shape and with the dimensions shown in Fig. 1. Bend the saw-toothed edges at right angles to the piece on the dotted lines. Bend the part that is marked 5½ in. in a half circle. Make a circle 3½ in. in diameter on another piece of tin, cut

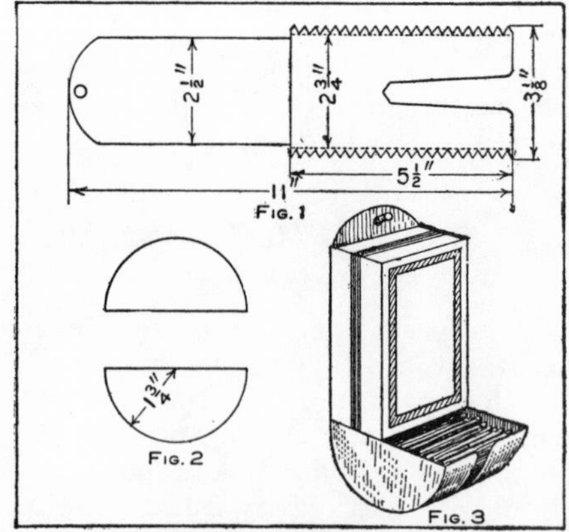

Details of the Match Safe

out the circle and cut the disk in two as shown in Fig. 2. These half circle pieces are soldered to the sides of the teeth of the half circle made in the long piece of tin. Remove one end from the inside box containing matches and slip the back of the match safe through between the bottom of the inside box and the open end box that forms the cover. The matches will fall into the half circle tray at the lower end of the box which will be kept full of matches until they are all used from the box.—Contributed by C. F. White, Denver, Colo.

An Electric Post Card Projector

A post card projector is an instrument for projecting on a screen in a darkened room picture post cards or any other pictures of a similar size. The lantern differs from the ordinary magic lantern in two features; first, it requires no expensive condensing lens, and second, the objects to be projected have no need of being transparent.

Two electric globes are made to cast the strongest possible light on the picture card set between them and in front of which a lens is placed to project the view on the screen, the whole being enclosed in a light-tight box. The box can be made of selected oak or mahogany. The lens to be used as a projector will determine the size of the box to some extent. The measurements given in these instructions are for a lens of about 5 in. focal length. The box should be constructed of well-seasoned wood and all joints made with care so they will be light-tight.

The portion shown carrying the lens in Fig. 1 is made to slide in the main body of the lantern for focusing. A box should first be made 5½ in. wide, 5½ in. high and 11 in. long. A hole is cut in the back of the box 4 by 6 in. represented by the dotted line in Fig. 2. This will be ¾ in. from the top and bottom and 2½ in. from each end of the outside of the box. Two strips of wood ½ in. wide and 6½ in. long are fastened along the top and bottom of the back. The door covering this hole in the back, and, which is also used as a carrier for the post cards, is made from a board 4½ in. wide and 6½ in. long. The door is hinged to the lower strip and held in position by a turn button on the upper strip. The slides for the picture cards are made from strips of tin bent as shown, and tacked to the inside surface of the door.

The runners to hold the part carrying the lens are two pieces 2¼ in. wide by 5 in. long and should be placed vertically, AA, as shown in Fig. 1, 3½ in. from each end. An open space 4 in. wide and 5 in. high in the center is for the part carrying the lens to slide for focusing. The part carrying the lens is a shallow box 4 by 5 in. and 2 in. deep in the center of which a hole is cut to admit the lens. If a camera lens is used, the flange should be fastened with screws to the front part of this shallow box. The sides of this box should be made quite smooth and a good, but not tight, fit into the runners. Plumbago can be rubbed on to prevent sticking and to dull any rays of light.

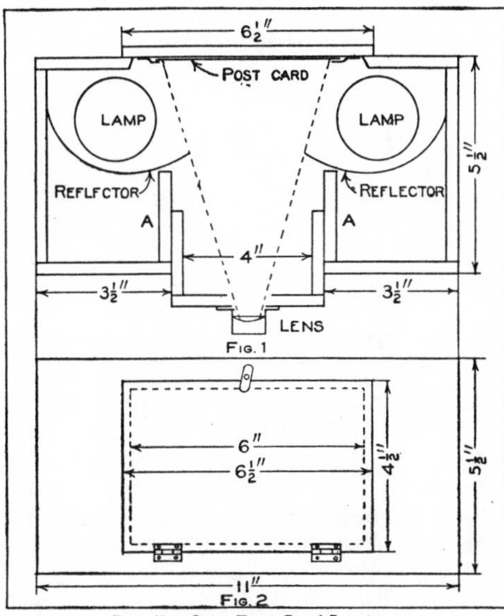

Details of the Post Card Lantern

Two keyless receptacles for electric globes are fastened to the under side of the top in the position shown and connected with wires from the outside. Two or three holes about 1 in. in diameter should be bored in the top between and in a line with the lights. These will provide ventilation to keep the pictures from being scorched or becoming buckled from the excessive heat. The holes must be covered over on the top with a piece of metal or wood to prevent the light from showing on the ceiling. This piece should not be more than ½ in. high and must

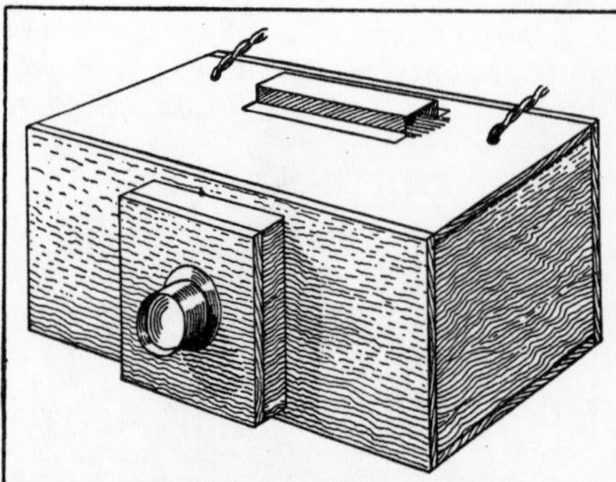

Post Card Lantern Complete

be colored dead black inside to cause no reflection.

The reflectors are made of sheet tin or nickel-plated metal bent to a curve as shown, and extending the whole height of the lantern. The length of these reflectors can be determined by the angle of the lens when covering the picture. This is clearly shown by the dotted lines in Fig. 1. The reflectors must not interfere with the light between the picture and the lens, but they must be sufficiently large to prevent any direct light reaching the lens from the lamps. In operation place the post card upside down in the slides and close the door. Sliding the shallow box carrying the lens will focus the picture on the screen.

A Handy Calendar

"Thirty days hath September, April, June and November," etc., and many other rhymes and devices are used to aid the memory to decide how many days are in each month of the year. Herewith is illustrated a very simple method to determine the number of days in any month. Place the first finger of your right hand on the first knuckle of your left hand, calling that knuckle January; then drop your finger into the depression between the first and second knuckles, calling this February; then the second knuckle will be March, and so on, until you reach July on the knuckle of the little finger, then begin over again with August on the first knuckle and continue until December is reached. Each month as it falls upon a knuckle will have 31 days and those down between the knuckles 30 days with the exception of February which has only 28 days.—Contributed by Chas. C. Bradley, West Toledo, Ohio.

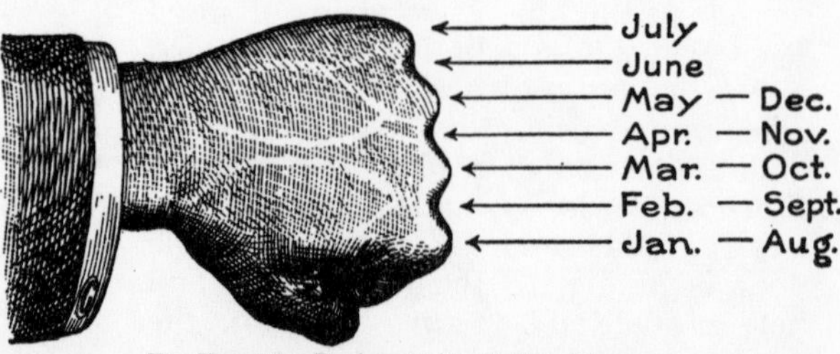

The Knuckles Designate the 31-Day Months

The Fuming of Oak

Darkened oak always has a better appearance when fumed with ammonia. This process is rather a difficult one, as it requires an airtight case, but the description herewith given may be entered into with as large a case as the builder cares to construct.

Oak articles can be treated in a case made from a tin biscuit box, or any other metal receptacle of good proportions, provided it is airtight. The oak to be fumed is arranged in the box so the fumes will entirely surround the piece; the article may be propped up with small sticks, or suspended by a string. The chief point is to see that no part of the wood is covered up and that all surfaces are exposed to the fumes. A saucer of ammonia is placed in the bottom of the box, the lid or cover closed, and all joints sealed up by pasting heavy brown paper over them. Any leakage will be detected if the nose is placed near the tin and farther application of the paper will stop the holes. A hole may be cut in the cover and a piece of glass fitted in, taking care to have all the edges closed. The process may be watched through the glass and the article removed when the oak is fumed to the desired shade. Wood stained in this manner should not be French polished or varnished, but waxed.

The process of waxing is simple: Cut some beeswax into fine shreds and place them in a small pot or jar. Pour in a little turpentine, and set aside for half a day, giving it an occasional stir. The wax must be thoroughly dissolved and then more turpentine added until the preparation has the consistency of a thick cream. This can be applied to the wood with a rag and afterward brushed up with a stiff brush.

How to Make an Electrolytic Rectifier

Many devices which will change alternating current to a direct current

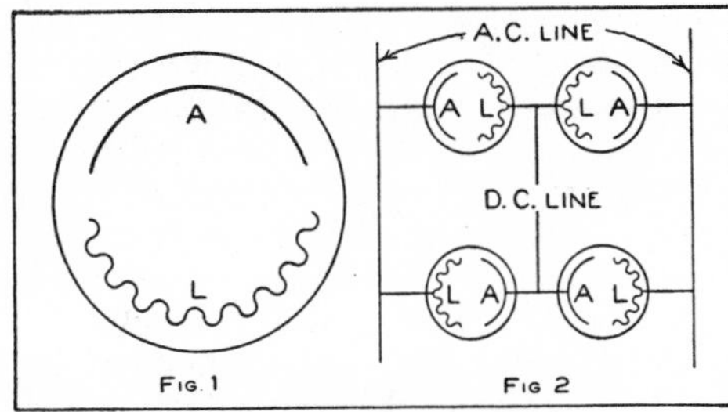

Electrolytic Rectifier and Connections

have been put on the market, but probably there is not one of them which suits the amateur's needs and pocketbook better than the electrolytic rectifier.

For the construction of such a rectifier four 2-qt. fruit jars are required. In each place two electrodes, one of lead and one of aluminum. The immersed surface of the aluminum should be about 15 sq. in. and the lead 24 sq. in. The immersed surface of the lead being greater than that of the aluminum, the lead will have to be crimped as shown in Fig. 1. In both Fig. 1 and 2, the lead is indicated by L and the aluminum by A.

The solution with which each jar is to be filled consists of the following:

Water	2 qt.
Sodium Carbonate	2 tablespoonfuls
Alum	3 tablespoonfuls

Care should be taken to leave the connections made as shown in Fig. 2. The alternating current comes in on the wires as shown, and the direct current is taken from the point indicated.

The capacity of this rectifier is from 3 to 5 amperes, which is sufficient for charging small storage batteries, running small motors and lighting small lamps.—Contributed by J. H. Crawford, Schenectady, N. Y.

The Rolling Marble

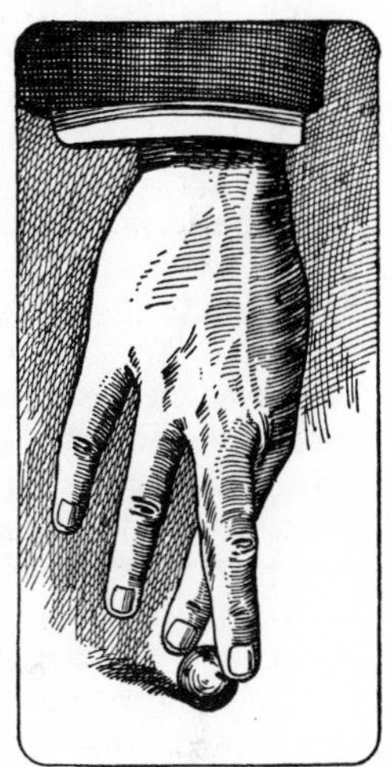

Take a marble and place it on a smooth surface, the top of a table will do. Ask some one to cross their first and second fingers and place them on the marble as shown in the illustration. Then have the person roll the marble about and at the same time close the eyes or look in another direction. The person will imagine that there are two marbles instead of one.

A Gas Cannon

If you have a small cannon with a bore of 1 or 1½ in., bore out the fuse hole large enough to tap and fit in a small sized spark plug such as used on a gasoline engine. Fill the cannon with gas from a gas jet and then push a

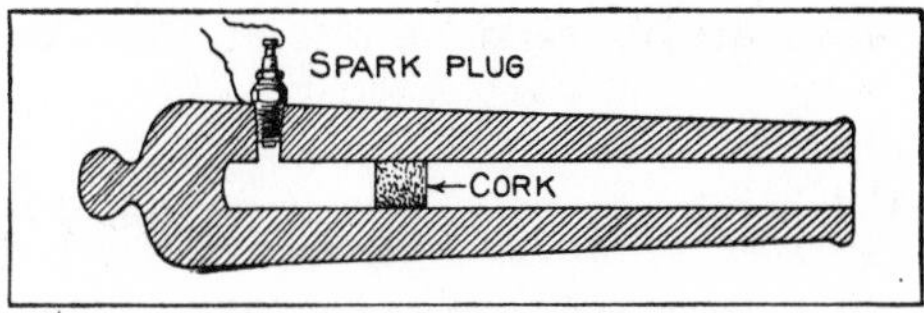

Gas Cannon Loaded

cork in the bore close up to the spark plug. Connect one of the wires from a battery to a spark coil and then to the spark plug. Attach the other wire to the cannon near the spark plug. Turn the switch to make a spark and a loud report will follow. Contributed by Cyril Tegner, Cleveland, O.

Old-Time Magic—Part VI

A Handkerchief Mended after Being Cut and Torn

Two persons are requested to come forward from the audience to hold the four corners of a handkerchief. Then beg several other handkerchiefs from the audience and place them on the one held by the two persons. When several handkerchiefs have been accumulated, have some one person draw out one from the bunch and examine for any marks that will determine that this handkerchief is the one to be mended after being mutilated. He, as well as others, are to cut off pieces from this handkerchief and to finally tear it to pieces.

The pieces are then all collected and some magic spirits thrown over the torn and cut parts; tie them in a small package with a ribbon and put them under a glass, which you warm with your hands. After a few seconds' time, you remove the glass, as you have held it all the time, and take the handkerchief and unfold it; everyone will recognize the mark and be amazed not to find a cut or tear in the texture.

This trick is very simple. You have an understanding with some one in the company, who has two handkerchiefs exactly alike and has given one of them to a person behind the curtain; he throws the other, at the time of request for handkerchiefs, on the handkerchiefs held for use in the performance of the trick. You manage to keep this handkerchief where it will be picked out in preference to the others, although pretending to thoroughly mix them up. The person selected to pick out a handkerchief naturally will take the handiest one. Be sure that this is the right one.

When the handkerchief has been torn and folded, put it under the glass, on a table, near a partition or curtain. The table should be made with a hole cut through the top and a small trap door fitted snugly in the hole, so it will appear to be a part of the table top. This trap door is hinged on the under side and opens into the drawer of the table and can be operated by the person behind the curtain who will remove the torn handkerchief and replace it with the good one and then close the trap door by reaching through the drawer of the table.

The Magic Knot

This is a very amusing trick which consists of tying one knot with two ends of a handkerchief, and pulling the ends only to untie them again. Take the two diagonal corners of a handkerchief, one in each hand and throw the main part of the handkerchief over the wrist of the left hand and tie the knot as shown in the illustration. Pull the ends quickly, allowing the loop over the left hand to slip freely, and you will have the handkerchief without any knot.

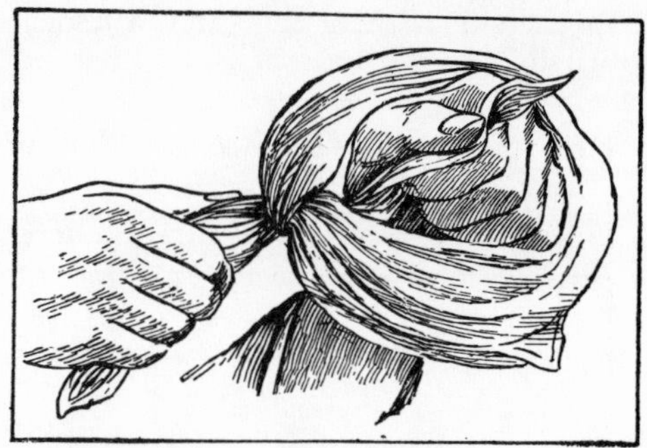

Tying and Untying a Knot

A Good Mouse Trap

When opening a tomato or other small can, cut the cover crossways from side to side making four triangular pieces in the top. Bend the four ends outward and remove the contents, wash clean and dry and then bend the four ends inward, leaving a hole about ¾ in. in diameter in the center. Drop in a piece of bread and lay the can down upon its side and the trap is ready for use. The mouse can get in but he cannot get out.—Contributed by E. J. Crocker, Victor, Colo.

Rubbing the surface of an aluminum plate with a steel brush will produce a satin finish.

How to Make a Sailing Canoe

A canvas canoe is easily made and light to handle, but in making one, it must be remembered that the cloth will tear, if any snags are encountered. Therefore such a craft cannot be used in all waters, but by being careful at shores, it can be used as safely as an ordinary sailing canoe. Be sure to select the best materials and when complete cover the seams well with paint.

The keelson, Fig. 1, is 14 ft. long, 8 in. wide in the center and tapered down from a point 4 ft. from each end to 1 in. at the ends. Both ends are mortised, one 6 in. for the stern piece, and the other 12 in. for the bow. Be sure to get the bow and stern pieces directly in the middle of the keelson and at right angles with the top edge. The stern and bow pieces are cut as shown in Fig. 2 and braced with an iron band,

Completed Sailing Canoe

The materials necessary for the construction of a sailing canoe, as illustrated in the engraving, are as follows:

1 keelson, 1 in. by 8 in. by 15 ft., selected pine.
14 rib bands, 1 in. square by 16 ft., clear pine.
2 gunwales, 1 in. by 2 in. by 16 ft.
1 piece for forms and bow pieces, 1 in. by 12 in. by 10 ft.
4 outwales, ¼ in. by 2 in. by 16 ft.
1 piece, 3 in. wide and 12 ft. long, for cockpit frame.
1 piece, 2 in. wide and 12 ft. long, for center deck braces.
11 yd. of 1½-yd. wide 12-oz. ducking.
8 yd. of 1-yd. wide unbleached muslin.
50 ft. of rope.
1 mast, 9 ft. long.
Paint, screws and cleats.

⅛ in. thick and ¾ in. wide, drilled and fastened with screws.

Study the sketches showing the details well before starting to cut out the pieces. Then there will be no trouble experienced later in putting the parts together. See that all the pieces fit their places as the work proceeds and apply the canvas with care.

Two forms are made as shown in Figs. 3 and 4; the smaller is placed 3 ft. from the bow and the large one, 7 ft. 3 in. from the stern. The larger mould is used temporarily while making the boat, and is removed after the ribs are in place. The gunwales are now placed over the forms and in the notches shown, and fastened with screws, and, after cutting the ends to fit the bow and stern pieces, they are fastened with bolts put through the three pieces. The sharp edges on one side of each rib-band are removed and seven of them fastened with screws to each side of the moulds, spacing them on the large mould 4 in. apart. The ribs are made of 28 good barrel hoops which should be well soaked in water for several hours before bending them in shape. These are put in 6 in. apart and are fastened to the rib-bands with 7/8-in. wood screws. The ribs should be put in straight and true to keep them from pulling the rib-bands out of shape. After the ribs are in place and fastened to the rib-bands, gunwales and keelson, put on the outwale strips and fasten them to the gunwales between every rib with 1½-in. screws.

Before making the deck, a block for the mast to rest in must be made and fastened to the keelson. This block, Fig. 5, is a cube having sides 6 in. square and is kept from splitting by an iron band tightly fitted around the outside. The block is fastened to the keelson, 3½ ft. from the bow, with bolts through countersunk holes from the under side.

There are three deck braces made as shown in Figs. 6, 7 and 8. Braces, Figs. 6 and 7, form the ends of the cockpit which is 20 in. wide. A 6-in. board is fitted into the mortises shown in these pieces; a center piece is fitted in the other mortises. The other deck braces slope down from the center piece and are placed 6 in. apart. They are 1 in. square and are mortised into the center piece and fastened to the gunwales with screws. The main deck braces are fastened to the gunwales with 4-in. corner braces and to the center piece with 2-in. corner braces. The mast hole on the deck is made as follows: Secure a piece of twine 1 in. thick, 6 in. wide and 3 ft. long. Cut this in halves and mortise for the center piece in the two halves and fasten to the gunwales. A block of pine, 4 in. thick and 12 in. long, is cut to fit under the top boards, Fig. 9, and fastened to them with bolts. With an expansive bit bore a hole 3 in. in diameter through the block. Be sure to get the block and hole directly over the block that is fastened to the keelson. Put on a coat of boiled linseed oil all over the frame before proceeding farther.

Putting on the canvas may be a diffi-

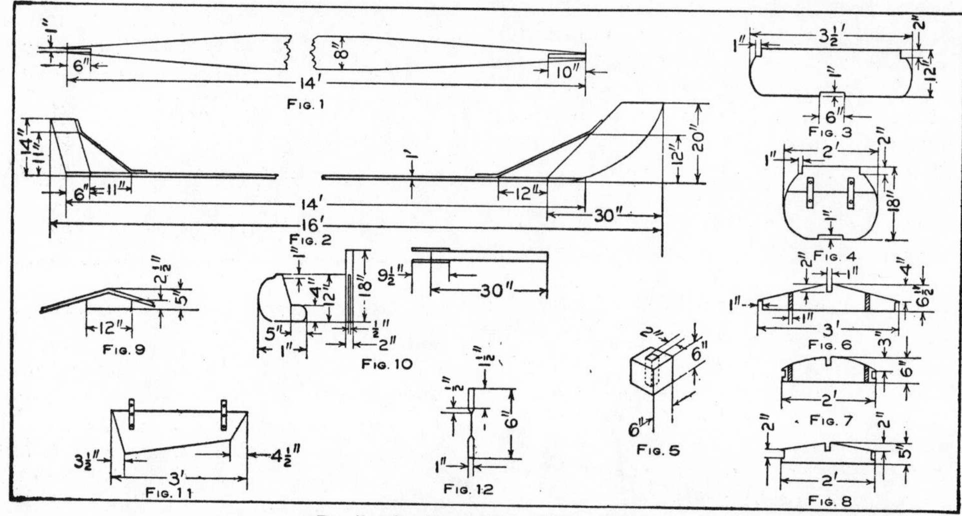

Details of a Home-Made Sailing Canoe

cult piece of work to do, yet if the following simple directions are followed out no trouble will be encountered. The 11-yd. length of canvas is cut in the center, doubled, and a seam made joining the two pieces together. Fill the seam with thick paint and tack it down with copper tacks along the center of the keelson. When this is well tacked commence stretching and pulling the canvas in the middle of the gunwales so as to make it as even and tight as possible and work toward each end, tacking the canvas as it is stretched to the outside of the gunwale. Seam the canvas along the stern and bow pieces as was done on the keelson. The deck is not so hard to do, but be careful to get the canvas tight and even. A seam should be made along the center piece. The trimming is wood, 1/4 in. thick and 1/2 in. wide. A strip of this is nailed along the center piece over the canvas. The outwales are nailed on over the canvas. A piece of oak, 1 in. thick 1 1/2 in. wide and 14 in. long, is fastened with screws over the canvas on the stern piece; also, a piece 1/4 in. thick, 1 in. wide and 24 in. long is well soaked in water, bent to the right shape and fastened over the canvas on the bow.

The rudder is made as shown in Fig. 10 with a movable handle. A strip 1 in. thick by 2 in. wide, is bolted to the keelson over the canvas for the outer keel. The keel, Fig. 11, is 6 in. wide at one end and 12 in. at the other, which is fastened to the outer keel with bolts having thumb nuts. The mast can be made of a young spruce tree having a diameter of 3 in. at the base with sufficient height to make it 9 ft. long. The canoe is driven by a lanteen sail and two curtain poles, each 1 in. in diameter and 10 ft. long, are used for the boom and gaff, which are held together with two pieces of iron bent as shown in Fig. 12. The sail is a triangle, 9 3/4 by 9 3/4 by 8 1/2 ft. which is held to the boom and gaff by cord lacings run through eyelets inserted in the muslin. The eyelets are of brass placed 4 in. apart in the muslin. The mast has two side and one front stay, each fitted with a turnbuckle for tightening. A pulley is placed at the top and bottom of the mast for the lift rope. The sail is held to the mast by an iron ring and the lift rope at the top of the mast. The boom rope is held in the hand and several cleats should be placed in the cockpit for convenience. A chock is placed at the bow for tying up to piers. Several coats of good paint complete the boat.—Contributed by O. E. Tronnes, Wilmette, Ill.

A Home-Made Hand Vise

A very useful little hand vise can easily be made from a hinge and a bolt carrying a wing nut. Get a fast

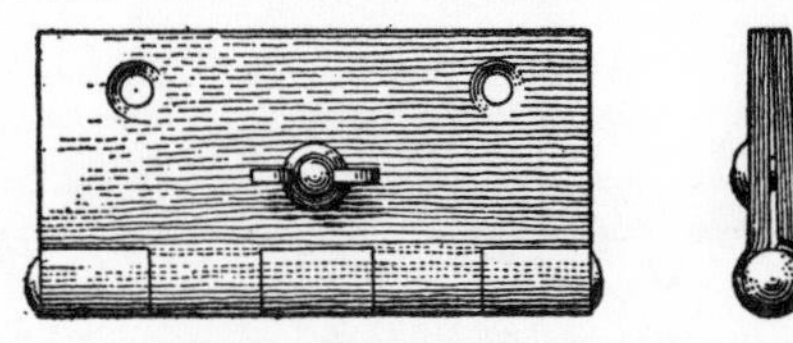

Hand Vise Made from a Hinge

joint hinge about 2 in. or more long and a bolt about 1/2 in. long that will fit the holes in the hinge. Put the bolt through the middle hole of the hinge and replace the nut as shown in the drawing. With this device any small object may be firmly held by simply placing it between the sides of the hinge and tightening the nut.

Proper Design for a Bird House

This bird house was designed and built to make a home for the American martin. The house will accommodate 20 families. All the holes are arranged so they will not be open to the cold winds from the north which often kill the birds which come in the early spring. Around each opening is an extra ring of wood to make a

longer passage which assists the martin inside in fighting off the English sparrow who tries to drive him out. The holes are made oval to allow all the little ones to get their heads out for fresh air. The long overhanging eaves protect the little birds from the hot summer sun.

The rooms are made up with partitions on the inside so each opening will have a room. The inside of the rooms should be stained black.

Boomerangs and How to Make Them

A boomerang is a weapon invented and used by the native Australians, who seemed to have the least intelligence of any race of mankind. The

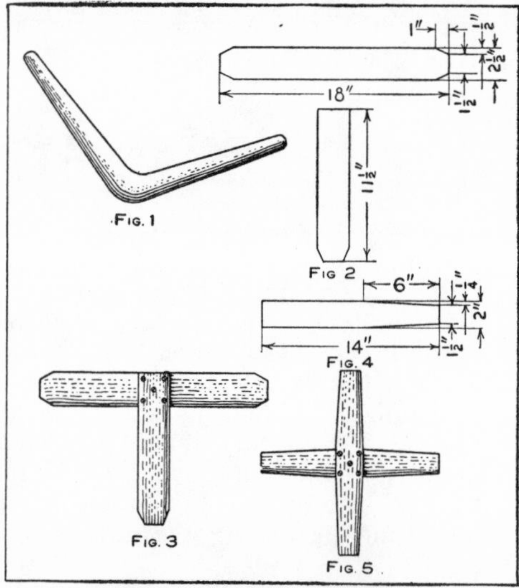

Details of Three Boomerangs

boomerang is a curved stick of hardwood, Fig. 1, about 5/16 in. thick, 2½ in. wide and 2 ft. long, flat on one side, with the ends and the other side rounding. One end of the stick is grasped in one hand with the convex edge forward and the flat side up and thrown upward. After going some distance and ascending slowly to a great height in the air with a quick rotary motion, it suddenly returns in an elliptical orbit to a spot near the starting point. If thrown down on the ground the boomerang rebounds in a straight line, pursuing a ricochet motion until the object is struck at which it was thrown.

Two other types of boomerangs are illustrated herewith and they can be made as described. The materials necessary for the T-shaped boomerang are: One piece of hard maple 5/16 in. thick, 2½ in. wide, and 3 ft. long; five ½-in. flat-headed screws. Cut the piece of hard maple into two pieces, one 11½ in. and the other 18 in. long. The corners are cut from these pieces as shown in Fig. 2, taking care to cut exactly the same amount from each corner. Bevel both sides of the pieces, making the edges very thin so they will cut the air better. Find the exact center of the long piece and make a line 1¼ in. on each side of the center and fasten the short length between the lines with the screws as shown in Fig. 3. The short piece should be fastened perfectly square and at right angles to the long one.

The materials necessary for the cross-shaped boomerang are one piece hard maple 5/16 in. thick, 2 in. wide and 30 in. long and five ½-in. flat-headed screws. Cut the maple into two 14-in. pieces and plane the edges of these pieces so the ends will be 1½ in. wide, as shown in Fig. 4. Bevel these pieces the same as the ones for the T-shaped boomerang. The two pieces are fastened together as shown in Fig. 5. All of the boomerangs when completed should be given several coats of linseed oil and thoroughly dried. This will keep the wood from absorbing water and becoming heavy. The last two boomerangs are thrown in a similar way to the first one, except that one of the pieces is grasped in the hand and the throw given with a quick underhand motion. A little practice is all that is necessary for one to become skillful in throwing them.—Contributed by O. E. Tronnes, Wilmette, Ill.

How to Make Water Wings

Purchase a piece of unbleached muslin, 1 yd. square. Take this and fold it over once, forming a double piece 1½ ft. wide and 3 ft. long. Make a double stitch all around the edge, leaving a small opening at one corner. Insert a piece of tape at this corner to be used for tying around the opening when the bag is blown up. The bag is then turned inside out, soaked with water and blown up. An occasional wetting all over will prevent it from leaking. As these wings are very large they will prevent the swimmer from sinking.—Contributed by W. C. Bliss, St. Louis, Mo.

How to Make an Ammeter

The outside case of this instrument is made of wood taken from old cigar boxes with the exception of the back. If carefully and neatly made, the finished instrument will be very satisfactory. The measurements here given need not be strictly followed out, but can be governed by circumstances. The case should first be made and varnished and while this is drying, the mechanical parts can be put together. turned into each three-cornered piece.

The front, which is a piece 5¼ in. wide and 6½ in. long, has a circular opening cut near the top through which the graduated scale may be seen. This front is centered and fastened the same as the back, and the four outside edges, as well as the edges around the opening, are rounded. The whole case can now be cleaned and stained with a light mahogany stain,

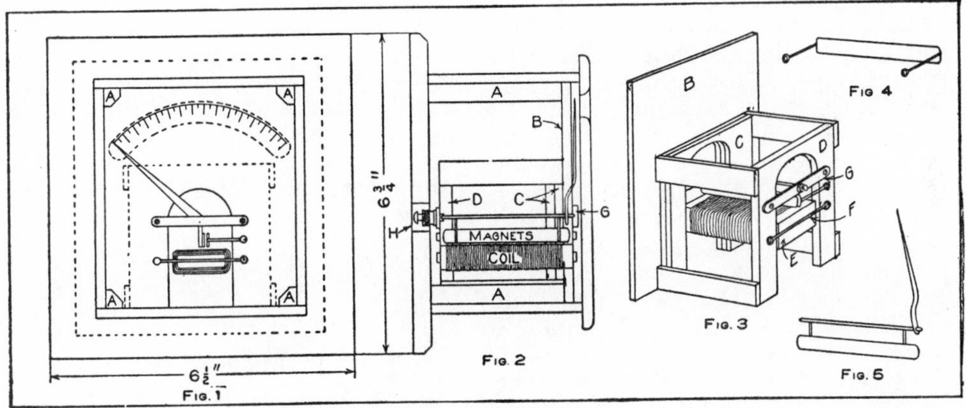

Details of an Ammeter

The back is a board ⅜ in. thick, 6½ in. wide and 6¾ in. long. The outer edges of this board are chamfered. The other parts of the case are made from the cigar box wood which should be well sandpapered to remove the labels. The sides are 3¼ in. wide and 5 in. long; the top and bottom, 3¼ in. wide and 4½ in. long. Glue a three-cornered piece, A, Fig. 1, at each end on the surface that is to be the inside of the top and bottom pieces. After the glue is set, fasten the sides to the pieces with glue, and take care that the pieces are all square. When the glue is set, this square box is well sandpapered, then centered, and fastened to the back with small screws and varnished. Cut another piece of board, B, Figs. 2 and 3, to just fit inside the case and rest on the ends of the three-cornered pieces, A, and glue to this board two smaller pieces, C, 3 in. square, with the grain of the wood in alternate directions to prevent warping. All of these pieces are made of the cigar box wood. Another piece, D, ⅜ in. thick and 3 in. square, is placed on the other pieces and a U-shaped opening 1¾ in. wide and 2½ in. high sawed out from all of the pieces as shown. The piece D is attached to the pieces C with four ½-in. pieces 2⅝ in. long.

A magnet is made from a soft piece of iron, E, about ⅜ in. thick, 1¼ in.

wide and 2¾ in. long. Solder across each end of the iron a piece of brass wire, F, and make a turn in each end of the wires, forming an eye for a screw. These wires are about 2½ in. long. Wind three layers of about No. 14 double cotton-covered copper wire on the soft iron and leave about 5 or 6 in. of each end unwound for connections.

The pointer is made as shown in Fig. 5 from 1/16-in. brass wire filed to make a point at both ends for a spindle. About ½ in. from each end of this wire are soldered two smaller brass wires which in turn are soldered to a strip of light tin ¼ in. wide and 2⅝ in. long. The lower edge of this tin should be about ½ in. from the spindle. The pointer is soldered to the spindle ¼ in. from one end. All of these parts should be brass with the exception of the strip of tin. Another strip of tin, the same size as the first, is soldered to two brass wires as shown in Fig. 4. These wires should be about 1 in. long.

The spindle of the pointer swings freely between two bars of brass, G, 1/16 in. thick, ¼ in. wide and 2½ in. long. A small hole is countersunk in one of the bars to receive one end of the spindle and a hole ⅛ in. in diameter is drilled in the other and a thumb nut taken from the binding-post of an old battery soldered over the hole so the screw will pass through when turned into the nut. The end of the screw is countersunk to receive the other end of the spindle. A lock nut is necessary to fasten the screw when proper adjustment is secured. A hole is drilled in both ends of the bars for screws to fasten them in place. The bar with the adjusting screw is fastened on the back so it can be readily adjusted through the hole H, bored in the back. The pointer is bent so it will pass through the U-shaped cut-out and up back of the board B. A brass pin is driven in the board B to hold the pointer from dropping down too far to the left. Place the tin, Fig. 4, so it will just clear the tin, Fig. 5, and fasten in place. The magnet is next placed with the ends of the coil to the back and the top just clearing the tin strips. Two binding screws are fitted to the bottom of the back and connected to the extending wires from the coil.

The instrument is now ready for calibrating. This is done by connecting it in series with another standard ammeter which has the scale marked in known quantities. In this series is also connected a variable resistance and a battery or some other source of current supply. The resistance is now adjusted to show .5 ampere on the standard ammeter and the position of the pointer marked on the scale. Change your resistance to all points and make the numbers until the entire scale is complete.

When the current flows through the coil, the two tinned strips of metal are magnetized, and being magnetized by the same lines of force they are both of the same polarity. Like poles repel each other, and as the part Fig. 4 is not movable, the part carrying the pointer moves away. The stronger the current, the greater the magnetism of the metal strips, and the farther apart they will be forced, showing a greater defection of the pointer.—Contributed by George Heimroth, Richmond Hill, L. I.

How to Make an Equatorial

Condensed from article contributed by J. R. Chapman, F. R. A. S. Austwick Hall, W. Yorkshire, England

This star finder can easily be made by anyone who can use a few tools as the parts are all wood and the only lathe work necessary is the turned shoulder on the polar axis and this could be dressed and sandpapered true enough for the purpose. The base is a board 5 in. wide and 9 in. long which is fitted with an ordinary wood screw in each corner for leveling. Two side pieces cut with an angle equal to the colatitude of the place are nailed to the base and on top of them is fastened another board on which is marked the hour circle as shown. The end of the polar axis B, that has the end turned with a shoulder, is fitted in a hole bored in the center of the hour circle. The polar axis B is secured to the board with a wooden collar and a pin underneath. The upper end of the polar axis is fitted with a 1/4-in. board, C, 5 1/2 in. in diameter. A thin compass card divided into degrees is fitted on the edge of this disk for the declination circle.

The hour circle A is half of a similar card with the hour marks divided into 20 minutes. An index pointer is fastened to the base of the polar axis. A pointer 12 in. long is fastened with a small bolt to the center of the declination circle. A small opening is made in the pointer into which an ordinary needle is inserted. This needle is adjusted to the degree to set the pointer in declination and when set, the pointer is clamped with the bolt at the center. A brass tube having a 1/4-in. hole is fastened to the pointer.

The first thing to do is to get a true N and S meridian mark. This can be approximately obtained by a good compass, and allowance made for the magnetic declination at your own place. Secure a slab of stone or some other solid flat surface, level this and have it firmly fixed facing due south with a line drawn through the center and put the equatorial on the surface with XII on the south end of the line. Then set the pointer D to the declination of the object, say Venus at the date of observation. You now want to know if this planet is east or west of your meridian at the time of observation. The following formula will show how this may be found. To find a celestial object by equatorial: Find the planet Venus May 21, 1881, at 9 hr. 10 min. A. M. Subtract right ascension of planet from the time shown by the clock, thus:

	hr.	min.	sec.
9 hr. 10 min. shows mean siderial...	1	0	0
Add 12 hrs....................	12	0	0
	13	0	0
Right ascension of Venus..........	2	10	0
Set hour circle to before meridian..	10	50	0

Again

	hr.	min.	sec.	
At 1 hr. 30 min. mean clock shows	5	20	0	siderial
Right ascension of Venus..	2	10	0	
Set hour circle to.........	3	10	0	afternoon

Books may be found in libraries that will give the right ascension and declination of most of the heavenly bodies.

The foregoing tables assume that you have a clock rated to siderial time,

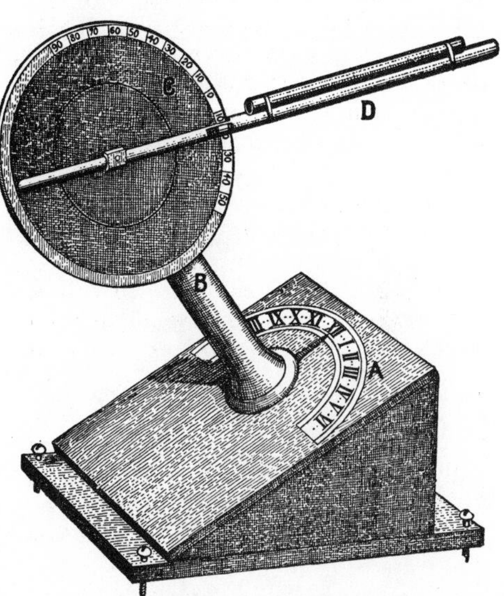

Home-Made Equatorial

but this is not absolutely necessary. If you can obtain the planet's declination on the day of observation and ascertain when it is due south, all you have to do is to set the pointer D by the needle point and note whether Venus has passed your meridian or not and set your hour index. There will be no difficulty in picking up Venus even in bright sunlight when the plant is visible to the naked eye.

Electric Light Turned On and Off from Different Places

How nice it would be to have an electric light at the turn in a stairway, or at the top that could be turned on before starting up the stair and on reaching the top turned out, and vice

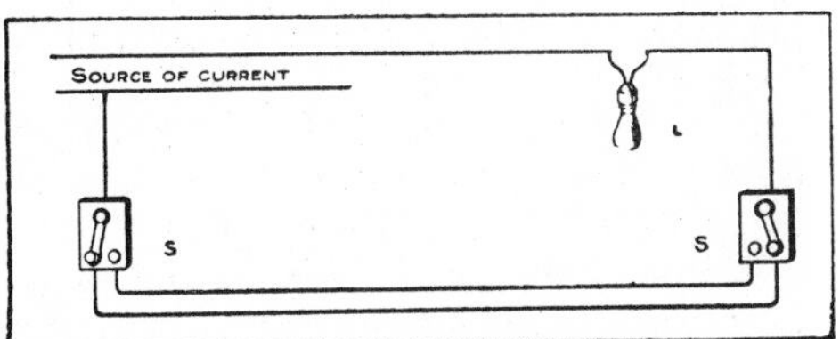

The Wiring Diagram

versa when coming down. The wiring diagram as shown in the illustration will make this a pleasant reality. This wiring may be applied in numerous like instances. The electric globe may be located at any desired place and the two point switches are connected in series with the source of current as shown in the sketch. The light may be turned on or off at either one of the switches.—Contributed by Robert W. Hall, New Haven, Conn.

How to Make a Bunsen Cell

This kind of a cell produces a high e. m. f. owing to the low internal resistance. Procure a glass jar such as used for a gravity battery, or, if one of these cannot be had, get a glazed vessel of similar construction. Take a piece of sheet zinc large enough so that when it is rolled up in the shape of a cylinder it will clear the edge of the jar by about ½ in. Solder a wire or binding-post to the edge of the cylinder for a connection. Secure a small unglazed vessel to fit inside of the zinc, or such a receptacle as used in a sal ammoniac cell, and fill it with a strong solution of nitric acid. Fill the outer jar with a solution of 16 parts water and 5 parts sulphuric acid. The connections are made from the zinc and carbon.

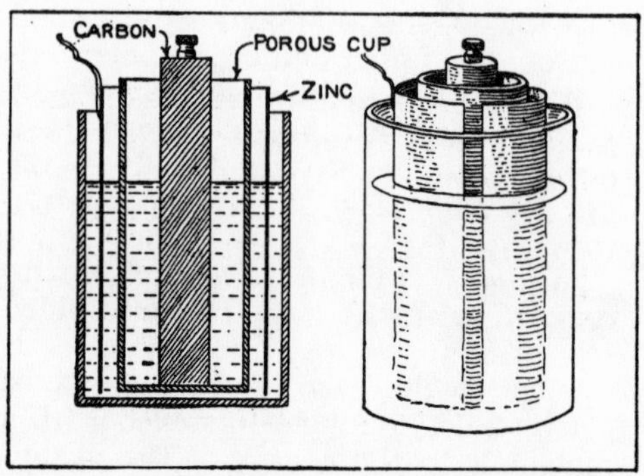

Cross Section and Completed Cell

Optical Illusion.—Can you tell which of these three figures is the tallest? Make a guess, and then verify its correctness by measurement.

One Way to Cook Fish

One of the best and easiest ways of cooking fish while out camping is told by a correspondent of Forest and Stream. A fire is built the size for the amount of food to be cooked and the wood allowed to burn down to a glowing mass of coals and ashes. Wash and season your fish well and then wrap them up in clean, fresh grass, leaves or bark. Then, after scraping away the greater part of the coals, put the fish among the ashes, cover up with the same, and heap the glowing coals on top. The fish cooks quickly—15 or 20 minutes—according to their size.

If you eat fish or game cooked after this fashion you will agree that it cannot be beaten by any method known to camp culinary savants. Clay also answers the purpose of protecting the fish or game from the fire if no other material is at hand, and for anything that requires more time for cooking it makes the best covering. Wet paper will answer, especially for cooking fish.

A successful method of hardening copper is to add 1 lb. of alum and 4 oz. arsenic to every 20 lb. of melted copper and stir for 10 minutes.

Packing Cut from Felt Hats

Felt from an old hat makes good packing for automobile water-circulating pumps. Strips should be cut to fit snugly in the stuffing box. When the follower is screwed down, it will expand the felt and make a watertight joint.

Homemade Gasoline Engine

The material used in the construction of the gasoline engine, as shown in the accompanying picture, was pieces found in a scrap pile that usually occupies a fence corner on almost every farm. The cylinder consists of an old pump cylinder, 3/8 in. thick, 1 3/4 in. inside diameter and about 5 in. long. This was fastened between some wooden blocks which were bolted on the tool carriage of a lathe and then bored out to a diameter of about 2 in. The boring bar, Fig. 1, consisted of an old shaft with a hole bored through the center and a tool inserted and held for each cut by a setscrew. A wood mandrel with a metal shaft to turn in the centers of a lathe was made to fit the bored-out cylinder. The cylinder was then placed on the mandrel, fastened with a pin, and threaded on both ends. Flanges were next made from couplings discarded from an old horsepower tumbling rod, to fit on the threaded ends of the cylinder casting. When these flanges were tightly screwed on the casting and faced off smooth the whole presented the appearance of a large spool.

The back cylinder head was made from a piece of cast iron, about 1/2 in. thick, turned to the same diameter as the flanges, and with a small projection to fit snugly inside the cylinder bore. Two holes were then drilled in this head and tapped for 3/4-in. pipe. Two pieces of 3/4-in. pipe were fitted to these holes so that, when they were turned in, a small part of the end of each pipe projected on the inside of the cylinder head. These pieces of pipe serve as valve cages and are reamed out on the inside ends to form a valve seat. The outlet for the exhaust and the inlet for the gas and air are through holes drilled in the side of each pipe respectively and tapped for 1/2-in. pipe. Two heads were then made to fit over the outer ends of the valve cages. These heads looked similar to a thread spool with one flange cut off, the remaining flange fitting on the

Complete Homemade Gasoline Engine

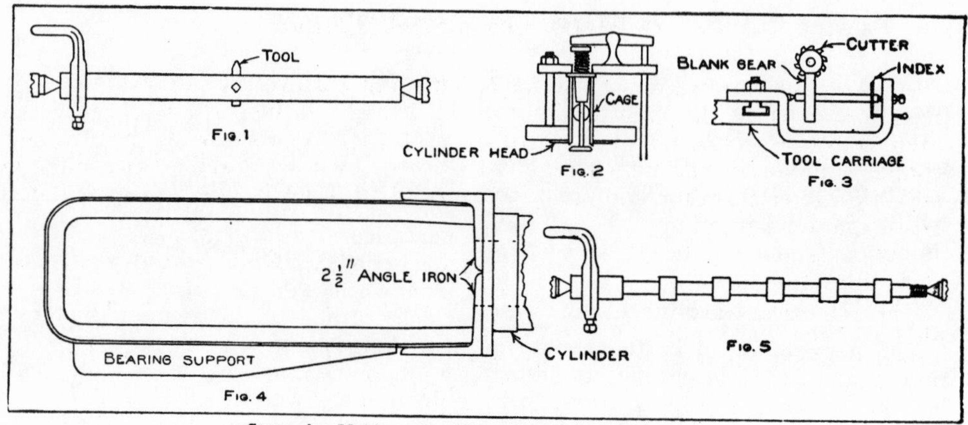

Steps in Making the Home-Made Gasoline Engine

end of the valve cage and the center extending down inside to make a long guide for the valve stems. These heads are held in place by a wrought-iron plate and two bolts, one of which is plainly shown in the picture. This plate also supports the rocker arms, Fig. 2, and the guides for the rods that operate the valves. Both valves are mechanically operated by one cam attached to a shaft running one turn to two of the crankshaft. The gears to run this shaft were cut from solid pieces on a small home-made gear-cutting attachment for the lathe as shown in Fig. 3. The gear on the crankshaft has 20 teeth meshing into a 40-tooth gear on the cam shaft.

The main part of the frame consists of a piece of ½-in. square iron, 30 in. long, bent in the shape of a U, and on the outside of this piece is riveted a bent piece of sheet metal ⅛ in. thick and 3 in. wide. The U-shaped iron is placed near one edge of the sheet metal. Two pieces of 2½-in. angle iron are riveted vertically on the ends of the U-shaped iron and a plate riveted on them to close the open end and to form a face on which to attach the cylinder with bolts or cap screws. A hole was cut through the angle irons and plate the same size as the bore of the cylinder so the piston could be taken out without removing the cylinder. A 1-in. angle iron was riveted to one side of the finished frame to make a support for the crankshaft bearing. The rough frame, Fig. 4, was then finished on an emery wheel. This long frame had to be made to accommodate the crosshead which was necessary for such a short cylinder.

The piston and rod were screwed together and turned in one operation on a lathe. The three rings were made from an old cast-iron pulley. The cap screws were made from steel pump rods. A piece of this rod was centered in a lathe and turned so as to shape six or more screws, Fig. 5, then removed and the first one threaded and cut off, then the second and so on until all of them were made into screws. The rod was held in a vise for this last operation. Studs were made by threading both ends of a proper length rod. Make-and-break ignition is used on the engine; however, a jump spark would be much better. The flywheel and mixing valve were purchased from a house dealing in these parts. The water jacket on the cylinder is a sheet of copper formed and soldered in place, and brass bands put on to cover the soldered joints.—Contributed by Peter J. Johnson, Clermont, Iowa.

If gasoline drips from the carburetor when the engine is not running, the needle valve connected with the float should be investigated. If the dripping stops when the valve is pressed down, the float is too high. If the valve keeps dripping, then it should be ground to a fit.

A Merry-Go-Round Thriller

As a home mechanic with a fondness for amusing the children I have seen many descriptions of merry-go-rounds, but never one which required so little material, labor and time, and which gave such satisfactory results, as the one illustrated herewith. It was erected in our back yard one afternoon, the materials being furnished by an accommodating lumber pile, and a little junk, and it has provided unlimited pleasure for "joy-riders," little and big, from all over the neighborhood. It looks like a toy, but once seat yourself in it and begin to go around. and, no matter what your age or size may be, you will have in a minute enough thrill and excitement to last the balance of the day.

The illustration largely explains itself, but a few dimensions will be a help to anyone wishing to construct the apparatus. The upright is a 4 by 4-in. timber, set 3 ft. in the ground with 8 ft. extending above. It is braced on four sides with pieces 2 in. square and 2 ft. long, butting against short stakes. The upper end of the post is wound with a few rounds of wire or an iron strap to prevent splitting. The crosspiece is 2 in. square, 12 ft. long, strengthened by a piece 4 in. square and 5 ft. long. These two pieces must be securely bolted or spiked together. A malleable iron bolt, ¾ in. in diameter and 15 in. long is the pivot. On this depends the safety of the contrivance, so it must be strong enough, and long enough to keep firmly in the post. Drive this bolt in a ⅜-in. hole bored in the post, which will make it a sufficiently tight fit. Make the hole for the bolt very loose through the crosspiece, so that there will be plenty of "wobble," as this is one of the mirth-making features of the machine. Use a heavy washer at the head. The seats are regular swing boards, supported by a stout and serviceable rope. A ¾-in. rope is not too heavy. One

Swinging on the Merry-Go-Round

set of ropes are passed through holes at the end of the crosspiece and knotted on top. The other set should be provided with loops at the top and slid over the crosspiece, being held in position by spikes as shown. This makes an easy adjustment. Seat the heavier of the riders on the latter seat, moving it toward the center until a balance with the lighter rider is reached. A rope tied to the crosspiece about 2 ft. from the center, for the "motive power" to grasp, completes the merry-go-round.

Put plenty of soap or grease between the crosspiece and upright. Be sure to have room for the ropes to swing out at high speed, with no trees or buildings in the way. The "wobble" mentioned will give an agreeable undulating motion, which adds greatly to the flying sensation. This will be found surprisingly evident for so small a machine. As there is no bracing, care must be taken to have the two riders sit at the same moment, or the iron bolt will be bent out of line. If it is to be used for adults, strong clear material only should be employed.—Contributed by C. W. Nieman.

How to Make and Fly a Chinese Kite

The Chinese boy is not satisfied with simply holding the end of a kite string and running up and down the block or field trying to raise a heavy paper kite with a half pound of rags for a tail. He makes a kite as light as possible without any tail which has the peculiar property of being able to move in every direction. Sometimes an expert can make one of these kites travel across the wind for several hundred feet; in fact, I have seen boys a full block apart bring their kites together and engage in a combat until one of their kites floated away with a broken string, or was punctured by the swift dives of the other, and sent to earth, a wreck.

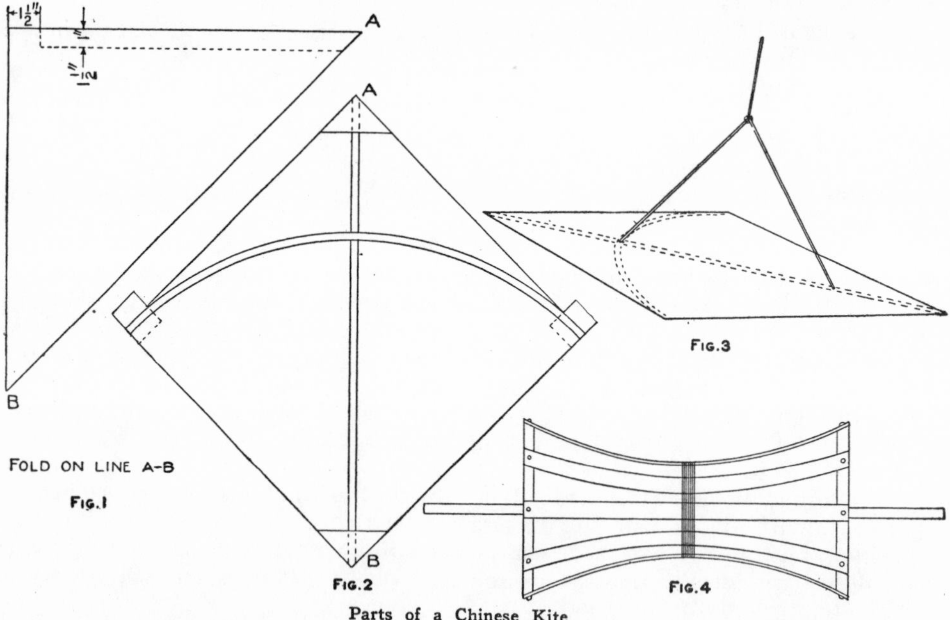

Parts of a Chinese Kite

The Chinese boy makes his kite as follows:

From a sheet of thin but tough tissue paper about 20 in. square, which he folds and cuts along the dotted line, as shown in Fig. 1, he gets a perfectly square kite having all the properties of a good flyer, light and strong. He shapes two pieces of bamboo, one for the backbone and one for the bow. The backbone is flat, 1/4 by 3/32 in. and 18 in. long. This he smears along one side with common boiled rice. Boiled rice is one of the best adhesives for use on paper that can be obtained and the Chinese have used it for centuries while we are just waking up to the fact that it makes fine photo paste. Having placed the backbone in position, paste two triangular pieces of paper over the ends of the stick to prevent tearing. The bow is now bent, and the lugs extending from the sides of the square paper are bent over the ends of the bow and pasted down. If the rice is quite dry or mealy it can be smeared on and will dry almost immediately, therefore no strings are needed to hold the bow bent while the paste dries.

After the sticks are in position the kite will appear as shown in Fig. 2. The dotted lines show the lugs bent over the ends of the bow and pasted down. Figure 3 shows how the band is put on and how the kite is balanced. This is the most important part and cannot be explained very well., This must be done by experimenting and it is enough to say that the kite must balance perfectly. The string is fastened by a slip-knot to the band and moved back and forth until the kite flies properly, then it is securely fastened.

A reel is next made. Two ends—the bottoms of two small peach baskets will do—are fastened to a dowel stick or broom handle, if nothing better is at hand. These ends are placed about 14 in. apart and strips nailed between them as shown in Fig. 4, and the centers drawn in and bound with a string. The kite string used is generally a heavy packing thread. This is run through a thin flour or rice paste until it is thoroughly coated, then it is run through a quantity of crushed glass. The glass should be beaten up fine and run through a fine sieve to make it about the same as No. 2 emery. The particles should be extremely sharp and full of splinters. These particles adhere to the pasted string and when dry are so sharp that it cannot be handled without scratching the fingers, therefore the kite is flown entirely from the reel. To wind the string upon the reel, all that is necessary is to lay one end of the reel stick in the bend of the left arm and twirl the other end between the fingers of the right hand.

A Chinese boy will be flying a gaily colored little kite from the roof of a house (if it be in one of the large cities where they have flat-roofed houses) and a second boy will appear on the roof of another house perhaps 200 ft. away. Both have large reels full of string, often several hundred yards of it. The first hundred feet or so is glass-covered string, the balance common packing thread, or glass-covered string. As soon as the second boy has his kite aloft, he begins maneuvering to drive it across the wind and over to the first kite. First, he pays out a large amount of string, then as the kite wabbles to one side with its nose pointing toward the first kite, he tightens his line and commences a steady quick pull. If properly done his kite crosses over to the other and above it. The string is now payed out until the second kite is hanging over the first one's line. The wind now tends to take the second kite back to its parallel and in so doing makes a turn about the first kite's string. If the second kite is close enough, the first tries to spear him by swift dives. The second boy in the meantime is see-sawing his string and presently the first kite's string is cut and it drifts away.

It is not considered sport to haul the other fellow's kite down as might be done and therefore a very interesting battle is often witnessed when the experts clash their kites.—Contributed by S. C. Bunker, Brooklyn, N. Y.

Home-Made Vise

An ordinary monkey wrench that has been discarded is used in making this vise. The wrench is supported by two L-shaped pieces of iron fastened with

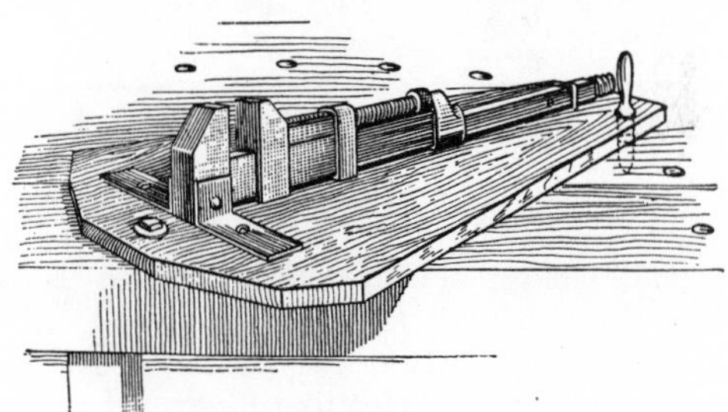

A Swivel Bench Vise

a rivet through the end jaw, and these in turn are bolted or screwed to the bench. The handle end is held down with a staple. The inside jaw is used in clamping and is operated with the thumb screw of the wrench. Two holes bored through the thumb piece will greatly facilitate setting up the jaws tightly by using a small rod in the holes as a lever.

The vise may be made into a swing vise if the wrench is mounted on a board which is swung on a bolt at one end and held with a pin at the other as shown in the illustration. Various holes bored in the bench on an arc will permit the board to be set at any angle. —Contributed by Harry S. Moody, Newburyport, Mass.

Home-Made Changing Bag for Plate Holders

A good bag for changing plates and loading plate holders and one that the operator can see well to work in can

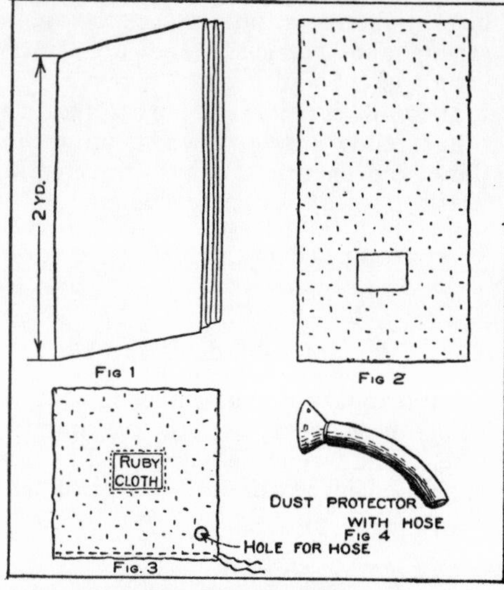

Made of Black Cambric

be made by anyone on a sewing machine. Ten yards of black cambric or other black cloth and a little ruby fabric will be required. Take the cambric and fold it into 2-yd. lengths (Fig. 1) which will make five layers of cloth, tack or fasten the layers together so they will not slip and cut an 8-in. square hole in the middle of one half (Fig. 2) and sew the ruby fabric over the opening. Be sure and make the seam light-tight and have enough layers of ruby fabric so no white light can get in. Fold the cloth up so it will be 1 yd. square (Fig. 3) and sew up the edges to make a bag with one side open. Put a drawstring in the edge of the cloth around the open side and the bag is complete ready for use.

Take the holders and plate boxes in the lap and put the bag over the head and down around the body, then draw the string up tight. A bag made up in this manner is for use only for a short time. If it is necessary to do considerable work at a time, then a dust protector, such as mill men use, must be attached to a 3-ft. length of 2-in. rubber hose and the hose run through a hole in the bag. This will make it possible to work in the bag as long as you wish.—Contributed by Earl R. Hastings, Corinth, Vt.

Home-Made Asbestos Table Pads

Asbestos table pads to prevent the marring of polished table tops from heated dishes can be easily made at home much cheaper than they can be bought. Procure a sheet of asbestos from a plumbing shop and cut it in the shape of the top of your table. If the table is round, make the pad as shown in the illustration, cutting the circular piece into quarters. Cut four pieces of canton flannel, each the size of half the table top. Two of the asbestos pieces are used to make one-half of the pad. Place the two pieces with their edges together so they will form half a circle disk and cover both sides with a piece of the flannel and pin them in place. A binding of white cotton tape is then basted around the edges to hold all the pieces together until they are stitched on a sewing machine. A line of machine stitching is made all around the outside and through the middle be-

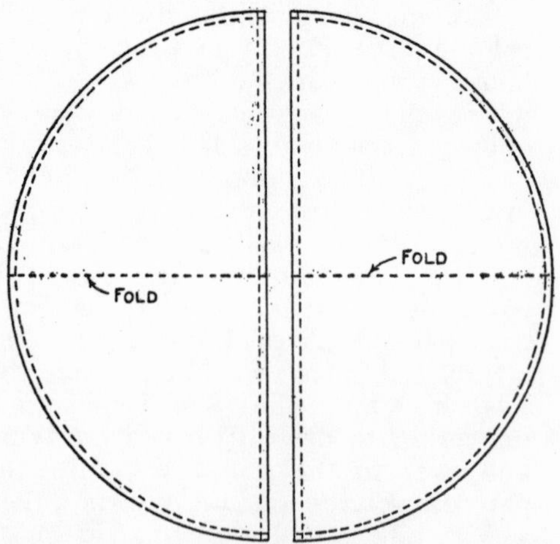

Pads Made of Asbestos

tween where the edges of the asbestos sheets join together. This will form a hinge so the two quarters may be folded for putting away. Make the other half circular disk in the same way. If leaves are wanted in extending the table, any number of pads can be made to cover them in the same manner with the hinge in the middle of each pad. The flannel is used with the nap side out so it will make the pad soft and noiseless. This kind of a pad furnishes perfect protection to the table from any heat or moisture.—Contributed by H. E. Wharton, Oakland, Calif.

How to Make a Ladies' Handbag

To make this bag, get a piece of Russian calf modeling leather. A shade of brown is the best as it does not soil easily and does not require coloring, which spoils the leather effect.

The dimensions of the full sized bag are: from A to B, 17½ in.; from C to D, 16¼ in.; from E to F, 9¼ in.; G to H, 6¼ in., and E to G, 2¼ in.

Enlarge the accompanying pattern to the given dimensions, trace this or some other appropriate design on it, and then cut the leather the size of the pattern.

Use a sponge to dampen the leather on the rough side, not so damp that the water will come through to the right side when working, but damp enough to allow the design to be well impressed

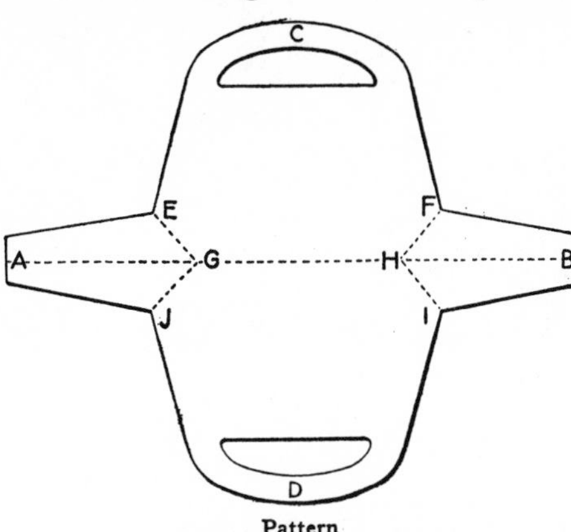

Pattern

on the leather. Use a smooth, non-absorbent surface to lay the leather on while at work.

Now lay the pattern on the right side of the leather and with the smallest end of the leather tool or a sharp, hard pencil, trace the design carefully on the leather. Moisten the leather as

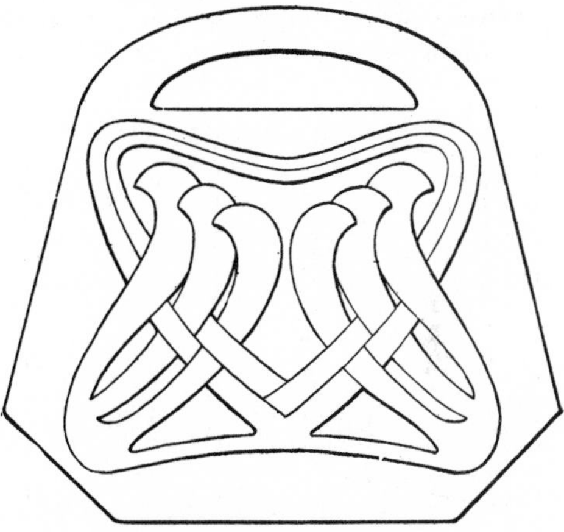
Design on the Leather

often as necessary to keep it sufficiently moist to work well. Trace the openings for the handles, also lines A-G, H-B, and E-G, G-J, and corresponding lines on the other side.

Remove pattern and trace the design directly on leather with the round point of tool, until it is made distinct and in marked contrast to the rest of the leather. Do not make sharp marks but round the edges of the lines nicely, with the rounded sides of the tools.

To complete the bag, get something with which to make a lining. A piece of oozed leather is the most satisfactory. Cut it the same size as the bag, place both together and with a leather punch, make holes all around the edge of the bag about ½ in. apart. Cut out the leather for the handle openings. Care should be taken not to cut the holes too near the edge of the bag lest the lacing pull out. Now cut narrow thongs, about ⅛ in. wide, and lace through the holes, lacing the sides of the end pieces in with the sides of the bag. Crease the lines A-G and B-H inward for ends of bag.

¶The claw of a hammer can be used for removing the insulation on copper wire, if not more than 1 in. is taken off at a time.

A Small Electric Motor

The drawing herewith shows a simple electric motor which can be easily constructed by any boy who is at all handy with tools. I made this motor

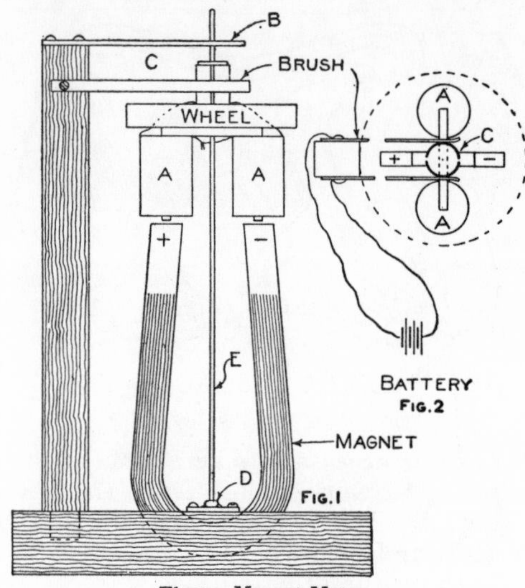

Electro-Magnet Motor

many times when a boy and can say that if carefully constructed it will run with greater rapidity than the more expensive ones.

A common magnet which can be purchased at any toy store is used. The one shown is 3½ in. in length. The armature core is a strip of $\frac{1}{16}$ by ¼-in. iron, 2¼ in. long, bent U-shaped and fastened to the wood flywheel. Each leg of the armature is wound with 10 ft. of No. 24 gauge magnet wire. The commutator is made from an old 22 cartridge filed into two equal parts, each being a half circle, both of which are made fast to a collar on the shaft E. Each half of the commutator must be insulated from the other half. The collar can be made by wrapping paper around the shaft until the required size is obtained.

The top end of the shaft runs in a hole bored in a brass support, B, which is screwed on the end of a piece of wood mortised in the base, as shown in Fig. 1. The lower end of the shaft runs in a glass bead, D, which is fastened to a small piece of brass with sealing wax. The small brass piece is fastened to the base with screws. The bead should not have an eye larger in diameter than the shaft. The shaft is made from an old discarded knitting needle. The brushes are fastened to each side of the upright piece of wood supporting the brass bearing B.

The connections to the battery are shown in Fig. 2. Each half of the commutator C is connected to the coils AA as shown in Fig. 1.—Contributed by J. M. Shannon, Pasadena, Calif.

Moving a Coin Under a Glass

Place a penny or a dime on a tablecloth, towel or napkin and cover it over with a glass in such a way that the glass will rest upon two 25 or 50-cent pieces as shown in the sketch. The coin is made to come forth without touching it or sliding a stick under the edge of the glass. It is only necessary to claw the cloth near the glass with the nail of the forefinger.

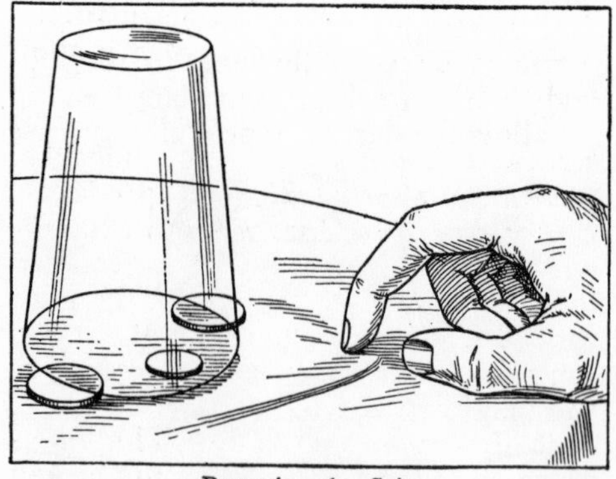
Removing the Coin

The cloth will produce a movement that will slide the coin to the edge and from under the glass.

When playing loud and harsh records on a phonograph the music is often spoiled by the vibration of the metal horn. This may be remedied by buckling a valise or shawl strap around the horn, near the center.

How to Make Paper Balloons

Balloons made spherical, or designed after the regular aeronaut's hot-air balloon, are the best kind to make. Those having an odd or unusual shape will not make good ascensions, and in most cases the paper will catch fire from the torch and burn before they have flown very far. The following description is for making a tissue-paper balloon about 6 ft. high.

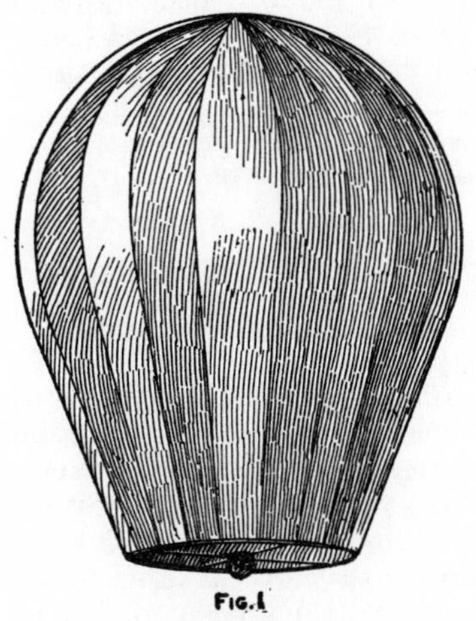

Paper Balloon

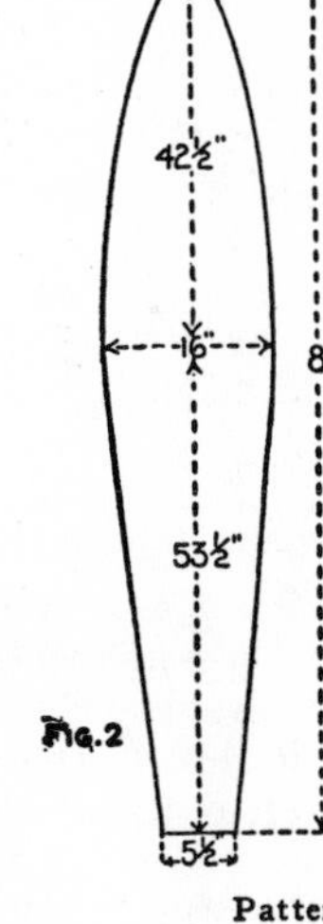

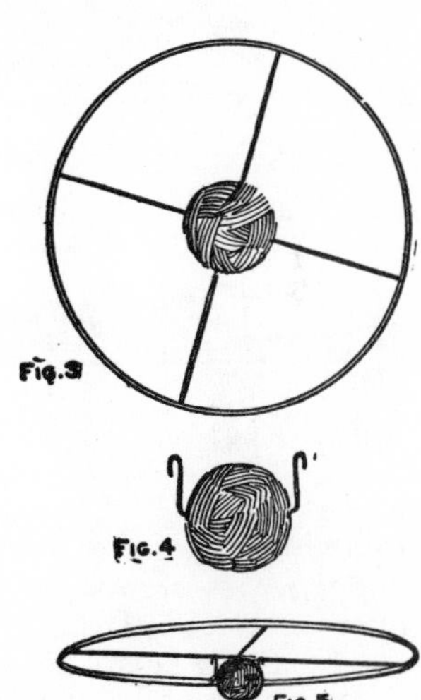

Pattern and Parts to Make Balloon

The paper may be selected in several colors, and the gores cut from these, pasted in alternately, will produce a pretty array of colors when the balloon is in flight. The shape of a good balloon is shown in Fig. 1. The gores for a 6-ft. balloon should be about 8 ft. long or about one-third longer than the height of the balloon. The widest part of each gore is 16 in. The widest place should be 53½ in. from the bottom end, or a little over half way from the bottom to the top. The bottom of the gore is one-third the width of the widest point. The dimensions and shape of each gore are shown in Fig. 2.

The balloon is made up of 13 gores pasted together, using about ½-in. lap on the edges. Any good paste will do—one that is made up of flour and water well cooked will serve the purpose. If the gores have been put together right, the pointed ends will close up the top entirely and the wider bottom ends will leave an opening about 20 in. in diameter. A light wood hoop having the same diameter as the opening is pasted to the bottom end of the gores. Two cross wires are fastened to the hoop, as shown in Fig. 3. These are to hold the wick ball, Fig. 4, so it will hang as shown in Fig. 5. The wick ball is made by winding wicking around a wire, having the ends bent into hooks as shown.

The balloon is filled with hot air in a manner similar to that used with the ordinary cloth balloon. A small trench or fireplace is made of brick having a chimney over which the mouth of the paper balloon is placed. Use fuel that will make heat with very little smoke. Hold the balloon so it will not catch fire from the flames coming out of the chimney. Have some alcohol ready to pour on the wick ball, saturating it thoroughly. When the balloon is well filled carry it away from the fireplace, attach the wick ball to the cross wires and light it.

In starting the balloon on its flight, take care that it leaves the ground as nearly upright as possible.—Contributed by R. E. Staunton.

A Simple Steamboat Model

The small boat shown in the accompanying sketch may have a length of 12 to 18 in. and is constructed in the

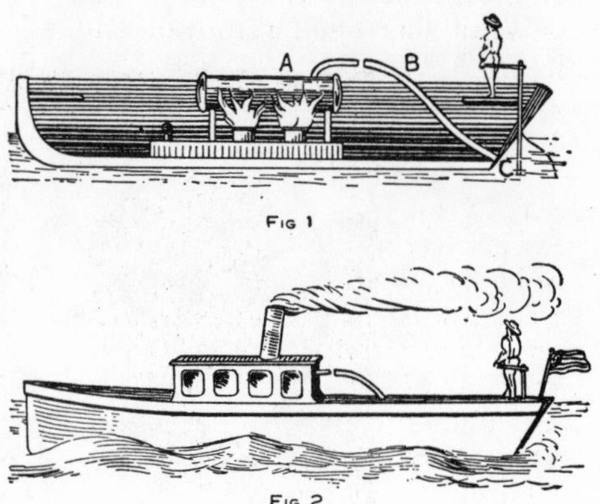

Sectional View and Completed Boat

following manner: A small steam boiler, A, is supported by two braces over an alcohol lamp in the middle of the boat. A small pipe is fastened to the top of the boiler in such a way that the open end will be opposite the open end of another pipe, B, somewhat larger in size. The pipe B opens into the stern of the boat at C, as shown in Fig. 1. The steam, coming through the small pipe A, is driven forcibly through the larger pipe B, and carries with it a certain amount of air out through the opening C into the water. As the boat is driven forward by this force, the steam arises to the surface in the form of bubbles. The boat soon attains considerable speed, leaving a long wake behind.

To Remove Grease from Machinery

A good way to remove grease or oil from machinery before painting is to brush slaked lime and water over the surface, leaving the solution on over night. After washing, the iron is dried and the paint will stick to it readily.

In removing grease from wood, common whitewash may be left on for a few hours and then washed off with warm water, after which the paint will adhere permanently.

A Game Played on the Ice

Two lines are drawn parallel on the ice from 50 to 100 ft. apart and blocks of wood are placed every 6 ft. apart on these lines. The player opening the game skates to the line and delivers, in bowling form, a sliding block similar to the blocks that are placed on the lines with the exception that it has a handle. The blocks are about 6 in. wide by 6 in. high and 8 in. long. The sliding blocks should be at least 1 ft. long and each provided with a handle. The handle is attached by boring a hole near one end in the middle of the block and driving in a wood pin. The hole is bored slanting so as to incline the handle. Two of these blocks are provided for the reason that when a player bowls one of the opposing player's blocks over the line he is entitled to another throw. The side wins that bowls over all of the opposing players' blocks first. This will prove an interesting and enjoyable pastime for skaters.

Bowling Over the Opponent's Blocks

Making Photo Silhouette Brass Plaques

Secure a brass plate having a smooth surface the right size for the photograph and cover it with a coat of paraffin. This is done by heating the paraffin in a vessel hot enough to make the wax run freely, then pouring the liquid over the entire surface of the brass.

When the paraffin has cooled sufficiently the outlines of the photograph must be drawn upon its surface. There are three ways of doing this: First, the photograph can be traced on tissue paper and then retraced on the paraffin surface. The exact outlines of the photograph can be obtained this way without destroying the print. Second, if you have several copies of the photograph, one can be utilized by tracing direct to the surface of the paraffin. In using either of the two methods described, carbon paper must be placed on the paraffin before the tissue paper or photograph is laid upon it. Third, cut out the outlines of the photograph and lay it on the paraffin surface, then trace around the edges with the point of a needle or sharp point of a knife. The outlines drawn by the first method are cut through the paraffin in the same way. The paraffin is carefully removed from the inside of the lines, leaving the brass surface perfectly clean, as is shown in Fig. 1.

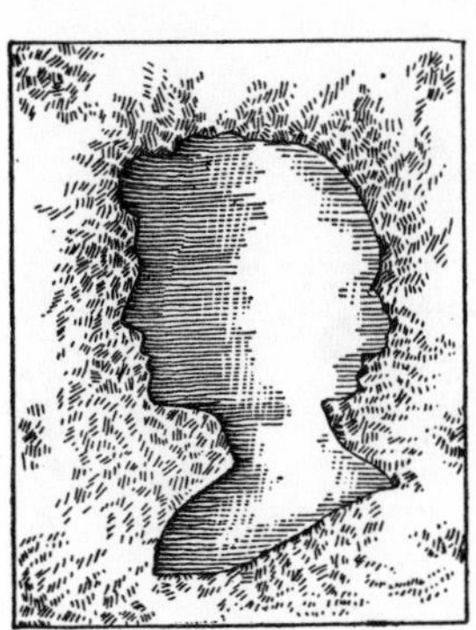

Fig. 1
Waxed Brass Plate

The exposed part of the plate is now ready to be etched or eaten away to the right depth with acid. The acid solution is made up of 1½ parts muriatic acid and 2 parts water. The mixture should be placed in a glass or earthenware vessel. If the plate is a small one a saucer will do for the acid solution. Pour the acid on the plate where the paraffin has been removed and allow it time to etch. The acid should be removed every five minutes to examine the etching. If any places show up where the paraffin has not been entirely removed they must be cleaned so the acid will eat out the metal. When the acid solution becomes weak new solution must be added until the proper depth is secured. Rinse the plate in cold water, stand in a tray and heat it sufficiently to run off all the paraffin. Polish the plate by rubbing it with a piece of flannel.

Fig. 2
Finished Plaque

The plaque can be given a real antique finish by painting the etched part with a dull black paint. Drill a small hole in each of the four corners, being careful not to dent the metal. The plaque is backed with a piece of wood ¾ in. thick, the dimensions of which should exceed those of the brass plate sufficiently to harmonize with the size of the plaque. The wood should be painted black with the same paint used in the plaque. Paint the heads of four thumb tacks black and use them in fastening the plaque to the board. The finished silhouette will appear as shown in Fig. 2.—Contributed by John A. Hellwig, Albany, N. Y.

¶Automobile headlights should be set to throw the light straight ahead, not pointed down at the road at an angle.

Telescope Stand and Holder

With the ordinary small telescope it is very difficult to keep the line of sight fixed upon any particular object. To meet the situation I constructed the

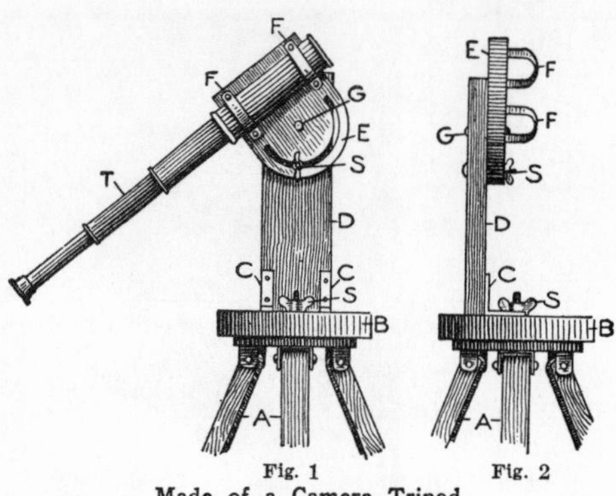

Fig. 1 Fig. 2
Made of a Camera Tripod

device illustrated herewith. A circular piece of wood, B, 6 in. in diameter, is fastened to a common camera tripod, A, with a set screw, S. Corner irons, CC, are screwed to the circular piece. These corner irons are also screwed to, and supported in a vertical position by the wood standard D, which is 4 in. wide and of any desired height. To this standard is secured the wood shield-shaped piece E by the screw G upon which it turns. A semi-circular slit is cut in the piece G, through which passes the set screw S. The telescope is secured to the piece G by means of the pipe straps FF. Rubber bands are put around the telescope to prevent rubbing at the places where the straps enclose it.

The wood pieces were made of ½-in. mahogany well rubbed with linseed oil to give them a finish. The corner irons and set screws or bolts with thumb-nuts can be purchased at any hardware store. The pipe straps of different sizes can be obtained from a plumber's or gas and steam fitter's store. With this device, either a vertical or a horizontal motion may be secured, and, after bringing the desired object into the line of sight, the set screws will hold the telescope in position. Any one owning a tripod can construct this device in three or four hours' time at a trifling cost. In Fig. 1 is shown the side view of the holder and stand, and Fig. 2 the front view.

It may be of interest to those owning telescopes without solar eyepieces to know that such an eyepiece can be obtained very cheaply by purchasing a pair of colored eyeglasses with very dark lenses and metal rims. Break off the frame, leaving the metal rims and nibs at each end. Place these over the eyepiece of the telescope and secure in place with rubber bands looped over the nibs and around the barrel of the instrument.—Contributed by R. A. Paine, Richmond, Va.

How to Make an Electrical Horn

Secure an empty syrup or fruit can, any kind having a smooth flat bottom will do. If the bottom is not perfectly flat, it will interfere with the regular tone vibrations, and not produce the right sound. Remove the label by soaking it in hot water. Take an ordinary electrical bell and remove the gong, clip off the striking ball and bend the rod at right angles. Cut a block of wood ¾ in. thick, 5 in. wide and 8 in. long for the base. Fasten the can on it with a piece of sheet brass or

Tin Can and Bell Parts

tin as shown in the sketch. Mount the bell vibrator on the base, using a small block of wood to elevate it to the level of the center of the can, and solder the end of the vibrator rod to the metal.

Connect two dry cells to the bell vibrator, and adjust the contact screw until a clear tone is obtained. The rapidly moving armature of the bell vibrator causes the bottom of the can to vibrate with it, thus producing sound waves. The pitch of the tone depends on the thickness of the bottom of the can. This horn, if carefully adjusted and using two cells of dry battery, will give a soft pleasant tone that can be heard a block away. If the two projecting parts of the vibrator are sawed off with a hacksaw, it can be mounted on the inside of the can. This will make a very compact electric horn, as only the can is visible.—Contributed by John Sidelmier, La Salle, Ill.

Driving a Washing Machine with Motorcycle Power

The halftone illustration shows how I rigged up my washing machine to be driven by the power from my motorcycle. I made a wheel 26 in. in diameter of some 1-in. pine boards, shrunk an iron band on it for a tire, and bolted it to the wheel on the washing machine. A long belt the same width as the motorcycle belt was used to drive the machine. The motorcycle was lined up and the engine started, then the motorcycle belt thrown off and the long belt run on, connecting the engine and washing machine wheel. —I. R. Kidder, Lake Preston, S. D.

Machine Belted to the Motorcycle

Home-Made Aquarium

A good aquarium can be made from a large-sized street lamp globe and a yellow pine block. Usually a lamp globe costs less than an aquarium globe of the same dimensions. Procure a yellow pine block 3 in. thick and 12 in. square. The more uneven and twisted the grain the better for the purpose, as it is then less liable to develop a continuous crack.

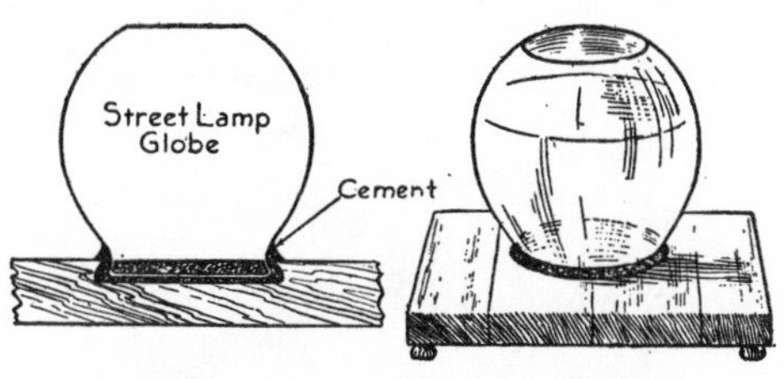

Lamp Globe as an Aquarium

Cut out a depression for the base of the globe as shown in Fig. 1. Pour in aquarium cement and embed the globe in it. Pour more cement inside of the globe until the cement is level with the top of the block. Finish with a ring of cement around the outside and sprinkle with fine sand while the cement is damp. Feet may be added to the base if desired. The weight of the pine block makes a very solid and substantial base for the globe and renders it less liable to be upset.—Contributed by James R. Kane, Doylestown, Pa.

¶Never allow lard oil to harden on a lathe.

Frame for Displaying Both Sides of Coins

It is quite important for coin collectors to have some convenient way to

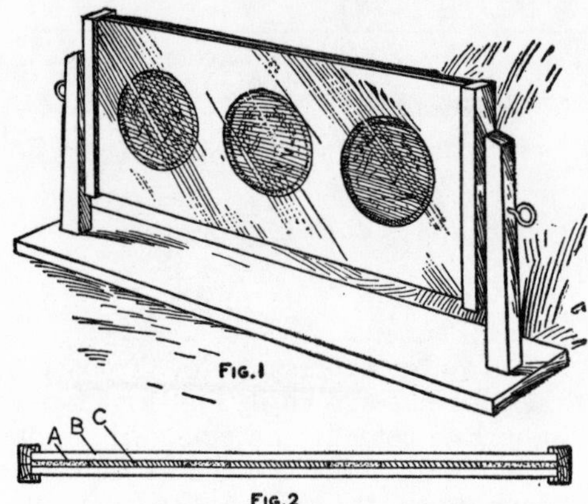

Holding Coins between Glasses

show both sides of coins without touching or handling them. If the collection consists of only a few coins, they can be arranged in a frame as shown in Fig. 1. The frame is made of a heavy card, A, Fig. 2, the same thickness as the coins, and covered over on each side with a piece of glass, B. Holes are cut in the card to receive the coins C. The frame is placed on bearings so it may be turned over to examine both sides. If there is a large collection of coins, the frame can be made in the same manner and used as drawers in a cabinet. The drawers can be taken out and turned over.—Contributed by C. Purdy, Ghent, O.

How to Make Lantern Slides

A great many persons who have magic lanterns do not use them very much, for after the slides have been shown a few times, they become uninteresting, and buying new ones or even making them from photographic negatives is expensive. But by the method described in the following paragraph any one can make new and interesting slides in a few minutes' time and at a very small cost.

Secure a number of glass plates of the size that will fit your lantern and clean them on both sides. Dissolve a piece of white rosin in a half-pint of gasoline and flow it over one side of the plates and allow to dry. Place the dried plate over a picture you wish to reproduce and draw the outline upon the thin film. A lead pencil, pen and ink or colored crayons can be used, as the rosin and gasoline give a surface that can be written upon as easily as upon paper. When the slide becomes uninteresting it can be cleaned with a little clear gasoline and used again to make another slide. A slide can be made in this way in five minutes and an interesting outline picture in even less time than that.

This solution also makes an ideal retouching varnish for negatives.—Contributed by J. E. Noble, Toronto, Canada.

How to Make a Developing Box

A box for developing 3¼ by 4¼-in. plates is shown in detail in the accompanying sketch. It is made of strips of wood ¼-in. thick, cut and grooved, and then glued together as indicated. If desired, a heavier piece can be placed on the bottom. Coat the inside of the box with paraffin or wax, melted and applied with a brush. Allow it to fill all crevices so that the developing box will be watertight. It will hold 4 oz. of developer. Boxes for larger plates

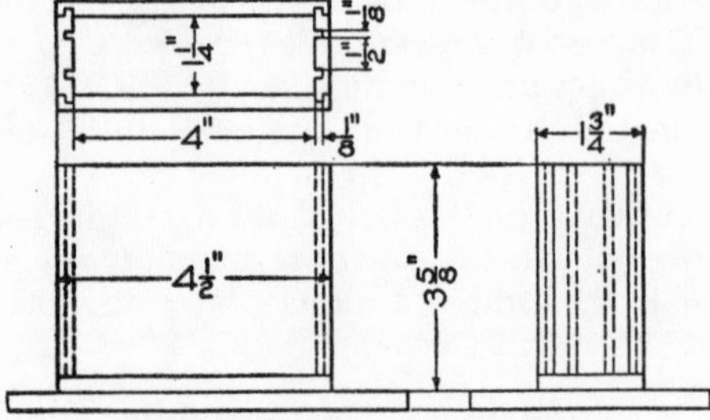

Details of the Developing Box

can be made in the same manner. Use a small wooden clip in taking the plates out of the box, being careful not to scratch the sensitive film.—Contributed by R. J. Smith, Milwaukee, Wis.

Staining Wood

A very good method of staining close-grained woods is to use muriatic acid. The acid is put on with a brush like any ordinary stain. The colors thus obtained are artistic and most beautiful, and cannot be duplicated by any known pigment. The more coats applied the darker the color will be. This method of staining has the advantage of requiring no wiping or rubbing. —Contributed by August T. Neyer, One Cloud, Cal.

Sheet-Metal Whisk-Broom Holder

A whisk-broom holder such as is shown in the accompanying picture may be easily made by the amateur. The tools needed are few: a pair of tin shears, a metal block of some kind upon which to pound when riveting, a hammer or mallet, several large nails, and a stout board upon which to work up the design. A rivet punch is desirable, though not absolutely necessary.

The material required is a sheet of No. 24 gauge copper or brass of a size equal to that of the proposed holder, plus a 3/8-in. border all around, into which to place the screws that are to be used to hold the metal to the board while pounding it. The design shown in the picture is 6 by 8 in. at the widest part and has proven a satisfactory holder for a small broom.

Carefully work out the design desired on a piece of drawing paper, both outline and decoration, avoiding sharp curves in the outline because they are hard to follow with the shears when cutting the metal. If the design is to be of two-part symmetry, like the one shown, draw one part, then fold on a center line and duplicate this by inserting double-surfaced carbon paper and tracing the part already drawn. With this same carbon paper transfer the design to the metal. Fasten the metal to the board firmly, using 1/2-in. screws placed about 1 in. apart in holes previously punched in the margin with a nail set or nail.

To flatten the metal preparatory to fastening it to the board, place a block of wood upon it and pound on this block, never upon the metal directly,

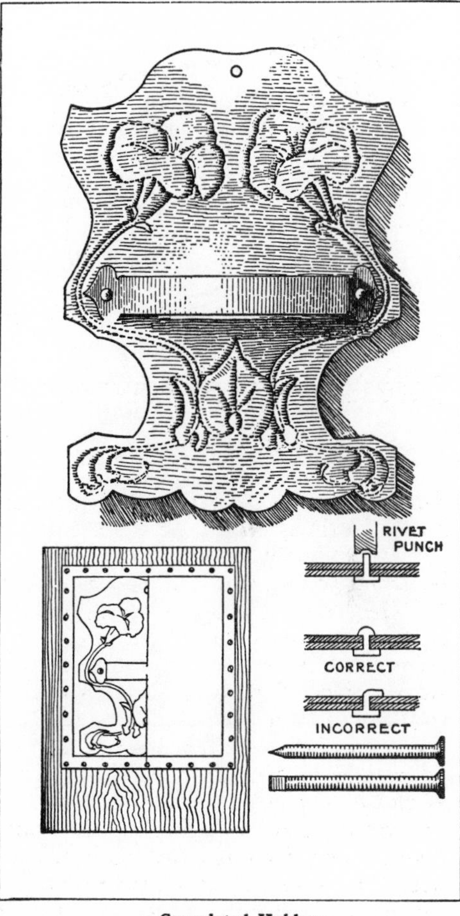

Completed Holder
Brass Fastened to Board—Method of Riveting

or the surface will be dented and look bad in the finished piece.

Take the nail, a 10 or 20-penny wire or cut, and file it to a chisel edge, rounding it just enough to take the sharpness off so that it will not cut the metal. This tool is used for indenting the metal so as to bring out the outline of the design on the surface.

There are several ways of working up the design. The simplest way is to take the nail and merely "chase" the outlines of holder design. Remove the screws, cut off the surplus metal.

and file the edges until they are smooth. Make a paper pattern for the metal band that is to hold the broom. Trace around this pattern on the metal and cut out the shape. Punch rivet holes in holder and band, also a hole by which to hang the whole upon the wall.

Rivet the band to the holder. Punch the rivet holes with a nail set and make the holes considerably larger than the diameter of the rivet, for in flattening the raised edges the holes will close. Do the riveting on a metal block and keep the head of the rivet on the back of the holder. Round up the "upset" end of the riveted part as shown in the picture. Do not bend it over or flatten it. This rounding is done by pounding around the outer edge of the rivet end and not flat upon the top as in driving a nail.

Clean the metal by scrubbing it off with a solution composed of one-half water and one-half nitric acid. Use a rag tied to a stick and do not allow the acid to touch either your hands or clothes. A metal lacquer may next be applied to keep the metal from early corrosion.

How to Make a Camp Stool

The stool, as shown in Fig. 1, is made of beech or any suitable wood

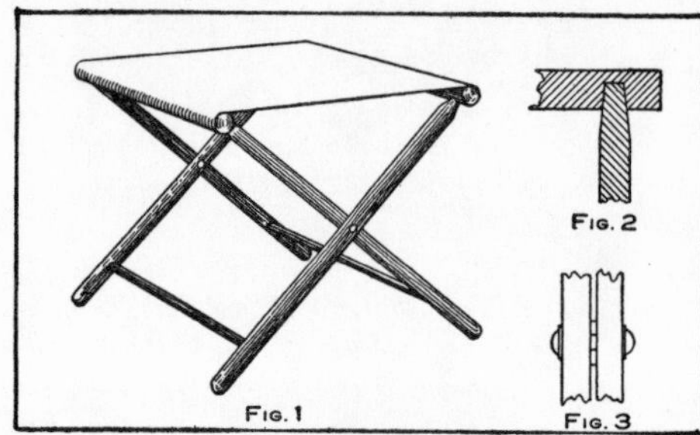

Camp Stool Details

with a canvas or carpet top. Provide four lengths for the legs, each 1 in. square and 18½ in. long; two lengths, 1⅛ in. square and 11 in. long, for the top, and two lengths, ¾ in. square, one 8½ and the other 10½ in. long, for the lower rails.

The legs are shaped at the ends to fit into a ⅝-in. hole bored in the top pieces as shown in Fig. 2, the distance between the centers of the holes being 7⅝ in. in one piece and 9⅝ in. in the other. The lower rails are fitted in the same way, using a ½-in. hole bored into each leg 2½ in. up from the lower end.

Each pair of legs has a joint for folding and this joint is made by boring a hole in the middle of each leg, inserting a bolt and riveting it over washers with a washer placed between the legs as shown in Fig. 3. The entire length of each part is rounded off for the sake of neatness as well as lightness.

About ½ yd. of 11-in. wide material will be required for the seat and each end of this is nailed securely on the under side of the top pieces. The woodwork may be stained and varnished or plain varnished and the cloth may be made to have a pleasing effect by stencilling in some neat pattern.

A Small Home-Made Electric Motor

The accompanying photographs show the construction of a very unique electric motor, the parts consisting of the frame from an old bicycle pedal wrapped with insulated wire to make the armature and three permanent magnets taken from an old telephone magneto. The pedal, being ball bearing, rotated with very little friction and at a surprisingly high rate of speed.

The Motor Complete

The dust cap on the end of the pedal was removed and a battery connection, having quite a length of threads, was soldered to it as shown in the photograph. The flanges were removed from an ordinary spool and two strips of brass fastened on its circumference for the commutator. The spool was held in position by a small binding

Commutator Parts

post nut. The shape of this nut made a good pulley for a cord belt.—Contributed by John Shahan, Attalla, Ala.

Rocker Blocks on Coaster Sleds

The accompanying sketch shows a coasting sled with rocker blocks attached on both front and rear runners. The runners and the other parts of the sled are made in the usual way, but instead of fastening the rear runners solid to the top board and the front runners to turn on a solid plane fifth wheel, they are pivoted so each pair of runners will rock when going over bumps.

The illustration will explain this construction without going into detail and giving dimensions for a certain size, as these rocker blocks can be attached to any coaster or toboggan sled. It will be noticed that the top board may bend as much as it will under the load without causing the front ends of the rear runners and the rear ends of the front runners gouging into the snow or ice.—Contributed by W. F. Quackenbush, New York City.

Coaster Sled with Rocker Runners

How to Make a Watch Fob

This novelty watch fob is made from felt, using class, college or lodge colors combined in the making with emblems or initials colored on the texture. Two pieces of felt, each 1¼ in. wide and 4¼ in. long, are cut V-shaped on one end of each piece about 1 in. in depth, and ⅜ in. in from the other end of one piece cut a slit ½ in. long; the end of the other piece is folded over, making a lap of about 1 in., and a slit is cut through the double thickness to match the one cut in the first piece. The desired emblem, initial, or pennant is stenciled on the outside of the folded piece with class, college or lodge colors. The strap is made from a strip of felt 3-16 in. wide and 8¼ in. long; stitched on both edges for appearance. Make a hole with a punch 1¼ in. from one end, and two holes in the other, one about 1 in. and the other 2¾ in. from the end. Purchase a ½-in. buckle from a harness maker and you will have all the parts necessary for the fob. Assemble as shown in the sketch. The end of the strap having the two holes is put through the slots cut in the wide pieces and the tongue of the buckle is run through both holes. The other end is passed through the ring of the watch and fastened in the buckle as in an ordinary belt.—Contributed by C. D. Luther, Ironwood, Mich.

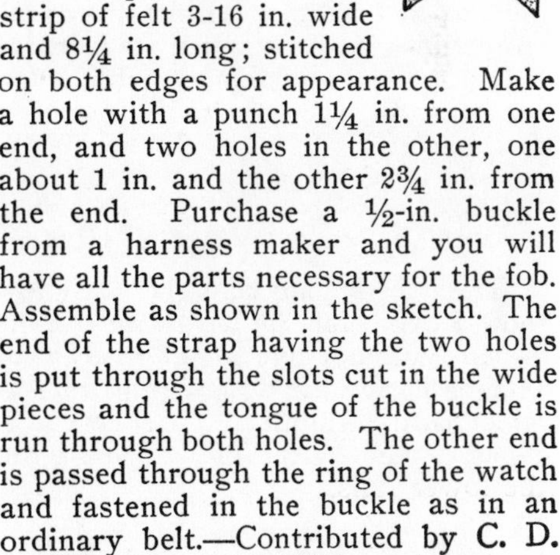

A good lubricant for drilling is made by dissolving ¾ to 1 lb. of sal-soda in one pailful of water.

New Way to Remove a Bottle Stopper

Take a bottle of liquid, something that is carbonated, and with the aid of a napkin form a pad which is applied

Removing the Stopper

to the lower end of the bottle. Strike hard with repeated blows against the solid surface of a wall, as shown in the sketch, and the cork will be driven out, sometimes with so much force that a part of the liquid comes with it and deluges the spectators, if desired by the operator.

Imitation Fancy Wings on Hinges

The accompanying sketch shows how I overcame the hardware troubles when I was not able to find ready-made hinges in antique design for a mission sideboard and buffet. This method allows a wide range of designs, which

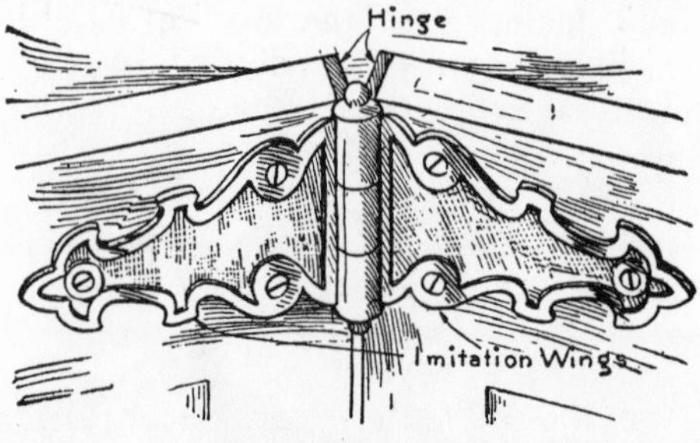

Fancy Hinge Wings

can be made at home with ordinary tools. The wings are made of copper or brass and finished in repoussé, or can be tarnished and the high places burnished with 000 sandpaper or steel wool, then lacquered with white shellac or banana bronzing liquid.—Contributed by John H. Schatz, Indianapolis, Ind.

How to Make a Child's Rolling Toy

Secure a tin can, or a pasteboard box, about 2 in. in diameter and 2 in. or more in height. Punch two holes A, Fig. 1, in the cover and the bottom, 1/4 in. from the center and opposite each other. Then cut a curved line from one hole to the other, as shown at B. A piece of lead, which can be procured from a plumber, is cut in the shape shown in Fig. 2, the size being 1 by 1 1/8 by 1 1/4 in. An ordinary rubber band is secured around the neck of the piece of

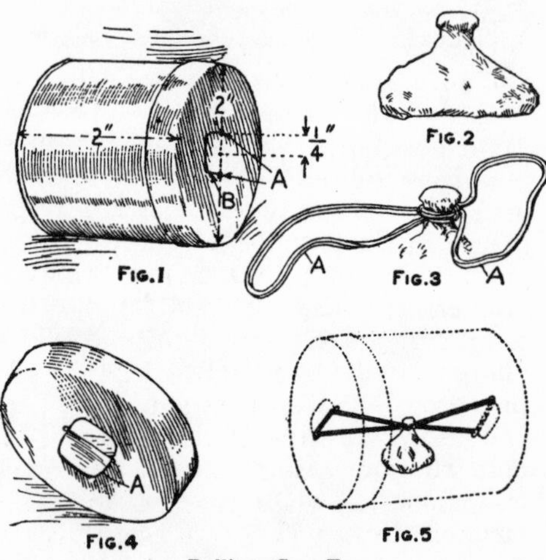

Rolling Can Toy

lead, as shown in Fig. 3, allowing the two ends to be free. The pieces of tin between the holes A, Fig. 1, on both top and bottom, are turned up as in Fig. 4, and the ends of the bands looped over them. The flaps are then turned down on the band and the can parts put together as in Fig. 5. The can may be decorated with brilliant colored stripes, made of paper strips pasted on the tin. When the can is rolled away from you, it winds up the rubber band, thus storing the propelling power which makes it return.—Contributed by Mack Wilson, Columbus, O.

How to Make a Portfolio

Secure a piece of Russian modeling calf leather of a size equal to 12 by 16 in. Make a paper pattern of the size indicated in the accompanying drawing, putting in the design.

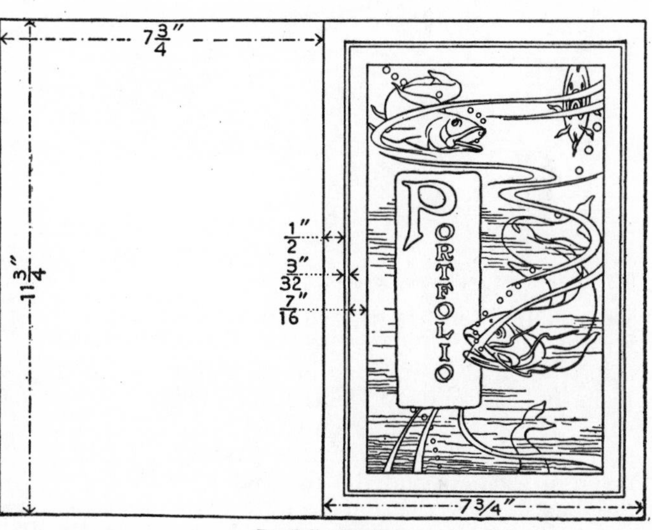

Portfolio Design

The necessary tools consist of a stick with a straight edge and a tool with an end shaped like that of a nutpick. A nutpick with a V-shaped point will do if the sharpness is smoothed off by means of a piece of emery paper, so that it will indent without cutting the leather. These tools can be bought for this special purpose, but are not essential for this piece if the nutpick is at hand. There will also be needed a level, non-absorbent surface upon which to lay the leather while working it. A piece of thick glass, metal, or marble will serve.

Begin work by moistening the leather on the back side with a sponge or cloth. Moisten as much as you dare and still not have the moisture show on the face side. Next place the leather on the glass, face up, and, holding the pattern firmly in place so that it will not slip—if possible get some one to hold the pattern for you—place the straight edge on the straight lines and mark out or indent. After this has been done, mark over the design. A pencil may be used the first time over.

The pattern is now to be removed and all the lines gone over with the tool to make them deep and uniform.

The surplus stock around the edges may not be cut off. A neat way to finish the edges is to punch a series of holes entirely around through which a thin leather thong may be laced. If it is desired to "line" the inside, this should be done before the holes are punched or the lacing done.

Gear for Model Work

When a gear is needed to drive a small pinion and there is none of the right size at hand, one can be made in the following manner: Turn up a wood disk to the proper diameter and $\frac{1}{4}$ in. thicker than the pinion, and cut a flat bottom groove $\frac{3}{16}$ in. deep in its face. The edges should be about $\frac{1}{8}$ in. or more thick on each side. Measure the distance between centers of two adjacent teeth in the pinion and step this off around the periphery in the bottom of the groove. Drill holes into the wood on each point stepped off and insert steel pins made of wire, allowing the end of each to protrude just far enough to act as a tooth. In this way a good gear for light work can be quickly and cheaply constructed.—Contributed by Henry Schaefer, New York City.

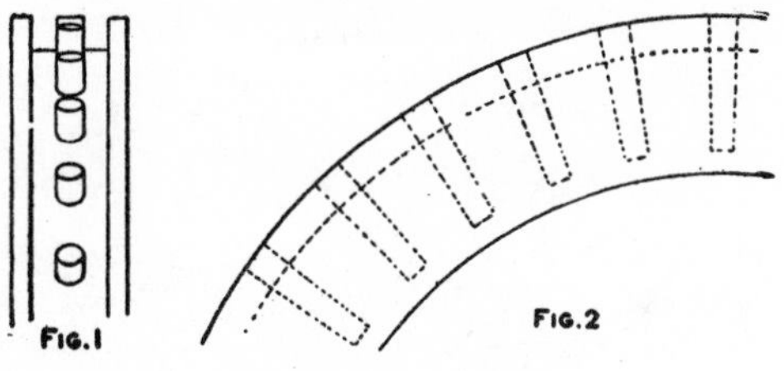

Steel Pins in Wood

A Home-Made Vise

While making a box I had some dovetailing to do, and as there was no

Vise on Bench

vise on the bench I rigged up a substitute. I secured a board 3/4 in. thick, 3 in. wide and 20 in. long and bored a 1/2-in. hole through it, 1 in. from each end. The board was then attached to the bench with two screws passing through washers and the two holes in the board into the bench top. The screws should be of a length suitable to take in the piece to be worked.—Contributed by A. M. Rice, Syracuse, New York.

Cardboard Spiral Turned by Heat

A novel attraction for a window display can be made from a piece of stiff cardboard cut in a spiral as shown in Fig. 1. The cardboard should be about 7 or 8 in. in diameter. Tie a piece of string to the center point of the spiral

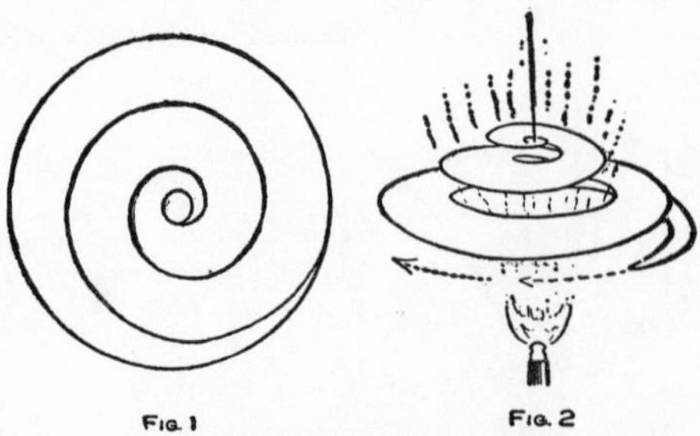

Spiral Cut from Cardboard

and fasten it so as to hang over a gas jet, Fig. 2. A small swivel must be put in the string at the top or near the cardboard, if it is desired to have the spiral run for any length of time. The cardboard will spin around rapidly and present quite an attraction.—Contributed by Harry Szerlip, Brooklyn, N. Y.

A Workbench for the Amateur

The accompanying detail drawing shows a design of a portable workbench suitable for the amateur woodworker. This bench can be made easily by anyone who has a few sharp tools and a little spare time. If the stock is purchased from the mill ready planed and cut to length, much of the hard labor will be saved. Birch or maple wood makes a very good bench. and the following pieces should be ordered:

4 legs, 3 by 3 by 36.
2 side rails, 3 by 3 by 62½ in.
2 end rails, 3 by 3 by 20 in.
1 back board, 1 by 9 by 80 in.
1 top board, 2 by 12 by 77 in.
1 top board, 1 by 12 by 77 in.
2 crosspieces, 1½ by 3 by 24 in.
1 piece for clamp, 1½ by 6½ by 12 in.
1 piece for clamp, 1½ by 6½ by 14 in.
4 guides, 2 by 2 by 18 in.
1 screw block, 3 by 3 by 6 in.
1 piece, 1½ by 4½ by 10½ in.

Make the lower frame first. Cut tenons on the rails and mortise the posts, then fasten them securely together with 3/8 by 5-in. lag screws as shown. Also fasten the 1½ by 3 by 24-in. pieces to the tops of the posts with screws. The heads should be countersunk or else holes bored in the top boards to fit over them. Fasten the front top board to the crosspieces by lag screws through from the under side. The screws can be put in from the top for the 1-in. thick top board.

Fasten the end pieces on with screws, countersinking the heads of the vise end. Cut the 2-in. square holes in the 1½ by 4½ by 10-in. pieces for the vise slides, and fit it in place for the side vise. Also cut square holes in the one end piece for the end vise slides as shown. Now fit up the two clamps. Fasten the slides to the front pieces with screws. Countersink the heads of the screws so they will not be in the way of the hands when the vise is used. The two clamp screws should be about 1½ in. in diameter. They can be purchased at a hardware store. A block should be fitted under the crosspiece to hold the nut for the end vise. After the better grade of tools should be purchased as they are the cheapest in

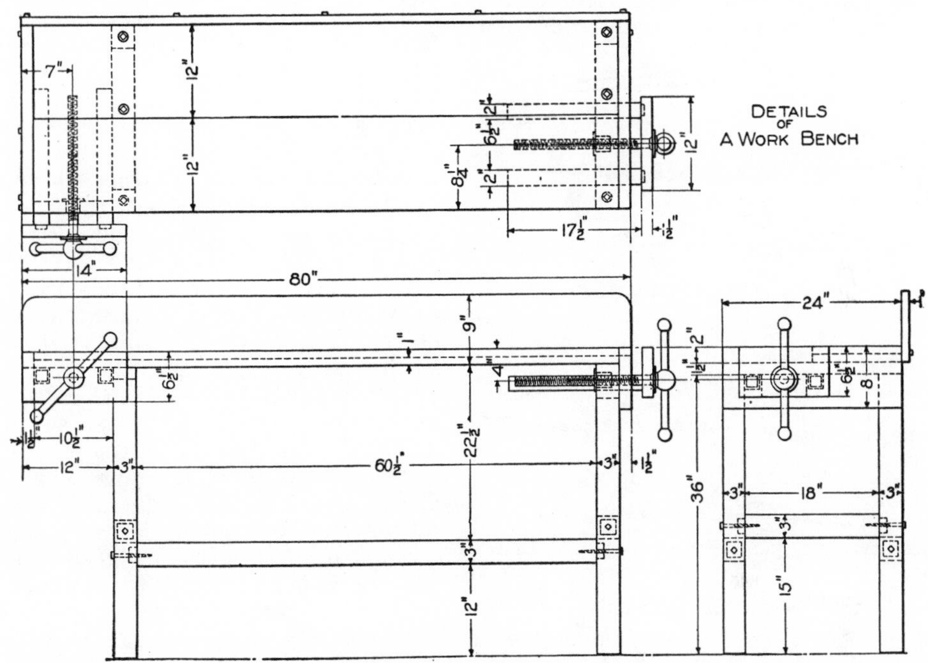

Detail of the Bench

you have the slides fitted, put them in place and bore the holes for the clamp screws.

The back board can now be fastened to the back with screws as shown in the top view. The bench is now complete, except for a couple of coats of oil which should be applied to give it a finish and preserve the wood. The amateur workman, as well as the patternmaker, will find this a very handy and serviceable bench for his workshop.

As the amateur workman does not always know just what tools he will need, a list is given which will answer for a general class of work. This list can be added to as the workman becomes more proficient in his line and has need for other tools. Only the better grade of tools should be purchased as they are the cheapest in the long run. If each tool is kept in a certain place, it can be easily found when wanted.

1 bench plane or jointer; 1 jack plane or smoother; 1 cross cut saw, 24 in.; 1 rip saw, 24 in.; 1 claw hammer; 1 set gimlets; 1 brace and set of bits; 2 screwdrivers, 3 and 6 in.; 1 countersink; 1 compass saw; 1 set chisels; 1 wood scraper; 1 monkey wrench; 1 2-ft. rule; 1 marking gauge; 1 pair pliers; 1 nail set; 1 pair dividers; 1 pocket level; 1 6-in. try square; 1 oilstone; No. 1, 2 and 00 sandpaper.

Workbench Complete

Repairing a Worn Knife Blade

When the blade of a favorite pocket knife, after constant use, becomes like A, Fig. 1, it is more dangerous than

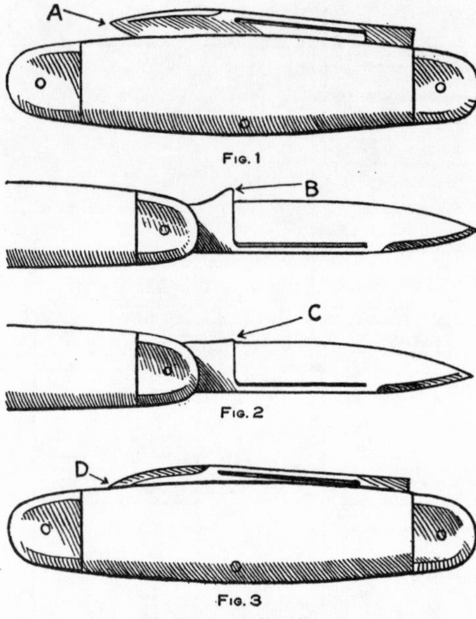

The Blade Is Cut Down

useful. To cut down the already worn blade would leave only a stump, but if the blade is fastened in a vise and the point B filed off until it is like C, Fig. 2, the projecting point A, Fig. 1, will sink into the handle as shown at D, Fig. 3, and the knife will be given a new lease of usefulness.—Contributed by James M. Kane, Doylestown, Pa.

How to Make a Leather Spectacle Case

The spectacle case shown in the accompanying illustration may be made of either calf or cow skin. The calf skin, being softer, will be easier to work, but will not make as rigid a case as the cow skin. If calf skin is to be used, secure a piece of modeling calf. The extreme width of the case is 2⅜ in. and the length 6⅝ in. Two pieces will be required of this size. Put on the design before the two parts are sewed together. First draw the design on paper, then prepare the leather. Place the leather on a small non-absorbent surface, such as copper or brass, and moisten the back side with as much water as it will take and still not show on the face side. Turn the leather, lay the design on the face, and hold it in place while both the outline and decoration are traced on the surface with a pencil or some tool that will make a sharp line without tearing the paper.

After the outlines are traced, go over the indentations a second time so as to make them sharp and distinct. There are special modeling tools that can be purchased for this purpose, but a V-shaped nut pick, if smoothed with emery paper so that it will not cut the leather, will do just as well.

Take a stippling tool—if no such tool is at hand, a cup-pointed nail set will do—and stamp the background. It is intended that the full design shall be placed on the back and the same design placed on the front as far as the material will allow. Be careful in stamping not to pound so hard as to cut the leather. A little rubbing on the point with emery will take off the sharpness always found on a new tool.

Having prepared the two sides, they may be placed together and sewed around the edges.

If cow hide is preferred, the same

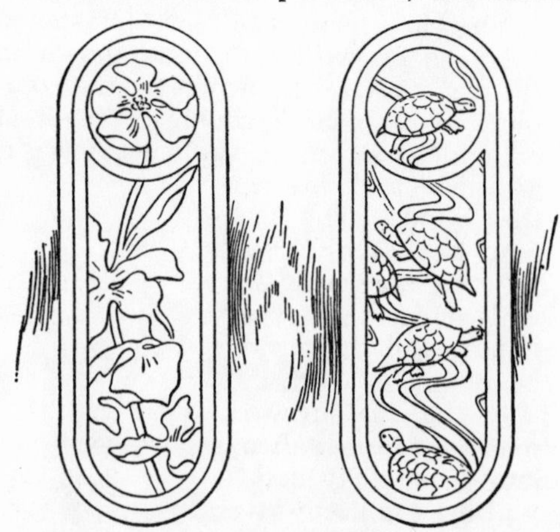

Two Designs of Cases

method of treatment is used, but a form will need to be made and placed inside the case while the leather is drying to give it the right shape. The form can be made of a stick of wood.

Waterproofing a Wall

The best way to make a tinted wall waterproof is to first use a material composed of cement properly tinted and with no glue in it—one that will not require a glue size on the wall. After this coating of cement is applied directly to the plaster, cover it completely with water enamel and, when dry, give the surface a thorough coating of varnish. This will make a perfectly impervious covering, which steam, water or heat will not affect.—Contributed by Julia A. White, New York City.

Polishing Flat Surfaces

The work of finishing a number of brass castings with flat sides was accomplished on an ordinary polishing wheel, from which the first few layers of cloth were removed and replaced with emery cloth. The emery surface of the cloth was placed outward and trimmed to the same diameter as the wheel. This made a sanding and polishing wheel in one.—Contributed by Chester L. Cobb, Portland, Maine.

Rubber Tip for Chair Legs

An inexpensive method of preventing a chair from scratching the floor is to bore a hole of the proper size in the bottom end of each chair leg and then procure four rubber stoppers of uniform size and press them into place.

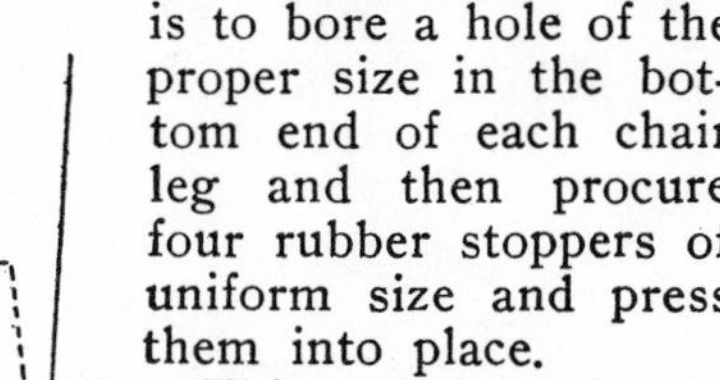

This cushion of rubber eliminates vibrations, and they will not slip nor mar the finest surface upon which they rest.—Contributed by W. A. Jaquythe, Richmond, Cal.

Adjusting a Plumb-Bob Line

When plumbing a piece of work, if there is no help at hand to hold the overhead line, it is common practice to fasten the plumb line to a nail or other suitable projection. On coming down to the lower floor it is often found that the bob has been secured either too high or too low. When fastening the line give it plenty of slack and when the lower floor is reached make a double loop in the line, as shown in the sketch. Tightening up on the parts A A will bind the loop bight B, and an adjustable friction-held loop, C, will be had for adjusting the bob accurately either up or down.—Contributed by Chas. Herrman, New York City.

Drier for Footwear

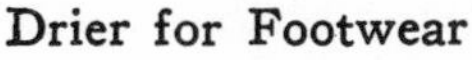

A drier for footwear can be readily made by a tinner, or anyone that can shape tin and solder. The drier consists of a pipe of sufficient length to enter the longest boot leg. Its top is bent at right angles and the other end is riveted to a base, an inverted stewpan, for instance, in whose bottom a few perforations have been made to let air in. The boot or stocking to be dried is placed over the pipe and the whole set on a heated surface. The heat will cause a rapid circulation of air which will dry the article quickly.—Contributed by Wm. Roberts, Cambridge, Mass.

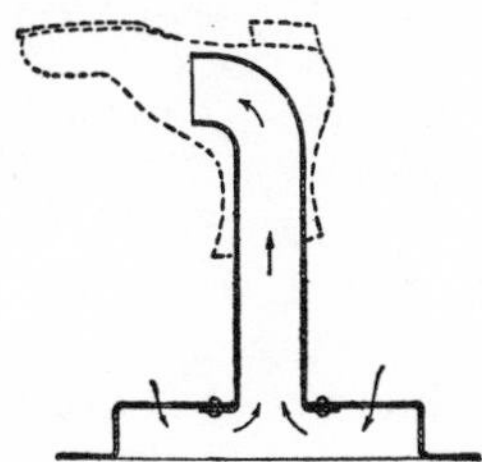

¶A very satisfactory repair can be made by using a good photographic paste to fasten a torn window shade to its roller.

A Shot Scoop

In the ammunition department of our hardware store the shot was kept in regular square bins and dished out

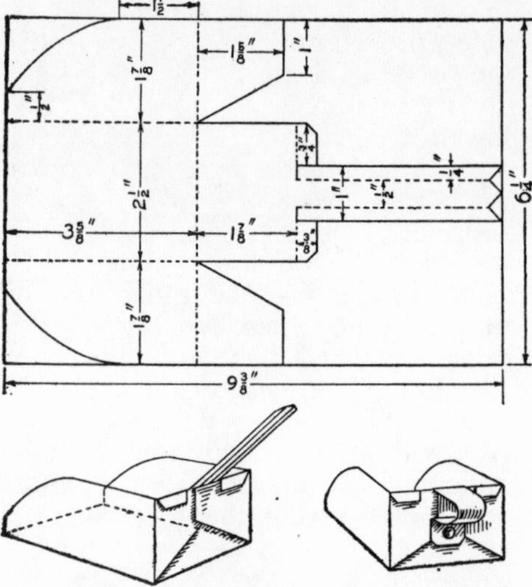

A Small Square Scoop Made of Tin for Dipping Up Shot Stored in a Square Bin

with a round-bottom scoop. This was very difficult, especially when the bottom of the bin was nearly reached, as the round scoop would roll over them and only pick up a few at a time. To overcome this difficulty I constructed a square-shaped scoop that gave entire satisfaction. The scoop can be used for other purposes as well.

A thick piece of tin, 6¼ by 9¾ in., was marked out as shown, the pattern being cut on the full lines and bent on the dotted ones. The strip for the handle was riveted to the end of the scoop.—Contributed by Geo. B. Wright, Middletown, Conn.

Removing Grease Stains from the Leaves of a Book

Happening to get a grease spot on a page of a valuable book, I found a way to remove it without injury to the paper, which has been tried out several times with success.

Heat an iron and hold it as near as possible to the stain without discoloring the paper, and the grease will disappear. If any traces of the grease are left, apply powdered calcined magnesia. Bone, well calcined and powdered, and plaster of Paris are also excellent absorbents of grease.

A beautifully bound book, and quite new, had oil from a lamp spilled over it. There was no quicklime to be had, so some bones were quickly calcined, pulverized and applied. The next morning there was no trace of oil, but only an odor which soon vanished.—Contributed by Paul Keller, Indianapolis, Ind.

Tightening Cane in Furniture

Split cane, used as part of furniture, such as chair seats, often becomes loose and the threads of cane pull out. This can be prevented by sponging with hot water, or by applying steaming cloths to the cane. This process also tightens the shreds of cane and does not injure ordinary furniture. If the article is highly polished, care should be taken to prevent the hot water from coming in contact with anything but the cane.

Cleaner for a Stovepipe

A long horizontal pipe for a stove soon fills with soot and must be cleaned. The usual method is to beat the pipe after taking it down to be cleaned, but a much better device for the purpose is shown in the sketch.

A scrub brush is procured and cut in two, the parts being hinged to a crosspiece fastened to a long broom handle. The brushes are pressed outward against the inside surfaces of the pipe with a wire and spring, as shown.—Contributed by C. L. Herbert, Chicago, Illinois.

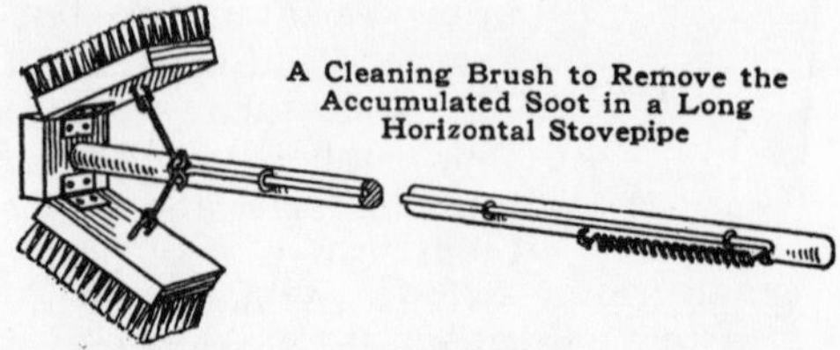

A Cleaning Brush to Remove the Accumulated Soot in a Long Horizontal Stovepipe

Mounting Photo Prints on Glass

Photograph prints can be mounted on glass with an adhesive made by soaking 1 oz. of sheet gelatine in cold water to saturation, then dissolving in 3½ oz. of boiling water. Let the solution cool to about 110 deg. F., then immerse the print in it and squeegee, face down, on a clear piece of glass. When dry, take a damp cloth or soft sponge and wipe off any surplus gelatine on the glass.

Dropping Coins in a Glass Full of Water

Take a glass and fill it to the brim with water, taking care that the surface of the water is raised a little above the edge of the glass, but not running over. Place a number of nickels or dimes on the table near the glass and ask your spectators how many coins can be put into the water without making it overflow. No doubt the reply will be that the water will run over before two coins are dropped in. But it is possible to put in ten or twelve of them. With a great deal of care the coins may be made to fall without disturbing the water, the surface of which will become more and more convex before the water overflows.

Hollow-Grinding Ice Skates

The accompanying sketch illustrates a practical method of clamping ice skates to hold them for grinding the small arc of a circle so much desired.

The U-shaped clamps are made of ¾-in. soft steel with the opening 6 in. deep and 5 in. high and are bolted to a block of wood, 2 in. thick, 6 in. wide and 12 in. long. The skate runner is adjusted to the proper height by ½-in. set and thumbscrews. The block

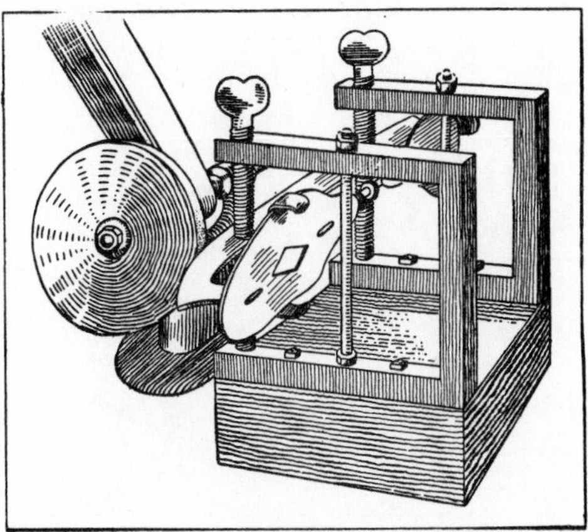

Skate Runner Fastened in Clamp

of wood holding the clamp and skate can be pushed along on the emery-wheel table in front of the revolving wheel.

If properly adjusted, a slight concave or hollow can be made full length of the runner, true and uniform, which will hold on the ice sideways and not retard the forward movement.—Contributed by Geo. A. Howe, Tarrytown, New York.

How to Make a Bicycle Coasting Sled

The accompanying drawing and sketch illustrate a new type of coasting sled built on the bicycle principle. This coaster is simple and easy to make, says Scientific American. It is constructed of a good quality of pine. The pieces marked S are single, and should be about 1 by 1½ in.; the pieces

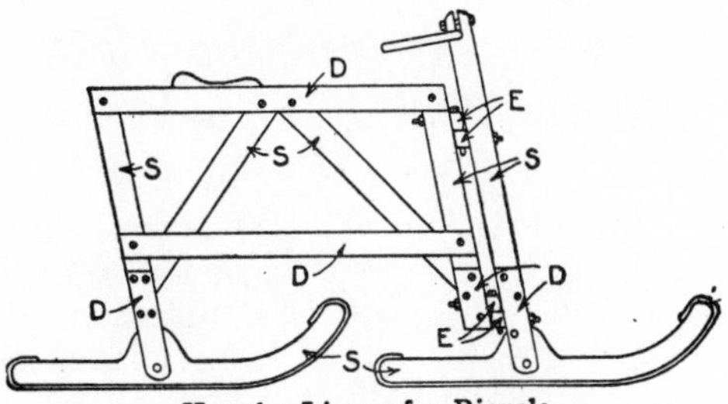

Has the Lines of a Bicycle

marked D are double or in duplicate, and should be ½ by 1½ in. The run-

Coasting

ners are shod with iron and are pivoted to the uprights as shown, double pieces being secured to the uprights to make a fork. The seat is a board, to the underside of which is a block, which drops down between the two top slats and is secured with a pin. A footrest is provided consisting of a short crosspiece secured to the front of the frame and resting on the two lower slats. The frame and front fork are hinged together with four short eyebolts, E, with a short bolt through each pair as shown.

Spelling Names with Photo Letters

There are, no doubt, many amateur photographers who make only occasional trips afield or through the more traveled thoroughfares with their cameras during the winter months. Each one is generally interested in working up the negatives that he or she made during the summer or on that last vacation into souvenir post cards, albums and the like, for sending to friends. Illustrated herewith is something different from the album or photographic calendar. The letters forming part of the word POPULAR are good examples of this work.

The masks which outline the letters are cut from the black paper in which plates come packed. Their size depends on the plate used. A sharp knife, a smooth board and a straightedge are all the tools needed, says Camera Craft. If the letters are all cut the same height, they will look remarkably uniform, even if one is not skilled in the work of forming them all in accordance with the rules. Be sure to have the prints a little larger than the letters to insure a sufficient margin in trimming, so as to have a white margin around the finished letters. The best method is to use a good pair of scissors or a sharp knife.

Many combinations can be made of these letter pictures to spell out the recipient's name or the season's greeting. During the holidays the letters may be made from winter scenes to spell "A Merry Christmas" or "A Happy New Year." An Easter greeting may have more springlike subjects and a birthday remembrance a fitting month. The prints are no more difficult to make than the ordinary kind. In cutting out an O, for example, do not forget to cut out a piece to correspond to the center. This piece can be

Letters Made from Photographs

placed on the printing paper after the outline mask has been laid down, using care to get it in the right position, and closing the frame carefully so that the small piece will not be disturbed. The letters should be of the kind to give as large an area of surface to have as much of the picture show as possible. What the printer calls black face letters are the most suitable.

By cutting the letters out of black paper in a solid form, and using these as a mask for a second printing after printing the full size of the negatives, these letter pictures can be made with a black border. So made, they can be trimmed to a uniform black line all around; and, mounted on a white card and photographed down to post card size, the greeting so spelled out makes a most unique souvenir. Another application of the letters in copying is to paste them on a white card as before, trim the card even with the bottoms of the letters, stand the strip of card on a mirror laid flat on a table, and then photograph both the letters and their reflections so as to nicely fill a post card. Still another suggestion is to cut out the letters, after pasting the prints on some thin card, and then arrange them in the desired order to spell out the name or greeting, but with flowers interspersed and forming a background, photographing them down to the desired size. A third means of securing a novel effect by photographing down an arrangement of the letters is to have them cut out in stiff form as in the last method; mount them on short pieces of corks, in turn fastened to a white card forming the background. So arranged, the letters will stand out from the card about ½ in. If they are now placed in a light falling from the side and slightly in front, each letter will cast a shadow upon the background, and in the finished print the letters will look as if suspended in the air in front of the surface of the card.

A piece of sheet lead put on each side of a screw will fill up and hold the threads in a too large hole.

A Checker Board Puzzle

Place eight checker men upon the checker board as shown in the first row in the sketch. The puzzle is to get

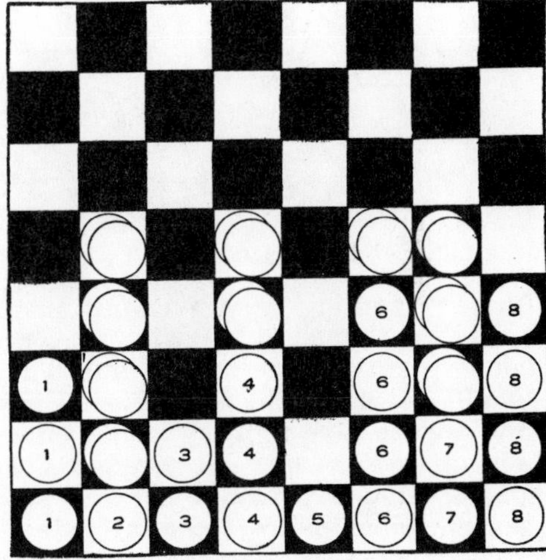

Placing the Checkers

them in four piles of two men each without omitting to jump over two checker men every time a move is made.

The first move is to jump 5 over 4 and 3 on 2 which is shown in the second row, then jump 3 over 4 and 6 on 7 and the positions will appear as shown in the third row; jump 1 over 2 and 5 on 4 to get the men placed like the fourth row and the last move is to jump 8 over 3 and 7 on 6 which will make the four piles of two men each as shown in the fifth row.—Contributed by I. G. Bayley, Cape May Point, N. J.

A Home-Made Rabbit Trap

A good serviceable rabbit trap can be made by sinking a common dry goods box in the ground to within 6 in. of its top. A hole 6 or 7 in. square is cut in each end level with the earth's surface and boxes 18 in. long that will just fit are set in, hung on pivots, with the longest end outside, so they will lie horizontal. A rabbit may now look through the two tubes, says the American Thresherman. The bait is hung on a string from the top of the large box so that it may be seen and smelled from the outside. The rabbit naturally goes into the holes and in this trap

Rabbit in the Trap

there is nothing to awaken his suspicion. He smells the bait, squeezes along past the center of the tube, when it tilts down and the game is shot into the pit, the tube righting itself at once for another catch. The top and sides of the large box may be covered with leaves, snow or anything to hide it. A door placed in the top will enable the trapper to take out the animals. By placing a little hay or other food in the bottom of the box the trap need not be visited oftener than once a week.

Old-Time Magic

Changing a Button into a Coin

Place a button in the palm of the left hand, then place a coin between the second and third fingers of the right hand. Keep the right hand faced down and the left hand faced up, so as to conceal the coin and expose the button. With a quick motion bring the left hand under the right, stop quick and

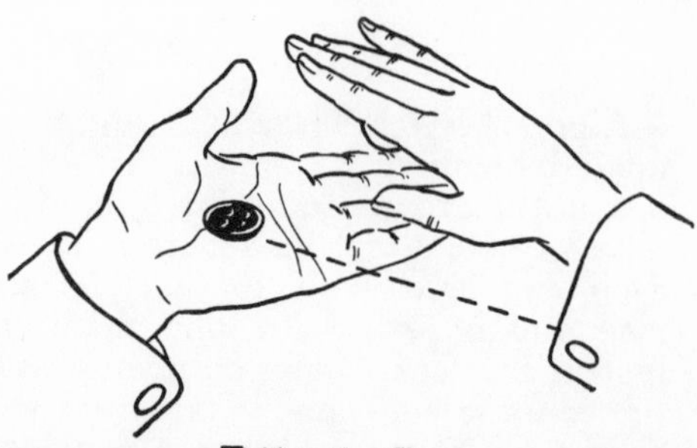

Making the Change

the button will go up the right-hand coat sleeve. Press the hands together, allowing the coin to drop into the left hand, then expose again, or rub the hands a little before doing so, saying that you are rubbing a button into a coin.—Contributed by L. E. Parker, Pocatello, Idaho.

Buttonhole Trick

This trick is performed with a small stick having a loop attached that is too small for the stick to pass through. Spread out the string and place it each side of the buttonhole, then draw the cloth around the hole through the string until it is far enough to pass the stick through the hole. Pull back the cloth and you have the string looped in the hole with a hitch the same as if the stick had been passed through the string.

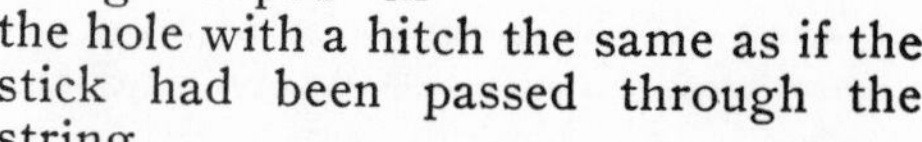

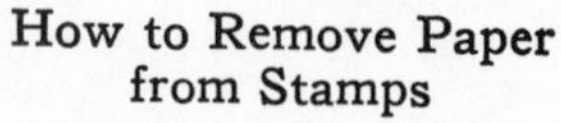

The stick may be removed by pulling up the loop as if you were passing the stick through it, putting the stick in the hole and leaving the string on the outside, then spread the string, pulling up the cloth and passing the stick through the hole as before.—Contributed by Charles Graham, Pawtucket, Rhode Island.

How to Remove Paper from Stamps

Old stamps as they are purchased usually have a part of the envelope from which they are taken sticking to them and in removing this paper many valuable stamps are torn or ruined. Place all the stamps that are stuck to pieces of envelopes in hot water and in a short time they can be separated without injury. Dry the stamps between two white blotters. Stamps removed in this way will have a much better appearance when placed in an album.—Contributed by L. Szerlip, Brooklyn, N. Y.

Imitation Arms and Armor

PART I

Genuine antique swords and armor, as used by the knights and soldiers in the days of old, are very expensive and at the present time practically impossible to obtain. The accompanying illustration shows four designs of swords that anyone can make, and if carefully made, they will look very much like the genuine article.

The drawings are so plain that the amateur armorer should have very little difficulty, if any, in building up his work from the illustrations, whether he requires a single sword only, or a complete suit of armor, full size.

The pieces or designs in this article are from authentic sources, says the English Mechanic, so that where names are given the amateur can so label them, and will thereby greatly add to their interest and value.

An executioners' sword of the fifteenth century is shown in Fig. 1. The blade should be about 27 in. long with a handle of sufficient length to be grasped by both hands. The width of the blade near the handle is about 2½ in., tapering down to 1½ in. near the point end. Several ridges are cut around the handle to permit a firm grip. The cross guard is flat and about 1 in. in width.

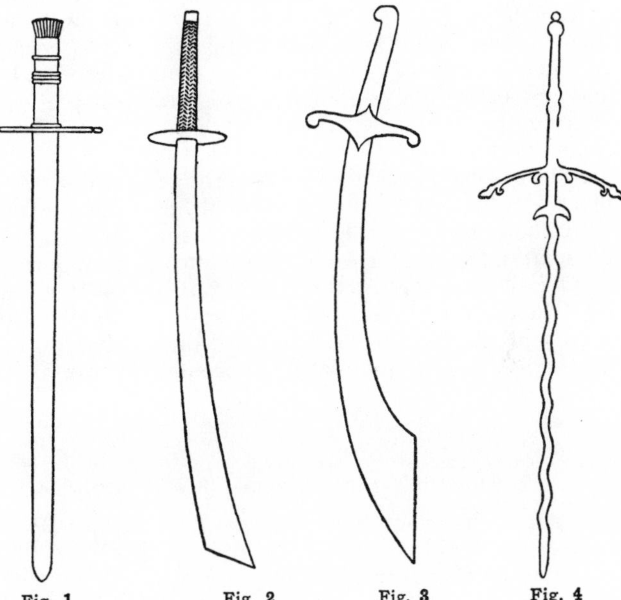

Fig. 1 Fig. 2 Fig. 3 Fig. 4

Mark out the shape and size of the blade on a piece of wood ⅛ in. thick, using a straightedge and a pencil, and allowing a few inches more in length on which to fasten the handle. Cut out the wood with a scroll saw or a keyhole saw, trim the edges down thin and smooth both surfaces with fine sandpaper. The end for the handle is cut about 1 in. wide and 2 in. long. The cross guard is cut out and a hole made in the center through which to pass the handle end of the blade. The handle is next made, and if the amateur does not possess a lathe on which to turn the shape of the handle, the ridges around the wood may be imitated by gluing and tacking on pieces of small rope. The handle is then mortised to receive the 1 by 2-in. end of the blade. The cross guard is now glued and placed on the blade, then the hole in the handle is well glued with glue that is not too thick and quite hot. The blade with the cross guard is inserted in the handle and allowed to set. When the glue is thoroughly dry, remove the surplus with a sharp knife and paint the handle with brown, dark red, or green oil paint. The blade is covered with tinfoil to give it the appearance of steel. Secure some pieces of tinfoil and cut one strip ½ in. wider than the blade and the other ¼ in. narrower. Quickly paint the blade well with thin glue on one side, then lay evenly and press on the narrow strip of tinfoil. Glue the other side of the blade, put on the wider strip of tinfoil and glue the overlapping edge and press it around and on the surface of the narrow strip. The cross guard must be covered with tinfoil in the same manner as the blade. When the whole is quite dry, wipe the blade with light strokes up and down several times, using a soft and dry piece of cloth. The sword is then ready to hang in its chosen place as a decoration, not for use only in cases of tableaux, for which this article will be especially useful to those who are arranging living pictures wherein swords and armor are part of the paraphernalia.

A Chinese scimitar is shown in Fig. 2. The handle of this sword is oval and covered with plaited cord. In making this scimitar, follow the directions as for Fig. 1, except that the handle has to be covered with a round black cord. If it is found difficult to plait the cord on the handle as in the illustration, wind it around in a continuous line closely together, and finish by fastening with a little glue and a small tack driven through the cord into the handle. The pommel is a circular piece of wood, 1/8 in. thick and 5 in. in diameter. The length of the handle, allowing for a good hold with both hands, should be about 9 in., the length of the blade 28 in., the width near the pommel 1½ in. and 3 in. in the widest part at the lower end. The sharp or cutting edge is only on the short side, the other is flat or half-round.

A Turkish sabre of ancient manufacture from Constantinople is shown in Fig. 3. The handle is painted a dull creamy white in imitation of ivory. The enamel paint sold in small tins will answer well for this purpose. The cross guard and blade are covered as described in Fig. 1. The sharp edge is on the longer curved side, the other is flat or half-round.

A two-handed sword used in the 14th and 15th centuries is shown in Fig. 4. This sword is about 68 in. long, has a cross guard and blade of steel with a round wood handle painted black. The ball or pommel on top of the handle is steel. Both edges of the blade are sharp. This sword is made in wood the same as described for Fig. 1.

A Dovetail Joint Puzzle

A simple but very ingenious example in joinery is illustrated. In the finished piece, Fig. 1, the dovetail appears on each side of the square stick of wood, the illustration, of course, shows only two sides, the other two are identical. The joint is separable and each part is solid and of one piece. In making, take two pieces of wood, preferably of contrasting colors, such as cherry and walnut or mahogany and boxwood, about 1½ in. square and of any length desired. Cut the dovetail on one end of each stick as shown in Fig. 2, drive together and then plane off the triangular corners marked A. The end of each piece after the dovetails are cut appear as shown in Fig. 3, the lines marking the path of the dovetail through the stick.

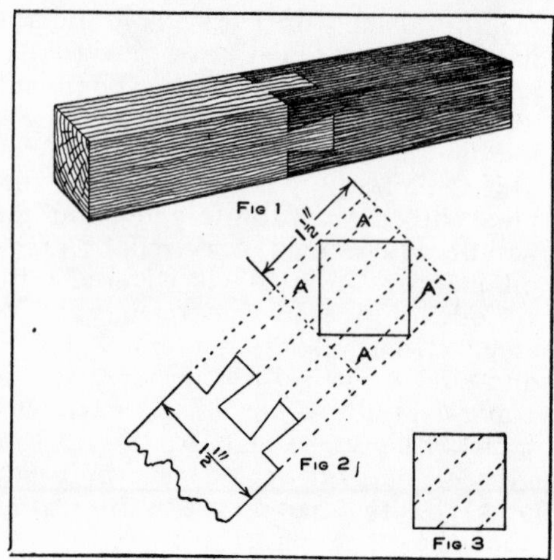

How the Joint Is Cut

Pure rain water is the best to use in a cooling system of an automobile engine, as it is free from the mineral substances which are deposited in the radiator, piping and jackets by hard water.

Springboard for Swimmers

A good springboard adds much to the fun of swimming. The boards are generally made so that the plank will bend, being dressed down thin at one end and fastened. The thinness of the plank, or an insecure fastening, causes many a plank to snap in two or come loose from its fastenings in a short time.

The accompanying sketch shows the method of constructing a springboard that does not depend upon the bending of the wood for its spring. It is made of a plank, 2 in. thick and from 14 to 16 ft. long, one end of which is secured with a hinge arrangement having a U-shaped rod whose ends are held with nuts. On each edge of the board, at the lower end, are fastened two pieces of strap iron, each about 1 ft. long and with the lower ends drilled to fit the horizontal of the U-shaped rod.

Buggy Springs Used beneath the Board

Secure a pair of light buggy springs from a discarded rig and attach them to the ends of a square bar of iron having a length equal to the width of the plank. Fasten this to the plank with bolts, as shown in the sketch. Should the springs be too high they can be moved forward.—Contributed by John Blake, Franklin, Mass.

Taking Button from a Child's Nostril

A three-year-old child snuffed a button up its nostril and the mother, in an attempt to remove it, had caused the button to be pushed farther up the channel. Doctors probed for the button without success. The distracted mother happened to think of snuff, and, as there was some at hand, took a pinch of snuff between the thumb and forefinger and held it close to the child's nose. The violent sneezing caused the button to be blown out. Such an accident may come under the observation of any parent, and if so, this method can be used to relieve the child when medical assistance is not at hand.—Contributed by Katharine D. Morse, Syracuse, N. Y.

Brass Frame in Repoussé

Punches can be purchased, as can the pitch bed or block. Both can be made easily, however. Several punches of different sizes and shapes will be needed. A piece of mild steel, about 3/8 in. square, can be easily worked into tools shaped as desired. A cold chisel will be needed to cut the metal to length; a file to reduce the ends to shape, and a piece of emery paper to smooth and polish the end of the tool so that it will not scar the metal.

A small metal box must be secured to hold the pitch. The illustration shows an iron receptacle. The pitch is prepared by heating the following materials in these proportions: pitch, 5 lb.; plaster of Paris, 5 lb.; tallow, 1/2

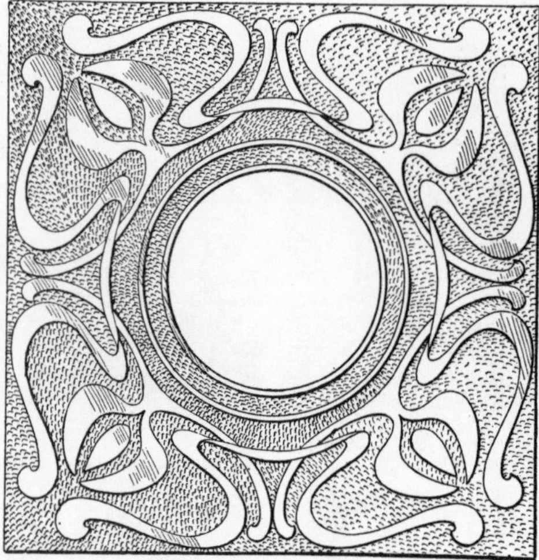
Design for the Frame

lb. To put it in another way, use pitch and plaster in equal parts with 1/10 part tallow. See that the pitch and plaster are dry so that the moisture will not cause the pitch to boil over. Keep stirring the mass so that it never boils. Melt the pitch first and add the plaster by degrees.

For a piece of repousse such as the frame shown, secure a piece of brass of about No. 18 gauge. With carbon paper trace the design on the brass. Place the metal on the pitch bed and work over the outline of the design. Use the chisel-edged tool and try to

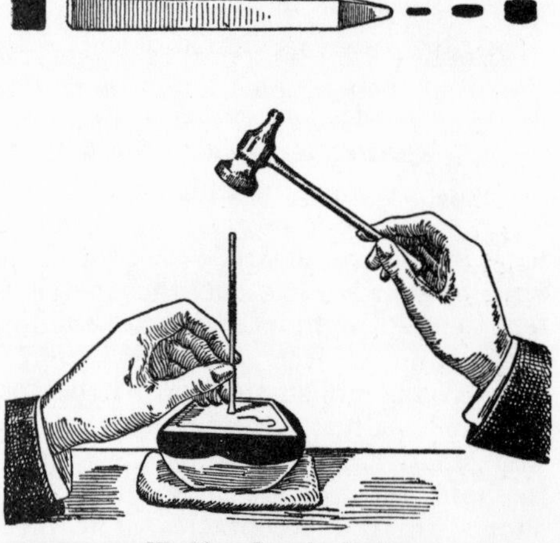
Working Out the Design

make the lines continuous. When this has been done, heat the pitch slightly and place the metal, design down, on the pitch, and with the raising punches work up the shape as desired after the pitch has hardened. When the desired form has been obtained, turn the metal over and "touch up" any places improperly raised. The metal will probably be warped somewhat. To remedy this, place a board on the metal and pound until the metal assumes a flat shape again. Next drill a hole in the center waste and saw out for the opening, using a small metal saw. Trim up the edges and file them smooth.

Clean the metal thoroughly, using powdered pumice with lye. Cotton batting fastened to the end of a stick will make a good brush. Upon the cleansed metal put a lacquer to prevent tarnishing. Metal clips may be soldered to the back to hold the picture in place and also a metal strip to hold the frame upright. These should be placed before the metal is lacquered.

Finding the Horsepower of Small Motors

A small motor often excites curiosity as to its true horsepower, or fraction of a horsepower. Guesses in this direction vary remarkably for the same motor or engine. It is comparatively easy to determine the horsepower put out by almost any machine by the following method which is intended for small battery motors and small steam engines.

Before giving the description, it may be well to know what horsepower means. Horsepower is the rate of work and a unit is equal to 33,000 ft. lb. per minute, or 550 ft. lb. per second. That is lifting 33,000 lb. 1 ft. in one minute or 550 lb. 1 ft. in one second. This may be applied to the problem of finding the horsepower of a motor by fastening a piece of twine about 25 ft. long to the shaft of the engine or motor to be tested in such a way that when the shaft revolves it will wind up the string similar to a windlass. Place the motor in such a position that the twine will hang freely without touching anything; out of a high window will do. Fasten a weight to the other end of the line as heavy as the motor or engine can lift and still run. It must weigh enough to slow the power down a little, but not to stop it. Mark the position of the weight and start the motor, at the same time accurately measuring time in minutes and seconds it takes to lift the weight from the lowest point to the highest. Next measure accurately the distance in feet covered by the weight in its ascent and obtain the correct weight in pounds of the weight.

Multiply the weight by the distance covered and divide the result by the number of minutes or fraction of a minute obtained and divide this last result by 33,000 and the quotient will be the horsepower of the motor or engine.

Perhaps an illustration will make this solution much plainer. Suppose the motor will lift a weight of 1 lb. and still revolve, 30 ft. in 10 seconds or 1/6 of a minute. Multiplying 1 by 30 we get 30, which divided by 1/6 gives 180. This in turn divided by 33,000 equals in round numbers 1/200 part of a horsepower.—Contributed by Harold H. Cutter.

Illusion for Window Attraction

Gold fish and canary birds, living together in what seems like one receptacle, make an unusual show window attraction. Secure two glass vessels having straight sides of the same height, one 18 in. in diameter (Fig. 1) and the other 12 in. in diameter (Fig. 2). The smaller is placed within the larger, the bottoms being covered with moss and aquarium decorations which can be purchased at a bird store. Fill the 3-in. space between the vessels with water. Cut a piece of galvanized screen into circular form to cover the larger vessel, and hang a bird swing, A, Fig. 3, in the center. Place the screen on top of the vessels so that the swing will hang in the center of the inner vessel. A weight—a box filled with sand will do—should be placed on top of the screen, over the smaller vessel, to keep it from floating. Moss should be put over the top of the screen so that the two separate vessels can not be seen.

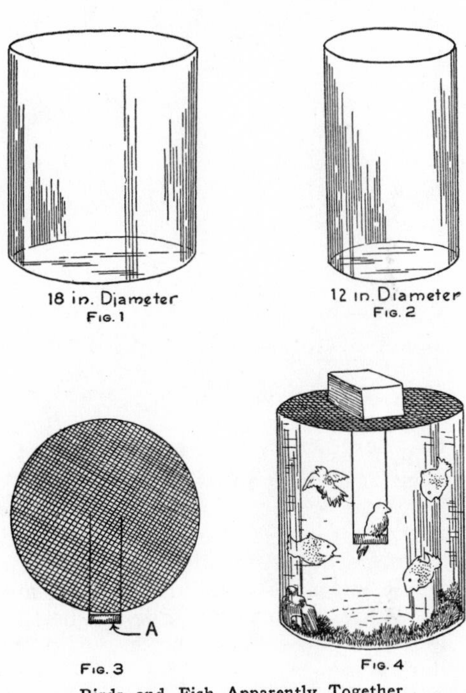

Birds and Fish Apparently Together

Place the birds in the inner vessel and the fish in the water. The effect is surprising. To complete the effect and aid the illusion the vessels can be set in a box lined with black velvet, or on a pedestal.—Contributed by J. F. Campbell, Somerville, Mass.

Cleaner for White Shoes

Finely ground whiting mixed with water to the consistency of paste makes a very good coating for white shoes. A brush can be used in applying the mixture which will dry in a few minutes. It is best to mix only as much paste as required for immediate use.—Contributed by L. Szerlip, Brooklyn, N. Y.

¶Belt laces should never cross on the side next to the pulley as they will cut themselves in two.

How to Make a Candlestick Holder

A candlestick of very simple construction and design can be made as follows: Secure a piece of brass or

Candle Holder Complete

copper of No. 23 gauge of a size sufficient to make the pieces detailed in the accompanying sketch. A riveting hammer and a pair of pliers will be needed, also a pair of tin shears and a piece of metal upon which to rivet.

Cut out a piece of metal for the base to a size of 5½ by 5½ in. Trim the sharp corners off slightly. Draw a pencil line all around the margin and ⅝ in. away from the edge. With the pliers shape the sides as shown in the illustration.

Next lay out the holding cup according to the plan of development shown, and cut out the shape with the shears. Polish both of these pieces, using any of the common metal polishes. Rivet the cup to the base, and then, with the pliers, shape the sides as shown in the photograph. The manner of making and fastening the handle is clearly illustrated. Use a file to smooth all the cut edges so that they will not injure the hands.

In riveting, care should be taken to round up the heads of the rivets nicely as a good mechanic would. Do not be content merely to bend them over. This rounding is easily accomplished by striking around the rivets' outer circumference, keeping the center high.

A good lacquer should be applied after the parts have been properly cleaned and polished, to keep the metal from tarnishing.

A Home-Made Duplicator

The usual gelatine pad, which is the principal part of the average hectograph or duplicator, is, as a rule, unsatisfactory, as it is apt to sour and mold in the summer and freeze in the winter, which, with other defects, often render it useless after a few months service.

A compound that is almost indestructible is the preparation sold at art stores as modeling clay. This clay is as easily worked as a putty and is spread into the tray, which may be of wood or tin, and the surface leveled by pounding with a mallet or hammer, then by drawing a straightedge over it.

The surface of the pad is now saturated with pure glycerine. This is poured upon the surface after it is slightly warmed, covering the same and then laying a cloth over the pad and allowing it to stand long enough for the clay to absorb the glycerine, after which it is ready for use.

The original copy is written with a copying pencil or typewritten through a hectograph ribbon. A sheet of newspaper is laid upon the pad and a round stick or pencil is passed over it

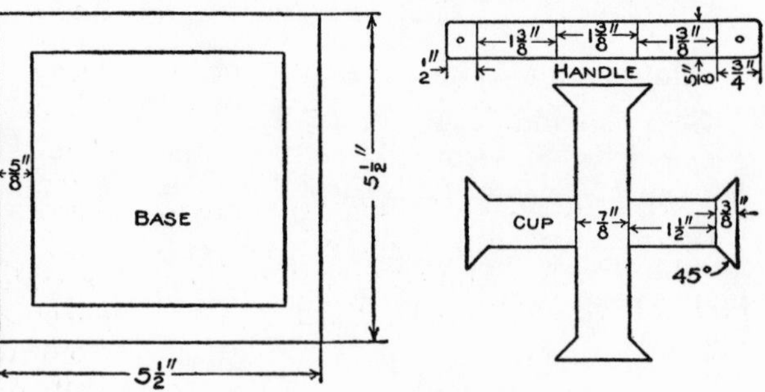

Details of Candle Holder

to make the surface level and smooth. Remove the newspaper and place the original copy face down on the leveled surface and smooth it out in the same way so that every part touches the pad. Remove the copy in about five minutes and place the clean sheets of paper one after another on the surface and remove them. From 50 to 75 copies of the original can be made in a short time.

This compound is impervious to water, so the negative print is removed by simply washing with a damp sponge, the same as removing writing from a slate. This makes it possible to place another original on the pad immediately without waiting for the ink to vanish by chemical action as in the original hectograph.

The action of the weather has no effect upon this compound and it is proof against accident, for the tray may be dropped and the pad dented or cut into pieces, and the clay can be pressed back and leveled. The only caution is to keep it covered with a cloth saturated in glycerine while not in use.—Contributed by A. A. Houghton, Northville, Mich.

Paper-Clip Bookmark

The combination of a paper clip and a calling card makes a good bookmark. The clip and card can be kept together by piercing the card and bending the ends of the wire to stick through the holes. The clip is attached to a page as shown in the sketch.—Contributed by Thos. DeLoof, Grand Rapids, Mich.

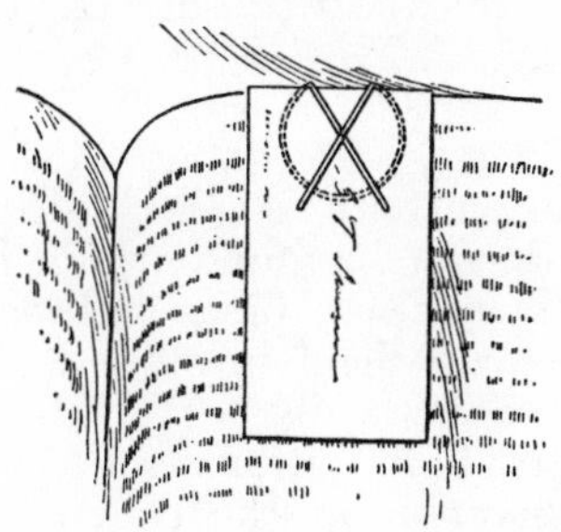

Aerating Water in a Small Tank

A simple way of producing air pressure sufficient to aerate water is by the use of a siphon as shown in Fig. 1. The siphon is made of glass tubes, the longer pieces being bent on one end as shown. The air receiver and regulating device are attached to the top end of the lower tube, as shown in Fig. 2. The receiver or air inlet is the most important part. It is made of a glass tube, $\frac{3}{4}$ in. in diameter and 5 in. long. A hole is filed or blown through one side of the glass for the admission of air. The ends of the smaller glass tubes are passed through corks having a diameter to fit the ends of this larger tube. The ends of these tubes should be so adjusted that the continuous drops of water from the upper will fall into the tube below. The succession of air bubbles thus imprisoned are driven down the tube and into the tank below.

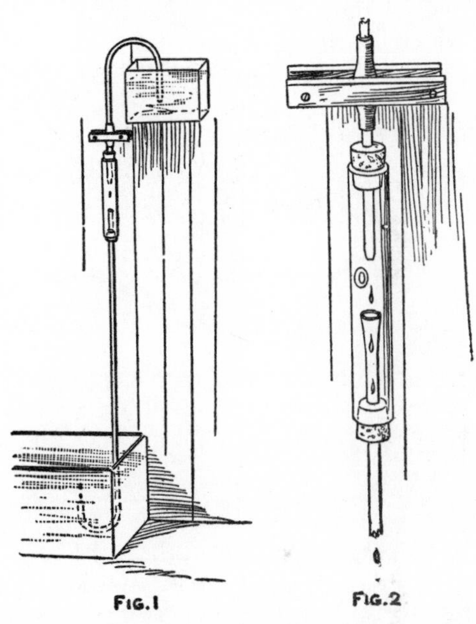

Forcing Air Through Water

The regulator is placed in the tube or siphon above the air receiver. Its purpose is to retard the flow of water from the siphon above and make it drop rapidly. It consists of a rubber connecting tube with two flat pieces of wood clamped over the center and adjusted with screws. The apparatus is started by clamping the rubber tube tightly and then exhausting the air in the siphon tube, then placing the end in the upper reservoir and releasing the clamp until the water begins to drop. If the reservoir is kept filled from the tank, the device will work for an indefinite time.—Contributed by John T. Dunlop, Shettleston, Scotland.

Imitation Arms and Armor—Part II

Imitation swords, stilettos and battle-axes, put up as ornaments, will look well if they are arranged on a shield which is hung high up on a wall of a room or hall, says the English Mechanic, London. The following described arms are authentic designs of the original articles. A German sword of the fifteenth century is shown in Fig. 1. This sword is 4 ft. long with the crossguard and blade of steel. The imitation sword is made of wood and covered with tinfoil to produce the steel color. The shape of the sword is marked out on a piece of wood that is about ⅛ in. thick with the aid of a straightedge and pencil, allowing a little extra length on which to fasten the handle. Cut the sword out with a saw and make both edges thin like a knife blade and smooth up with sandpaper. The extra length for the handle is cut about 1 in. in width and 2 in. long. The handle is next carved and a mortise cut in one end to receive the handle end of the blade. As the handle is to represent copper, the ornamentations can be built up of wire, string, small rope and round-headed nails, the whole finally having a thin coat of glue worked over it with a stiff bristle brush and finished with bronze paint.

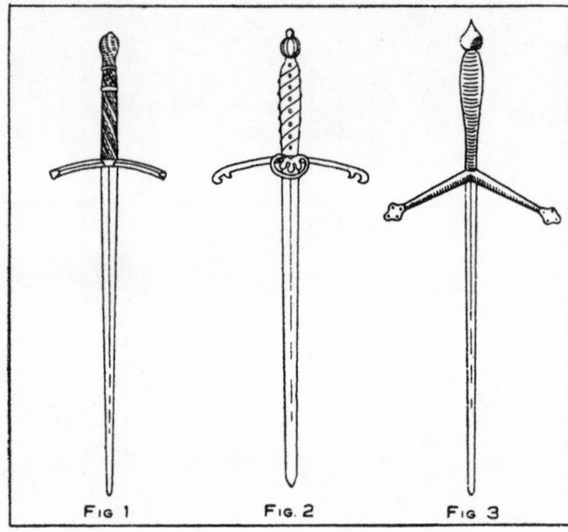

Three Fifteenth Century Swords

The crossbar is flat and about 1 in. in width. Cut this out of a piece of wood and make a center hole to fit over the extra length on the blade, glue and put it in place. Fill the hole in the handle with glue and put it on the blade. When the glue is thoroughly dry, remove all the surplus with a sharp knife. Sheets of tinfoil are secured for covering the blade. Cut two strips of tinfoil, one about ½ in. wider than the blade and the other ¼ in. narrower. Quickly cover one side of the blade with a thin coat of glue and evenly lay on and press down the narrow strip of tinfoil. Stick the wider strip on the other side in the same way, allowing equal margin of tinfoil to overlap the edges of the blade. Glue the overlapping edges and press them around on the surface of the narrow strip. The crossguard must be covered in the same manner as the blade. When the whole is quite dry, wipe the blade up and down several times with light strokes using a soft rag.

The sword shown in Fig. 2 is a two-handed Swiss sword about 4 ft. in length, sharp on both edges with a handle of dark wood around which is wound spirally a heavy piece of brass or copper wire and held in place with round-headed brass nails. The blade and crossbar are in imitation steel. The projecting ornament in the center of the crossguard may be cut from heavy pasteboard and bent into shape, then glued on the blade as shown.

In Fig. 3 is shown a claymore, or Scottish sword of the fifteenth century. This sword is about 4 ft. long and has a wood handle bound closely around with heavy cord. The crossbar and blade are steel, with both edges sharp. A German poniard is shown in Fig. 4. This weapon is about 1 ft. long, very broad, with wire or string bound handle, sharp edges on both sides. Another poniard of the fourteenth century is shown in Fig. 5. This weapon is also about 1 ft. long with wood handle and steel embossed blade. A sixteenth century German poniard is shown in Fig. 6. The blade and ornamental crossbar is of steel, with both edges of the blade sharp. The handle is of wood. A German stiletto, sometimes called cuirass breakers, is shown in Fig. 7. This stiletto has a wood handle, steel crossbar and blade of steel with both edges sharp.

In Fig. 8 is shown a short-handled flail, which is about 2½ ft. long with a dark handle of wood, studded with brass or steel nails. A steel band is placed around the handle near the top. The imitation of the steel band is made by gluing a piece of tinfoil on a strip of cardboard and tacking it to the handle. A large screweye is screwed into the top of the handle. The spiked ball may be made of wood or clay. Cover the ball with some pieces of linen, firmly glued on. When dry, paint it a dark brown or black. A large screweye must be inserted in this ball, the same as used on the end of the handle, and both eyes connected with a small piece of rope twisted into shape. The rope is finished by covering with tinfoil. Some short and heavy spike-headed nails are driven into the ball to give it the appearance shown in the illustration.

A Russian knout is shown in Fig. 9. The lower half of the handle is of wood, the upper part iron or steel, which can be imitated by covering a piece of wood that is properly shaped with tinfoil. The whole handle can be made of wood in one piece, the lower part painted black and the upper part covered with tinfoil. A screweye is screwed into the upper end. A length of real iron or steel chain is used to connect the handle with the ball. The ball is made as described in Fig. 8. The spikes in the ball are about 1 in. in length. These must be cut from pieces of wood, leaving a small peg at the end and in the center about the size of a No. 20 spike. The pegs are glued and inserted into holes drilled into the ball.

In Fig. 10 is shown a Sclavonic horseman's battle-axe which has a handle of wood painted dark gray or light brown; the axe is of steel. The blade is cut from a piece of ¼-in. wood with a keyhole saw. The round part is made thin and sharp on the edge. The thick hammer side of the axe is built up to the necessary thickness to cover

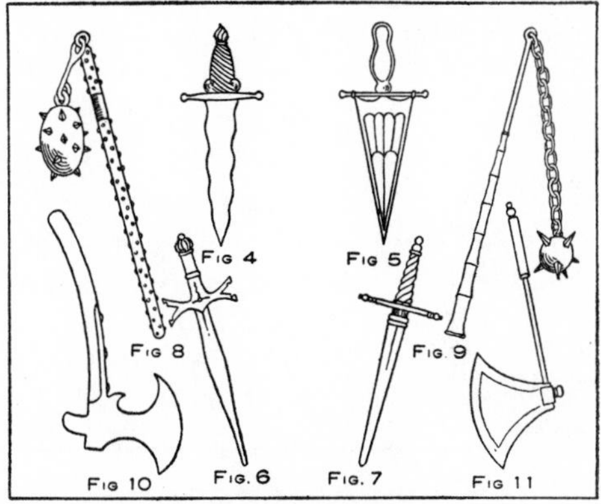

Ancient Weapons

the handle by gluing on pieces of wood the same thickness as used for the blade, and gradually shaping off to the middle of the axe by the use of a chisel, finishing with sandpaper and covering with tinfoil. Three large, round-headed brass or iron nails fixed into the front side of the handle will complete the axe.

At the beginning of the sixteenth century horseman's battle-axes shaped as shown in Fig. 11 were used. Both handle and axe are of steel. This axe is made similar to the one described in Fig. 10. When the woodwork is finished the handle and axe are covered with tinfoil.

How to Make a Round Belt Without Ends

A very good belt may be made by laying several strands of strong cord, such as braided fishline, together as shown in Fig. 1 and wrapping them as

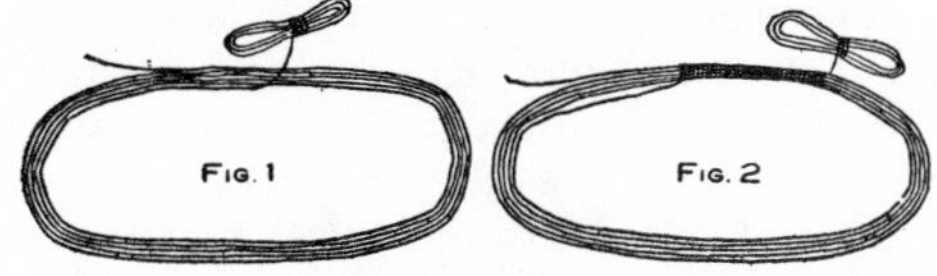

Method of Forming the Belt

shown in Fig. 2. When wrapped all the way around, the ends are tied and cut off. This will make a very good flexible belt; will pull where other belts slip, and as the tension members are all protected from wear, will last until the wrapping member is worn through without being weakened.—Contributed by E. W. Davis, Chicago.

Old-Time Magic

The Growing Flower

This trick is performed with a wide-mouthed jar which is about 10 in. high. If an earthern jar of this kind is not at hand, use a glass fruit jar and cover it with black cloth or paper, so the contents cannot be seen. Two pieces of wire are bent as shown in Fig. 1 and put together as in Fig. 2. These wires are put in the jar, about one-third the way down from the top, with the circle centrally located. The wires can be held in place by carefully bending the ends, or using small wedges of wood.

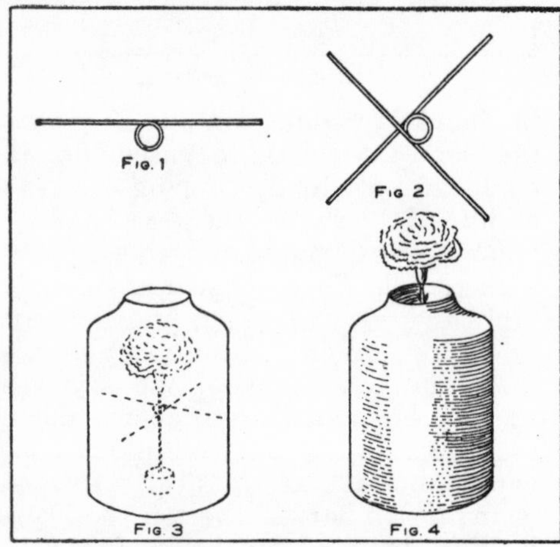

Flower Grows Instantly

Cut a wire shorter in length than the height of the jar and tie a rose or several flowers on one end. Put a cork in the bottom of the jar and stick the opposite end of the wire from where the flowers are tied through the circle of the two wires and into the cork. The dotted lines in Fig. 3 show the position of the wires and flowers.

To make the flowers grow in an instant, pour water into the jar at one side of the wide mouth. The cork will float and carry the wire with the flowers attached upward, causing the flowers to grow, apparently, in a few seconds' time. Do not pour in too much water to raise the flowers so far that the wire will be seen.—Contributed by A. S. Macdonald, Oakland, Calif.

Water and Wine Trick

This is an interesting trick based on the chemical properties of acids and alkalies. The materials needed are: One glass pitcher, filled with water, four glass tumblers, an acid, an alkali and some phenolphthalein solution which can be obtained from your local druggist. Before the performance, add a few drops of the phenolphthalein to the water in the pitcher and rub a small quantity of the alkali solution on the sides of two of the tumblers and repeat, only using as large a quantity of the acid as will escape notice on the remaining tumblers. Set the tumblers so you will know which is which and proceed as follows: Take hold of a prepared tumbler with the left hand and pour from the pitcher, held in the right hand, some of the liquid. The liquid turned into the glass will become red like wine. Set this full tumbler aside and take the pitcher in the left hand and pour some of the liquid in one of the tumblers containing the acid as it is held in the right hand. There will be no change in color. Repeat both parts in the same order then begin to pour the liquids contained in the tumblers back into the pitcher in the order reversed and the excess of acid will neutralize the alkali and cause it to lose its color and in the end the pitcher will contain a colorless liquid. —Contributed by Kenneth Weeks, Bridgeton, N. J.

The life of iron shingle nails is about 6 years. An iron nail cannot be used again in putting on a new roof. Solid zinc nails last forever and can be used as often as necessary. As zinc is much lighter than iron, the cost of zinc nails is only about 2½ times that of iron nails.

Cutting Lantern Slide Masks

It has long been a puzzle to me why round cornered masks are almost invariably used for lantern slides, when most works of art are included within rectangular spaces, says a correspondent of Photo Era. Certainly the present commercial masks are in very poor taste. The worker who wishes to make the most of every slide will do well to cut his own masks, not only because of the fact just mentioned, but also because he can suit the size of the opening to the requirements of each slide. Slides can be works of art just as much as prints; so that masking a slide becomes just as important as trimming a print, and equally worthy of individual treatment. It is folly to give each slide a mask opening of uniform size and shape.

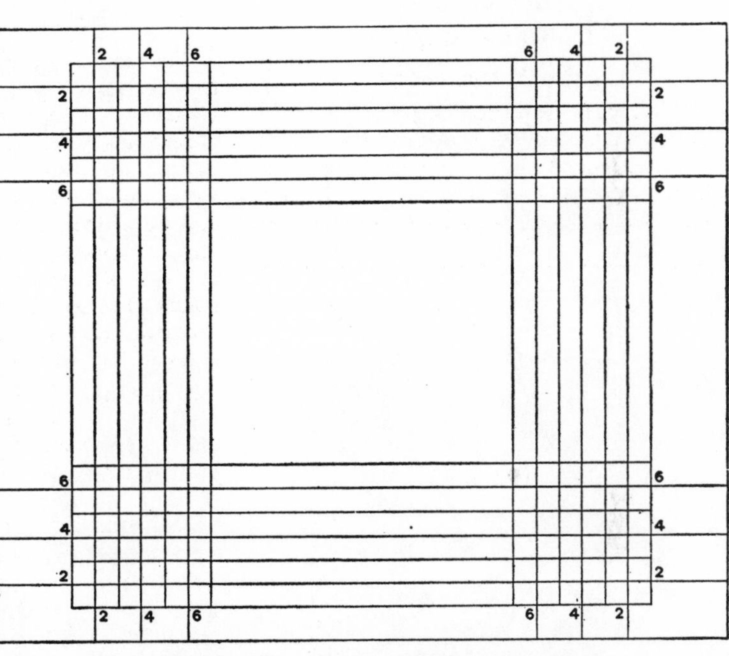

Form for Marking Out Rectangular Lantern Slide Masks

When many slides are to be masked, it becomes tedious work to treat each one separately, unless some special device is used. The accompanying drawing shows a way to mark masks which is simple, practical and costs nothing. The drawing is exactly lantern slide size.

Lay the slide over such a guide and note the size of the opening best suited to the picture. This will be determined by the intersection of the ruled lines, which are numbered for convenience in working. If the size wanted is No. 4 for width and No. 2 for height, place the guide over a piece of black mask paper and prick through the proper intersections with the point of a pin. This outlines the desired opening, which may then be cut out easily with a knife and straight edge.

The black paper from plate boxes and film rolls is excellent for making masks. It should be cut up in pieces $3\frac{1}{4}$ by 4 in. and kept ready for use at any time.

Relieving the Weight of a Talking-Machine Reproducer

Too loud reproduction from a record, the scratching noise sometimes heard and the forcing of the needle into a soft record, because the extension arm and reproducer are too heavy, can be remedied in the following manner: Attach a small ring to the under side of the horn and use a rubber band to lift the extending arm slightly.—Contributed by W. A. Jaquythe, Richmond, Cal.

How to Make a Thermometer Back in Etched Copper

Etching copper is not a very difficult process. Secure a sheet of No. 16 gauge copper of the width and length

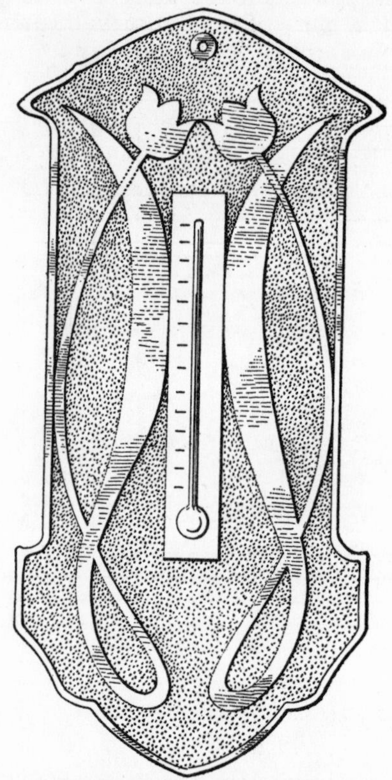

Copper Thermometer Holder

wanted for the back of the thermometer. In the design shown the extreme width is 3½ in. and the extreme length 7 in.

Draw a design. The one shown is merely suggestive. The worker may change the outline or proportions as desired. The decoration, too, may be changed. The essential thing is to keep a space upon which to place the thermometer. This design is in what is known as two-part symmetry. A line is drawn down the paper and one-half of the outline and decoration worked out. This done, the paper is folded along the center line, a piece of carbon paper is inserted between the folds and the design transferred on the inner surfaces by tracing with a pencil over the half of the outline previously drawn. Trace the design and outline upon the metal, using the carbon paper.

Cut out the outline with metal shears and file the edges smooth.

With a small brush and ordinary asphaltum or black varnish, paint the design, the margin and the entire back of the metal. When this coat has dried put on a second and then a third. The asphaltum is to keep the acid into which the metal is to be immersed later from eating any part of the metal but the background. Two coats or more are needed to withstand the action of the acid.

The acid bath is composed of nitric acid and water, about half and half, or, possibly, a little less acid than water, the mixture being made by pouring the acid into the water, not the water into the acid, which is dangerous. Keep this solution off the hands and clothes, and do not inhale the fumes.

Put the asphalt-coated metal in the bath and allow it to remain for four or five hours, depending upon the thickness of the metal and the strength of the acid. With a stick, or a pair of old tongs, take the metal out of the acid occasionally and examine it to see how deep the acid has eaten it—$\frac{1}{32}$ in. is about right for the No. 16 gauge.

When etched to the desired depth, remove the piece and with an old knife scrape off the asphaltum. Finish the cleaning by scrubbing with turpentine and a brush having stiff bristles.

If the metal is first covered with turpentine and then heated over a flame, all the colors of the rainbow will appear on its surface. These colors fade away in the course of a long time, but they can be easily revived. Another way to get these colors is to heat the metal and then plunge it into the acid bath quickly.

A green finish is obtained by painting the background with an acid stain composed as follows: 1 part ammonia muriate; 3 parts ammonia carbonate; 24 parts water. If one coat does not give the depth of color desired, repeat as many times as is necessary, allowing each coat time to dry before applying the next.

To "fix" this color so that it will not rub off, and to keep the metal from tarnishing, apply a coat of banana oil or lacquer.

Thermometers of suitable size can be bought in either brass or nickel. They have holes through their top and bottom ends through which metal paper fasteners can be inserted, and these in turn put through holes punched in the copper back.

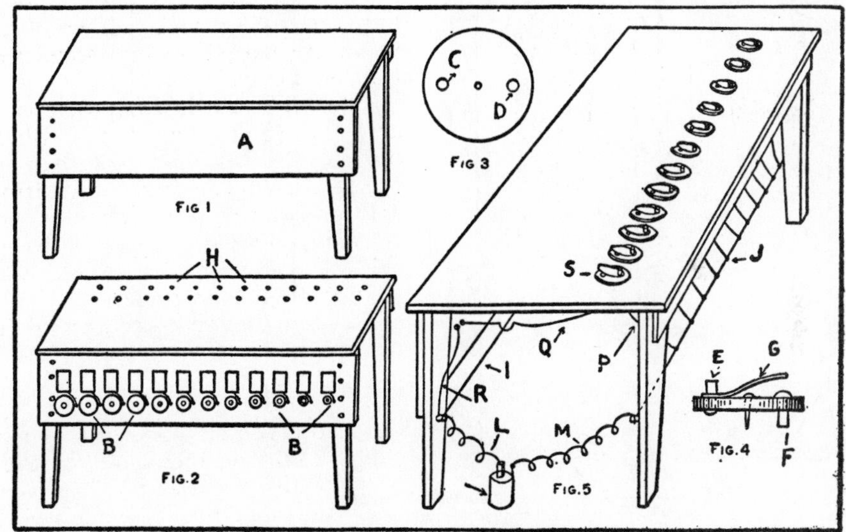

How the Electric Piano is Constructed

To Make an Electric Piano

Make or buy a table, about 3 ft. long and 1 ft. or more wide, and about 2½ ft. high. Nail a board, A, Fig. 1, about 8 in. wide and of the same length as the table, to the table, as shown in the illustration. Paint the table any color desired.

Purchase a dozen or so battery electric bells (they are cheaper if bought by the dozen) and screw them to the board, as in Fig. 2. Arrange the bells in the scale shown at B, Fig. 2. Bore two holes near the posts of each bell for the wires to pass through.

Buttons for the bells may be purchased, but it is cheaper to make them in the following way: Take a piece of wood and cut it round, about 2½ in. in diameter and ¼ in. thick, Fig. 3, and bore two holes, C and D, through it. Then get two posts, about 1 in. long, (battery posts will do) and put them through the holes as in Fig. 4. Cut out a piece of tin, ⅜ in. wide, punch a hole through it and put in under post E, so that when it is pressed down, it will touch post F. It may be either nailed or screwed down.

Make two holes in the table for each button and its wires, as at H, Fig. 2. Nail or screw the buttons to the table, as shown in Fig. 5, with the wires underneath. The connections are simple: I, Fig. 5, is a wire running from one end of the table to the other end, attached to a post at each end; J is another wire attached in the same way; L is the carbon wire running from the batteries to I; M is the zinc wire running from the batteries to wire J; O indicates the batteries; P is a wire running from J to one post of a button; Q is another wire running from the other post of the button to one of the posts of the bell; R is a wire running from I to one post of the bell. When the button S is pressed, the bell will ring. Each button should be connected with its bell in the same way.—Contributed by Vincent de Ybarrondo.

Imitation Arms and Armor

PART III

Maces and battle-axes patterned after and made in imitation of the ancient weapons which were used from the fourteenth to the sixteenth century produce fine ornaments for the hall or den, says the English Mechanic. The imitation articles are made of wood, the steel parts represented by tinfoil stuck on with glue and the ornaments carved out with a carving tool.

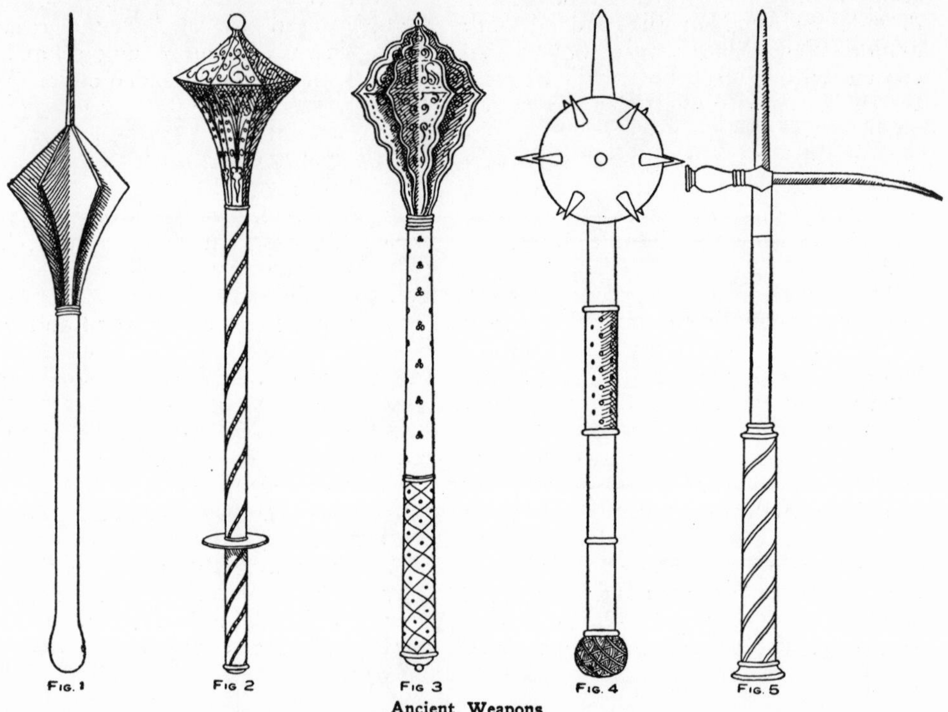

Ancient Weapons

An English mace used about the middle of the fifteenth century is shown in Fig. 1. The entire length of this weapon is about 24 in.; the handle is round with a four-sided sharp spike extending out from the points of six triangular shaped wings. Cut the handle and spike from one piece of wood and glue the wings on at equal distances apart around the base of the spike. The two bands or wings can be made by gluing two pieces of rope around the handle and fastening it with tacks. These rings can be carved out, but they are somewhat difficult to make. After the glue is dry, remove all the surplus that has been pressed out from the joints with the point of a sharp knife blade and then sandpaper the surface of the wood to make it smooth. Secure some tinfoil to cover the parts in imitation of steel. A thin coat of glue is quickly applied to the surface of the wood and the tinfoil laid on evenly so there will be no wrinkles and without making any more seams than is necessary. The entire weapon, handle and all, is to appear as steel.

An engraved iron mace of the fifteenth century is shown in Fig. 2. This weapon is about 22 in. long, mounted with an eight-sided or octagonal head. It will be easier to make this mace in three pieces, the octagonal head in one piece and the handle in two parts, so that the circular shield shown at the lower end of the handle can be easily placed between the parts. The circular piece or shield can be cut from a piece of wood about ¼ in. thick. The circle is marked out with a compass. A hole is made through the center for the dowel of the two handle parts when they are put together. A wood peg about 2 in. long serves as the dowel. A hole is bored in the end of both handle pieces and these holes well coated with glue, the wood peg inserted in one of them, the shield put on in place and handle parts put together and left for the glue to set. The head is fastened on the end of the handle with a dowel in the same manner as putting the handle parts together.

The head must have a pattern sketched upon each side in pencil marks, such as ornamental scrolls, leaves, flowers, etc. These ornaments must be carved out to a depth of about ¼ in. with a sharp carving tool. If such a tool is not at hand, or the amateur cannot use it well, an excellent substitute will be found in using a sharp-pointed and red-hot poker, or pieces of heavy wire heated to burn out the pattern to the desired depth. The handle also has a scroll to be engraved. When the whole is finished and cleaned and firmly pressed into the engraved parts with the finger tips or thumb.

A French mace used in the sixteenth century is shown in Fig. 3. This weapon is about 22 in. long and has a wood handle covered with dark red cloth or velvet, the lower part to have a gold or red silk cord wound around it, as shown, the whole handle finished off with small brass-headed nails. The top has six ornamental carved wings which are cut out, fastened on the handle and covered with tinfoil, as described in Fig. 2.

Figure 4 shows a Morning Star which is about 26 in. long. The spiked ball and the four-sided and sharp-pointed spike are of steel. The ball may be made of clay or wood and covered with tinfoil. The spikes are cut out of wood, sharp-pointed and cone-shaped, the base having a brad to stick into the ball. The wood spikes are also covered with tinfoil. The handle is of steel imitation, covered in the middle with red cloth or velvet and studded with large-headed steel nails.

A war hammer of the fifteenth century is shown in Fig. 5. Its length is about 3 ft. The lower half of the handle is wood, covered with red vel-

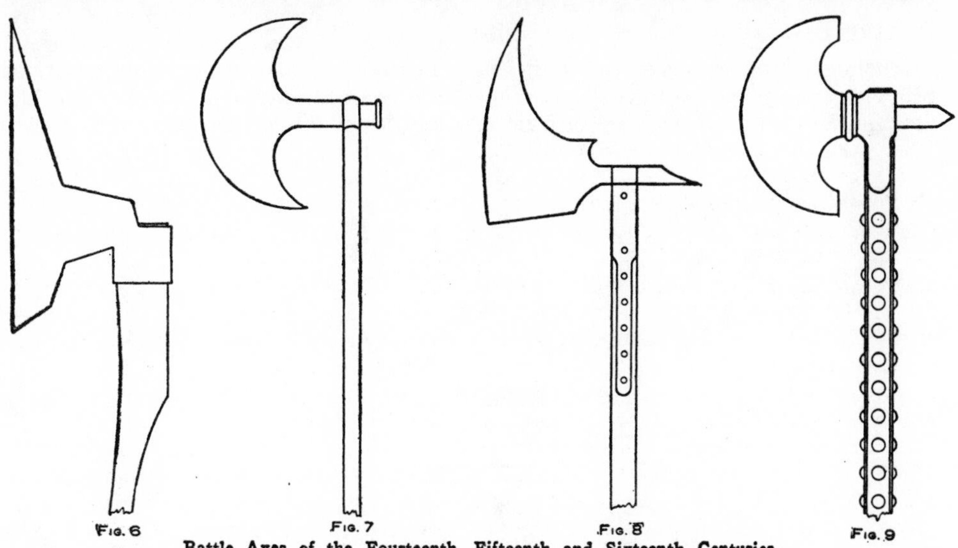

Battle Axes of the Fourteenth, Fifteenth and Sixteenth Centuries

up, it is covered with tinfoil in imitation of steel. The tinfoil should be applied carefully, as before mentioned, vet, with a golden or yellow cord wound spirally over the cloth. The upper half of the handle is steel, also, the hammer and spike. The entire handle should be made of one piece, then the hammer put on the base of the spike. The spike made with a peg in its lower end and well glued, can be firmly placed in position by the peg fitting in a hole made for its reception in the top of the handle. Finish up the steel parts with tinfoil.

The following described weapons can be constructed of the same materials and built up in the same way as described in the foregoing articles: A horseman's short-handled battle-axe, used at the end of the fifteenth century, is shown in Fig. 6. The handle is of wood and the axe in imitation steel. Figure 7 shows an English horseman's battle-axe used at the beginning of the reign of Queen Elizabeth. The handle and axe both are to be shown in steel. A German foot soldier's poleaxe used at the end of the fourteenth century is shown in Fig. 8. The handle is made of dark wood and the axe covered with tinfoil. Figure 9 shows an English foot soldier's jedburgh axe of the sixteenth century. The handle is of wood, studded with large brass or steel nails. The axe is shown in steel. All of these axes are about the same length.

Playing Baseball with a Pocket Knife

An interesting game of baseball can be played by two persons with a common pocket knife on a rainy day or in the winter time when the regular game cannot be played outdoors. The knife is opened and loosely stuck into a board, as in Fig. 1, and with a quick upward movement of the forefinger it is thrown into the air to fall and land in one of the positions shown. The plays are determined by the position of the knife after the fall.

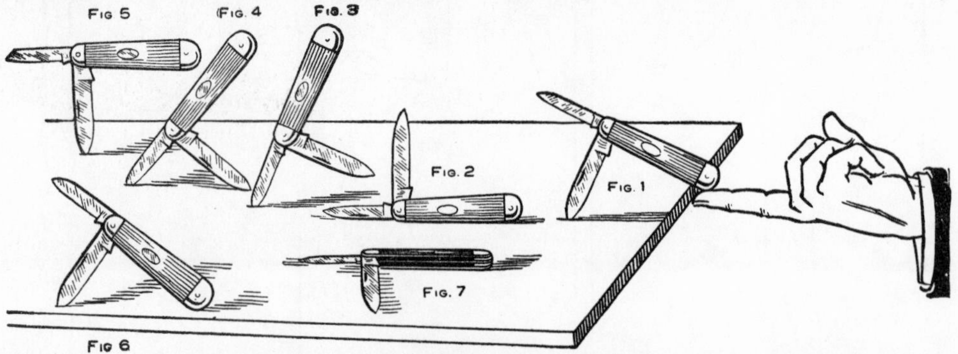

Positions of the Knife Indicate the Plays

A foul ball is indicated by Fig. 2, the knife resting on its back. The small blade sticking in the board which holds the handle in an upright position, as shown in Fig. 3, calls for a home run. Both blades sticking in the board (Fig. 4), a three-base hit. A two-base hit is made when the large blade sticks in the board, Fig. 5. A one-base hit is secured when the large blade and the end of the handle touch the board as in Fig. 6. The knife falling on its side (Fig. 7) calls for one out. Each person plays until three outs have been made, then the other plays, and so on for nine innings.—Contributed by Herbert Hahn, Chicago.

How to Remove Paper Stuck to a Negative

When making photographic prints from a negative, sometimes a drop of moisture will cause the print to stick to the gelatine film on the glass. Remove as much of the paper as can be readily torn off and soak the negative in a fresh hypo bath of 3 or 4 oz. hypo to 1 pt. of water for an hour or two. Then a little gentle rubbing with the finger—not the finger nail—will remove anything adhering to the film. It may be found that the negative is not colored. If it is spotted at all, the negative must be washed for a few minutes and placed in a combined toning and fixing bath, which will remove the spots in a couple of hours. The negative must be well washed after going through the solutions to take away any trace of hypo.

Old-Time Magic

A Sack Trick

The magician appears accompanied by his assistant. He has a sack similar to a meal bag only on a large scale. The upper end of this bag is shown in Fig. 1, with the rope laced in the cloth. He then selects several people from the audience as a committee to examine the sack to see that there is absolutely no deception whatever in its makeup. When they are satisfied that the bag or sack is all right, the magician places his assistant inside and drawing the bag around him he allows the committee to tie him up with as many knots as they choose to make, as shown in Fig. 2.

The bag with its occupant is placed in a small cabinet which the committee surround to see that there is no outside help. The magician then takes his watch and shows the audience that in less than 30 seconds his assistant will emerge from the cabinet with the sack in his hand. This he does, the sack is again examined and found to be the same as when it was first seen.

The solution is when the assistant enters the bag he pulls in about 15 in. of the rope and holds it, as shown in Fig. 3, while the committee is tying him up. As soon as he is in the cabinet he merely lets out the slack thus making enough room for his body to pass through. When he is out of the bag he quickly unties the knots and then steps from his cabinet.—Contributed by J. F. Campbell, Somerville, Mass.

The Invisible Light

The magician places two common wax candles on a table, one of them burning brightly, the other without a light. Members of the audience are allowed to inspect both the table and the candles.

The magician walks over to the burning candle, shades the light for a few seconds, turns to the audience with his hands a few inches apart, showing that there is nothing between them, at the

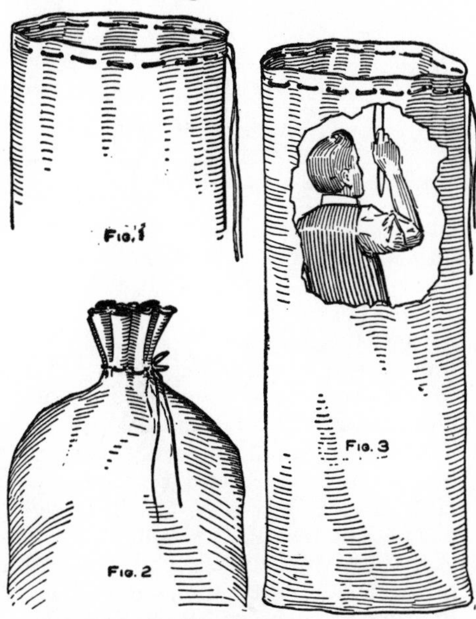

Sack Trick—Holding the Rope Inside the Bag

same time saying that he has a light between his hands, invisible to them (the audience), with which he is going to light the other candle. He then walks over to the other candle, and, in plain sight of the audience lights the candle apparently with nothing.

In reality the magician has a very fine wire in his hand which he is heating while he bends over the lighted candle, and the audience gaze on and see nothing. He turns to the other candle and touches a grain of phosphorus that has been previously concealed in the wick with the heated wire, thus causing it to light.—Contributed by C. Brown, New York City.

Using the Sun's Light in a Magic Lantern

The light furnished with a small magic lantern does very well for evening exhibitions, but the lantern can be used in the daytime with good results by directing sunlight through the lens instead of using the oil lamp.

A window facing the sun is selected

and the shade is drawn almost down, the remaining space being covered by a piece of heavy paper. A small hole is

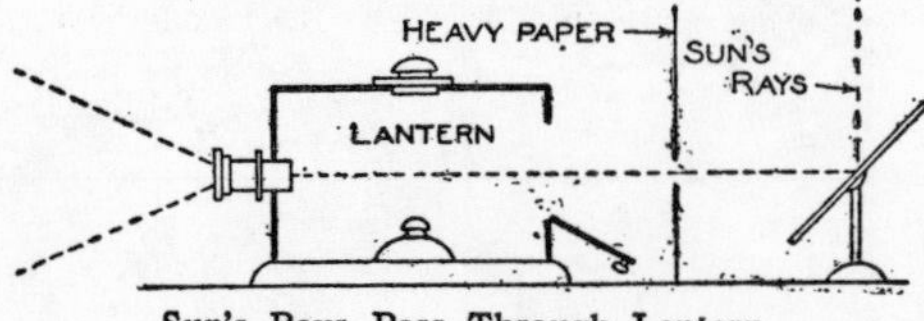

Sun's Rays Pass Through Lantern

cut in the paper and the lantern placed on a table in front of the hole, the lamp having been removed and the back opened. The lantern must be arranged so that the lens will be on a horizontal line with the hole in the paper. A mirror is then placed just outside of the window and at such an angle that the beam of light is thrown through the hole in the paper and the lens of the lantern.

The shades of the remaining windows are then drawn and the lantern is operated in the usual way.—Contributed by L. B. Evans, Lebanon, Ky.

A Handy Drill Gauge

The accompanying sketch shows a simple drill gauge which will be found very handy for amateurs. The gauge consists of a piece of hard wood, 3/4 in. thick, with a width and length that will be suitable for the size and number of drills you have on hand. Drill a hole through the wood with each drill you have and place a screweye in one end to be used as a hanger. When you want to drill a hole for a pipe, bolt,

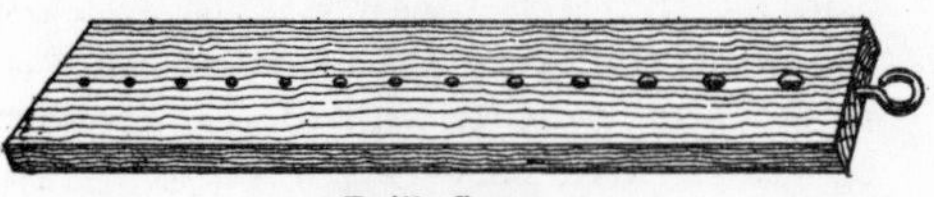
Drill Gauge

screw, etc., you take the gauge and find what size drill must be used in drilling the hole.—Contributed by Andrew G. Thome, Louisville, Ky.

A good stove polish can be made by mixing together 1 lb. of plumbago, 4 oz. of turpentine, 4 oz. of water and 1 oz. of sugar. Mix well and apply with a cloth or brush.

A Home-Made Daniell Cell

An effective Daniell galvanic cell may be constructed from material costing very little money. A common tin tomato can with a copper wire soldered to the top forms the jar and positive electrode. A piece of discarded stove zinc rolled into an open cylinder of about 1 1/2-in. diameter, 5 in. long, with a copper wire soldered at one end forms the negative electrode.

To make the porous cell, roll a piece of heavy brown wrapping paper, or blotting paper, into a tube of several thicknesses, about 5 in. long with an internal diameter of 2 in. Tie the paper firmly to prevent unrolling and close up one end with plaster of paris 1/2 in. thick. It is well to slightly choke the tube to better retain the plaster. The paper used must be unsized so that the solutions can mingle through the pores.

Two liquids are necessary for the cell. Make a strong solution in a glass or wooden vessel of blue vitriol in water. Dilute some oil of vitriol (sulphuric acid) with about 12 times its measure of water and keep in a bottle when not in use. In making up the solution, add the acid to the water with constant stirring. *Do not add water to the acid.*

The cell is charged by placing the zinc in the paper tube and both placed into the tin can. Connect the two wires and pour the dilute acid into the porous cell around the zinc, and then immediately turn the blue vitriol solution into the can outside the paper cup.

A current generates at once and metallic copper begins to deposit on the inside of the can. It is best to let the action continue for a half hour or so before putting the cell into use.

Several hours working will be required before the film of copper becomes sufficiently thick to protect the tin from corrosion when the cell stands idle. For this reason it will be necessary to pour out the blue vitriol solution into another receptacle immediately after through using, as otherwise the tin would be soon eaten full of holes. The porous cup should always be emptied after using to prevent the diffusion of the blue vitriol solution into the cup, and the paper tube must be well rinsed before putting away to dry.

This makes one of the most satisfactory battery cells on account of the constancy of its current, running for hours at a time without materially losing strength, and the low cost of maintenance makes it especially adapted for amateurs' use. Its current strength is about one volt, but can be made up into any required voltage in series. A battery of a dozen cells should cost not to exceed 50 cts. for the material, which will give a strong, steady current, amply sufficient for all ordinary experimental work.

A strong solution of common salt may be used in place of the oil of vitriol in the porous cup, but is not so good.—Contributed by C. H. Denniston, Pulteney, N. Y.

A Home-Made Equatorial

By Harry Clark

The ordinary equatorial is designed and built for the latitude of the observatory where it is to be used. This is necessary since the hour axis must point to the north pole of the heavens whose elevation above the horizon is equal to the latitude of the observer's station. The final adjustment of an ordinary equatorial is very tedious so that when once set up it is not to be moved. This calls for a suitable house to protect the instrument. It has been the aim of the writer to build a very simple instrument for amateur work which would be adjustable to any latitude, so easily set up ready for work and so portable that it need not be left out of doors from one evening until the next.

The instrument is mounted on a tripod or piece of iron pipe carrying a

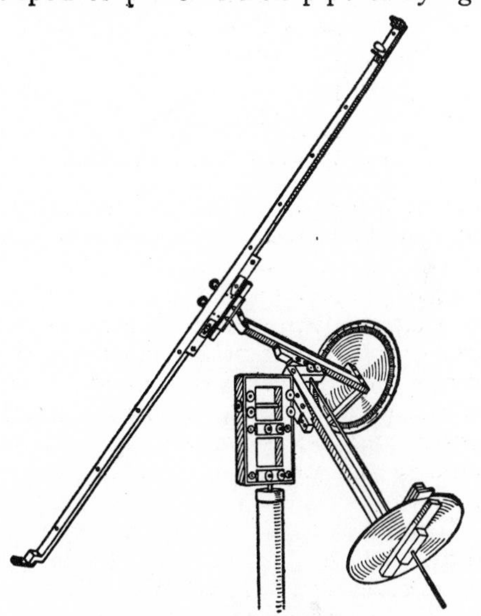

Instrument for Locating Stars

short vertical rod of 3/8-in. steel. A rectangular wooden frame with suitable bearings rotates about this shaft. The frame has also two horizontal bearings carrying a short shaft to the end of which the frame carrying the hour axis is firmly clamped. By this arrangement of two perpendicular shafts the hour axis may be directed to any point in the heavens without care as to how the tripod or pipe is set up.

The frame for the hour axis is about 12 in. long with a bearing at each end. The shaft which it carries is 1/4-in. steel, carrying the hour circle at one end, and at the other the frame for the declination axis which is similar to the other, but somewhat lighter. The declination axis is also of 1/4-in. steel, carrying at one end the declination circle and the pointer at the other.

The entire frame of the instrument is made of cherry and it will save the builder much time if he will purchase cherry "furniture" which is used by printers and can be obtained from any printers' supply company. It is best quality wood free from imperfections in straight strips one yard long and of a uniform width of about 5/8 in. As to thickness, any multiple of 12-point (about 1/8 in.) may be obtained, thus saving much work in fitting up joints. Fifty cents will buy enough wood for an entire instrument. All corners are carefully mortised and braced with small brass angle-pieces. The frame is held together by small brass machine screws. After much experimentation with bearings, it was found best to make them in halves as metal bearings are usually made. The loose half is held in place by guides on all four sides and is tightened by two screws with milled nuts. A great deal of trouble was experienced in boring out the bearings until the following method was devised. One hole was bored as well as possible. The bearing was then loosened and a bit run through it to bore the other. Finally, a piece of shafting was roughened by rolling it on a file; placed in both bearings and turned with a brace. The bearings were gradually tightened until perfectly ground.

The declination axis must be perpendicular to both the hour axis and the line of sight over the pointer. To insure this, a positive adjustment was provided. The end of the shaft is clamped in a short block of wood by means of a bearing like the ones described. One end of the block is hinged to the axis frame, while the other end is attached by two screws, one drawing them together, the other holding them apart. The axis is adjusted by turning these screws. Each shaft, save the one in the pipe, is provided with this adjustment.

The pointer is of two very thin strips placed at right angles and tapered slightly at each end. The clamp is attached as shown in the illustration. The eye piece is a black iron washer supported on a small strip of wood. The aperture should be 1/4 in., since the pupil of the eye dilates very much in darkness. The error due to large aperture is reduced by using a very long pointer which also makes it possible to focus the eye upon the front sight and the star simultaneously. The forward sight is a bright brass peg illuminated by a tiny electric lamp with a reflector to shield the eye. The pointer arranged in this way is a great improvement over the hollow tube sometimes used, since it allows an unobstructed view of the heavens while indicating the exact point in question.

The circles of the instrument are of aluminum, attached to the shafts by means of wooden clamps. They were nicely graduated by a home-made dividing engine of very simple construction, and the figures were engraved with a pantograph. The reading is indicated by a cut on a small aluminum plate attached to a pointer. The hour circle is divided into 24 parts and subdivided to every four minutes. The figures are arranged so that when the instrument is set up, the number of hours increases while the pointer travels oppositely to the stars. The declination circle is graduated from zero to 90 deg. in each direction from two points 180 deg. apart. It is adjusted to read zero when the pointer and two axes are mutually perpendicular as shown in the picture.

To adjust the instrument it is set up on the iron pipe and the pointer directed to some distant object. All set screws, excepting those on the declination axis, are tightened. Then the pointer is carefully turned through 180 deg. and if it is not again directed to the same point, it is not perpendicular to the declination axis. When properly set it will describe a great circle. With the declination axis in an approximately horizontal position the place where the pointer cuts the horizon is noted. The declination axis is then turned through 180 deg., when the pointer should again cut at the same place. Proper adjustment will cause it to do so. It is desirable that the hour circle should read approximately zero when the declination axis is horizontal, but this is not necessary for a reason soon to be explained. All these adjustments, once carefully made, need not be changed.

In using the instrument the hour axis can be directed to the north pole by the following method. Point it approximately to the north star. The pole is 1 deg. and 15 min. from the star on a straight line from the star to "Mizar," the star at the bend of the handle in the Big Dipper. Turn the hour circle into a position where the pointer can describe a circle through "Mizar." Only a rough setting is necessary. Now turn the pointer so that a reading of 88 deg. 45 min. shows on the declination circle on that side of 90 which is toward "Mizar." When this is done, clamp both axes and turn the shafts in the base until the pointer is directed accurately to the north star. It is evident from a study of the picture that the position of the small pointer which indicates the reading on the hour circle is not independent of the way in which the tripod or pipe is set up. It would then be useless to adjust it carefully to zero when the pointer cuts the "zenith" as is done with a large equatorial. Instead, the adjustment is made by setting the clock or watch which is part of the outfit. The pointer is directed to Alpha, Cassiopiæ, and the hour reading subtracted from 24 hours (the approximate right ascension of the star) gives the time which the clock should be set to indicate. All of these settings should require not more than five minutes.

To find a star in the heavens, look up its declination and right ascension in an atlas. Set the declination circle to its reading. Subtract the clock time from the right ascension (plus 24 if necessary) and set the hour circle to the result. The star will then be seen on the tip of the pointer.

To locate a known star on the map, turn the pointer to the star. Declination is read directly. Add the clock time to the hour reading to get right ascension. If the result is more than 24 hours, subtract 24.

A Ground Glass Substitute

Ordinary plain glass coated with the following mixture will make a good ground glass substitute: Dissolve 18 gr. of gum sandarac and 4 gr. of gum mastic in 3½ dr. of ether, then add 1 2-3 dr. benzole. If this will be too transparent, add a little more benzole, taking care not to add too much. Cover one side of a clear glass and after drying it will produce a perfect surface for use as a ground glass in cameras.—Contributed by Ray E. Strosnider, Plain City, Ohio.

A Miniature War Dance

A piece of paper, 3 or 4 in. long, is folded several times, as shown in the sketch, and the first fold marked out to represent one-half of an Indian. Cut out all the folds at one time on the dotted line and you will have as many men joined together as there were folds in the paper. Join the hands of the two end men with a little paste so as to form a circle of Indians holding hands.

The next thing to do is to punch holes in heavy cardboard that is large enough to cover a pot or stew pan, and

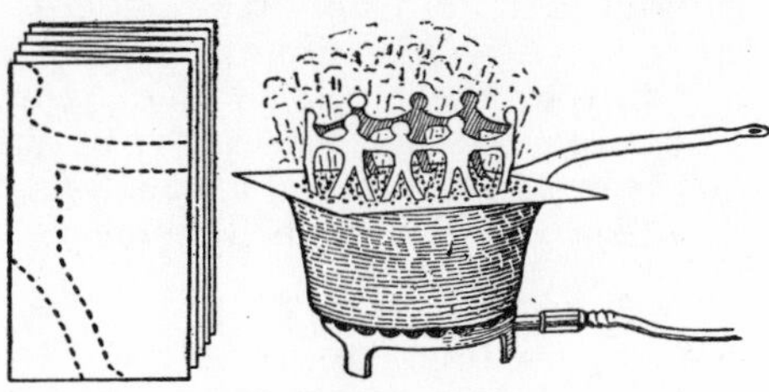

Indian War Dance

partially fill the vessel with water. Set this covered vessel over a heat and bring the water to a boiling point and then set the miniature Indians on the perforated cover. The dance will begin.

If the Indians are decked out with small feathers to represent the head gear and trailing plumes, a great effect will be produced.—Contributed by Maurice Baudier, New Orleans, La.

Turning the water on before starting the gas engine may prevent breaking a cylinder on a cold day.

OLD-TIME MAGIC

Removing 36 Cannon Balls from a Handbag

The magician produces a small handbag and informs the audience that he has it filled with 20-lb. cannon balls. He opens up the bag and takes out a ball which he passes to the audience

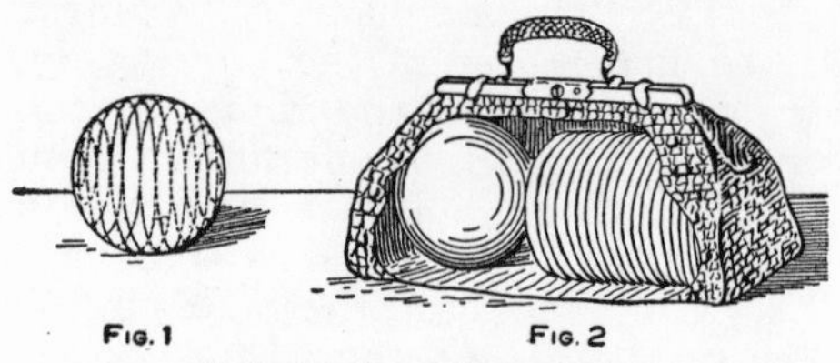

Balls Made of Spring Wire

for examination. The ball is found to be the genuine article. He makes a few passes with the wand and produces another ball, and so on until 36 of them lie on the floor.

In reality the first ball, which is the one examined, is the real cannon ball, the others are spiral-spherical springs covered with black cloth (Fig. 1). These balls can be pressed together in flat disks and put in the bag, Fig. 2, without taking up any great amount of space. When the spring is released it will fill out the black cloth to represent a cannon ball that cannot be distinguished from the real article.—Contributed by J. F. Campbell, Somerville, Mass.

A Rising Card Trick

A rising card trick can be accomplished with very little skill by using the simple device illustrated. The only

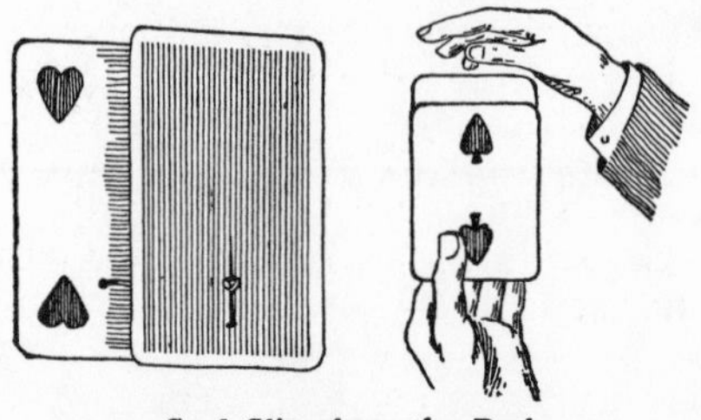
Card Slips from the Pack

things needed are four ordinary playing cards and a short rubber band. Pass one end of the rubber band through one card and the other end through the other card, as shown in the illustration, drawing the cards close together and fastening the ends by putting a pin through them. The remaining two cards are pasted to the first two so as to conceal the pins and ends of the rubber band.

Put the cards with the rubber band in a pack of cards; take any other card from the pack and show it to the audience in such a way that you do not see and know the card shown. Return the card to the pack, but be sure and place it between the cards tied together with the rubber band. Grasp the pack between your thumb and finger tightly at first, and by gradually loosening your hold the card previously shown to the audience will slowly rise out of the pack.—Contributed by Tomi O'Kawara, San Francisco, Cal.

Sliding Box Cover Fastener

While traveling through the country as a watchmaker I found it quite convenient to keep my small drills, taps, small brooches, etc., in boxes having a sliding cover. To keep the contents from spilling or getting mixed in my case I used a small fastener as shown in the accompanying illustration. The fastener is made of steel or brass and fastened by means of small screws or tacks on the outside of the box. A hole is drilled on the upper part to receive the pin that is driven into the sliding cover. This pin should not stick out beyond the thickness of the spring, which is bent up at the point so the pin will freely pass under it. The pin can be driven through the cover to prevent it from being pulled entirely out of the box.—Contributed by Herm Grabemann, Milwaukee, Wis.

How to Chain a Dog

A good way to chain a dog and give him plenty of ground for exercise is to stretch a clothesline or a galvanized wire between the house and barn on which is placed a ring large enough to slide freely. The chain from the dog's collar is fastened to the ring. This method can also be used for tethering a cow or horse, the advantage being the use of a short tie rope eliminating the possibility of the animal becoming entangled.

The Dog Has Plenty of Room for Exercise

Water-Color Box

There are many different trays in the market for the purpose of holding water colors, but they are either too expensive for the average person or too small to be convenient. I do a great deal of water-color work and always felt the need of a suitable color dish. At last I found something that filled my want and suited my pocketbook. I bought 22 individual salt dishes and made a box to hold them, as shown in the illustration. This box has done good service.

Some of the advantages are: Each color is in a separate dish which can be easily taken out and cleaned; the dishes are deep enough to prevent spilling the colors into the adjoining ones, and the box can be made as big or as small as individual needs require. The tray containing the color dishes and brushes rests on 1/4-in. round pieces 2 1/4 in. from the bottom of the box, thus giving ample store room for colors, prints, slides and extra brushes.

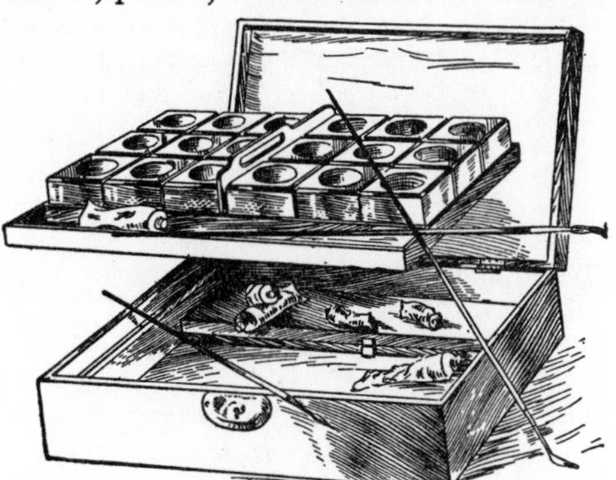

Color Trays Made of Salt Dishes

—Contributed by B. Beller, Hartford, Connecticut.

Ink usually corrodes pens in a short time. This can be prevented by placing pieces of steel pens or steel wire in the ink, which will absorb the acid and prevent it from corroding the pens.

A Plant-Food Percolator

Obtain two butter tubs and bore a large number of ¼-in. holes in the bottom of one, then cover the perforated part with a piece of fine brass gauze (Fig. 1), tacking the gauze well at the corners. The other tub should be fitted with a faucet of some kind—a wood faucet, costing 5 cents, will answer the purpose. Put the first tub on top of the other with two narrow strips between them (Fig. 2). Fill the upper tub, about three-fourths full, with well packed horse manure, and pour water on it until it is well soaked. When the water has percolated through into the lower tub, it is ready to use on house and garden plants and is better than plain water, as it adds both fertilizer and moisture.—Contributed by C. O. Darke, West Lynn, Mass.

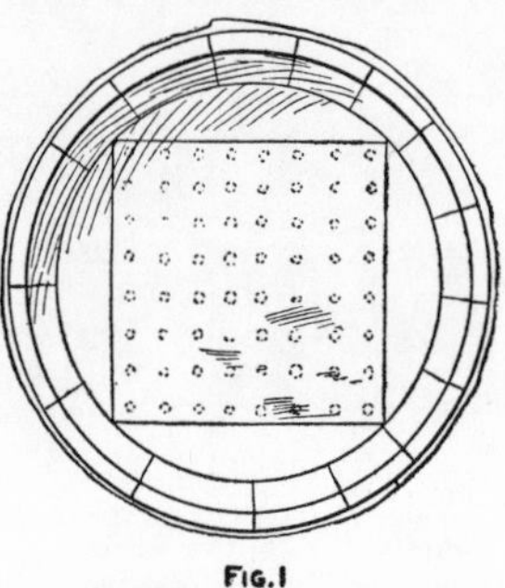

Fig. 1

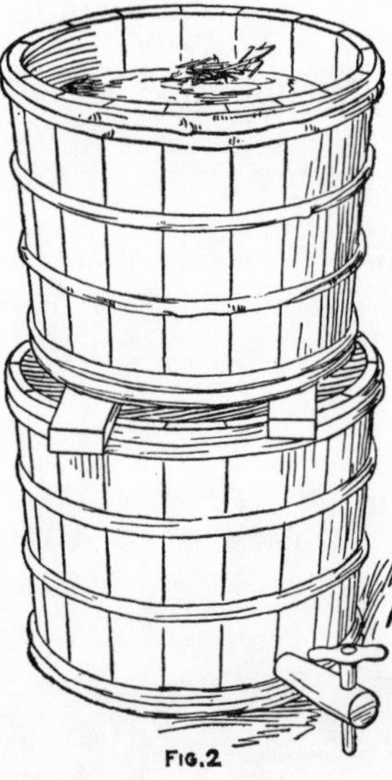

Fig. 2

ℭAlways caliper the work in a lathe while it is standing still.

ℭNever use the ways of a lathe for an anvil or storage platform.

Folding Quilting-Frames

The frame in which the material is kept stretched when making a quilt is usually too large to be put out of the way conveniently when other duties must be attended to; and especially are the end pieces objectionable. This can be remedied by hinging the ends so they will fold underneath to the center. The end pieces are cut in two at one-fourth their distance from each end, a hinge screwed to the under side to hold them together, and a hook and eye fastened on the other side to hold the parts rigid when they are in use. When the ends are turned under, the frame is narrow enough to be easily carried from one room to another, or placed against a wall.

A Drip Shield for the Arms

When working with the hands in a pan of water, oil or other fluid, it is very disagreeable to have the liquid run down the arms, when they are raised from the pan, often to soil the sleeves of a clean garment. A drip shield which will stop the fluid and cause it to run back into the pan can be easily made from a piece of sheet rubber or, if this is not available, from a piece of the inner tube of a bicycle tire. Cut a washer with the hole large enough to fit snugly about the wrist, but not so tight as to stop the circulation of the blood. A pair of these shields will always come in handy.—Contributed by L. M. Eifel, Chicago.

Shields for the Arms

How to Cane Chairs

There are but few households that do not have at least one or two chairs without a seat or back. The same households may have some one who would enjoy recaning the chairs if he only knew how to do it, and also make considerable pin money by repairing chairs for the neighbors. If the following directions are carried out, new cane seats and backs can easily be put in chairs where they are broken or sagged to an uncomfortable position.

The first thing necessary is to remove the old cane. This can be done by turning the chair upside down and, with the aid of a sharp knife or chisel, cutting the cane between the holes. After this is done the old bottom can be pulled out. If plugs are found in any of the holes, they should be knocked out. If the beginner is in doubt about finding which holes along any curved sides should be used for the cane running nearly parallel to the edge, he may find it to his advantage to mark the holes on the under side of the frame before removing the old cane.

The worker should be provided with a small sample of the old cane. At any first-class hardware store a bundle of similar material may be secured.

The cane usually comes in lengths of about 15 ft. and each bundle contains enough to reseat several chairs. In addition to the cane, the worker should provide himself with a piece of bacon rind, a square pointed wedge, as shown in Fig. 1, and 8 or 10 round wood plugs, which are used for temporarily holding the ends of the cane in the holes.

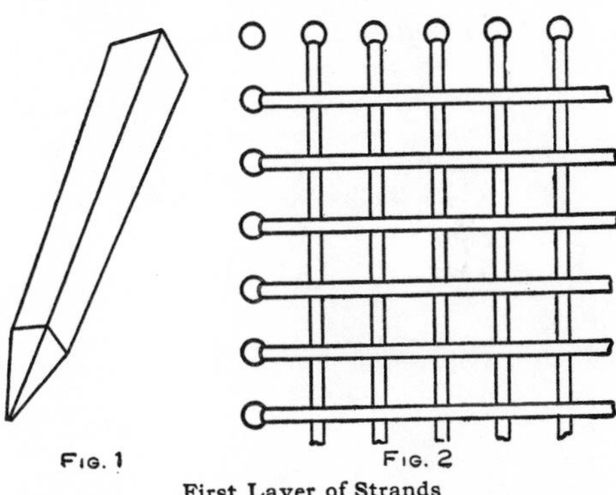

First Layer of Strands

A bucket of water should be supplied in which to soak the cane just before weaving it. Several minutes before you are ready to begin work, take four or five strands of the cane, and, after having doubled them up singly into convenient lengths and tied each one into a single knot, put them into the water to soak. The cane is much more pliable and is less liable to crack in bending when worked while wet. As fast as the soaked cane is used, more of it should be put into the water.

Untie one of the strands which has been well soaked, put about 3 or 4 in. down through the hole at one end of what is to be the outside strand of

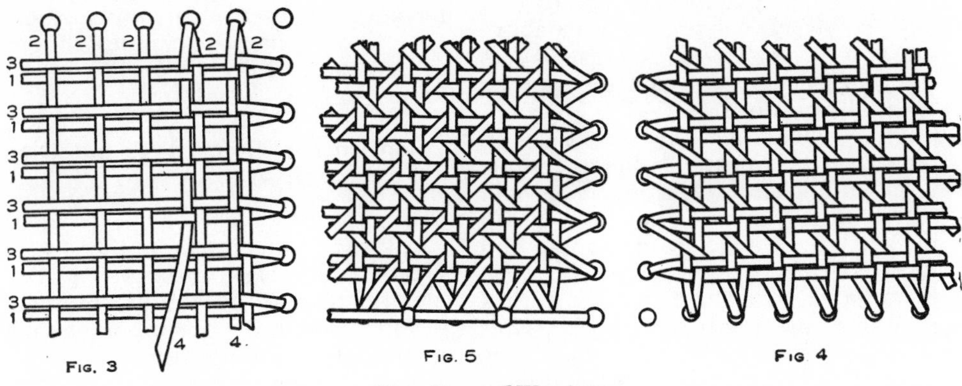

Three Stages of Weaving

one side and secure it in this hole by means of one of the small plugs mentioned. The plug should not be forced in too hard nor cut off, as it must be re-

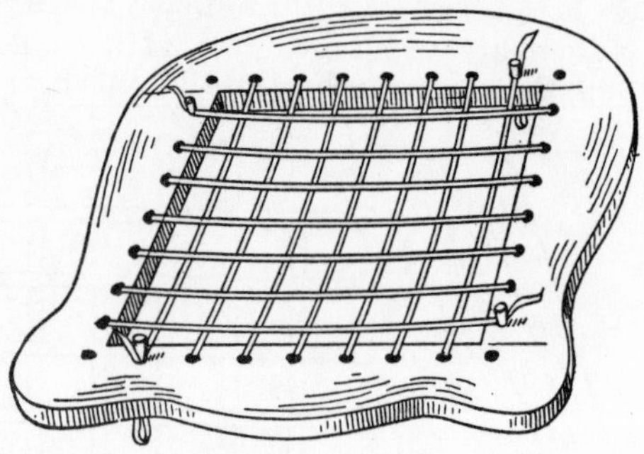

First Two Layers in Place

moved again. The other end of the strand should be made pointed and passed down through the hole at the opposite side, and, after having been pulled tight, held there by inserting another plug. Pass the end up through the next hole, then across and down, and hold while the second plug is moved to the last hole through which the cane was drawn. In the same manner proceed across the chair bottom. Whenever the end of one strand is reached, it should be held by a plug, and a new one started in the next hole as in the beginning. No plugs should be permanently removed until another strand of cane is through the same hole to hold the first strand in place. After laying the strands across the seat in one direction, put in another layer at right angles and lying entirely above the first layer. Both of these layers when in place appear as shown in one of the illustrations.

After completing the second layer, stretch the third one, using the same holes as for the first layer. This will make three layers, the first being hidden by the third while the second layer is at right angles to and between the first and third. No weaving has been done up to this time, nothing but stretching and threading the cane through the holes. The cane will have the appearance shown in Fig. 3. The next thing to do is to start the cane across in the same direction as the second layer and begin the weaving. The top or third layer strands should be pushed toward the end from which the weaving starts, so that the strand being woven may be pushed down between the first and third layers and up again between pairs. The two first strands of the fourth layer are shown woven in Fig. 3. During the weaving, the strands should be lubricated with the rind of bacon to make them pass through with ease. Even with this lubrication, one can seldom weave more than half way across the seat with the pointed end before finding it advisable to pull the remainder of the strand through. After finishing this fourth layer of strands, it is quite probable that each strand will be about midway between its two neighbors instead of lying close to its mate as desired, and here is where the square and pointed wedge is used. The wedge is driven down between the proper strands to move them into place.

Start at one corner and weave diagonally, as shown in Fig. 4, making sure that the strand will slip in between the two which form the corner of the square in each case. One more weave across on the diagonal and the seat will be finished except for the binding, as shown in Fig. 5. The binding consists of one strand that covers the row of holes while it is held down with another strand, a loop over the first being made every second or third hole as desired. It will be of great assistance to keep another chair with a cane bottom at hand to examine while recaning the first chair.—Contributed by M. R. W.

Repairing a Cracked Composition Developing Tray

Fill the crack with some powdered rosin and heap it up on the outside. Heat a soldering-iron or any piece of metal enough to melt the rosin and let it flow through the break. When cool, trim off the surplus rosin. If handled with a little care, a tray repaired in this manner will last a long time. The chemicals will not affect the rosin.—Contributed by E. D. Patrick, Detroit, Michigan.

How to Lay Out a Sundial

The sundial is an instrument for measuring time by using the shadow of the sun. They were quite common in ancient times before clocks and watches were invented. At the present time they are used more as an ornamentation than as a means of measuring time, although they are quite accurate if properly constructed. There are several different designs of sundials, but the most common, and the one we shall describe in this article, is the horizontal dial. It consists of a flat circular table, placed firmly on a solid pedestal and having a triangular plate of metal, Fig. 1, called the gnomon, rising from its center and inclined toward the meridian line of the dial at an angle equal to the latitude of the place where the dial is to be used. The shadow of the edge of the triangular plate moves around the northern part of the dial from morning to afternoon, and thus supplies a rough measurement of the hour of the day.

The style or gnomon, as it always equals the latitude of the place, can be laid out as follows: Draw a line AB, Fig. 1, 5 in. long and at the one end erect a perpendicular BC, the height of which is taken from table No. 1. It may be necessary to interpolate for a given latitude, as for example, lat. 41°-30′. From table No. 1 lat. 42° is 4.5 in. and for lat. 40°, the next smallest, it is 4.2 in. Their difference is .3 in. for 2°, and for 1° it would be .15 in. For 30′ it would be ½ of 1° or .075 in. All added to the lesser or 40°, we have 4.2 + .15 + .075 in.= 4.42 in. as the height of the line BC for lat. 41°-30′. If you have a table of natural functions, the height of the line BC, or the style, is the base (5 in. in this case) times the tangent of the degree of latitude. Draw the line AD, and the angle BAD is the correct angle for the style for the given

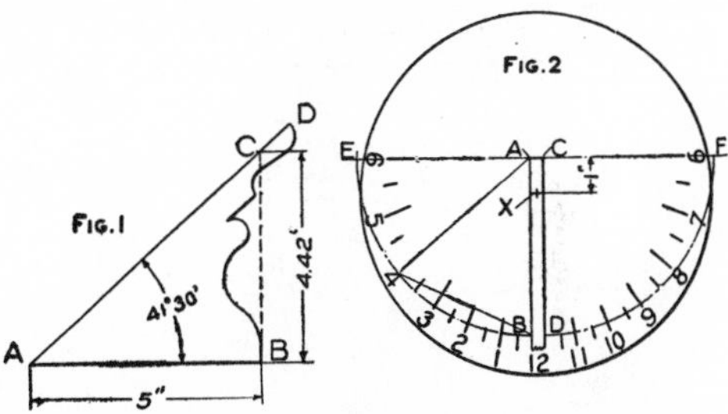

Details of Dial

latitude. Its thickness, if of metal, may be conveniently from ⅛ to ¼ in.; or if of stone, an inch or two, or more, according to the size of the dial. Usually for neatness of appearance the back of the style is hollowed as shown. The upper edges which cast the shadows must be sharp and straight, and for this size dial (10 in. in diameter) they should be about 7½ in. long.

To lay out the hour circle, draw two parallel lines AB and CD, Fig. 2, which will represent the base in length and thickness. Draw two semi-circles, using the points A and C as centers, with a radius of 5 in. The points of intersection with the lines AB and CD will be the 12-o'clock marks. A line EF drawn through the points A and C, and perpendicular to the base or style, and intersecting the semi-circles, gives the 6-o'clock points. The point marked X is to be used as the center of the dial. The intermediate hour and half-hour lines can be plotted by using table No. 2 for given lati-

TABLE NO. I.
Height of stile in inches for a 5 in. base, for various latitudes.

Latitude	Height	Latitude	Height
25°	2.33	42°	4.50
26°	2.44	44°	4.83
27°	2.55	46°	5.18
28°	2.66	48°	5.55
30°	2.89	50°	5.96
32°	3.12	52°	6.40
34°	3.37	54°	6.88
36°	3.63	56°	7.41
38°	3.91	58°	8.00
40°	4.20	60°	8.66

tudes, placing them to the right or left of the 12-o'clock points. For latitudes not given, interpolate in the same manner as for the height of the style. The

TABLE No.2.
Chords in inches for a 10in. circle Sundial.

Latitude	Hours of Day										
	12-30	1	1-30	2	2-30	3	3-30	4	4-30	5	5-30
	11-30	11	10-30	10	9-30	9	8-30	8	7-30	7	6-30
25°	.28	.56	.87	1.19	1.57	1.99	2.49	3.11	3.87	4.82	5.93
30°	.33	.66	1.02	1.40	1.82	2.30	2.85	3.49	4.26	5.14	6.10
35°	.38	.76	1.16	1.59	2.06	2.57	3.16	3.81	4.55	5.37	6.23
40°	.42	.85	1.30	1.77	2.27	2.82	3.42	4.07	4.79	5.55	6.32
45°	.46	.94	1.42	1.93	2.46	3.03	3.64	4.29	4.97	5.68	6.39
50°	.50	1.01	1.53	2.06	2.68	3.21	3.82	4.46	5.12	5.79	6.46
55°	.54	1.08	1.63	2.19	2.77	3.37	3.98	4.60	5.24	5.87	6.49
60°	.57	1.14	1.71	2.30	2.89	3.49	4.10	4.72	5.34	5.93	6.52

¼-hour and the 5 and 10-minute divisions may be spaced with the eye or they may be computed.

When placing the dial in position, care must be taken to get it perfectly level and have the style at right angles to the dial face, with its sloping side pointing to the North Pole. An ordinary compass, after allowing for the declination, will enable one to set the dial, or it may be set by placing it as near north and south as one may judge and comparing with a watch set at standard time. The dial time and the watch time should agree after the watch has been corrected for the equation of time from table No. 3, and for the difference between standard and local time, changing the position of the dial until an agreement is reached. Sun time and standard time agree only four times a year, April 16, June 15, Sept. 2 and Dec. 25, and on these dates the dial needs no correction. The corrections for the various days of the month can be taken from Table 3. The + means that the clock is faster, and the — means that the dial is faster than the sun. Still another correction must be made which is constant for each given locality. Standard time is the correct time for longitude 75° New York, 90° Chicago, 105° Denver and 120° for San Francisco. Ascertain in degrees of longitude how far your dial is east or west of the nearest standard meridian and divide this by 15, reducing the answer to minutes and seconds, which will be the correction in minutes and seconds of time. If the dial is east of the meridian chosen, then the watch is slower; if west, it will be faster. This correction can be added to the values in table No. 3, making each value slower when it is east of the standard meridian and faster when it is west.

The style or gnomon with its base can be made in cement and set on a cement pedestal which has sufficient base placed in the ground to make it solid.

The design of the sundial is left to the ingenuity of the maker.—Contributed by J. E. Mitchell, Sioux City, Iowa.

TABLE No.3
Corrections in minutes to change Sun time to local mean time,– add those marked +, subtract those marked –, from Sundial time.

Day of month	1	10	20	30
January	+3	+7	+11	+13
February	+14	+14	+14	
March	+13	+11	+8	+5
April	+4	+2	−1	−3
May	−3	−4	−4	−3
June	−3	−1	+1	+3
July	+3	+5	+6	+6
August	+6	+5	+3	+1
September	+0	−3	−6	−10
October	−10	−13	−15	−16
November	−16	−16	−14	−11
December	−11	−7	−3	+2

Imitation Arms and Armor—Part IV

The ancient arms of defense as shown in the accompanying illustrations make good ornaments for the den if they are cut from wood and finished in imitation of the real weapon. The designs shown represent original arms of the sixteenth and seventeenth centuries. As they are the genuine reproductions, each article can be labelled with the name, adding to each piece interest and value, says the English Mechanic, London.

Each weapon is cut from wood. The blades of the axes and the cutting edges of the swords are dressed down and finished with sandpaper and the steel parts represented by covering the wood with tinfoil. When putting on the tinfoil, brush a thin coat of glue on the part to be covered and quickly lay on the foil. If a cutting edge is to be covered the tinfoil on one side of the blade must overlap the edge which is pasted on the opposite side. The other side is then covered with the tinfoil of a size that will not quite cover to the cutting edge. After laying the foil and allowing time for the glue to dry, wipe the surface with light strokes up and down several times using a soft piece of cloth.

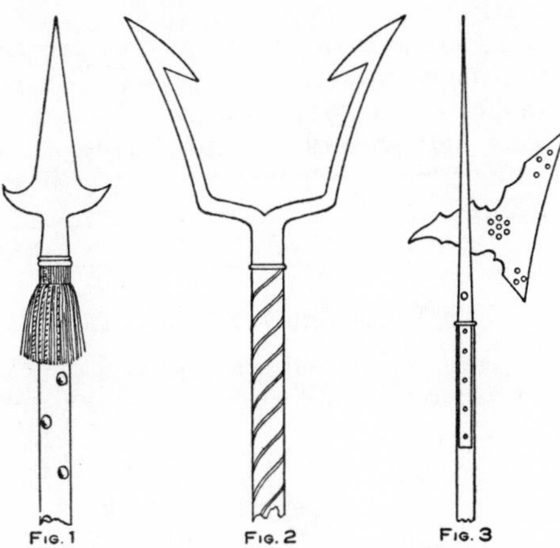

Partisan, Fork and Halberd

A French partisan of the sixteenth century is shown in Fig. 1. The weapon is 6½ ft. long with a round handle having the same circumference for the entire length which is covered with crimson cloth or velvet and studded all over with round-headed brass nails. The spear head is of steel about 15 in. long from the point where it is attached to the handle. The widest part of the blade from spear to spear is about 8 in. The length of the tassel or fringe is about 4 in.

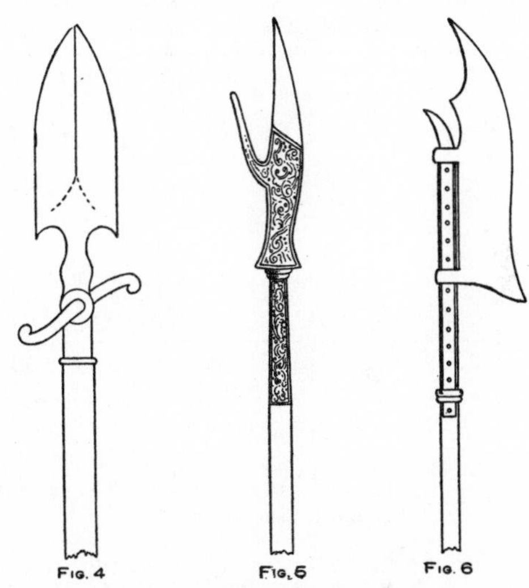

Spontoon, Glaive and Voulge

Figure 2 shows a German military fork of the sixteenth century, the length of which is about 5 ft. with a handle of wood bound with heavy cord in a spiral form and the whole painted a dark color. The entire length of the fork from the handle to the points is about 10 in., and is covered with tinfoil in imitation of steel.

A Swiss halberd of the sixteenth century is shown in Fig. 3. This combination of an axe and spear is about 7 ft. long from the point of the spear to the end of the handle, which is square. The spear and axe is of steel with a handle of plain dark wood. The holes in the axe can be bored or burned out with red-hot iron rods, the holes being about ¼ in. in diameter.

Figure 4 shows an Austrian officers' spontoon, used about the seventeenth century. It is about 6 ft. long with a round wooden handle. The spear head from its point to where fixed on the handle is about 9 in. long. The edges are sharp. The cross bar which runs through the lower end of the spear can

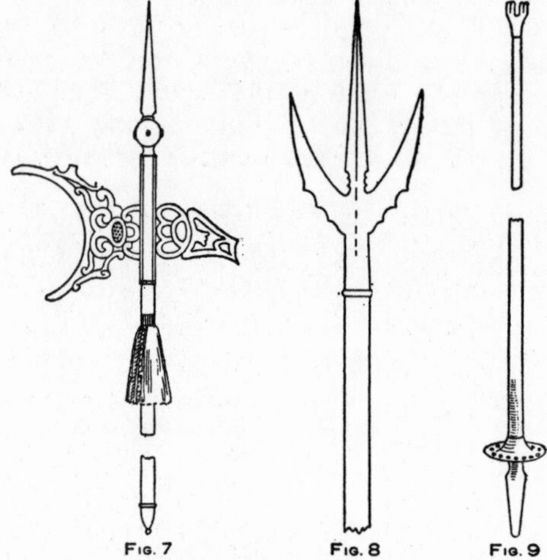

Fig. 7 Fig. 8 Fig. 9

Halberd, Ranseur and Lance

be made in two pieces and glued into a hole on each side. The length of this bar is about 5 in. The small circular plate through which the bar is fixed can be cut from a piece of cardboard and glued on the wooden spear.

A gisarm or glaive, used by Italians in the sixteenth century, is shown in Fig. 5. The entire length is about 6½ ft. The blade is engraved steel with a length of metal work from the point of the spear to where it joins the handle or staff of about 18 in. It has a round wooden handle painted black or dark brown. The engraved work must be carved in the wood and when putting the tinfoil on, press it well into the carved depressions.

Figure 6 shows a Saxon voulge of the sixteenth century, 6 ft. long, with a round wood handle and a steel axe or blade, sharp on the outer edge and held to the handle by two steel bands, which are a part of the axe. The bands can be made of cardboard and glued on to the wood axe. These bands can be made very strong by reinforcing the cardboard with a piece of canvas. A small curved spear point is carved from a piece of wood, covered with tinfoil and fastened on the end of the handle as shown. The band of metal on the side is cut from cardboard, covered with tinfoil and fastened on with round-headed brass or steel nails.

A very handsome weapon is the German halberd of the sixteenth century which is shown in Fig. 7. The entire length is about 6½ ft., with a round wooden handle fitted at the lower end with a steel ornament. The length of the spear point to the lower end where it joins on to the handle is 14 in. The extreme width of the axe is 16 or 17 in. The outer and inner edges of the crescent-shaped part of the axe are sharp. This axe is cut out with a scroll or keyhole saw and covered with tinfoil.

An Italian ranseur of the sixteenth century is shown in Fig. 8. This weapon is about 6 ft. long with a round staff or handle. The entire length of the metal part from the point of the spear to where it joins the staff is 15 in. The spear is steel, sharp on the outer edges.

Figure 9 shows a tilting lance with vamplate used in tournaments in the sixteenth century. The wood pole is covered with cloth or painted a dark color. At the end is a four-pronged piece of steel. The vamplate can be made of cardboard covered with tinfoil to represent steel and studded with brass nails. The extreme length is 9 ft.

The tassels or fringe used in decorating the handles can be made from a few inches of worsted fringe, about 4 in. long and wound around the handle or staff twice and fastened with brass-headed nails.

An Emergency Babbitt Ladle

Take an old stove leg and rivet a handle on it and then break the piece off which fastens on the stove. The large and rounding part of the leg makes the bowl of the ladle. This ladle will be found convenient for melting babbitt or lead.—Contributed by R. H. Workman, Loudonville, Ohio.

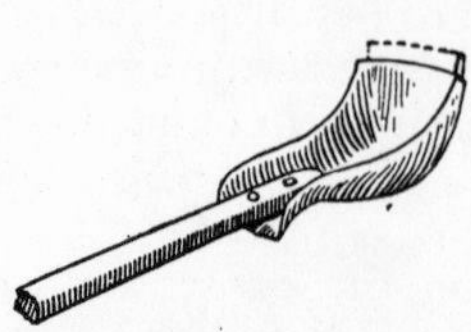

How to Make Japanese Portieres

These very useful and ornamental draperies can be easily made at home by anyone possessing a little ingenuity. They can be made of various materials, the most durable being bamboo, although beads of glass or rolled paper will produce good results. Substances such as straw, while readily adaptable and having a neat appearance, are less durable and will quickly show wear. The paper beads are easily made, as shown in Figs. 1, 2 and 3. In Figs. 1 and 2 are shown how the paper is cut tapering, and as it appears after rolling and gluing down the ends. A straight paper bead is shown in Fig. 3.

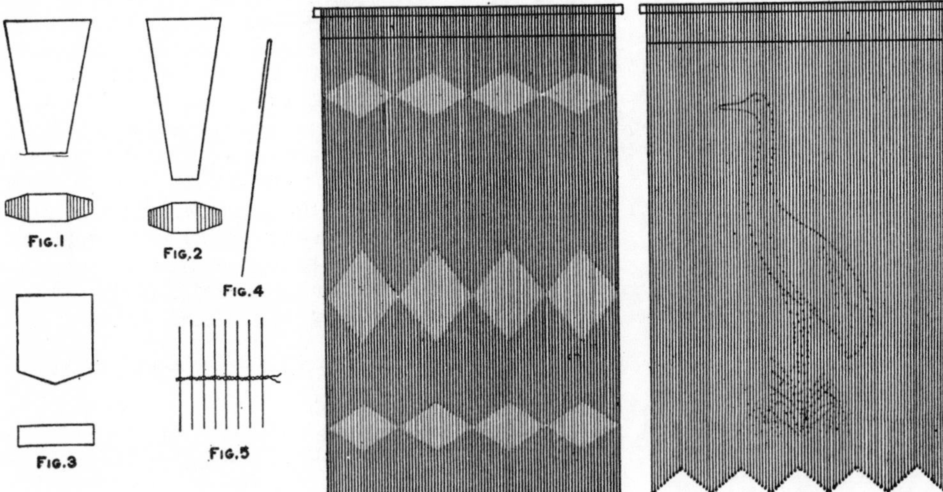

Bamboo and Straw Portieres

The first step is to select the kind of beads desired for stringing and then procure the hanging cord. Be sure to get a cord of such size that the beads will slip on readily and yet have the least possible lateral movement. This is important to secure neatness. One end of each cord is tied to a round piece of wood, or in holes punched in a leather strap. Iron or brass rings can be used if desired.

Cut all the cords the same length, making allowance for the number of knots necessary to produce the design selected. Some designs require only one knot at the bottom. It is best to make a rough sketch of the design on paper. This will greatly aid the maker in carrying on the work.

When the main part of the screen is finished, the cross cords, used for spacing and binding the whole together, are put in place. This is done with a needle made from a piece of small wire, as shown in Fig. 4. The cross cords are woven in as shown in Fig. 5. As many of these cross cords can be put in as desired, and if placed from 6 to 12 in. apart, a solid screen will be made instead of a portière. The twisted cross cords should be of such material, and put through in such manner that they will not be readily seen. If paper beads are used they can be colored to suit and hardened by varnishing.

The first design shown is for using bamboo. The cords are knotted to hold the bamboo pieces in place. The finished portière will resemble drawn work in cloth. Many beautiful hangings can be easily fashioned.

The second design is to be constructed with a plain ground of either straw, bamboo or rolled paper. The cords are hung upon a round stick with rings of metal to make the sliding easy. The design is made by stringing beads of colored glass at the right

ished portiere will resemble drawn work in cloth. Many beautiful hangings can be easily fashioned.

The second design is to be constructed with a plain ground of either straw, bamboo or rolled paper. The cords are hung upon a round stick with rings of metal to make the sliding easy. The design is made by stringing beads of colored glass at the right places between the lengths of ground material. One bead is placed at the extreme end of each cord. The rows of twisted cord placed at the top keep the strings properly spaced.—Contributed by Geo. M. Harrer, Lockport, N. Y.

Makeshift Camper's Lantern

While out camping, our only lantern was accidentally smashed beyond repair and it was necessary for us to devise something that would take its

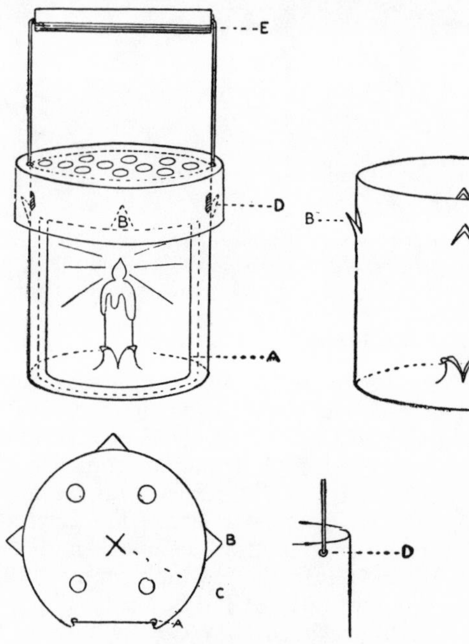

Lantern Made of Old Cans

place. We took an empty tomato can and cut out the tin 3 in. wide for a length extending from a point 2 in. below the top and to within 1/4 in. of the bottom. Each side of the cut-out A was bent inward in the shape of a letter S, in which was placed a piece of glass. Four V-shaped notches were cut as shown at B near the top of the can and their points turned outward. A slit was cut in the bottom, shaped as shown at C, and the pointed ends thus formed were turned up to make a place for holding the base of a candle. A larger can was secured and the bottom perforated. This was turned over the top of the other can. A heavy wire was run through the perforations and a short piece of broom handle used to make a bail.—Contributed by Maurice Baudier, New Orleans, La.

New Tires for Carpet-Sweeper Wheels

The rubber tires on carpet-sweeper wheels often become so badly worn and stretched that they fail to grip the carpet firmly enough to run the sweeper. To remedy this, procure some rubber tape a little wider than the rims of the old wheels, remove the old rubber tires and wind the tape on the rims to the proper thickness. Trim the edges with a sharp knife and rub on some chalk or soapstone powder to prevent the tape from sticking to the carpet. A sweeper treated in this manner will work as well as a new one.—Contributed by W. H. Shay, Newburgh, N. Y.

How to Make an Ornamental Brass Flag

The outlines of the flag—which may be of any size to suit the metal at hand—and the name, are first drawn on a sheet of thin paper and then transferred to the brass by tracing through a sheet of carbon paper. The brass should be somewhat larger than the design.

The brass is fastened to a block of soft wood with small nails driven through the edges. Indent the name and outline of the flag with a small chisel with the face ground flat, about $\frac{1}{16}$ in. wide. This should be done gradually, sinking the lines deeper and deeper by going over them a number of times. After this is finished, the brass is loosened from the block, turned over but not fastened, and the whole outside of and between the letters is indented with the rounded end of a nail, giving the appearance of hammered brass.

The edges are now cut off and four holes drilled, two for the chain by which to hang the flag to the wall, and two along the side for attaching the staff. The staff is a small brass rod with a knob attached to the top end.

It would be well to polish the brass at first, if the finished work is to be

The Finished Flag

bright, as it cannot be done after the flag is completed. A coat of lacquer is applied to keep it from tarnishing. This is done by heating the brass and quickly applying a coat of shellac.—Contributed by Chas. Schaffner, Maywood, Ill.

An Adjustable Punching-Bag Platform

A punching-bag platform, suitable for the tall athlete as well as the small boy, is shown in the accompanying sketch. The platform is securely fastened to two strong wooden arms or braces, which in turn are nailed to a 2 by 12-in. plank as long as the diameter of the platform. This plank, as shown in the small drawing at the

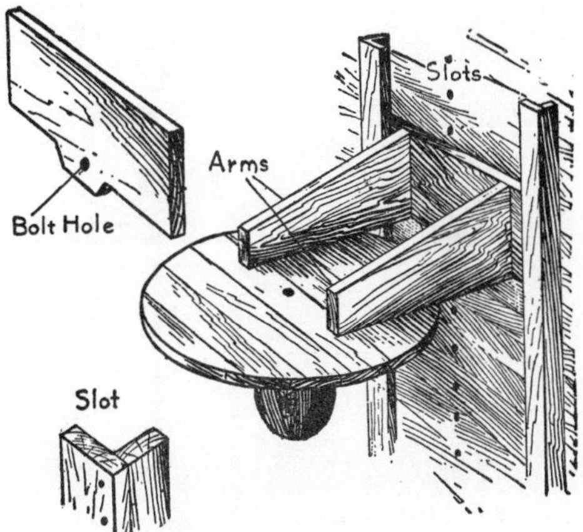

Adjustable Platform

upper left-hand corner of the sketch, is placed in grooves or slots fastened against the side of a wall. The plank with the platform attached may be raised or lowered to the desired height and held there by a pin or bolt put through the bolt-hole of the plank and into a hole in the wall.—Contributed by W. A. Jaquythe, Richmond, Cal.

Clasp for Holding Flexible Lamp Cords

A very easily made drop-light adjuster is shown in the illustration. It consists of a piece of copper wire ⅛ in. in diameter, bent as shown. This clasp is capable of standing a strong pull and will hold the

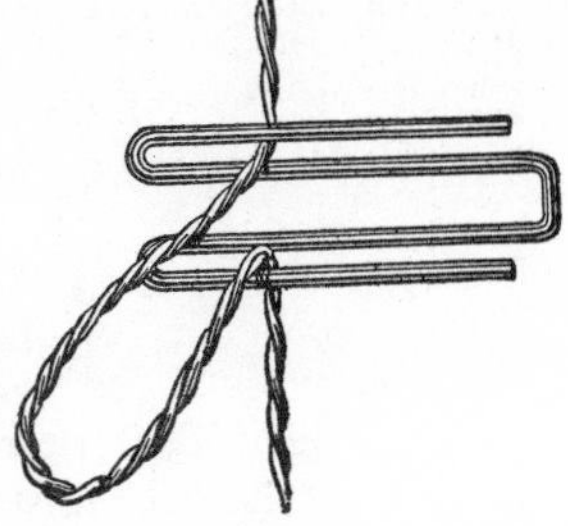

lamp and socket with a glass shade.—E. K. Marshall, Oak Park, Ill.

Camel hair brushes for painters' use should never be allowed to come in contact with water.

Home-Made Electric Clock

The clock illustrated herewith is driven by means of electromagnets acting directly on the pendulum bob. Unlike most clocks, the pendulum swings forward and backward instead of laterally. The construction is very simple, and the result is not only novel but well worth while, because one does not have to bother about winding a clock, such as this one, says the Scientific American.

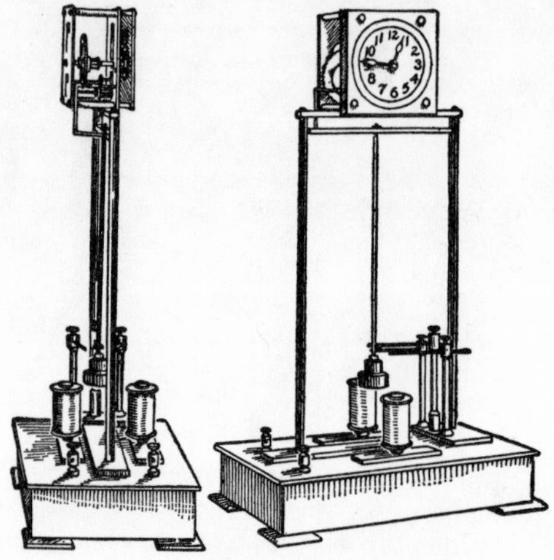

Magnetic Clock

The clock is mounted on a wooden base measuring 3¾ by 6½ in., by $1\frac{5}{16}$ in. thick. Secured centrally on this base is a ⅛ by ¾-in. bar, 6 in. long and at each side of this, $\frac{5}{16}$ in. away, is an electromagnet, ¾ in. in diameter and $1\frac{7}{16}$ in. high. Two uprights, 7½ in. high and ¼ in. in diameter, are secured in the base bar, and are connected at the top by a brass yoke piece on which the clock frame is supported. Just below the yoke piece a hole is drilled in each upright to receive the pivot pins of the crosspiece secured to the upper end of the pendulum rod. The pendulum bob at the lower end is adjusted to swing just clear of the electromagnets. Mounted at the right-hand side of the base are three tall binding-posts, the center one being 2¾ in. high, and the other two 2⅝ in. high. Each is fitted with a piece of copper wire provided with a small brass spring tip. These springs lie in the plane of the pendulum, which serves to swing the central tip first against one and then against the other of the side tips, thereby closing the circuit of first one magnet and then the other. Each magnet attracts the pendulum until its circuit is broken by release of the center tip, and on the return swing of the pendulum the circuit of the other magnet is similarly closed. Thus the pendulum is kept in motion by the alternate magnetic impulses. The clock train is taken from a standard clock and the motion of the pendulum is imparted to the escape wheel by means of a pawl, bearing on the latter, which is lifted at each forward stroke of the pendulum by an arm projecting forward from the pivotal end of the pendulum rod.

Method of Joining Boards

The amateur wood-worker often has trouble in joining two boards together so that they will fit square and tight. The accompanying sketch shows a simple and effective method of doing this. Secure a board, A, about 12 in. wide that is perfectly flat.

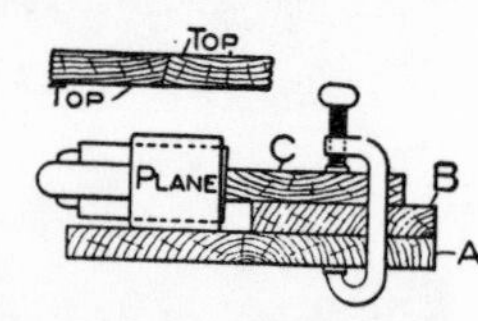

Fasten another board, B, about 6 in. wide, to the first one with screws or glue. Now place the board to be joined, C, on the board B, letting it extend over the inside edge about 1 in. and fastening it to the others with clamps at each end. Lay the plane on its side and plane the edge straight. Place the second board in the clamps in the same manner as the first, only have the opposite side up. If the cutting edge of the blade is not vertical, the boards planed in this manner will fit as shown in the upper sketch. In using this method, first-class joints can be made without much trouble.—Contributed by V. Metzech, Chicago.

Toy Gun for Throwing Cardboard Squares

The parts of the gun are attached to a thin piece of wood 1 in. wide and 5 in. long. It is best to use a piece of wood cut from the side or cover of a cigar box. A rectangular hole $\frac{3}{16}$ in. wide and 1 in. long is cut in the wood longitudinally along its axis and 1⅜ in. from one end, as shown at A, Fig. 1. A small notch is made with the point of a knife blade at B and notches are cut in the end of the wood as shown at C. Rubber bands are fastened in these notches as shown in Fig. 2. The trigger, whose dimensions are given in Fig. 3, is fastened in the hole A, Fig. 1, by driving a pin through the wood. The assembled parts are shown in Fig. 4.

Place the cardboard square in the nick B, attach the rubber bands and pull the trigger. The top rubber band will fly off and drive the cardboard

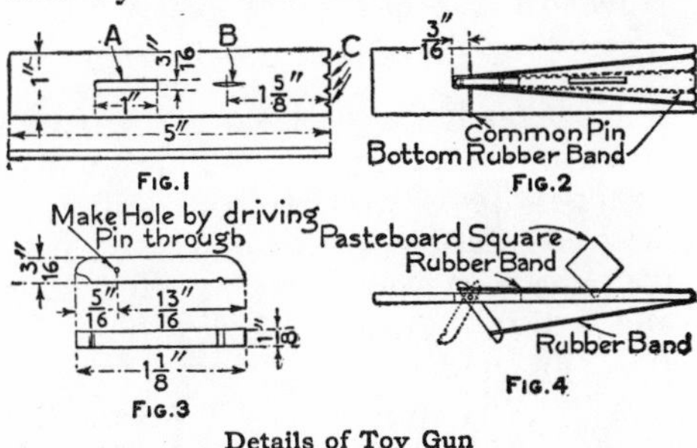

Details of Toy Gun

square 75 ft. or more. The cardboard should be about ½ in. square. These can be cut from any old pasteboard box.—Contributed by Elmer A. Vanderslice, Phoenixville, Pa.

Photographic Developing Tray

Plates developed in an ordinary tray must be removed from the bath occasionally for examination. The film when in a chemical-soaked condition is easily damaged. The tray illustrated herewith was made for the purpose of developing plates without having to take hold of them until the bath had completed its work, the examination being made through the plate and the bottom of the tray.

A pocket is provided for the liquid developer in one end of the tray when it

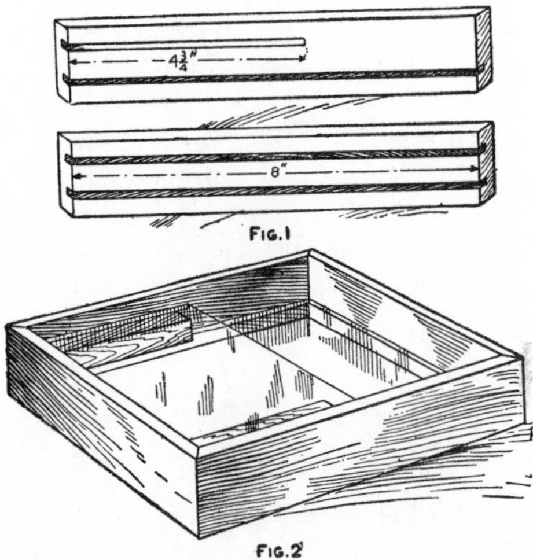

Developing Tray with Glass Bottom

is turned up in a vertical position. A tray for developing 5 by 7-in. plates should be made 8 in. square inside. The side pieces with the grooves for the glass are shown in Fig. 1. Two of each of these pieces are made with mitered ends. The short groove shown in the top piece of the illustration is for inserting the plate covering on the pocket end of the tray.

Two blocks, one-half the length of the side pieces, are put in between the glass plates to hold the plate being developed from dropping down when the tray is tipped up in a vertical position. The glass bottom of the tray is 8½ in. square, which allows ¼ in. on all edges to set in the grooves of the side pieces. The wood pieces should be well soaked in hot paraffin, and the mitered corners well glued and nailed. —Contributed by J. A. Simonis, Fostoria, Ohio.

¶A good filler used as a putty on iron castings may be made as follows: Take, by weight, 3 parts of stiff keg lead, 5 parts of black filler, 2 parts of whiting, 5 parts of pulverized silica and make into a paste with a mixture of one part each of coach japan, rubbing varnish and turpentine.

Rubber Bands in Kite Balancing Strings

Kite flyers will find it to their advantage to place rubber bands of suit-

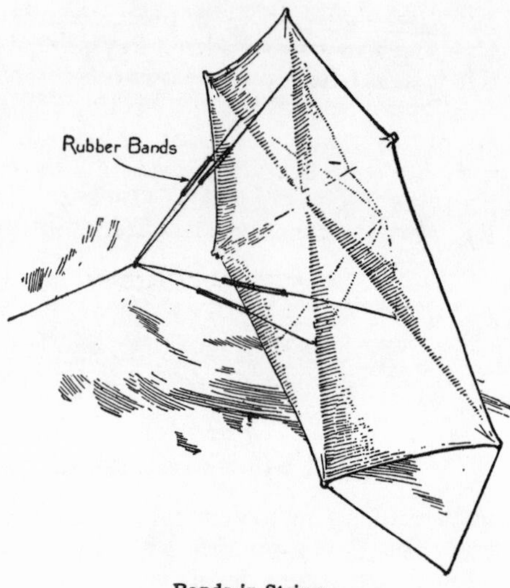

Bands in String

able size in the balancing strings to the kite, as shown in the illustration. This will prevent a "break-away" and also make the right pull, if only two bands are put in the lower strings.—Contributed by Thos. DeLoof, Grand Rapids, Michigan.

An Aid in Sketching

Sketching requires some little training, but with the apparatus here illustrated an inexperienced person can

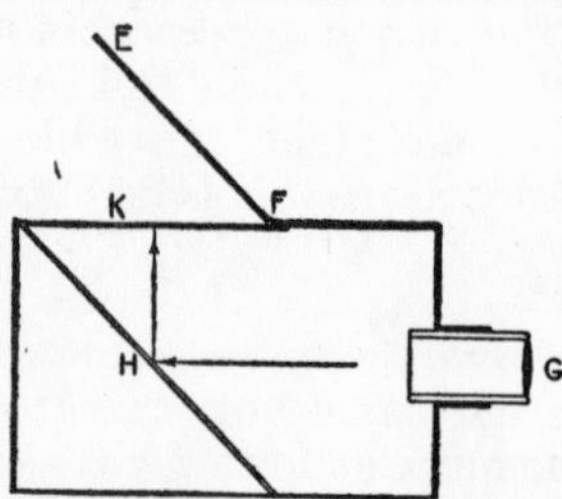

obtain excellent results. The apparatus is made of a box 8 in. deep, 8 in. wide and about 1 ft. long. A double convex lens, G, is fitted in a brass tube which should have a sliding fit in another shorter and larger tube fastened to the end of the box. A mirror, H, is set at an angle of 45 deg. in the opposite end of the box. This reflects the rays of light passing through the lens to the surface K, which may be either of ground or plain glass. The lid or cover E F protects the glass and keeps the strong light out when sketching. The inside of the box and brass tube are painted a dull black.

In use, the device is set with the lens tube directed toward the scene to be painted or sketched and the lens focused so the reflected picture will be seen in sharp detail on the glass. Select your colors and put them on the respective colors depicted on the glass. If you wish to make a pencil drawing, all you have to do is to fill in the lines in the picture on the ground glass. If a plain glass is used, place tracing paper on its surface, and the picture can be drawn as described.

How to Make Miniature Electric Lamp Sockets

A socket for a miniature lamp can be made as shown in the sketch. A brass spring wire is wound around the base of the threads on the lamp and an eye turned on each end to receive a screw and a binding-post, as shown in Fig. 1. A piece of metal, preferably copper, is attached to a wood base as shown in Fig. 2 and the coil-spring socket fastened across it in the opposite direction. Bend the wire so that the spring presses the lamp against the metal. If the wire fits the lamp loosely, remove the lamp and press the sides of the coil closer together. The metal parts can

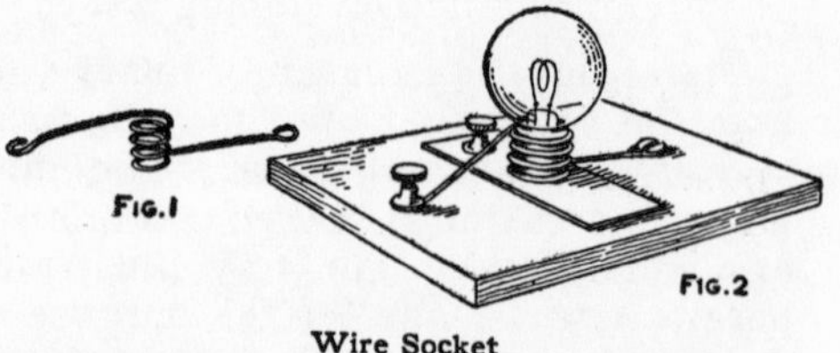

Wire Socket

be attached to any smooth surface of wood without making a regular base. —Contributed by Abner B. Shaw, No. Dartmouth, Mass.

Imitation Arms and Armor—Part V

The preceeding chapters gave descriptions of making arms in imitation of ancient weapons, and now the amateur armorer must have some helmets to add to his collection. There is no limit to the size of the helmet, and it may be made as a model or full sized. In constructing helmets, a mass of clay of any kind that is easily workable and fairly stiff, is necessary, says the English Mechanic, London. It must be kept moist and well kneaded. A large board or several planks, joined closely together, on which to place the clay, will be necessary. The size of this board will depend on the size of the work that is intended to be modeled upon it.

The way to make a helmet is described in the following method of producing a German morion, shown in Fig. 1. This helmet has fleur-de-lis in embossed work, and on each side is a badge of the civic regiment of the city of Munich. The side view of the helmet is shown in Fig. 1.

The clay is put on the board and modeled into the shape shown in Fig. 2. This is done with the aid of a pair of compasses, a few clay-modeling tools, and the deft use of the fingers. The fleur-de-lis are slightly raised, as in bas-relief. To aid in getting the helmet in correct proportion on both sides, and over the crest on top, cut out the shape from a piece of wood, as shown in Fig. 3, with a keyhole saw. This wood being passed carefully and firmly over the clay will bring it into shape, and will also show where there may be any deficiencies in the modeling, which can then be easily remedied by adding more clay. The cut-out pattern shown in Fig. 4 is the side outline of the helmet.

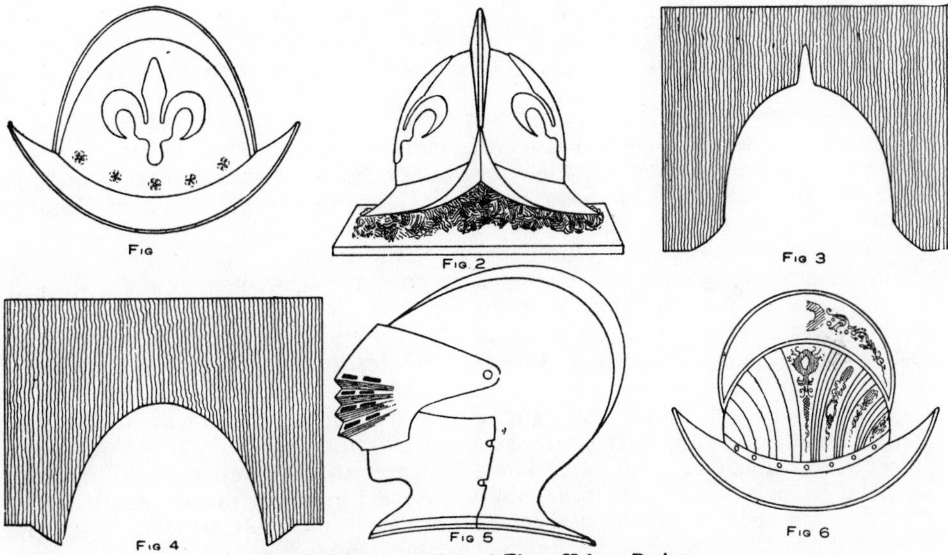

Making the Clay Model and Three Helmet Designs

Scraps of thin, brown, wrapping paper are put to soak in a basin of water to which has been added about a tablespoonful of size melted and well stirred, or some thin glue, and left over night to soak. The paper should be torn in irregular shapes about as large as the palm of the hand. After the clay model is finished, give it a thin coat of oil—sweet or olive oil will answer the purpose very well. All being ready, the clay model oiled, and the basin of soaked paper near to hand, take up one piece of paper at a time and very carefully place it upon the model, pressing it well on the clay and into and around any crevices and patterns, and continue until the clay is completely covered.

This being done, give the paper a thin and even coating of glue, which must be quite hot and put on as quickly as possible. Put on a second layer of paper as carefully as before, then another coating of glue, and so on, until there are from four to six coats of glue and paper. When dry, the paper coating should be quite stout and strong enough for the helmet to be used for ornamental purposes. Before taking it off the model, which should be no difficult matter, owing to the clay being oiled, trim off any ragged edges of paper with a sharp knife, and smooth and finish all over with some fine sandpaper. The paper is then given a thin coat of glue and sections of tinfoil stuck on to give it a finished appearance. When the helmet is off the model, make holes with a small awl at equal distances, through which to insert some fancy brass nails, bending the points over and flat against the inside of the helmet.

A vizor helmet is shown in Fig. 5. This helmet has a movable vizor in the front that can be lifted up, a crest on top, and around the neck a narrow gorget which rests upon the wearer's shoulders. The whole helmet, with the exception of the vizor, should be modeled and made in one piece. The vizor can then be made and put in place with a brass-headed nail on each side. The oblong slits in front of the vizor must be carefully marked out with a pencil and cut through with a knife or chisel.

In Fig. 6 is shown an Italian casque of a foot soldier of the sixteenth century. This helmet may have the appearance of being richly engraved as shown in one-half of the drawing, or, a few lines running down, as seen in the other part of the sketch, will make it look neat. The band is decorated with brass studs.

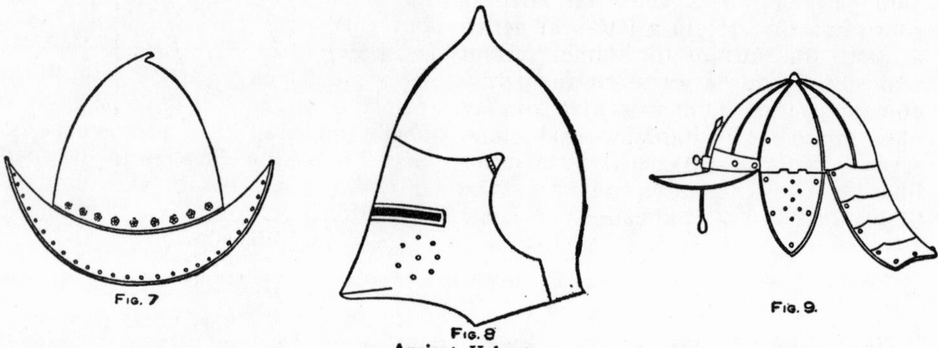

Ancient Helmets

An Italian cabasset of the sixteenth century is shown in Fig. 7. This helmet is elaborately decorated with fancy and round-headed nails, as shown in the design.

In Fig. 8 is shown a large bassinet with a hinged vizor which comes very much forward, so as to allow the wearer to breathe freely. This helmet was worn about the sixteenth century, and was probably used for tilting and tournaments.

A burgonet skull-cap of the seventeenth century is shown in Fig. 9. The vizor is composed of a single bar of metal, square in shape, which slides up and down in an iron socket attached to the front of the helmet, and is held in any position by a thumbscrew as shown in the illustration.

A hole in the peak of the helmet allows it to hang in front of the wearer's face. This contrivance should be made of wood, the helmet to be modeled in three pieces, the skullcap, peak and lobster shell neck guard in one piece, and the ear guards in two pieces, one for each side. The center of the ear guards are perforated. All of the helmets are made in the same manner as described for Fig. 1. They are all covered with tinfoil.

How to Repair Linoleum

A deep crack or fissure right in front of the kitchen cabinet spoiled the appearance of the new linoleum. The damaged spot was removed with a sharp knife and from a left-over scrap a piece was cut of the same outline and size. The edges were varnished and then the patch was set in the open space. The linoleum was given a good coat of varnish making it more durable. When perfectly dry, the piecing could not be detected.—Contributed by Paul Keller, Indianapolis, Indiana.

How to Make an Electric Stove

The parts necessary for making an electric stove are: Two metal pie plates of the same size; 4 lb. of fire clay; two ordinary binding posts; about 1 lb. of mineral wool, or, if this cannot be obtained, thick sheet asbestos; one oblong piece of wood, 1 in. thick, 12 in. wide and 15 in. long; one small switch; one fuse block; about 80 ft. of No. 22 gauge resistance wire,—German-silver wire is better, as it stands a higher temperature; two middle-sized stove bolts with nuts; one glass tube, about 1/4 in. in diameter and 9 in. long, which can be bought from a local druggist, and two large 3-in. screws.

If a neat appearance is desired, the wood can be thoroughly sandpapered on one side and the corners and edges rounded off on the upper side. Punch holes in one of the pie plates, as shown in Fig. 1. The two holes, E and F, are on the rim and should be exactly on a line with the hole D punched in the center. The holes B and C are about 3 in. apart and should be at equal distances from the center hole D. The rim of the second plate is drilled to make two holes, AA, Fig. 2, that will match the holes E and F in the first plate, Fig. 1. A round collar of galvanized iron, FF, Fig. 4, 3 in. high, is made with a diameter to receive the first plate snugly. Two small flaps are cut and turned out and holes punched in their centers, AA, to receive screws for holding it to the base. Two bolts are soldered in the holes E and F, Fig. 1, and used to hold the

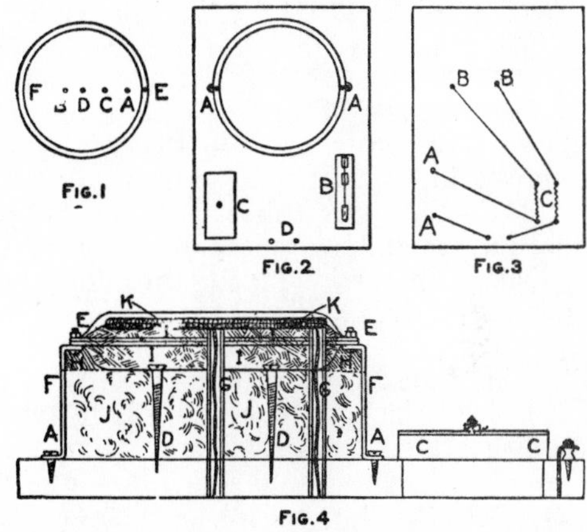

Details of Electric Stove

rims of both plates together, when they are placed in opposite positions, as shown in Fig. 4. This will make an open space between the plates. The collar is then screwed to one end of the base, as shown in Fig. 2.

Two holes are bored through the base to correspond with the holes D and A in the bottom plate. The glass tube is cut to make two pieces, each 4 1/2 in. long. This can be done easily by filing a nick in the tube at the proper point and breaking it. These tubes are forced into the holes bored in the base, and, if the measurements are correct, should extend about 1/4 in. above the collar. The mineral wool, JJ, Fig. 4, is then packed down inside the collar, until it is within 1 in. of the top. This will allow the plate, Fig. 1, to rest on the wool and the ends of the glass tubes, GG, Fig. 4, to project through the holes D and A of the plate, Fig. 1. The rim of the plate should be level with the top edge of the collar. If asbestos is used, the sheets should be cut into disks having the same diameter as the inside of the collar, and holes cut to coincide with the holes D and A of the plate. The small scraps should be dampened and made into pulp to fill the space H, Fig. 4. The plate, Fig. 1, is held to the base by two screws which are run through the holes BC and take the position shown by DD, Fig. 4.

The two binding-posts are attached on the base at D, Fig. 2, also the switch B and the fuse block C, holes being bored in the base to make the wire connections. The reverse side of the base, with slits cut for the wires, is shown in Fig. 3. The points marked BB are the glass tubes; AA, the holes leading to the switch; and C, the fuse block. The wires run through the glass tubes GG, Fig. 4, are allowed to project about 1 in. for connections.

The best way to find the correct length of the resistance wire is to take a large clay or drain tile and wind the wire tightly around it, allowing a space between each turn. The tile is then set on its side with a block or brick under each end. It should not be set on end, as the turns of the wires, when heated, will slip and come in contact with each other, causing a short circuit. When the tile is in place, a short piece of fuse wire is fastened to each of its two ends. A 5-ampere fuse wire is about strong enough. A connection is made to these two wires from an electric-light socket. The wire will get hot but probably remain the same color. If this is the case, one of the feed wires is disconnected from the fuse wire and gradually moved farther down the coil until a point is found where the resistance wire glows a dull red. This point marks the proper length to cut it, as the wire should not be allowed to become any hotter. If the wire gets bright hot when the current is turned on, more wire should be added. The wire is then made into a long coil by winding it around a large wire nail. The coils should be open and about 1/8 in. apart.

Next, the fire clay is moistened and well mixed, using care not to get it too wet. It should have the proper consistency to mould well. The clay, II, Fig. 4, is then packed in the first plate to a height of about 1/4 in. above the rim. While the clay is damp, one end of the coil is connected with the wire in the central glass tube, and the coil laid in a spiral winding on the damp clay, KK, and pressed into it. When this is done, the other end is connected to the wire projecting from the outer glass tube. As these connections cannot be soldered, the ends of the wires should be twisted closely together, so that the circuit will not become broken. Make sure that the coils of wire do not touch each other or the top plate. The fuse wire (about 5 amperes) is put into the fuse block, and wires with a socket adapter connected to the two binding-posts. The top plate is put in place and screwed down. This completes the stove.

It should be set aside in a warm place for a few days to dry out the packing. If it is not thoroughly dry, steam will form when the current is applied. It should not be left heated in this condition. The top plate is used when cooking and removed when making toast.—Contributed by R. H. Cnonyn, St. Catherines, Can.

How to Make Weights for Athletes

Many times boys would like to make their own shots and weights for athletic stunts, but do not know how to go about it to cast the metal. In making a lead sphere as shown in the illustration, it is not necessary to know the method of molding. The round lead weight for shot-putting or hammer-throwing can be cast in a hollow cardboard or pressed-paper ball, sold in department and toy stores for 10 cents. Cut a 1/2-in. hole in the ball as shown in Fig. 1 and place it with the hole up

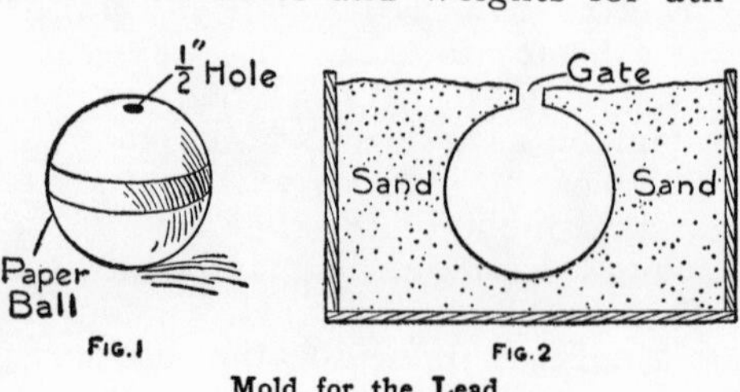

Mold for the Lead

in damp sand and press or tamp the sand lightly around the ball as shown in the section, Fig. 2. Cover over about 1 in. deep. A wood plug inserted in the hole will prevent any sand falling inside. When the sand is tamped in and the plug removed, it leaves a gate for the metal. Pour melted lead into the gate until it is full, then, when cool, shake it out from the sand and remove the charred paper. A file can be used to remove any rough places. The dry paper ball prevents any sputtering of the hot lead.—Contributed by W. A. Jaquythe, Richmond, Cal.

Removing Pies from Pans

Sometimes the juices from a hot pie make it stick to the pan so tightly that a knife blade must be run under to cut it loose. If a knife with a flexible blade is not used, the pie will be damaged. If the pie pans are provided with the simple attachment shown in the accompanying sketch, the baked dough can be separated from the tin with one revolution of the cutter. The cutter is made from a piece of heavy tin, bent to the same outline as the inside of the pan and pivoted at its center.

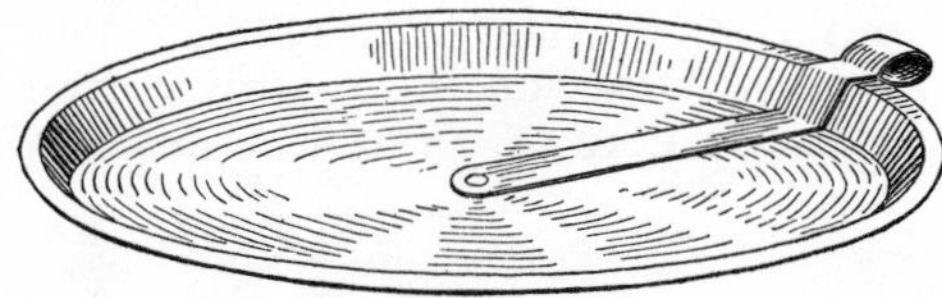

Separating Pies from Pans

Stretcher for Drying Photograph Prints

A quick and convenient way to dry prints is to place them on a cheesecloth stretcher. Such a stretcher can be made on a light wood frame, constructed of ¾-in. square material in any size, but 12 by 24 in. is large enough. The end pieces B are fastened on top of the long side pieces A, and the cheesecloth C stretched and tacked over them, as shown.

The prints should be placed face up on the cloth, and the frame set near a window. If the stretcher is made in this way, the air can enter from both top and bottom, and the prints will dry rapidly. Several of these frames can be stacked and a large number of prints thus dried at the same time.—Contributed by Andrew G. Thorne, Louisville, Ky.

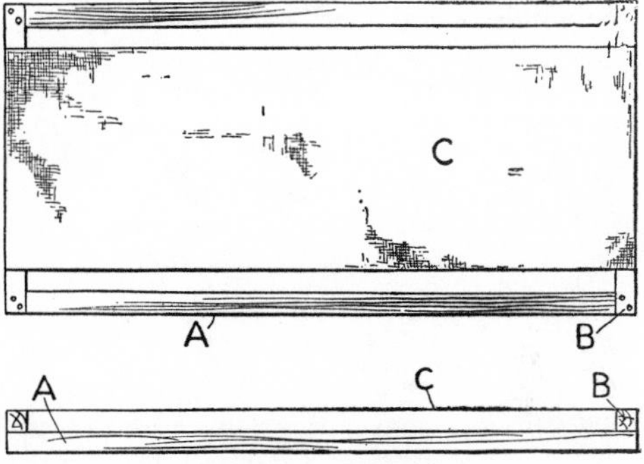

Cloth on the Frame

A Temporary Funnel

The amateur photographer often has some solution which he desires to put into a bottle which his glass funnel will not fit, says the Photographic Times. The funnel made by rolling up a piece of paper usually allows half of the solution to run down the outside of the bottle, thereby causing the amateur to be dubbed a "musser." A better way is to take an ordinary envelope and cut it off as shown by the dotted lines. Then clip a little off the point, open out, and you have a funnel that will not give any trouble. It is cheap and you can afford to throw it away when dirty, thereby saving time and washing.

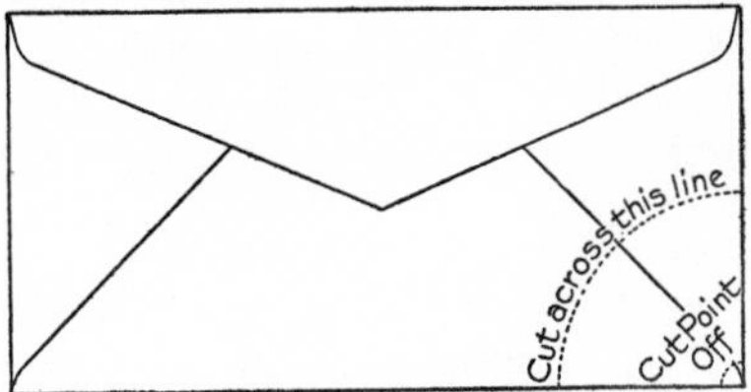

Paper Funnel

An Electric Engine

The parts of this engine are supported on a base ¾ in. thick, 4 in. wide and 7 in. long. The upright B, Fig. 1,

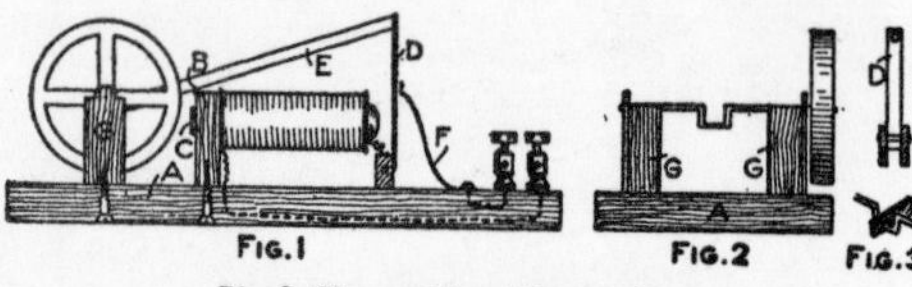

Shaft Turned by Magnetism

which is ½ in. thick and 3 in. high, is secured across the base about one-third of the distance from one end and fastened with a wood screw put through from the under side. The magnet core C is made of a carriage bolt, 2½ in. long, which is fastened in a hole in the top part of the upright B so that the end C will protrude slightly. Before placing the bolt in the hole of the upright, slip on two cardboard washers, each 1 in. in diameter, one at the head end and the other against the upright B. Wrap a thin piece of paper around the bolt between the washers and wind the space full of No. 22-gauge magnet wire, allowing each end to project for connections.

The driving arm D, Figs. 1 and 3, is made of a piece of soft sheet iron, ½ in. wide and 3 in. long. A small block is fastened to the lower end of the metal and pivoted between two uprights, ½ in. high, which are fastened to the base. The uprights on each side of the block are better shown in Fig. 3.

Two supports, each ½ in. thick and 3 in. high, are fastened with screws about half way between the end of the base and the upright B, Fig. 1. The end view of these supports is shown in Fig. 2, at GG. A ⅛-in. hole is bored through the top part of each support so they will be in a line for the axle. The axle is made of a piece of steel ⅛ in. in diameter and about 4 in. long. An offset is bent in the center, as shown, for the crank. A small flywheel is attached to one end of the shaft. The connecting rod E, Fig. 1, is made of wood and fastened to the upper end of the driving arm D with a small screw or nail. The contact F is made of a strip of copper, ¼ in. wide. This is to open and close the circuit when the engine is running. The connections are made as shown in Fig. 1.

Connect two dry cells to the binding-posts and turn the flywheel. The current passing through the magnet pulls the driving arm toward the bolt head, which gives the shaft a half turn. The turning of the shaft pulls the arm away from the copper piece F, causing a break in the current. As the shaft revolves, the arm is again brought back against the copper strip F, thus the current is broken and applied at each revolution of the shaft.—Contributed by S. W. Herron, Le Mars, Iowa.

Child's Home-Made Swing Seat

A very useful swing or seat for children can be made from a box or packing case. Procure a box of the right size and saw it out in the shape shown in the illustration. The apron or board in front slides on the two front ropes. The board can be raised to place the

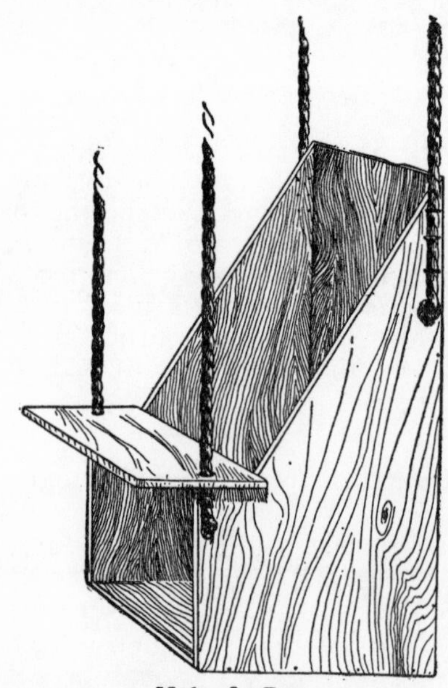
Made of a Box

child in the box and to remove him. The ropes are fastened to the box by tying knots in their ends and driving staples over them.

Clay Flower Pots Used for Bird Houses

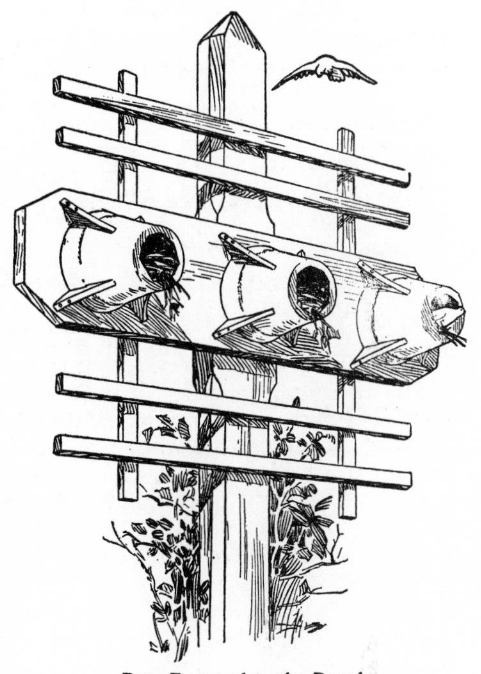
Pots Fastened to the Board

A novel use of the common garden flower pot may be made by enlarging the small opening at the bottom with a pair of pliers, and carefully breaking the clay away until the opening is large enough to admit a small bird.

Place the pot, bottom side up, on a board, 3 in. wider than the diameter of the largest pot used, and fasten it to the board with wood cleats and brass screws. Fit the cleats as close as possible to the sides of the pot. One or more pots may be used, as shown in the sketch.

The board on which the pots are fastened is nailed or screwed to a post or pole 10 or 12 ft. in height. The board is braced with lath or similar strips of wood, making a framework suitable for a roost. In designing the roost, the lath can be arranged to make it quite attractive, or the braces may be of twigs and branches of a tree to make a rustic effect.—Contributed by William F. Stecher, Dorchester, Mass.

Location of a Gas Meter

The gas meter should not be located in a warm place or the gas will expand before the meter measures it and the gas bill will be proportionately increased. Gas expands by about 1-491 part of its volume for each deg. F. that it is heated. If the meter is warmed 10 deg. F., it will make the gas cost over 2 per cent more, without any corresponding benefit.

How to Make Rope Grills

Beautiful and useful household ornaments, grills and gratings for doors, windows, shelves, odd corners, etc., can be made by the following method at a slight cost and by anyone possessing a little ingenuity. The materials required are rope or, preferably, common window cord (called sash cord) about $\frac{5}{16}$ in. in diameter; ordinary glue, paraffin and paint or varnish. A few strips of wood or molding are very handy to use around the edges.

The design must be considered first and when one is selected, if it is other than straight lines, adopt the method described.

Take a smooth flat board and lay out the design or designs which, when combined, will produce the pattern desired. Drive finishing nails at the angle points or along curves as required. Coat the board along the lines of the patterns with melted paraffin, using an ordinary painter's brush to prevent the ropes from sticking to the boards after they are soaked in glue and run around the nails.

Soak the sash cord in common glue sizing for a short time, then bend or twist it along or around the lines desired, as shown in Fig. 1, and give it time to dry. The bottom part of the sketch, Fig. 1, shows a method of winding the rope on a round stick to make circular objects. Wind the de-

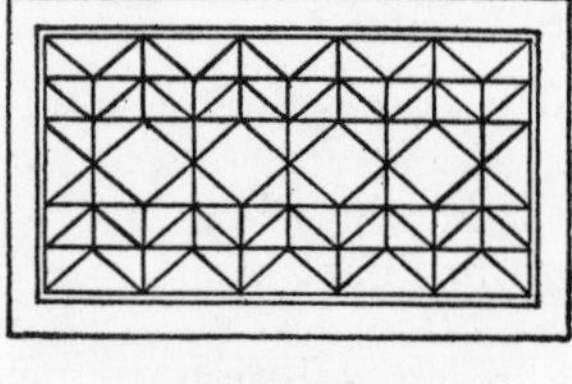

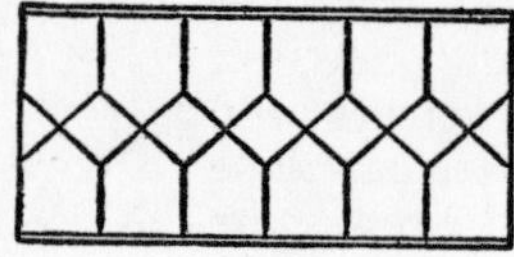
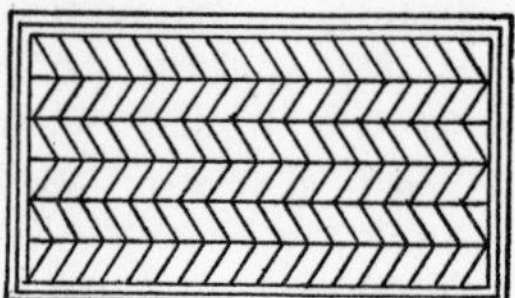

Fig. 2—Designs for Grills

sired number of turns and when dry, cut and glue them together.

Fig. 1—Method of Forming the Rope

In Fig. 2, six designs are shown. These suggest ideas in making up combinations or in plain figures and the number is limited only by the ingenuity of the designer.—Contributed by Geo. M. Harrer, Lockport, N. Y.

A Simple and Effective Filter

Procure an ordinary lamp chimney and fit two or three thicknesses of cheesecloth over the end of it. Press a tuft of absorbent cotton into the small part of the neck to a depth of about 3 in. Insert the chimney in a hole cut in a wood shelf used as a support. Pour the water in until the filter is filled, when it will be observed that any organic matter, chips of iron rust, etc., will be retained by the cotton. The fine organic matter may penetrate the cotton for about 1 in., but no farther. The resultant filtered water will be clear and pure.

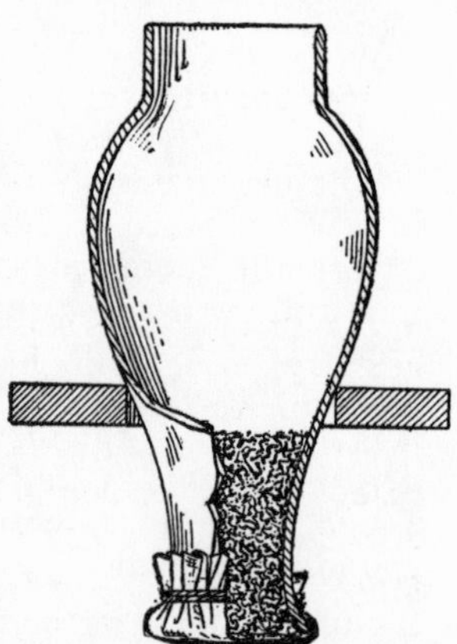

¶The cutting point of a tool should never be below the centers.

Imitation Arms and Armor—Part VI

A mass of any kind of clay that is easily modeled and fairly stiff must be prepared and kept moist and well kneaded for making the models over which paper is formed to make the shape of the articles illustrated in these sketches. A modeling board must be made of one large board or several pieces joined closely together upon which to work the clay, says the English Mechanic, London. The size of the board depends upon the size of the work to be made.

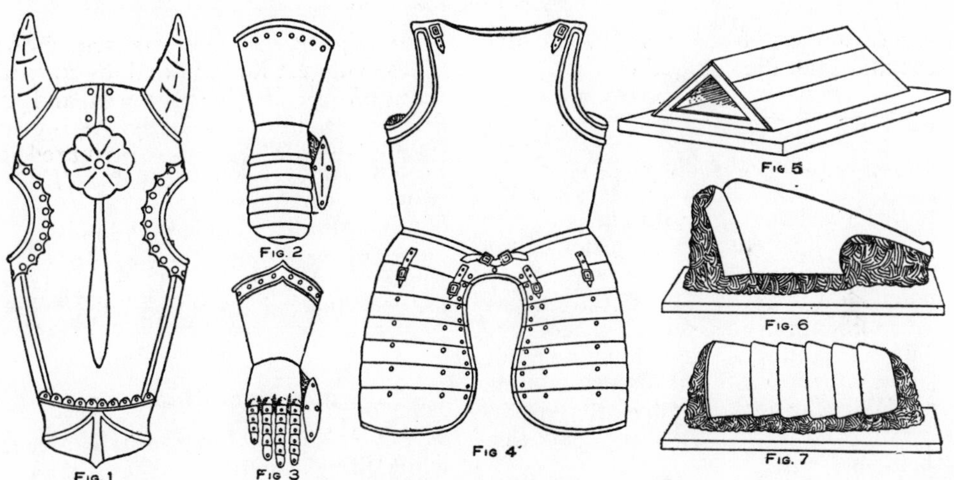

Armor and Clay Models

An open chamfron of the fifteenth century is shown in Fig. 1. This piece of horse armor, which was used in front of a horse's head, makes a splendid center for a shield on which are fixed the swords, etc., and is a good piece for the amateur armorer to try his hand on in the way of modeling in clay or papier maché work. The opening for the animal to put his head into is semicircular, and the sides do not cover the jaws. As the main part of this armor is worn in front of the head the extreme depth is about 4 in. The entire head piece must be modeled in clay with the hands, after which it is covered with a thin and even coating of sweet or pure olive oil. A day before making the clay model some pieces of thin, brown wrapping paper are torn in irregular shapes to the size of the palm of the hand and put to soak in a basin of water in which a tablespoonful of size has been dissolved. If size cannot be obtained from your local painter, a weak solution of glue will do equally well. All being ready, and the clay model oiled, take up one piece of paper at a time and very carefully place it on the surface of the model, pressing it on well and into and around any crevices and patterns. Continue this operation until the clay model is completely covered on every part. This being done, give the paper a thin and even coating of glue, which must be quite hot and laid on as quickly as possible. Lay on a second layer of paper as carefully as before, then another coat of glue, and so on until there are five or six coats of glue and paper. When this is dry it will be strong enough for all ornamental purposes. The ragged edges of the paper are trimmed off with a sharp knife and the whole surface smoothed with fine sandpaper. Then carefully glue on sections of tinfoil to give the armor the appearance of steel. The armor is now removed from the model.

A mitten gauntlet of the fifteenth century is shown in Fig. 2. This can be made in one piece, with the exception of the thumb shield, which is separate. The thumb shield is attached to the thumb of an old glove which is fastened with round headed nails on the inside of the gauntlet.

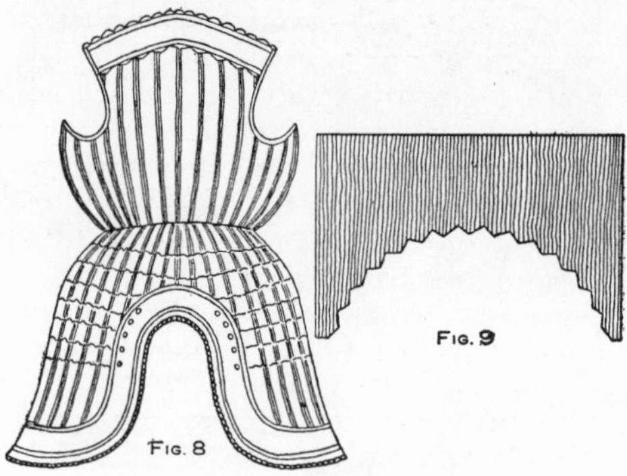

Corrugated Breastplate and Former

The part covering the wrist is a circular piece, but the back is not necessary as it would not be seen when the gauntlet is hanging in its place.

In Fig. 3 is shown a gauntlet of the seventeenth century with separately articulated fingers. This gauntlet may be molded in one piece, except the thumb and fingers, which must be made separately and fastened with the thumb shield to the leather glove that is attached to the inside of the gauntlet, the same as in Fig. 2.

A breastplate and tassets of the sixteenth century are shown in Fig. 4. The tassets are separate and attached to the front plate with straps and buckles, as shown in the sketch. There is a belt around the waist which helps to hold the back plate on. Attached to the back of the plate would be two short straps at the shoulder. These are passed through the buckles shown at the top right and left-hand corners of the front plate. For decorative purposes the back plate need not be made, and therefore it is not described. The method of making armor is the same as of making helmets, but as larger pieces are formed it is well to use less clay owing to the bulk and weight.

An arrangement is shown in Fig. 5 to reduce the amount of clay used. This triangular-shaped support, which can be made in any size, is placed on the modeling board or bench and covered with clay. This will make the model light and easy to move around, and will require less clay. It is not necessary to have smooth boards; the rougher the better, as the surface will hold the clay. The clay forms modeled up ready to receive the patches of brown paper on the surface are shown in Figs. 6 and 7.

A German fluted armor used at the beginning of the sixteenth century is shown in Fig. 8. The breastplate and tassets of this armor are supposed to be in one piece, but for convenience in making it will be found best to make them separately and then glue them together after they are taken from the model. A narrow leather belt placed around the armor will cover the joint. Fluted armor takes its name from a series of corrugated grooves, ½ in. in depth, running down the plate. A piece of board, cut into the shape shown in Fig. 9, will be very useful for marking out the fluted lines.

Home-Made Hand Vise

A vise for holding small articles while filing can be made as shown in the illustration. The vise consists of three pieces of wood, two for the jaws and one a wedge.

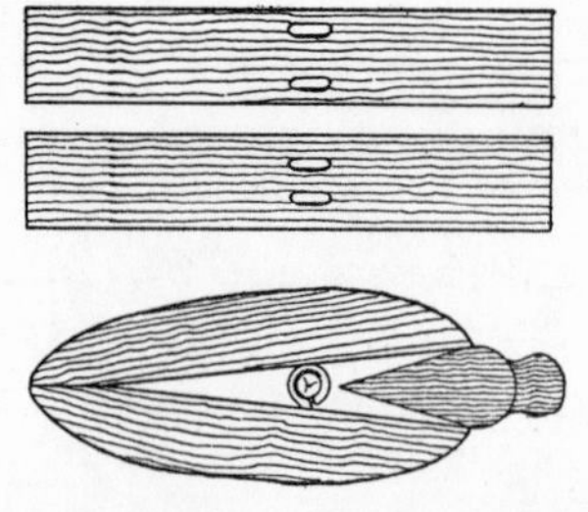

The hinge for connecting the two jaws is made of four small screw eyes, two in each jaw. When locating the place for the screw eyes, place the two in one jaw so they will fit between the two of the other jaw. Put a nail through the eyes when the jaws are matched together and they are ready for the wedge in clamping the article to be filed.—Contributed by John G. Buxton, Redondo Beach, Calif.

Detector for Slight Electrical Charges

A thin glass bottle is thoroughly cleaned and fitted with a rubber stopper. A hole is made through the center of the stopper large enough to admit a small brass rod. The length of this rod will be governed by the shape of the bottle, but 3½ in. will be about right. The bottom of the rod is bent and two pieces of aluminum foil, each about ¼ in. wide and ½ in. long, are glued to it. The two pieces of foil, fastened to the rod, are better shown in Fig. 2. Fasten a polished brass ball to the top of the rod, and the instrument is ready for use. Place the article which you wish to test near the ball, and if it holds a slight electrical charge, the two pieces of foil will draw together. If it does not hold a charge, the foils will not move.—Contributed by Ralph L. La Rue, Goshen, N. Y.

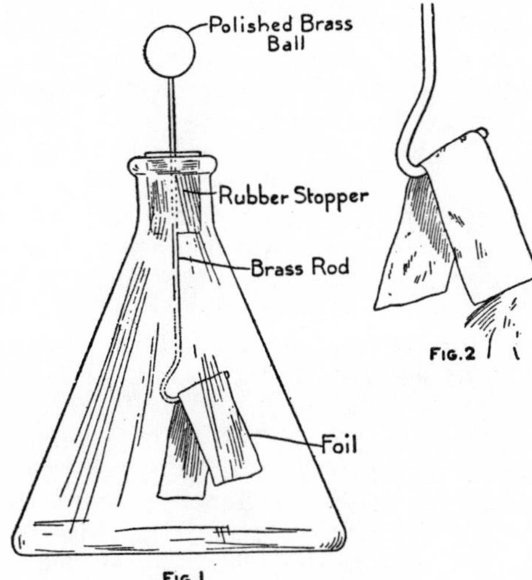

Aluminum Foil in a Bottle

Fishing through Ice with a Tip-Up

The tip-up, used for signaling the fisherman when a fish is caught, is made of a ¼-in. pine board, about 15 in. long, 2½ in. wide at one end and narrowing down to about 1 in at the other. At a point 6 in. from the smaller end, the board should be cut slightly wider and a ½-in. hole bored through it. Two or three wrappings of fine copper wire may be wound around the board on each side of the hole to give added strength. Both ends of the board should be notched deeply.

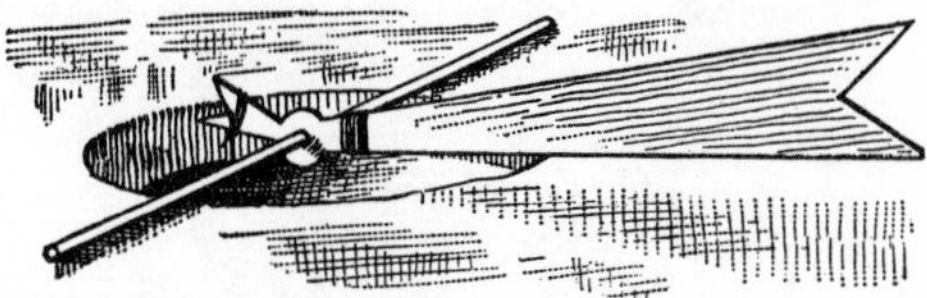
Tip-Up in Place

A long gash is cut in the ice and then a round hole is made with a chisel, as this will cut under the water without splashing. The chipped ice can be removed with a pail. A rod or round stick of wood is passed through the hole in the tip-up and placed across the round hole, as shown in the illustration.

The fishhook is baited in the usual way and hung on a line from the short end of the tip-up. When a fish is hooked, the other end will tip up and signal the fisherman. Any number of holes can be cut in the ice and a tip-up used in each, thus enabling one person to take care of as many lines.

Home-Made Candle Holder

The candlestick or holder shown in the illustration is made of an ordinary tin can, such as is used for canning salmon or potted ham. Three triangular cuts are made in the cover or bottom of the can and the points turned up about the candle. The can may be bronzed, silvered, enameled or otherwise decorated, thus making it ornamental as well as useful.—Contributed by Mrs. A. M. Bryan, Corsicana, Texas.

How to Make a Match Holder of Wood and Metal

A very simple piece of art craft work is easily made, as follows: Secure a piece of paper and upon it draw the outline and design, as indicated in the accompanying sketch. The size may be made to suit the taste of the worker. A good size is 5 in. wide by 6 in. long over all. The metal holder should be proportioned to this size, as shown.

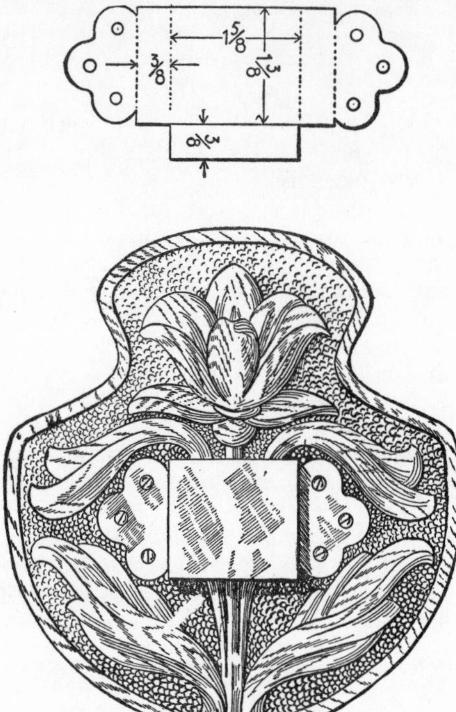

Match Holder

Having completed the drawing, take a piece of thin wood, ⅜ or ¼ in. thick, and trace upon it the design and outline, using a piece of carbon paper. A couple of thumb tacks should be used to fasten the paper and design in place. Put the tacks in the lines of the design so that the holes will not show in the finished piece. Any kind of wood will do. Basswood or butternut, or even pine, will do as well as the more expensive woods.

Next prepare the metal holder. This may be made of brass or copper and need not be of very heavy gauge—No. 22 is plenty heavy enough. The easiest way to get the shape of the metal is to make a paper pattern of the development. The illustration shows how this will look and the size of the parts for the back dimensioned above. Trace this shape on the metal with the carbon paper and cut it out by means of metal shears. Polish the metal, using powdered pumice and lye, then with a nail, punch the holes, through which small round-head brass screws are to be placed to hold the metal to the wood back. Carefully bend the metal to shape by placing it on the edge of a board and putting another board on top and over the lower edge so as to keep the bending true.

The wood back may be treated in quite a variety of ways. If soft wood, such as basswood or pine was used, it may be treated by burning with the pyrography outfit. If no outfit is at hand a very satisfactory way is to take a knife and cut a very small V-shaped groove around the design and border so as to keep the colors from "running." Next stain the leaves of the conventional plant with a little green wood dye and with another dye stain the petals of the flower red. Malachite and mahogany are the colors to use. Rub a coat of weathered oil stain over the whole back and wipe dry with a cloth. The green and red are barbarously brilliant when first put on, but by covering them at the same time the background is colored brown, they are "greyed" in a most pleasing manner. When it has dried over night, put a coat or two of wax and polish over the wood as the directions on the can suggest.

The metal holder may next be fastened in place.

If one has some insight in carving, the background might be lowered and the plant modeled, the whole being finished in linseed oil. If carving is contemplated, hard woods such as cherry or mahogany should be used.

Protecting the Fingers from Chemicals

The finger nails and fingers may be easily protected from stains of chemicals by coating them with a wax made up as follows: Melt white wax in the same manner as melting glue. This may be done by cutting the wax into small pieces, placing them in a vessel and setting the vessel in boiling water. To each ounce of melted wax thoroughly stir in 1 dr. of pure olive oil. The fingers should be dipped into the wax while it is in a liquid state. This will form a coating that will permit the free use of the fingers, yet protects the skin from the chemicals. It is useful for photographers.

Combined Turning Rings and Swings

This trapeze, with rings for the large boys and a swing for the smaller ones, can be made on the same standards. Instead of the usual two short ropes, tied and bolted through the top crosstimber, bore two holes large enough for the ropes to pass through easily. Pass the rope along the crosspiece and down the post and tie it to cleats nailed at a height that can be easily reached.

At the ends of the crosspiece drive two nails, allowing them to project 1 or 2 in. This will keep the rope from slipping off when the rings and swing are raised and lowered. All sharp edges should be sandpapered to prevent the rope from being cut. A board with notches cut in the ends will make a good swing board which can be removed instantly.—Contributed by W. A. Jaquythe, Richmond, Cal.

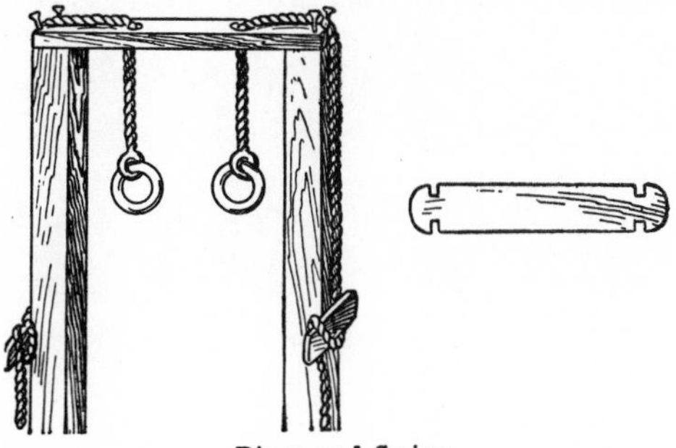

Rings and Swing

Homemade Telegraph Key

A piece of wood, ½ in. thick, 2 in. wide and 5 in. long, is used for the base of this instrument. Two wire nails, each 1 in. long, are used for the cores of the magnets. Each nail is wound with three or four layers of fine insulated magnet wire, about No. 25 gauge, similar to that used in electric bells, leaving about ¼ in. of the end bare so that they may be driven into the wood base. The connections for the coils are shown in the sketch, at A.

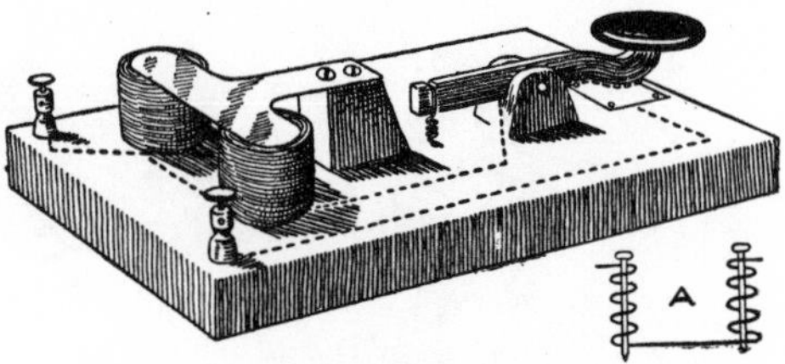

Key and Connections

About 1 in. behind the coils is fastened a small block of wood, the top of which is just even with the top of the nails in the coils. A piece of tin, cut in the shape of the letter T, is fastened with two screws to the top of this block, and the end bent slightly so as to clear the top of the nails about $\frac{1}{32}$ in.

The key lever is cut from a thin piece of wood, in the shape shown in the sketch, and pivoted in a slotted block which is used as a base for the key. A piece of bare copper wire is fastened along the under side of the key, as shown by the dotted lines. A rubber band, passing over the end of the key and attached to the base with a tack, acts as a spring to keep the key open. A small piece of tin is fastened to the base under the knob of the key. This is for making the contact between the copper on the key and the wires from the coils, when the key is pushed down.—Contributed by W. H. Lynas.

¶Bicycle trousers-guards make excellent sleeve bands when the cuffs are turned back and rolled above the elbows.

Imitation Arms and Armor—Part VII

The helmets, breastplates and gauntlets described in parts V and VI can be used in making up a complete model

Full Suit of Armor

for a full suit of armor of any size, as shown in Fig. 1. All of the parts for the armor have been described, except that for the legs. Figure 2 shows how the armor is modeled on the side of the left leg. The clay is modeled as described in previous chapters, the paper covering put on, and the tinfoil applied in imitation of steel. The chain mail seen between and behind the tassets is made by sewing small steel rings on a piece of cloth as shown in Fig. 3. These rings may be purchased at a hardware store or harness shop.

The whole figure when completed is placed on a square box covered with red or green baize. The armor should be supported by a light frame of wood built up on the inside, says the English Mechanic, London. Two vertical pieces are firmly attached to the box so they will extend up inside the legs, and at the top of them is attached a crosspiece on which is placed a vertical stick high enough to carry the helmet. The two lower pieces must be built up and padded out with straw, then covered with red cloth or baize to represent the legs.

In making up the various pieces for a full model it will be found very convenient to use rope, a stout cord or strings in making up the patterns on the parts. Instead of using brass-headed nails, brass paper fasteners will be found useful. These can be purchased at a stationery store. Secure the kind having a round brass head from which hang two brass tongues. These are pushed through a hole and spread out flat on the opposite side. Other materials can be used in the place of tinfoil to represent steel. Silver paper will do very well, but if either the tinfoil or silver paper are found difficult to manipulate, go over the armor with a coat of silver paint put on with a brush. When dry give the surface a coat of varnish.

A Home-Made Tripod Holder

An inexpensive tripod holder, one that will prevent the tripod from slipping on a smooth floor, and prevent the points from doing damage to the polished surface or puncturing an expensive rug or carpet, can be made in a few minutes' time, says Camera Craft.

Secure two strips of wood, or ordinary plaster laths will do, and plane them down to a thickness of 3/16 in., for the sake of lightness. Cut them to a length of 40 in. and round off the ends to improve their appearance. Take the piece shown in Fig. 1 and drill a ¼-in. hole in the center, and eight small holes, 1 in. apart, at each end. In one end of the piece, Fig. 2, make the same series of eight small holes and, in the other end, drill six ¼-in. holes, 3 in. apart. A ¼-in. flat-headed carriage bolt, about 1 in. long, completes the equipment.

The two pieces are bolted together, not too tight, and the points of the tripod legs inserted in their respective small holes. So set up, there is absolutely no danger of one of the legs slipping out of position. By moving the position of the bolt from one to another of the larger holes in the strip, Fig. 2, almost any desired inclination of the camera can be secured.

The same sort of simple apparatus built slightly stronger, and with a small caster under each of the three series of small holes, makes an excellent tripod clamp for use when the camera has to be shifted about, as in portraiture and the like.

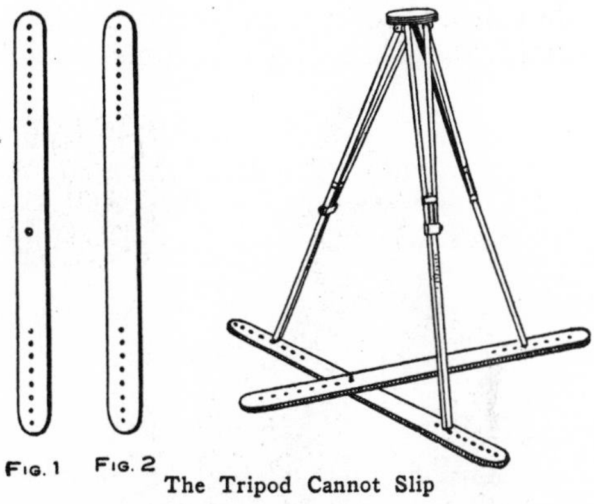

The Tripod Cannot Slip

How to Weave a Shoestring Watch Fob

Having procured a pair of ordinary shoestrings, take both ends of one of them and force the ends through the middle of the other, leaving a loop 1½ in. long, as shown in Fig. 2. In this sketch, A is the first string and B is the second, doubled and run through the web of A. Take hold of the loop and turn it as shown in Fig. 2, allowing the four ends to hang in four directions. Start with one end, the one marked A, in Fig. 1, for instance, and lay it over the one to the right. Then take B and lay it over A, and the one beneath C; lay C over B and the one under D, and then lay D over C and stick the end under A. Then draw all four ends up snugly. Commence the next layer by laying the end A back over B and D; D over A and C; C over D and B, then B over C and the end stuck under A. Proceed in the same manner and keep on until about 1½ in. of the ends remain unwoven. Four pins stuck through each corner and into the layers will hold the ends from coming apart. The ends of the strings are raveled out so as to make a tassel. This will make a square fob which will appear as shown in Fig. 4.

A round fob is made in a similar way, taking the same start as for the square fob, but instead of reversing the ends of each alternate layer, always lap one string, as at A in Fig. 3, over the one to its right, as B, slipping

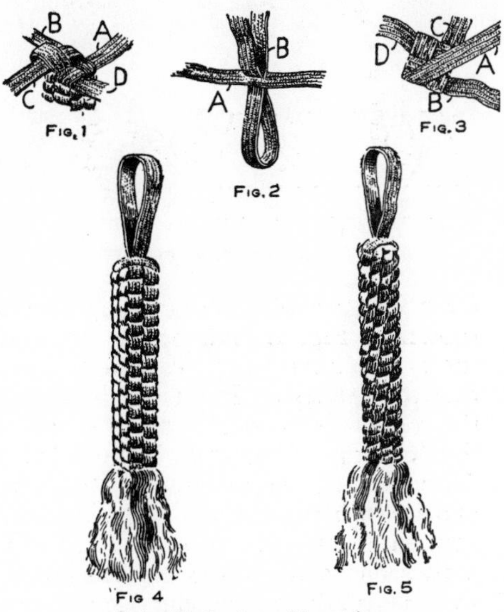

Fobs Made from Shoestrings

the last end of the four strings under and tightening all, as in making the square fob. Fasten the ends with pins and ravel out for a tassel. The round fob is shown in Fig. 5.

A fob in the shape of a horseshoe can be made by taking four shoestrings and tying a small string around the middle of them, then weaving the layers both ways from the point where the strings are tied. A loop, $1\frac{1}{2}$ in. long, is left out at the center before starting on one side. The loop is for attaching the fob to the watch. After the weaving is complete and the tassel ends made, a small stiff wire is forced through the center to form the shape of a horseshoe.

Other designs can be made in the same manner. Strings of different colors will make up a very pretty fob, especially if silk strings are used.—Contributed by John P. Rupp, Monroeville, Ohio.

How to Make a Table Mat of Leather

The table mat, the design of which is shown herewith, is to be made of leather. It may be made of Russian calf and the background modeled down

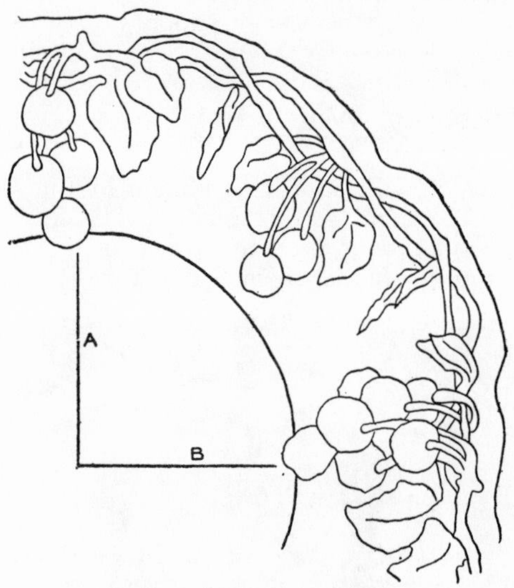

Pattern for the Table Mat

as has been described in several previous articles dealing with leather work. To do this the leather is moistened on the back side just enough to make the leather take the impression of the tool, but not enough to make the moisture show through on the face. Any smooth piece of steel, such as a nut pick, that will not cut or scratch the leather and will make a V-shaped depression will do.

A second method is to secure a piece of sheepskin and, using the reverse side, outline the design by means of a pyrographer's outfit. This manner of treating leather is so common that it needs no description.

A third method is to secure a piece of sheep or goat skin, trace the design on the reverse side by means of carbon paper, and put the outline and design in with brush and stains such as are sold for this purpose.

The accompanying pattern shows but one-fourth of the mat. Draw the one-fourth on paper to the size desired and then fold on lines A and B, tracing this one-fourth on the other parts by the insertion of double-surfaced carbon paper.

On the calfskin the pattern is to be held on the leather and the tool worked over the pattern to get the outline transferred. After this the pattern is to be removed and the leather modeled.

Sad Iron Polisher

A small amount of wax is necessary on an iron for successful work. The wax is usually applied by hand to the heated surface of the iron. A much better and handier way is to bore five or six holes in one end of

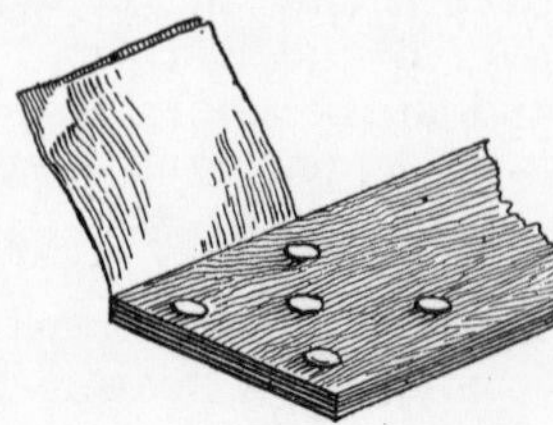

the ironing board to a depth of half

its thickness, filling them with wax, beeswax or paraffin, and covering them over with two thicknesses of muslin.

The rubbing of the hot iron over this cloth absorbs just enough of the wax to make the iron work smoothly. When the supply of wax is exhausted, it can be easily renewed.—Contributed by A. A. Houghton, Northville, Mich.

Making Coins Stick to Wood by Vacuum

Take a quarter and place it flat against a vertical surface of wood such as the side of a bookcase, door facing or door panel, and strike it hard with a downward sliding motion, pressing it against the wood. Take the hand away and the coin will remain on the woodwork. The striking and pressure expel the air between the quarter and the wood, thus forming a vacuum sufficient to hold the coin.

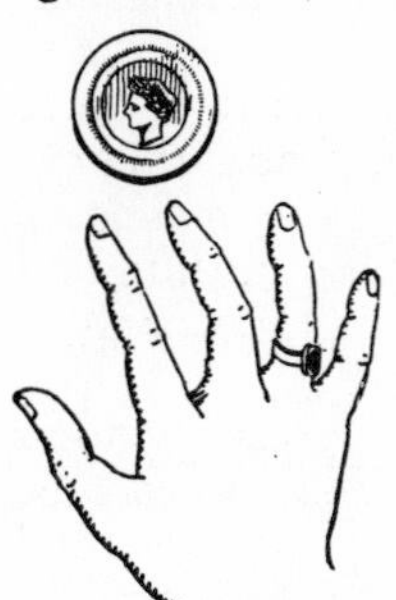

Simple and Safe Method for Sending Coins by Mail

Sending coins by mail is not as a rule advisable, but sometimes it becomes necessary, and usually a regular coin mailer is not available. A very simple and secure way to wrap a coin or coins for mailing is as follows: Procure a piece of heavy paper, nearly as wide as the envelope is long, and about 12 in. long. Fold on the dotted lines shown by A and B in the sketch, and slip the coin in the pocket thus formed. Fold together on lines C, D, E and F, making the last two folds wide enough to fit snugly in the envelope. This method holds the coin in the center of the envelope where it cannot work around and cut through the edges.—Contributed by O. J. Thompson, Petersburg, Ill.

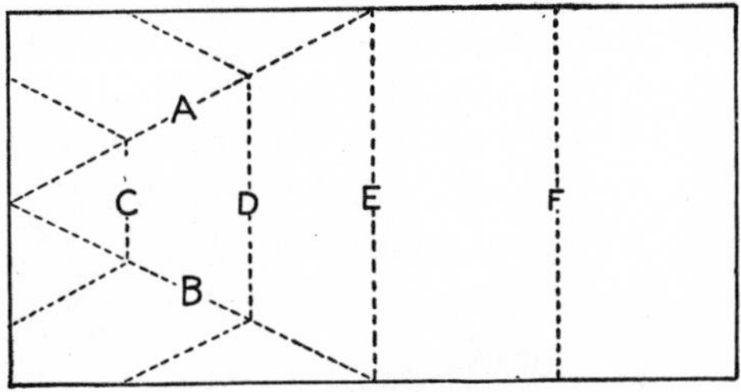

How the Paper is Folded

Mounting Photographs in Plaster Plaques

Purchase a few pounds of plaster of paris from your local druggist and select a dish of the desired shape in which to make your cast. The size of the dish will depend on the size of the print to be mounted. Select the print you wish to mount, those on matte paper will work best, and after wetting, place it face down in the dish, press into place and remove all drops of water with a soft cloth. Be sure and have the print in the center of the dish. Earthen dishes will be found more convenient, although tin ones can be used with good success, says Photographic Times.

Mix some of the plaster in clear water so it will be a little thick. Enough plaster should be mixed to cover the bottom of the dish about ½ in. thick. Pour the plaster into the dish over the print and allow to stand until it becomes quite hard. The cast can then be removed and the print should be fast to it. If the print or plaster is inclined to stick, take a knife and gently pry around the edges and it can be removed without breaking.

Prints of any size may be used by having the mold or dish large enough to leave a good margin. This is a very important point as it is the margin that adds richness to all prints. Platinum or blueprint papers work well, but any kind that will not stick may be used. After the plaster has thoroughly dried, any tint may be worked on the margin by the use of water colors; if blueprints are used, it is best to leave a plain white margin.

Iron Rest for an Ironing Board

A flatiron rest can be made on an ironing-board by driving a number of large tacks into one end of the board. The tacks should be about 1 in. apart and driven in only part way, leaving about 1/4 in. remaining above the surface of the board. The hot iron will not burn the wood and it cannot slip off the tacks. This iron rest is always with the board and ready when wanted.—Contributed by Beatrice Oliver, New York, N. Y.

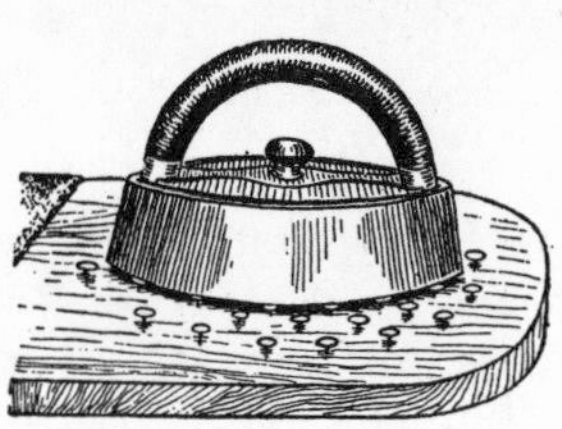

Instantaneous Crystallization

Dissolve 150 parts of hyposulphite of soda in 15 parts of water and pour the solution slowly into a test tube which has been warmed in boiling water, filling the same about one-half full. Dissolve in another glass 100 parts of acetate of soda in 15 parts of boiling water. Pour this solution slowly on top of the first in such a way that it forms an upper layer, without mixing the solutions. The two solutions are then covered over with a thin layer of boiling water and allowed to cool.

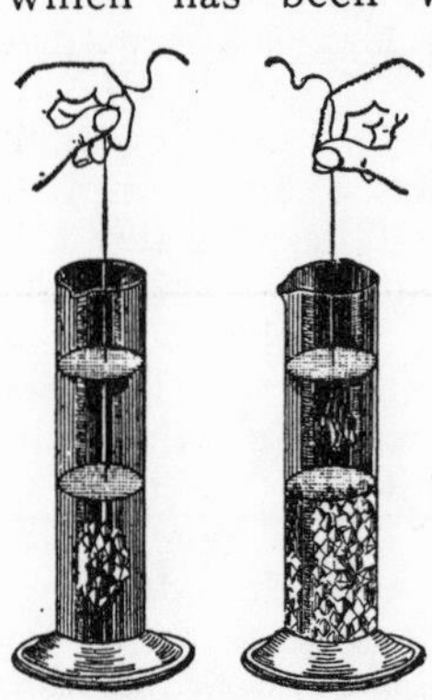

Lower into the test tube a wire, at the extremity of which is fixed a small crystal of hyposulphite of soda. The crystal traverses the solution of acetate without causing trouble, but crystallization will immediaely set in as soon as it touches the lower hyposulphite of soda solution, as shown at the left in the sketch.

When the hyposulphite of soda solution becomes crystallized, lower in the upper solution a crystal of acetate of soda suspended by another wire, as shown in the right of the sketch, and this will crystallize the same as the other solution.

Decoloration of Flowers by Fumes of Sulphur

Dissolve some sulphur in a small dish which will inflame by contact with air thus forming sulphuric acid fumes. Cover the dish with a conical chimney made of tin and expose to the upper opening the flowers that are to be decolored. The action is very rapid and in a short time myrtle, violets, bell flowers, roses, etc., will be rendered perfectly white.

How to Preserve Egg Shells

Many naturalists experience difficulty in preserving valuable egg shells. One of the most effective ways of preserving them is as follows: After the egg is blown, melt common beeswax and force it into the shell with a discarded fountain pen filler. Set in a cool place until the wax hardens. The most delicate shells treated in this manner can be handled without fear of breaking, and the transparency of the wax will not alter the color, shading, or delicate tints of the egg.—Contributed by L. L. Shabino, Millstown, South Dakota.

Homemade Phonograph

Make a box large enough to hold four dry cells and use it as a base to mount the motor on and to support the revolving cylinder. Anyone of the various battery motors may be used to supply the power. The support for the cylinder is first made and located on the cover of the box in such a position that it will give ample room for the motor. The motor base and the support are fastened by screws turned up through the cover or top of the box. The location of these parts is shown in Fig. 1.

The core for holding the cylindrical wax records is 4½ in. long and made of wood, turned a little tapering, the diameter at the small or outer end being 1⅝ in., and at the larger end, 1⅞ in. A wood wheel with a V-shaped groove on its edge is nailed to the larger end of the cylinder. The hole in the core is fitted with a brass tube, driven in tightly to serve as a bearing. A rod that will fit the brass tube, not too tightly, but which will not wabble loose, is threaded and turned into the upper end of the support. The core with its attached driving wheel is shown in Fig. 3. The dotted lines show the brass bearing and rod axle. The end of the axle should be provided with a thread over which a washer and nut are placed, to keep the core from coming off in turning.

The sound box, Fig. 2, is about 2½ in. in diameter and 1 in. thick, made of heavy tin. The diaphragm, which should be of thin ferrotype tin, should be soldered to the box. The needle is made of a piece of sewing needle, about ⅛ in. long, and soldered to the center of the diaphragm. The first point should be ground blunt, as shown in the sketch. When soldering these parts together, take care to have the diaphragm lie perfectly flat and not made warping by any pressure applied while the solder is cooling.

The tin horn can be easily made, attached to the sound box with a piece of rubber hose and held so it will swing the length of the record by a rod attached to the top of the box, as shown. The motor can be controlled by a small three or four-point battery rheostat.—

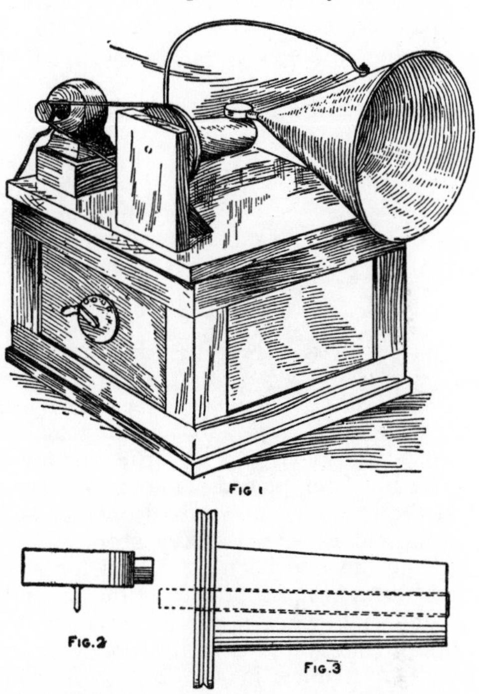

Phonograph and Construction of Parts

Contributed by Herbert Hahn, Chicago, Ill.

A Substitute for a Compass

An easy way to make a pencil compass when one is not at hand, is to take a knife with two blades at one end, open one to the full extent and the other only halfway. Stick the point end of the fully open blade into the side of a lead pencil and use the half-

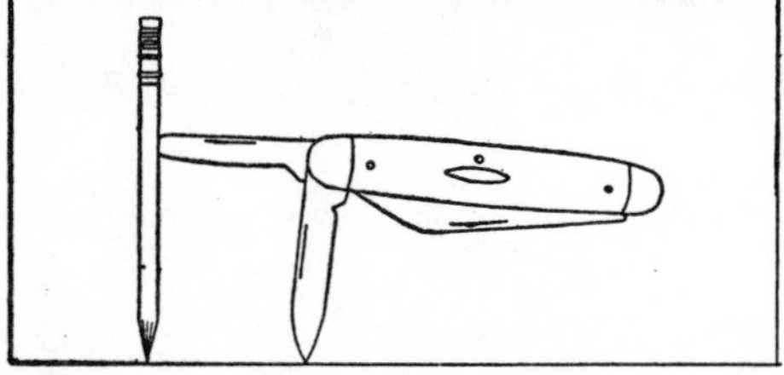

Pencil on the Knife Blade

open blade as the center leg of the compass. Turn with the knife handle to make the circle.—Contributed by E. E. Gold, Jr., Victor, Colo.

A Novel Rat Trap

A boy, while playing in the yard close to a grain house, dug a hole and buried an old-fashioned fruit jug or jar that

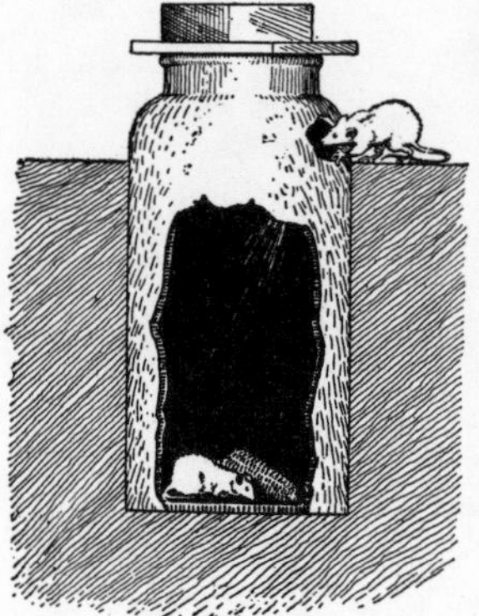

his mother had thrown away, says the Iowa Homestead. The top part of the jug was left uncovered as shown in the sketch, and a hole was broken in it just above the ground. The boy then placed some shelled corn in the bottom, put a board on top, and weighted it with a heavy stone.

The jug had been forgotten for several days when a farmer found it, and, wondering what it was, he raised the board and found nine full-grown rats and four mice in the bottom. The trap has been in use for some time and is opened every day or two and never fails to have from one to six rats or mice in it.

A Nut-Cracking Block

In the sketch herewith is shown an appliance for cracking nuts which will prevent many a bruised thumb. To

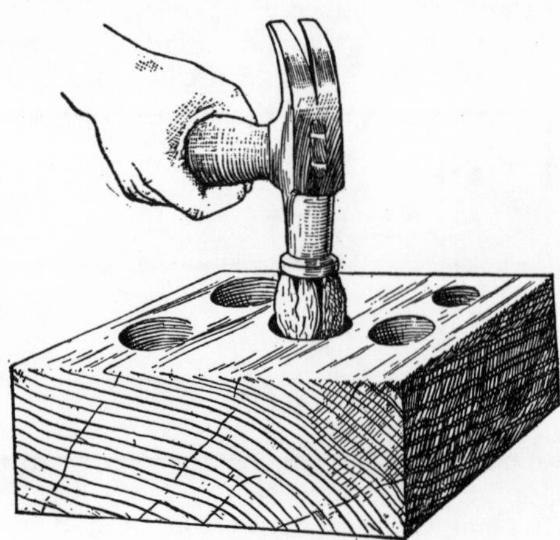

Holes in Block for Nuts

anyone who has ever tried to crack butternuts it needs no further recommendation. The device is nothing more than a good block of hardwood with a few holes bored in it to fit the different sized nuts. There is no need of holding the nut with the fingers, and as hard a blow may be struck as desired. Make the depth of the hole two-thirds the height of the nut and the broken pieces will not scatter.—Contributed by Albert O'Brien, Buffalo, N. Y.

A Jelly-Making Stand

Every housewife who makes jelly is only too well acquainted with the inconvenience and danger of upsets when using the old method of balancing a

Cheesecloth Strainer on Stand

jelly-bag on a couple of chairs stood on the kitchen table, with the additional inconvenience of having a couple of chairs on the kitchen table out of commission for such a length of time.

The accompanying sketch shows how a stand can be made from a few pieces of boards that will help jelly makers and prevent the old-time dangers and disadvantages. The stand can be stood in the corner of the kitchen, or under the kitchen table where it will be out of danger of being upset.—Contributed by Lyndwode, Pereira, Ottawa, Can.

How to Make an Egg-Beater

There is no reason why any cook or housewife should be without this egg-beater, as it can be made quickly in any size. All that is needed is an ordinary can with a tight-fitting cover—a baking-powder can will do. Cut a round piece of wood 3 in. longer than the length of the can. Cut a neat hole in the cover of the can to allow the stick to pass through, and at one end of the stick fasten, by means of a flat-headed tack, a piece of tin, cut round, through which several holes have been punched. Secure another piece of heavier tin of the same size, and make

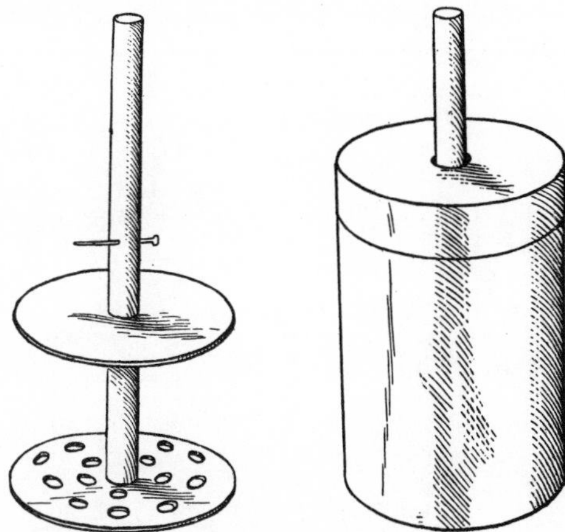

Made Like a Churn

a hole in the center to pass the stick through. Put a small nail 2 in. above the end of the dasher, which allows the second tin to pass up and down in the opposite direction to the dasher. This beater will do the work in less time than the regular kitchen utensil.—Contributed by W. A. Jaquythe, Richmond, Cal.

Cart Without an Axle

The boy who has a couple of cart wheels is not always lucky enough to have an axle of the proper length to fit the wheels. In such a case the cart can be constructed as shown in the illustration. This cart has no axle, each wheel being attached with a short pin for an axle, on the side and at the lower edge of the box. The outer end of the pin is carried on a piece of wood extending the full length of the box and

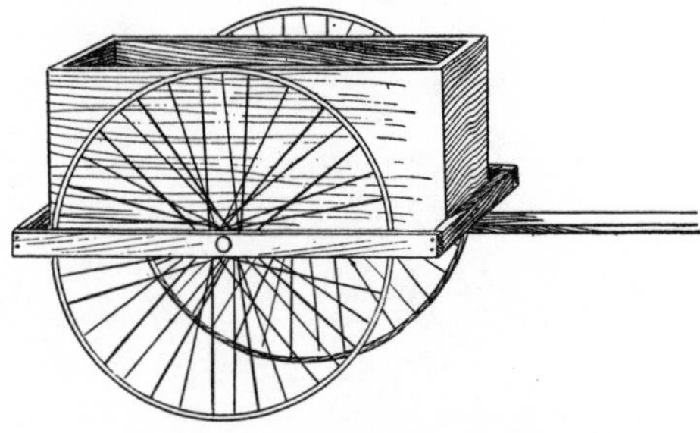

Wheels Fastened to the Box

supported by crosspieces nailed to the ends, as shown.—Contributed by Thos. De Loof, Grand Rapids, Mich.

An Illuminated Target

My youthful nephews some time ago were presented with an air rifle and it worked so well that it became necessary for me to construct a target that would allow the fun to be carried on at night.

I reversed a door gong, screwed it on the inside of a store box, and fitted two candles on the inside to illuminate the bullseye. The candles, of course, were below the level of the bullseye. The position of the candles and gong are shown in Fig. 1. At night the illuminated interior of the bell could be

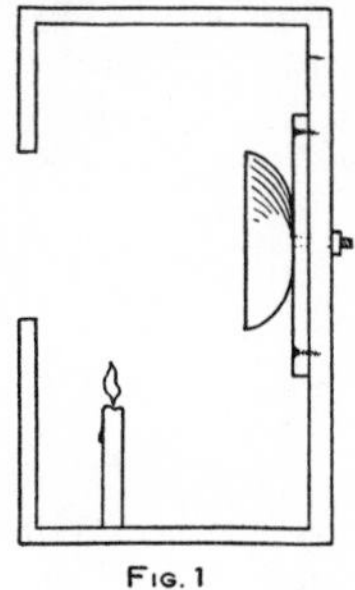

Fig. 1

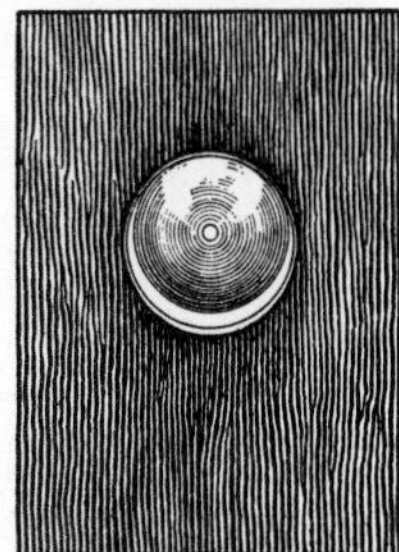

Fig. 2

Target for Night Shooting

plainly seen as shown in Fig. 2.—Contributed by James M. Kane, Doylestown, Pa.

¶Sheet metal placed between two boards in the jaws of a vise and clamped tightly, can be sawed easily with a hacksaw.

Feed Box for Chickens

The sketch shows the construction of a feed box designed to prevent the scattering of feed and give the coward

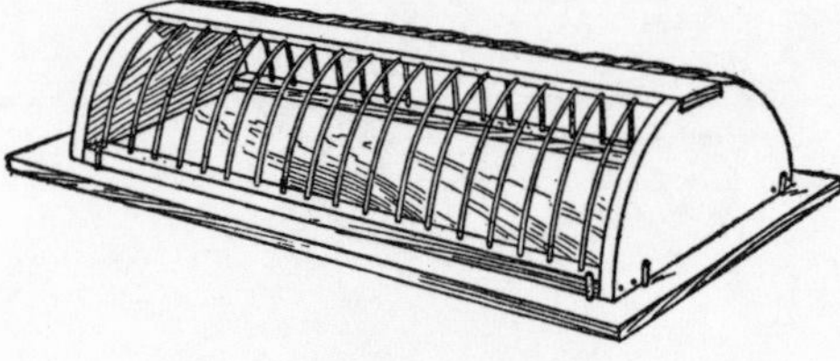

Chicken Feed Box

rooster as much chance to fatten as the game cock. The base may be made of a ½-in. board, 1 ft. wide and 3 ft. long, although any of the dimensions may be varied to suit special requirements. The ends are semi-circular pieces with a notch, ¼ in. deep and 3 in. wide, cut in the center of the rounding edge. The ends are connected together with a piece of wood set in the notches. The strip of wood is ¼ in. thick, 2 in. wide and as long as the box. Notches ⅛ in. wide and ⅛ in. deep are cut on the under side of this piece of wood, 1½ in. apart. Heavy pieces of wire are bent in the form of a semicircle, as shown. The wires are set in the ⅛-in. notches cut on the under side of the top piece of wood. The ends of the wires are set in holes in wood pieces joining the bases of the end pieces. The baseboard and top are separable.—Contributed by Maurice Baudier, New Orleans, La.

A Book Rest

A book that does not open flat is rather inconvenient to write in when one of its sides is in the position shown in Fig. 2. A wedge-shaped piece of

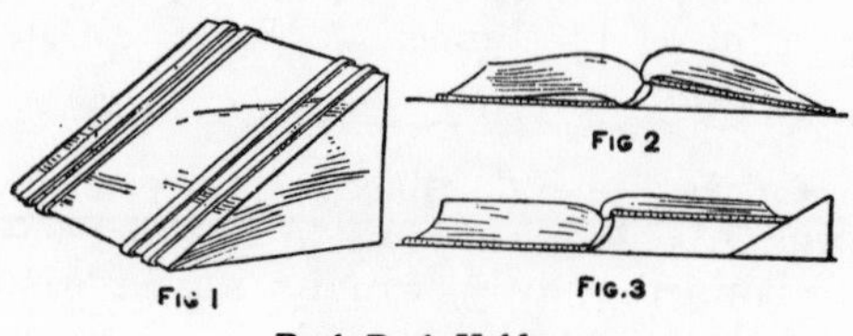

Book Back Holders

metal, stone or wood, as shown in Fig. 1, will, when placed as in Fig. 3, raise the sloping half to the level of the other pages. Cover the block with rubber, wide rubber bands or felt, to prevent its scratching the desk top. The block can also be used as a paperweight.

Window Shelf for Flower Pots

On the ledge formed by the top part of the lower sash of the window I fitted a board 7 in. wide into each side of the casing, by cutting away the ends. I placed a small bracket at each end of the shelf, so that it would fit solidly against the lower window sash to support the weight of the plants.

Shelf in Window

One of the brackets I nailed to the shelf and the other I held in place with a hinge, the reason being that if both were solid, the shelf could not be put on the window, as one end must be dropped in place before the other. Such a shelf will hold all the plants a person can put on it. When not in use, it can be removed without marring the casing.—Contributed by G. A. Wood, West Union, Ia.

Magnet for the Work Basket

Tie a ribbon or strong string to the work basket and fasten a large magnet to the other end. Needles, scissors, etc., can be picked up without any trouble. This device is very convenient for invalids.—Contributed by Nellie Conlon, Worcester, Mass.

Knife Made from a Hack-Saw Blade

A very serviceable knife with excellent cutting qualities can be made easily from a discarded hack-saw blade. The dimensions given in the sketch make a knife of convenient size.

The saw teeth are ground off on an emery wheel or grindstone to a smooth edge parallel with the back edge. For the handle, take two pieces of hard wood, dressing one surface of each piece, and cut a groove as wide and thick as the saw blade. Place the blade in the groove and glue the two dressed sides of the wood together. After the glue has dried, the blade can be pulled out of the groove and the wood shaped to any desired form. A small wood-screw is put through one side of the handle to prevent the blade from sliding. After completing the

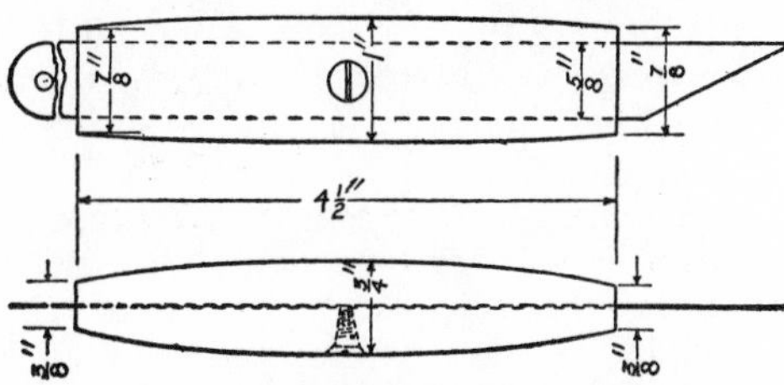

Details of Handle

handle, the blade is put back into the groove and sharpened to a cutting edge.—Contributed by H. A. Hutchins, Cleveland, Ohio.

Killing Mice and Rats

A simple and inexpensive means for killing mice and rats is to leave yeast cakes lying around where they can eat them.—Contributed by Maud McKee, Erie, Pa.

Roller Coaster Illusion Traveling Up an Incline

A toy car with a paddle wheel and a shaft on both ends traveling upward on a chute in which water is flowing down, is shown in the accompanying sketch. The paddle wheels travel in a reverse direction causing the ends of the axles to roll on the edge of the chute, thus carrying the car up the incline. If a rack is used on each side of the chute and a small pinion on the

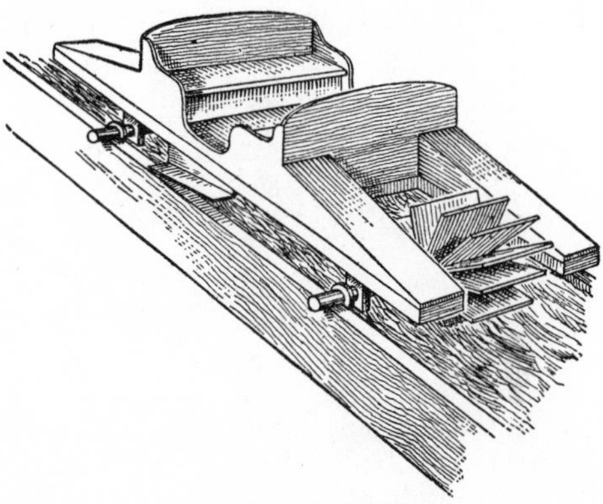

Car Travels Uphill

ends of the axles, a positive upward movement of the car will be obtained.—Contributed by W. S. Jacobs, Malden, Mass.

Block for Planing Octagonal Wood Pieces

The little device shown in the illustration will be found very useful in any workshop. Two or three of them will be necessary for planing long pieces. Each one is made of a hardwood block, 1 in. square and 4 in. long. A notch is cut in one side, as shown in Fig. 1, so a piece of wood which has been planed square will fit in it. Put a screw in the end of each piece and fasten it down to the bench. If desired, a tenon may be made on the bottom of each block, as shown in Fig. 2, to fit a mortise cut in the bench. Place the blocks far enough apart so the board to be planed will rest firmly in the notches.

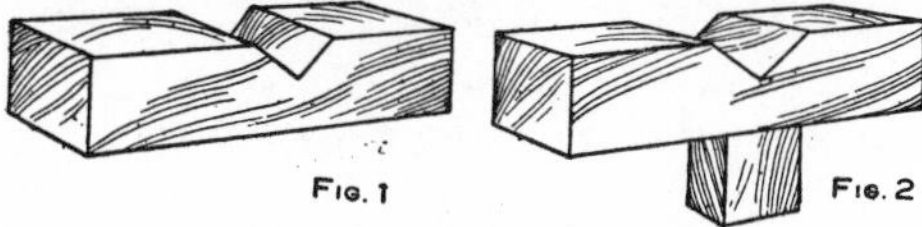

The Notch Holds the Wood

Plane the board square first and then place it in the notches and plane the corners down to the proper dimensions.—Contributed by Willie Woolsen, Cape May Point, N. J.

A Letter Holder of Pierced Metal

The letter holder shown in the illustration will be found convenient for holding out-going letters that await the postman's coming. It can be made of either copper or brass and need not

Finished Letter Holder

be of very heavy material. Gauge 22 will be sufficiently heavy. One sheet of metal, 6 by 9½ in., a board on which to work it, and an awl and hammer, will be needed.

Prepare a design for the front. If one such as is shown is to be used,

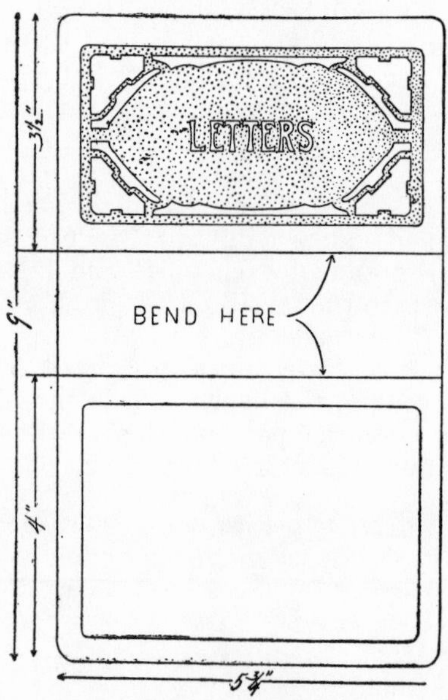

Layout for the Metal

make one-quarter of it first, and then get the other parts by folding on the center lines and tracing. This will insure having all parts alike. The letters can be put on afterward.

Fasten the metal to the board, using tacks and nailing outside of the required space, in the waste metal. Trace the design on the metal with carbon paper; or, if desired, paste the paper design right on the metal. With an awl pierce the metal between the marginal line and the design, as shown. The holes should be uniform along the outlines but should be pierced promiscuously otherwise. On the back, only the marginal line is to be pierced.

Remove the metal, together with the paper if the latter was pasted to the metal, and trim off the surplus metal where the tacks had been placed. File off any sharpness so that the hand may not be injured in handling it. Place the metal on the edge of a table or between two boards, and bend on the two lines indicated in the drawing, to right angles.

A good finish is obtained by just letting the copper age with its natural color. If any polishing is required, it should be done before the metal is fastened to the board and pierced.

Imitating Ground Glass

Make a mixture of white lead in oil, 1 part; varnish, ¾ part; turpentine, ¼ part, and add sugar of lead as a dryer. Make a very thin paint of this and use a broad, flat brush, says Master Painter. With care you may succeed in getting the paint on quite evenly all over, which is desirable. One coat will do. If it becomes necessary to remove this coating for renewal, it may be effected by an application of potash lye, or the old may be renewed by a coating of a mixture of 2 parts hydrochloric acid, 2 parts white vitriol, 1 part sulphate of copper (blue vitriol) and 1 part of gum arabic, applied by means of a brush.

¶A detail drawing made of a piece of furniture before starting the work will often save time and mistakes.

Making "Spirits" Play a Violin

A very pretty trick, that can be worked in your own parlor, will produce as much sensation as a fake "medium." In all appearance, a violin, mandolin or guitar, placed on a table, will begin to produce music simply through stamping the foot and a few passes of the hand. The music will not sound natural, but weird and distant.

The trick is done by placing the end of a small stick on a music box in the basement of the house and allowing the other end to pass up through the floor and table top so it will project about $\frac{1}{16}$ in. The stick may be placed by the side of, behind or through the center of a table leg. Be careful not to have any obstruction in the way of the stick. The instrument is placed sideways on the protruding end of the stick. The "fake" work of invoking the "spirit" is performed and ended by stamping the foot, which signals the operator in the basement to start the machine, and the violin seemingly produces music without anyone touching it.

So impressive are the results, that many people really think the spirits of the departed are playing the violin with unseen hands. The music is transmitted through the stick from the music box to the violin.

The Music Produced by the Phonograph is Transmitted to the Violin on the Second Floor by the Aid of a Long Stick

Sizing a Threaded Hole

It sometimes becomes necessary to transfer the size of a threaded hole from some out-of-the-way place to the shop in order to make a piece to fit it. With proper tools this is easy; without them, it might be difficult. One thing is always at hand and that is wood. Whittle a stick tapering until it starts in the hole. Then turn it into the hole and a fair thread will be made on the wood. The stick can be carried in the pocket without risk of changing the size, as would be the case with ordinary calipers.

Leaded-Glass Fire Screen

The main frame of the fire screen shown in Fig. 1 is made from two pieces of ½-in. square bar iron. The longest piece, which should be about 5½ ft. long, is bent square so as to form two uprights, each 28 in. long and measuring 26 in. across the top. The bottom crosspiece can be either riveted or welded to the uprights. Two pairs of feet, each 6 in. long and spread about 8 in. apart, are shaped as shown in Fig. 2. These are welded to the lower end of the uprights.

The ornamental scrollwork on the

frame is simple and effective, and is easy to construct, says Work, London. The scrolls are attached to the frame by means of $\frac{3}{16}$-in. round-head machine screws. The leaf ornament at the termination of the scroll is shaped and embossed as shown in Fig. 3. The metal used for the scrolls is $\frac{3}{16}$ in. thick by ½ in. wide. The leaf ornament is formed by turning over the end of a piece of metal and working it together at a welding heat, and then shaping out the leaf with a chisel and files, after which they are embossed with a ball-peen hammer.

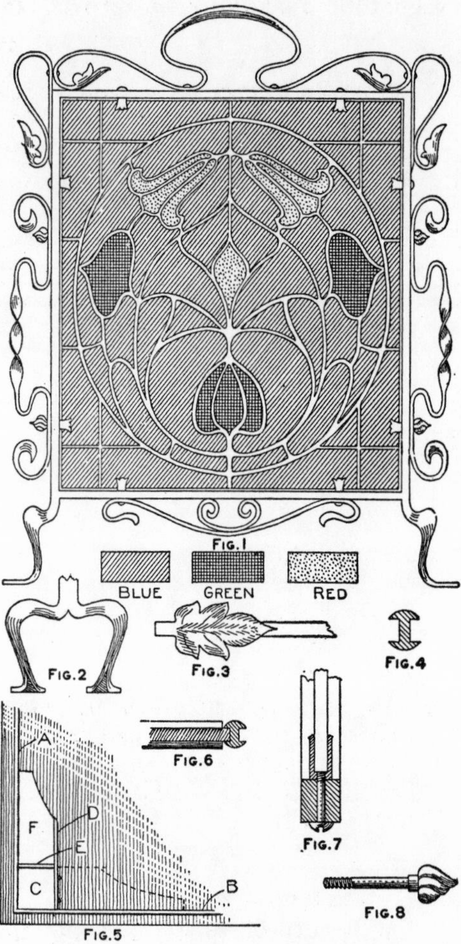

Completed Fire Screen and Parts

The center is made from colored glass of special make for leaded work. The design is formed in the lead, of which a cross section is shown in Fig. 4. Use care to give the lead a symmetrical outline. The design should be drawn full size on a large sheet of heavy paper and the spaces to be occupied by the lead cut out so as to leave the exact size and shape of each piece of paper the same as wanted for each piece of glass. These are used as patterns in marking the glass for cutting. The glass is cut the same as ordinary window glass. The glass, lead, border and special flux can be purchased from an art glass shop.

After the glass is cut, the work of putting the pieces together with the lead between them is begun. Secure a board as wide as the screen—several narrow boards put together will do—and begin by placing one vertical side border, A, Fig. 5, and the base border, B, on it as shown. Place the corner piece of glass, C, in the grooves of the borders, cut a long piece of lead, D, and hold it in place with two or three brads or glazier's points. The piece of lead E is cut and a small tenon joint made as shown in Fig. 6. While the piece of lead D, Fig. 5, is held by the brads, the piece E can be fitted and soldered. The soldering is done with a hot soldering iron and wire solder, using rosin as a flux, or, better still, special flux purchased for this purpose. After the joints are soldered, the piece of glass F is put in place and the lead held with brads as before until the cross leads are fitted and soldered. The brads are then removed, the glass piece as shown by the dotted lines put in, and the leads around it held with brads until the crosspieces are put in and soldered. This method is pursued until the glass is complete, then the two remaining vertical and top pieces of border are put on and all corners soldered.

The leaded glass is held in the iron frame by means of eight U-shaped clips, as shown in Fig. 7. A hole is drilled in the frame for the retaining screw, the latter being tapped to the base of the clip. Special screws may be made with ornamental heads, as shown in Fig. 8, and used for securing the side scrolls and clips together.

A Revolving Teeter Board

The accompanying sketch shows the details of a revolving teeter board for the children's playground that can be constructed in a few hours. Secure a post, not less than 4 in. square and of the length given in the drawing, and round the corners of one end for a ring. This ring can be made of 1-in. strap iron and it should be shrunk on the post. Bore a ¾-in. hole in the end of the post for the center pin to rest in. Make three washers 3 in. in diameter and ¼ in. thick and drill ¾-in. holes through their centers. Drill and countersink two smaller holes for 2-in. wood screws in each washer. Fasten one of these washers to the top of the post as shown. The post is now ready to be set in the ground. Coarse gravel should be packed tightly about it to make it solid. Concrete is much better if it can be secured.

To make the swivel you will need two ¼ by 5 by 8-in. plates, rounded at the top as shown, and two wood blocks, A and B, each 3½ by 5 by 10 in. Drill the lower ends of the plates for four 2½-in. lag screws and the upper ends for a ⅝-in. bolt. Fasten the plates to the block B, then drill a ¾-in. hole as shown and fasten the two remaining washers to the block, one on each side and central with the hole. Bore a ⅝-in. hole lengthwise through the block A for the ⅝-in. rocker bolt. This bolt should be 11½ in. long.

The teeter board is made of a 2 by 12-in. plank about 12 ft. long. It should be slightly tapered from the center to the ends. Two styles of hand holds are shown, but the one on the left is the one most generally used. The handles are rounded at the ends and are fastened to the board with lag screws or bolts. The block A is fastened to the board with lag screws and should be a working fit between the

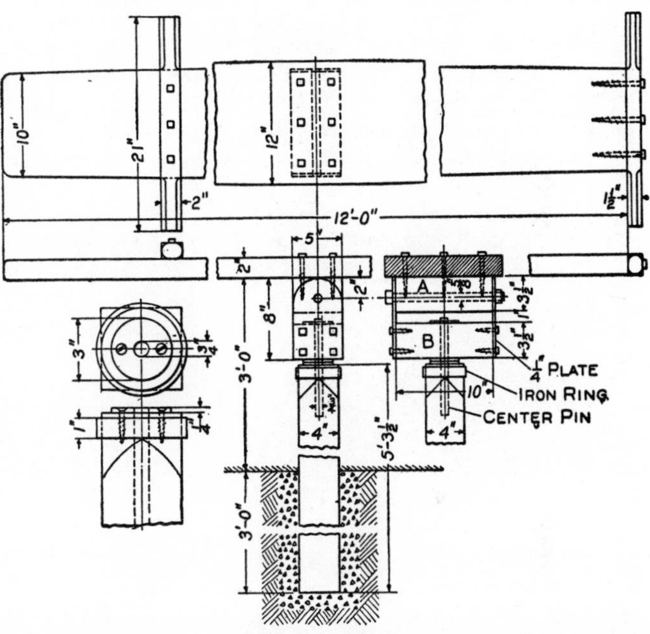

Details of Teeter Board

two plates where it is held by means of the ⅝-in. bolt. The center pin is ¾ in. in diameter and about 9 in. long. —Contributed by W. H. Dreier, Jr., Camden, N. J.

Home-Made Pot Covers

Empty thread spools and the tins used as extra inside covers in lard cans are usually thrown away, but these can be put to good use as kettle covers, if they are made up as follows:

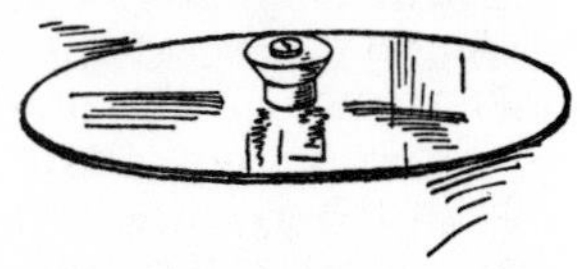

Saw the spool in half as shown, make a hole in the center of the tin and run a screw or nail through the spool and the tin; then flatten its end on the under side. This will make an excellent cover for a pot.—Contributed by Maurice Baudier, New Orleans, La.

An Outdoor Gymnasium

Part I—The Horizontal Bar

Gymnastic apparatus costs money and needs to be housed, because it will not stand the weather. Gymnasiums are not always available for the average boy who likes exercise and who would like to learn the tricks on horizontal and parallel bars, horse and rings, which all young athletes are taught in regular gymnastic courses.

Any small crowd of boys—even two—having a few simple tools, a will to use them and the small amount of money required to buy the necessary 4 filler pieces, 3/4 by 3 in. by 3 ft. 9 in. long and 1 piece, 2½ in. square by 5 ft. 7 in. long. This latter piece is for the bar and should be of well seasoned, straight-grained hickory. It makes no difference what kind of wood is used for the other pieces, but it is best to use cedar for the heavy pieces that are set in the ground as it will take years for this wood to rot. Ordinary yellow pine will do very well. The four 7-in. boards should be of some hard wood if possible such as oak, hickory, maple, chest-

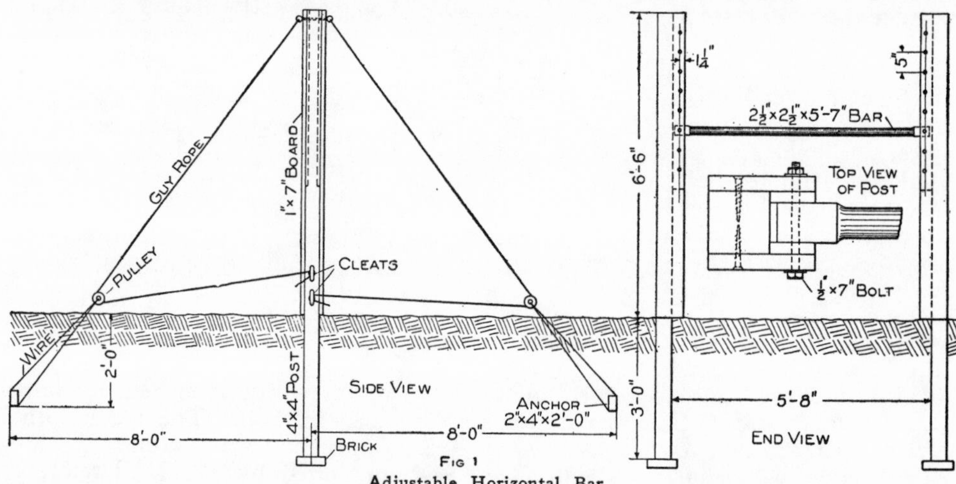

Fig 1
Adjustable Horizontal Bar

wood, bolts and rope, can make a first-class gymnasium. If trees are convenient, and some one can swing an axe, the money outlay will be almost nothing. The following plans are for material purchased from a mill squared and cut to length. To substitute small, straight trees for the squared timbers requires but little changes in the plans.

The most important piece of apparatus in the gymnasium is the horizontal bar. Most gymnasiums have two: one adjustable bar for various exercises and a high bar for gymnastic work. The outdoor gymnasium combines the two. The material required is as follows: 2 pieces of wood, 4 in. square by 9½ ft. long; 4 pieces, 2 by 4 in. by 2 ft. long; 4 pieces, 1 by 7 in. by 6½ ft. long; nut or ash. The other material necessary consists of 2 bolts, ½ in. in diameter and 7 in. long; 16 screws, 3 in. long; 4 heavy screw eyes with two ½-in. shanks; 50 ft. of heavy galvanized wire: 80 ft. of ¼-in. manila rope and 4 pulley blocks. Four cleats are also required but these can be made of wood at home.

Draw a line on the four 7-in. boards along the side of each from end to end, 1¼ in. from one edge. Beginning at one end of each board make pencil dots on this line 5 in. apart for a distance of 3 ft. 4 in. Bore holes through the boards on these marks with a $\frac{9}{16}$-in. bit. Fasten two of these boards on each post with the 3-in. screws, as shown in the top view of the post Fig. 1, forming a channel of the edges in which the holes were bored. Two of the filler pieces are fastened in each channel as shown, so as to make the space fit the squared end of the bar snugly. The ends of the boards with the holes should be flush with the top of the post. This will make each pair of holes in the 7-in. boards coincide, so the ½-in. bolt can be put through them and the squared end of the bar.

Select a level place where the apparatus is to be placed and dig two holes 6 ft. apart, each 3 ft. deep and remove all loose dirt. The ends of the posts not covered with the boards are set in these holes on bricks or small stones. The channels formed by the boards must be set facing each other with the inner surfaces of the posts parallel and 5 ft. 8 in. apart. The holes around the posts are filled with earth and well tamped.

The hickory piece which is to form the bar should be planed, scraped and sandpapered until it is perfectly smooth and round except for 3 in. at each end. Bore a $\frac{9}{16}$-in. hole through each square end 1¼ in. from the end. The bar may be fastened at any desired height by slipping the ½-in. bolts through the holes bored in both the bar and channel.

Each post must be well braced to keep it rigid while a person is swinging on the bar. Four anchors are placed in the ground at the corners of an imaginary rectangle 9 by 16 ft., in the center of which the posts stand as shown in Fig. 2. Each anchor is made of one 2-ft. piece of wood, around the center of which four strands of the heavy galvanized wire are twisted, then buried to a depth of 2 ft., the extending ends of the wires coming up to the surface at an angle.

The heavy screw eyes are turned into the posts at the top and lengths of ropes tied to each. These ropes or guys pass through the pulley blocks, which are fastened to the projecting ends of the anchor wire, and return to the posts where they are tied to cleats. Do not tighten the guy ropes without the bar in place, as to do so will strain the posts in the ground. Do not change the elevation of the bar without slacking up on the ropes. It takes but little pull on the guy ropes to make them taut, and once tightened the bar will be rigid.

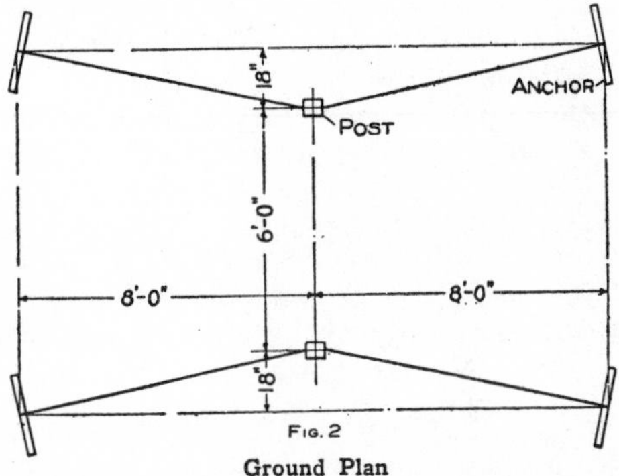

Ground Plan

Oil the bar when it is finished and remove it during the winter. It is well to oil the wood occasionally during the summer and reverse the bar at times to prevent its becoming curved. The wood parts should be well painted to protect them from the weather.

Electrostatic Illumination

Any one having the use of a static machine can perform the following experiment which gives a striking result. A common tumbler is mounted on a revolving platform and a narrow strip of tinfoil is fastened with shellac varnish to the surface of the glass as follows: Starting beneath the foot of the glass from a point immediately below the stem, it is taken to the edge of the foot; it follows the edge for about 1 in. and then passes in a curve across the base, and ascends the stem; then it passes

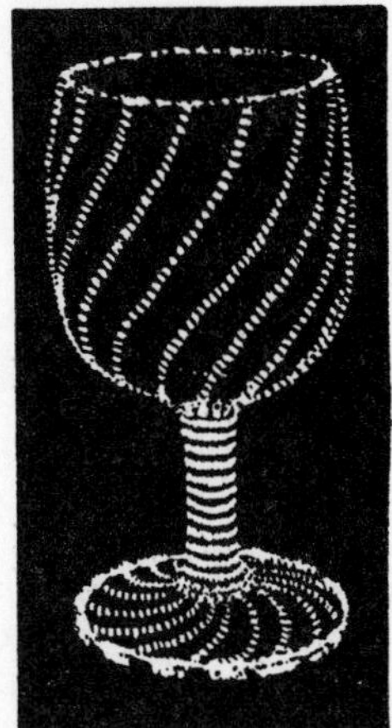

around the bowl in a sinuous course to the rim, which it follows for about one-third of its circumference; after which it descends on the inside and terminates at the bottom. The tinfoil on the outside of the glass is divided by cutting with a knife every ⅛ in., the parts inside and beneath the glass being left undivided. Current is then led from a static machine to two terminals, one terminal being connected to one end of the tinfoil strip, and similarly the second terminal makes contact with the other end. As soon as the current is led into the apparatus, a spark is seen at each place where the knife has cut through the tinfoil. If the tumbler is rotated, the effect will be as shown in the illustration. A variety of small and peculiar effects can be obtained by making some of the gaps in the tinfoil larger than others, in which case larger sparks would be produced at these points. The experiment should be carried out in a darkened room, and under these circumstances when nothing is visible, not even the tumbler, the effect is very striking.

Balloon Ascension Illusion

By C. W. Nieman

In these days of startling revelations in air-craft flight we are prepared to see any day some marvelous machine-driven bird cutting figure-eights all over the sky above our heads. One boy recently took advantage of this state of expectancy to have an evening's harmless amusement, through an illusion which deceived even the most incredulous. He caused a whole hotel-full of people to gaze open mouthed at a sort of "Zeppelin XXIII," which skimmed along the distant horizon, just visible against the dark evening sky, disappearing only to reappear again, and working the whole crowd up to a frenzy of excitement. And all he used was a black thread, a big piece of cardboard and a pair of field glasses.

He stretched the thread between two buildings, about 100 ft. apart, in an endless belt, passing through a screw-eye at either end. On this thread he fastened a cardboard "cut-out" of a dirigible, not much to look at in daytime, but most deceptive at dusk. By pulling one or the other string he moved the "airship" in either direction. He took the precaution of stretching his thread just beyond a blackberry hedge and thus kept over-inquisitive persons at a safe distance. He also saw to it that there was a black background at either end so that the reversing of the direction of the craft would not be noticed.

In attracting the crowd he had a confederate stand looking at the moving ship through a field glass, which at once gave the suggestion of distance, and materially heightened the illusion. When the interest of the crowd, which at once gathered, was at its height, the "aeronaut" pulled his craft out of sight and let the disillusion come when the light of day laid bare his fraud.

A Cork Extractor

The device shown in the sketch is for removing a cork or stopper from a bottle whether full or empty where the cork has been pushed inside. A wire about No. 14 gauge is bent as shown at B, Fig. 1, to fit the index finger and the other end filed to a point C, and turned in a spiral D, so the point will be on top. Insert this tool in the bottle as shown in Fig. 2 and place the end D under the cork and pull up. The cork will come out easily.—Contributed by Maurice Baudier, New Orleans, La.

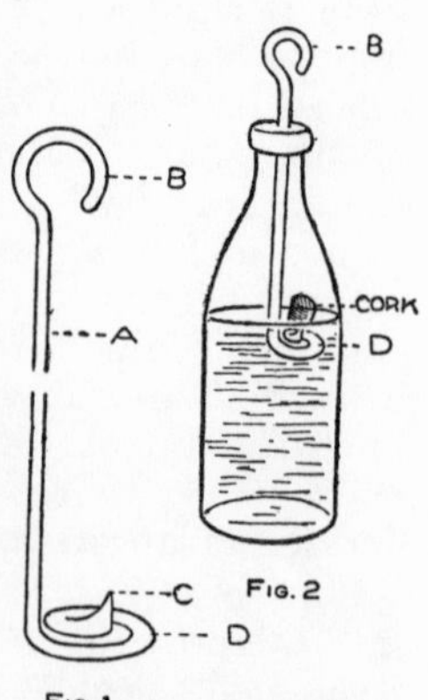

An Outdoor Gymnasium

Part II—Parallel Bars

Parallel bars hold a high place in the affection of those who frequent gymnasiums as the best apparatus for development of the back and shoulder muscles, as well as a promoter of ease and grace of movement. The outdoor "gym" can have a set of these bars with very little more labor than was required for the horizontal bar.

The material required is as follows: 4 posts, preferably cedar, 4 in. square and 6 ft. long; 2 base pieces, 4 in. square and 5½ ft. long; 2 cross braces, 2 by 4 in. by 2 ft. 2 in. long; 2 side braces, 2 by 4 in. by 7 ft. 8 in. long; 4 knee braces, 2 by 4 in. by 3 ft. 8 in. long; 2 bars of straight grained hickory, 2 by 3 in. by 10 ft. long; 4 wood screws, 6 in. long; 4 bolts, 8 in. long; 8 bolts, 7 in. long and 1 doz. large spikes.

To make the apparatus, lay off the bases as shown in the end view and bevel the ends at an angle of 60 deg. Chisel out two notches 4 in. wide and 1 in. deep, beginning at a point 9 in. from either side of the center. These are to receive the lower ends of the posts. Bevel two sides of one end of each post down to the width of the finished bar—a little less than 2 in. Cut notches in these ends to receive the oval bars. Bevel the ends of the knee braces, as shown in the diagram, and fasten the lower ends to the beveled ends of the bases with the spikes. Fasten the upper ends of the knee braces to the uprights with the 8-in. bolts put through the holes bored for that purpose, and countersinking the heads. Lay the whole end flat on the ground and make a mark 2½ ft. from the bottom of the base up along the posts, and fasten the end braces with their top edges flush with the marks, using four of the 7-in. bolts. Finally toe-nail the base into the ends of the posts merely to hold them in position while the whole structure is being handled.

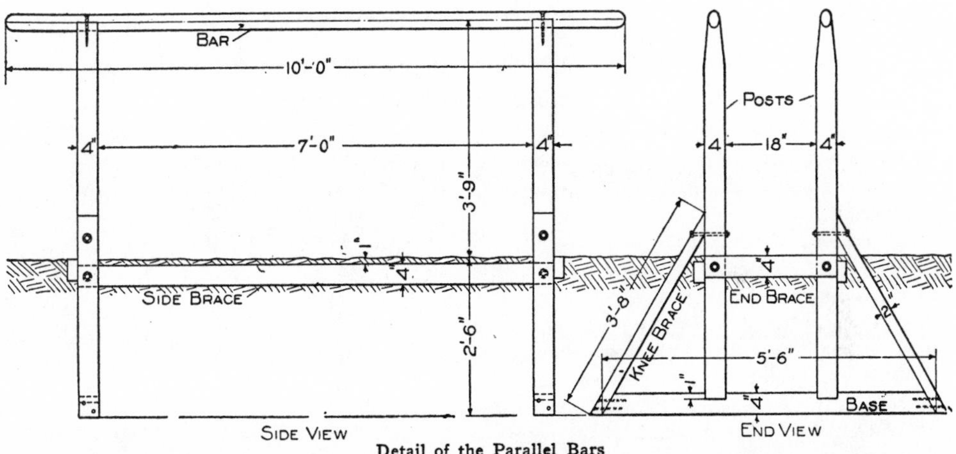

Detail of the Parallel Bars

Two endpieces must be made. These sets or ends of the apparatus are to be buried in trenches dug to the depth of 2½ ft., with the distance between the two inner surfaces of the posts, which face each other, of 7 ft. After the trenches are dug, additional long, shallow trenches must be made connecting the posts to receive the side braces. The function of these side braces is to hold both ends together solidly. It is necessary to bury these braces so they will be out of the way of the performer. The side braces are bolted to the posts just below the cross braces, so the bolts in both will not meet. The bars are dressed down so that a cross section is oval as shown in the end view. They are to be screwed to the notched ends of the uprights with the 6-in. screws. The holes should be countersunk so they can be filled with putty after the screws are in place. The bars should be well oiled with linseed oil to protect them from the weather, and in the winter they should be removed and stored.

Every piece of wood in this apparatus can be round and cut from trees, except the bars. If using mill-cut lumber, leave it undressed, and if using round timber leave the bark upon it as a protection from the weather. It is well to paint the entire apparatus, save the bars, before burying the lower part of the end pieces. The wood so treated will last for years, but even unpainted they are very durable. Be sure to tamp down the earth well about the posts. A smooth piece of ground should be selected on which to erect the apparatus.

(*To be Continued.*)

Combined Ladle and Strainer

When using a strainer in connection with a ladle the operation requires both

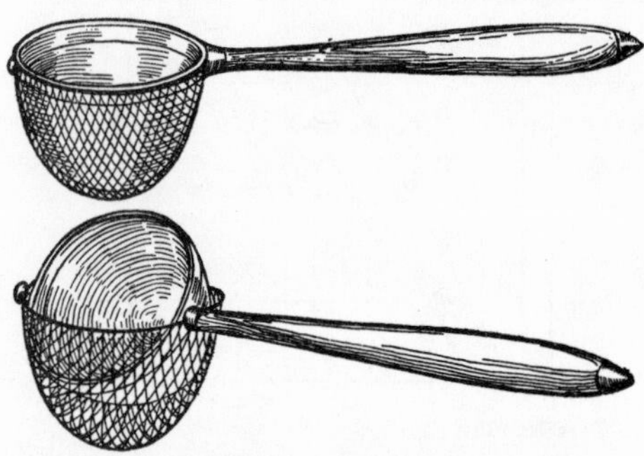

Ladle and Strainer

hands. A convenient article where a ladle and strainer are needed is to swing a cup-shaped strainer under the bowl of a ladle as shown in the illustration. The strainer can be held in place with small bands that fit loosely over the handle, and a small tip soldered to the ladle. These will allow the ladle to be turned, leaving the strainer always in position. A large sized ladle, equipped with a strainer, is just the thing for painters to dip and strain paint, while a small one is of great assistance to the housewife for dipping and straining soups, jellies, etc.—Contributed by W. A. Jaquythe, Richmond, Cal.

ℭA solution consisting of 1 dr. of sodium carbonate and 1 qt. of milk makes an excellent cleaner for motorists' gloves.

Turpentine in Cutting Oil

When cutting steel or wrought iron in a lathe, milling machine, drill press or planer, it is sometimes necessary to leave a smooth surface. Oil, or various cutting compounds of oil, is used for this purpose and to keep the surface cool. If a little turpentine is added to the oil, it will greatly assist in leaving a smooth surface. A proportion of one-quarter turpentine is good.

Center of Gravity Experiment

This experiment consists of suspending a pail of water from a stick placed upon a table as shown in the accompanying sketch. In order to accomplish this experiment, which seems impossible, it is necessary to place a stick, A, of sufficient length, between the end of the stick on the table and the bottom of the pail. This makes the center of gravity somewhere near the middle of the stick on the table, thus holding the pail as shown.

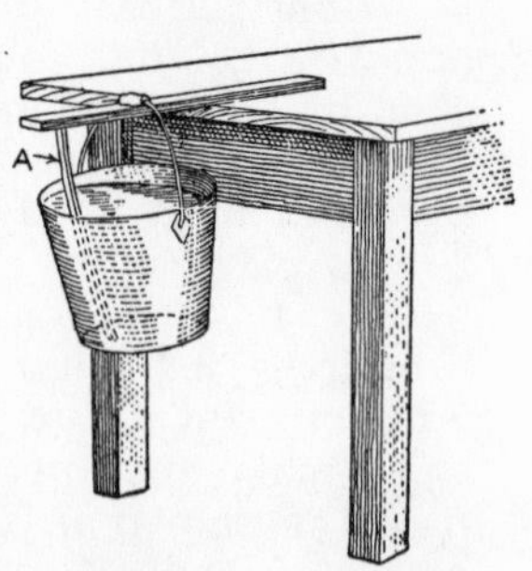

ℭA heavy lathe cut will not do accurate work.

An Outdoor Gymnasium

PART III—The Horse

The German horse is that peculiar piece of apparatus which is partly a horizontal obstruction to leap over, partly a barrier for jumps, partly a smooth surface of long and narrow dimensions over and about which the body may slide and swing, and partly an artificial back for the purpose of a peculiar style of leap frog.

The round part of this log must be planed, scraped and sandpapered until it is perfectly smooth, and free from knots, projections and splinters. Hand holds must be provided next. These are placed 18 in. apart in a central position on the horse. Make two parallel saw cuts 2 in. apart, straight down in the round surface of the horse until

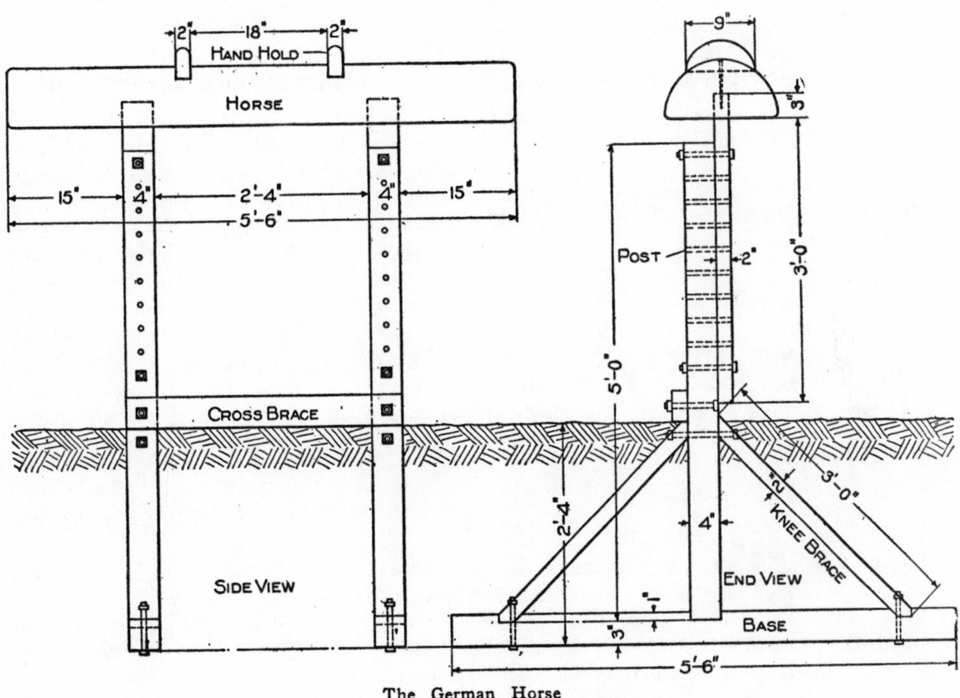

The German Horse

To make a horse for the outdoor "gym" requires no difficult work save the preparation of the top or body of the horse. The making of the regular gymnasium horse requires a very elaborate wood-working and leather upholstering plant, but the one used for outdoor work can be made of a log of wood. Procure from a saw mill, wood yard or from the woods, one-half of a tree trunk from a tree 9 to 15 in. in diameter—the larger the better. The length may be anywhere from 4 to 7 ft., but 5½ ft. is a good length.

each cut is 9 in. long. Chisel out the wood between the cuts and in the mortises thus made insert the hand holds. Each hand hold is made of a 9-in. piece of 2 by 4-in. stud cut rounding on one edge. These are well nailed in place.

The body of the horse is to be fastened on top of posts so that it may be adjusted for height. It is not as difficult to make as the horizontal and parallel bars. The material required is as follows: Two posts, 4 in. square by 5 ft. long; 2 adjusting pieces, 2 by 4 in. by 3 ft. 3 in. long; 1 cross brace,

2 by 4 in. by 3 ft. long; 2 bases, 4 in. square by 5½ ft. long; 4 knee braces, 2 by 4 in. by 3 ft. long; two ½-in. bolts, 9 in. long, to fasten the knee braces at the top; ten ½-in. bolts, 7 in. long, 4 to fasten the knee braces at the bottom, 2 to fasten the cross brace and 4 to be used in fastening the adjusting pieces to the posts.

To construct, lay out the bases as shown in the drawing, making the mortises to receive the bottom ends of the posts exactly in the center, and cut a slanting mortise 6 in. from each end to receive the ends of the knee braces. Bevel the ends of the knee braces and fasten the upper ends of each pair to the post with one 9-in. bolt. Fasten the lower ends to the base with the 7-in. bolts.

The upper end of each post should have ⅝-in. holes bored through it parallel to the base at intervals of 3 in., beginning 1½ in. from the top and extending down its length for 2 ft. 4½ in. The adjusting pieces are to be bored in a similar manner after which they are to be mortised into the under side of the horse top 15 in. from each end, and secured with screws put through the top and into the end of the adjusting pieces.

The bases with their posts and knee braces are buried 2 ft. 4 in. in the ground, parallel to each other and the same distance apart as the adjusting pieces are mortised in the horse top. When the ground has been filled in and tamped hard, the cross brace should be bolted in position with its lower edge resting on the ground and connecting the two posts.

The height of the horse from the ground is adjusted by changing the bolts in the different holes connecting the two adjusting pieces with the two posts. Much pleasant and healthful gymnastic exercise can be had in competitive horse jumping and leaping, the handles providing a way to make many different leaps through, over and around, including not only those made to see who can go over the horse from a standing or running start at the greatest height, but who can go over at the greatest height when starting from the "toeing off mark" farthest away from the horse. This horse should be located on level ground having smooth space about it for several feet.

Spoon Rest for Kettles

A rest for keeping spoons from slipping into kettles can be made from a strip of metal bent as shown in the illustration. The spring of the metal will make it easy to apply to the kettle. The spoon placed in the rest will drain back into the kettle. The cover can be placed on without removing the spoon.—Contributed by W. A. Jaquythe, Richmond, Cal.

Reason for Bursting of Gun Barrels

Gun barrels do not burst without a cause and usually that cause is one of which the shooter is entirely ignorant, but nevertheless, no one is responsible but himself, says the Sporting Goods Dealer. Gun barrels can only burst by having some obstruction in the barrel or by overloading with powder. Any gun barrel can be burst by misuse or by carelessly loading smokeless powder, but no barrel will burst by using factory loaded ammunition, provided there is no obstruction or foreign substance inside the barrel. When a gun barrel bursts at the breech or chamber, it is caused by an overloaded shell, and when it bursts in the center or near the muzzle, it is caused by some obstruction, such as a dent, snow, water, etc.

Hand Sled Made of Pipe and Fittings

The accompanying sketch shows how an ordinary hand sled can be made of ¾-in. pipe and fittings. Each runner is made of one piece of pipe bent to the proper shape. This can be accomplished by filling the pipe with melted rosin or lead, then bending to the shape desired, and afterward removing the rosin or lead by heating. Each joint is turned up tightly and well pinned or brazed. One of the top crosspieces should have right-hand and left-hand threads or be fitted with a union. Also, one of the top pieces connecting the rear part to the front part of each runner must be fitted in the same way. The top is fastened to the two crosspieces.

Such a hand sled can be made in a

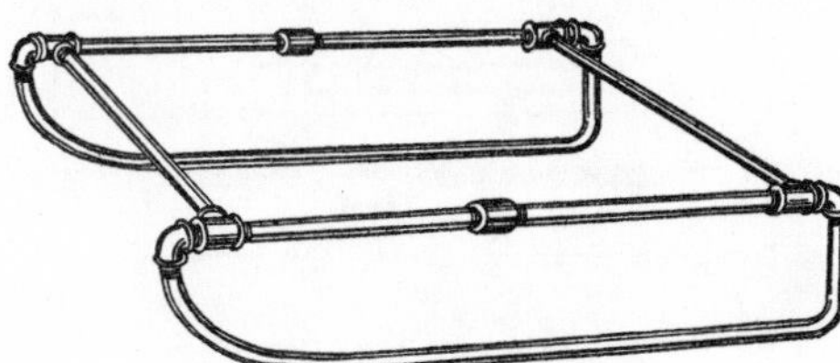

Parts Made of Pipe Fittings

few hours' time and, when complete, is much better than a wood sled.—Contributed by James E. Noble, Toronto, Ontario.

Emergency Magnifying Glass

When in need of a microscope in the study of botany, one may be made in the following manner: Bend a small wire or the stem of a leaf so as to form a small loop not larger than the ordi-

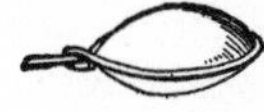

Loop Inclosing a Drop of Water

nary drop of water. When this is done place a drop of clear water in the loop and the microscope is complete. This temporary device will prove valuable where a strong magnifying glass is not at hand.—Contributed by Arthur E. Joerin, Paris, France.

Bent-Iron Pipe Rack

Strips of soft iron, ¼ or $\frac{3}{16}$ in. in width and $\frac{1}{32}$ in. thick, are used in

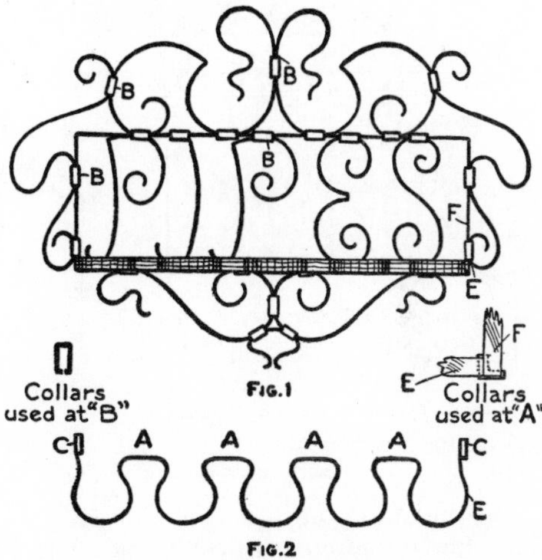

Design of a Rack

making the pipe rack shown in Fig. 1. This material can be obtained from any local hardware dealer who carries bar iron in stock.

Draw a full-size sketch of the design on paper, then run a string over each part, which, when straightened out, will give the length. The scrolls are bent with a pair of round-nose pliers. These, with a pair of flat-nose pliers, are all the tools necessary. The part for holding the pipes is shown in Fig. 2. The end elevation, at E and F, shows how the rack is fastened to the main frame of the rack.—Contributed by J. W. Vener, Boston, Mass.

To Clean Silver

A good method to clean silver of any kind is to place the articles in an aluminum vessel and add a few pieces of zinc. Hot water is added and the silver boiled until clean. It is best to use soft water. The tarnish is removed by the electrolytic action of the zinc on the aluminum and the silver, and the latter will take on a bright luster. This method of cleaning will not injure oxidized or black silver, nor that which is partly oxidized.

Sharpening Skates with a File

Two methods are shown in the sketches for filing skates—one for hollow filing and the other for filing flat

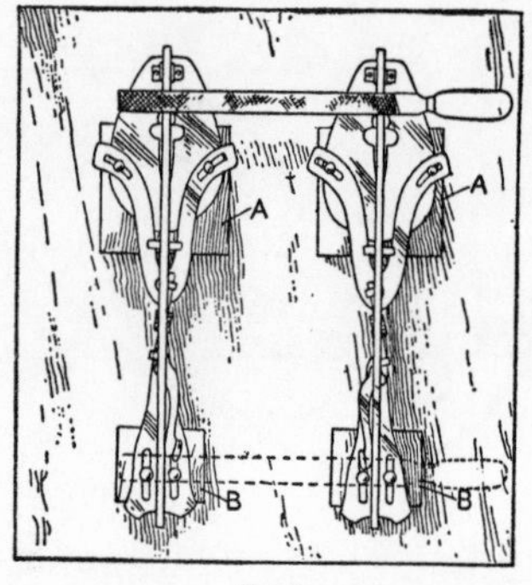

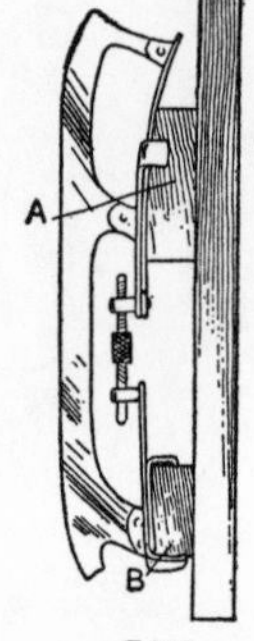

Filing a Flat Surface

and straight across the blade. The method shown in Figs. 1 and 2 is for filing the blade flat. The device for holding the skates consists of a board on which four blocks, AA and BB, are nailed. These blocks are fastened on the board in the relative positions of the heel and sole on a shoe. The skates are clamped on them in the same manner as on a shoe. A flat file is drawn across both blades of the skates as shown. After the roundness is cut down on the edges of the blades the skates are removed and the file is drawn along the sides to remove the

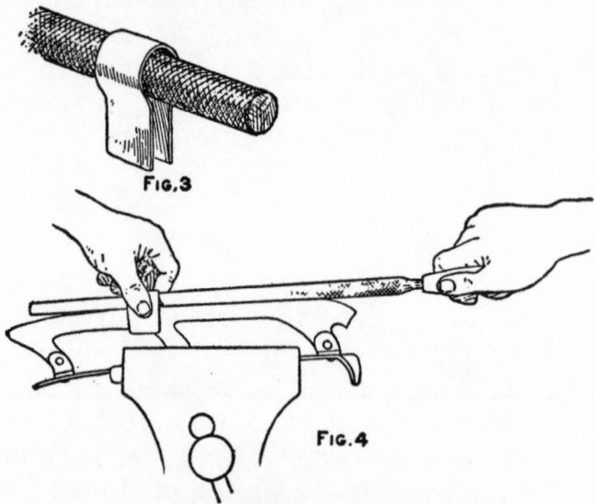

Filing a Curved Surface

burr. Skates filed in this way have flat surfaces with sharp edges.

Some skaters like a hollow-ground skate and the method shown in Figs. 3 and 4 can be used for filing a slightly curved surface in the blade. A piece of tin or sheet metal is shaped over a round file as shown in Fig. 3. The manner of filing the curves is shown in Fig. 4. The piece of metal is held over the file and blade of the skate as the file is worked.

Lines and Letters Made with a Carpenter's Pencil

The sketch shows some unusual work made with a carpenter's pencil. If the flat lead is notched with a three-cornered file (Fig. 1), two parallel lines may be drawn at one stroke, or various rulings may be made, as shown in Fig. 2. Broad lines can be made, as shown in Fig. 3, or unequal widths as in Fig. 4.

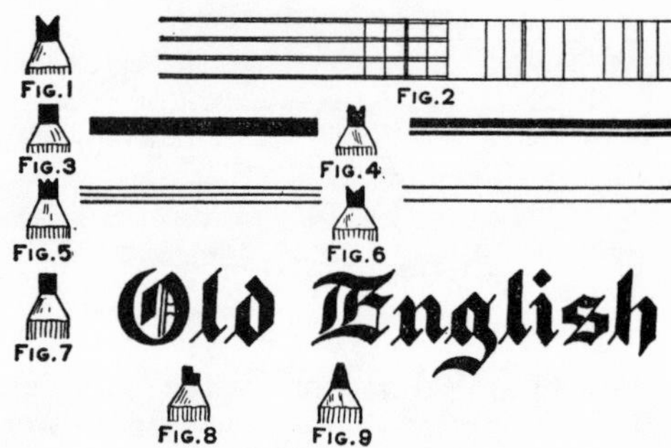

Pencil Points and Their Work

In Figs. 2, 5 and 6 are shown lines especially adapted for the bookkeeper or draftsman. If one lacks the ability to draw old English letters with a pen, the letters may be first drawn with a carpenter's pencil (Fig. 7) and the outlines marked with ink and finally filled in. Narrow lines are made with points cut as in Figs. 8 and 9. A little practice with the carpenter's pencil in making these letters will enable the student to finally produce them with the pen used for the purpose.

Aluminum wire plunged hot into a cold solution of carbonate of soda becomes coated with a strong layer of oxide which forms an excellent insulator to electricity.

How to Build an Ice-Yacht*

The plans and specifications shown in the illustrations are for making a 400-ft. class ice-yacht, having a double cockpit to accommodate four persons. The weight of the persons in the forward cockpit keeps the boat from rearing when in a stiff breeze. The forward cockpit can be removed if necessary.

The materials used are: backbone, white pine; center, clear spruce; sides, white oak caps; runner plank, basswood, butternut or oak; cockpit, oak; runners, chocks, etc., quartered white oak. All the iron work should be first-grade Swedish iron, with the exception of the runners, which are soft cast iron.

It is not necessary to go into detail with the measurements as they are plainly shown in the sketches. The backbone is 37½ ft. over all, 12 in. in the center, 5 in. stern, 3½ in. at the nose; width 4¼ in. All wood should be selected from the best grades, well seasoned and free from checks. In Fig. 1 is shown the complete ice-yacht with general dimensions for the sail and main parts. Other dimensions are shown in Fig. 2. The backbone is capped on the upper and lower edges full length with strips of oak, 4¼ in. wide and ⅝ in. thick. The lengthwise side strips of spruce are 1¼ in. thick. The filling-in pieces placed between the side pieces are of seasoned white pine, leaving the open places as shown in Fig. 2. The parts are put together with hot glue and brass screws.

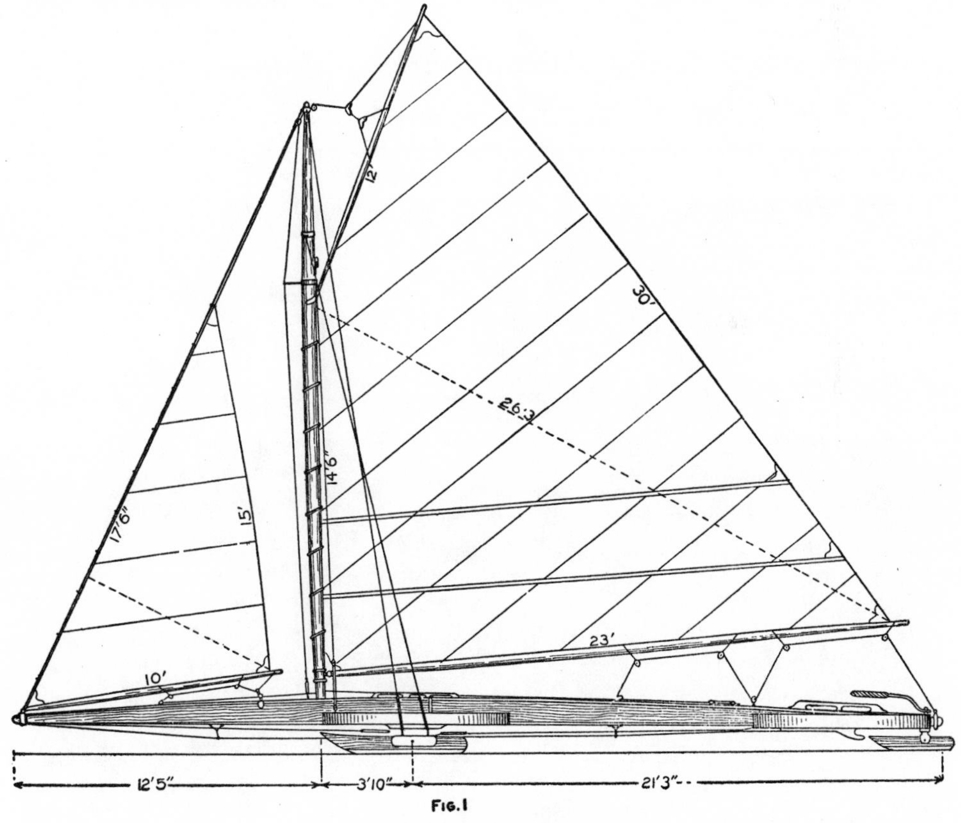

Fig. 1
Ice-Yacht Complete

The runner plank should be placed

*Condensed from an article by H. Percy Ashley in Rudder.

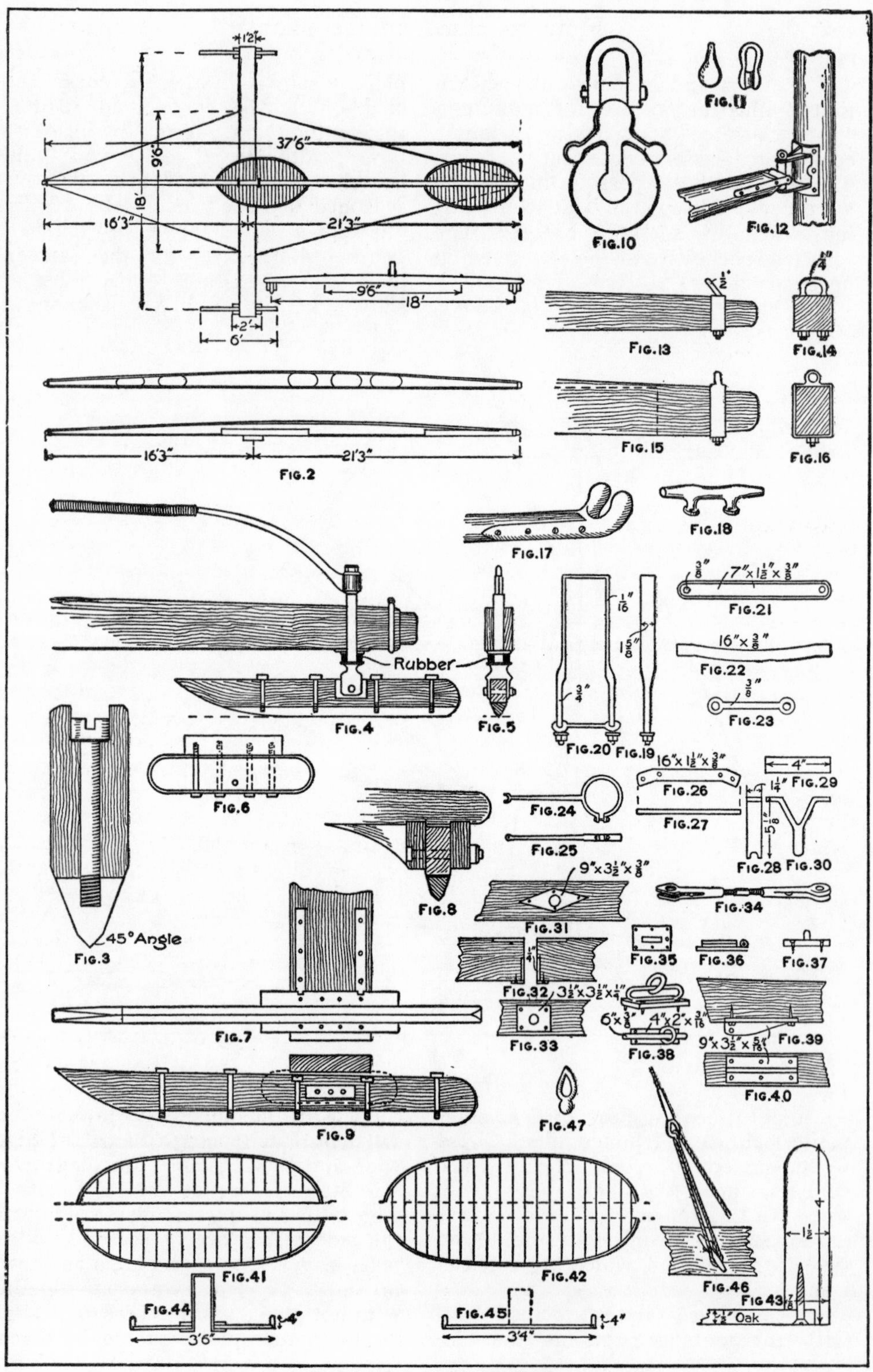

Details of the Ice-Yacht Parts

with the heart of the wood up, so as to give the natural curve from the ice so that it will act as a spring. The plank is 16 in. wide in the center, 14 in. at the ends; 4⅛ in. thick at the center and 2¾ in. at the ends.

Details of the runners are shown in Figs. 3, 4, 5, 6, 7, 8 and 9. The cast iron shoes are filed and finished with emery paper, making the angle on the cutting edge 45 deg. on both sides. The runners are 7¼ in. wide over all and 2⅛ in. thick. The soft iron casting is 2¼ in. deep. The shoes are fastened by ⅝-in. machine bolts. These are shown in Figs. 3 and 9. The rudder is 2¾ in. thick, 5 in. deep, including wood and iron, and 3 ft. long. The cast iron shoe is 1⅞ in. deep and fastened on with four ½-in. machine bolts. A brass plate, ¼ in. thick, 2 in. wide and 7 in. long, is inserted on each side of the runners as shown in Fig. 9. Three holes are drilled through for a ¾-in. riding bolt that can be shifted as desired for rough or smooth ice. The runner chocks and guides are 1⅞ in. thick and 4½ in. deep. They are set in the runner plank ¼ in. and fastened with glue and ½-in. lag screws. These are shown in Figs. 6 and 7.

The aft cockpit is stationary, while the fore or passenger cockpit can be removed at will. Both cockpits are the same size, 42 in. wide and 7 ft. long over all. Each one has a bent rail, 1½ in. by 4 in., grooved ½ in. by ⅞ in. before bending. The flooring is of oak, 1½ in. thick and 4 in. wide, tongue-and-grooved. The forward cockpit is made in halves and hung on the backbone with wrought-iron straps and bolts. These are shown in Figs. 41, 43 and 44. Two pieces of oak, ½ in. by 4 in. are fastened with screws to the flooring, parallel with the backbone in the forward cockpit. The runner plank which passes under this cockpit gives it stability.

The spars should be hollow and have the following dimensions: Mast, 23 ft. 3 in.; heel, 3¾ in.; center, 5¼ in.; tip, 4 in.; boom 23½ ft.; heel, 3¾ in.; center, 4 in.; tip, 2⅞ in. at ends; gaff, 12½ ft.; center, 3½ in.; ends, 2½ in.; jib-boom, 10½ ft.; 1¾ in. at the ends, 2⅛ in. at the center. The gaff is furnished with bent jaws of oak, Fig. 17, and the main boom with gooseneck, Fig. 12.

Galvanized cast-steel yacht rigging, $\frac{5}{16}$ in. in diameter, is used for the shrouds; jibstay, ⅜ in. in diameter; runner plank guys, $\frac{5}{16}$ in. in diameter; bobstay, ⅜ in. in diameter; martingale stay, ¼ in. in diameter. The throat and peak halyards are ⅜ in. in diameter; jib halyards, ¼ in. in diameter.

The main sheet rigging is $\frac{9}{16}$-in. Russian bolt rope; jibs, $\frac{7}{16}$-in. manila bolt rope, 4-strand; jib-sheet, ⅜-in. manila bolt rope. Four ½-in. bronze turnbuckles, Fig. 34, are used for the shrouds; one ⅝-in. turnbuckle for the jibstay and one for the bobstay; four ⅜-in. turnbuckles for the runner plank stays, and one for the martingale stay.

Two rope blocks for ⅜-in. wire rope, Fig. 10, are used for the peak and throat, and one block for the wire rope ¼ in. in diameter for the jib halyard. Four 6-in. and one 7-in. cleats, Fig. 18, are used. The blocks shown in Fig. 11 are used for the main and jib sheets. The steering arrangement is shown in Figs. 4 and 5. The tiller is 3½ ft. long; rudder post, 1¼ in. in diameter; shoulder to lower end of jaws, 4 in.; depth of jaws, 2⅞ in.; length of post including screw top, 12 in. The rubber washer acts as a spring on rough ice.

In Figs. 13, 14, 15 and 16 are shown metal bands for the nose of the backbone, and Figs. 19, 20, 21, 22 and 23 show the saddles that fit over the backbone and hold the runner plank in place. There are two sets of these. A chock should be sunk in the runner plank at each side to connect with the backbone to keep it from slipping sidewise as the boat rises in the air. The martingale spreader is shown in Figs. 24 and 25. Straps through which the ring bolts for the shrouds pass on the ends to fasten the turnbuckles for the runner plank guys are shown in Figs. 26 and 27. The bobstay spreaders are shown in Figs. 28, 29 and 30. In Fig. 31 is shown the top plate for the rudder post and in Figs. 32 and 33, the lower plate for same. The mast step is shown in Figs. 35, 36 and 37. Two positions of the jib traveler are shown in Fig. 38. The anchor plate for the bobstay under the cockpit is shown in Figs. 39 and 40.

At the nose and heel the runner plank guys end in a loop. The bobstay has a loop at the nose and ends in a turnbuckle that fastens to the anchor plate under the cockpit, aft. The shrouds, jibstay and martingale have loops at the masthead and are spliced bare over solid thimbles. The loops are finished in pigskin and served with soft cotton twine over the splice and varnished. The parceling is done with insulating tape. Serve the tiller with soft cotton twine and ride a second serving over the first. For the halyards hoisting use a jig shown in Fig. 46. The thimble shown in Fig. 47 is made by splicing the rope to the thimble at running part of halyard and passing back and forth through cleat and thimble. This gives a quick and strong purchase and does away with cumbersome blocks of the old-fashioned jig. The jib-sheet leads aft to the steering cockpit. The main-sheet ends in a jig of a single block and a single block with becket. Be sure that your sail covers are large enough—the sail maker always makes them too tight. The cockpit covers must fit tightly around the cockpit rail. Many boats have sail and cockpit covers in one piece.

The woodwork may be finished as desired by the builder. The dimensions of the sails are given in the general drawing, Fig. 1.

Turning Lights On and Off from Any Number of Places

This can be done by the use of any number of reversing switches such as

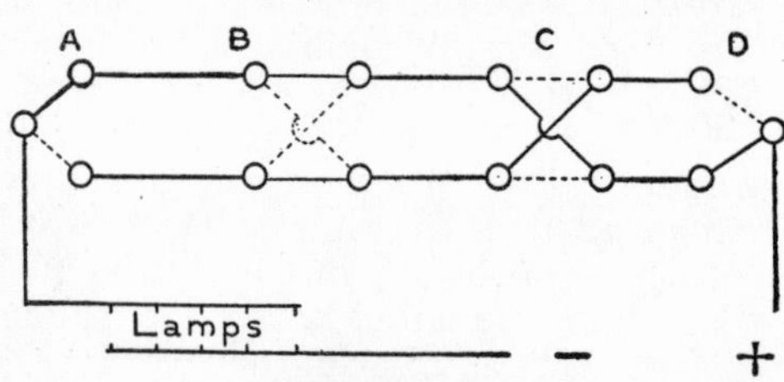

Wiring Diagram

those shown at B and C. These are inserted between the two-way switches A and D. Turning such a switch up or down connects the four contact pieces either diagonally as at C, or lengthwise as at B. The diagram shows connection from A to D, when the lamps will be on, but by turning either of these four switches into its alternative position, shown by the dotted lines, the circuit will be broken and the lights extinguished. When this has been done, the circuit may be restored and the lamps lighted again by altering either of the four switches in exactly the same way, and so on.

It will be observed that a reversing switch used in this way practically undoes whatever is done by the other switches. In the accompanying diagram only two reversing switches are shown and the lights can be independently controlled from four distinct positions. Any number of reversing switches can be placed between the two-way switches A and D to increase the number of places from which the lights could be turned on and off.—Contributed by J. S. Dow, Mayfield, London.

How to Make an Electric Pendant Switch

It is often desired to use a pendant switch for controlling clusters of incandescent lamps. When such a switch is not at hand, a very good substitute can be made by screwing a common fuse plug into a key socket and connecting the socket in series with the lamps to be controlled. In this way you get a safe, reliable, fused switch.—Contributed by C. C. Heyder, Hansford, W. Va.

¶Never guess the length of a piece ot work—measure it.

Home-Made Water Motor

The small water motor shown in the illustration is constructed in the same manner as a German toy steam turbine. The wheel, which is made of aluminum $\frac{1}{16}$ in. thick and 7 in. in diameter, has 24 blades attached to it.

The lugs or extensions carrying the rim must be made from the metal of the wheel, therefore a circle 8 in. in diameter must be first described on the aluminum plate, then another circle 7 in. in diameter within the first and then a circle for the base of the blades, 3½ in. in diameter. Twenty-four radial lines at equal distances apart are drawn between the two smaller circles and a ¼-in. hole drilled at the intersecting points of the radial lines and the innermost circle.

Centrally between each pair of radial lines and between the two outer circles, ½ by ⅜-in. lugs are marked out and the metal cut away as shown in Fig. 1. A ⅛-in. hole is then drilled in the center of each lug. Each division is separated by cutting down each radial line to the ¼-in. hole with a hacksaw. Each arm is then given a quarter turn, as shown by the dotted lines in Fig. 2, and the lug bent over at right angles to receive the rim. The rim is made of the same material as the disk and contains twenty-four ⅛-in. holes corresponding to those in the lugs to receive brass bolts ¼-in. long.

The disks PP were taken from the ends of a discarded typewriter platen, but if these cannot be readily obtained, they can be turned from metal or a heavy flat disk used instead.

The casing was made from two aluminum cake pans whose diameter was 8 in. at the base, increasing to 9 in. at the rim. The centers of these were located and a ¼-in. hole drilled for the shaft. The disks P are the same as used on the wheel. Six holes ⅛-in. in diameter were drilled through the flat part of the rims while the two halves were held together in a vise. Bolts were placed through these holes to join the casing when ready for assembling. One side of the casing was then bolted to two 4-in. ordinary metal shelf brackets which were

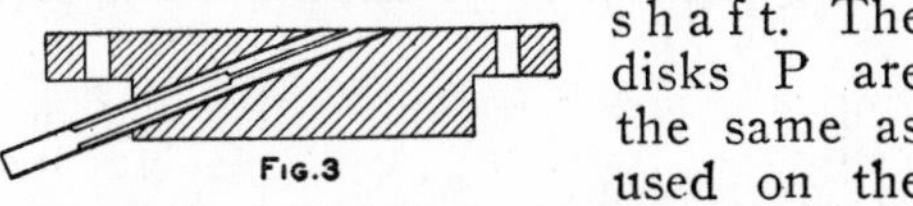

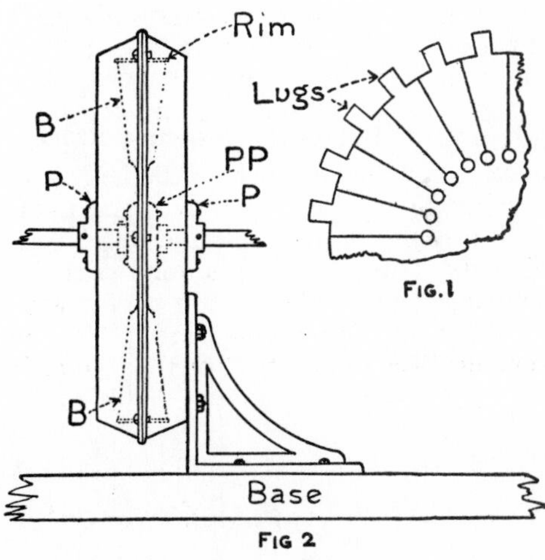

Details of Motor

screwed to a substantial wood base. This kept one-half of the casing independent of the main structure so that the wheel is easily accessible.

The nozzle was made of ½-in. brass pipe which was first filled with molten babbitt metal. When the metal was cool, a ¼-in. hole was drilled halfway through the length of the tube, the hole being continued through to the other end by means of a ⅛-in. drill. The lower orifice was then slightly enlarged with a small taper reamer, and the upper portion of the bore was reamed out almost to the brass to make a smooth entrance for the water.

A fixture to hold this nozzle is shown in Fig. 3. It was cast of babbitt metal in a wood mold. The hole for the nozzle was drilled at an angle of 20 deg. to the plate part. An alternative and perhaps easier way would be to insert the nozzle in the mold at the proper angle and cast the metal around it. A hole was then cut in one of the sides of the casing at a point 2⅞ in. along a horizontal line from the center. The nozzle fixture was then bolted on with the exit orifice of the nozzle pointing downward and through the hole in the casing.

Six 1/8-in. holes were drilled through the flat portions of the rims while the two halves of the casing were held securely together in a vise. Bolts were used in these holes to join the casing.

The wheel was used on the drip-board of a kitchen sink and no provision was made to carry off the spent water except to cut two 1/2-in. holes in the bottom of the casing and allowing the waste to flow off directly into the sink.—Contributed by Harry F. Lowe, Washington, D. C.

Device for Baseball Throwing Practice

Anyone training to be a baseball player will find the device shown in the accompanying illustration a great help

Ball Bounding on Concrete Slabs

when practicing alone. It consists of two cement slabs, one flat and upright, the other curved and on the ground. The vertical slab is fastened securely against a fence, barn or shed. The barn or the shed is preferable, for if the slab is fastened to a fence, the ball will bound over a great many times and much time will be lost in finding it.

The player stands as far as he cares from the slabs and throws the ball against the lower slab. The ball immediately rebounds to the upright slab and returns with almost as great a force as it was delivered. If the thrower does not throw the ball exactly in the same spot each time, the ball will not rebound to the same place, consequently the eye and muscles are trained to act quickly, especially if the player stands within 15 or 20 ft. of the slabs and throws the ball with great force.

This apparatus also teaches a person to throw accurately, as a difference in aim of a few inches on the lower slab may cause the ball to fly away over the player's head on the rebound.—Contributed by F. L. Oilar, La Fayette, Indiana.

How to Mail Photographs

Cut a piece of cardboard 1 in. longer and 1 in. wider than the mount of the photograph and lay the picture on it in the center. This allows a 1/2-in. border on all sides of the photograph. Punch two holes 1 in. apart at A, B, C and D, Fig. 1, in the cardboard border close to the edge of the picture. Put a string up through the hole B, Fig. 2, then across the corner of the photograph and down through the hole C and up through hole D, then to E, etc., until the starting point A is reached, and tie the ends.

The photograph will not get damaged, if it is covered with tissue paper and placed with the face to the cardboard. The extension border of cardboard prevents the edges of the mount from being damaged and the corners

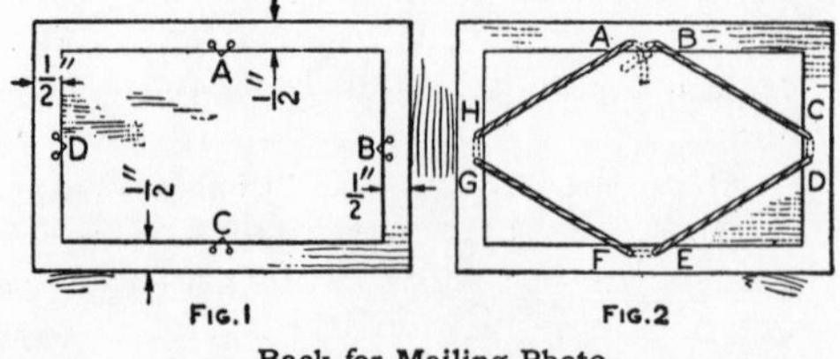

Back for Mailing Photo

from wearing. Both cardboard and photograph are wrapped together in paper, and the package is ready for mailing.—Contributed by Earl R. Hastings, Corinth, Vt.

A Mystifying Watch Trick

Borrow a watch from one of the audience and allow the owner to place it in the box, as shown in Fig. 1. This box should be about 3 in. long, 4 in. wide and 2½ in. deep, says the Scientific American. It should be provided with a hinged cover, M, with a lock, N. The tricky part of this box is the side S, which is pivoted at T by driving two short nails into it, one through the front side and the other through the back, so that when S is pushed in at the top, it swings around as shown in Fig. 1 and allows the watch to slide out into the performer's hand. The side S should fit tightly when closed, so that the box may be examined without betraying the secret. As the side S extends down to the bottom of the box, it facilitates the use of the fingers in pulling outward at the lower part while the thumb is pressing inward at the top part. The side of the box opposite S should be built up in the same way, but not pivoted.

Use a flat-bottom tumbler, A, Fig. 2, containing an inner cone, B, for the reproduction of the watch. The cone is made of cardboard pasted together so it fits snugly inside of the tumbler. The cone is closed except at the bottom, then bran is pasted on the outside surfaces to make the tumbler appear as if filled with bran when it is in place. Place the tumbler with the cone inside on a table somewhat in the background. Put some loose bran on top of the cone and allow the cork, attached as shown in B, Fig. 2, to hang down on the outside of the tumbler, away from the audience. A large handkerchief should be laid beside the tumbler.

After the watch has been placed in the box, Fig. 1, the performer takes the box in his left hand, and while in the act of locking it with his right hand secures possession of the watch as previously explained. Tossing the key to the owner of the watch, the performer places the box on a chair or table near the audience and, with the watch securely palmed, walks back to get the tumbler. Standing directly in front of the tumbler with his back toward the audience, the performer

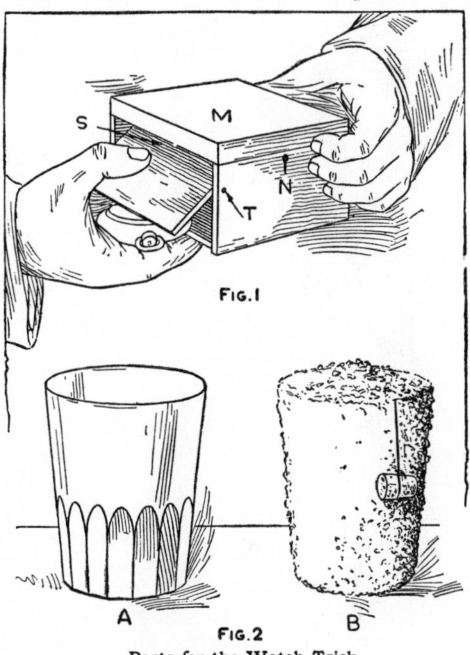

Parts for the Watch Trick

quickly raises the cone with his right hand, lays the watch in the bottom of the tumbler and replaces the cone.

The loaded tumbler and the handkerchief are then brought forward, and the former is placed in full view of the audience with the cork hanging down behind it. The performer calls attention to the tumbler being full of bran and picks up some of it from the top to substantiate his statement. He then spreads the handkerchief over the tumbler, commands the watch to pass from the box into the tumbler and the bran to disappear.

The box is then handed to the owner of the watch so that he may unlock it with the key he holds. As soon as the box is found to be empty, the performer grasps the handkerchief spread over the tumbler, also the cork tied to the cone. Raising the handkerchief, he carries up the cone within it, leaving the watch in the bottom to be returned to its owner.

Locking Several Drawers with One Lock

A series or row of drawers can be secured with one lock by using the device shown in the sketch. This method takes away several dangling locks and the carrying of many keys. A rod is used through the various staples over the hasps. The rod is upset on one end and flattened to make sufficient metal for drilling a hole large enough to insert the bar of a padlock. If the bar is made of steel and hardened, it is almost impossible to cut it in two.—Contributed by F. W. Bentley, Huron, S. Dak.

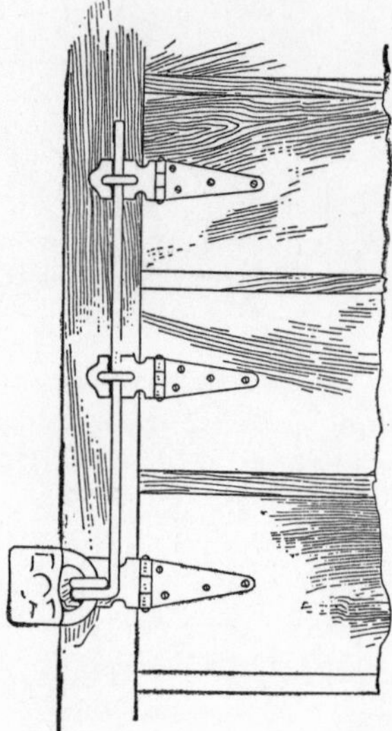

Testing Small Electric Lamps

The accompanying sketch shows the construction of a handy device for testing miniature electric lights. The base is made to take in an electric flash lamp battery. Two strips of brass, C and D, are connected to the battery. The lamp is tested by putting the metal end on the lower brass strip and the side against the upper one. A great number of lamps can be tested in a short time by means of this device.—Contributed by Abner B. Shaw, North Dartmouth, Mass.

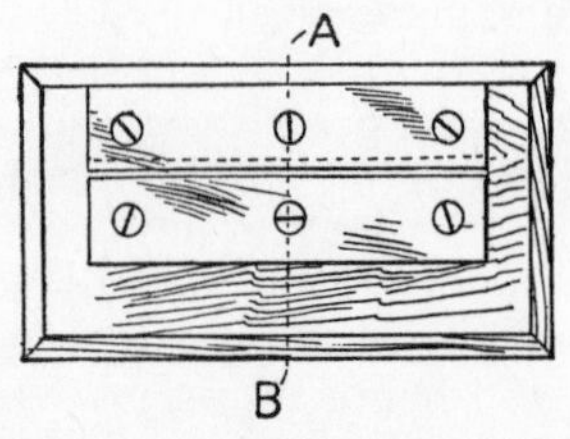

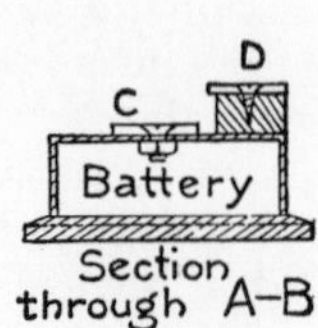

Lamp Tester

How to Make a Pin Ball

The pin ball shown in the illustration is made of calfskin modeling leather and saddler's felt. Two pieces of leather are used, and one piece of felt, all three being cut circular to a diameter of about 3 in. The felt may be about ½ in. thick, and leather of a deep brown color is recommended.

Moisten the leather on the back side with as much water as it will take without showing through the face. Lay it on a sheet of heavy glass or copper, or other hard, smooth, nonabsorbent material. Place the design, which has been previously prepared, over the face of the leather. Indent the outline of the design with a nutpick or any other pointed tool that will not cut the leather. Remove the pattern, and go over the outline again to deepen the tool marks.

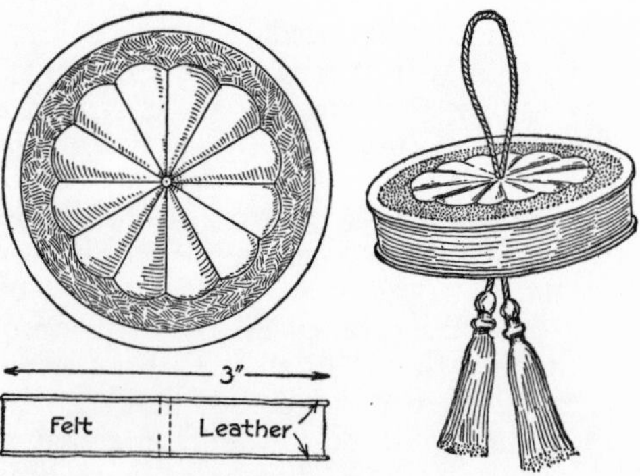

Made of Leather and Felt

The space between the border and the design is now stamped with a cup-pointed nail set, care being taken not to cut the leather, especially if the tool be new. Rubbing the edges of the nail set over a piece of emery paper will serve to dull them, if they are too sharp.

When the designs have been worked on the leather, paste or glue the leather to the two sides of the belt, and punch a hole in the center through which to place a cord for hanging up the ball.

Cleaning Woodwork

An easy method of removing the dirt and old varnish at the same time around a kitchen sink is told by a correspondent of National Magazine as follows:

Make a soft soap from common yellow laundry soap, and when it is almost cold stir in one tablespoonful of concentrated lye and one-half cupful of kerosene. When the mixture becomes a heavy paste, it is ready to be spread over the woodwork with a paint brush. Allow the soap to remain for a day and a half, then wash it off with plenty of hot water. The woodwork will be clean and ready for varnishing when it dries out.

Bill File Made of Corkscrews

An ordinary corkscrew makes a convenient file for small bills or memoranda. It may be thrown in any position without danger of the papers slipping off. A rack to hold a number of files can be made of a wood strip (Fig. 1) fitted with hooks or screweyes cut in a hook shape, as shown in Fig. 2.

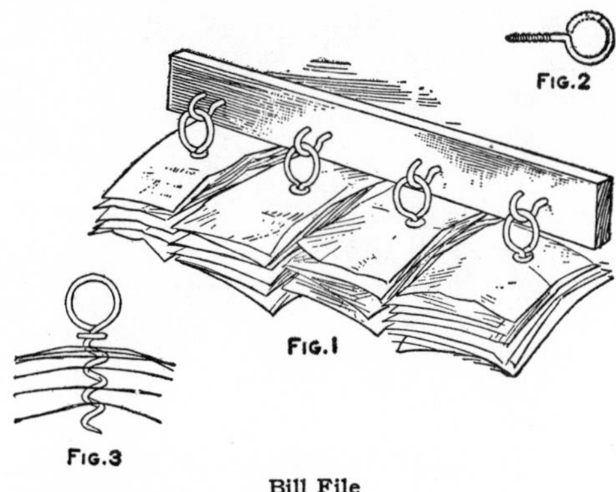

Bill File

Single bills may be separated from the others and will remain separated as in Fig. 3.—Contributed by James M. Kane, Doylestown, Pa.

Ornamental Metal Inkstand

The metal required for making this stand is $\frac{3}{16}$ in. in width and may be

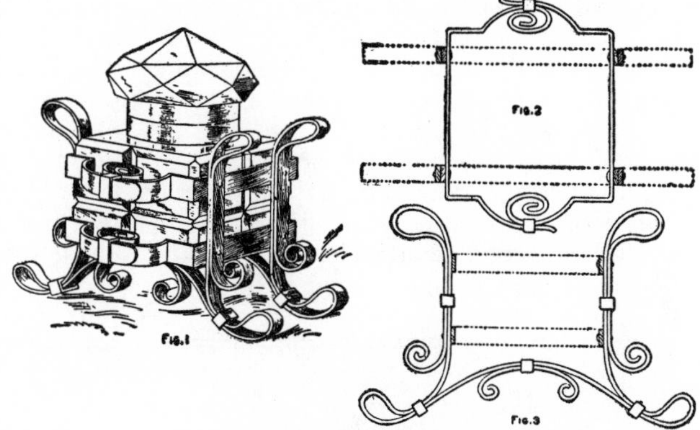

Inkstand and Details of Frame

steel, brass or copper. The shaping is done as shown in Figs. 2 and 3. There are, in all, eight pieces to be bent. The two supports are each formed of one piece of metal with the exception that the end scroll pieces on the under side are made separately. Eight rivets are required to fasten the two horizontal rings to the supports. The glass receptacle can be purchased at a stationery store.

Holding Eyeglasses Firm

Persons who wear noseglasses and who are troubled with excessive perspiration, should chalk the sides of the bridge of the nose before putting on the glasses. The latter will then never slip, even in the warmest weather. If the chalk shows, use a pink stick, which can be purchased from any art school or supply store.

Substitute for Gummed Paper

Gummed paper is a great convenience in the home especially for labels, but it is not always found among the household supplies. The gummed portions of unsealed envelopes in which circulars are received can be utilized for this purpose. Quite a large label may be made from these envelope flaps.

Repairing a Broken Phonograph Spring

As I live a great distance from a railroad station, I did not care to pay the price, and await the time necessary to deliver a new phonograph spring to replace one that broke in my machine, and I repaired the old one in a creditable manner as follows:

I forced the two ends of the break out where I could get at them, then heated each end separately with a pair of redhot tongs and turned a hook or lap on them the same as the joints in knock-down stovepipes. When the ends were hooked together, the spring worked as good as new. The heated portion did not affect the strength of the spring.—Contributed by Marion P. Wheeler, Greenleaf, Oregon.

If you wish to know whether or not the door or telephone bell rings during your absence, place a little rider of paper or cardboard on the clapper in such a way that it will be dislodged if the bell rings.

A Small Bench Lathe Made of Pipe Fittings

The most important machine in use in the modern machine or wood-working shop is the lathe. The uses to which this wonderful machine can be put would be too numerous to describe, but there is hardly a mechanical operation in which the turning lathe does not figure. For this reason every amateur mechanic and wood-worker who has a workshop, no matter how small, is anxious to possess a lathe of some sort. A good and substantial home-made lathe, which is suitable for wood-turning and light metal work, may be constructed from pipe and pipe fittings as shown in the accompanying sketch.

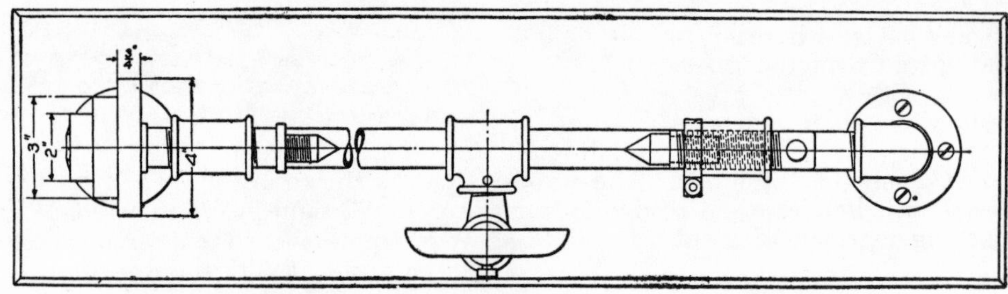

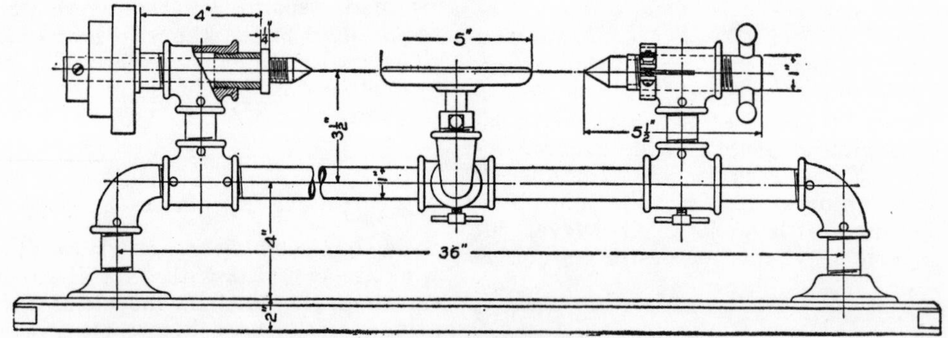

Fig. 1—Details of Lathe

The bed of this lathe is made of a piece of 1-in. pipe, about 30 in. long. It can be made longer or shorter, but if it is made much longer, a larger size of pipe should be used. The headstock is made of two tees, joined by a standard long nipple as shown in Fig. 1. All the joints should be screwed up tight and then fastened with $\frac{3}{16}$-in. pins to keep them from turning. The ends of the bed are fixed to the baseboard by means of elbows, nipples and flanges arranged as shown. The two bearings in the headstock are of brass. The spindle hole should be drilled and reamed after they are screwed in place in the tee. The spindle should be of steel and long enough to reach through the bearing and pulley and have enough end left for the center point. The point should extend about 1½ in. out from the collar. The collar can be turned or shrunk on the spindle as desired. The end of the spindle should be threaded to receive a chuck.

The tailstock is also made of two tees joined by a nipple. The lower tee should be bored out for a sliding fit on the bed pipe. The upper one should be tapped with a machine tap for the spindle which is threaded to fit it. The spindle has a handle fitted at one end and has the other end bored out for the tailstock center.

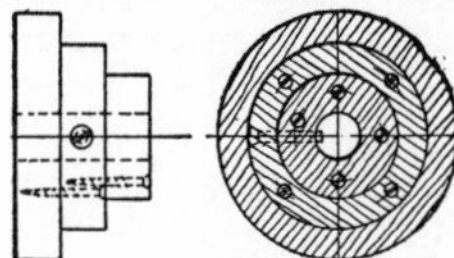
Fig. 2

Both the tailstock and the headstock centerpoints should be hardened. A clamp for holding the tailstock spindle is made of a piece of strap iron, bent and drilled as shown. It is held together by means of a small machine screw and a knurled nut. The tee should have a slot cut in it about one-half its length and it should also have one bead filed away so that the clamp will fit tightly over it.

The hand rest is made from a tapering elbow, a tee and a forging. The forging can be made by a blacksmith at a small expense. Both the lower tees of the hand-rest and the tailstock should be provided with screw clamps to hold them in place.

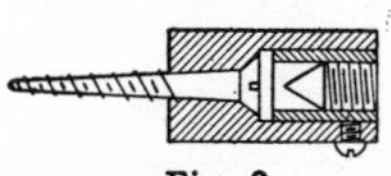
Fig. 3

The pulley is made of hardwood pieces, ¾ or 1 in. thick as desired. It is fastened to the spindle by means of a screw, as shown in Fig. 2, or a key can be used as well.

Care must be taken to get the tailstock center vertically over the bed, else taper turning will result. To do this, a straight line should be scratched

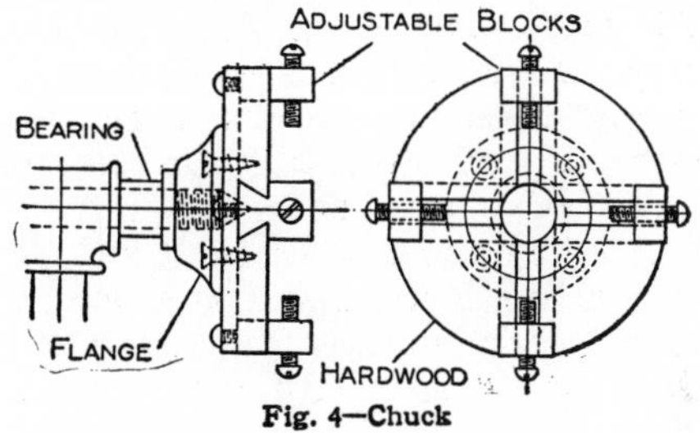

Fig. 4—Chuck

on the top of the bed pipe, and when the tailstock is set exactly vertical, a corresponding line made on this. This will save a great deal of time and trouble and possibly some errors.

The two designs of chucks shown in Figs. 3 and 4 are very easy to make, and will answer for a great variety of work.

As the details are clearly shown and the general dimensions given on the accompanying sketches, it should not be a difficult matter for the young mechanic to construct this machine.—Contributed by W. M. Held, Laporte, Indiana.

Holder for Flexible Lamp-Cord

The holder is made of a round stick—a piece of a broom handle will do—as shown in Fig. 1. It is about 1 in. long with two notches cut out for the strands of the cord. These holders are easily made and will answer the purpose almost as well as the ones made in porcelain. Painting or enameling will improve not only their appearance, but also their insulating properties. Several of them can be used along a line, as shown in Fig. 2.—Contributed by M. Musgrove, Boissevain, Man.

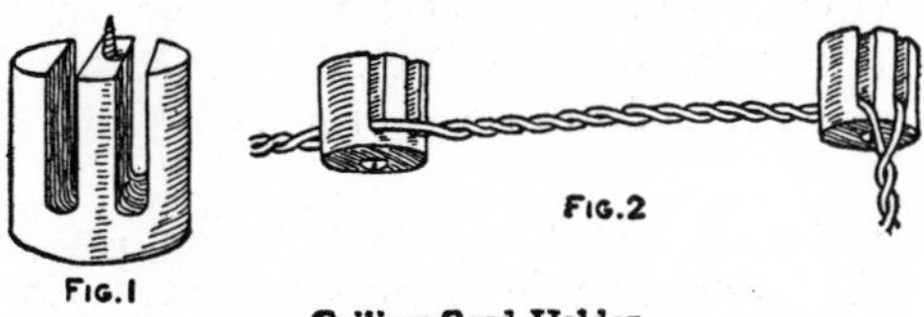

Ceiling-Cord Holder

Support for Double Clotheslines

Anyone using a double clothesline over pulleys will find the arrangement shown in Fig. 1 for supporting the

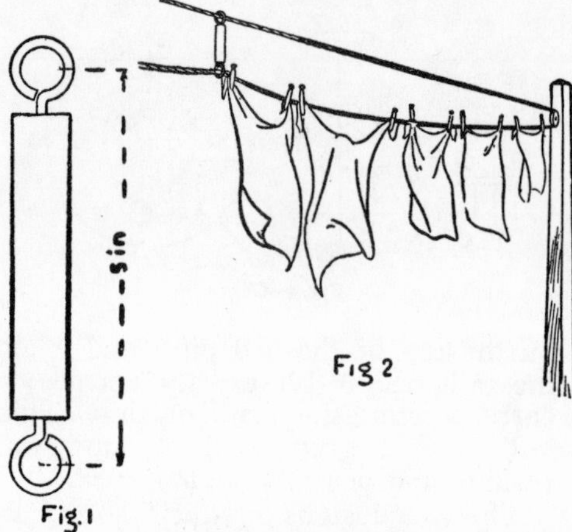

Holder on a Clothesline

lower line quite convenient. The support is made of a piece of ¾-in. square or round wood which has a screw-eye turned into each end. The line is run through these screw-eyes as shown in Fig. 2.—Contributed by W. W. UpDeGraff, Fruitvale, Cal.

Hot Pan or Plate Lifter

Unless a person uses considerable caution, bad burns may be suffered when taking hot pies from an oven. If one reaches in and takes hold of the pie pan with a cloth, the arm is liable to touch the oven door and receive a

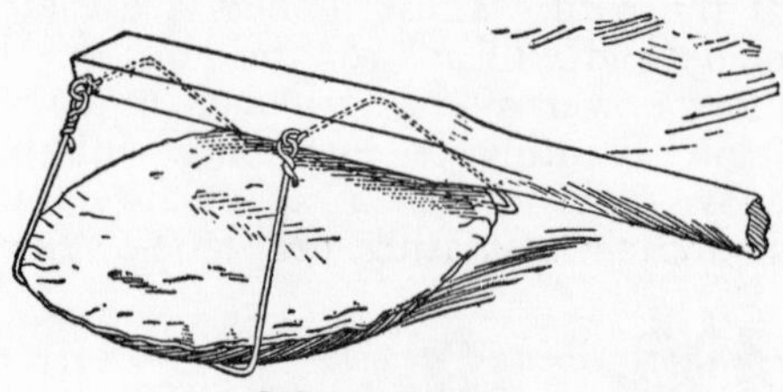

Lifter on Pie Pan

burn. To obviate this, I made the device shown in the sketch for lifting hot pie pans and plates. The handle is of pine about 18 in. long, and the two loops are made of heavy wire. The ends of the first loop of wire are put through the handle from the back, as shown, and then bent so as to stand out at an angle. The second loop is hinged to swing free on the opposite side of the handle. In use, the hinged side of the loop is dropped under one edge of a plate or pan and the rigid loop is then hooked under the opposite side. The weight of the pan or dish draws the loops together and there is little or no danger of a spill. The same lifter will pick up any size of plate or pan from a saucer to the largest pie plates.—Contributed by E. J. Cline, Ft. Smith, Ark.

Weighting Indian Clubs

An ordinary Indian club can be fixed so that different weights may be had without changing clubs. Each club is bored to receive lead washers which are held in place by a spiral spring. A bolt is run through from the handle end and fastened with a round nut. The lead washers and spring slip over the bolt as shown in the illustration. Changing the number of washers changes the weight of the club.—Contributed by Walter W. White, Denver, Colo.

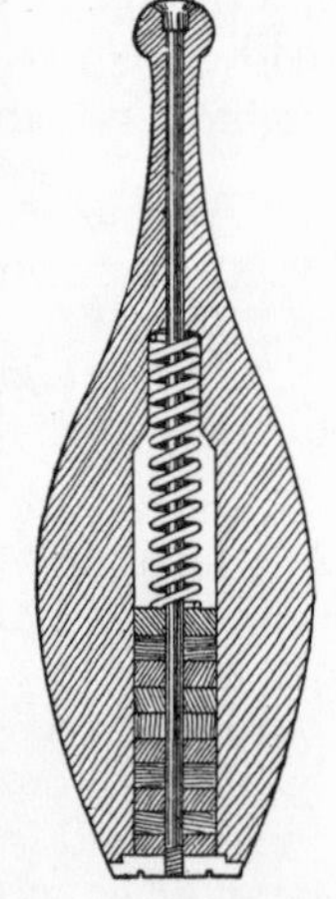

Venting a Funnel

When using a tight-fitting funnel in a small-neck bottle, trouble is usually experienced by the air causing a spill. This can be easily remedied by splitting a match in half and tying the parts on the sides of the stem with thread.—Contributed by Maurice Baudier, New Orleans, La.

A screw may be turned into hardwood easily, by boring a small hole and lubricating the screw threads with soft soap.

To Make "Centering" Unnecessary

For drilling a hole in a chucked piece, centering is just one operation too many, if this method is followed:

First, face off the end of the piece, making a true spot at least as big as the diameter of the drill. Put a center punch mark where the tool lines indicate the center of revolution. This serves as a rough guide for placing the drill between the tailstock center and the work as usual. Clamp a tool in the tool-post and, on starting the lathe, bring it in contact with the drill and keep it firmly so until the drill is in fully up to the lips. This prevents the drill from wobbling, and when once in true up to its size, it cannot change any more than under any other starting conditions. After being entered, the drill does not need the tool, which should be backed out of contact.

Fountain Pen Cap Used as a Ruler

When it is necessary to draw a short line and there is no ruler at hand, take

Ruling Lines

off the cap of your fountain pen and use it as a ruler. If the cap is fitted with a retaining clip, all the better, as this will prove a safeguard against slipping.

Vanishing Handkerchief Trick

The necessary articles used in performing this trick are the handkerchief,

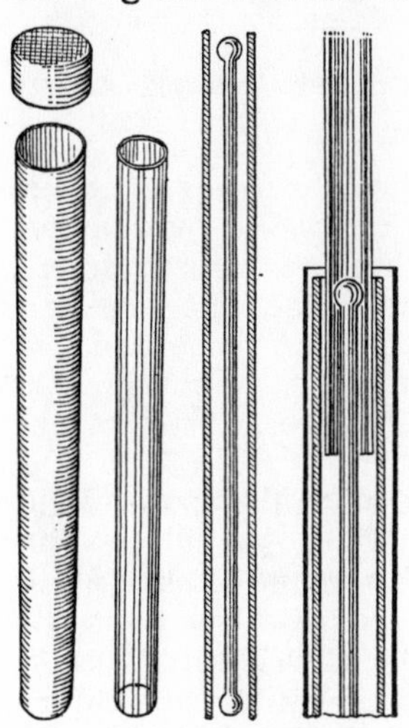

vanishing wand, a long piece of glass tubing, about ½ in. shorter than the wand, and a paper tube closed at one end and covered with a cap at the other, says the Sphinx. The handkerchief rod, shown at C, is concealed in the paper tube A before the performance. The glass tube B, after being shown empty, is put into the paper tube A, so that the handkerchief rod now is within it, unknown to the spectators. The handkerchief is then placed over the opening of the tube and pushed in by means of the wand. In doing this, the handkerchief and the rod are pushed into the wand, as shown in D. After the wand is removed, the cap is placed over the paper tube, and this given to someone to hold. The command for the handkerchief to vanish is given, and it is found to be gone when the glass tube is taken out of the paper cover. This is a novel way of making a handkerchief vanish. It can be used in a great number of tricks, and can be varied to suit the performer.

Removing Glass Letters from Windows

Glass letters are removed in the same way as metal letters, by applying caustic soda or potash around the edges of the letters. As the cement softens, manipulate the point of a pocket knife under the edges of the letter until the caustic works completely under and makes it easy to lift the letters. With care and patience, every letter may be thus taken off without breakage.

A Guitar That Is Easy to Make

A guitar having straight lines, giving it an old-fashioned appearance, can be made by the home mechanic, and if care is taken in selecting the material, and having it thoroughly seasoned, the finished instrument will have a fine tone. The sides, ends and bottom are made of hard wood, preferably hard maple, and the top should be made of a thoroughly seasoned piece of soft pine. The dimensioned pieces required are as follows:

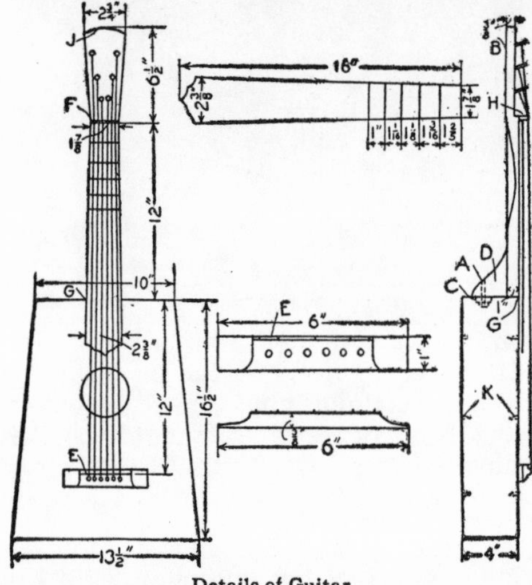

Details of Guitar

1 Top, $\frac{3}{16}$ by 14 by 17 in.
1 Bottom, $\frac{3}{16}$ by 14 by 17 in.
2 Sides, $\frac{3}{16}$ by 3⅝ by 16¾ in.
1 End, $\frac{3}{16}$ by 3⅝ by 13⅛ in.
1 End, $\frac{3}{16}$ by 3⅝ by 9⅝ in.
1 Neck, 1 by 2$\frac{3}{8}$ by 18½ in.
1 Fingerboard, $\frac{3}{16}$ by 2⅝ by 16 in.

Cut the fingerboard tapering and fasten pieces cut from hatpins with small wire staples for frets. All dimensions for cutting and setting are shown in the sketch. The neck is cut tapering from G to F and from J to F, with the back side rounding. A drawknife is the proper tool for shaping the neck. Cut a piece of hard wood, ¼ in. square and 1⅞ in. long, and glue it to the neck at F. Glue the fingerboard to the neck and hold it secure with clamps while the glue sets.

The brace at D is 1 in. thick, cut to any shape desired. The sides are glued together and then the front is glued on them. Place some heavy weights on top and give the glue time to dry. Fasten pieces of soft wood in the corners for braces. Glue the neck to the box, making it secure by the addition of a carriage bolt at A. A small block C is glued to the end to reinforce it for the bolt. Glue strips of soft wood, as shown by K, across the front and back to strengthen them. The back is then glued on and the outside smoothed with sandpaper.

Make the bottom bridge by using an old hatpin or wire of the same size for E secured with pin staples. Glue the bridge on the top at a place that will make the distance from the bridge F to the bottom bridge E just 24 in. This dimension and those for the frets should be made accurately. Six holes, $\frac{3}{16}$ in. in diameter, are drilled in the bottom bridge for pins. The turning plugs B and strings can be purchased at any music store.—Contributed by J. H. Stoddard, Carbondale, Pa.

Greasing the Front Wheels of an Automobile

The front wheel bearings of an automobile can be greased without removing the wheels in the following manner: Remove the hub caps and fill them with heavy grease and then screw them in place. Continue this operation until the grease is forced between all the bearings and out through the small clearance on the opposite side of the wheels. This should be done at least once every month to keep bearings well lubricated and free from grit. Dirt cannot enter a well filled bearing as easily as muddy water can enter a dry bearing.—Contributed by Chas. E. Frary, Norwalk, O.

¶Mold on wallpaper can be removed at once by applying a solution of 1 part salicylic acid in 4 parts of 95-percent alcohol.

The Paper Boat Is Light and Easy to Propel

HOW TO MAKE A PAPER BOAT

A Light Boat That Can Be Easily Carried

Now you might think it absurd to advise making a paper boat, but it is not, and you will find it in some respects and for some purposes better than the wooden boat. When it is completed you will have a canoe, probably equal to the Indian's bark canoe. Not only will it serve as an ideal fishing boat, but when you want to combine hunting and fishing you can put your boat on your shoulders and carry it from place to place wherever you want to go and at the same time carry your gun in your hand. The material used in its construction is inexpensive and can be purchased for a few dollars.

Make a frame (Fig. 1) on which to stretch the paper. A board 1 in. thick and about 1 ft. wide and 11½ ft. long is used for a keel, or backbone, and is cut tapering for about a third of its length, toward each end, and beveled on the outer edges (A, Fig. 2). The cross-boards (B, B, Fig. 2) are next sawed from a pine board 1 in. thick. Shape these as shown by A, Fig. 4, 13 in. wide by 26 in. long, and cut away in the center to avoid useless weight. Fasten them cross-wise to the bottom-board as shown in Fig. 1 and 2, with long stout screws, so as to divide the keel into three nearly equal parts. Then add the stem and stern pieces (C, C, Fig. 2). These are better, probably, when made of green elm. Screw the pieces to the bottom-board and bend them, as shown in Fig. 2, by means of a string or wire, fastened to a nail driven into the bottom. Any tough, light wood that is not easily broken when bending will do. Green wood is preferable, because it will retain the shape in which it has been bent better after drying. For the gunwales (a, a, Fig. 3), procure at a carriage factory,

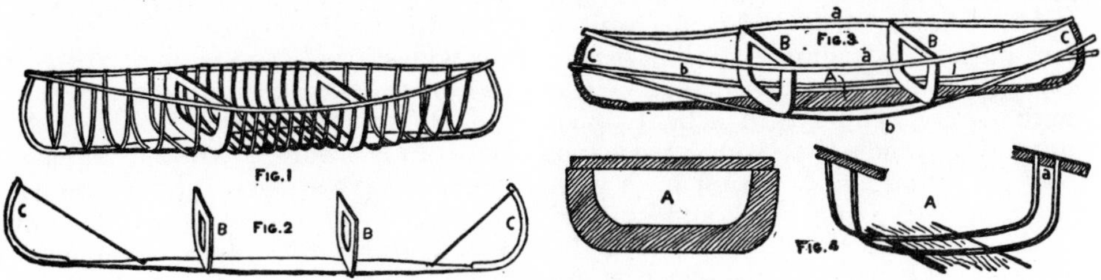

Details of Framework Construction

or other place, some light strips of ash, ⅜ in. thick. Nail them to the cross-boards and fasten to the end pieces (C, C,) in notches, by several wrappings of annealed iron wire or copper wire, as shown in Fig. 3. Copper wire is better because it is less apt to rust. For fastening the gunwales to the crossboards use nails instead of screws, because the nails are not apt to loosen and come out. The ribs, which are easily made of long, slender switches of osier willow, or similar material, are next put in, but before doing this, two strips of wood (b, b, Fig. 3) should be bent and placed as in Fig. 3. They are used only temporarily as a guide in putting in the ribs, and are not fastened, the elasticity of the wood being sufficient to cause them to retain their position. The osiers may average a little more than ½ in. in thickness and should be cut, stripped of leaves and bark and put in place while green and fresh. They are attached to the bottom by means of shingle nails driven through holes previously made in them with an awl, and are then bent down until they touch the strips of ash (b, b, Fig. 3), and finally cut off even with the tops of the gunwales, and notched at the end to receive them (B, Fig. 4). Between the cross-boards the ribs are placed at intervals of 2 or 3 in., while in other parts they are as much as 5 or 6 in. apart. The ribs having all been fastened in place as described, the loose strips of ash (b, b, Fig. 3) are withdrawn and the framework will appear somewhat as in Fig. 1. In order to make all firm and to prevent the ribs from changing position, as they are apt to do, buy some split cane or rattan, such as is used for making chair-bottoms, and, after soaking it in water for a short time to render it soft and pliable, wind it tightly around the gunwales and ribs where they join, and also interweave it among the ribs in other places, winding it about them and forming an irregular network over the whole frame. Osiers probably make the best ribs, but twigs of some other trees, such as hazel or birch, will answer nearly as well. For the ribs near the middle of the boat, twigs 5 or 6 ft. long are required. It is often quite difficult to get these of sufficient thickness throughout, and so, in such cases, two twigs may be used to make one rib, fastening the butts side by side on the bottom-board, and the smaller ends to the gunwales, as before described. In drying, the rattan becomes very tight and the twigs hard and stiff.

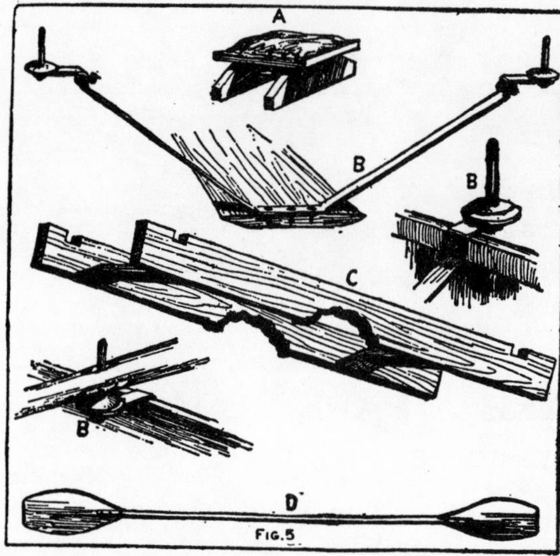

Important Features of Construction

The frame-work is now complete and ready to be covered. For this purpose buy about 18 yd. of very strong wrapping-paper. It should be smooth on the surface, and very tough, but neither stiff nor very thick. Being made in long rolls, it can be obtained in almost any length desired. If the paper be 1 yd. wide, it will require about two breadths to reach around the frame in the widest part. Cut enough of the roll to cover the frame and then soak it for a few minutes in water. Then turn the frame upside down and fasten the edges of the two strips of paper to it, by lapping them carefully on the under side of the bottom-board and tacking them to it so that the paper hangs down loosely on all sides. The paper is then trimmed, lapped and doubled over as smoothly as possible at the ends of the frame, and held in place by means of small clamps. It should be drawn tight along the edges, trimmed and doubled down over the gunwale, where it is firmly held by slipping the strips of ash (b, b) just inside of the gunwales into notches which should have been cut at the ends of the cross-boards. The shrinkage caused by the drying will stretch the paper tightly over the framework. When thoroughly dry, varnish inside and out with asphaltum varnish thinned with turpentine, and as soon as that has soaked in, apply a second coat of the same varnish, but with less turpentine; and finally cover the laps or joints of the paper with pieces of muslin stuck on with thick varnish. Now remove the loose strips of ash and put on another layer of paper, fastening it along the edge of the boat by replacing the strips as before. When the paper is dry, cover the laps with muslin as was done with the first covering. Then varnish the whole outside of the boat several times until it presents a smooth shining surface. Then take some of the split rattan and, after wetting it, wind it firmly around both gunwales and inside strip, passing it through small holes punched in the paper just below the gunwale, until the inside and outside strips are bound together into one strong gunwale. Then put a piece of oil-cloth in the boat between the cross-boards, tacking it to the bottom-board. This is done to protect the bottom of the boat.

Now you may already have a canoe that is perfectly water-tight, and steady in the water, if it has been properly constructed of good material. If not, however, in a few days you may be disappointed to find that it is becoming leaky. Then the best remedy is to cover the whole boat with unbleached muslin, sewed at the ends and tacked along the gunwales. Then tighten it by shrinking and finally give it at least three coats of a mixture of varnish and paint. This will doubtless stop the leaking entirely and will add but little to either the weight or cost.

Rig the boat with wooden or iron rowlocks (B, B, Fig. 5), preferably iron, and light oars. You may put in several extra thwarts or cross-sticks, fore and aft, and make a movable seat (A, Fig. 5.) With this you will doubtless find your boat so satisfactory that you will make no more changes.

Off for a Hunt

For carrying the boat it is convenient to make a sort of short yoke (C, Fig. 5), which brings all the weight upon the shoulders, and thus lightens the labor and makes it very handy to carry.

To Hang Heavy Things on a Nail

Boys will find many places around the house, where a hook to hang things on will be a great convenience. Instead of buying hooks use wire nails, and if driven as shown in the cut, they will support very heavy weights. Drive the lower nail first.

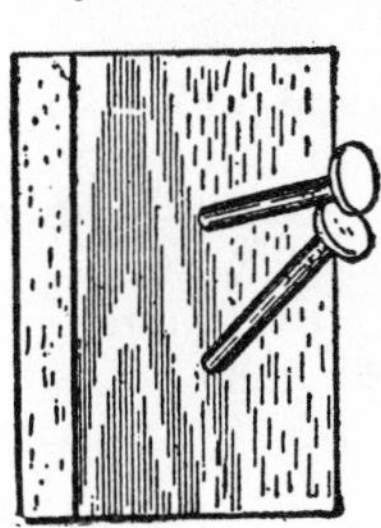

A Home-Made Elderberry Huller

As we had only one day to pick elderberries, we wanted to get as many of them as we could in that time. We could pick them faster than they could

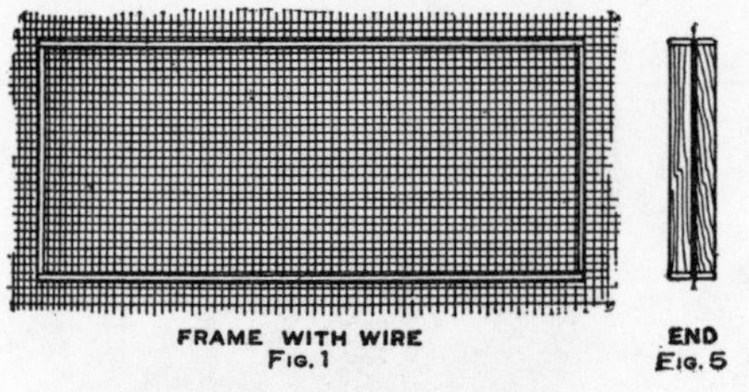

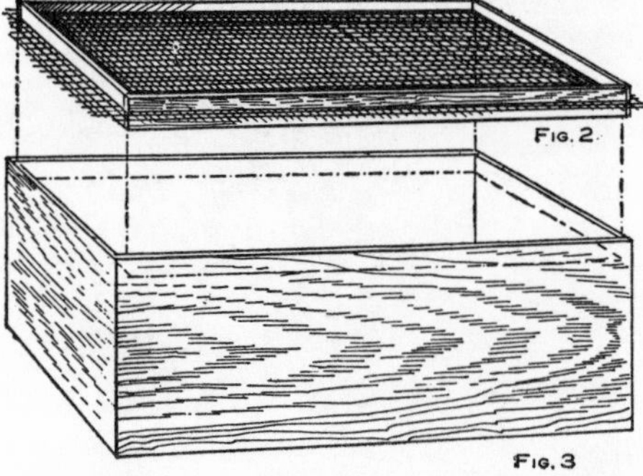

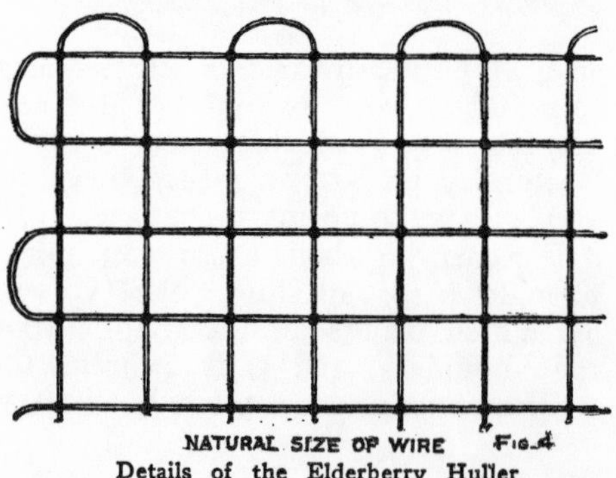

Details of the Elderberry Huller

be hulled by hand so we made a huller to take along with us to hull the berries as fast as they were picked. We procured a box and made a frame, Fig. 1, to fit it easily, then made another frame the same size and put a piece of wire mesh between them as shown in Fig. 2, allowing a small portion of the mesh to stick out of the frames. The top frame would keep the berries from rolling or jumping off, and the bottom frame kept the wire mesh and frame from being shaken off the box. The projecting edges of the mesh would keep the frame on the top edge of the box. The top view of the frame is shown in Fig. 1 and the end in Fig. 5, and the box on which the frame rests in Fig. 3. The actual size of the wire mesh used is shown in Fig. 4. One person could hull with this huller as many berries as two persons would pick.—Contributed by Albert Niemann, Pittsburg, Pa.

How to Make a Bulb on a Glass Tube

As a great many persons during the winter months are taking advantage of the long evenings to experiment in one way or another, the following method of forming bulbs on glass tubes may be of interest. A common method is to heat the part to be formed and by blowing in one end of the tube gradually expand the glass. This way has its drawbacks, as many are not sufficiently familiar with the work to blow a uniform blast, and the result is, a hole is blown through the side of the tube by uneven heating or blowing.

A good way to handle this work, is to take the tube and 1 or 2 in. more in length than the finished article is to be and place one end over an alcohol flame, and by holding a spare piece of tubing against the end allow them both to come to a melting heat, then pull apart and instead of breaking off the long thread thus formed, simply hold it in the flame at an angle of 45 deg. and melt it down and close the end at the same time. Close the other end with the same operation; this makes the tube airtight.

Gradually heat the tube at the point where the bulb is to be formed, slowly turning the tube to get a uniform heat. The air inside of the tube becoming heated will expand, and the glass, being softer where the flame has been applied, will be pushed out in the shape of a bulb. A great deal of care should be taken not to go to extremes, as the bulb will burst with a loud report if the heat is applied too long. The best results are obtained by heating the glass slowly and then the bulb can be formed with regularity. This is an easy way to make a thermometer tube. After the bulb is formed, the other end of the tube can be opened by heating, drawing out and breaking the thread like glass.—Contributed by A. Oswald.

How to Make a Sconce

A sconce is a candlestick holder, so made that it has a reflector of brass or copper and is to hang upon the wall. The tools necessary are a riveting hammer, file, metal shears, rivet punch, flat and round-nosed pliers, screwdriver and sheet brass or copper No. 23 gauge.

To make the sconce proceed as follows: First, cut off a piece of brass so that it shall have ½ in. extra metal all around; second, with a piece of carbon paper, trace upon the brass lines that shall represent the margin of the sconce proper, also trace the decorative design; third, with a nailset make a series of holes in the extra margin about ¾ in. apart and large enough to take in a ¾-in. thin screw; fourth, fasten the metal to a thick board by inserting screws in these holes; fifth, with a twenty-penny wire nail that has had the sharpness of its point filed off, stamp the background of the design promiscuously. By holding the nail about ¼ in. above the work and striking it with the hammer, at the same time striving to keep its point at ¼ in. above the metal, very rapid progress can be made. This stamping lowers the background and at the same time raises the design. Sixth, chase or stamp along the border of the design and background using a nail filed to a chisel edge. This is to make a clean sharp division between background and design. Seventh, when the stamping is complete remove the screws and metal from the board and cut off the extra margin with the metal shears. File the edges until they are smooth to the touch.

The drip cup is a piece of brass cut circular and shaped by placing the brass over a hollow in one end of a block. Give the metal a circular motion, at the same time beat it with a round-nosed mallet. Work from the center along concentric rings outward, then reverse.

The candle holders may have two, three, four, or six arms, and are bent to shape by means of the round-nosed pliers. The form of the brackets which support the drip cups may be seen in the illustration.

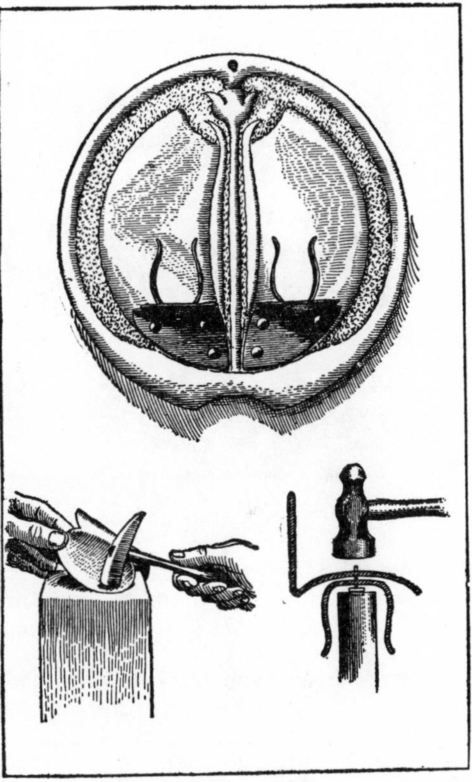

Completed Sconce
Shaping the Holders Riveting

Having pierced the bracket, drip cup, and holder, these three parts are riveted together as indicated in the drawing. It will be found easier usually if the holder is not shaped until after the riveting is done. The bracket is then riveted to the back of the sconce. Small copper rivets are used.

It is better to polish all the pieces before fastening any of them together. Metal polish of any kind will do. After the parts have been assembled a lacquer may be applied to keep the metal from tarnishing.

How To Make a Hectograph

A hectograph is very simply and easily made and by means of it many copies of writing can be obtained from a single original.

Make a tray of either tin or pasteboard, a little larger than the sheet of paper you ordinarily use and about ½ in. deep. Soak 1 oz. of gelatine in cold water over night and in the morning pour off the water. Heat 6½ oz. of glycerine to about 200 deg. F. on a water bath, and add the gelatine. This should give a clear glycerine solution of gelatine.

Making Copies with the Hectograph

Place the tray so that it is perfectly level and pour in the gelatinous composition until it is nearly level with the edge of the tray. Cover it so the cover does not touch the surface of the composition and let it stand six hours, when it will be ready for use.

Make the copy to be reproduced on ordinary paper with aniline ink; using a steel pen, and making the lines rather heavy so they have a greenish color in the light. A good ink may be made of methyl violet 2 parts, alcohol 2 parts, sugar 1 part, glycerine 4 parts, and water 24 parts. Dissolve the violet in the alcohol mixed with the glycerine; dissolve the sugar in the water and mix both solutions.

When the original copy of the writing is ready moisten the surface of the hectograph slightly with a sponge, lay the copy face down upon it and smooth down, being careful to exclude all air bubbles and not shifting the paper. Leave it nearly a minute and raise one corner and strip it from the pad, where will remain a reversed copy of the inscription.

Immediately lay a piece of writing paper of the right size on the pad, smooth it down and then remove as before. It will bear a perfect copy of the original. Repeat the operation until the number of copies desired is obtained or until the ink on the pad is exhausted. Fifty or more copies can be obtained from a single original.

When through using the hectograph wash it off with a moist sponge, and it will be ready for future use. If the surface is impaired at any time it can be remelted in a water bath and poured into a tray as before, if it has not absorbed too much ink.

How to Make a Sailomobile

By Frank Mulford, Shiloh, N. J.

I had read of the beach automobiles used on the Florida coast; they were like an ice boat with a sail, except they had wheels instead of runners. So I set to work to make something to take me over the country roads.

I found and used seven fence pickets for the frame work, and other things as they were needed. I spliced two rake handles together for the mast, winding the ends where they came together with wire. A single piece would be better if you can get one long enough. The gaff, which is the stick to which the upper end of the sail is fastened, is a broomstick. The boom, the stick at the bottom of the sail, was made of a rake handle with a broomstick spliced to make it long enough. Mother let me have a sheet, which I put down on the floor and cut in the shape of a mainsail. The wind was the cheapest power to be found, thus it was utilized; the three wheels were cast-off bicycle wheels.

I steer with the front wheel, which was the front wheel of an old bicycle with the fork left on. The axle between the rear wheels is an iron bar which cost me 15 cents, and the pulley which raises and lowers the sail cost 5 cents. Twenty cents was all I spent, all the rest I found.

A saw, hammer, and brace and bit were the tools used. Slats made the seat and a cushion from the house made it comfortable, and in a week everything was ready for sailing.

Sailomobile for Use on Country Roads

Once it was started with only my little cousin in it and I had to run fast to catch up.

A Home-Made Magic Lantern

The essential parts of a magic lantern are a condensing lens to make the beam of light converge upon the slide to illuminate it evenly, a projecting lens

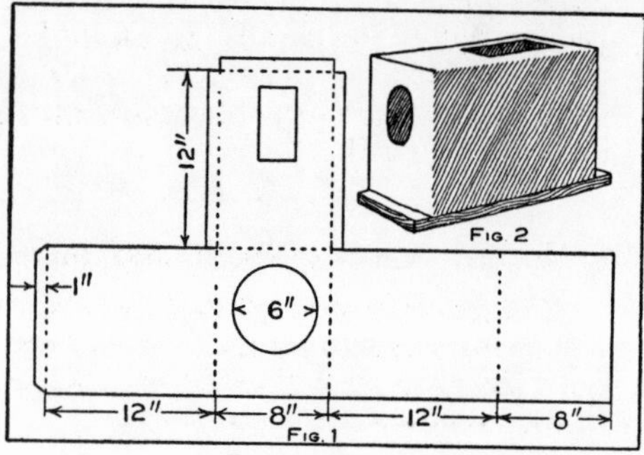

Lantern House

with which to throw an enlarged picture of the illuminated slide upon a screen and some appliances for preserving the proper relation of these parts to each other. The best of materials should be used and the parts put together with care to produce a clear picture on the screen.

The first to make is the lamp house or box to hold the light. Our illustration shows the construction for an electric light, yet the same box may be used for gas or an oil lamp, provided the material is of metal. A tin box having dimensions somewhere near those given in the diagrammatic sketch may be secured from your local grocer, but if such a box is not found, one can be made from a piece of tin cut as shown in Fig. 1. When this metal is bent at right angles on the dotted lines it will form a box as shown in Fig. 2 which is placed on a baseboard, ½ to ¾ in. thick, 8 in. wide, and 14 in. long. This box should be provided with a reflector located just back of the lamp.

Procure a plano-convex or a bi-convex 6-in. lens with a focal length of from 15 to 20 in. and a projecting lens 2 in. in diameter with such a focal length that will give a picture of the required size, or a lens of 12-in. focus enlarging a 3-in. slide to about 6 ft. at a distance of 24 ft.

The woodwork of the lantern should be of ½-in., well seasoned pine, white wood or walnut and the parts fastened together with wood screws, wire brads, or glue, as desired. The board in which to mount the condensing lens is 16 in. wide and 15 in. high, battened on both ends to keep the wood from warping. The board is centered both ways, and, at a point 1 in. above the center, describe a 9-in. circle with a compass and saw the wood out with a scroll or keyhole saw. If a small saw is used, and the work carefully done, the circular piece removed will serve to make the smaller portion of the ring for holding the condensing lens. This ring is made up from two rings, A and B, Fig. 3. The inside and outside diameters of the ring B are ⅜ in. greater than the corresponding diameters of ring A, so when fastened together concentrically an inner rabbet is formed for the reception of the lens and an outer rabbet to fit against the board C in and against which it rotates being held in place by buttons, DD.

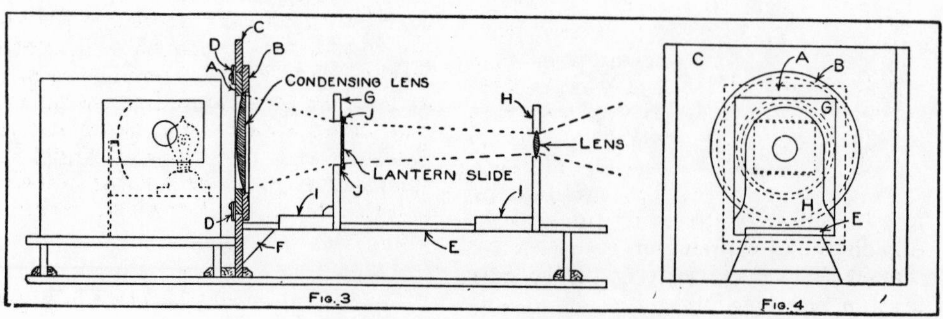

Magic Lantern Details

A table, E, about 2 ft. long is fastened to the board C with brackets F and supported at the outer end with a standard. The slide support, G, and the lens slide, H, are constructed to slip easily on the table, E, the strips II serving as guides. Small strips of tin, JJ, are bent as shown and fastened at the top and bottom of the rectangular opening cut in the support G for holding the lantern slides.

All the parts should be joined together snugly and the movable parts made to slide freely and when all is complete and well sandpapered, apply two coats of shellac varnish. Place the lamphouse on the bottom board behind the condensing lens and the lantern is ready for use.

The proper light and focus may be obtained by slipping the movable parts on the board E, and when the right position is found for each, all lantern slides will produce a clear picture on the screen, if the position of the lantern and screen is not changed.—Contributed by Stuart Mason Kerr, St. Paul, Minn.

A Quickly Made Lamp

A very simple lamp can be made from materials which are available in practically every household in the following manner: A cheap glass tumbler is partly filled with water and then about ½ in. of safe, light burning oil, placed on the water. Cut a thin strip from an ordinary cork and make a hole in the center to carry a short piece of wick. The wick should be of such a length as to dip into the oil, but not long enough to reach the water. The upper surface of the cork may be protected from the flame with a small piece of tin bent over the edges and a hole punched in the center for the wick. The weight of the tin will force the cork down into the oil. The level of the oil should be such as to make the flame below the top of the tumbler and the light then will not be blown out with draughts. The arrangement is quite safe as, should the glass happen to upset, the water at once extinguishes the flame.—Contributed by G. P. B.

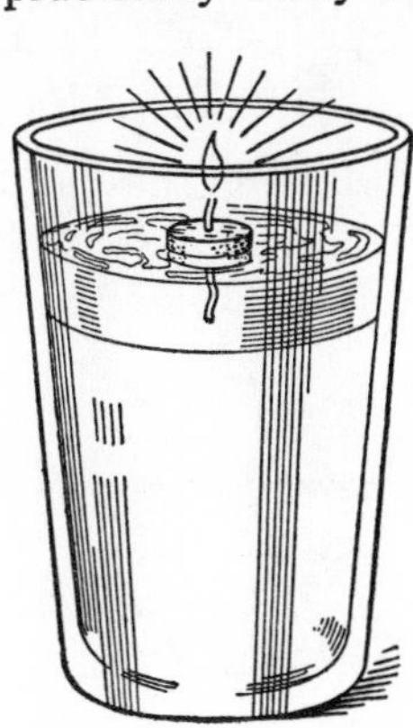

How to Make a Paper Aeroplane

A very interesting and instructive toy aeroplane can be made as shown in the accompanying illustrations. A sheet of paper is first folded, Fig. 1, then the corners on one end are doubled over, Fig. 2, and the whole piece finished up and held together with a paper clip as in Fig. 3. The paper clip to be used should be like the one shown in Fig. 4. If one of these clips is not at hand, form a piece of wire in the same shape, as it will be needed for balancing purposes as well as for holding the paper together. Grasp the aeroplane between the thumb and forefinger at the place marked A in Fig. 3, keeping the paper as level as possible and throwing it as you would a dart. The aeroplane will make an easy and graceful flight in a room where no air will strike it.—Contributed by J. H. Crawford, Schenectady, N. Y.

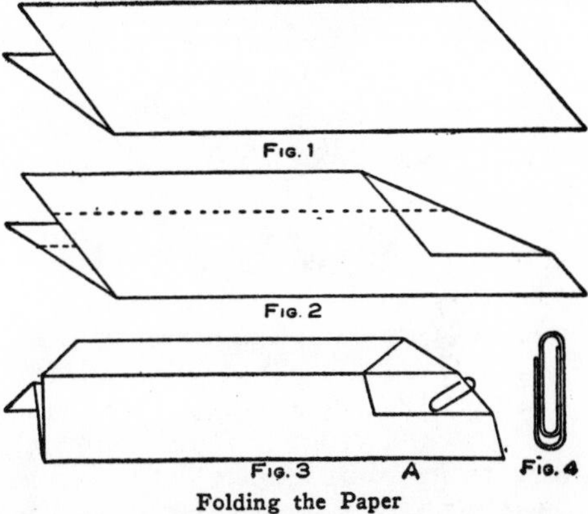

Folding the Paper

Banana oil or amyl acetate is a good bronze liquid.

A Wrestling Mat

The cost of a wrestling mat is so great that few small clubs can afford to own one. As we did not see our way

Made of Bed Mattresses

clear to purchase such a mat, I made one of six used bed mattresses (Fig. 1) purchased from a second-hand dealer. I ordered a canvas bag, 12 ft. 3 in. by 12 ft. 9 in., from a tent company, to cover the mattresses. The bag consisted of two pieces with the seam along each edge. The mattresses were laid side by side and end to end and the bag placed on and laced up as shown in Fig. 2.—Contributed by Walter W. White, Denver, Colo.

A Pocket Voltammeter

Remove the works and stem from a discarded dollar watch, drill two $\frac{3}{16}$-in. holes in the edge, ¾ in. apart, and insert two binding-posts, Fig. 1, insulating them from the case with cardboard. Fold two strips of light cardboard, ½ in. wide, so as to form two oblong boxes, ½ in. long and $\frac{3}{16}$ in. thick, open on the edges. On one of these forms wind evenly the wire taken from a bell magnet to the depth of ⅛ in. and on the other wind some 20-gauge wire to the same depth. Fasten the wire with gummed label to keep it from unwinding.

Glue the coils to the back of the case and connect one wire from each binding-post as shown in Fig. 2, while the other two wires are connected to an induction coil lead which is inserted in the hole from which the stem was removed. Fasten a brass-headed tack to the case at the point F with sealing wax or solder and bend a wire in the shape shown in Fig. 3 to swing freely on the tack. Attach - piece of steel rod, ¾ in. long, in the center coil, C, Fig. 2.

A rubber band, D, connects the steel rod C with the top of the watch case. The ends of the rubber are fastened with sealing wax. The rubber keeps the pointer at zero or in the middle of the scale. Do not use too strong a rubber. A dial may be made by cutting a piece of stiff white paper so it will fit under the crystal of the watch. An arc is cut in the paper, as shown in Fig. 1, through which the indicator works.

To calibrate the instrument, first mark the binding-post A, which is connected to the coil of heavy wire, for amperes and the other post, V, to the coil of small wire for volts. Connect the lead and the post marked A to one, two and three cells and each time mark the place of the pointer on the dial. Take corresponding readings on a standard ammeter and mark the figures on the dial. The volt side of the dial may be calibrated in the same manner, using a voltmeter instead of the ammeter. The place where the

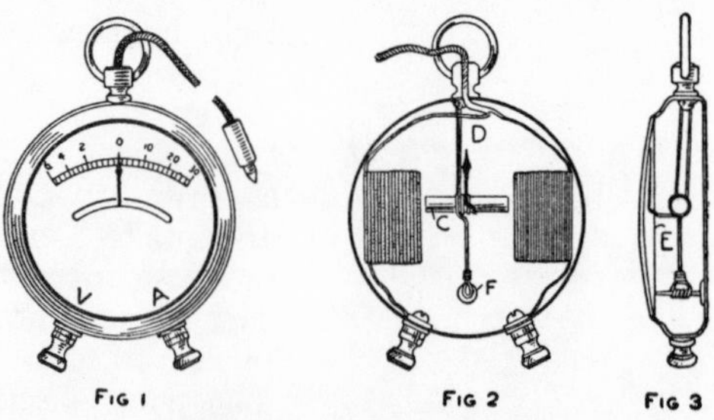

Voltammeter in a Watch Case

indicator comes to rest after disconnecting the current is marked zero.—Contributed by Edward M. Teasdale, Warren, Pa.

A Film Washing Trough

The washing of films without scratching them after they are developed and fixed is very difficult in hot weather. A convenient washing trough for washing full length films is shown in the accompanying sketch. The trough must be made for the size of the film to be washed. Cut a 1/4-in. board as long as the film and a trifle wider than the film's width. Attach strips to the edges of the board to keep the water from spilling over the sides.

Cut a hole in one side of a baking-powder can about half way between the top and bottom, large enough to admit a fair-sized stream of water from a faucet. Then solder the cover to the can and punch a number of holes about 1/4 in. apart along the opposite side from where the large hole was cut. Place this can on one end of the trough, as shown, with the large hole up.

Some heavy wire bent in the shape of a U and fastened to the under side of the trough at the can end will furnish supports to keep that end of the trough the highest and place the opening in the can close beneath the water faucet. A common pin stuck through one end of the film and then in the trough close to the can will hold it in position for washing. Five minutes' washing with this device is sufficient to remove all traces of the hypo from the film.—Contributed by M. M. Hunting, Dayton, O.

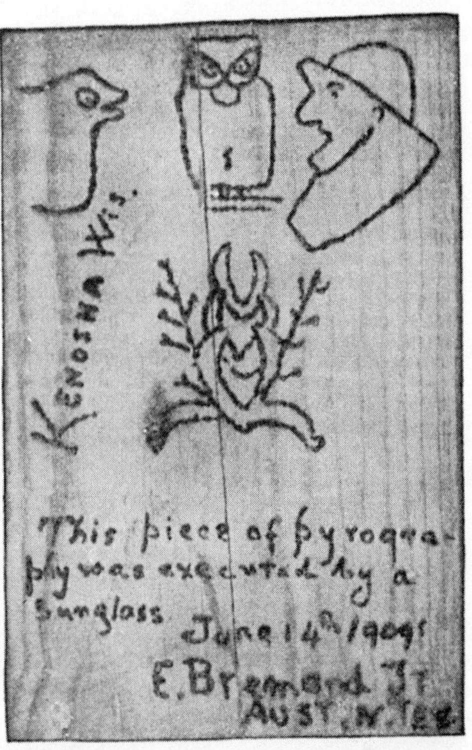

Burnt wood work done with an ordinary reading glass and the sun's rays.

Washing a Negative Film

The Diving Bottle

This is a very interesting and easily performed experiment illustrating the transmission of pressure by liquids. Take a wide-mouthed bottle and fill almost full of water; then into this bottle place, mouth downward, a small vial or bottle having just enough air in the bottle to keep it barely afloat. Put a sheet of rubber over the mouth of the large bottle, draw the edge down over the neck and wrap securely with a piece of string thus forming a tightly stretched diaphragm over the top. When a finger is pressed on the rubber the small bottle will slowly descend until the pressure is released when the

Pressure Experiments

small bottle will ascend. The moving of the small bottle is caused by the pressure transmitted through the water, thus causing the volume of air in the small tube to decrease and the bottle to descend and ascend when released as the air increases to the original volume.

This experiment can be performed with a narrow-necked bottle, provided the bottle is wide, but not very thick. Place the small bottle in as before, taking care not to have too much air in the bottom. If the cork is adjusted properly, the bottle may be held in the hand and the sides pressed with the fingers, thus causing the small bottle to descend and ascend at will. If the small bottle used is opaque, or an opaque tube such as the cap of a fountain pen, many puzzling effects may be obtained.—Contributed by John Shahan, Auburn, Ala.

How to Make an Inexpensive Wooden Fan

Select a nice straight-grained piece of white pine about ¼ in. thick, ¾ in. wide and 4 in. long. Lay out the design desired and cut as shown in Fig. 1, and then soak the wood in hot water to make it soft and easy to split. Cut the divisions very thin with a sharp knife down to the point A, as shown in the sketch, taking care not to split the wood through the part left for the handle. The fan is then finished by placing each piece over the other as in Fig. 2. This will make a very pretty ornament.—Contributed by Fred W. Whitehouse, Upper Troy, N. Y.

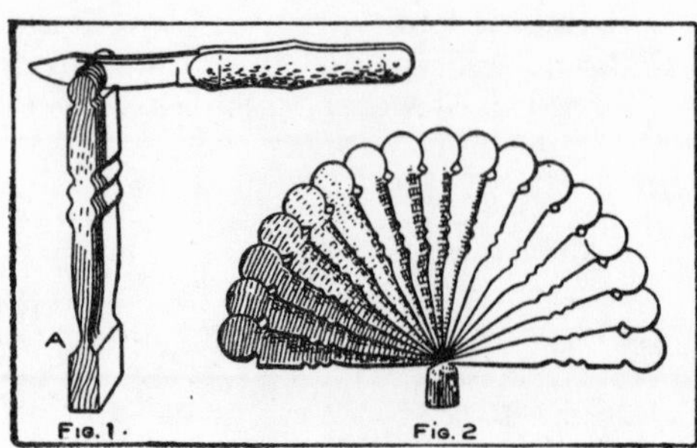

Cutting the Wood and Complete Fan

Combination Telegraph and Telephone Line

The accompanying diagrams show connections for a short line system

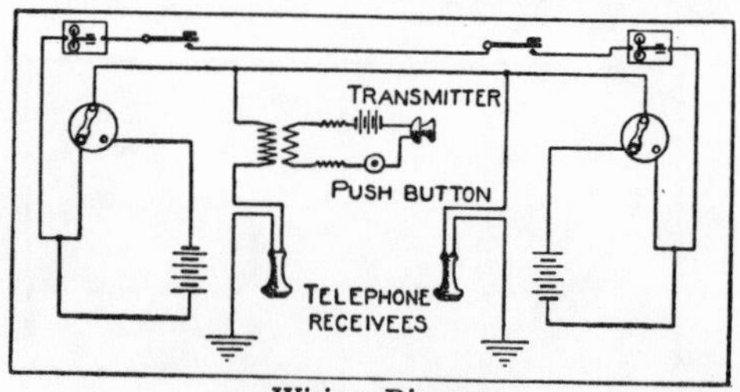

Wiring Diagram

(metallic circuit) of telegraph where a telephone may be used in combination on the line. The telephone receivers can be used both as receivers and transmitters, or ordinary telephone transmitters, induction coils and battery may be used in the circuit with a receiver. If a transmitter is used, its batteries may be connected in circuit with a common push button which is held down when using the telephone. On a 1000-ft. line, four dry cells will be sufficient for the telegraph instruments and two cells for the telephone.—Contributed by D. W. Miller.

How to Make a Miniature Windmill

The following description is how a miniature windmill was made, which gave considerable power for its size, even in a light breeze. Its smaller parts, such as blades and pulleys, were constructed of 1-in. sugar pine on account of its softness.

The eight blades were made from pieces 1 by 1½ by 12 in. Two opposite edges were cut away until the blade was about ⅛ in. thick. Two inches were left uncut at the hub end. They were then nailed to the circular face plate A, Fig. 1, which was 6 in. in diameter and 1 in. thick. The center of the hub was lengthened by the wooden disk, B, Fig. 1, which was nailed to the face plate. The shaft C, Fig. 1, was ¼-in. iron rod, 2 ft. long, and turned in the bearings detailed in Fig. 2. J was a nut from a wagon bolt and was placed in the bearing to insure easy running. The bearing blocks were 3 in. wide, 1 in. thick and 3 in. high without the upper half. Both bearings were made in this manner.

The shaft C was keyed to the hub of the wheel, by the method shown in Fig. 3. A staple, K, held the shaft from revolving in the hub. This method was also applied in keying the 5-in. pulley F, to the shaft, G, Fig. 1, which extended to the ground. The 2½-in. pulley, I, Fig. 1, was keyed to shaft C, as shown in Fig. 4. The wire L was put through the hole in the axle and the two ends curved so as to pass through the two holes in the pulley, after which they were given a final bend to keep the pulley in place. The method by which the shaft C was kept from working forward is shown in Fig. 5. The washer M intervened between the bearing block and the wire N, which was passed through the axle and then bent to prevent its falling out. Two washers were placed on shaft C, between the forward bearing and the hub of the wheel to lessen the friction.

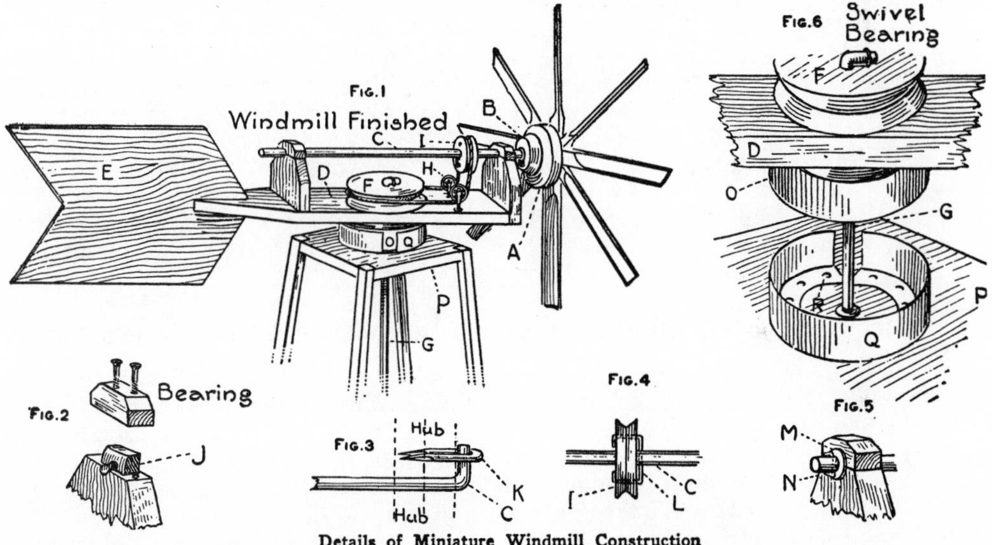

Details of Miniature Windmill Construction

The bed plate D, Fig. 1, was 2 ft. long, 3 in. wide and 1 in. thick and was tapered from the rear bearing to the slot in which the fan E was nailed. This fan was made of ¼-in. pine 18 by 12 in. and was cut the shape shown.

The two small iron pulleys with screw bases, H, Fig. 1, were obtained for a small sum from a hardware dealer. Their diameter was 1¼ in. The belt which transferred the power from shaft C to shaft G was top string, with a section of rubber in it to take up slack. To prevent it from slipping on the two wooden pulleys a rubber band was placed in the grooves of each.

The point for the swivel bearing was determined by balancing the bed plate, with all parts in place, across the thin edge of a board. There a ¼-in. hole was bored in which shaft G turned. To lessen the friction here, washers were placed under pulley F. The swivel bearing was made from two lids of baking powder cans. A section was cut out of one to permit its being enlarged enough to admit the other. The smaller one, O, Fig. 6, was nailed top down, with the sharp edge to the underside of the bed plate, so that the ¼-in. hole for the shaft G was in the center. The other lid, G, was tacked, top down also, in the center of the board P, with brass headed furniture tacks, R, Fig. 6, which acted as a smooth surface for the other tin to revolve upon. Holes for shaft G were cut through both lids. Shaft G was but ¼ in. in diameter, but to keep it from rubbing against the board P, a ½-in. hole was bored for it, through the latter.

The tower was made of four 1 by 1-in. strips, 25 ft. long. They converged from points on the ground forming an 8-ft. square to the board P at the top of the tower. This board was 12 in. square and the corners were notched to admit the strips as shown, Fig. 1. Laths were nailed diagonally between the strips to strengthen the tower laterally. Each strip was screwed to a stake in the ground so that by disconnecting two of them the other two could be used as hinges and the tower could be tipped over and lowered to the ground, as, for instance, when the windmill needed oiling. Bearings for the shaft G were placed 5 ft. apart in the tower. The power was put to various uses.

How to Make a Telegraph Instrument and Buzzer

The only expenditure necessary in constructing this telegraph instrument is the price of a dry cell, providing one has a few old materials on hand.

Procure a block of wood about 6 in. long and 3 in. wide and take the coils out of an old electric bell. If you have no bell, one may be had at the dealers for a small sum. Fasten these coils on the blocks at one end as in Fig. 1.

Cut a piece of tin 2 in. long and ½ in. wide and bend it so the end of the tin shown in the illustration. This completes the receiver or sounder.

To make the key, cut out another piece of tin (X, Fig. 1) 4 in. long and bend it as shown. Before tacking it to the board, cut off the head of a nail and drive it in the board at a point where the loose end of the tin will cover it. Then tack the key to the board and connect the wires of the battery as in Fig. 1. Now, move the coils back and forth until the click sounds just the way

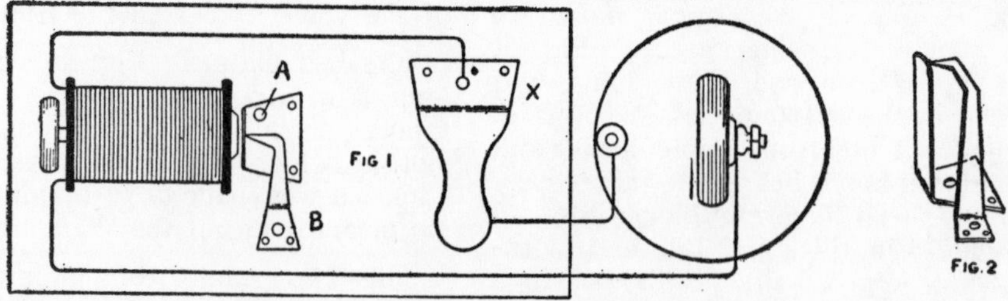

Home-Made Telegraph Instrument

when fastened to the block will come just above the core of the coil. Cut another piece of tin 3 in. long and bend it as shown at A, Fig. 2. Tack these two pieces of tin in front of the coils as you wish and you are ready to begin on the Morse code.

When tired of this instrument, connect the wire from the coils to the key to point A and the one connected at the point under the key to B, leaving the other wire as it is. By adjusting the coils the receiver will begin to vibrate rapidly, causing a buzzing sound.—Contributed by John R. McConnell.

How To Make a Water Bicycle

Water bicycles afford fine sport, and, like many another device boys make, can be made of material often cast off by their people as rubbish. The principal material necessary for the construction of a water bicycle is oil barrels. Flour barrels will not do—they are not strong enough, nor can they be made perfectly airtight. The grocer can furnish you with oil barrels at a very small cost, probably let you have them for making a few deliveries for him. Three barrels are required for the water bicycle, although it can be made with but two. Figure 1 shows the method of arranging the barrels; after the manner of bicycle wheels.

Procure an old bicycle frame and make for it a board platform about 3 ft. wide at the rear end and tapering to about 2 ft. at the front, using cleats to hold the board frame, as shown at

Water Bicycle Complete

the shaded portion K. The construction of the barrel part is shown in Fig. 2. Bore holes in the center of the heads of the two rear barrels and also in the heads of the first barrel and put a shaft of wood through the rear barrels and one through the front barrel, adjusting the side pieces to the shafts, as indicated.

Next place the platform of the bicycle frame and connections thereon. Going back to Fig. 1 we see that the driving chain passes from the sprocket driver L of the bicycle frame to the place downward between the slits in the platform to the driven sprocket on the shaft between the two barrels. Thus a center drive is made. The rear barrels are fitted with paddles as at M, consisting of four pieces of board nailed

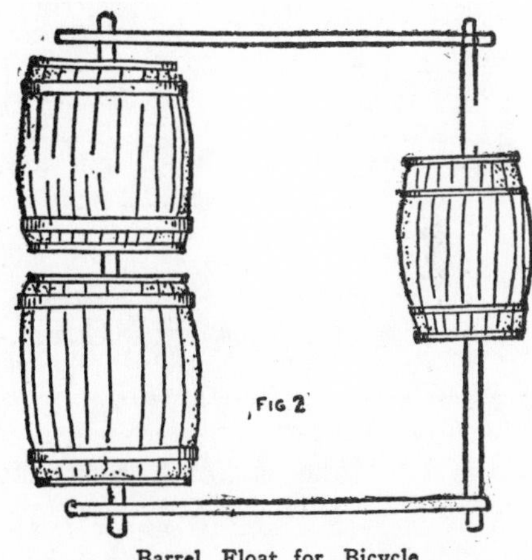

Barrel Float for Bicycle

and cleated about the circumference of the barrels, as shown in Fig. 1.

The new craft is now ready for a first voyage. To propel it, seat yourself on the bicycle seat, feet on the pedals, just as you would were you on a bicycle out in the street. The steering is effected by simply bending the body to the right or left, which causes the craft to dip to the inclined side and the affair turns in the dipped direction. The speed is slow at first, but increases as the force is generated and as one becomes familiar with the working of the affair. There is no danger, as the airtight barrels cannot possibly sink.

Another mode of putting together the set of barrels, using one large one in the rear and a small one in the front is presented in Fig. 3. These two barrels are empty oil barrels like the others. The head holes are bored and the proper wooden shafts are inserted and the entrance to the bores closed tight by calking with hemp and putty or clay. The ends of the shafts turn in the wooden frame where the required bores are made to receive the same. If the journals thus made are well oiled, there will not be much friction. Such a frame can be fitted with a platform and a raft to suit one's individual fancy built upon it, which can

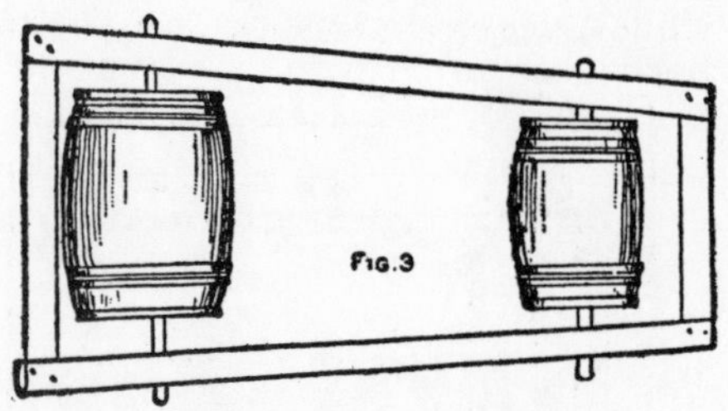

Another Type of Float

be paddled about with ease and safety on any pond. A sail can be rigged up by using a mast and some sheeting; or even a little houseboat, which will give any amount of pleasure, can be built.

How To Make a Small Searchlight

The materials required for a small searchlight are a 4-volt lamp of the loop variety, thin sheet brass for the cylinder, copper piping and brass tubing for base. When completed the searchlight may be fitted to a small boat and will afford a great amount of pleasure for a little work, or it may be put to other uses if desired.

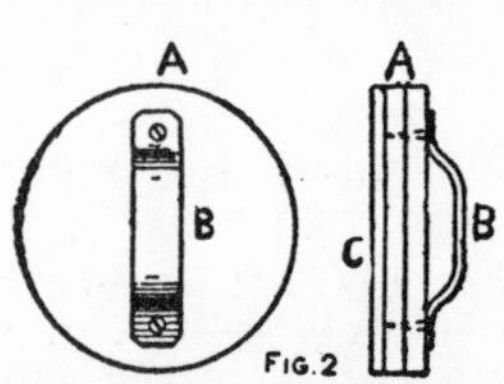

Make a cylinder of wood of the required size and bend a sheet of thin brass around it. Shape small blocks of boxwood, D, Fig. 1, to fit the sides and pass stout pieces of brass wire through the middle of the blocks for trunnions. Exactly through the middle of the sides of the cylinder drill holes just so large that when the blocks containing the trunnions are cemented to the cylinder there is no chance of contact between cylinder and trunnion, and so creating a false circuit.

The trunnion should project slightly into the cylinder, and after the lamp has been placed in position by means of the small wood blocks shown in Fig. 1, the wires from the lamp should be soldered to the trunnions. It is best to solder the wire to the trunnions before cementing the side blocks inside the cylinder.

Turn a small circle of wood, A, Fig. 2, inside the cylinder to fit exactly and fasten to it a piece of mirror, C, Fig. 2, exactly the same size to serve as a reflector. Painting the wood with white enamel or a piece of brightly polished metal will serve the purpose. On the back of the piece of wood fasten a small brass handle, B, Fig. 2, so that it may readily be removed for cleaning.

In front of cylinder place a piece of magnifying glass for a lens. If a piece

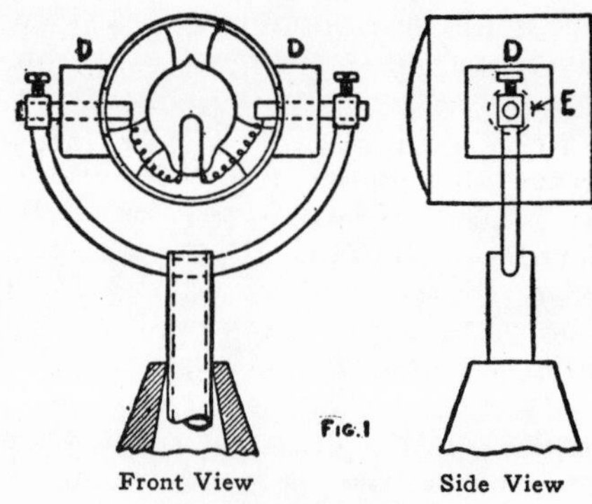

Front View Side View

to fit cannot be obtained, fit a glass like a linen tester to a small disc of wood or brass to fit the cylinder. If magnifying glass cannot be had, use plain glass and fit them as follows:

Make two rings of brass wire to fit tightly into the cylinder, trace a circle (inside diameter of cylinder) on a piece of cardboard; place cardboard on glass and cut out glass with a glass cutter; break off odd corners with notches on cutters and grind the edge of the glass on an ordinary red brick using plenty of water. Place one brass ring in cylinder, then the glass disc and then the other ring.

For the stand fill a piece of copper piping with melted rosin or lead. When hard bend the pipe around a piece of wood which has been sawed to the shape of bend desired. Then melt out the rosin or lead. Make an incision with a half-round file in the under side of the tube for the wires to come through. Make the base of wood as shown in Fig. 1. One-half inch from the top bore a hole large enough to admit the copper pipe and a larger hole up the center to meet it for the wires to come down.

If it is desired to make the light very complete, make the base of two pieces of brass tube—one being a sliding fit in the other and with projecting pieces to prevent the cylinder from going too far. The light may then be elevated or lowered as wished. On two ordinary brass terminals twist or solder some flexible wire, but before doing so fix a little bone washer on the screws of the terminal so as to insulate it from the tube. When the wires have been secured to the terminals cover the joint with a piece of very thin india rubber tubing, such as is used for cycle valves. The two wires may now be threaded down the copper tube into the base, and pulled tight, the terminals firmly fixed into the tubes; if too small, some glue will secure them. To get the cylinder into its carriage, put one trunnion into the terminal as far as it will go and this will allow room for the other trunnion to go in its terminal.

Electric Alarm that Rings a Bell and Turns on a Light

The illustration shows an alarm clock connected up to ring an electric bell, and at the same time turn on an electric light to show the time. The parts indicated are as follows: A, key of alarm clock; B, contact post, 4 in. long; C, shelf, 5¼ by 10 in.; D, bracket; E, electric bulb (3½ volts); S, brass strip, 4¼ in. long, ⅜ in. wide and 1/16 in. thick; T, switch; F, wire from batteries to switch; G, wire from bell to switch; H, wire from light to switch; I, dry batteries; J, bell; X, point where a splice is made from the light to wire leading to batteries from brass strip under clock. Push the switch lever to the right before retiring.

To operate this, set alarm key as shown in diagram, after two turns have been made on the key. When alarm goes off, it turns till it forms a connection by striking the contact post and starts the electric bell ringing. Throw lever off from the right to center, which stops bell ringing. To throw on light throw levers to the left. The bell is then cut out but the light remains on till lever is again thrown in the center.

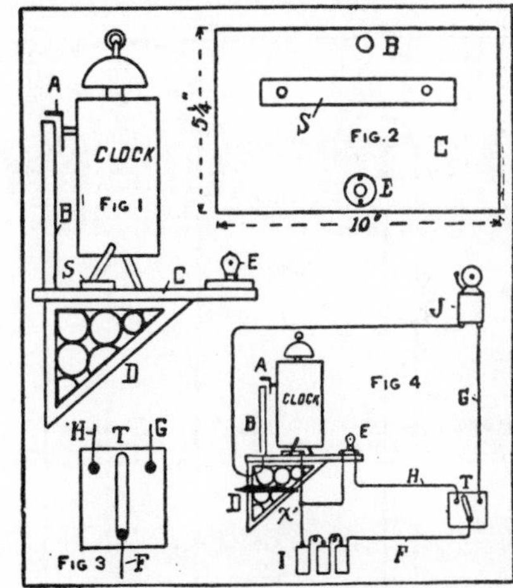

Details of Alarm Construction

In placing clock on shelf, after setting alarm, be sure that the legs of clock are on the brass strip and that the alarm key is in position so it will come in contact with the contact post in back of clock. The contact post may be of ¼-in. copper tubing, or ¼-in. brass rod.

The advantage of this is that one can control the bell and light, while lying in bed, by having the switch on the baseboard, near the bed, so it can be reached without getting out of bed.—Contributed by Geo. C. Brinkerhoff, Swissvale, Pa.

How to Hold a Screw on a Screwdriver

A screw that is taken from a place almost inaccessible with the fingers requires considerable patience to return it with an ordinary screwdriver unless some holding-on device is used. I have found that by putting a piece of cardboard or thick paper with the blade of the screwdriver in the screw head slot, the screw may be held and turned into places that it would be impossible with the screwdriver alone.—Contributed by C. Chatland, Ogden, Utah.

How to Make a Lead Cannon

Any boy who has a little mechanical ability can make a very reliable cannon for his Fourth-of-July celebration by following the instructions given here:

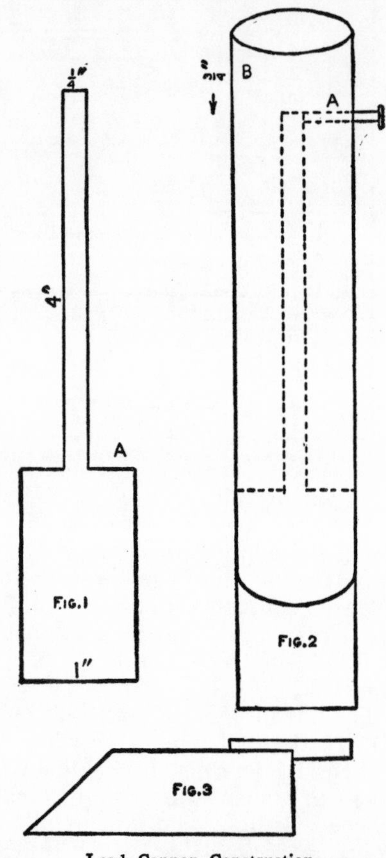

Lead Cannon Construction

Take a stick—a piece of curtain roller will do—7 in. long. Make a shoulder, as at A, Fig. 1, 4 in. from one end, making it as true and smooth as possible, as this is to be the muzzle of the cannon. Make the spindle as in Fig. 1, ¼ in. in diameter. Procure a good quality of stiff paper, about 6 in. wide, and wrap it around the shoulder of the stick, letting it extend ¾ in. beyond the end of the spindle, as at B, Fig. 2. Push an ordinary shingle nail through the paper and into the extreme end of the spindle, as at A, Fig. 2. This is to form the fuse hole.

Having finished this, place stick and all in a pail of sand, being careful not to get the sand in it, and letting the opening at the top extend a little above the surface of the sand. Then fill the paper cylinder with melted lead and let cool. Pull out the nail and stick, scrape off the paper and the cannon is ready for mounting, as in Fig. 3.—Contributed by Chas. S. Chapman, Lanesboro, Minn.

Homemade Electric Bed Warmer

The heat developed by a carbon-filament lamp is sufficiently high to allow its use as a heating element of, for instance, a bed warmer. There are a number of other small heaters which can be easily made and for which lamps form very suitable heating elements, but the bed warmer is probably the best example. All that is required is a tin covering, which can be made of an old can, about 3½ in. in diameter. The top is cut out and the edge filed smooth. The lamp-socket end of the flexible cord is inserted in the can and the shade holder gripped over the opening. A small lamp of about 5 cp. will do the heating.

A flannel bag, large enough to slip over the tin can and provided with a neck that can be drawn together by means of a cord, gives the heater a more finished appearance, as well as making it more pleasant to the touch.

Making a Fire with the Aid of Ice

Take a piece of very clear ice and melt it down into the hollow of your hands so as to form a large lens. The illustration shows how this is done. With the lens-shaped ice used in the same manner as a reading glass to di-

Forming the Ice Lens

rect the sun's rays on paper or shavings you can start a fire.—Contributed by Arthur E. Joerin.

How to Make a Crossbow and Arrow Sling

In the making of this crossbow it is best to use maple for the stock, but if this wood cannot be procured, good straight-grained pine will do. The opposite end, which should be slanting a little as shown by the dotted lines. A spring, Fig. 2, is made from a good piece of oak and fastened to the stock

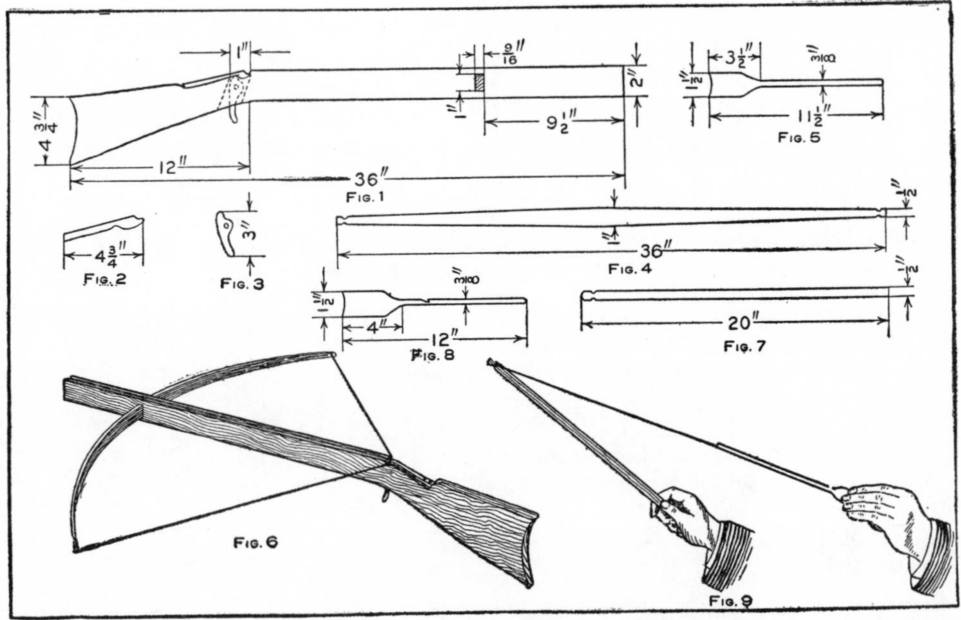

Details of the Bow-Gun and Arrow Sling

material must be 1½ in. thick, 6 in. wide and a trifle over 3 ft. long. The bow is made from straight-grained oak, ash, or hickory, ⅝ in. thick, 1 in. wide and 3 ft. long. A piece of oak, ⅜ in. thick, 1½ in. wide and 6 ft. long, will be sufficient to make the trigger, spring and arrows. A piece of tin, some nails and a good cord will complete the materials necessary to make the crossbow.

The piece of maple or pine selected for the stock must be planed and sandpapered on both sides, and then marked and cut as shown in Fig. 1. A groove is cut for the arrows in the top straight edge ⅜ in. wide and ⅜ in. deep. The tin is bent and fastened on the wood at the back end of the groove where the cord slips out of the notch; this is to keep the edges from splitting.

A mortise is cut for the bow at a point 9½ in. from the end of the stock, and one for the trigger 12 in. from the

with two screws. The trigger, Fig. 3, which is ¼ in. thick, is inserted in the mortise in the position when pulled back, and adjusted so as to raise the spring to the proper height, and then a pin is put through both stock and trigger, having the latter swing quite freely. When the trigger is pulled, it lifts the spring up, which in turn lifts the cord off the tin notch.

The stick for the bow, Fig. 4, is dressed down from a point ¾ in. on each side of the center line to ½ in. wide at each end. Notches are cut in the ends for the cord. The bow is not fastened in the stock, it is wrapped with a piece of canvas 1½ in. wide on the center line to make a tight fit in the mortise. A stout cord is now tied in the notches cut in the ends of the bow making the cord taut when the wood is straight.

The design of the arrows is shown in Fig. 5 and they are made with the blades much thinner than the round part.

To shoot the crossbow, pull the cord back and down in the notch as shown in Fig. 6, place the arrow in the groove, sight and pull the trigger as in shooting an ordinary gun.

The arrow sling is made from a branch of ash about ½ in. in diameter, the bark removed and a notch cut in one end, as shown in Fig. 7. A stout cord about 2½ ft. long is tied in the notch and a large knot made in the other or loose end. The arrows are practically the same as those used on the crossbow, with the exception of a small notch which is cut in them as shown in Fig. 8.

To throw the arrow, insert the cord near the knot in the notch of the arrow, then grasping the stick with the right hand and holding the wing of the arrow with the left, as shown in Fig. 9, throw the arrow with a quick slinging motion. The arrow may be thrown several hundred feet after a little practice.—Contributed by O. E. Trownes, Wilmette, Ill.

A Home-Made Vise

Cut two pieces of wood in the shape shown in the sketch and bore a ⅜-in. hole through both of them for a common carriage bolt. Fasten one of the pieces to the edge of the bench with a large wood screw and attach the other piece to the first one with a piece of leather nailed across the bottom of both pieces. The nut on the carriage bolt may be tightened with a wrench, or, better still, a key filed out of a piece of soft steel to fit the nut. The edges of the jaws are faced with sheet metal which can be copper or steel suitable for the work it is intended to hold.

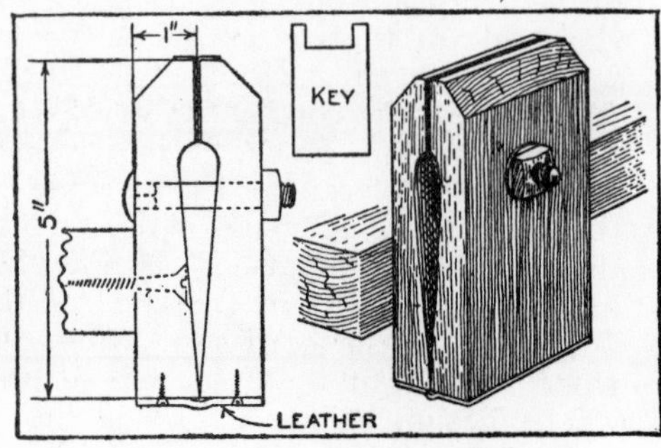

Details of a Home-Made Bench Vise

Temporary Dark Room Lantern

Occasionally through some accident to the regular ruby lamp, or through the necessity of developing while out of reach of a properly equipped dark room, some makeshift of illumination must be improvised. Such a temporary safe light may be made from an empty cigar box in a short time.

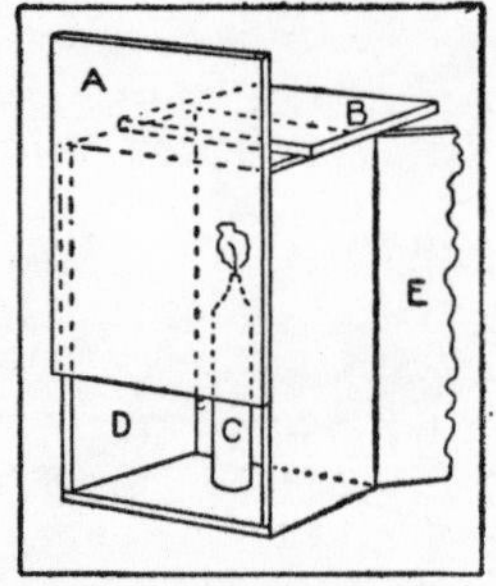

Remove the bottom of the box, and nail it in position as shown at A. Remove one end, and replace as shown at B. Drive a short wire nail through the center of the opposite end to serve as a seat for the candle, C. The lamp is finished by tacking two or more layers of yellow post-office paper over the aperture D, bringing the paper well around to the sides and bottom of the box to prevent light leakage from the cracks around the edges, says Photo Era. The hinged cover E, is used as a door, making lighting and trimming convenient. The door may be fastened with a nail or piece of wire. It is well to reinforce the hinge by gluing on a strip of cloth if the lamp is to be in use more than once or twice. This lamp is safe, for the projecting edges of A and B form light-shields for the ventilation orifice and the crack at the top of the hinged cover, respectively. Moreover, since the flame of the candle is above A, only reflected and transmitted light reaches the plate, while the danger of igniting the paper is reduced to a minimum.

The paint will sag and run if too much oil is put in white lead.

Camps and How to Build Them

There are several ways of building a temporary camp from material that is always to be found in the woods, and whether these improvised shelters are intended to last until a permanent camp is built, or only as a camp on a short excursion, a great deal of fun can be had in their construction. The Indian camp is the easiest to make. An evergreen tree with branches growing well down toward the ground furnishes all the material. By chopping the trunk almost through, so that when the tree falls the upper part will still remain attached to the stump, a serviceable shelter can be quickly provided. The cut should be about 5 ft. from the ground. Then the boughs and branches on the under side of the fallen top are chopped away and piled on top. There is room for several persons under this sort of shelter, which offers fairly good protection against any but the most drenching rains.

The Indian wigwam sheds rain better, and where there are no suitable trees that can be cut, it is the easiest camp to make. Three long poles with the tops tied together and the lower ends spaced 8 or 10 ft. apart, make the frame of the wigwam. Branches and brush can easily be piled up, and woven in and out on these poles so as to shed a very heavy rain.

The brush camp is shaped like an ordinary "A" tent. The ridge pole should be about 8 ft. long and supported by crotched uprights about 6 ft. from the ground. Often the ridge pole can be laid from one small tree to another. Avoid tall trees on account of lightning. Eight or ten long poles are then laid slanting against the ridge pole on each side. Cedar or hemlock boughs make the best thatch for the brush camp. They should be piled up to a thickness of a foot or more over the slanting poles and woven in and out to keep them from slipping. Then a number of poles should be laid over them to prevent them from blowing away.

In woods where there is plenty of bark available in large slabs, the bark lean-to is a quickly constructed and serviceable camp. The ridge pole is set up like that of the brush camp. Three or four other poles are laid slanting to the ground on one side only. The ends of these poles should be pushed into the earth and fastened with crotched sticks. Long poles are then laid crossways of these slanting poles, and the whole can be covered with brush as in the case of the brush camp or with strips of bark laid overlapping each other like shingles. Where bark is used, nails are necessary to hold it in place. Bark may also be used for a wigwam and it can be held in place by a cord wrapped tightly around the whole structure, running spiralwise from the ground to the peak. In the early summer, the bark can easily be removed from most trees by making two circular cuts around the trunk and joining them with another vertical cut. The bark is easily pried off with an ax, and if laid on the ground under heavy stones, will dry flat. Sheets of bark, 6 ft. long and 2 or 3 ft. wide, are a convenient size for camp construction.

The small boughs and twigs of hemlock, spruce, and cedar, piled 2 or 3 ft. deep and covered with blankets, make the best kind of a camp bed. For a permanent camp, a bunk can be made by laying small poles close together across two larger poles on a rude framework easily constructed. Evergreen twigs or dried leaves are piled on this, and a blanket or a piece of canvas stretched across and fastened down to the poles at the sides. A bed like this is soft and springy and will last through an ordinary camping season without renewal. A portable cot that does not take up much room in the camp outfit is made of a piece of heavy canvas 40 in. wide and 6 ft. long. Four-inch hems are sewed in each side of the canvas, and when the camp is pitched, a 2-in. pole is run through each hem and the ends of the pole supported on crotched sticks.

The Wigwam
The Brush Camp
The Indian Camp
Tongs
A Closed Lean-to, Thatched with Bark
Broom of Hemlock Twigs
Table and Chairs Combined
Packing Box Cupboard
Stool Made of a Block
Bunk with Mattress of Springy Boughs

Fresh water close at hand and shade for the middle of the day are two points that should always be looked for in selecting a site for a camp. If the camp is to be occupied for any length of time, useful implements for many purposes can be made out of such material as the woods afford. The simplest way to build a crane for hanging kettles over the campfire is to drive two posts into the ground, each of them a foot or more from one end of the fire space, and split the tops with an ax, so that a pole laid from one to the other across the fire will be securely held in the split. Tongs are very useful in camp. A piece of elm or hickory, 3 ft. long and 1½ in. thick, makes a good pair of tongs. For a foot in the middle of the stick, cut half of the thickness away and hold this part over the fire until it can be bent easily to bring the two ends together, then fasten a crosspiece to hold the ends close together, shape the ends so that anything that drops into the fire can be seized by them, and a serviceable pair of tongs is the result. Any sort of a stick that is easily handled will serve as a poker. Hemlock twigs tied around one end of a stick make an excellent broom. Movable seats for a permanent camp are easily made by splitting a log, boring holes in the rounded side of the slab and driving pegs into them to serve as legs. A short slab or plank can easily be made into a three-legged stool in the same way.

Campers usually have boxes in which their provisions have been carried. Such a packing box is easily made into a cupboard, and it is not difficult to improvise shelves, hinges, or even a rough lock for the camp larder.

A good way to make a camp table is to set four posts into the ground and nail crosspieces to support slabs cut from chopped wood logs to form a top. Pieces can be nailed onto the legs of the table to hold other slabs to serve as seats, and affording accommodation for several persons.

Brooder for Small Chicks

A very simple brooder can be constructed by cutting a sugar barrel in half and using one part in the manner

Brooder for Young Chicks Kept Warm with a Jug of Boiling Water

described. Line the inside of the half barrel with paper and then cover this with old flannel cloth. Make a cover for the top and line it in the same manner. At the bottom cut a hole in the edge, about 4 in. deep and 4 in. wide, and provide a cover or door. The inside is kept warm by filling a jug with boiling water and setting it within, changing the water both morning and night. When the temperature outside is 10 deg. the interior can be kept at 90 or 100 deg., but the jug must be refilled with boiling water at least twice a day.

Faucet Used as an Emergency Plug

A brass faucet split as shown at A during a cold spell, and as no suitable plug to screw into the elbow after removing the faucet was at hand, I drove a small cork, B, into the end of the faucet and screwed it back in place. The cork converted the faucet into an

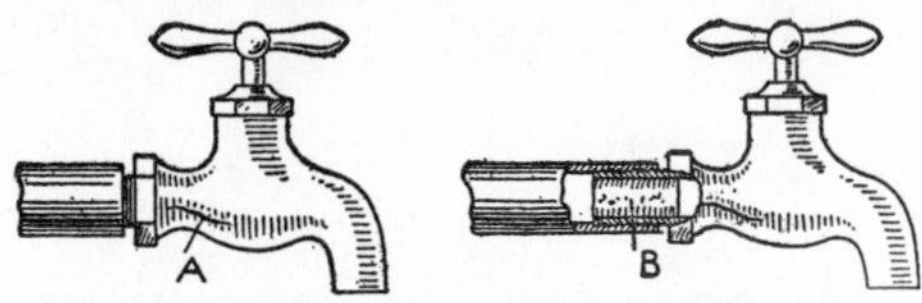

A Tight-Fitting Cork Driven into a Cracked Faucet Converted It into an Emergency Plug

emergency plug which prevented leakage until the proper fitting to take its place could be secured.—Contributed by James M. Kane, Doylestown, Pa.

Automatic Electric Heat Regulator

It is composed of a closed glass tube, A, Fig. 1, connected by means of a very small lead pipe, B, to another

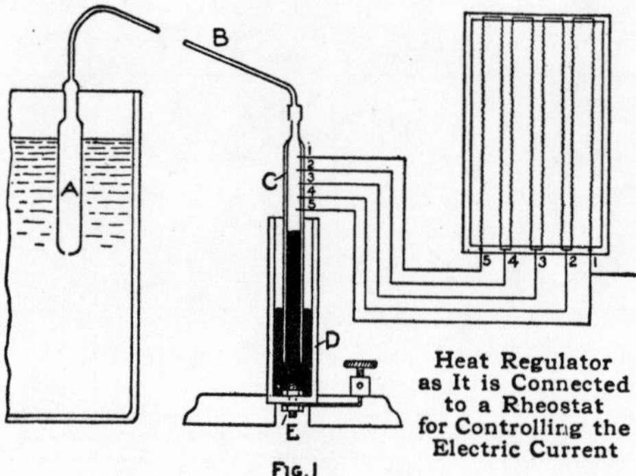

Heat Regulator as It is Connected to a Rheostat for Controlling the Electric Current

Fig. 1

glass tube, C, open at the bottom and having five pieces of platinum wire (1, 2, 3, 4 and 5), which project inside and outside of the tube, fused into one side. This tube is plunged into an ebonite vessel of somewhat larger diameter, which is fastened to the base by a copper screw, E. The tube C is filled to a certain height with mercury and then petroleum. The outer ends of the five platinum wires are soldered to ordinary copper wires and connections made to various points on a rheostat as shown. The diagram, Fig. 2, shows how the connections to the supply current are made.

The apparatus operates as follows: The tube is immersed in the matter to be heated, a liquid, for instance. As

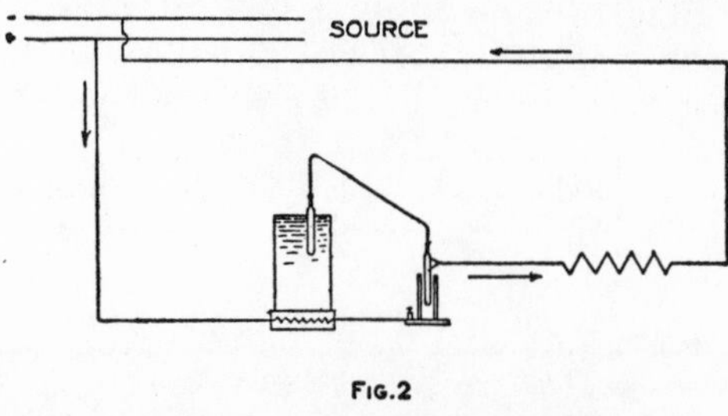

Fig. 2

Wiring Diagram Showing How the Connections to a Source of Current Supply are Made

the temperature of this rises, the air expands and exerts pressure on the petroleum in the tube C so that the level of the mercury is lowered. The current is thus compelled, as the platinum wires with the fall of the mercury are brought out of circuit, to pass through an increasing resistance, until, if necessary, the flow is entirely stopped when the mercury falls below the wire 5.

With this very simple apparatus the temperature can be kept constant within a 10-deg. limit, and it can be made much more sensitive by increasing the number of platinum wires and placing them closer together, and by filling the tube A with some very volatile substance, such as ether, for instance. The petroleum above the mercury prevents sparking between the platinum wire and the mercury when the latter falls below any one of them.

Repairing a Washer on a Flush Valve

When the rubber washer on the copper flush valve of a soil-basin tank becomes loose it can be set by pouring a small quantity of paraffin between the rubber and the copper while the valve is inverted, care being taken to have the rubber ring centered. This makes a repair that will not allow a drop of water to leak out of the tank.—Contributed by Frank Jermin, Alpena, Michigan.

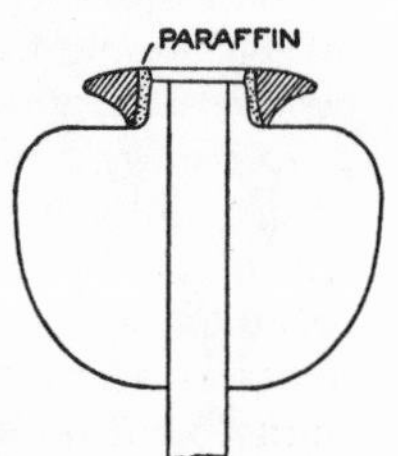

Cleaning Discolored Silver

A very quick way to clean silver when it is not tarnished, but merely discolored, is to wash the articles in a weak solution of ammonia water. This removes the black stains caused by sulphur in the air. After cleaning them with the solution, they should be washed and polished in magnesia powder or with a cloth. This method works well on silver spoons tarnished by eggs and can be used every day while other methods require much time and, therefore, cannot be used so often.

How to Make a Small Electric Motor

By W. A. ROBERTSON

The field frame of the motor, Fig. 1, is composed of wrought sheet iron, which may be of any thickness so that, when several pieces are placed together, they will make a frame 3/4 in. thick. It is necessary to lay out a template of the frame as shown, making it 1/16 in. larger than the dimensions given, to allow for filing to shape after the parts are fastened together. After the template is marked out, drill the four rivet holes, clamp the template, or pattern, to the sheet iron and mark carefully with a scriber. The bore can be marked with a pair of dividers, set at 1/8 in. This will mark a line for the center of the holes to be drilled with a 1/4-in. drill for removing the unnecessary metal. The points formed by drilling the holes can be filed to the pattern size. Be sure to mark and cut out a sufficient number of plates to make a frame 3/4 in. thick, or even 1/16 in. thicker, to allow for finishing.

After the plates are cut out and the rivet holes drilled, assemble and rivet them solidly, then bore it out to a diameter of 2 3/4 in. on a lathe. If the thickness is sufficient, a slight finishing cut can be taken on the face. Before removing the field from the lathe, mark off a space, 3 3/8 in. in diameter, for the field core with a sharp-pointed tool, and for the outside of the frame, 4 1/2 in. in diameter, by turning the lathe with the hand. Then the field can be finished to these marks, which will make it uniform in size. When the frame is finished so far, two holes, 3 5/8 in. between centers, are drilled and tapped with a 3/8-in. tap. These holes are for the bearing studs. Two holes are also drilled and tapped for 1/4-in. screws, which fasten the holding-down lugs or feet to the frame. These lugs are made of a piece of 1/8-in. brass or iron, bent at right angles as shown.

The bearing studs are now made, as shown in Fig. 2, and turned into the threaded holes in the frame. The bearing supports are made of two pieces of 1/8-in. brass, as shown in the left-hand sketch, Fig. 3, which are fitted on the studs in the frame. A 5/8-in. hole is

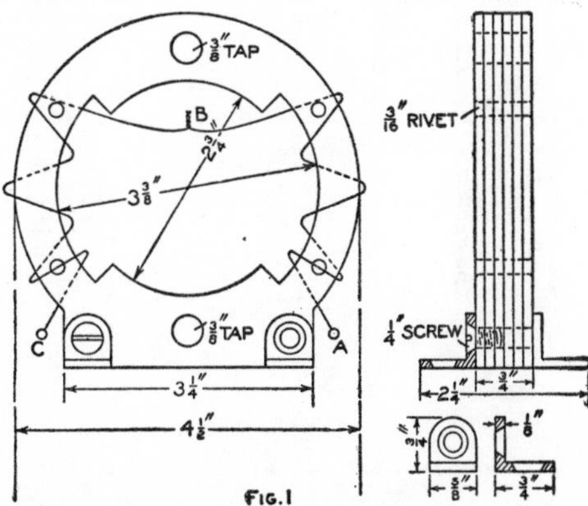

The Field-Coil Core is Built Up of Laminated Wrought Iron Riveted Together

drilled in the center of each of these supports, into which a piece of 5/8-in. brass rod is inserted, soldered into place, and drilled to receive the armature shaft. These bearings should be fitted and soldered in place after the armature is constructed. The manner of doing this is to wrap a piece of paper on the outside of the finished armature ring and place it through the opening in the field, then slip the bearings on the ends of the shaft. If the holes in the bearing support should be out of line, file them out to make the proper adjustment. When the bearings are located, solder them to the supports, and build up the solder well. Remove

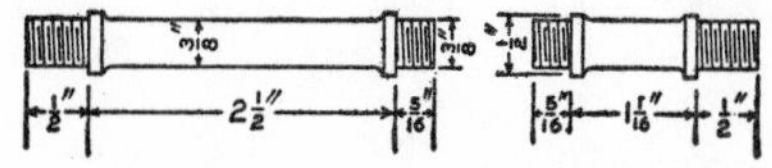

The Bearing Studs are Turned from Machine Steel Two of Each Length being Required

the paper from the armature ring and see that the armature revolves freely in the bearings without touching the inside of the field at any point. The supports are then removed and the solder turned up in a lathe, or otherwise finished. The shaft of the armature, Fig. 4, is turned up from machine steel, leaving the finish of the bearings until the armature is completed and fastened to the shaft.

The armature core is made up as fol-

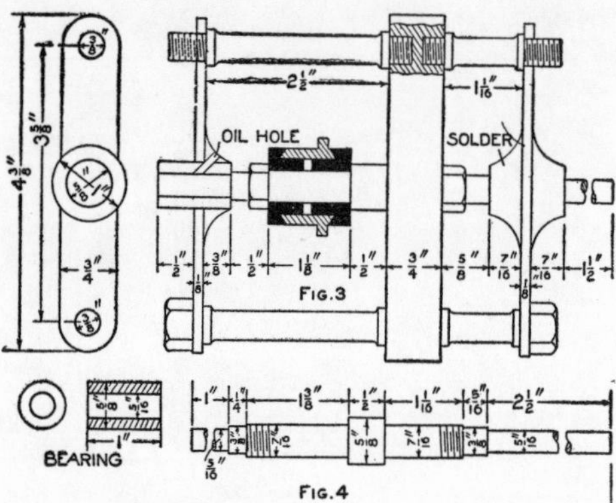

The Assembled Bearing Frame on the Field Core and the Armature Shaft Made of Machine Steel

lows: Two pieces of wrought sheet iron, 1/8 in. thick, are cut out a little larger than called for by the dimensions given in Fig. 5, to allow for finishing to size. These are used for the outside plates and enough pieces of No. 24 gauge sheet iron to fill up the part between until the whole is over 3/4 in. thick are cut like the pattern. After the pieces are cut out, clamp them together and drill six 1/8-in. holes through them for rivets. Rivet them together, and anneal the whole piece by placing it in a fire and heating the metal to a cherry red, then allowing it to cool in the ashes. When annealed, bore out the inside to 1 11/16 in. in diameter and fit in a brass spider, which is made as follows: Procure a piece of brass, 3/4 in. thick, and turn it up to the size shown and file out the metal between the arms. Slip the spider on the armature shaft and secure it solidly with the setscrew so that the shaft will not turn in the spider when truing up the armature core. File grooves or slots in the armature ring so that it will fit on the arms of the spider. Be sure to have the inside of the armature core run true. When this is accomplished, solder the arms of the spider to the metal of the armature core. The shaft with the core is then put in a lathe and the outside turned off to the proper size. The sides are also faced off and finished. Make the core 3/4 in. thick. Remove the core from the lathe and file out slots 1/4 in. deep and 7/16 in. wide.

The commutator is turned from a piece of brass pipe, 3/4 in. inside diameter, as shown in Fig. 6. The piece is placed on a mandrel and turned to 3/4 in. in length and both ends chamfered to an angle of 60 deg. Divide the surface into 12 equal parts, or segments. Find the centers of each segment at one end, then drill a 1/8-in. hole and tap it for a pin. The pins are made of brass, threaded, turned into place and the ends turned in a lathe to an outside diameter of 1 1/4 in. Make a slit with a small saw blade in the end of each pin for the ends of the wires coming from the commutator coils. Saw the ring into the 12 parts on the lines between the pins.

The two insulating ends for holding these segments are made of fiber turned to fit the bore of the brass tubing, as shown in Fig. 7. Procure 12 strips of mica, the same thickness as the width of the saw cut made between the segments, and use them as a filler and insulation between the commuta-

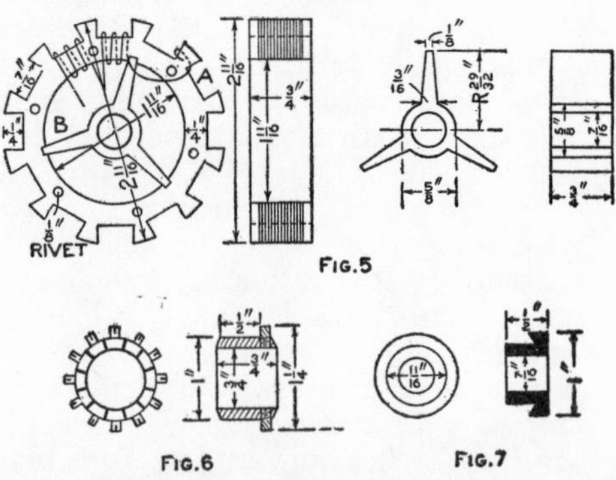

Armature-Ring Core, Its Hub and the Construction of the Commutator and Its Insulation

tor bars. Place them on the fiber hub and slip the hub on the shaft, then clamp the whole in place with the nut, as shown in Fig. 3. True up the commutator in a lathe to the size given in Fig. 6.

The brush holder is shaped from a

piece of fiber, as shown in Fig. 8. The studs for holding the brushes are cut from $\frac{5}{16}$-in. brass rod, as shown in Fig. 9. The brushes consist of brass or copper wire gauze, rolled up and flattened out to 1/8 in. thick and 1/4 in. wide, one end being soldered to keep the wires in place. The holder is slipped on the projecting outside end of the bearing, as shown in Fig. 3, and held with a setscrew.

The field core is insulated before winding with 1/64-in. sheet fiber, washers, 1 1/8 in. by 1 1/2 in., being formed for the ends, with a hole cut in them to fit over the insulation placed on the cores. A slit is cut through from the hole to the outside, and then they are soaked in warm water, until they become flexible enough to be put in place. After they have dried, they are glued to the core insulation.

The field is wound with No. 18 gauge double-cotton-covered magnet wire, about 100 ft. being required. Drill a small hole through each of the lower-end insulating washers. In starting to wind, insert the end of the wire through the hole from the inside, at A, Fig. 1, and wind on four layers, which will take 50 ft. of the wire, and bring the end of the wire out at B. After one coil, or side, is wound start at C in the same manner as at A, using the same number of turns and the same length of wire. The two ends are joined at B.

The armature ring is insulated by covering the inside and brass spider with $\frac{1}{16}$-in. sheet fiber. Two rings of $\frac{1}{16}$-in. sheet fiber are cut and glued to the sides of the ring. When the glue is set, cut out the part within the slot ends and make 12 channel pieces from 1/64-in. sheet fiber, which are glued in the slots and to the fiber washers. Be sure to have the ring and spider covered so the wire will not touch the iron or brass.

Each slot of the armature is wound with about 12 ft. of No. 21 gauge double-cotton-covered magnet wire. The winding is started at A, Fig. 5, by bending the end around one of the projections, then wind the coil in one of the slots as shown, making 40 turns, or four layers of 10 turns each, shellacking each layer as it is wound. After the coil is completed in one slot, allow about 2 in. of the end to protrude, to

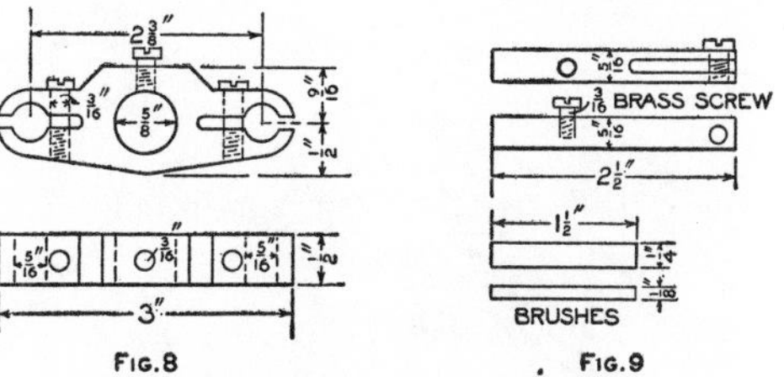

The Insulated Brush Holder and Its Studs for Holding the Brushes on the Commutator

fasten to the commutator segment. Wind the next slot with the same number of turns in the same manner, and so on, until the 12 slots are filled. The protruding ends of the coils are connected to the pins in the commutator segments after the starting end of one coil is joined to the finishing end of the next adjacent. All connections should be securely soldered.

The whole motor is fastened with screws to a wood base, 8 in. long, 6 in. wide and 1 in. thick. Two terminals are fastened at one side on the base, and a switch at the other side.

To connect the wires, after the motor is on the stand, the two ends of the wire, shown at B, Fig. 1, are soldered together. Run one end of the field wire, shown at A, through a small hole in the base and make a groove on the under side so that the wire end can be connected to one of the terminals. The other end of the field wire C is connected to the brass screw in the brass brush stud. Connect a wire from the other brush stud, run it through a small hole in the base and cut a groove for it on the under side so that it can be connected through the switch and the other terminal. This winding is for a series motor. The source of current is connected to the terminals. The motor can be run on a 110-volt direct current, but a resistance must be placed in series with it.

¶New tinware rubbed over with fresh lard and heated will never rust.

Another Optical Illusion

After taking a look at the accompanying illustration you will be positive that the cords shown run in a spiral toward the center, yet it shows a series of per-

The Cord Is Not a Spiral

fect circles of cords placed one inside the other. You can test this for yourself in a moment with a pair of compasses, or, still more simply, by laying a point of a pencil on any part of the cord and following it round. Instead of approaching or receding from the center in a continuous line, as in the case of a spiral, you will find the pencil returning to the point from which it started.

Substitute for Insulating Cleats

In wiring up door bells, alarms and telephones, as well as experimental work the use of common felt gun wads make a very good cleat for the wires. They are used in the manner illustrated in the accompanying sketch. The insulated wire is placed between two wads and fastened with two nails or screws. If one wad on the back is not thick enough to keep the wire away from the support, put on two wads behind and one in front of the wire and fasten in the same manner as described.

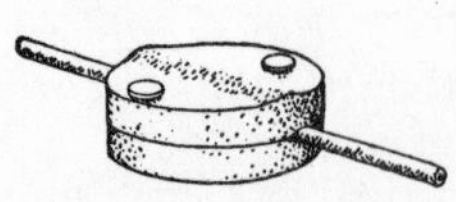

Electrically Operated Indicator for a Wind Vane

The accompanying photograph shows a wind vane connected with electric wires to an instrument at considerable distance which indicates by means of a magnetic needle the direction of the wind. The bearings of the vane consist of the head of a wornout bicycle. A ½-in. iron pipe extends from the vane and is held in place by the clamp originally used to secure the handle bar of the bicycle. In place of the forks is attached an eight-cylinder gas engine timer which is slightly altered in such a manner that the brush is at all times in contact, and when pointing between two contacts connects them both. Nine wires run from the timer, one from each of the eight contacts, and one, which serves as the ground wire, is fastened to the metallic body. The timer is set at such a position that when the vane points directly north, the brush of the timer makes a connection in the middle of a contact. When the timer is held in this position the brush will make connections with each of the contacts as the vane revolves.

The indicating device which is placed in a convenient place in the house consists of eight 4-ohm magnets fastened upon a 1-in. board. These magnets are placed in a 10-in. circle, 45 deg. apart and with their faces pointing toward the center. Covering these is a thin, wood board upon which is fastened a neatly drawn dial resembling a mariner's compass card. This is placed over the magnets in such a manner that there will be a magnet under each of the eight principal points marked on the dial. Over this dial is a magnetic needle or pointer, 6 in. long, perfectly balanced on the end of a standard and above all is placed a cover having a glass top. The eight wires from the timer contacts connect with the outside wires of the eight magnets separately and the inside wires from the magnets connect with the metal brace which holds the magnets in place. A wire is then connected from the metal brace to a push button, two or three cells of dry battery and to the ground wire in connection with the timer. The wires are connected in such a manner that when the vane is pointing in a certain direction the battery will be connected in series with the coil under that part of the dial representing the direction in which the vane is pointing, thus magnetizing the core of the magnet which attracts the opposite pole of the needle toward the face of the magnet and indicating the way the wind is blowing. The pointer end of the needle is painted black.

If the vane points in such a direction that the timer brush connects two contacts, two magnets will be magnetized and the needle will point midway between the two lines represented on the dial, thus giving 16 different directions. Around the pointer end of the needle is wound a fine copper wire, one end of which extends down to about $\frac{1}{32}$ in. of the dial. This wire holds the needle in place when the pointer end is directly over the magnet attracting it; the magnet causing the needle to "dip" will bring the wire in contact with the paper dial. Without this attachment, the needle would swing a few seconds before coming to a standstill.

The Wind Vane, Magnets and Indicator

The vane itself is easily constructed as can be seen in the illustration. It should be about 6 ft. long to give the best results. The magnets used can be purchased from any electrical store in pairs which are called "instrument magnets." Any automobile garage can supply the timer and an old valueless bicycle frame is not hard to find. The cover is easily made from a picture frame with four small boards arranged to take the place of the picture as shown.

The outfit is valuable to a person who is situated where a vane could not be placed so as to be seen from a window and especially at night when it is hard to determine the direction of the wind. By simply pressing the push button on the side of the cover, the needle will instantly point to the part of the dial from which the wind is blowing.—Contributed by James L. Blackmer, Buffalo, N. Y.

A Home-Made Floor Polisher

An inexpensive floor polisher can be made as follows: Secure a wooden box with a base 8 by 12 in. and about 6 in. high, also a piece of new carpet, 14 by 18 in. Cut 3-in. squares out of the four corners of the carpet and place the box squarely on it. Turn three of the flaps of the carpet up and tack them securely to the sides of the box. Before tacking the fourth side, fold a couple of newspapers to the right size and shove them in between the carpet and the bottom of the box for a cushion. Fill the box with any handy ballast, making it heavy or light, according to who is going to use it, and securely nail on the top of the box. The handle can be made from an old broom handle the whole of which will be none too long. Drive a heavy screweye into the big end of the handle and fasten to the polisher by a staple driven through the eye into the center of the cover, thus making a universal joint. The size of the box given here is the best although any size near that, if not too high, will answer the purpose just as well. The box is pushed or pulled over the floor and the padded side will produce a fine polish.

How to Make a Lady's Card-Case

A card-case such as is shown here makes a very appropriate present for any lady. To make it, secure a piece of "ooze" calf skin leather 4½ by 10½ in. The one shown in the accompanying picture was made of a rich tan ooze of light weight and was lined with a grey-green goat skin. The design was stenciled and the open parts backed with a green silk plush having a rather heavy nap. The lining of goat skin need not cover more than the central part—not the flies. A piece 4½ by 5

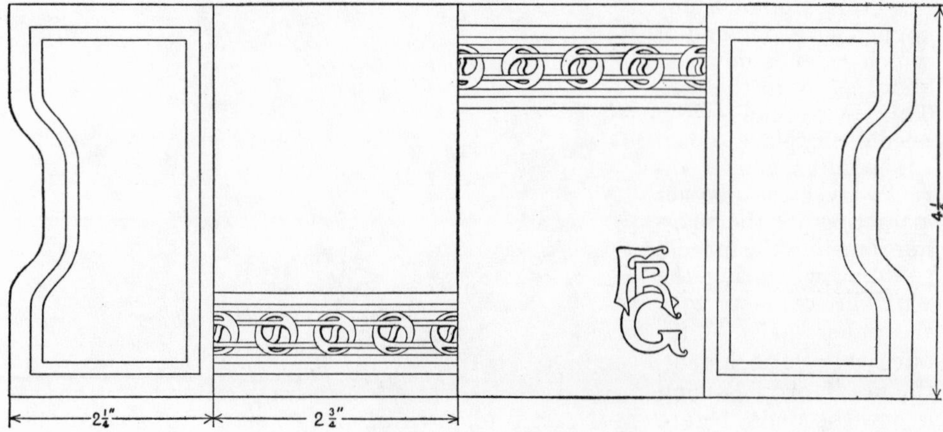

Design for the Cover of Lady's Card-Case

in. will be sufficient. A piece of plush $1\frac{1}{4}$ by 6 in. will be enough for the two sides.

Begin work by shaping the larger piece of leather as shown in the drawing. Allow a little margin at the top and bottom, however, to permit trimming the edges slightly after the parts have been sewed together. A knife or a pair of scissors will do to cut the leather with, though a special knife, called a chip carving knife, is most satisfactory.

The next thing is to put in the marks for the outline of the designs and the borders. A tool having a point shaped as in the illustration is commonly used. It is called a modeling tool for leather and may be purchased, or, one can be made from an ordinary nut pick by taking off the sharpness with fine emery paper so that it will not cut the leather. To work these outlines, first moisten the leather on the back with as much water as it will take and still not show through on the face side. Place the leather on some level, nonabsorbent surface and with the tool—and a straightedge on the straight lines—indent the leather as shown. The easiest way is to place the paper pattern on the leather and mark on the paper. The indentations will be transferred without the necessity of putting any lines on the leather.

With the knife cut out the stencils as shown. Paste the silk plush to the inner side, being careful not to get any of the paste so far out that it will show. A good leather paste will be required.

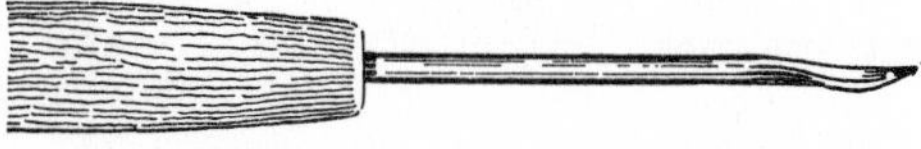

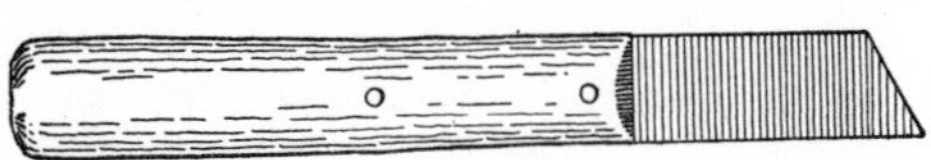

Leather Tools

Next place the lining, fold the flies along the lines indicated in the drawing. Hold the parts together and stitch them on a sewing-machine. An ordinary sewing-machine will do if a good stout needle is used. A silk thread that will match the leather should be used. Keep the ooze side of the lining

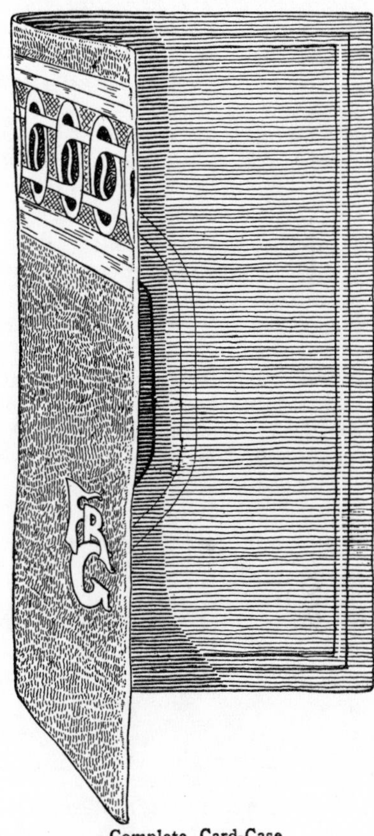

Complete Card-Case

out so that it will show, rather than the smooth side. With the knife and straightedge trim off the surplus material at the top and bottom and the book is ready for use.

Home-Made Fire Extinguisher

Dissolve 20 lb. of common salt and 10 lb. of sal ammoniac in 7 gal. of water, and put the solution in thin glass bottles, cork tightly and seal to prevent evaporation. The bottles should hold about 1 qt. If a fire breaks out, throw one of the bottles in or near the flames, or break off the neck and scatter the contents on the fire. It may be necessary to use several bottles to quench the flames.

Crutch Made of an Old Broom

An emergency crutch made of a worn-out broom is an excellent substitute for a wood crutch, especially when one or more crutches are needed for a short time, as in cases of a sprained ankle, temporary lameness, or a hip that has been wrenched.

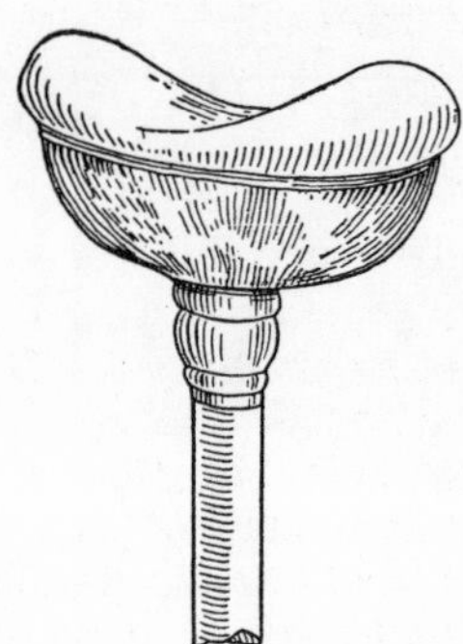

Shorten and hollow out the brush of the broom and then pad the hollow part with cotton batting, covering it with a piece of cloth sewed in place. Such a crutch does not heat the arm pit and there is an elasticity about it not to be had in the wooden crutch. The crutch can be made to fit either child or adult, and, owing to its cheapness, can be thrown away when no longer needed.—Contributed by Katharine D. Morse, Syracuse, N. Y.

Toy Darts and Parachutes

A dart (Fig. 1) is made of a cork having a tin cap, a needle and some feathers. The needle is run through the center of the cork A and a pin or piece of steel is put through the eye of the needle. Take a quantity of small

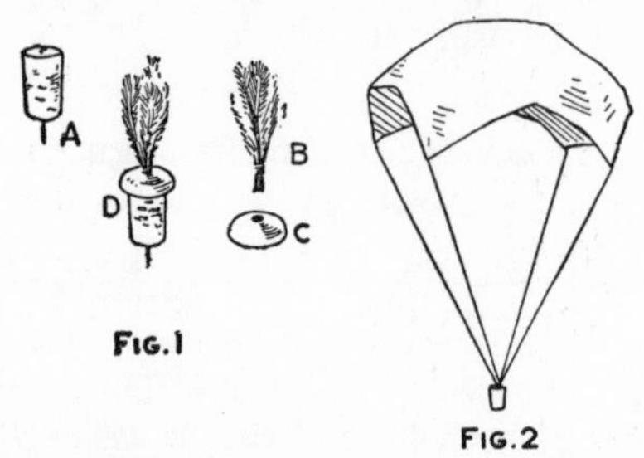

Dart Parts and Paper Parachute

feathers, B, and tie them together securely at the bottom. Bore a hole in the center of the cap C, and fasten the feathers inside of it. Fasten the cap on the cork and the dart is ready for use. When throwing the dart at a target stand from 6 to 10 ft. away from it.

The parachute is made by cutting a piece of paper 15 in. square and tying a piece of string to each corner. The strings should be about 15 in. long. Tie all four strings together in a knot at the end and fasten them in the top of a cork with a small tack. It is best to be as high as possible when flying the parachute as the air currents will sail it high and fast. Take hold of the parachute by the cork and run it through the air with the wind, letting it go at arm's length.—Contributed by J. Gordon Dempsey, Paterson, N. J.

A Tool for Lifting Can Covers

A handy tool for prying up varnish, paint, syrup and similar can covers can be made from an old fork filed down

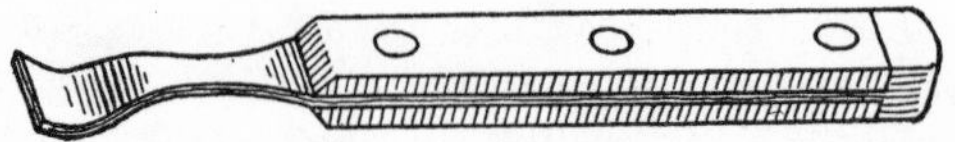

Made of an Old Fork

to the shape shown in the illustration. The end is filed to an edge, but not sharp.—Contributed by Ben Grebin, Ashland, Wis.

Keeping Rats from a Chicken Coop

After trying for months to keep the rats from tunneling their way into my chicken coop by filling in the holes, laying poisoned meat and meal, setting traps, etc., I devised a simple and effective method to prevent them from doing harm.

My roosting coop is 5 by 15 ft. There is a 1-in. board all around the bottom on the inside. I used wire mesh having ½-in. openings and formed it into the shape of a large tray with edges 6 in. high, the corners being wired, and tacked it to the boards. This not only keeps the rats out, but prevents the chickens from digging holes, thus helping the rats to enter.—Contributed by John A. Hellwig, Albany, N. Y.

Homemade Telephone Receiver

The receiver illustrated herewith is to be used in connection with the transmitter described elsewhere in this volume. The body of the receiver, A, is made of a large wooden ribbon spool. One end is removed entirely, the other sawed in two on the line C and a flange, F, is cut on the wood, 1/8 in. wide and 1/16 in. deep. A flange of the same size is made on the end D that was sawed off, and the outside part tapered toward the hole as shown. The magnet is made of a 30-penny nail, B, cut to the length of the spool, and a coil of wire, E, wound on the head end. The coil is 1 in. long, made up of four layers of No. 22 gauge copper magnet wire, allowing the ends to extend out about 6 in. The nail with the coil is then put into the hole of the spool as shown. The diaphragm C, which is the essential part of the instrument, should be made as carefully as possible from ferrotype tin, commonly called tintype tin. The diaphragm is placed between the flanges on the spool and the end D that was sawed off. The end piece and diaphragm are both fastened to the spool with two or three slender wood screws, as shown.

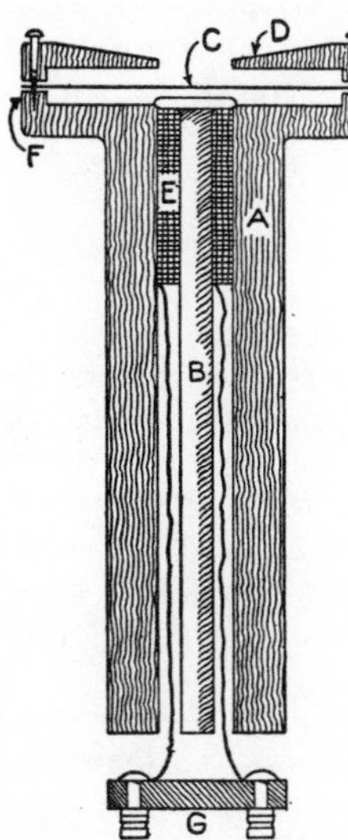

A small wooden or fiber end, G, is fitted with two binding posts which are connected to the ends of the wire left projecting from the magnet winding. The binding posts are attached to the line and a trial given. The proper distance must be found between the diaphragm and the head of the nail. This can be accomplished by moving the nail and magnet in the hole of the spool. When the distance to produce the right sound is found, the nail and magnet can be made fast by filling the open space with melted sealing wax. The end G is now fastened to the end of the spool, and the receiver is ready for use.

How to Clean Jewelry

To cleanse articles of silver, gold, bronze and brass use a saturated solution of cyanide of potassium. To clean small articles, dip each one into the solution and rinse immediately in hot water; then dry and polish with a linen cloth. Larger articles are cleaned by rubbing the surface with a small tuft of cotton saturated in the solution. As cyanide of potassium is a deadly poison, care must be taken not to have it touch any sore spot on the flesh.

Ornamental Iron Flower Stand

The illustration shows an ornamental iron stand constructed to hold a glass or china vase. This stand can be made by first drawing an outline of the vase on a heavy piece of paper. The vase is to have three supports. The shape of the scrolls forming each support should be drawn on the paper

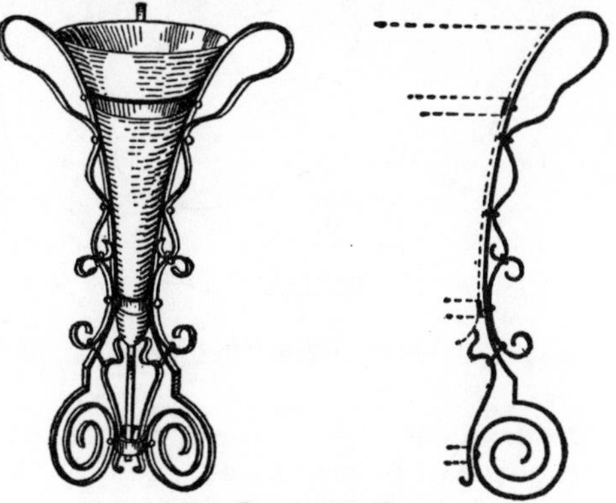

The Stand with Vase

around the shape of the vase. A single line will be sufficient, but care must be taken to get the shapes of the scrolls true. Take a piece of string or, better still, a piece of small wire, and pass it around the scroll shape on the paper.

This will give the exact length of the iron required to make the scroll. As sheet metal is used for making the scrolls, it can be cut in the right lengths with a pair of tinner's shears. Take a pair of round-nose pliers, begin with the smallest scrolls, and bend each strip in shape, using the flat-nose pliers when necessary to keep the iron straight, placing it on the sketch from time to time to see that the scrolls are kept to the shape required. The scrolls are riveted and bolted together. The supports are fastened together with rings of strip iron 3/8 in. wide, to which the supports are fastened with rivets. The metal can be covered with any desired color of enamel paint.

How to Make a Coin Purse

The dimensions for a leather coin purse are as follows: from A to B, as shown in the sketch, 6 3/8 in.; from C to D, 4 1/4 in.; from E to F, 3 1/2 in. and from G to H, 3 1/4 in. Russian calf modeling leather is the material used. A shade of brown is best as it does not soil easily, and does not require coloring.

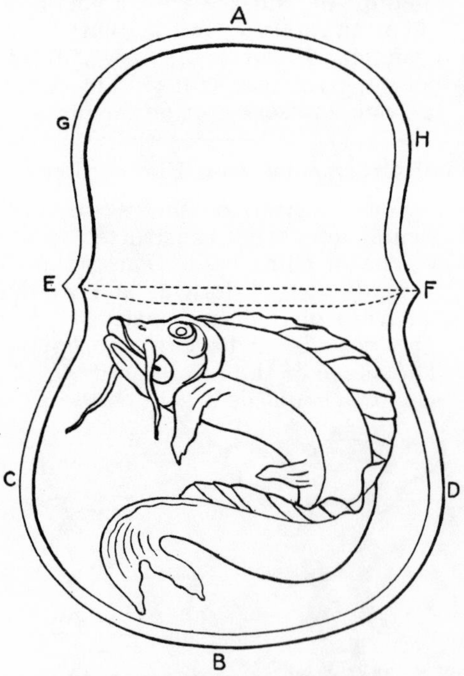

Leather Design for a Purse

Cut out the leather to the size of the pattern, then moisten the surface on the rough side with a sponge soaked in water. Be careful not to moisten the leather too much or the water will go through to the smooth side. Have the design drawn or traced on the pattern. Then lay the pattern on the smooth side of the leather and trace over the design with the small end of the leather tool or a hard, sharp pencil. Trace also the line around the purse. Dampen the leather as often as is necessary to keep it properly moistened.

After taking off the pattern, retrace the design directly on the leather to make it more distinct, using a duller point of the tool. Press or model down the leather all around the design, making it as smooth as possible with the round side of the tool. Work down the outside line of the design, thus raising it.

Fold the leather on the line EF. Cut another piece of leather the size of the side ECBD of the purse, and after putting the wrong sides of the leather together, stitch around the edge as designated by the letters above mentioned. Do not make this piece come quite up to the line EF, so that the coins may be more easily put in and taken out. About 1 in. from the lines EF on the piece, stitch in a strip of leather about 1/4 in. wide when stitching up the purse, through which to slip the fly AGH.

A window glass may be kept from frosting by rubbing over the inner surface a solution of 55 parts of glycerine and 1,000 parts of 60 per cent alcohol. The odor may be improved by adding a little oil of amber. This solution will also prevent a glass from sweating in warm weather.

How to Make a Turbine Engine

In the following article is described a machine which anyone can make, and which will be very interesting, as well as useful. It can be made without the use of a lathe, or other tools usually out of reach of the amateur mechanic. It is neat and efficient, and a model for speed and power. Babbitt metal is the material used in its construction, being cast in wooden molds. The casing for the wheel is cast in halves—a fact which must be kept in mind.

First, procure a planed pine board 1 by 12 in. by 12 ft. long. Cut off six

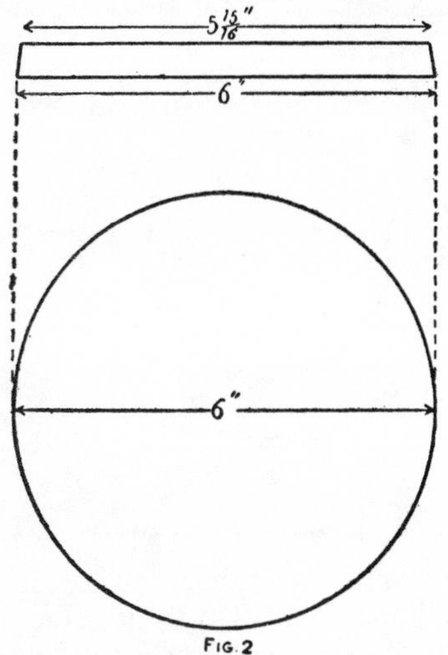

Fig. 2

pieces 12 in. square, and, with a compass saw, cut out one piece as shown in Fig. 1, following the dotted lines, leaving the lug a, and the projections B and b to be cut out with a pocket knife. Make the lug ¼ in. deep, and the projections B, b, ½ in. deep. The entire cut should be slightly beveled.

Now take another piece of wood, and cut out a wheel, as shown in Fig. 2. This also should be slightly beveled. When it is finished, place it on one of the square pieces of wood, with the largest side down, then place the square piece out of which Fig. 1 was cut, around the wheel, with the open side down. (We shall call that side of a mold out of which a casting is drawn, the "open" side.) Place it so that it is even at the edge with the under square piece and place the wheel so that the space between the wheel and

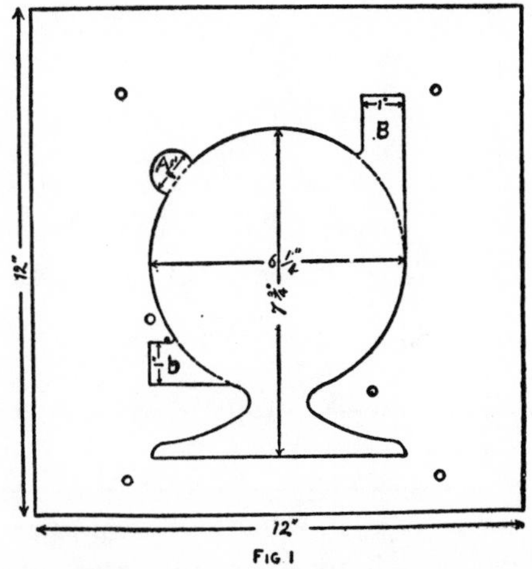

Fig. 1

the other piece of wood is an even ⅛ in. all the way around. Then nail the wheel down firmly, and tack the other piece slightly.

Procure a thin board ¼ in. thick, and cut it out as shown in Fig. 3; then nail it, with pins or small nails, on the center of one of the square pieces of wood. Fit this to the two pieces just finished, with the thin wheel down—but first boring a ¾-in. hole ¼ in. deep, in the center of it; and boring a ⅜-in.

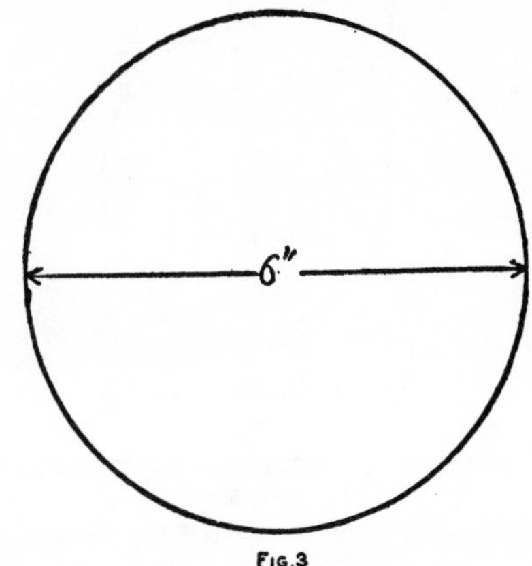

Fig. 3

hole entirely through at the same place. Now put mold No. 1 (for that is what we shall call this mold) in a vise, and bore six ¼-in. holes through it. Be careful to keep these holes well out in the solid part, as shown by the black dots in Fig. 1. Take the mold apart, and clean all the shavings out of it;

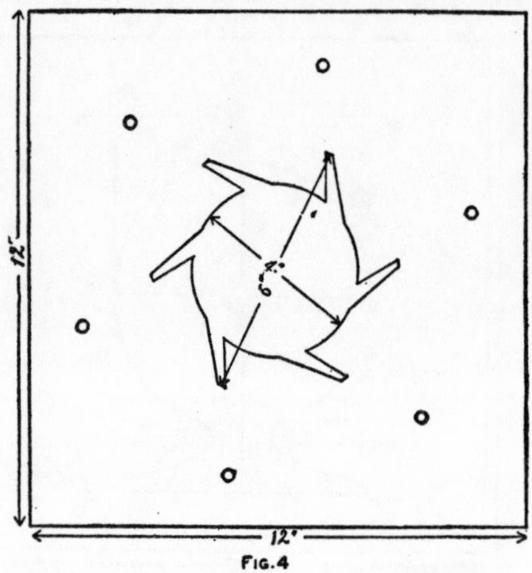

Fig. 4

then bolt it together, and lay it away to dry.

Now take another of the 12-in. square pieces of wood, and cut it out as shown in Fig. 4, slightly beveled. After it is finished, place it between two of the 12-in. square pieces of wood, one of which should have a ⅜-in. hole bored through its center. Then bolt together with six ¼-in. bolts, as shown by the

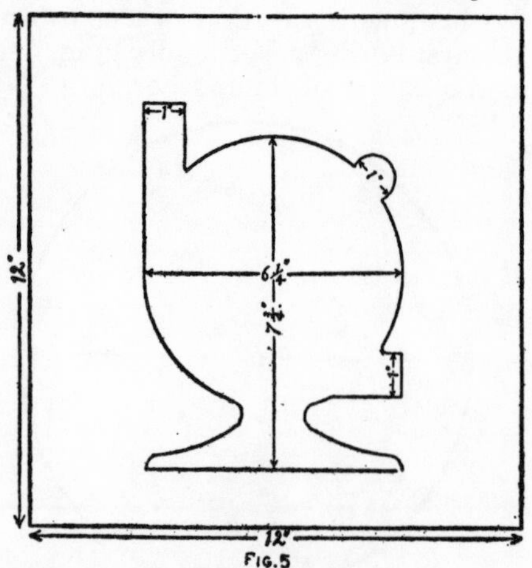

Fig. 5

black dots in Fig. 4, and lay it away to dry. This is mold No. 2.

Now take mold No. 1; see that the bolts are all tight; lay it on a level place, and pour babbitt metal into it, until it is full. Let it stand for half an hour, then loosen the bolts and remove the casting.

Now cut out one of the 12-in.-square pieces of wood as shown in Fig. 5. This is the same as Fig. 1, only the one is left-handed, the other right-handed. Put this together in mold No. 1, instead of the right-handed piece; and run in babbitt metal again. The casting thus made will face together with the casting previously made.

Pour metal into mold No. 2. This will cast a paddle-wheel, which is intended to turn inside of the casting already made.

If there should happen to be any

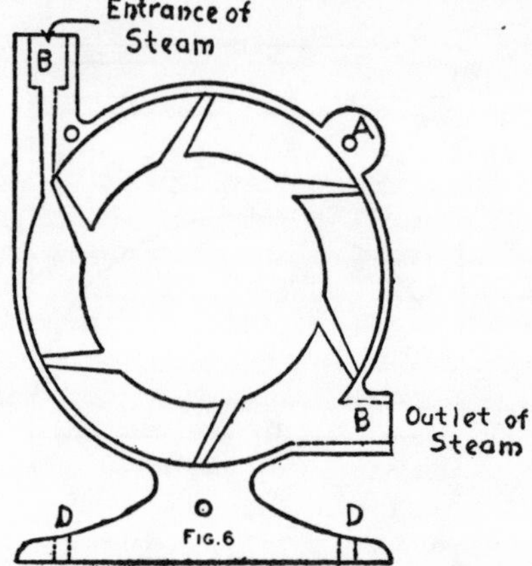

Fig. 6

holes or spots, where the casting did not fill out, fill them by placing a small piece of wood with a hole in it, over the defective part, and pouring metal in to fill it up.

If you cannot obtain the use of a drill press, take an ordinary brace, fasten a ⅜-in. drill in it, and bore a hole through the end of a strip about 2 in. wide and 16 in. long; put the top of the brace through this hole, and fasten the other end of the strip to a bench, as shown in illustration. Find the center of the paddle-wheel, place it under the drill, true it up with a square; and drill it entirely through. Find the centers of the insides of the other two castings, and drill them in the same manner.

A piece of mild steel 5 in. long, and ⅜ in. in diameter must now be obtained. This is for a shaft. Commencing 1½ in. from the one end, file the shaft off flat for a distance of 1 in. Then cut a slot in the paddle-wheel, and place the shaft inside of the paddle-wheel, with the flat part of the shaft turned to face the slot in the wheel. Pour metal into the slot to key the wheel on to the shaft.

The paddle-wheel is now ready to be fitted inside of the casing. It may be necessary to file some of the ends off the paddles, in order to let the paddle-wheel go into the casing. After it is fitted in, so that it will turn easily, place the entire machine in a vise, and bore three ¼-in. holes, one in the lug, one in the projections, B, b, and the other in the base, as shown by the black dots in Fig. 6. Also bore the port-hole in projection B, and the exhaust hole in projection b, and two ¼-in. holes at d, d, Fig. 6. Cut out a piece of gasket and fit it between the two castings. Then bolt the castings together, screw down, and connect to the boiler.

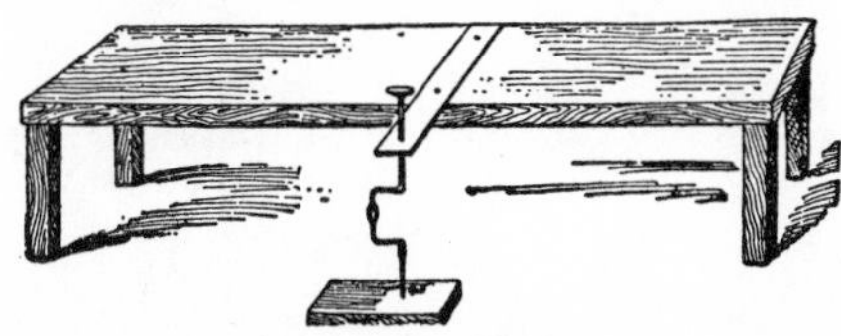

Using the Brace

The reader must either cast a pulley out of babbitt metal, or else go to a machinist and get a collar turned, with a boss and a set screw, and with three small screw holes around the edge. Cut out a small wood wheel and screw the collar fast to it, fasten it to the shaft of the turbine and turn on the steam. Then take a knife or a chisel, and, while it is running at full speed, turn the wheel to the shape desired.

Your turbine engine is now ready for work, and if instructions have been carefully followed, will do good service.

When painting the automobile body and chassis be sure to stuff the oil holes with felt or waste before applying the paint. If this caution is not observed the holes will become clogged with paint which will prevent any oil reaching the bearing.

How To Build An Ice Boat

The ice boat is each year becoming more popular. Any one with even small experience in using tools can construct such a craft, and the pleasure many times repays the effort.

A Four-Runner Ice Yacht

Take two pieces of wood 2 by 6 in., one 6 ft. and the other 8 ft. long. At each end of the 6-ft. piece and at right angles to it, bolt a piece of hardwood 2 by 4 by 12 in. Round off the lower edge of each piece to fit an old skate. Have a blacksmith bore holes through the top of the skates and screw one of them to each of the pieces of hardwood.

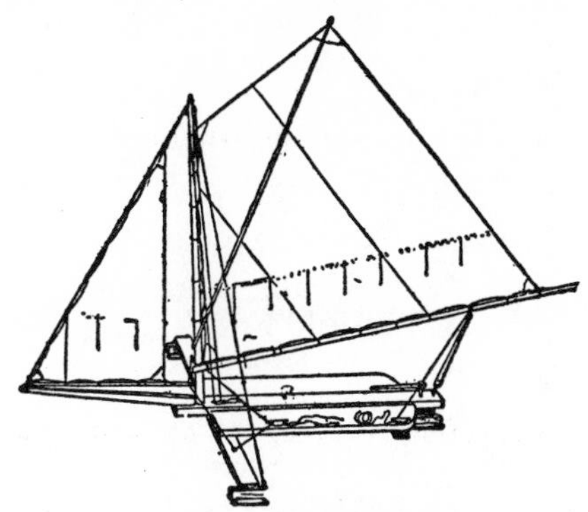

Plan of Ice Boat

These skates must be exactly parallel or there will be trouble the first time the craft is used.

Over the middle of the 6-ft. piece and

at right angles to it, bolt the 8-ft. plank, leaving 1 ft. projecting as in Fig. 1.

The rudder skate is fastened to a piece of hardwood 2 by 2 by 12 in. as the runners were fastened. This piece should be mortised 3 by 3 by 4 in. in the top before the skate is put on. Figure 2 shows the rudder post.

A piece of hardwood 1 by 6 by 6 in. should be screwed to the under side of the 8-ft. plank at the end with the grain running crosswise. Through this bore a hole 1½ in. in diameter in order that the rudder post may fit nicely. The tiller, Fig. 3, should be of hardwood, and about 8 in. long.

To the under side of the 8-ft. plank bolt a piece of timber 2 by 4 by 22 in. in front of the rudder block, and to this cross piece and the 6-ft. plank nail 8-in. boards to make the platform.

The spar should be 9 ft. long and 2½ in. in diameter at the base, tapering to 1½ in. at the top. This fits in the square hole, Fig. 1. The horn should be 5½ ft. long, 2 by 3 in. at the butt and 1 in. at the end.

Figure 4 gives the shape and dimensions of the mainsail which can be made of muslin. Run the seam on a machine, put a stout cord in the hem and make loops at the corners.

Figure 6 shows the way of rigging the gaff to the spar. Figure 7 shows the method of crotching the main boom and Fig. 8 a reef point knot, which may come in handy in heavy winds.

Make your runners as long as possible, and if a blacksmith will make an iron or steel runner for you, so much the better will be your boat.

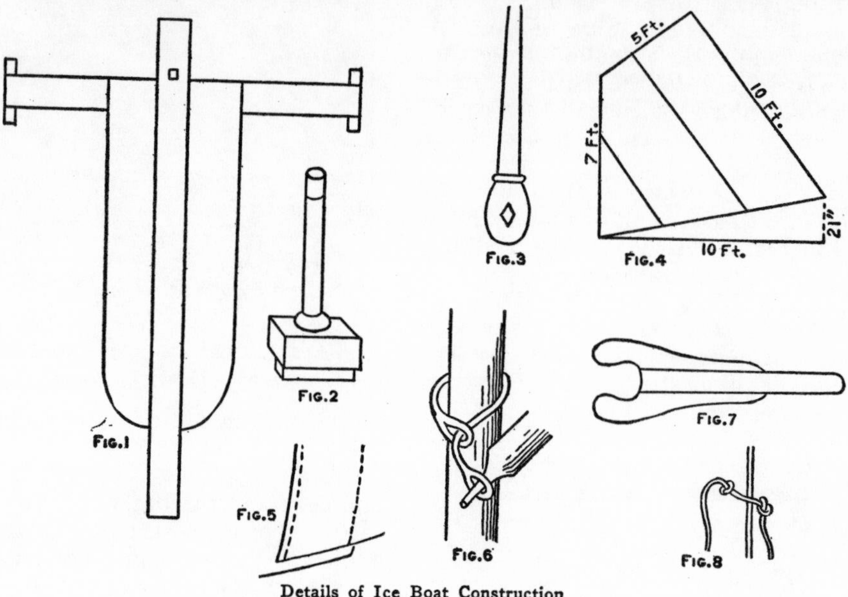

Details of Ice Boat Construction

Electric Rat Exterminator

Some time ago we were troubled by numerous large rats around the shop, particularly in a storehouse about 100 ft. distant, where they often did considerable damage. One of the boys thought he would try a plan of electrical extermination, and in order to carry out his plan he picked up an old zinc floor plate that had been used under a stove and mounted a wooden disk 6 in. in diameter in the center. On this disk he placed a small tin pan about 6 in. in diameter, being careful that none of the fastening nails made an electrical connection between the zinc plate and the tin pan.

This apparatus was placed on the floor of the warehouse where it was plainly visible from a window in the shop where we worked and a wire was run from the pan and another from the zinc plate through the intervening yard and into the shop. A good sized induction coil was through connected with these wires and about six dry batteries were used to run the induction coil whenever a push button was manipulated.

It is quite evident that when a rat put its two fore feet on the edge of the pan in order to eat the mush which it contained, that an electrical connection would be made through the body of the rat, and when we pushed the button up in the shop the rat would be thrown

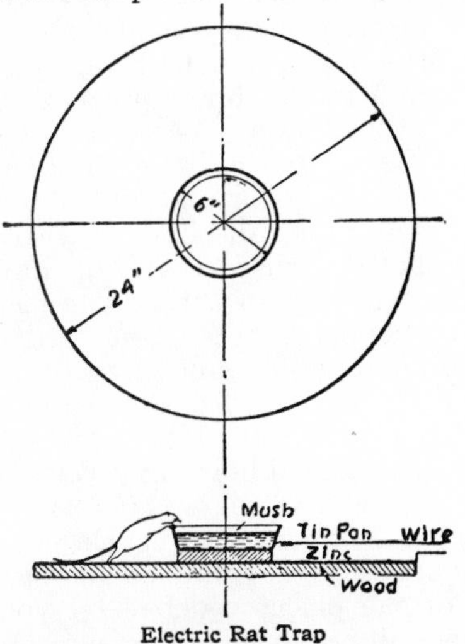

Electric Rat Trap

2 or 3 ft. in the air and let out a terrific squeak. The arrangement proved quite too effective, for after a week the rats all departed and the boys all regretted that their fun was at an end.—Contributed by John D. Adams, Phoenix, Ariz.

How to Make a Simple Fire Alarm

A fire alarm which is both inexpensive and simple in construction is shown in the illustration. Its parts are as follows:

A, small piece of wood; B, block of wood nailed to A; S S, two pieces of sheet brass about 1/4 in. wide, bent into a hook at each end; P, P, binding-posts fastening the springs S S, to block B, so that they come in contact at C. W is a piece of wax crayon just long enough to break the contact at C when inserted as shown in the illustration.

When these parts have been put together in the manner described, connect the device in circuit with an electric bell, and place it behind a stove.

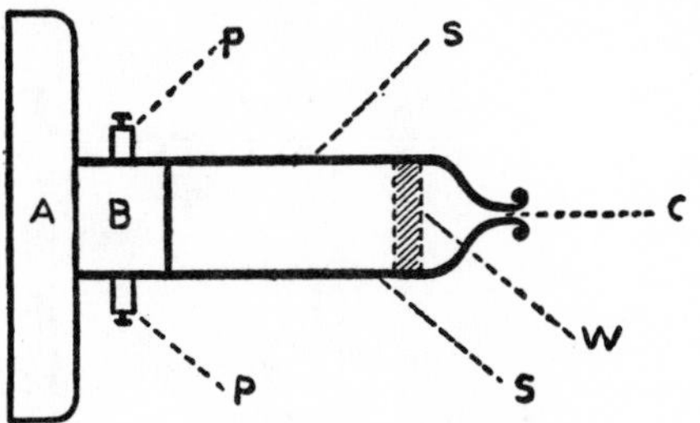

Simple Fire Alarm

When the stove becomes too hot the wax will melt at the ends, allowing the springs to contact at C, and the alarm bell will ring.—Contributed by J. R. Comstock, Mechanicsburg, Pa.

To Build a Merry-Go-Round

This is a very simple device, but one that will afford any amount of amusement. The center post rests in an auger hole bored in an old stump or in a post set in the ground. The stump makes the best support. The center pole should be 10 ft. high. An old wheel is mounted at the top of the pole, and the pole works in the wheel as an axle, says the American Boy. The wheel is anchored out by several guy

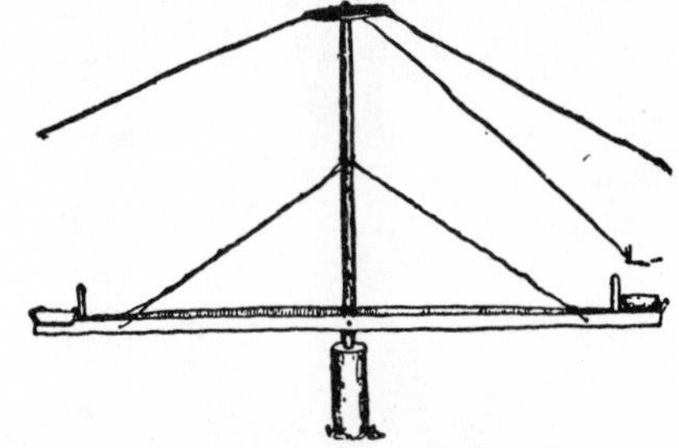

Home-Made Merry-Go-Round

wires. The seat arms may be any length desired. A passenger rides in each seat and the motorman takes his station at the middle.

Emery wheel arbors should be fitted with flanges or washers having a slight concave to their face.

Novelty Clock for the Kitchen

An inexpensive and easy way to make an unique ornament of a clock

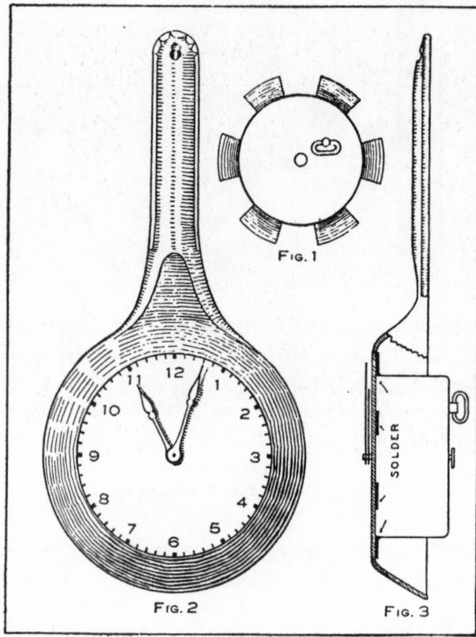

The Clock with Holder

for kitchen use is to take an old alarm clock or a new one if preferred, and make it into a clock to hang on the wall. Take the glass, dial and works out of the shell and cut some pieces out of the metal so that when the pieces left are turned back it will have the appearance as in Fig. 1. Then get a 10-cent frying pan, 6 in. in diameter, and drill a hole in the center so the shaft for the hands will easily pass through and extend out far enough to replace the two hands. Put the works back in the metal shell and solder it to the frying pan by the pieces turned out as in Fig. 2. Gild the pan all over, including the handle, and print black figures in the small circles. Calendar figures can be pasted on small circles and these pasted on the frying pan. The parts can be divided into minutes with small lines the same as shown in the drawing. Make new hands that are long enough to reach the figures from sheet brass or tin and paint them black.—Contributed by Carl P. Herd, Davenport, Iowa.

How to Make a Small Silver Plating Outfit

Take an ordinary glass fruit jar or any other receptacle in glass, not metal, which will hold 1 qt. of liquid and fill it with rain or distilled water and then add 3/4 oz. of silver chloride and 1 1/2 oz. of c. p. potassium cyanide. Let this dissolve and incorporate well with the water before using. Take an ordinary wet battery and fasten two copper wires to the terminals and fasten the other ends of the wires to two pieces of heavy copper wire or 1/4-in. brass pipe. The wires must be well soldered to the brass pipe to make a good connection. When the solution is made up and entirely dissolved the outfit is ready for plating.

Procure a small piece of silver, a silver button, ring, chain or anything made entirely of silver and fasten a small copper wire to it and hang on the brass pipe with connections to the carbon of the battery. Clean the article to be plated well with pumice and a brush saturated in water. When cleaning any article there should be a copper wire attached to it. Do not touch the article after you once start to clean it, or the places touched by your fingers will cause the silver plate to peel off when finished. When well scoured, run clear, cold water over the article and if it appears greasy, place in hot water. When well cleaned place in the plating bath and carefully watch the results. If small bubbles come to the surface you will know that you have too much of the anode or the piece of silver hanging in the solution and you

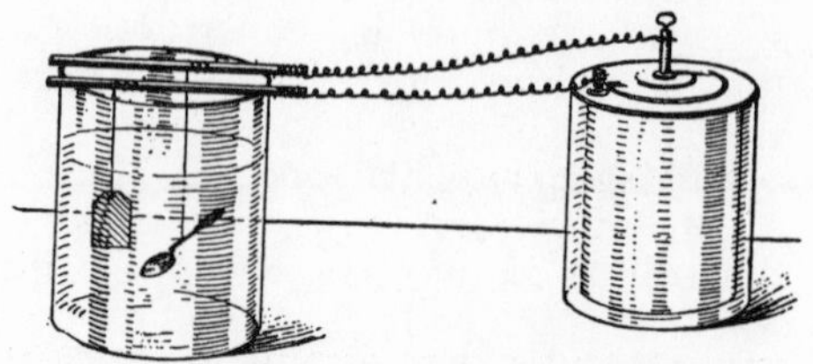
Plating Jar and Battery

must draw out enough of the piece until you can see no more bubbles. Leave the piece to be plated in the solution for about one-half hour, then take the article out and with a tooth brush and some pumice, clean the yellowish scum off, rinse in clear water and dry in sawdust. When thoroughly dry, take a cotton flannel rag and some polishing powder and polish the article. The article must have a fine polish before plating if it is desired to have a finely polished surface after the plate is put on.

In order to see if your battery is working, take a small copper wire and touch one end to the anode pipe and the other end to the pipe holding the article to be plated. When these two parts touch there will be a small spark. Always take the zincs out of the solution when not in use and the batteries will last longer. This description applies only to silver plating. Articles of lead, pewter, tin or any soft metal cannot be silver plated unless the article is first copper plated.

Removing a Tight-Fitting Ring from a Finger

When a ring cannot be removed easily from the finger, take a string or thread and draw one end through between the ring and the flesh. Coil the other end of the string around the finger covering the part from the ring to and over the finger joint. Uncoil the string by taking the end placed through the ring and at the same time keep the ring close up to the string. In this way the ring can be easily slipped over the knuckle and off from the finger.—Contributed by J. K. Miller, Marietta, Penn.

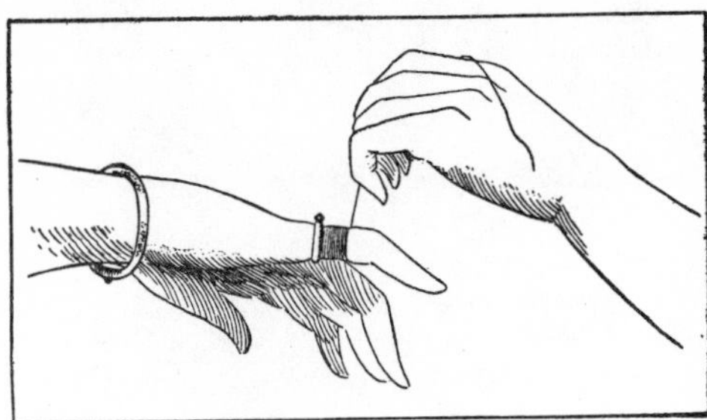

Wrapping the Finger

A Photographic Jig-Saw Puzzle

Take any photographic print and mount it on heavy cardboard, or, if you have a jig saw, a thin smooth wood board and mark out various shaped pieces as shown in the accompanying cut. If the picture is mounted on cardboard, the lines can be cut through with a sharp pointed knife. If you have a jig saw, you can make a bromide enlargement from the negative you have selected and mount the print on a smooth board that is not too thick. This wood-mounted picture can be sawed out making all shapes of blocks, which forms a perfect jig-saw puzzle. —Contributed by Erich Lehmann, New York City.

Picture Marked for Cutting

Rolling Uphill Illusion

This interesting as well as entertaining illusion, can be made by anyone having a wood-turning lathe. A solid, similar to two cones placed base to base, is accurately turned in a lathe, the sides sloping to an angle of 45 deg. The spindle can be turned out of the solid at the same time as the cone; or, after turning the cone, drive an iron or wood shaft through the center making a tight fit.

The boards for the track are made with a sloping edge on which the cone is to roll. This slope will depend on the diameter of the cone, which can be any size from 3 to 12 in. The slope should not be too flat, or the cone will not roll, and it should be such that the

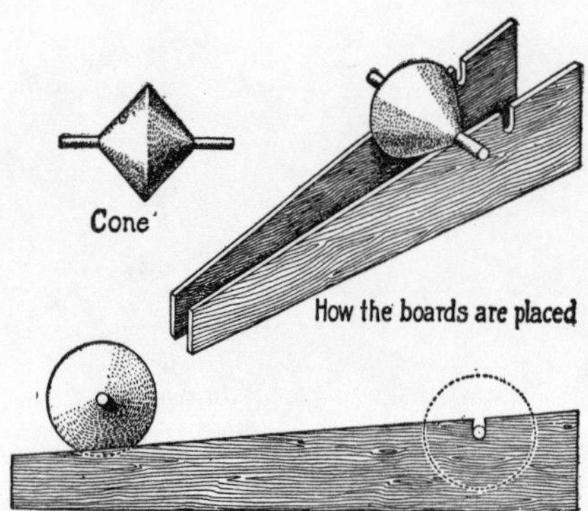

The Illusion

one end will be higher than the other by a little less than half the diameter of the cone. Thus it will be seen that the diameter of the cone determines the length of the slope of the tracks. A notch should be cut in the tracks, as indicated, for the shaft to drop into at the end of the course.

The lower end of the tracks are closed until the high edge of the cone rests upon the inside edges of the tracks and the high end spread sufficiently to take the full width of the cone and to allow the shaft to fall into the notches. When the cone and tracks are viewed from the broadside the deception will be more perfect, and will not be discovered until the construction of the model is seen from all sides. Should it be difficult to make the cone from wood, a good substitute can be made from two funnels.—Contributed by I. G. Bayley, Cape May Point, N. J.

Annealing Chisel Steel

Persons who have occasion to use tool or carbon steel now and then and do not have access to an assorted stock of this material find that the kind most readily obtained at the hardware store is the unannealed steel known as chisel steel. Machining or filing such steel is exceedingly slow and difficult, besides the destruction of tools; as a matter of fact this steel is intended for chisels, drills, and like tools which require only forging and filing. If this steel is annealed, it can be worked as easily as the more expensive annealed steel.

Annealing may be done by heating the steel to a cherry red, not any more, and burying it in a box of slaked lime, where it is allowed to remain until all the heat is gone. If well done, the metal will be comparatively soft and in a condition to machine easily and rapidly. In lieu of lime, bury in ashes, sand, loam, or any substance not inflammable, but fine enough to closely surround the steel and exclude the air so that the steel cools very slowly.

If possible, keep the steel red hot in the fire several hours, the longer the better. In certain processes, like that of file manufacturing, the steel blanks are kept hot for 48 hours or more. Where it is impossible to wait so long as the foregoing method takes, then a cold water anneal may be used with less time. This method consists of heating the work as slowly and thoroughly as the time will permit, then

The above photograph was made by first printing a maple leaf on the paper, not too dark, then printing on top the picture from the negative, and finished in the usual way.

removing the steel from the fire and allowing it to cool in the air until black and then quenching in water.

In addition to softening the steel, annealing benefits the metal by relieving strains in the piece. Should a particularly accurate job be called for, the steel should be annealed again after the roughing cuts have been taken and before machining to the final size. This will insure a true job and diminishes the danger of spring in the final hardening.—Contributed by Donald A. Hampson, Middletown, N. Y.

How to Make a Post Card Holder

This holder is designed to lay flat on the counter or to stack one on top of the other, keeping each variety of cards separate, or a number of them can be fastened on any upright surface to display either horizontal or vertical cards.

The holders can be made from sheet tin, zinc, brass or aluminum. The dimensions for the right size are given in Fig. 1; the dotted line showing where the bends are made. The completed holder is shown in Fig. 2 as fastened to a wall.—Contributed by John F. Williamson, Daytona, Fla.

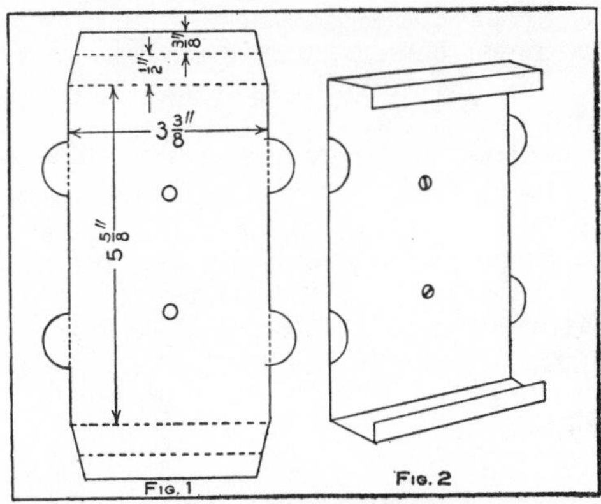

Pattern for Cutting the Metal

Do not allow paint that is left over from a job to stand uncovered. The can should be tightly sealed and the paint will be found suitable for use for several days.

Perfume-Making Outfit

The real perfume from the flowers is not always contained in the liquid purchased for perfume. The most expensive perfume can be made at home for less than 10 cents an ounce. The outfit necessary is a large bottle or glass jar with a smaller bottle to fit snugly into the open mouth of the large one. Secure a small piece of very fine sponge and wash it clean to thoroughly remove all grit and sand. Saturate the sponge with pure olive oil, do not use strong oil, and place it inside of the smaller bottle.

Fill the large bottle or jar with flowers, such as roses, carnations, pansies, honeysuckles or any flower having a strong and sweet odor. Place the small bottle containing the sponge upside down in the large one, as shown in the illustration.

The bottle is now placed in the sun and kept there for a day and then the flowers are removed and fresh ones put in. Change the flowers each day as long as they bloom. Remove the sponge and squeeze out the oil. For each drop of oil add 2 oz. of grain alcohol. If stronger perfume is desired add only 1 oz. alcohol to each drop of oil.

Home-Made Duplicator for Box Cameras

The projecting tube of the lens on a hand camera can be easily fitted with a duplicator while the box camera with its lens set on the inside and nothing but a hole in the box does not have such advantages. A small piece of heavy cardboard can be made to produce the same results on a box camera as a first-class duplicator applied to a hand camera. The cardboard is cut triangular and attached to the front end of the camera as shown in Fig. 1 with a pin about 1 in. above the lens opening. A rubber band placed around the lower end of the cardboard and camera holds the former at any position it is placed. A slight pressure of the finger on the point A, Fig. 2, will push the cardboard over and expose one-half of the plate and the same pressure at B, Fig. 3, will reverse the operation and expose the other one-half. Pins can be stuck in the end of the camera on each side of the lens opening at the right place to stop the cardboard for the exposure. With this device one can duplicate the picture of a person on the same negative.—Contributed by Maurice Baudier, New Orleans, La.

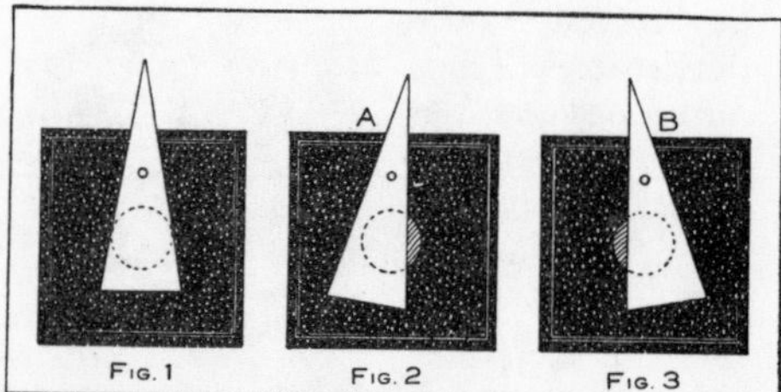

Duplicator Attached to a Camera

Optical Illusions

The accompanying sketch shows two optical illusions, the first having a perfect circle on the outside edge appears to be flattened at the points A, and the arcs of the circle, B, appear to be more rounding. In the second figure the circle appears to have an oval form with the distance from C to C greater than from D to D. A compass applied to the circles in either figures will show that they are perfectly round.—Contributed by Norman S. Brown, Chippewa Falls, Wis.

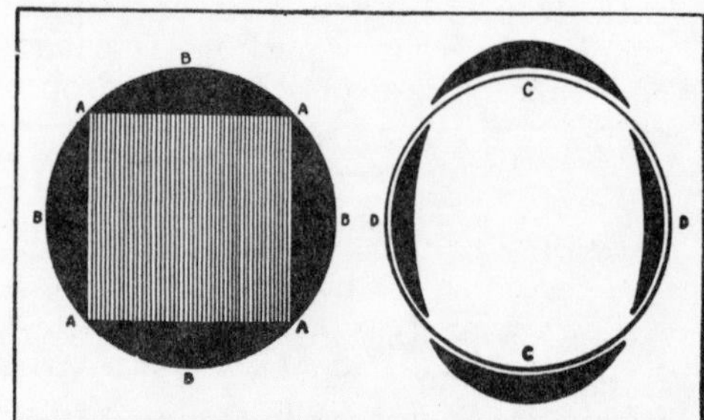

The Two Illusions

Use of Kerosene in Polishing Metals

Anyone who has polished a flat iron or steel surface with emery cloth knows how soon the cloth gums and fills up. The cloth in this condition will do little or no cutting. A simple remedy for this trouble is to use kerosene on the surface. The oil floats away a large part of the gumming substance and leaves the emery cloth sharp and clean to do the best work, also, it seems to act as a lubricant to keep particles of metal from collecting on the cloth and scratching or digging in the surface of the metal. A very light lard oil is equally good for this purpose, but not always easily obtained. A surface polished where oil or kerosene is used does not rust so easily as one polished dry, for the reason that a little oil remains on the metal.

Kerosene is the best to use on oil stones, being better than heavier oil. This oil readily floats away all particles of the feather edge that are liable to become loosened and forced into the stone. These particles of metal when stuck to the stone are the cause of spoiling it, as well as nicking the tools that are being sharpened. Keep the surface of the stone well oiled at all times to make the cutting free.—Contributed by Donald A. Hampson, Middletown, N. Y.

How to Make Lamps Burn Brightly

For a good, steady light there is nothing better than a lamp, but like most everything it must have attention. After cleaning well and fitting it, place a small lump of camphor in the oil vessel. This will greatly improve the light and make the flame clearer and brighter. If there is no camphor at hand add a few drops of vinegar occasionally.

A Practical Camera for Fifty Cents

By C. H. Claudy

I say for fifty cents, but really this is an outside estimate. If you possess a few tools and the rudiments of a shop, by which is meant a few odds and ends of screws, brass and nails, you can really make this camera for nothing.

The camera box is the first consideration, and for this a cigar box answers every purpose. It is better to use one of the long boxes which contain a hundred cigars and which have square ends. This box should be cut down, by means of a saw and a plate, until the ends are 4 in. square. Leave the lid hinged as it is when it comes. Clean all the paper from the outside and inside of the box—which may be readily done with a piece of glass for a scraper and a damp cloth—and paint the interior of the box a dead black, either with carriage makers' black or black ink.

Now bore in the center of one end a small hole, 1/4 in. or less in diameter. Finally insert on the inside of the box, on the sides, two small strips of wood, 1/8 by 1/4 in. and fasten them with glue, 1/8 in. from the other end of the box. Examine Fig. 1, and see the location of these strips, which are lettered EE. Their purpose is to hold the plate, which may be any size desired up to 4 in. square. Commercially, plates come 3½ by 3½ in., or, in the lantern slide plate, 3¼ by 4 in. If it is desired to use the 3½ by 3½ in. plates, which is advised, the box should measure that size in its internal dimensions.

We now come to the construction of the most essential part of the camera —the pin hole and the shutter, which take the place of the lens and shutter used in more expensive outfits. This construction is illustrated in Fig. 4. Take a piece of brass, about 1/16 in. thick and 1½ in. square. Bore a hole in each corner, to take a small screw, which will fasten it to the front of the camera. With 1/4-in. drill bore nearly through the plate in the center, but be careful that the point of the drill does not come through. This will produce the recess shown in the first section in Fig. 4. Now take a No. 10 needle, insert the eye end in a piece of wood and very carefully and gently twirl it in the center of the brass where it is the thinnest, until it goes through. This pin hole, as it is called, is what produces the image on the sensitive plate, in a manner which I shall presently describe. The shutter consists of a little swinging piece of brass completely covering the recess and pin hole, and provided with a little knob at its lower end. See Fig. 3, in which F is the front of the camera, B the brass plate and C the shutter. This is also illustrated in the second cross section in Fig. 4. In the latter I have depicted it as swung from a pivot in the brass, and in Fig. 3 as hung from a screw in the wood of

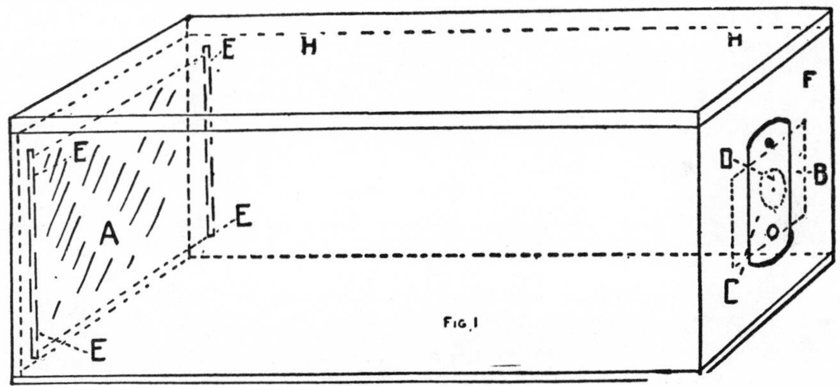

Construction of Camera Box

the front board; either construction will be effective.

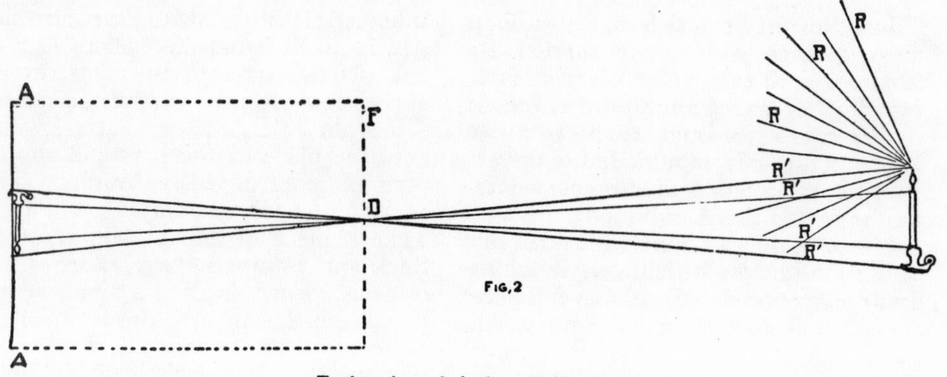

Explanation of Action of Pin Hole

Lastly, it is necessary to provide a finder for this camera in order to know what picture you are taking. Make a little frame of wire, the size of the plate you are using, and mount it upright (see Fig. 5) on top of the camera as close to the end where the pin hole is as you can. At the other end, in the center, erect a little pole of wire half the height of the plate. If now you look along the top of this little pole, through the wire frame and see that the top of the little pole appears in the center of the frame, everything that you see beyond will be

Fig. 5

Constructing a Finder for Camera

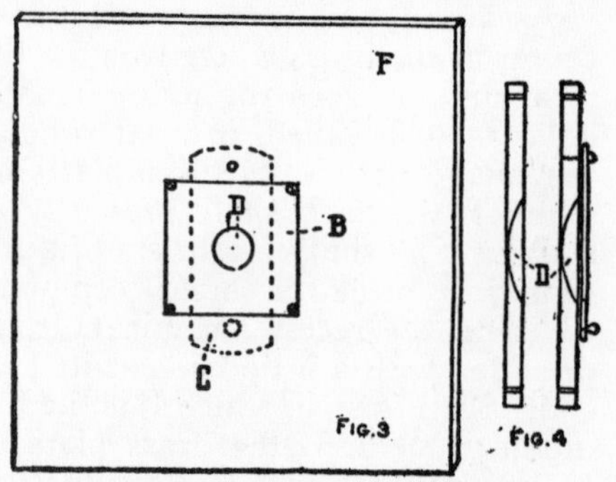

Pin Hole and Shutter Construction

taken on the plate, as will be made plain by looking at the dotted lines in Fig. 5, which represents the outer limits of your vision when confined within the little frame.

When you want to use this camera, take it into an absolutely dark room and insert a plate (which you can buy at any supply store for photographers) in the end where the slides of wood are, and between them and the back of the box. Close the lid and secure it with a couple of rubber bands. See that the little shutter covers the hole. Now take the camera to where you wish to take a photograph, and rest it securely on some solid surface. The exposure will be, in bright sunlight and supposing that your camera is 10 in. long, about six to eight seconds. This exposure is made by lifting the little brass shutter until the hole is uncovered, keeping it up the required time, and then letting it drop back into place. It is important that the camera be held rigid during the exposure, and that it does not move and is not jarred —otherwise the picture will be blurred. Remove the plate in the dark room and pack it carefully in a pasteboard box and several wrappings of paper to protect it absolutely from the light. It is now ready to be carried to some one who knows how to do developing and printing.

To explain the action of the pin hole I would direct attention to Fig. 2. Here F represents the front of the camera, D the pin hole, AA the plate and the letters RR, rays from a lighted candle. These rays of course, radiate in all directions, an infinite multitude of them. Similar rays radiate from every point of the object, from light reflected from these points. Certain of these rays strike the pin hole in the front of the camera, represented here by RRRR. These rays pass through the pin hole, and as light travels only in straight lines, reach the plate AA, forming an inverted image of the object, in this case a candle in a candlestick. Millions of rays are given off by every point in every object which is lighted by either direct or reflected light. To all practical purposes only one of these rays from each point in an object can pass through a minute opening like a pin hole. This being so, any screen which interrupts these selected rays of light will show upon it a picture of the object, only inverted. If that screen happens to be a photographically sensitive plate, which is protected from all other light by being in a dark box, upon it will be imprinted a photographic image which can be made visible by the application of certain chemicals, when it becomes a negative, from which may be printed positives. This camera is not a theoretical possibility, but an actual fact. I have made and used one successfully, as a demonstration of pin-hole photography.

Use for an Old Clock

Remove the hair spring of the clock, and fasten a spring to one end of the pawl and a small wire to the other end. Make a slit in the case of the clock opposite the pawl. Fasten the spring on the outside in any convenient way and pass the wire through the slit to an eccentric or other oscillating body.

To make the dial, paste a piece of paper over the old dial, pull the wire back and forth one hundred times, and make a mark where the minute hand stops. Using this for a unit divide up the whole dial. The hour hand has an inner circle of its own. Put the alarm hand at a little before twelve and wind the alarm. When the alarm is un-

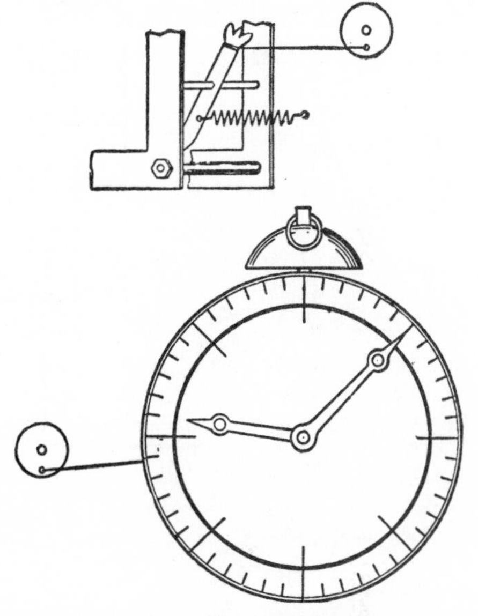

Revolution Recorder

wound the hour hand starts on a new trip. The clock I used was put on an amateur windmill and when the hour hand went around once 86,400 revolutions or jerks on the wire were made, while the minute hand recorded one-twelfth of this number, or 7,200.—Contributed by Richard H. Ranger, Indianapolis, Ind.

Renewing Dry Batteries

Dry batteries, if not too far gone, can be renewed by simply boring a small hole through the composition on top of each carbon and pouring some strong salt water or sal ammoniac solution into the holes. This kink is sent us by a reader who says that the process will make the battery nearly as good as new if it is not too far gone beforehand.

If a round brush spreads too much, slip a rubber band over the upper part of the bristles.

How to Make a Simple Burglar Alarm

Take a piece of any wood about 6 by 8 in. for the base. This may be finished in any way desired. For the contact points use brass or any sheet metal

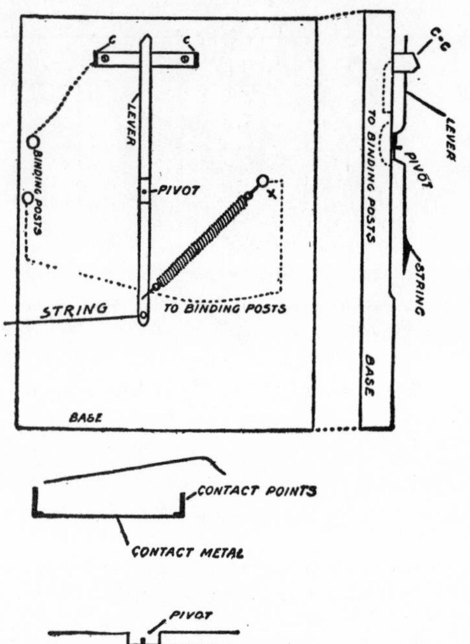

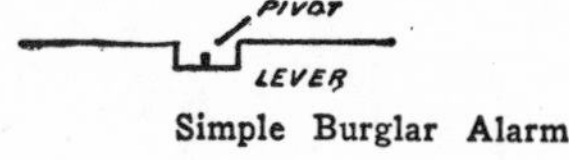

Simple Burglar Alarm

which will be satisfactory. Take a piece about 2½ or 3 in. in length and bend the ends up about ½ in. in a vertical position as shown. Fasten this to the top of the board using screws or nails. Under this strip of metal fasten a copper wire which can be connected to a binding-post on the board if desired. Take another piece of metal about 4½ in. in length and make a lever of it in the shape shown in the diagram. Fasten this so that one end of it will swing freely, but not loosely between the ends of the other piece marked C-C. Near the end fasten a spiral spring, S, which can be obtained almost anywhere. Fasten the end of this to the screw marked X. Also fasten to this screw a copper wire leading to the binding-post. In the lower end of the lever make a small hole to fasten a string through.

This string may be fastened across a door or window and any movement of it will pull it to the contact point on the right. If the string is cut or broken the spring will pull the lever to the contact point on the left and thus complete the circuit. If the string is burned it will also act as a fire alarm.

How to Fit Corks

Occasionally odd-sized bottles are received in stores which require corks cut to fit them. No matter how sharp a knife may be, it will leave some sharp edges after cutting the cork, which will cause leakage. The illustration shows three very effective methods of reducing the size of corks. The one shown in Fig. 1 is made from two pieces of ½-in. wood fastened together at one end with a common hinge. Two or three grooves are cut cross-wise in sizes desired. The cork is put into the groove and both pieces are pressed together, which will make the cork smaller.

Rolling the cork between two flat

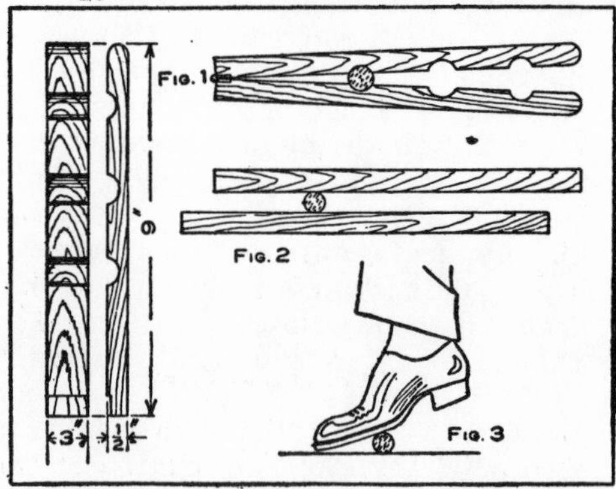

Three Methods for Reducing Size of Corks

surfaces (Fig. 2) is simple and almost as good as pressing in the grooves. A cork rolled on the floor (Fig. 3) is a quick and effective way. A slower and equally as good way is to soak the cork in hot water for a short time.—Contributed by L. Szerlip, Brooklyn, N. Y.

Standing at the cylinder end and looking toward the flywheel of an engine, the wheel will be at the right if the engine is right-hand.

Home-Made Crutch

While a fractured bone was healing in the limb of my boy he needed a pair of crutches and not being able to secure the right length, I set about to make the crutches from two broom handles. I split the handles to within 1 ft. of the end (Fig. 1) with a rip saw, and then stuck them in a barrel of water for three days to make the wood pliable for bending. A grip for each stick was made as long as the hand is wide and a hole bored through the center the size of a No. 10 gauge wire. These grips were placed between the two halves of each stick at the right distance for the length of the boy's arm and a wire run through both split

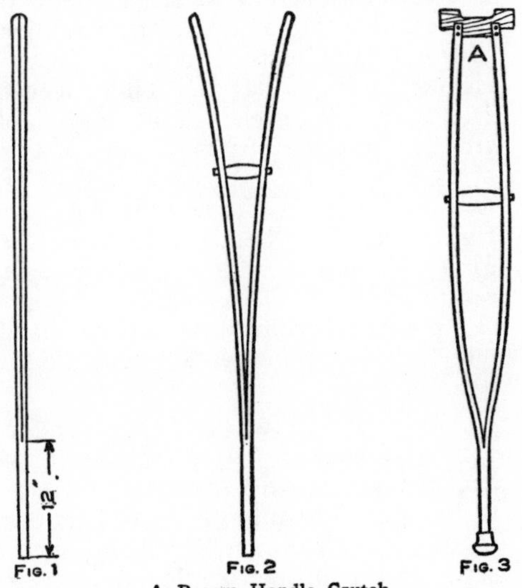

A Broom Handle Crutch

pieces and the handle then riveted as shown in Fig. 2. Another piece was cut as shown at A, Fig. 3, and nailed to the upper ends of each half of the broom handle.—Contributed by Geo. P. Grehore, Nashville, Tenn.

Home-Made Necktie Holder

The gas bracket is considered a good place to hang neckties, even if it does crowd them together. The illustration shows a better method, a curtain rod attached to one end of a bureau. Two long-shanked, square-hooked screws should be used, so they may be screwed beneath and close up to the projecting top. When removed they will leave no

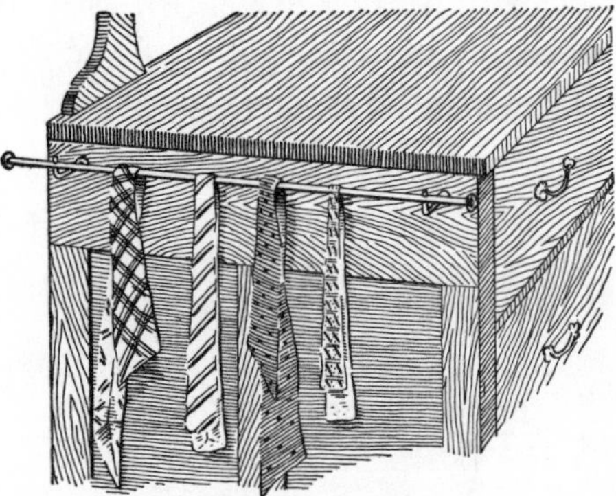
Hanger for Ties

disfiguring holes.—Contributed by C. W. Neiman, New York City.

How to Make a Trousers Hanger

Secure from your tinsmith a piece of sheet metal 7 in. wide and 12 in. long. Cut the metal as shown in Fig. 1 and make a close bend at the point A, but not too close to cause it to break. The piece will then appear as shown in Fig. 2. Cut a piece from the waste material ½ in. wide and 2¼ in. long and bend it around the two pieces B, Fig. 2, so it will slide freely on their length. Bend the edges C in for ⅛ in. to hold the trousers firmly. Drill a hole through the top end of B and attach a wire formed into a hook for use in hanging on a nail. The bottom end of the trousers is inserted between the jaws C and the small ferrule pushed

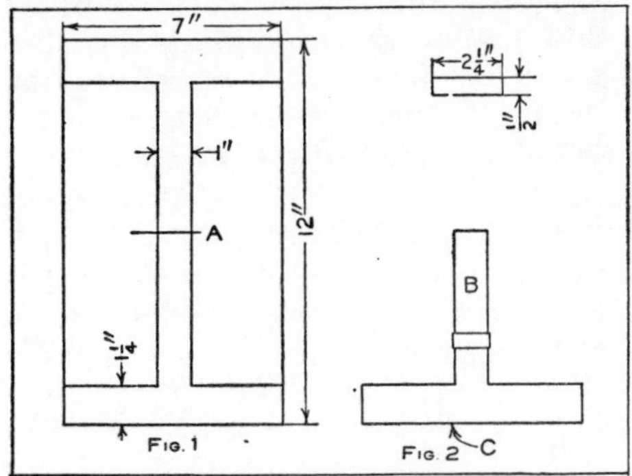

Cut from Sheet Metal

down to clamp them on the cloth.—Contributed by A. Levinson, Saginaw, Michigan.

Easy Designs in Ornamental Iron Work

Many an industrious lad has made money manufacturing the common forms of wood brackets, shelves, boxes, stands, etc., but the day of the scroll

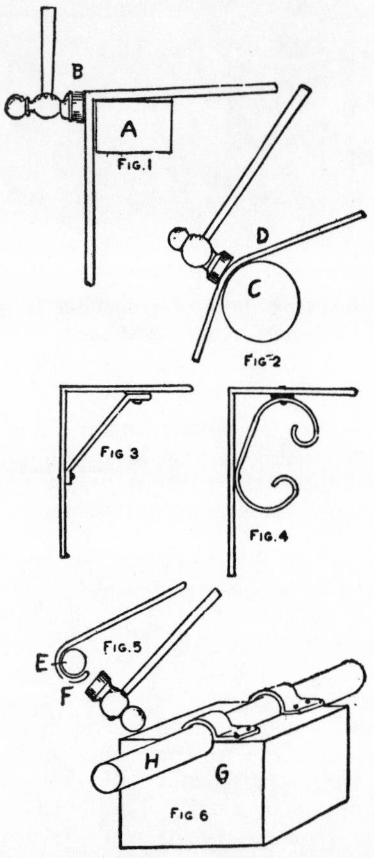

saw and the cigar-box wood bracket and picture frame has given way to the more advanced and more profitable work of metal construction. Metal brackets, stands for lamps, gates, parts of artistic fences for gardens, supporting arms for signs, etc., are among the articles of modern times that come under the head of things possible to construct of iron in the back room or attic shop. The accompanying sketches present some of the articles possible to manufacture.

First, it is essential that a light room be available, or a portion of the cellar where there is light, or a workshop may be built in the yard. Buy a moderate sized anvil, a vise and a few other tools, including bell hammer, and this is all required for cold bending. If you go into a forge for hot bending, other devices will be needed. Figure 1 shows how to make the square bend, getting the shoulder even. The strip metal is secured at the hardware store or the iron works. Often the strips can be secured at low cost from junk dealers. Metal strips about ½ in. wide and ⅛ in. thick are preferable. The letter A indicates a square section of iron, though an anvil would do, or the base of a section of railroad iron. The bend is worked on the corner as at B, cold. If a rounded bend is desired, the same process is applied on the circular piece of iron or the horn of an anvil. This is shown in Fig. 2, at C. This piece of iron can be purchased at any junk store, where various pieces are always strewn about. A piece about 20 in. long and 4 in. in diameter is about the right size. The bend in the metal begins at D and is made according to the requirements. Occasionally where sharp bends or abrupt corners are needed, the metal is heated previous to bending.

Although the worker may produce various forms of strip-metal work, the bracket is, as a rule, the most profitable to handle. The plain bracket is shown in Fig. 3, and is made by bending the strip at the proper angle on form A, after which the brace is adjusted by means of rivets. A rivet hole boring tool will be needed. A small metal turning or drilling lathe can be purchased for a few dollars and operated by hand for the boring, or a common hand drill can be used. Sometimes the bracket is improved in design by adding a few curves to the end pieces of the brace, making the effect as shown in Fig. 4. After these brackets are made they are coated with asphaltum or Japan; or the brackets may be painted or stained any desired shade.

In some of the work required, it is necessary to shape a complete loop or circle at the end of the piece. This may be wrought out as in Fig. 5. The use of a bar of iron or steel is as shown. The bar is usually about 2 in. in diameter and several feet in length, so that it will rest firmly on a base of wood or stone. Then the bending is effected as at F, about the bar E, by repeated blows with the hammer. After a little practice, it is possible to describe almost any kind of a circle with the tools. The bar can be bought at an iron dealers for about 40 cents. From the junk pile of junk shop one may get a like bar for a few cents.

A convenient form for shaping strip-metal into pieces required for brackets, fences, gates, arches, and general trimmings is illustrated at Fig. 6. First there ought to be a base block, G, of hard wood, say about 2 ft. square. With a round point or gouging chisel work out the groove to the size of the bar, forming a seat, by sinking the bar, H, one-half its depth into the wood as shown. In order to retain the bar securely in position in the groove, there should be two caps fitted over it and set-screwed to the wooden base. These caps may be found in junk dealers' heaps, having been cast off from 2-in. shaft boxes. Or if caps are not available, the caps can be constructed from sheet metal by bending to the form of the bar, allowing side portions or lips for boring, so that the caps can be set-screwed to the wood. Thus we get a tool which can be used on the bench for the purpose of effecting series of bends in strips of metal.

Since the introduction of the laws requiring that signs of certain size and projection be removed from public thoroughfares in cities, there has been quite a call for short sign brackets, so termed, of the order exhibited in Fig. 7. These sign-supporting brackets do not extend more than 3 ft. out from the building. A boy can take orders for these signs in almost any city or large town with a little canvassing. The sign supporting bracket shown is merely a suggestion. Other designs may be wrought out in endless variety. A hook or eye is needed to sustain the ring in the sign.

The young man who undertakes to construct any sort of bracket, supports, frames or the like, will find that he will get many orders for lamp-supporting contrivances, such as shown at Fig. 8. It is hardly necessary to go into details

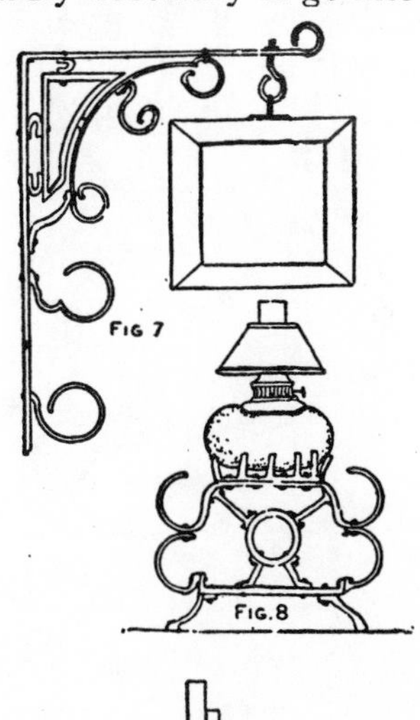

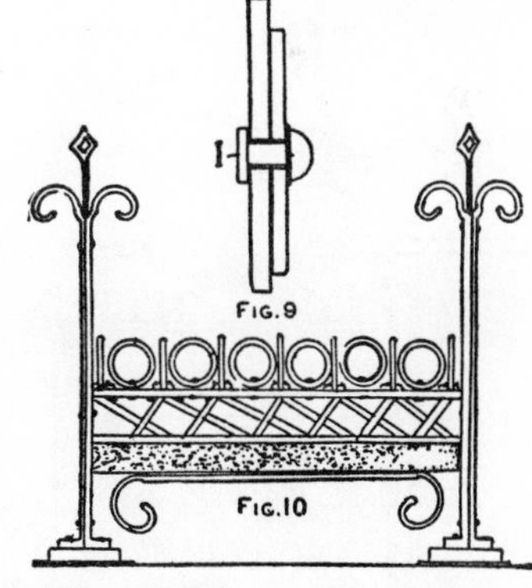

for making these stands, as every part is bent as described in connection with the bending forms, and the portions are simply riveted at the different junctures. Both iron and copper rivets are used as at I, in Fig. 9, a cross sectional view.

The best way is to bore straight through both pieces and insert the rivet. In some cases the rivet is headed up in the bore and again washers are used and the heading effected on the washer. Copper rivets are soft and easily handled, but are costly as compared with iron rivets.

Good prices are obtained for the guards for open fireplaces made in many varieties in these days. The return of the open fireplace in modern houses has created a demand for these guards and in Fig. 10 we show a design for one of them. The posts are made sufficiently stiff by uniting two sides with rivets. The ends at top are looped as shown, while the ends or butts at the base are opened out to make the feet. Rings are shaped on forms and are then riveted to the base cross-piece as illustrated. Crosses are made to describe to central design and the plan is worked out quite readily with the different shapes.

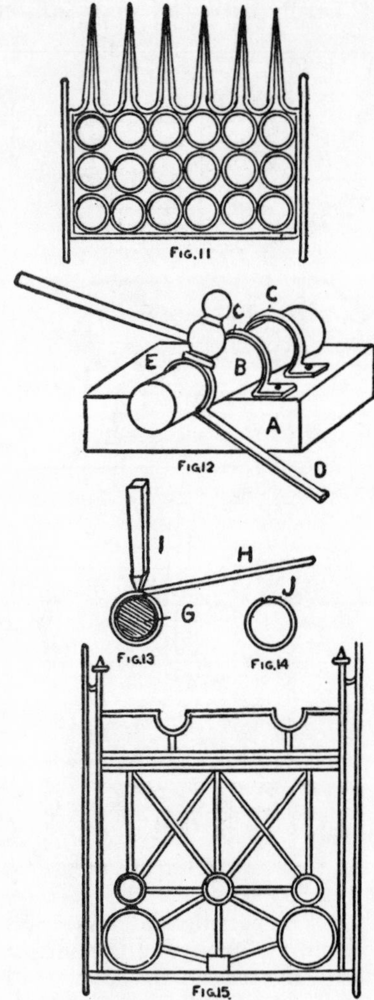

The making of metal fire grate fronts has proven to be a very interesting and profitable occupation for boys in recent times. Not long ago it was sufficient for the ingenious youth to turn out juvenile windmills, toy houses and various little knickknacks for amusement. The modern lad wants more than this. He desires to turn some of his product into cash. Therefore we present some of the patterns of fire grates which boys have made and can make again from scrap iron, with few tools and devices, and find a ready market for the same as soon as they are made. Figure 11 is a sketch of a form of fire grate bar or front that is constructed with a series of circles of strip metal. The best way is to go to the hardware store or iron dealer's and buy a quantity of $\frac{1}{4}$-in., $\frac{1}{2}$-in., and $\frac{3}{4}$-in. iron, about $\frac{1}{8}$ to $\frac{3}{16}$-in. thick. In fact $\frac{1}{16}$-in. metal would do in many cases where the parts are worked out small in size. The $\frac{1}{8}$-in. metal is very strong. Then after getting the supply of strip metal in stock, procure the usual type of metal worker's hammer, a cheap anvil, a 9-lb. vise, a cold chisel, a file or two, and a round piece of shaft iron, about 3 in. diameter and 2 to 3 ft. long. This piece of iron is represented at B, Fig. 12.

The iron is held in position by means of the straps of metal C, C, which are bent over the shaft tightly and grip the board base with set or lag screws as shown. The wooden base should be about 2 in. thick and large enough to make a good support for the iron shaft. The process of bending the rings in this way is as shown. The piece of strip iron is grasped at D. Then with the hammer the iron is gradually worked cold about the mandrel as at E until the perfect form is acquired. After the form is finished, the strip at the terminus of the ring is cut off. In order to get a steady base the wooden part may be bolted to a bench. In Fig. 13 is shown the method of clipping off the completed ring. The cold chisel is held upright, and by delivering several blows with the hammer upon the same, the point is caused to chip through the metal and release the ring. The shaft or mandrel is marked G. The cold chisel is indicated at I and the position where the hand grasps the strip is at H. The final operation in shaping the ring is by driving the protruding cut, lip down, to the common level of the opposite point, thus giving us the finished ring with the lips closed on the mandrel as at J, Fig. 14. These rings can be turned out in this way very speedily. The next operation involves the process of uniting the rings in the plan to shape the design. The design work is often worked out ahead and followed. Some become so proficient that they can develop a design as they proceed.

Figure 11 is a design of grate front used for various purposes in connection with grate fires. The series of rings are united by a rivet between each at the joining point. With thin metal the holes can be punched with an iron punch and hammer on an anvil where there is a hole to receive the point of the punch after the punch penetrates the metal. For the heavier forms of metal a drill is necessary. A metal drill and brace can be purchased very cheaply for this work. After drilling the holes, the parts are erected and the rivets inserted and headed up as each addition is made. Thus the series of rings are united and then the side pieces are similarly riveted. The points at the top are then worked out and joined on. These points are filed down to the necessary taper after the union is effected. The finishing work involves smoothing rough places with a file and painting. Asphaltum makes a good black finish. Some of the best designs of grates are bronzed. Some are silvered. The different designs are finished as desired by customers.

Figure 15 is another design of grate in which the process of shaping the rings is like that in the first design. There are some half circles in this pattern and these are framed by shaping the same about the mandrel with the hammer. In order to get the shoulders close and the circle complete it is necessary to heat the metal. A coke fire can be made in a hole in the ground. Then procure a tin blowpipe and blow the flame against the metal at the point to be bent. This metal will become red hot very soon, and can be bent readily against the anvil and the circular form. Let the metal cool off on the ground after heating. Fig. 16 is another design

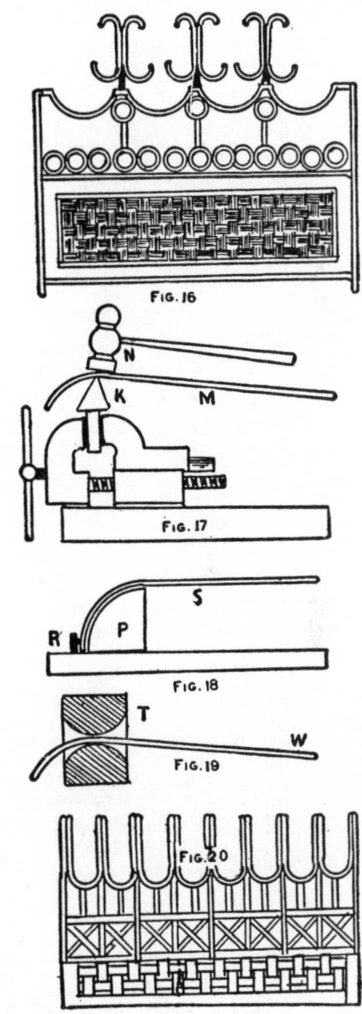

FIG. 16

FIG. 17

FIG. 18

FIG. 19

FIG. 20

which can be wrought out. The middle adjustment is wire screen work which may be bought at a hardware store and set into the position shown. Fig. 17 shows a chipping off device useful in connection with this work. Metal chippers can be bought at any tool store. The chipper is placed in the jaws of the vise as at K, and secured there. The strip of metal in process of cutting is marked M. The hammer head is caused to strike the metal just over the cutting edge of the chipper. The quick, hard blow causes the cutting edge to penetrate far enough to sever the piece. Bending cold with a wooden form is done as in Fig. 18. The wooden form is marked P and is about 8 in. wide and 7 in. high, forming a one-sided oval shape. There is a pin R set into the base board of the oval form and the strip of metal for bending is grasped at S and the other end is inserted back of the pin R. By applying pressure, the strip of metal is bent to the form.

Figure 19 shows the hour-glass wood bending form, made by selecting a piece of hard wood block, about 6 in. square and boring through with an inch bit. Then the hole is shaped hour-glass like. The view is a sectional one. The block is placed in a vise and the strip for bending is inserted as at T.

The strip of metal is grasped at W and can be bent to various forms by exerting pressure. Fig. 20 is another type of fireplace front, constructed by uniting the shaped metal pieces. In fact an almost endless variety of designs can be wrought out after the start is once made. A good way to figure the price on the grate is to add up the costs of the parts and charge about 12 cents per hour for the work.

How to Make a Water Wheel

Considerable power can be developed with an overshot water wheel erected as in Fig. 1. This wheel is made with blocks of wood cut out in sections as indicated by the lines, so as to form the circle properly. The wheel can be

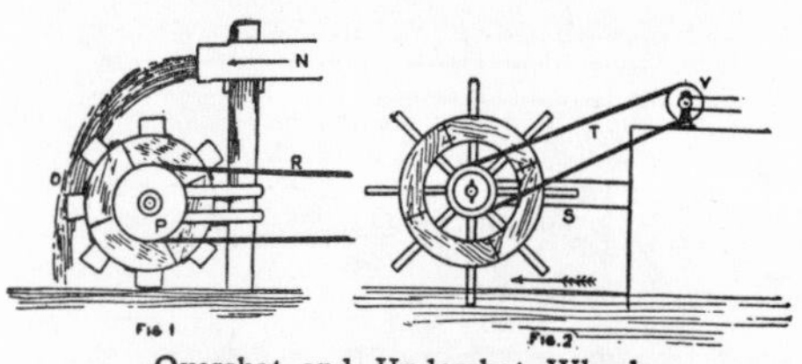

Overshot and Undershot Wheels

about 24 in. in diameter to produce results and about 10 in. wide. Get some tin cans and attach them around the wheel as shown. Bore the wheel center out and put on the grooved wood wheel, P, and a rope for driving, R. This rope runs to a wooden frame in the manner illustrated. The water is carried in a sluice affair, N, to the fall, O, where the water dippers are struck by the volume and from 2 to 4 hp. will be produced with this size of wheel if there is sufficient flow of water. This power can be used for running two or three sewing machines, fans, fret-saws, and the like. Another form of water wheel is shown in Fig. 2. This is driven by an underflow of current. This type of wheel can be made on lines similar to the other, only that the paddles are of wood and extend outward as shown. The wheel is supported in a bearing on the piece S. A belt, T, communicates the power to the wheel V and from here the power is carried to any desired point.

How To Build An Imitation Street Car Line

An imitation street car line may sound like a big undertaking, but, in fact, it is one of the easiest things a boy can construct, does not take much time and the expense is not great. A boy who lives on a farm can find many fine places to run such a line, and one in town can have a line between the house and the barn, if they are some distance apart.

Often all the boards and blocks required can be had for helping a carpenter clear away the rubbish around a new building. Wheels and parts of old bicycles, which can be used in so many ways, can be found at a junk shop at very low prices, wheels in good repair are not expensive. For the car for the street car line try to find a set of wheels having axles, but if you cannot find such, make shafts of hard wood, about 3 in. by 2½ in. and by means of a jack-knife turn, or shave down the ends to receive the hub bearings of the wheels. Fasten the wheel hubs securely over the ends of the wood with pins or little bolts, or if the wheel bearing is of such a nature that it revolves on its own journal, the journal can be fastened to the end of the wood piece. Each of the wheels should be provided with a sprocket; any chain sprocket of a bicycle may be used. Fasten these sprockets on the outside of the wheels as shown in Fig. 1. They can be set on over the bearing end and secured with a set screw, or the original key can be employed. It is best in cases like this to use the original parts. Make the floor of the car of pieces of boards placed on the axles and nailed, screwed or bolted, as shown at A. To erect the frame, place uprights, C C C C, in position as shown, fastening the ends to the base-boards, and making the roof line as at B, then put in the cross - pieces, G G. Seats, E E, are simply boxes. The drive of the car is effected by using the driving sprockets, D D, fitted to the crosspieces, G G, with the original bearings. The parts are thereby secured to the car and the chain placed on.

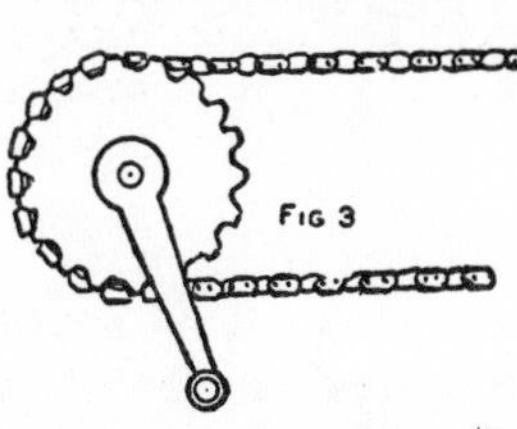

Key the cranks for turning to the upper sprocket's shaft and all is ready. If there are sprocket gears and cranks on either side, four boys may propel the car at one time. Considerable speed can be made on smooth roads, but it is the best amusement to run a car line on wooden tracks with a brake consisting of a piece of wooden shaft, passing through a bore in the car floor, and fitted with a leather covered pad as at H. A spiral spring holds up the brake until pressure is applied by foot power, when the brake contacts with the wooden track and checks the car.

The track plan is illustrated in Fig. 2. Get some boards and place them end for end on other pieces set as ties. The main boards or tracks, J J, can be about 6 in. wide, to the edges of which nail strips about ¾ in. wide and about the

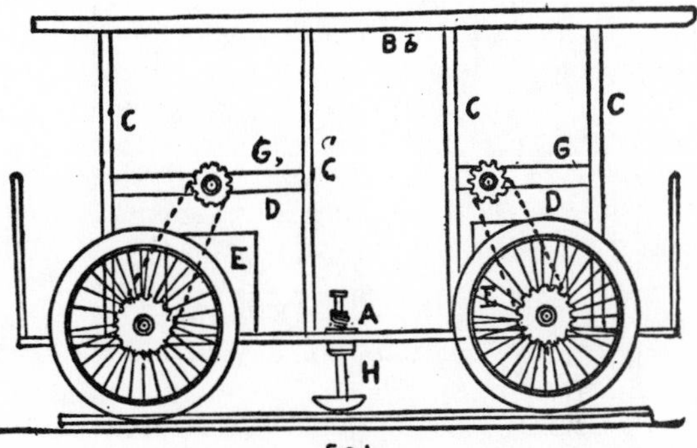

Construction of Car

same height. The ties, I I, can be almost any box boards. Wire nails are the best to use in putting the tracks together. The sprocket connection with the chain is shown in Fig. 3. This consists of the sprocket gear on the propelling shaft, and the crank. The pedals may be removed and a chisel handle, or any tool handle, substituted, so as to afford means for turning the

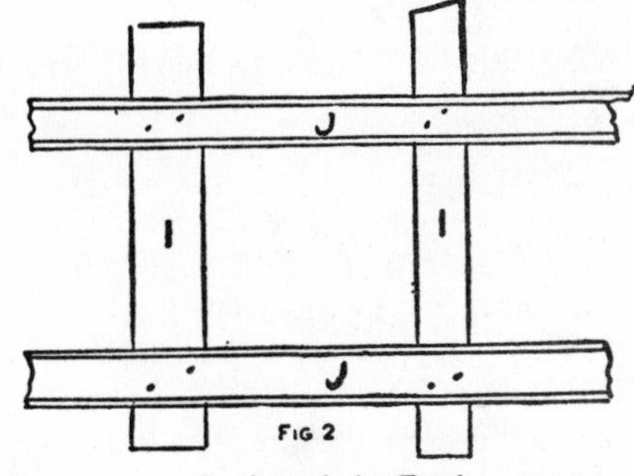

Section of the Track

crank by hand power. Great fun can be had with the road, and, furthermore, it can be made renumerative, as boys and girls can be given rides for a penny each.

Apply a coat of raw starch water to a dirty wall before painting; this, when dry, may be brushed or wiped off.

A good varnish for electric terminals is made of sealing wax dissolved in gasoline. To prevent brittleness add a little linseed oil.

Method of Applying the Triangle Measure

Measuring the Height of a Tree

"Near the end of the season our boy announced the height of our tall maple tree to be 33 ft.

" 'Why, how do you know?' was the general question.

" 'Measured it.'

" 'How?'

" 'Foot rule and yardstick.'

" 'You didn't climb that tall tree?' his mother asked anxiously.

" 'No'm; I found the length of the shadow and measured that.'

" 'But the length of the shadow changes.'

" 'Yes'm; but twice a day the shadows are just as long as the things themselves. I've been trying it all summer. I drove a stick into the ground, and when its shadow was just as long as the stick I knew that the shadow of the tree would be just as long as the tree, and that's 33 ft.' "

The above paragraph appeared in one of the daily papers which come to our office. The item was headed, "A Clever Boy." Now we do not know who this advertised boy was, but we knew quite as clever a boy, one who could have got the approximate height of the tree without waiting for the sun to shine at a particular angle or to shine at all for that matter. The way boy No. 2 went about the same problem was this: He got a stick and planted it in the ground and then cut it off just at the level of his eyes. Then he went out and took a look at the tree and made a rough estimate of the tree's height in his mind, and judging the same distance along the ground from the tree trunk, he planted his stick in the ground. Then he lay down on his back with his feet against the standing stick and looked at the top of the tree over the stick.

If he found the top of stick and tree did not agree he tried a new position and kept at it until he could just see the tree top over the end of the upright stick. Then all he had to do was to measure along the ground to where his eye had been when lying down and that gave him the height of the tree.

The point about this method is that the boy and stick made a right-angled triangle with boy for base, stick for perpendicular, both of the same length, and the "line of sight" the hypotenuse or long line of the triangle. When he got into the position which enabled him to just see the tree top over the top of the stick he again had a right-angled triangle with tree as perpendicular, his eye's distance away from the trunk, the base, and the line of sight the hypotenuse. He could measure the base line along the ground and knew it must equal the vertical height, and he could do this without reference to the sun. It was an ingenious application of the well known properties of a right-angled triangle.—Railway and Locomotive Engineer.

White putty on a black window frame can be made to harmonize by rubbing the fresh putty with a piece of cotton dipped in lampblack.

Sandpaper may be kept from slipping under the hand by chalking the back.

An Interesting Electrical Experiment

Anyone possessing a battery having an electromotive force of from 4 to 20 volts can perform the following experiment, which is particularly interesting on account of the variation of results with apparently the same conditions.

Immerse two pieces of brass in a strong solution of common salt and water. Connect one piece to the positive wire and the other to the negative, taking care that the brass pieces do not touch each other.

After the current has passed one or two minutes, the solution will become colored, and if the process is continued a colored pigment will be precipitated. The precipitate varies considerably in color and may be either yellow, blue, orange, green or brown, depending on the strength of the current, the strength of the solution, and the composition of the brass.

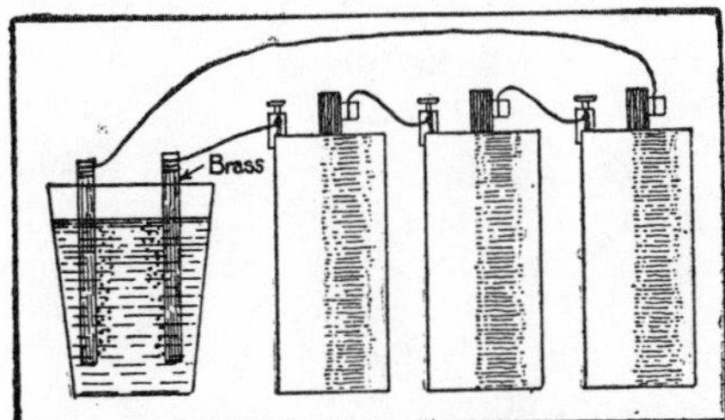

How Wires are Connected

Novelty Chain Made from a Match

The accompanying engraving shows what is possible to do with a penknife.

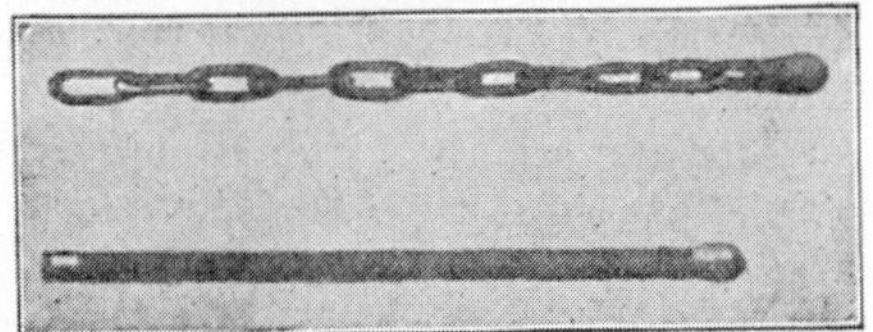
Lay a Match on the Picture

A small chain composed of several links was cut from the wood that forms the match.

¶Glass doors in bookcases may be kept from swinging open by boring a hole, about 1/4 in. deep, either at the top or bottom in the edge of the door, 2 in. from the closing edge, and inserting an ordinary cork, allowing a small portion to project and rub on the facing.

Restoring Broken Negatives

Whoever has the misfortune to break a valuable negative need not despair, for the damage can be repaired most effectively. In case the negative be broken into many pieces, take a clean glass, the same size as the broken negative, and put upon this the pieces, joining them accurately, says Camera Craft. Put another clean glass on top of this and bind the three together with passe-partout binding or gummed strips of ordinary paper, as one would a lantern slide, and cover the glass edges.

Next make a transparency of this—in the camera, of course—and if it is done right, the positive will only show the cracks as dark and light lines. The

Before and after Mending

dark lines are removed with the etching knife and the light ones with the retouching pencil. From this transparency another negative can be made, or as many negatives as necessary, by either contact or in the camera, and if the work on the glass positive was done carefully, no trace of the break should be seen on the finished negative. If the negative is broken in two or three larger pieces only, a contact positive may be made in the printing frame without binding, by using a clean glass in the latter, upon which the pieces are put together, face up, and a dry plate exposed in contact with them in the dark room. The accompanying engravings show a print before and after repairing a broken negative in this manner.

Coin and Tumbler Trick

The accompanying sketch shows how a good trick may be easily performed by any one. Lay a piece of

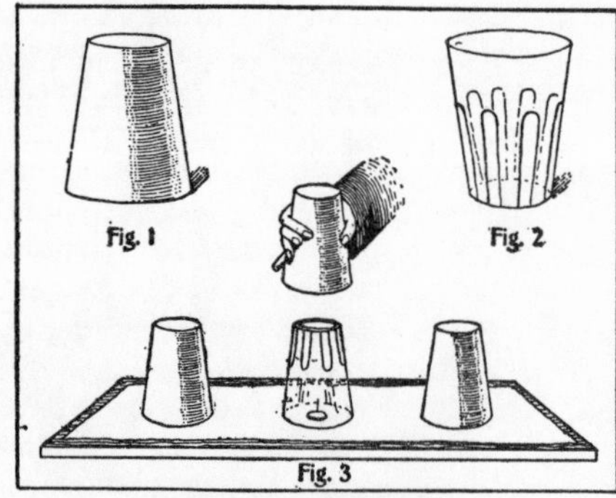

This is a Good Trick

heavy paper that is free from creases on a board or table. Secure three tumblers that are alike and stick a piece of the same heavy paper over the openings in two of them, neatly trimming it all around the edges so as to leave nothing of the paper for any one to see. Make three covers of paper as shown in Fig. 1 to put over the tumblers. Place three coins on the sheet of paper, then the tumblers with covers on top of the coins, the unprepared tumbler being in the middle. Now lift the covers off the end tumblers, and you will see that the paper on the openings covers the coins. Replace the covers, lift the middle one, and a coin will be seen under the tumbler, as the opening of this tumbler is not covered. Drop the cover back again and lift the other tumblers and covers bodily, so that the spectators can see the coins, remarking at the same time that you can make them vanish from one to the other. The openings of the tumblers must never be exposed so that any one can see them, and a safe way to do this is to keep them level with the table.

Another Way to Renew Dry Batteries

There are many methods of renewing dry batteries, and I have used several of them, but I found the following the best: Remove the paper cover and with a 1/4-in. drill make about six holes around the side of the zinc, about 1/2 in. from the bottom. Then drill another row of holes about half way up the side and put the battery to soak in a solution of sal ammoniac for 48 hours. Then remove and plug the holes up with hard soap, and replace in the paper box, when it will give nearly as strong a current as when new.

Simply Made Wire Puzzle

The object of this simply made wire puzzle is to get the ring off, which is not easy unless you know how. To do so it is necessary to move the triangle with ring to one of the hinge joints and fold the puzzle. Then slip the ring off the triangle over the hinge joint and it will slip all around and off at the other hinge.

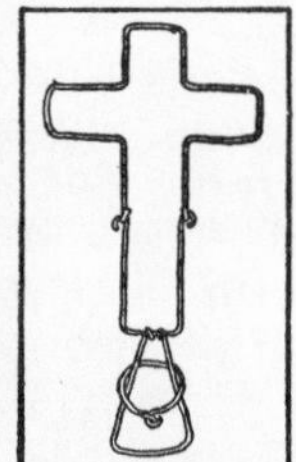

Diabolo is pronounced Dee-ab-lo.

Repairing Box Cameras

In repairing the inner part of box cameras which have been broken loose, use a binding of strong black cloth well glued in place. This will materially strengthen the joints where the wooden pieces are so thin that it is impossible to use brads in holding them together.

Do not forget to thoroughly clean all the old glue or cement from the joints with a rasp or sandpaper before attempting a repair.

A Fishhook Box

A box that may be used to hold fishhooks, sinkers, matches or any small articles, can be made from two empty shot-gun cartridges as shown in the sketch. The paper is cut from the brass part of one shell at the place marked A, Fig. 1, and the brass part, Fig. 2, is used for a cap on the other

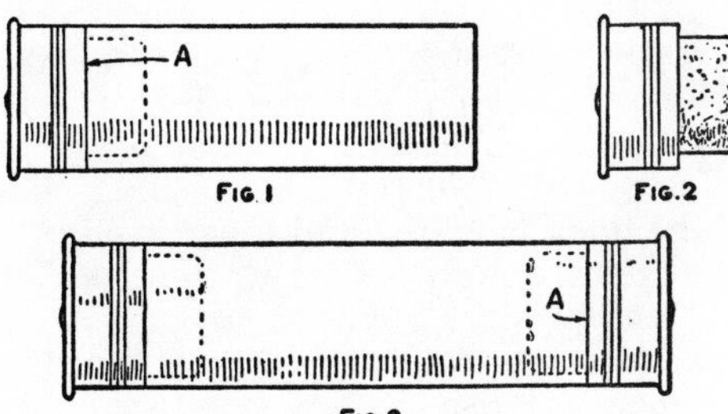

Made of Shotgun Shells

shell (Fig. 3). Coating the box with shellac will improve its appearance.—Contributed by Abner B. Shaw, N. Dartmouth, Mass.

A Tin Drinking Cup for the Camp

If in need of a drinking cup while camping, a temporary cup can be made of a tomato or baking-powder can. Punch two holes near the top of the can; bend a piece of wire and place the ends through the holes as shown at A in the sketch. Pull the ends to draw the loop close up on the inside of the tin and then twist the ends to form a handle as shown at B. When there is enough wire twisted to form a good handle, pass the ends around the can

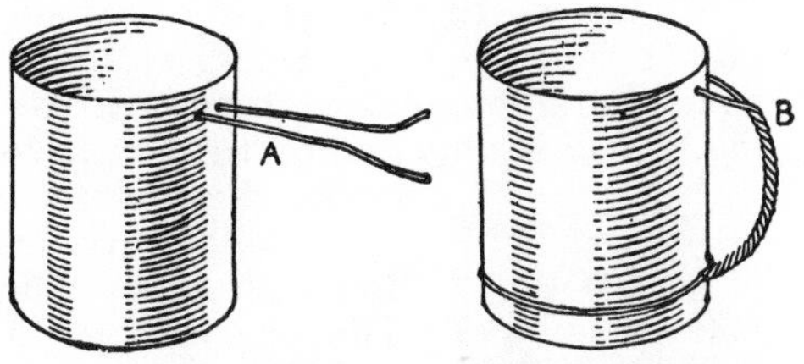

Handle on a Tin Can

at the bottom and twist them together on the opposite side.—Contributed by W. A. Lane, El Paso, Tex.

A Bookmark

A very handy bookmark can be made by attaching a narrow ribbon to an ordinary paper clip and using it as shown in the sketch. The clip is slipped over the binding in the back of the book as shown in the sketch.—Contributed by Chester E. Warner, Kalamazoo, Mich.

Kitchen Knife Sharpener

A good serviceable knife sharpener may be made from a piece of steel cut as shown with two screw holes drilled for fastening it to a piece of wood or to a table. The knife is drawn through and sharpened on either side. Both positions of the knife are shown. The

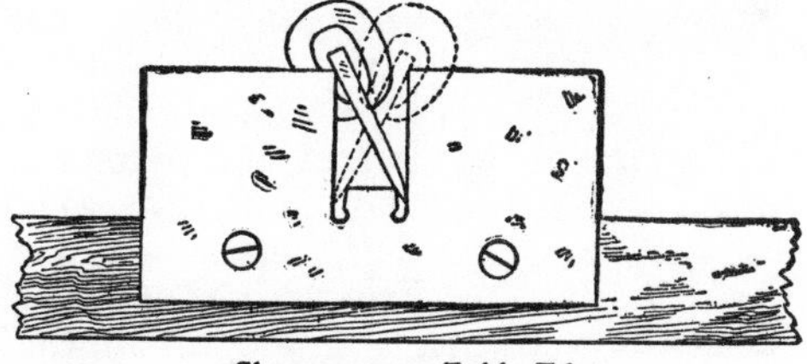
Sharpener on Table Edge

steel is hardened before fastening it in place.—Contributed by George Madsen, Chicago, Ill.

Devices of Winter Sports—How to Make and Use Them

In the north the red-cheeked boy digs a hole in the ice and while he amuses and invigorates himself at skating, the fish underneath the icy sheet fasten themselves to the hook he has let down through a hole. The boy used to sit over the hole in the ice and wait for the fish to bite, but that became too slow and detracted too much from his pleasure at skating. So his inventive genius set itself to work and the "tip-up" and "signal" shown in the illustration was the result. When the fish is not biting the flag lies flat on the ice, but as soon as a fish has swallowed the hook the flag pole stands straight up wafting its bright colored flag to the breezes and all the boys on the skating pond read the word "fish." The fish is drawn up, the hook rebaited and the youthful fisherman resumes his pleasures on the ice. Often a score or more of these "tip-ups" are planted about the edges of the ice pond, each boy bringing his fishing tackle with his skates and thus finding a double source of amusement. Maybe one boy will thus have a half dozen different lines in the water at once, it being easy to watch them all together.

"Tip-Up Pole"

The device by which the fish is made to give its own signal when caught is exceedingly simple and any boy can make it. Procure a light rod about 2 ft. in length and to one end fasten a small flag, made of any bright colored cloth. Bind the rod at right angles to another stick which is placed across the hole, so that a short piece of the flagrod projects over the cross stick. To this short end fasten the fishing line. Be sure and use strong string in binding the two rods together, and also take care that the cross stick is long enough to permit several inches of each end to rest on the ice. After fastening the line to the short end of the rod, bait the hook with a live minnow or other suitable bait and let it down through the hole. When the fish is hooked the flag will instantly raise and wave about strenuously until the fish is taken from the water.

"Tip-Up" Fish Caught

"Jumping-Jack" Fisherman

If the small boy has a "jumping-jack" left over from Christmas, he may make this do his fishing for him and serve as well as the "tip-up," or he can easily make the jumping-jack himself independent of Santa Claus. The string which is pulled to make the joints move is tied securely to the fishing line; the hook is baited and lowered into the water through a hole in the ice. The "jumping-jack" waves his legs and arms frantically to notify the boys when the fish is biting. The "jumping-jack" is also used for fishing in summer time by placing it on a float which is cast into the water.

Jumping-Jack Fisherman

Merry-Go-Round Whirl on Ice

A German device for the amusement of children is a whirl on an ice merry-go-round. It is made by placing a vertical shaft or stake, provided with a couple of old cart-wheels, in a hole in the ice. One wheel acts as a turning base and prevents the shaft from sinking into the pond, and the other forms a support for the long sweep attached for propulsion purposes, and should be fastened to the shaft about 3 ft. above the base wheel. The sleds are made fast in a string to the long end of the sweep, which when turned rapidly causes the sleds to slide over the ice in a circle at a high speed.

If the sweep is long enough to have each end from the shaft the same length, two strings of sleds may be attached, which will balance the device and make the turning much easier.

The Running Sleigh

Another winter sport, very popular in Sweden, and which has already reached America, is the "running sleigh," shown in the illustration. A light sleigh is equipped with long double runners and is propelled by foot power. The person using the sleigh stands with one foot upon a rest attached to one of the braces connecting the runners and propels the sleigh by pushing backward with the other foot. To steady the body an upright support is attached to the runners. The contrivance can be used upon hard frozen ground, thin ice and snow-covered surfaces, and under favorable conditions moves with remarkable speed. The "running sleigh" has a decided advantage over skis, because the two foot supports are braced so that they cannot come apart. Any boy can make the sleigh.

Running Sleigh

The Winged Skater

With the actual speed of the wind a skater may be hurled along the ice if he is aided by sails. He has been known to travel at the rate of 40 miles an hour, and the sport while affording the limit of excitement, is not attended with danger. The sails are easily made, as the illustrations and description will show.

Secure two large thin hoops about 4 ft. in diameter. They may be obtained from an old hogshead or by bending thin strips. For each hoop select a piece of strong cane about ¾ in. in diameter to constitute the fore and main masts or cross-yards. Extend these across the center of the hoop and fasten each end firmly to the hoop's sides. For the middle of each cross-spar make a cleat and lash it on firmly. The main spar should also be made of two pieces of strong cane, each about 9½ ft. long. Bind them together at each end so that the large end of one is fastened to the small end of the other.

Next comes the attaching of the sails to the separate masts. The sails should be made of strong sheeting or thin canvas. Tack the cloth to the hoop on the inner side after it has been wrapped around the hoop two or three times.

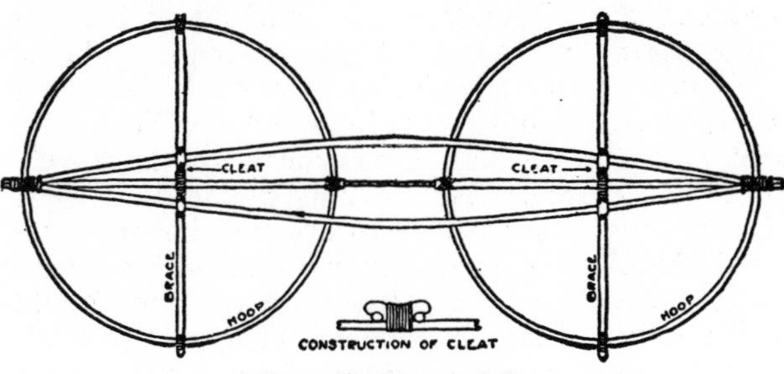

Frame for Skater's Sails

Now the main spar should be attached by springing it apart and slipping the cleats of the cross-spar between the two pieces. Bind the inner sides of the hoops tightly together by means of a very strong double cord, as shown in the figure. Then your sail is ready for the ice pond. See that your skates are securely fastened, raise your

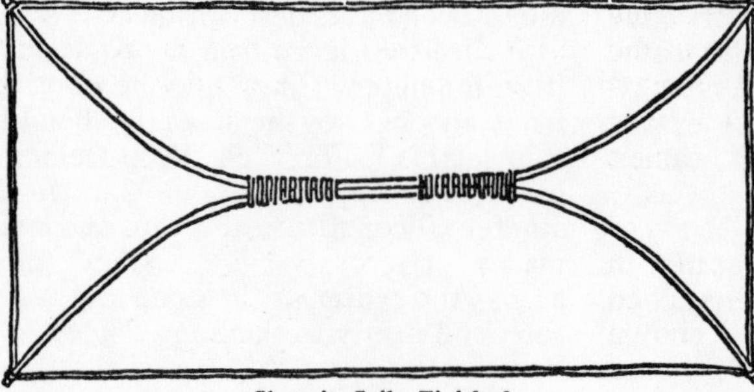
Skater's Sails Finished

sail and you will skim along the ice as lightly as a bird on the wing. With a little practice you will learn to tack and guide yourself as desired.

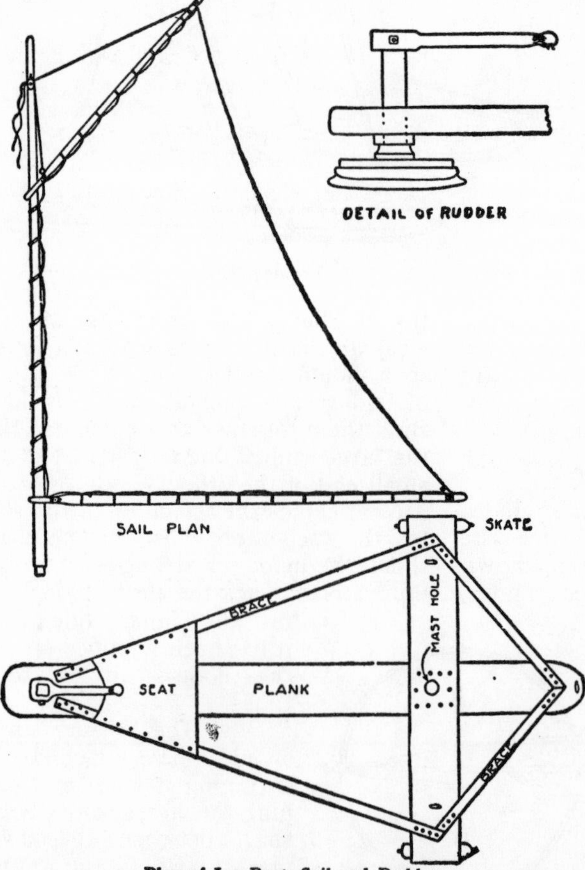

Plan of Ice Boat, Sail and Rudder

If the hoops cannot be easily obtained the sails may be made equally effective by using the main spar and fore and main masts as herein described, making the sails square shaped instead of round and leaving off the hoops. In this case the sails should be securely bound with strong tape. Attach a corner to each end of the cross-spar, and a corner to the outer end of the main spar. The remaining corner of each then appears opposite to each other, and should be fastened together by strong cord in the same manner as the hoops. In this case the sails may be left off until after the frame is entirely put together and then fastened on to the spars by buttons.

A more simple sail may be made according to the plans illustrated in the lower drawing. It is made by binding together in the center the halves of two strong hogshead hoops, or two bent poles are better. If possible the sail should be about 8 ft. long and 4 ft. wide. Fasten on the sail at the four corners. The rig will convey two persons and is more easily constructed than any other.

Ice Boating

But the sport that is greatest of all, the one that used to be part of the life of every northern boy, and which is being revived in popularity after years of stagnation, is ice boating. With the aid of old skates, pieces of board and an old sheet or a small bit of canvas, any boy possessed of ordinary mechanical genius may make an ice boat. The frame of the boat should be made something in the form of a kite. The centerboard should be 4 or 5 ft. long, 6 in. wide and 2 in. thick. The cross board may be of a piece of 1 by 6-in. plank 3 ft.

long. Fasten these with braces of small stout strip, as shown in the drawing, and screw the cross-piece securely to the center-board. Bore a hole in the center of the intersection for the mast pole. The seat may be made of a piece of strong cloth or leather. Three skates are fastened on to either side of the cross-board and one to the rear end of the center-board, the latter of which is to operate as a rudder. In attaching the skates first make a couple of runner blocks, each 6 in. long and 3 in. wide. Bore holes in them for the straps of the skates to pass through and fasten them securely. Nail the runner blocks firmly to the cross-board about 1½ in. from each end.

Boy's Ice Boat

In making the rudder hew down a piece of scantling 1 ft. long until it assumes the shape of a club with a flat base. Nail a strip of wood firmly to this base, and to the strip fasten the skate. Run the top of the club through a hole bored in the stern of the center-board. Then make the helm by boring a hole in one end of a strip of soft board about 1 ft. long, and through this hole pass the club or rubber-pole and fasten it so it may be shifted when desired. Make the sail out of an old sheet, if it be strong enough, piece of canvas, or any such substance and attach it to the mast and sprit as shown in the illustration, and guide it by a stout string attached to the lower outer corner. As

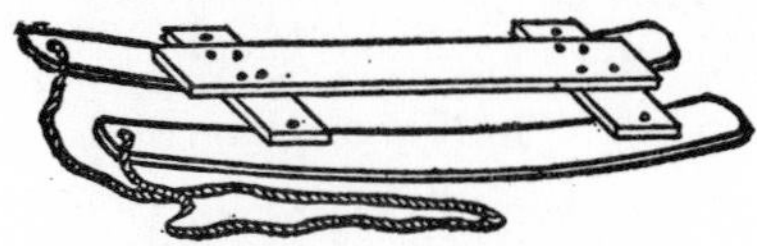
Fig. 1—Barrel Stave Sled

an ice boat will travel faster than the wind, some care and considerable skill is necessary. Unless you are accustomed to managing a sail boat, do not select a place in which to learn where there are air holes or open water. To stop the boat throw the head around into the wind, same as you would with a sail boat. If the wind is strong the

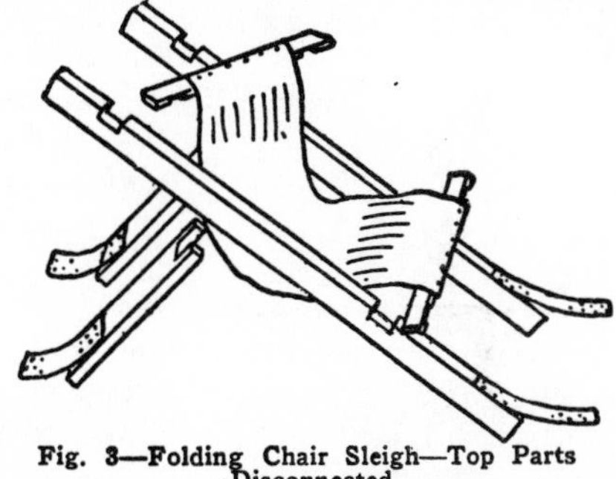
Fig. 3—Folding Chair Sleigh—Top Parts Disconnected

occupants of the boat should lie flat on their stomach.

Coasters and Chair Sleighs

Make your own sled, boys! There is no use in buying them, because your hand-made sled is probably better than any purchased one and then you can take so much more pride in it when you know it is of your own construction. There are so many different designs of sleds that can be made by hand that the matter can be left almost entirely to your own ingenuity. You can make one like the bought sleds and face the runners with pieces of an iron hoop which will answer every purpose. A

Chair Sleigh

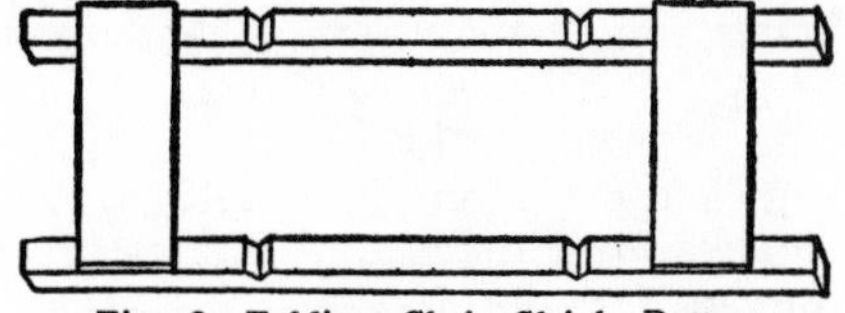
Fig. 2—Folding Chair Sleigh Bottom

good sled for coasting consists simply of two barrel staves and three pieces of board as shown in the picture, Fig. 1. No bought sled will equal it for coasting and it is also just the thing for carrying loads of snow for building snow houses. The method of its construction is so simple that no other description is needed than the picture. You can make a chair-sleigh out of this by fitting a chair on the cross board instead of the long top board or it will be still stronger if the top board is allowed to remain, and then you will have a device that can readily again be transformed into a coasting sled. In making the chair-sleigh it is necessary, in order to hold the chair in place, to nail four L-shaped blocks on the cross boards, one for each leg of the chair. Skating along over the ice and pushing the chair in front of him the proud possessor of a chair-sleigh may take his mother, grown sister or lady friend with him on his outings, and permit her to ride in the chair.

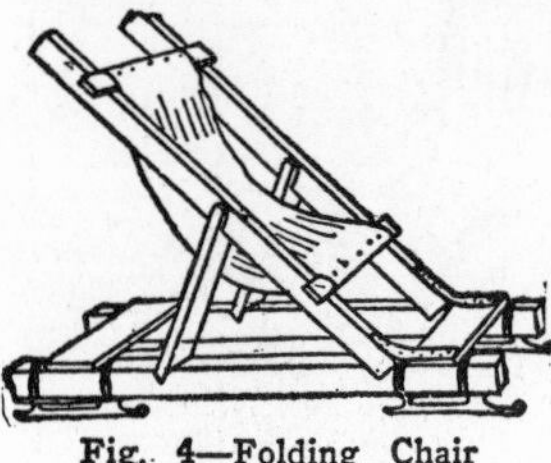

Fig. 4—Folding Chair Sleigh Open

Folding Chair Sleigh

A folding chair sleigh is even more enjoyable and convenient than the device just described. If the ice pond is far from home this may be placed under your arm and carried where you like.

The illustrations, Figs. 2 and 3, show all the parts as they should look before

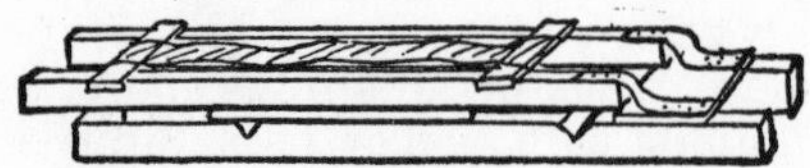

Fig. 5—Folding Chair Sleigh Closed

being joined together. The seat may be made of a piece of canvas or carpet. The hinges are of leather. Figure 4 shows the folding chair sleigh after it has been put together. Skates are employed for the runners. The skates may be strapped on or taken off whenever desired. When the chair is lifted the supports slip from the notches on the side bars and fall on the runner bars. The chair is then folded up so that it can be carried by a small boy. With regular metal hinges and light timbers a very handsome chair can be constructed that will also afford an ornamental lawn chair for summer.

The Toboggan Sled

When the snow is very deep a toboggan sled is the thing for real sport. The runners of the ordinary sled break through the crust of the deep snow, blocking the progress, and spoiling the fun. The toboggan sled, with its broad, smooth bottom, glides along over the soft surface with perfect ease.

To make the toboggan sled, secure two boards each 10 ft. long and 1 ft. wide and so thin that they can be easily bent. Place the boards beside each other and join them together with cross sticks. Screw the boards to the cross stick from the bottom and be sure that the heads of the screws are buried deep enough in the wood to not protrude, so

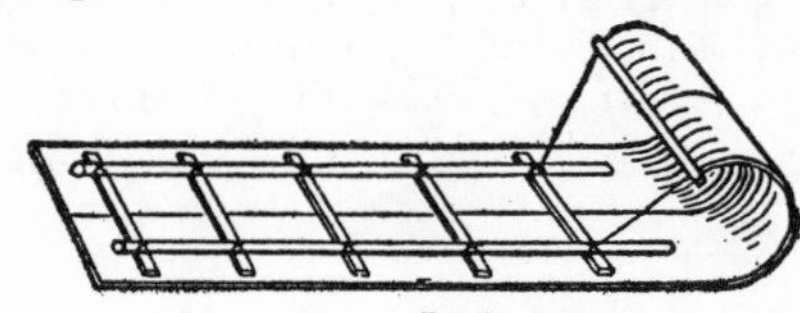

FIG 6

Fig. 6—The Toboggan

that the bottom will present an absolutely smooth surface to the snow. Fasten two side bars to the top of the cross sticks and screw them firmly. In some instances the timbers are fastened together by strings, a groove being cut in the bottom of the boards so as to keep the strings from protruding and being ground to pieces. After the side bars are securely fastened, bend the ends of the boards over and tie them to the ends of the front cross bar to hold them in position. See Fig. 6. The strings for keeping the boards bent must be very strong. Pieces of stout wire, or a slender steel rod, are even better. The toboggan slide is the favored device of sport among the boys in Canada, where nearly every boy knows how to make them.

The Norwegian Ski.

You have often read of the ski, the snowshoe used by the Norwegians and other people living in the far north. With them the men and women glide down the snow-covered mountain sides, leap across ditches, run races and have all kinds of sport. They are just as amusing to the American boy who has ever learned to manipulate them, and it is wonderful how much skill can be attained in their use. Any boy with a little mechanical ingenuity can make a pair of skis (pronounced skees). They can be made from two barrel staves. Select staves of straight grained wood. Sharpen the ends of each and score each end by cutting grooves in the wood, as shown in the cut, Fig. 7. A pocket knife or small gouge will suffice for this work. Then smear the end of the staves with oil and hold them close to a hot fire until they can be bent so as to tip the toes upward, as shown in the picture, Fig. 7. Then with a cord bind the staves as they are bent and permit them to remain thus tied until they retain the curved form of their own accord. Now screw on top of each ski a little block, just broad and high enough to fit in front of the heels of your shoe. Fasten a strap in front of

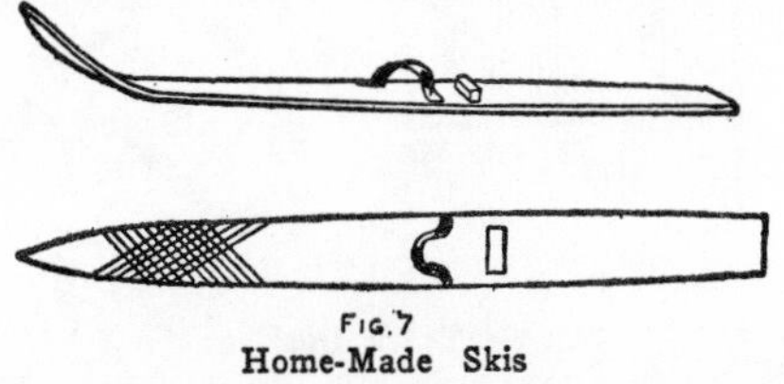

Fig. 7
Home-Made Skis

each block through which to slip your toes, and the skis are made. The inside of the shoe heel should press firmly against the block and the toe be held tightly under the strap. This will keep the skis on your feet. Now procure a stick with which to steer and hunt a snow bank. At first you will afford more amusement to onlookers than to yourself, for the skis have a way of trying to run in opposite directions, crosswise and various ways, but with practice you will soon become expert in their manipulation.

Home-Made Settee

Many people have old wooden beds stored away which can easily be made into handy settees like the one shown in the accompanying photograph. A few nails and one-half dozen 3-in. screws are all the materials necessary besides the old bed. The tools needed are a saw, hammer and a screwdriver. The head-board, if too high, can be cut

Settee Made from Old Wooden Bed

off and some of the ornaments replaced. The footboard must be cut in two to make the ends or arms of the settee. The side rails and a few of the slats are used in making the seat.—Contributed by Wm. F. Hild, Lake Forest, Ill.

Enameling a Bicycle Frame

Make an enamel by mixing 2 oz. burnt umber with 1 qt. boiled oil, heating, and then adding 1 oz. asphaltum. Keep the mass hot until thoroughly mixed, says the Master Painter. Thin with turpentine while still hot.

Use a camel's hair brush for applying the enamel and allow it to set; then place the article in an oven, bake for six or eight hours at a temperature of 250 deg. F. When cool rub down with steel wool. Apply a finishing coat and allow it to bake eight hours at 250 deg. F. Rub down with a soft rag, varnish and bake again at 200 deg. F. Heat and cool the frame gradually each time. Black enamel is easiest to apply and bakes hardest, but requires a temperature of 300 deg. Colors can be baked at from 200 to 250 deg.

How to Make a Sewing Bag

A very practical and novel sewing bag for odds and ends necessary for mending, etc., can be made of a folding camp stool. If an old stool is not

Camp-Stool Work Bag

at hand, a new one can be purchased for 25 cents. Remove the top or seat, which is usually made of a piece of carpet, then make a bag as shown in Fig. 1 and stitch a heavy cord around the top to make it strong. Make pockets on the inside as shown and nail the bag to the two crosspieces on which the ends of the carpet were tacked. Large, brass furniture nails should be used. Attach a small hook and eye on each end and fasten two leather handles to the crosspieces.

Such a bag requires little room when folded and can be stored in a closet when not in use.—Contributed by Joseph Ledwinka, Philadelphia, Pa.

Home-Made Roller Skates

The rubber-tired wheels of an old carpet sweeper can be used to advantage in making a pair of roller skates. In Fig. 1 is shown how an iron washer or two may be fastened to the wood with a piece of sheet metal to support

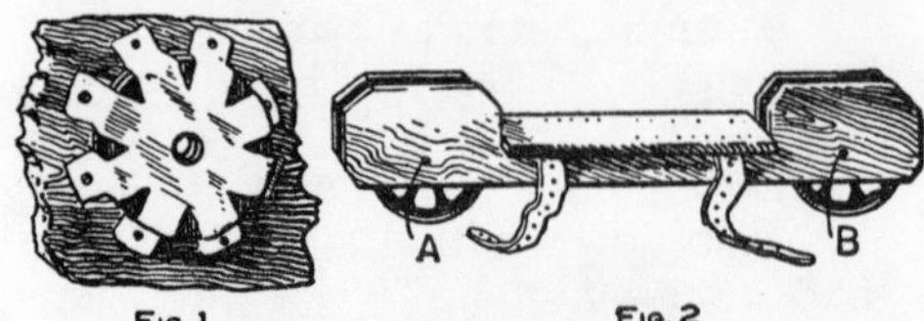

Rubber Tired Roller Skate

the short axles of the wheels. The wheels are oiled through the holes A and B, Fig. 2. These holes should be smaller than the axles. The two side pieces are fastened together with a board nailed on the top edges, as shown. This board also furnishes the flat top for the shoe sole. Two straps are attached for fastening the skate to the shoe.—Contributed by Thos. De Loof, Grand Rapids, Mich.

Adjuster for Flexible Electric Wires

The accompanying illustration shows an adjuster for changing the drop of an electric light. The main feature of this adjuster is that it can be removed from the cord at any time. The adjuster is made from a piece of wood, 3/8 in. thick, 2 in. wide and 3 in. long. A 1/4-in. hole is bored in the center near each end of the wood and a slot cut from

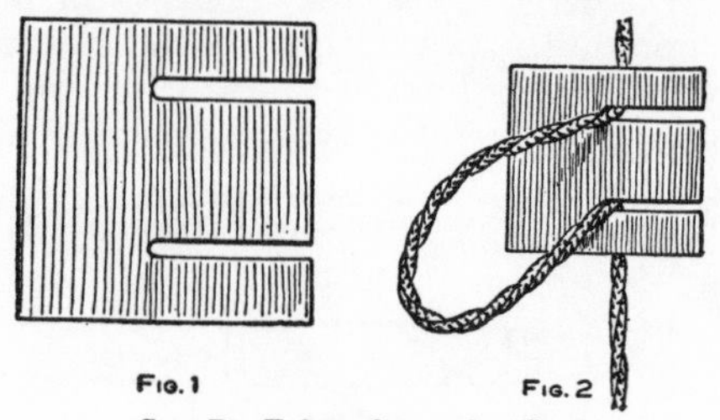

Can Be Taken from the Cord

the holes to the outside edge, as shown in Fig. 1. It is attached to the flexible cord as shown in Fig. 2.—Contributed by J. J. Voelcker, Decatur, Ill.

Making Photographs on Watch Dials

Beat to a foam the white of an egg, with the addition of a little ammonia. Add 9 oz. and 3 dr. of water and beat again. After the egg has settled, filter and let the liquid run over the dial, which has been previously cleaned with ammonia. When the surplus has run off, coat with the mixture and allow to dry.

A sensitive collodion is now produced as follows: Dissolve 9 gr. of chloride of zinc in 5 dr. of alcohol; add 7 1/2 gr. of collodion cotton and 6 1/2 dr. of ether. Shake the whole forcibly.

Dissolve 23 gr. of nitrate of silver in hot water, add 1½ dr. of alcohol and keep the whole solution by heating. The silver solution is now added in small quantities at a time to the collodion, which must be well settled. This, of course, is done in the dark room. After 24 hours the emulsion is filtered by passing it through cotton moistened with alcohol. This durable collodion emulsion is now flowed thinly upon the prepared watch dial, which, after the collodion has coagulated, is moved up and down in distilled water until the fatty stripes disappear. The water is then changed once, and after a short immersion, the dial is left to dry on a piece of blotting paper. It is now ready for exposure. Expose under magnesium light and develop with a citrate oxalic developer, or in the following hydroquinone developer:

Hydroquinone	1 dr.
Bromide of potassium	6 dr.
Sulphite of soda	1½ oz.
Carbonate of soda	2 2/3 dr.
Water	14 oz.

After fixing and drying, coat with a transparent positive varnish.

Home-Made Overhead Trolley Coaster

The accompanying sketch shows a playground trolley line which furnished a great deal of amusement to many children at a minimum cost. The wire, which is 3/16 in. in diameter, was stretched between a tree and a barn across a vacant quarter block. The strength of the wire was first tested by a heavy man. When not in use the wire is unhooked from the tree and hauled into the barn and coiled loosely in the hay loft. The wire was made taut for use by a rope which was fastened to the beams in the barn. The trolley was made, as shown in Figs. 1 and 2, of strips of wood bolted with stove bolts on two grooved pulleys. The middle wide board was made of hardwood. The wheels were taken from light pulley blocks and stove bolts were purchased from a local hardware store to accurately fit the hubs. As it was necessary to keep the bearings greased, we used vaseline. This coaster made great sport for the youngsters and at no time were they in danger of a serious fall as the line was hung low and the slant of the wire was moderate.—Contributed by H. J. Holden, Palm Springs, Calif.

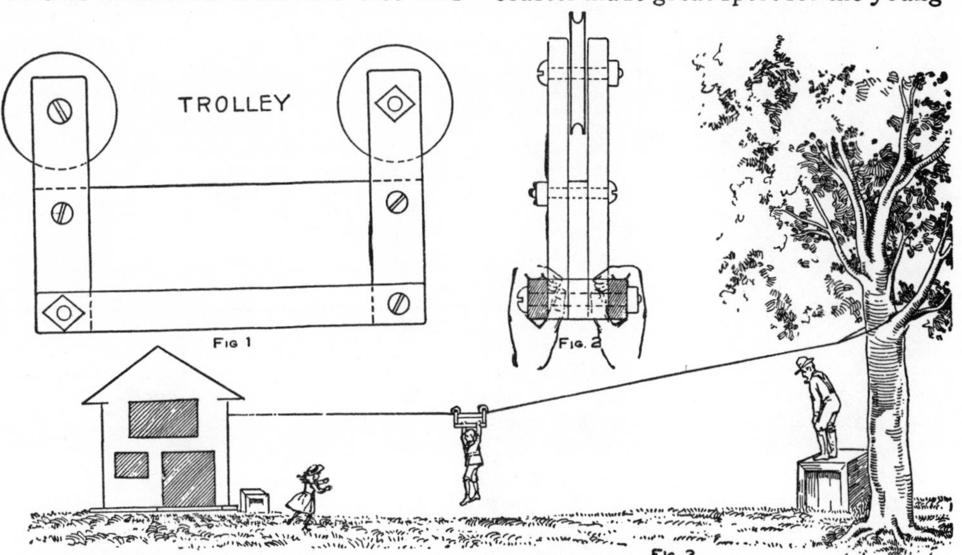

Details of the Trolley and How It Is Used

How to Make an Electric Furnace Regulator

We have a furnace in our house and a part of my work each evening last winter was to go down in the basement at 9 o'clock, fill the furnace with coal for the night and stay there until it was burning in good shape, then to close the draft door. As this performance requires from twenty to thirty minutes I concluded to make a self-acting device which would close the draft and leave the furnace safe, without any further attention on my part, after putting in the coal and opening it up to burn. As some other boys may like to build the same regulator I will tell just how to make one and how it operates.

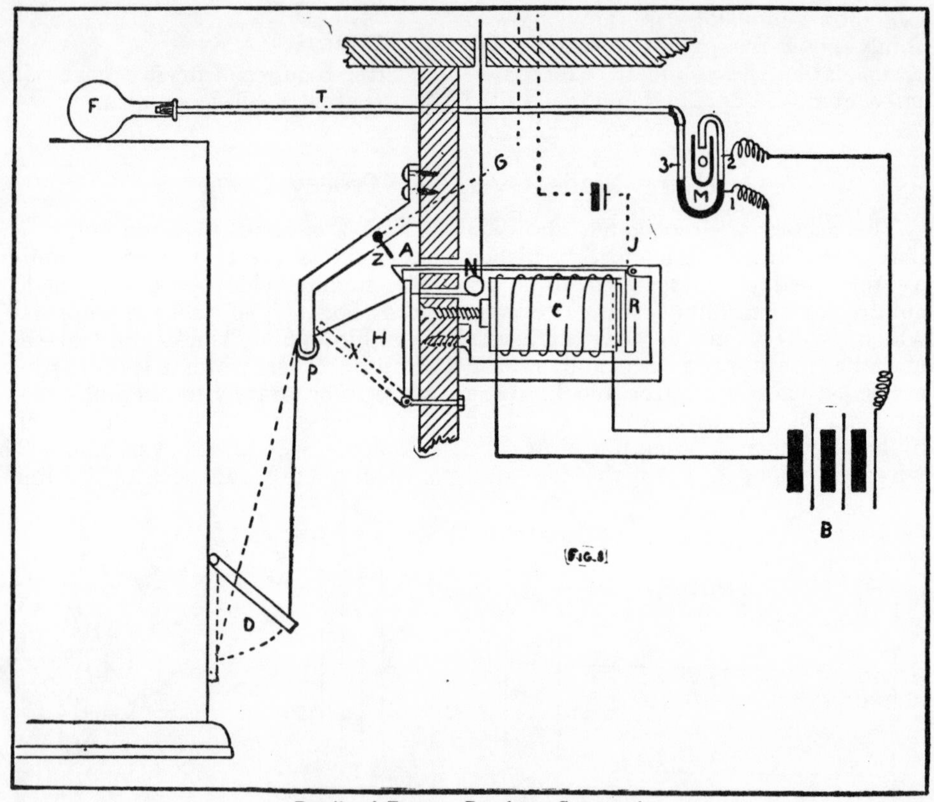

Details of Furnace Regulator Construction

Referring to Fig. 1, you will see a straight cord is attached to the draft door of the furnace, D, and is run over the pulley P and finally is attached to a small piece of iron, H. This piece of iron is hinged to I. To the other side of H another cord G is fastened, which passes over the pulley N and terminates in any convenient place in the rooms above. This piece of iron H is held in place by the release A. Now C is a coil of wire from a door bell. R is an armature which works A on pivot J. M is a U-tube, filled with mercury, one end being connected to a half liter glass flask F by the tube T, and the other end terminates in an overflow tube O. B is a battery of three bichromate cells which are connected up with the C and the platinum points 1—2, which are fused into the U-tube.

On fixing the furnace the iron piece H takes position X, this being the normal position when draft door D is closed. On arriving upstairs I pull the cord G, which causes the piece H to become fixed in the vertical position by means of A. This opens the draft door at the same time. Now when the furnace heats up sufficiently it causes the air to expand in F, which causes the mercury in M to rise a little above the point 2. This immediately causes a current to flow through C which in turn draws R towards it, raises A and causes H to drop to position X. This shuts the furnace door. Now the furnace, of course, cools down, thus causing the air in F to contract and consequently opening the circuit through C. If at any time the furnace should overheat, the raising of A, on which is grounded a wire from a signal bell upstairs, will make a circuit through the bell by means of the point Z and wire leading therefrom. This bell also serves to tell me whether H has dropped or not. This same device of regulating the draft D can be used to regulate the damper, found on the coal doors of most furnaces, by simply fusing a platinum point on the other side of M and changing the cord which is attached to D. A two-contact switch could also be inserted to throw connections from 2 to 3. It would work in this manner: The damper door, of course, which keeps a low fire, would be up in a position similar to D; on the furnace cooling too much, connection, due to contracting of air in F, would be made through 3 and C, causing H to drop, thus closing door. This simple device worked very well all last winter and gave me no trouble whatever.

If you cannot readily procure a U-tube, you can make one, as I did, and the work is interesting.

The U-tube is constructed in the following manner. A glass tube is closed at one end. This is done by holding the tube in one corner of a gas flame, somewhat near the dark area (A, Fig. 2), and constantly turning the tube, when it will be found that the glass has melted together. Now, after it is cool, about 3 or 4 in. from the sealed end, the tube is held steadily so that the flame will heat one small portion (B, Fig. 2). After this small portion is heated blow into the tube, not very hard, but just enough to cause tube to bulge out. Allow to cool. Then reheat the small bulged portion, blow quite hard, so that the glass will be blown out at this point, forming a small hole. Now insert about ½ in. of platinum wire and reheat, holding platinum

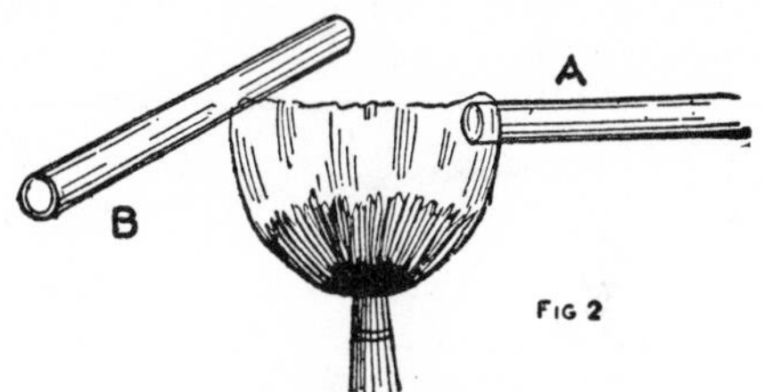

Making the U-Tube

wire by means of a small pliers so that it will be partly in the tube and partly without. The platinum will stick to the glass, and if glass is sufficiently heated one will be able to pull it, by means of pliers, from one side of the hole to the other, thus sealing the wire into the tube. Another wire is sealed in the same way about 1 in. from the first. Now, to bend the tube, one must hold it, with both hands, in the flame and turn constantly until soft. Quickly withdraw from flame and bend, just as you would a piece of copper wire. Allow to cool slowly.

The several tubes are connected with a short piece of rubber tubing.

The total cost of materials for constructing the apparatus complete will not amount to more than one dollar.—Contributed by M. G. Kopf, Lewis Institute, Chicago.

Weatherproofing for Tents

Dissolve 4 oz. sulphate of zinc in 10 gal. water; add ½ lb. sal-soda; stir well until dissolved, and add ½ oz. tartaric acid. Put the tent cover in this solution and let lie 24 hrs. Take out (do not wring it) and hang up to dry.—Grinnell's Hand Book on Painting.

Sheet metal placed between two boards in the jaws of a vise and clamped tightly, can be sawed easily with a hacksaw.

A Monoplane Weather Vane

The toy windmill or weather vane shown in the sketch is made to represent a Blériot monoplane. The propeller is turned by the wind. The frame is made of heavy wire and connected with straps of tin. The construction is plainly shown in the illustration. The windmill vane can be made in any size to suit the builder.—Contributed by W. C. Bliss, St. Louis, Missouri.

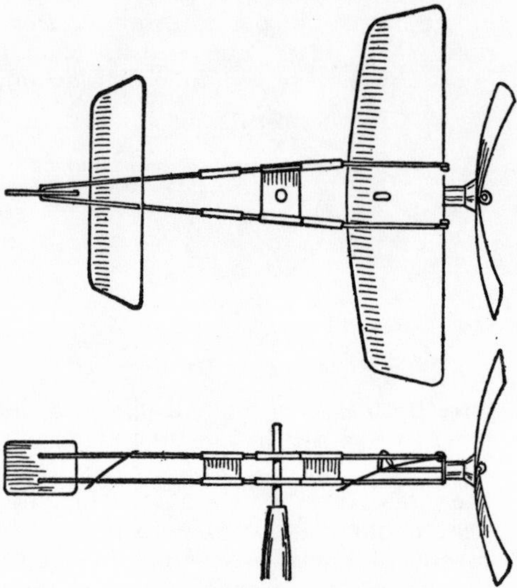

Wire and Sheet-Metal Vane

How to Make a Minnow Trap

Glass minnow traps that will give as good service as those purchased at the tackle store can be made without difficulty. If a trap should be banged carelessly against the side of the boat or some other obstruction and smashed, instead of spending several dollars to replace it, a half hour's time will turn out a new one just as good, says a correspondent of Outing.

A trap of this kind can be made from an ordinary fruit jar such as used in putting up preserves, either of one or two-quart capacity. A one-quart jar gives good results, but if the bait to be caught is of fairly large size, the two-quart size may be used. As the jars have the same style top they can be used interchangeably with one mouthpiece.

The mouthpiece is made of a round-neck bottle of which the glass is colorless and rather thin. If the neck of the bottle is cut at the right point, it makes a glass funnel that will just fit into the fruit jar. The funnel forms the mouth of the trap. Put the neck of the bottle into the fruit jar and mark the glass with a file where the bottle and jar meet. Make as deep a cut as possible with a file around the bottle on the mark and place two turns of a yarn string saturated in kerosene around just below the cut when the bottle is standing in an upright position. Set fire to the string and turn the bottle from side to side to distribute the heat evenly, then when the string has burned out, plunge the bottle in cold water and it will separate on the cut.

Bind some copper wire around the neck of the jar so that three ends will project ½ in. or more. These are bent down over the funnel when put into the jar, forming clamps to hold it in place. The copper wire can be bent many times in emptying or baiting the trap without breaking.

Two copper wire bands are tied tightly around the jar about 3 in. apart. They should be twisted tight with a pair of pliers and the ends joined, forming a ring for attaching a cord.

For catching "kellies" or "killies," bait the trap with crushed clams or salt-water mussels and for fresh water shiners use mincemeat or bread crumbs and do not spill any bait outside of the trap. Leave the trap down ten to fifteen minutes and when resetting it after emptying, put back one or two of the victims, as the others enter more readily if they see some of their companions ahead of them.

A Remedy for Leaking Fountain Pens

Fountain-pen leaks may often be prevented by unscrewing the joint and lightly smearing the screw with vaseline. This also makes it easy to unscrew the joint for filling.

Kites of Many Kinds and How to Make Them

One of the prettiest of all is the butterfly kite. To make this get two thin kite sticks of equal length. Bend each in an arc, tying one end of a strong string to one end of each stick and the other end of the string to a point about 3 in. from the other end of the stick. This leaves one end of each stick free, hooking over the hemisphere described by the thread and the stick. Now tie another thread to each of these free ends and tie the other end of the thread to a point near the other end of the stick, corresponding with the distance from the end at which the first strings were tied on the opposite side. This done, you should have two arched frames, each an exact counterpart of the other in size, curvature and weight. Now fasten the two frames together so that the arcs will overlap each other as shown in the sketch. Bind the intersecting points securely with thread. To make the butterfly's head, secure two heavy broom straws or two short wires, and attach them to the top part of the wing frames near where the sticks intersect, so that the straws or wires will cross. These form the antennae, or the "smellers." Then select the color of paper you want, yellow, brown, blue, white or any other color; lay it on a flat surface and place the frame on top of it, holding the frame down securely with a weight. Then with a pair of scissors cut the paper around the frame, leaving about a ½-in. margin for pasting. Cut slits in the paper about 2 in. apart around the curves and at all angles to keep the paper from wrinkling when it is pasted.

Boy Kite

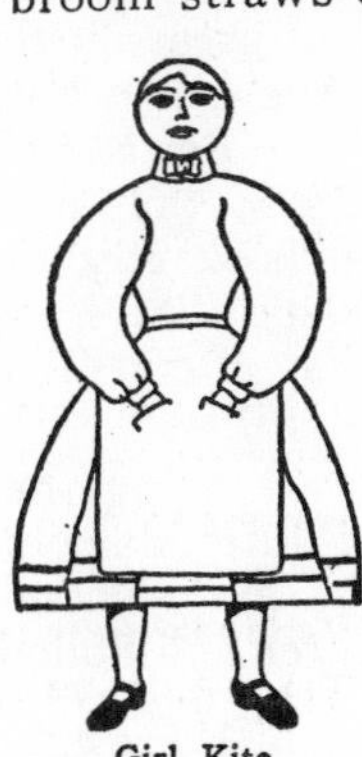

Girl Kite

Distribute the paste with a small brush and make the overlaps a little more than ¼ in. wide and press them together with a soft cloth. When the kite is dry decorate it with paint or strips of colored paper in any design you may fancy. The best effects are produced by pasting pieces of colored paper on top of the other paper. Black paper decorations show up to fine advantage when the kite is in flight. Attach the "belly-band" to the curved sticks by punching a hole in the paper in the same manner as it is attached to the common hexagonal or coffin-shaped kite. With a tail, your kite is ready to fly.

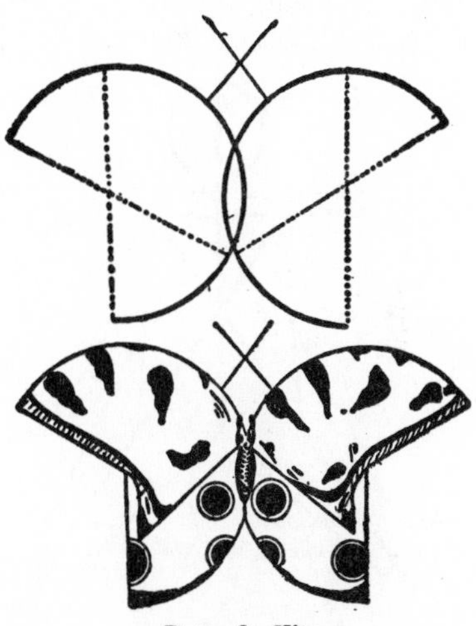

Butterfly Kite

Another interesting design is the boy kite. With light colored coat and vest and gay striped trousers, the kite standing high in the air always attracts at-

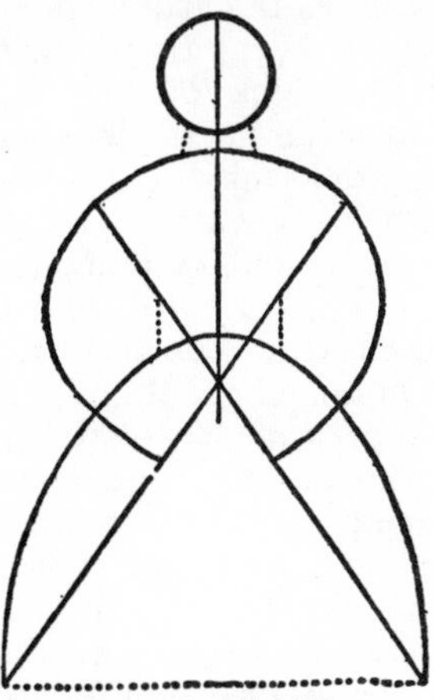

Frame for Girl Kite

tention and affords splendid sport for the American youth in springtime.

In making a boy kite it should be remembered that the larger the boy is the better he will fly. To construct the frame, two straight sticks, say 3½ ft. long, should serve for the legs and

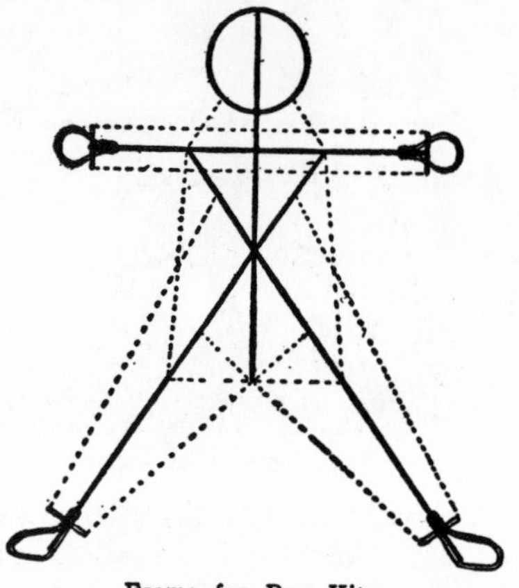

Frame for Boy Kite

body; another straight stick forms the spine and should be about 2 ft. 4 in. long. For the arms, get a fourth straight stick about 3 ft. 3 in. long. Make the frame for the head by bending a light tough stick in a circle about 7 in. in diameter. Bind it tightly with a strong thread and through its center run the spine. Then tack on the arm stick 3 in. under the circle so that the spinal column crosses the arm stick exactly in the center. Wrap tightly with strong thread and tack on the two sticks that are to serve for the legs and body. The leg sticks should be fastened to the arm stick about 6 in. on either side of the spinal column, and crossed so that the other ends are 3 ft. apart. Tack them and the arm stick together at the point where they intersect. Small hoops and cross stick of the same material as the head frame should be fastened to both extremities of the arm stick and the lower ends of the leg stick for the hands and feet. See that both hand frames are exactly alike and exercise equal caution regarding the foot frames; also see that the arm stick is at exact right angles with the spine stick and that the kite joints are all firmly tied and the kite evenly balanced; otherwise it may be lopsided. Fasten on the strings of the frame, beginning at the neck at equal distances from the spine, as indicated by the dotted lines in the diagram. Extend a string slantingly from the armstick to the head on both sides of the spinal column, and run all the other strings as shown in the cut, being careful that both sides of the frame correspond in measurements.

To cover the kite, select different colors of paper to suit your taste, and after pasting them together, lay the paper on the floor and placing the frame on it, cut out the pattern. Leave an edge of ½ in. all around and make a slit in this edge every 6 in. and at each angle; make the slits 2 in. apart around the head. After the kite is pasted and dry, paint the buttons, hair, eyes, hands, feet, etc., as you desire. Arrange the "belly band" and tail band and attach the kite string in the same manner as in the ordinary coffin-shaped kite.

The "lady kite" is made on the same principle as the boy kite. The frame may be made exactly as the boy kite and then "dressed" with tissue paper to represent a girl, or it may be made on the special frame, page 81. Remember the dotted lines represent the strings or thread, and the other lines indicate the kite sticks. Be careful with your measurements so that each side of the kite corresponds exactly and is well balanced. Also see that every point where the sticks intersect is firmly tacked and bound.

To cover the kite, first paste together pieces of tissue paper of different color to suit your taste. The paste should be made of flour and water and boiled. Make the seams or overlaps not quite ⅜ in. wide. Lay the paper on the floor, using weights to hold it down, and place the frame of the kite upon it. Then cut out the paper around the frame, leaving an edge of ½ in. Don't forget to make a slit in the edge every 6 or 7 in. and at each angle. Around the head the slits are cut 2 in. apart, as in the case of the boy kite. After the kite is dry, paint the paper as your fancy dictates.

To make the breast band, punch holes through the paper, one upon each side of the leg sticks, just above the bottom, and one upon each side of the arm sticks at the shoulder. Run one end of the string through the hole at the bottom of the left limb and tie it to the leg stick; tie the other end at the right shoulder. Fasten one end of another string of the same length at the bottom of the right leg; pass the string up across the first band and tie the other end at the left shoulder. Attach the kite string to the breast band at the point where the two strings intersect. Tie the knot so that you can slide the kite string up or down until it is properly adjusted. The tail band is made by tying a string to the leg sticks at the bottom of the breast band. Let the string hang slack below the skirt and attach the tail to the center. The same general rules apply in attaching the string and tail to the boy kite.

You can make the lady look as if dancing and kicking in the clouds by making the feet of stiff pasteboard and allowing them to hang loose from the line which forms the bottom of the skirt. The feet will move and sway with each motion of the kite.

How to Make Rubber Stamps

India rubber, especially prepared for stamp-making, should be procured from a dealer or manufacturer, if good results are to be obtained. As an experiment, it is possible for an amateur to prepare the rubber, but, in such cases, it is always attended with uncertain results. The mixed uncured rubber comes in white sheets, strong, firm and about 1/8 in. thick, and for its manipulation a press is indispensable, but can be home-made.

For the base of the press use a piece of iron, having two holes drilled in it at the middle of opposite sides, through which pass bolts, letting the thread ends extend upward and counter-sinking places for the bolt heads to keep the under side of the base level. Solder the bolts in place at the base. The upper part of the press, or the platen, is also of iron, cut so it can be swung

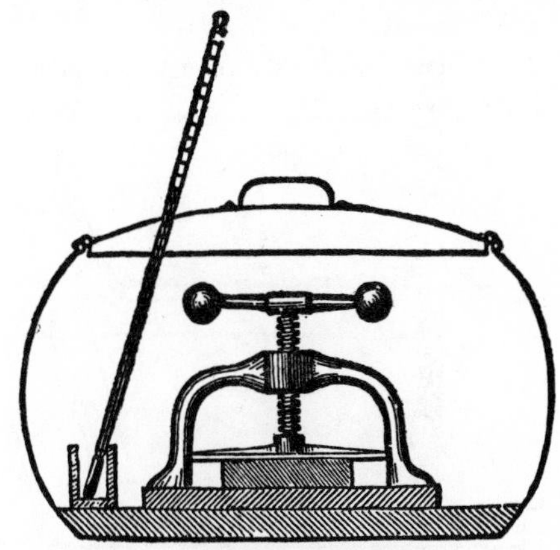

Fish Kettle Vulcanizer

off the bolts, rather than by removing the nuts and lifting it off. String a half dozen nuts, larger than those which screw on, on each bolt, so that when the upper nut on each is screwed to the extent of the thread the pressure will be communicated through the nuts wedged in between the platen and the upper nut. The bolt holes in the platen should be directly over those in the base. Distance pieces of an exact thickness should be provided for use on the base; these serve to keep the pressure even.

In preparing the mould, if type is to be copied, use rather large type with wide spaces and set up with high quads and spaces, or the type faces may be filled up by rubbing with either wax, or soap, lightly brushing off any that remains loose. The type so set should be locked into a frame. This may be made of two pieces of wood bolted together at both ends, or of printer's furniture. Place it on a flat surface (marble is good, but any perfectly smooth surface will do) and place distance pieces 1/8 in. higher than its upper surface on either side of it. Apply olive oil to the type faces and wipe off any excess. To form the matrix or reverse of the model, take a piece of iron larger than the inscription to be copied, and spread upon it to a depth of 1/4 in, a putty made by mixing plaster of paris and water to the right consistency. By means of a table knife spread the plaster smoothly and then invert the plate upon the model and press down until

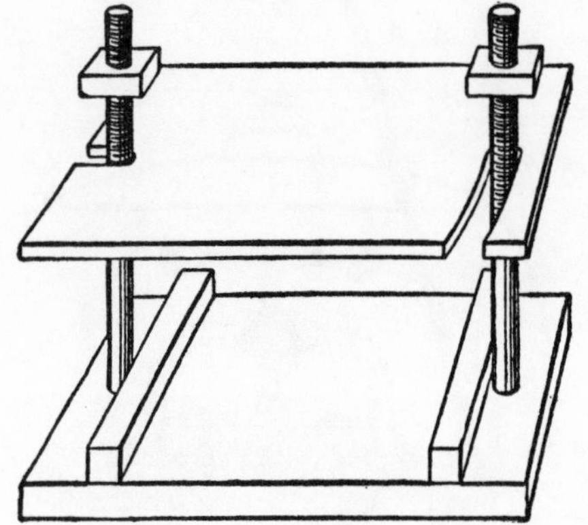

Vulcanizing Press for Rubber Stamps

the distance pieces are struck. Let it set 10 minutes and then remove. If care has been taken the matrix will be perfect. After it has thoroughly dried, preferably in an oven, saturate it with an alcoholic solution of shellac to strengthen it.

Cut a piece of smooth rubber, large enough to cover the matrix, from the sheet, throw this into a box of talc, or powdered soapstone, so that it receives a coating on both sides; dust a little of the powder over the matrix, also. Place the press on a support over a gas burner, or a kerosene lamp, and apply the heat. Place the matrix on the base of the press, dust off the piece of india rubber and place in the press upon the matrix and screw down the platen. Heat the press to 284 deg. F. and keep screwing down the platen so that the rubber, now soft and putty-like, is forced into every recess of the matrix. A thermometer is not necessary; some rubber always protrudes and the stage of the process can be told from that. At first it is quite elastic, then as the heat increases it becomes soft, then the curing begins and it again becomes elastic, so that, if a point of a knife blade is pressed against it, it resumes its shape when the point is removed. When this takes place it is then thoroughly vulcanized and the sheet can be removed from the matrix. Ten minutes, under favorable conditions, is sufficient time for moulding the rubber. By means of common glue, or bicycle tire cement, fasten the rubber stamp to a wooden handle.

It is possible to dispense with the press in making stamps, where the work is not done in quantities, and use a hot flat-iron. The matrix is placed on a stove at low heat, the rubber laid on and the hot iron applied. But a few moments are required to mould it.

An old letter press if it be inclosed in a tin oven makes a good press, or all the necessary materials and apparatus can be purchased from a dealer. Any type such as all printers use will answer.

To Light a Gaslight Without Matches

It is probably well known that if you rub your feet briskly over a carpet on a dry, cold day and then touch any metallic object with your finger it will emit a small spark. The following amusing experiment may be done on the same principle:

Take any small piece of wire about 2 in. long and twist it around a gas-burner as shown at A in the sketch. Have the tip of the burner about $1/8$ in. below the end of the wire. The wire must be just far enough away from the center of the burner to keep it out of the flame, or else it will melt.

Now get a friend to turn on the gas when you are ready for it. Go around the room once or twice rubbing your feet along the carpet. When you come around to the gaslight touch the point of the wire and if the gas is turned on, the light will flare right up as if it had been lit with a match.

This experiment cannot be done on a damp day or without shoes, and works best in cold weather.—Contributed by E. H. Klipstein.

How To Make a Trap For Rabbits, Rats and Mice

From an old 6-in. pine fence board cut off four pieces 2½ ft. long and one 6 in. square for the end of the trap and another 4 in. by 8 in. for the door. Use old boards, as new boards scare rabbits.

Figure 1 shows how the box is made. It should be 4 in. wide and 6 in. high on the inside. The top and bottom boards project 1 in. beyond the side boards at the back and the end board is set in. The top board should be 2 in. shorter than the sides at the front. Nail a strip on the top board back of the door and one on the bottom board so the game cannot push the door open from inside the trap and get out.

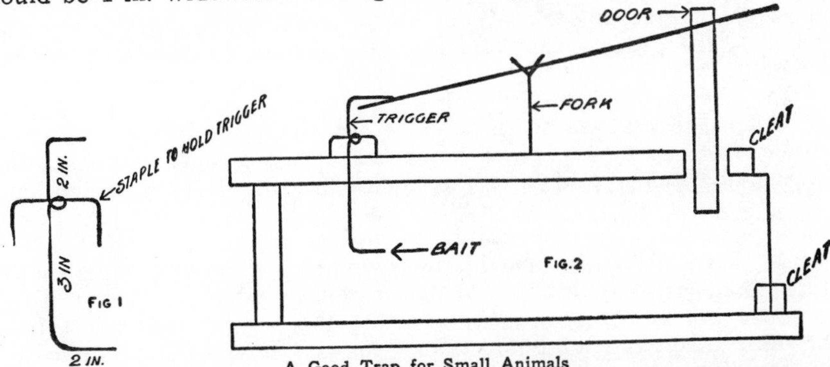

A Good Trap for Small Animals

In the middle of the top board bore a hole and put a crotched stick in for the lever to rest on. Bore another hole in the top of the door for the lever to pass through. Two inches from the back of the box bore a hole for the trigger, which should be made out of heavy wire in the manner shown in Fig. 2. The door of the trap must work easily and loosely.

Novel Electric Motor

The materials necessary to make this motor are an old electric bell of the "buzzer" type and a cogwheel from an old clock.

Remove the hammer-head and gong from the bell, then bend the end of the hammer into a loop, as in Fig. 1. Now make a little wire catch like Fig. 2, and fasten its loop into the loop of the hammer. Mount the bell on a small board as in Fig. 3 and fasten the cogwheel almost on a line with it. Now press down the hammer and place a nail in the position shown in the diagram so that the catch touches one of the teeth.

Fasten the board in an upright position and attach two dry batteries to the binding-posts. If properly connected, the fly-wheel will turn quite rapidly and with amazing force for so small a machine. The machine, however, has a fixed direction as shown by the arrow, but the belting can be arranged so as to send the models in a reversed direction if required. The materials for the motor should not cost more than 25c for the bell and if you have an old bell it will cost next to nothing.—Contributed by Fred C. Curry, Brockville, Ontario.

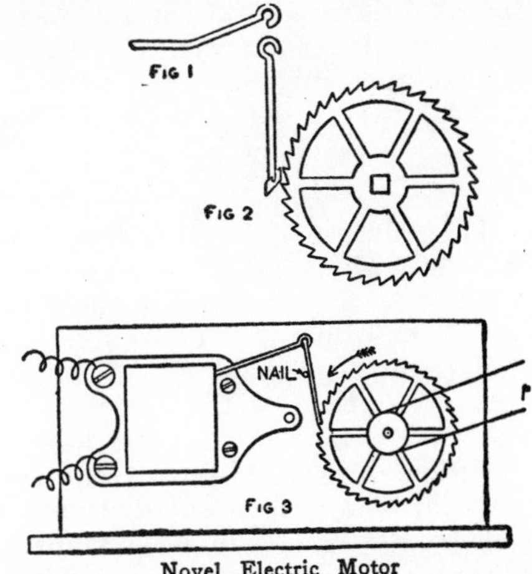

Novel Electric Motor

How to Print Photographs on Silk

Silk, satin or any other fine material can be used to make photographic prints, but the most attractive results for the amateur are obtained on silk, the best color for this purpose being either cream or white, says Photography. The chemicals required are only four in number, and a comparatively small amount of each will suffice, so that the process can be tried without any very great outlay.

A dram of dextrine is mixed with 2 oz. of water and allowed to dissolve. It is then made up to 4 oz. with boiling water, and, when cold, a solution of 1 dr. of ammonium chloride in 2 oz. of water is added. As this mixture does not keep well, it should be used as soon as possible after being made up.

The silk is soaked in the liquid until it is thoroughly saturated, which should take about four or five minutes, and it is then hung up to dry, suspending it, tightly stretched, from its two top corners. The fabric when "salted," as this operation is termed, will keep indefinitely. All these operations can be done in daylight.

The next stage is the application of the sensitizer, for which purpose the two following solutions must be made up and then mixed:

Silver nitrate	120 gr.
Water	1 oz.
Citric acid	50 gr.
Water	1 oz.

The mixture is spread evenly over the silk with a soft camel's-hair brush. There must be no metal in the mounting of the brush that is used.

Particular care must be taken to see that no particle of the surface of the silk is left uncovered. The best way to insure this is to brush the liquid over the silk, first in one direction and then crosswise. The process of sensitizing must be done in a weak artificial light, such as at night by ordinary gas or lamp light, or in the very feeblest daylight.

The silk is then again fastened up and allowed to dry, but it is now sensitive to the light and the drying must therefore be done in the dark. It is ready for printing as soon as it is dry, and as it does not keep well in the sensitive condition, it should be used up within a few days at the most.

The printing, which is done in daylight, is carried on in the same way as for printing-out papers, except that the silk should be printed a little darker than usual. It will be found convenient to gum the edges slightly, and then to fix the silk on a stiff piece of paper before putting it into the printing frame. If this precaution is not adopted there is a tendency for the silk to slip or crease when it is being examined. The silk must be handled carefully while in the printing frame for this reason, but apart from that, there is no particular difficulty. The paper can be taken off when the printing is finished.

Prints on silk are toned, fixed and washed in the same way as ordinary silver prints. The washing should be thorough, and before the prints are quite dry, they should be ironed to remove all creases.

Removing Old Paint

A chair more than a hundred years old came to me by inheritance. It was originally painted green and had been given two coats of dark paint or varnish within the last 30 years. Desiring to improve the appearance of the relic, I decided to remove the paint and give it a mahogany stain. The usual paint removers would readily take off the two latter coats but had no effect upon the first. I tried to remove the troublesome green in various ways, but with little success until I applied a hot, saturated solution of concentrated lye. By coating the paint with this repeatedly, applying one coat upon another for two days, and then using a stiff brush, the layer was easily and completely removed.—Contributed by Thos. R. Baker, Chicago, Ill.

A Window Lock

Bore a hole through the sash of the lower window and halfway through the sash of the upper window, where they meet in the center, and insert a heavy nail or spike. This will fasten the sash together so well that nothing short of a crowbar can pry them apart. The nail can be easily removed when the windows are to be opened.

Fig. 1—Trailer Attached to a Bicycle

Homemade Magnifying Glass

A very good magnifying glass can be made from an ordinary incandescent lamp of about 16-cp. size which has been rendered useless by being burned out or having the filament broken. Grind or break off the tip end of the globe and fill with water. Put in clear water and plug or cork up the hole.

Trailer for a Bicycle

Instead of using a seat on the handlebars or frame of a bicycle for my little girl, I made a trailer, as shown in Fig. 1, to attach to the rear axle. I made it from old bicycle parts. The handlebars, which form the back of the seat, fasten into the seat post of an old bicycle attached to the trailer axle. The trailer is attached to the rear axle of the bicycle with two arms or forks, on the ends of which are two forgings, formerly used on the rear ends of a bicycle frame, brazed in, and one of the tube projections cut off from each to make a hook, as shown in Fig. 2. The piece marked E shows one of these forgings or hooks in section. The original axle of the bicycle was removed and one $1\frac{5}{16}$ in. longer supplied, which was turned below the threads for clearance, as shown at A. A washer, D, with a hexagon hole was fitted over the regular nut C, on the axle, and filed tapering so the forging or hook E, on the trailer attachment, could be kept in position. The washer F is held tightly against the hook by pressure from a spring, G. The spring is held in place by a small nut, H, and cotter pin, I. This attachment makes a flexible joint for turning corners. When turning from right to left the left hook on the trailer fork stays in

Fig. 2—The Hook in Position

position, while the right hook pushes the washer F outward and relieves the strain on the fork. This attachment also makes it easy to remove the trailer from the bicycle. The washers F are pushed outward and the hook raised off the axle.—Contributed by John F. Grieves, Providence, R. I.

Home-Made Telephone Transmitter

The parts for transmitting the sound are encased in a covering, H, made from the gong of an old electric bell. A round button, D, is turned or filed from the carbon electrode of an old dry cell and a hole drilled through the center to fit in a binding-post taken from the same battery cell. This button must be carefully insulated from the shell, H, by running the binding-post through a piece of small rubber tube where it passes through the hole and placing a rubber or paper washer, F, under the carbon button, and an insulating washer under the nut on the outside. This will provide one of the terminals of the instrument. Construct a paper tube having the same diameter as the button and with a length equal to the depth of the bell case, less 1/8 in. Glue or paste this tube to the button so it will form a paper cup with a carbon bottom.

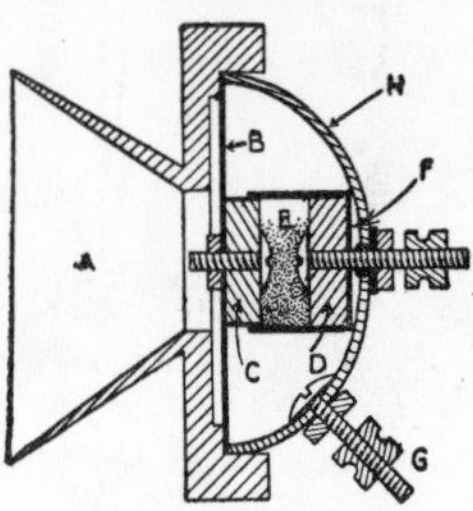

The diaphragm, B, which is the essential part of the instrument, should be made as carefully as possible from ferrotype tin, commonly called tintype tin. Cut a circular piece from this metal the exact size of the outside of the shell. A hole is made in the center of the disk a little larger than a binding-post that is taken from another old battery cell. When making the hole in the disk be careful not to bend or crease the tin. Scrape the black coating from the tin around the outside about 1/4 in. wide and a place about 1 in. in diameter at the center.

The second electrode, C, is made the same as D, and fastened to the tin diaphragm with the binding-post without using any insulation. A third binding-post, G, is fastened to the shell through a drilled hole to make the other terminal. The mouthpiece, A, may be turned from wood in any shape desired, but have a flange on the back side that will make a tight fit with the outside of the shell.

Fill the paper tube with powdered carbon, E, which can be made by pounding and breaking up pieces of carbon to about the size of pin heads. Powdered carbon can be purchased, but if you make it be sure to sift out all the very fine particles. Assemble the parts as shown and the transmitter is ready for use. If speech is not heard distinctly, put in a little more, or remove some of the carbon and try it out until you get the instrument working nicely.—Contributed by Harold H. Cutter, Springfield, Mass.

Quickly Made Lawn Tent

A very simple way of erecting a lawn tent for the children is to take a large umbrella such as used on delivery wagons and drive the handle into the ground deep enough to hold it solid. Fasten canvas or cotton cloth to the ends of the ribs and let it hang so that the bottom edge will touch the ground. Light ropes can be tied to the ends of the ribs and fastened to stakes driven in the ground in a tent-like manner to make the whole more substantial and to stand against a heavy wind. This makes an exceptionally fine tent, as the umbrella is waterproof; also, there is more room to stand up in than in a tent that is in the shape of a wigwam.—Contributed by J. A. Whamer, Schenectady, N. Y.

Lawn Tent Complete

How to Make a Windmill of One or Two Horsepower for Practical Purposes

A windmill for developing from ½ to 2 hp. may be constructed at home, the expense being very small and the results highly satisfactory.

The hub for the revolving fan wheel is first constructed. One good way to get both the hub, lining, shaft and spokes for the blades, is to go to a wheelwright's and purchase the wheel and axle of some old rig. There are always a number of discarded carriages, wagons or parts thereof in the rear of the average blacksmith's shop. Sometimes for half a dollar, and often for nothing, you can get a wheel, an axle, and connected parts. Remove from the wheel, all but the four spokes needed for the fans as in Fig. 1. The same hub, axle and bearings will do. In case you cannot secure a wheel and shaft, the hub may be made from a piece of hardwood, about 4 in. in diameter and 6 in. long. A 2-in. hole should be bored through for a wooden shaft, or a 1½-in. hole for a metal shaft. The hub may be secured by putting two or three metal pins through hub and shaft. Adjust the spokes by boring holes for them and arrange them so that they extend from the center A, like B. The wheel is then ready for the blades. These

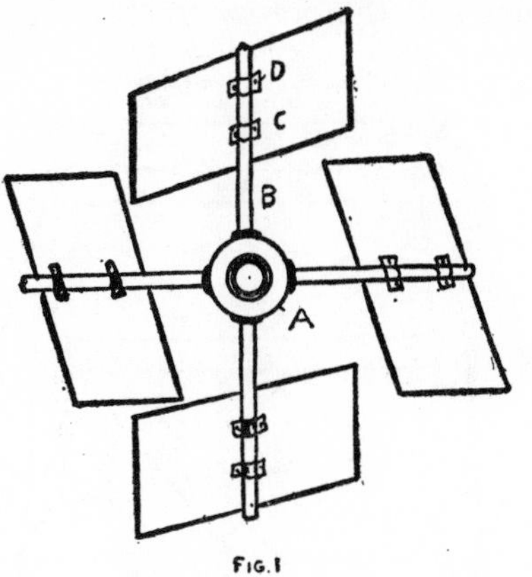

Fig. 1

blades should be of sheet metal or thin hardwood. The sizes may vary according to the capacity of the wheel and amount of room for the blades on the spokes. Each one is tilted so as to receive the force of the wind at an angle, which adjustment causes the wheel to revolve when the wind pressure is

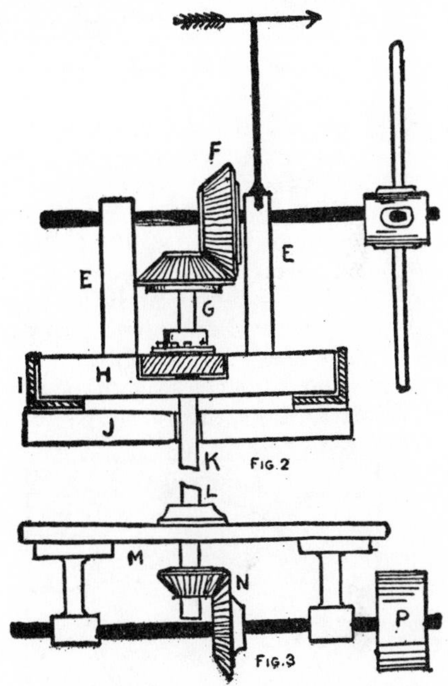

strong enough. Secure the blades to the spokes by using little metal cleats, C and D. Bend these metal strips to suit the form of the spokes and flatten against the blades and then insert the screws to fasten the cleats to the wood. If sheet metal blades are used, rivets should be used for fastening them.

The stand for the wheel shaft is shown in Fig. 2. Arrange the base piece in platform order, (J). This is more fully shown in Fig. 5. On top of this base piece, which is about 36 in. long, place the seat or ring for the revolving table. The circular seat is indicated at I, Fig. 1. This ring is like an inverted cheese box cover with the center cut out. It can be made by a tinner. Size of ring outside, 35 in. The shoulders are 4 in. high and made of tin also. Form the shoulder by soldering the piece on. Thus we get a smooth surface with sides for the mill base to turn in so as to receive the wind at each point to advantage. The X-shaped piece H rests in the tin rim. The X-form, however, does not show in this sketch, but in Fig. 5, where it is marked S. This part is made of two pieces of

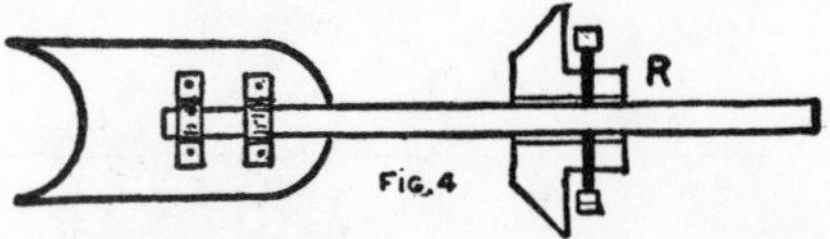

Fig. 4

2-in. plank, about 3 in. wide, arranged so that the two pieces cross to make a letter X. When the pieces join, mortise them one into the other so as to secure a good joint. Adjust the uprights for sustaining the wheel shaft to the X-pieces as shown at E, E, Fig. 2. These are 4 by 4 in. pieces of wood, hard pine preferred, planed and securely set up in the X-pieces by mortising into the same. Make the bearings for the

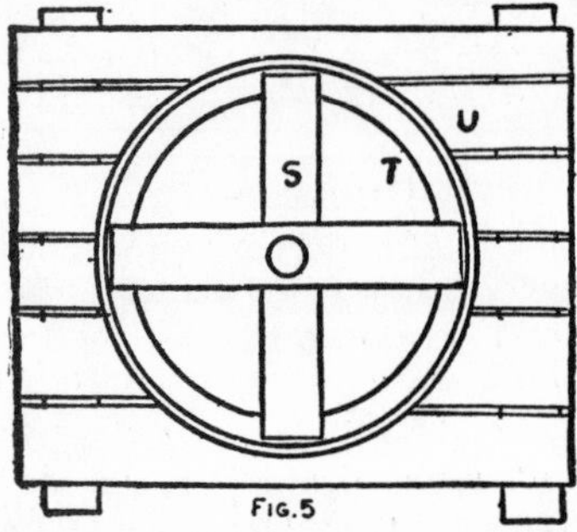

Fig. 5

wheel shaft in the uprights and insert the shaft.

The gearing for the transmission of the power from the wheel shaft to the shaft calculated for the delivery of the power at an accessible point below must next be adjusted. The windmill is intended for installation on top of a building, and the power may be transmitted below, or to the top of a stand specially erected for the purpose. It is a good plan to visit some of the second-hand machinery dealers and get four gears, a pulley and a shaft. Gears about 5 in. in diameter and beveled will be required. Adjust the first pair of the beveled gears as at F and G. If the wheel shaft is metal, the gear may be set-screwed to the shaft, or keyed to it. If the shaft is hardwood, it will be necessary to arrange for a special connection. The shaft may be wrapped with sheet metal and this metal fastened on with screws. Then the gear may be attached by passing a pin through the set-screw hole and through the shaft. The upright shaft like the wheel shaft is best when of metal. This shaft is shown extending from the gear, G, to a point below. The object is to have the shaft reach to the point where the power is received for the service below. The shaft is shown cut off at K. Passing to Fig. 3 the shaft is again taken up at L. It now passes through the arrangement shown, which device is rigged up to hold the shaft and delivery wheel P in place. This shaft should also be metal. Secure the beveled gears M and N as shown. These transmit the power from the upright shaft to the lower horizontal shaft. Provide the wheel or pulley, P, with the necessary belt to carry the power from this shaft to the point of use.

The tail board of the windmill is illustrated in Fig. 4. A good way to make this board is to use a section of thin lumber and attach it to the rear upright, E of Fig. 2. This may be done by boring a hole in the upright and inserting the shaft of the tail-piece. In Fig. 4 is also shown the process of fastening a gear, R, to the shaft. The set screws enter the hub from the two sides and the points are pressed upon

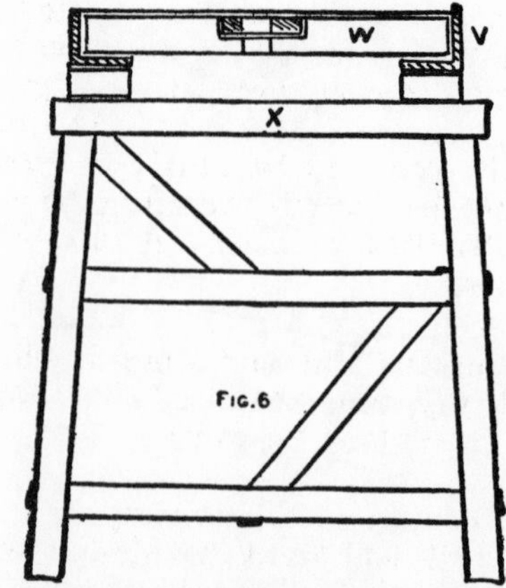

Fig. 6

the shaft, thus holding the gear firmly in place. The platform for the entire wheel device is shown in Fig. 5. The

X-piece S is bored through in the middle and the upright shaft passes through. The tin run-way or ring is marked T, and the X-piece very readily revolves in this ring, whenever the wind alters and causes the wheel's position to change. The ring and ring base are secured to the platform, U. The latter is made of boards nailed to the timbers of the staging for supporting the mill. This staging is shown in Fig. 6, in a sectional view. The ring with its X-piece is marked V, the X-piece is marked W, and the base for the part, and the top of the stage is marked X. The stage is made of 2 by 4-in. stock. The height may vary, according to the requirements. If the affair is set up on a barn or shed, the staging will be sufficient to support the device. But if the stage is constructed direct from the ground, it will be necessary to use some long timbers to get the wheel up high enough to receive the benefit of the force of the wind. Proceeding on the plan of the derrick stand, as shown in Fig. 6, a stage of considerable height can be obtained.

To Renew Old Dry Batteries

Remove the paper that covers the cell and knock several good-sized holes in the zinc shell. Place the battery in a glass jar, fill it two-thirds full of strong sal ammoniac (or salt) solution and connect the terminals to whatever apparatus the current is to be used for. A few drops of sulphuric acid quickens and improves the action. The output of the cell will be nearly as great as when the battery was first bought.—Contributed by C. W. Arbitt, Austin, Texas.

Prussian blue and Chinese blue are both the same chemically but they do not cut or look the same.

When an acetylene lamp is in good order it will light up slowly with a hissing noise followed by a pure white flame. Should the lamp light up quickly with a yellowish flame, it is a sign of a leak somewhere.

Another Electric Motor

This form of electric motor is used largely in England in the form of an indicator. It is very easily made and

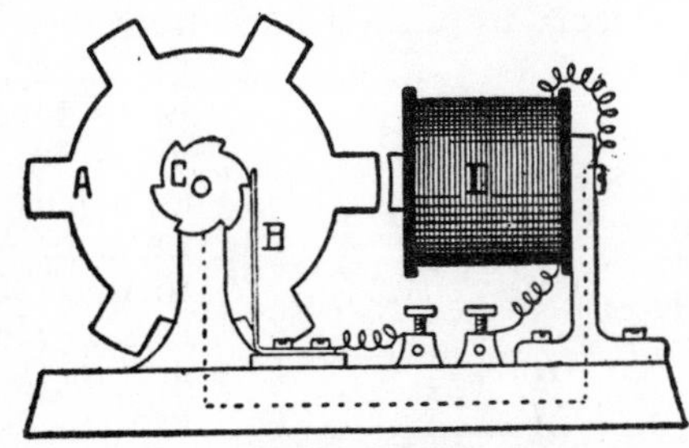

Electric Motor

if you have an old electro-magnet will cost practically nothing.

A large soft-iron wheel is mounted on an axle with a pulley-wheel on one end and a circuit breaker on the other end. The teeth on the circuit-breaker must be the same number as on the soft-iron wheel.

The electro-magnet is mounted so that its core is level with the axle and in a line with the wheel. One wire from it is attached to one binding screw and the other end is grounded to the iron frame that supports it. This frame is connected to the frame supporting the wheel. A small brush presses on the circuit-breaker and is connected to the other binding screw.

In the diagram A represents the iron wheel; B, the brush; C, the circuit-breaker; D, the magnet. The wire connecting the two frames is shown by a dotted line.

To start the motor, attach your battery to the screws and turn the wheel a little. The magnet attracts one of the teeth on the wheel, but as soon as it is parallel with the core of the magnet the circuit is broken and the momentum of the wheel brings another tooth to be attracted.

To reverse the motor reverse the connections and start the wheel the other way. Be sure that the frames are screwed down well or the motor will run jerkily and destroy the connections.—Contributed by F. Crawford Curry, Brockville, Ontario.

How to Make a Propelling Vehicle

Any boy, with a little knack and a few odd tools, can rig up various contrivances which will be a source of pleasure to himself and oftentimes can be sold, to less ingenious boys, for a snug little sum. Any tool a boy can obtain is apt to be of use to him, chisel, bit, jack-knife or hammer.

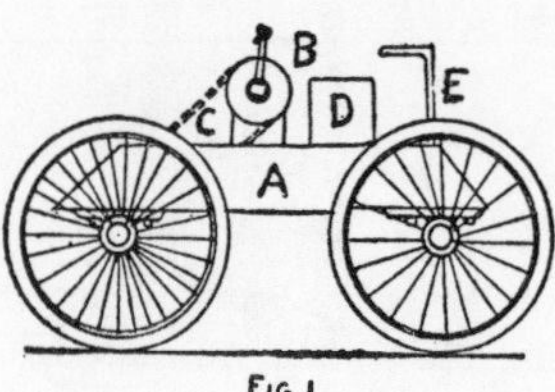

Fig 1

Figure 1 shows what two boys did with old cycle wheels. They went to some junk shops where the concerns had purchased cast-away bicycles and noticed that there were numerous wheels in very good order that could be selected from among the sets of wheels with broken or bent rims, spokes, burst tires, etc. In fact, the lads had no trouble in getting several sets of bicycle wheels in good condition for very little money. These wheels were taken to the back-yard shop of the boys where the young fellows had rigged up a shed-like affair and put in a bench. The previous Christmas one of the boys received a box of tools as a gift, in which was included a little hand vise and the required tools for general boy's handiwork.

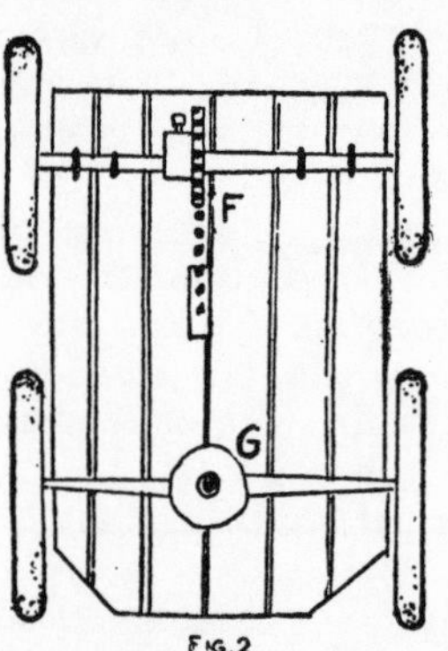

Fig.2

Four of the cycle wheels they used in making the hand-propelled vehicle shown at Fig. 1.

A wooden body, A, made of smooth boards rests upon shafts. Fixed on this body is an upright carrying the sprocket B. The upright is a piece of wood about 10 in. high and 4 in. wide, fitted with one of the bearings from the cycle. The regular cycle chain sprocket is used at B as well as upon the shaft. The regular chain of the cycle is likewise employed, so, when buying the wheels, it is well to select one or more chains with corresponding sprockets from the junk heap. The detail of the adjustment of the parts is shown in next views. The letter D signifies the seat which is a box. The steering gear is a bent iron rod, also found in the waste pile of the junk shop, and is bent to right form by heating and bending over on a rock or any solid matter. The steering rod is marked E. It fits into a socket in the shaft of the forward wheels.

Figure 2 shows the construction of the cart below. The cog is keyed or set-screwed to the driving shaft of the wheels with either key or set-screw used in original fastening, as the case may be. The chain is marked F, and there is a slot cut in the floor of the cart to let the chain pass up and through to the cog on the propelling shaft crank. The disk which receives the steering rod is at G. The forward shaft bears only at the center upon a disk of metal, consisting of any circular piece found among the pieces of iron or brass at the junk store. One can get nearly all the mechanical parts in junk establishments that purchase parts of out-of-date or cast-away bicycles. The detail of the driving shaft is shown at Fig. 3. The sprocket wheel is at H and this is just as it is taken from the original bicycle shaft. The bearings consist of wires looped around the shaft and inserted into holes bored in metal plates as shown. These plates are screwed to the bottom of the cart.

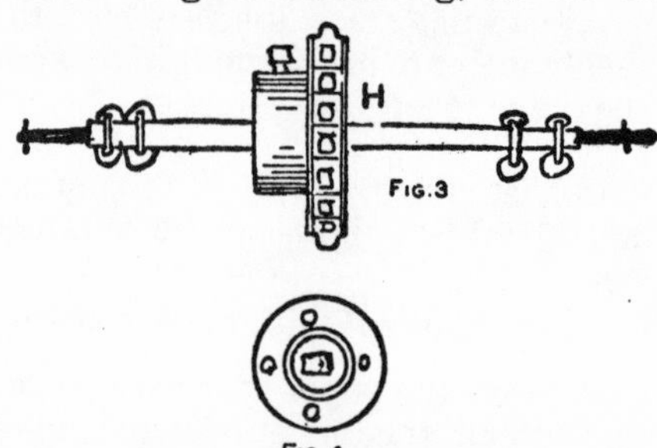

Driving Shaft and Disk for Steering Gear

The shaft itself is found in rods or even cast-away metal axles which are commonly found in most any carriage works, cycle shops or junk dealer's. Figure 4 shows the disk that receives the steering gear. The disk is bored around edges for the securing screws, while the center is open for the steering rod. When put together, three boys usually ride. One steers and the other two turn the crank. Freight can be carried and some boys do quite an express business in their town with one of the carts like this that they made.

Ringing a Bell by Touching a Gas Jet

The experiment of scuffling the feet over a carpet and then producing a spark which will light the gas by touching the chandelier is described on another page. One of our correspondents says that if a wire is connected to the chandelier and led to one terminal of the coherer of a wireless telegraph outfit the bell will ring every time the

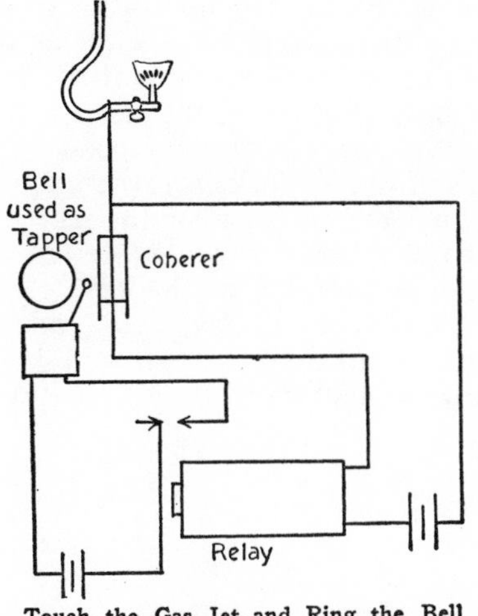

Touch the Gas Jet and Ring the Bell

spark is produced by touching the chandelier, and that, as the chandeliers are all connected by the gas-pipe, the bell will ring, no matter in which room the spark is produced.

The covering quality will be greatly improved if some dry red lead is added to the shellac varnish used for killing knots.

How to Make a Wood-Turning Lathe Out of an Old Sewing Machine

With a hack-saw, cut off the arm containing the needle on line AB, Fig. 1, leaving the shaft only. On the end of the shaft will be found a round plate,

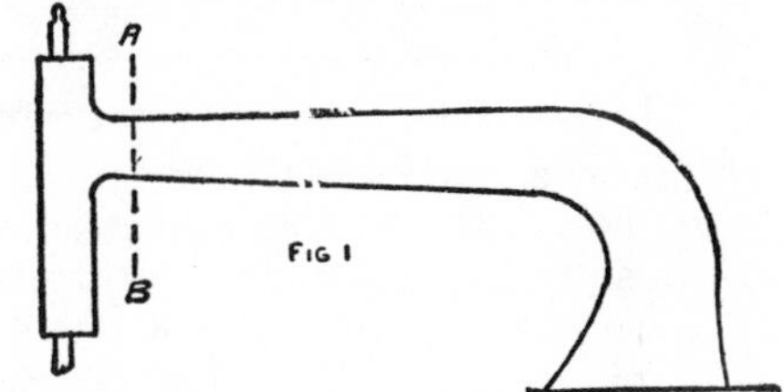

in which drill four 3/16-in. holes. Now secure, or have turned, a piece of iron or steel 1½ in. in diameter, Fig. 2. Drill and countersink four 3/16-in. holes in it to fit the holes on the shaft plate. File a spur center 5/16 in. long, and two side points 3/16 in. long. Bolt this plate to the shaft plate with four flat-headed stove bolts, 3/16 in. in diameter by ⅝ or ¾ in. long, Fig. 3.

For the bed, use a board 32 in. long and as wide as the base of the machine arm. This gives a limit of 2 ft. between spur and dead centers. Let this board be made level with the rest of machine table by making a pair of legs if needed. Next make a T-rail, Fig. 4, of two boards, one 5 by ¾ by 32 in., the other 3½ by ¾ by 32 in. Three-quarter inch of the wider board projects over each of the smaller boards. Nail firmly and clinch nails, or screw together. Screw this rail on the machine board so that its center coincides exactly with the machine centers. Bore a number of ⅜-in. holes with centers 2¾ in. apart along the center line of this rail, beginning 6 in. from the end nearest the machine. Make another T-rail for slide tool rest, of two pieces 32 by 3 by ¾ in., and 32 by 1½ by ¾ in. Fasten this in front of the larger T-rail and parallel to it, the center lines being 6½ in. apart.

To make the tail-piece, that is, the part to hold wood to be turned, get a board 6½ by 7 by ¾ in., and on the edges, Fig. 5, A, screw two pieces 7 by ¾ by 1½ in. so that the cap thus made will fit snugly over the large T-rail. Fasten to these last two pieces,

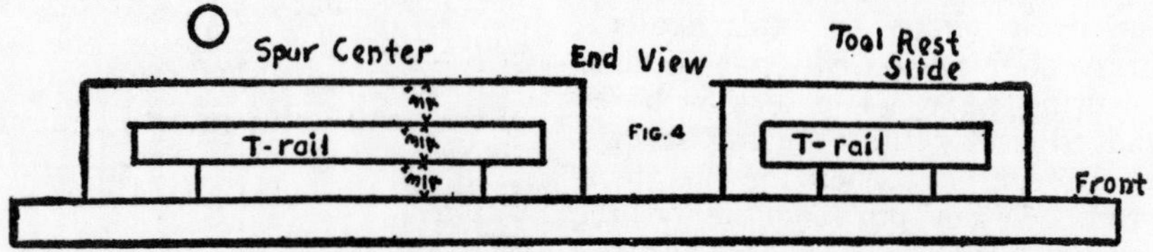

with screws, two more pieces 7 by ¾ by ¾ in., Fig. 5, B. This tail-piece should move smoothly back and forth with no side motion. Now get a block of hardwood 4 by 2¼ in., and 1¾ in. higher than the spur center when mounted on the middle of the tail-piece just described. At exactly the height of the spur center bore through this block a ¾-in. hole, Fig. 5. Have a blacksmith make a crank 8 in. long, threaded for 5 in. as shown. At the dead center end taper the crank and make a cup center, out of which allow a 3/16-in. point to project. The cup prevents the point from boring into

Fig. 2

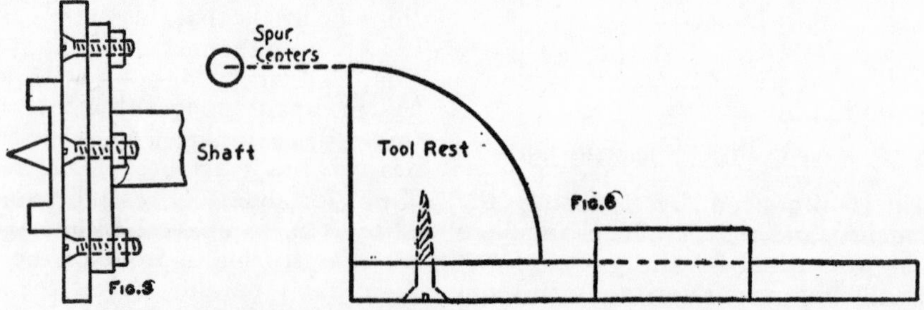

wood too rapidly. One inch from the outer end of the crank block, Fig. 5, bore a 3/16-in. hole, and force a ¼-in. bolt to cut its thread in the wood. This is a set screw to hold the crank in any position desired. Place a strap nut, threaded to fit the crank, on the head end of the crank block, and a plain nut to act as a bearing, on the crank end. One and one-half inches from the back of the tail-piece bore a ⅜-in. hole. Make a peg ⅜ by 2 in. To put in a piece of wood to turn, move the tail-piece back until the head end is over the center of the hole nearest the end of the block, then the peg will slip into second hole from the head end of the tail-piece, and into a corresponding T-rail hole, pinning the two together. Insert wood and screw up dead center to hold it.

For a tool rest make a second piece like the base of the tail-piece, 11 in. long and fitting the small T-rail. Cut out two blocks 1½ by 2¼ by ¾ in. and screw them, one on each end of the base of the tool rest, covering the half farthest from the centers, and having an 8-in. space between blocks. On the tops of these blocks screw a strip 11 by 2¼ by ¾ in. Now for the rest proper, cut out a board 8 by 11/16 by 9 in. to slide in the slot of the rest. Take a piece of oak 11 by 2 in., and high enough so that the top will be level with the centers of the lathe, and bevel as shown in Fig. 6. Screw on one end of the 8 by 9-in. piece exactly in the middle. This piece will slide in and out, closer or farther from the centers as desired, and also along the T-rail.

A center for turning rosettes, saucers,

etc., may be made as follows: Remove the spur center and bolt in its place a 1-in. circular board of the same diameter, using longer 3/16-in. stove bolts with heads countersunk. Rotate the lathe, and with a gimlet bore a hole at the exact center and through the board. Now take off the board and countersink on the back a place for the head of a coarse threaded screw. Turn in a 1¾-in. screw, replace the board and any block held on the end of the rotating screw will turn on and be held while being turned.—Contributed by L. L. Winans, Mexico, Mo.

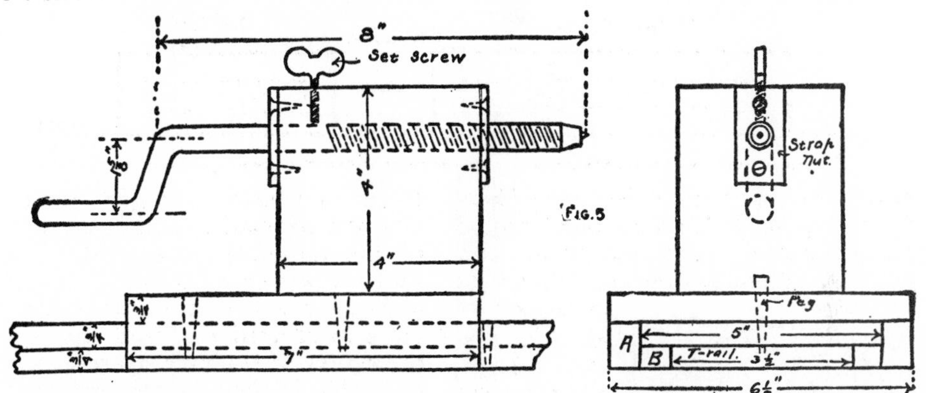

and 4. Hold the brass strips apart by means of the hard rubber strip and screws. Do not let the screws come all the way through the rubber strip or you are liable to get a shock in case you should touch both screws simultaneously. Screw a rubber handle onto the rubber strip to move the lever back and forth with. Fig. 2 shows the arrangement of strips, handle, screws, etc., in detail. Fig. 3 is an end view of the same.—Contributed by Eugene F. Tuttle, Jr., Newark, Ohio.

Bronze bearings may be cleaned with a solution of washing powder and water run through the oil cups while the machine is running without any load. The solution, cutting out the dirt and grime, will come from the bearing very black. About 1 pt. of this mixture should be run through each bearing, then clean thoroughly with clear water.

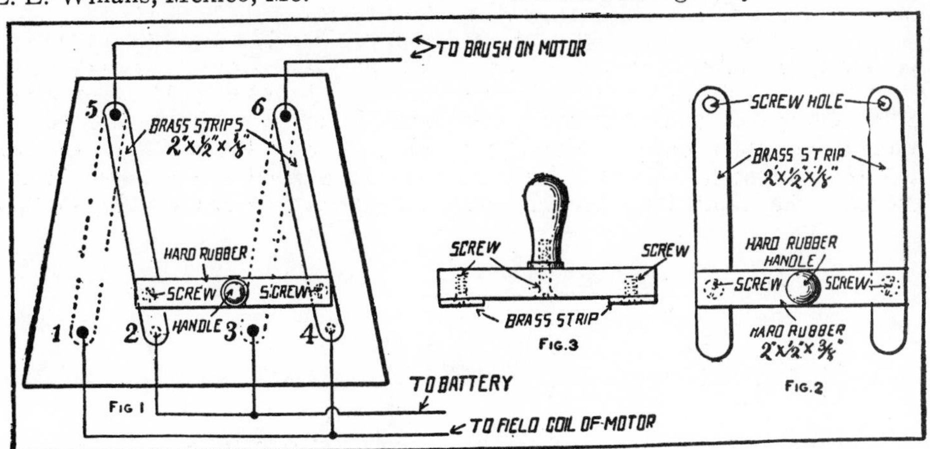

Reversing Small Battery Motor

Make the switch out of a piece of slate (for the base) two strips of brass, a rubber strip and handle and some binding-posts from old dry batteries. Fasten the brass strips at 5 and 6, Fig. 1, so they can swing from 1 and 3 to 2

A Water Candlestick

A glass of water makes a fine emergency candlestick. Weight one end of the candle with a nail just large enough to hold the candle in the water so that the water comes near its top edge, but does not touch the wick, and then light the candle.

It will burn until the last vestige of wick is gone and the flame will not flicker. The melted tallow that runs down but serves to hold the candle more stationary.

To Make a Magazine Binder

Get ½ yd. of cloth, one shoestring, a pasteboard box for covers, and some heavy paper. Cut the pasteboard into two covers, ¼ in. larger all around than the magazine, except at the back with which they should be even. Next cut a strip 1 in. wide off the back of each cover. Place the covers on the cloth, Fig. 1, with the back edges ¼ in. farther apart than the thickness of the volume to be bound. Cut the cloth around the covers, leaving 1½ in. margin. Paste the cloth on the covers as they lay, and turn over the 1½ in. margin, pasting down smoothly. Cut a piece of stiff paper to fit and paste on the back. Take a piece of cloth as wide as the cover, and long enough to extend over the back and 1½ in. beyond each "strip." Paste on to hold all together. Two pieces of paper the exact size of the magazine, pasted on the inside of each cover protects the edges of the cloth, and adds to the appearance. Let dry slowly.

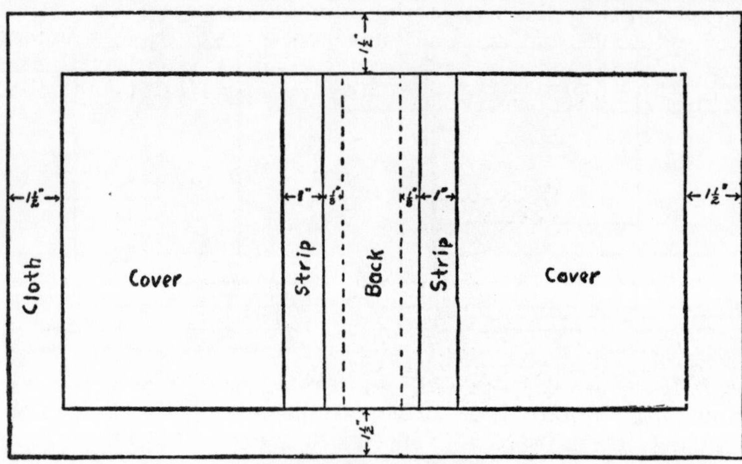

Plan of Magazine Binder

With backs and edges of magazines even, place in a vise and set up tight allowing ¾ in. from back to show above the vise. Bore three 3/16-in. holes ½ in. from the back, one in the middle, the other two 1½ in. from each end. Make corresponding holes in the strips of the binder and use the shoestring to complete as in Fig. 2.

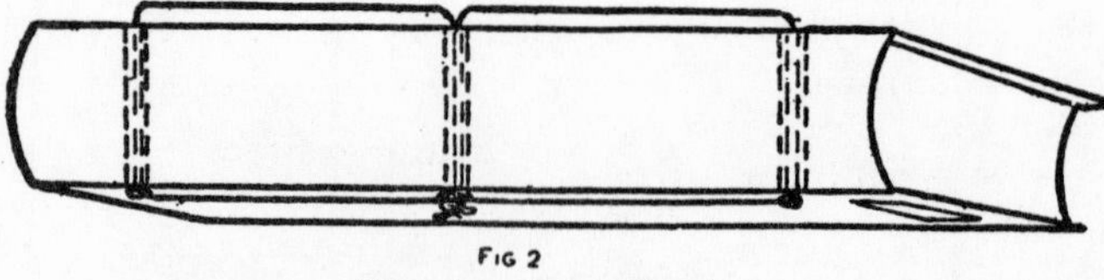

Magazine Binder Complete

How to File Soft Metals

When filing soft metals, such as solder or babbitt metal, the file, after a few strokes, will become filled with metal, causing scratches on the surface being filed. The surface may be filed smooth, provided the file has been well oiled. The oil prevents the cutters from clogging and also allows the metal to yield easily. Oil the file every few minutes and use a card frequently in cleaning and the work will be smooth.—Contributed by Jno. E. Ganaway, Paducah, Ky.

A piece of wire solder makes a good temporary spline for the draftsman.

A Library Set in Pyro-Carving

By HELEN WESTINGHOUSE

The multitude of indifferently executed small articles which followed the introduction of pyrography is beginning to disappear. People are considering the art more seriously and applying it to more dignified uses. Pyro-carving is one of the new methods of decorating furniture which is both beautiful and practical, two qualities which do not always go together.

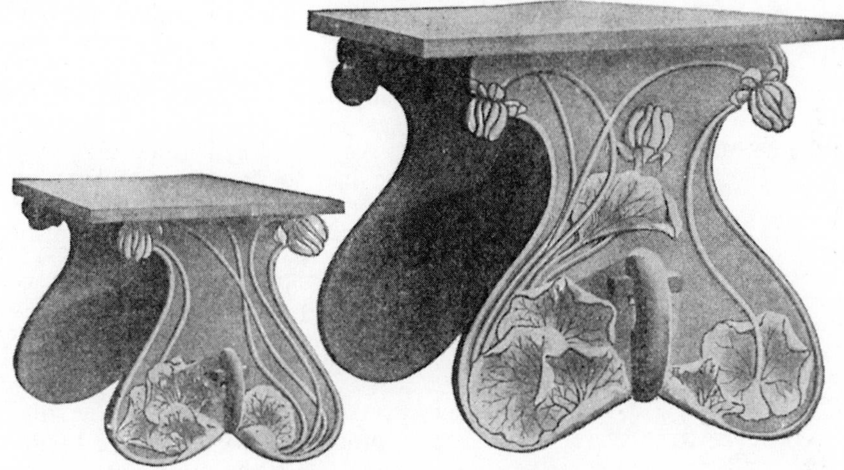

Table and Seat Decorated in Pyro-Carving

The library set illustrated consists of a table, 30 to 50 in., with two benches, 14 in. wide, of the same length. The supports are made of selected white pine, which must be absolutely free from pitch. The pine is soft enough to work easily with the point and stands wear much better than basswood. The tops and braces are made of curly fir. All of the material must be 2-in. lumber, which dresses to about 1½ in. All surfaces, except the faces of the supports, are given a well rubbed coat of oil with a little burnt umber, the stain to be applied directly to the wood without a filler.

On the outside of the supports the design is drawn in with pencil, the background is then cut out smoothly with a chisel to the depth of an eighth of an inch, leaving the decoration in relief. It is then burned deeply, the background in straight flat strokes, the outlines having the effect of a sloping, dark edge. The shadows are burned in as deeply as possible and the shading is put in with the flat of the point.

A wax or eggshell oil-varnish finish is most suitable for this set, but any other finish may be applied, as the builder may desire, to make it harmonize with other furnishings.

Cleaning Brass

Small brass castings can be cleaned by heating them slightly and then dipping them in a solution of sal ammoniac. The pieces will come out as bright and clean as if new. This cleaning process is the same as that used in cleaning a soldering iron.

A Phoneidoscope

The phoneidoscope has many and varied forms, but the simplest can be made by bending the forefinger and thumb so as to form a circle and then drawing a soap film across the opening. This is done in a manner similar to the blowing of soap bubbles.

The angle with the direction of the light may be readily adjusted by turning the wrist, a motion of the elbow alters the distance from the mouth and the tension of the film can be regulated by moving the thumb and forefinger. Singing or speaking at the film when under proper tension will cause beautiful figures to appear, which may be reflected from the film directly on the screen.—Contributed by Robt. E. Bradley, Winchester, Mass.

A Home-Made Yankee Bobsled

A good coasting sled, which I call a Yankee bob, can be made from two hardwood barrel staves, two pieces of

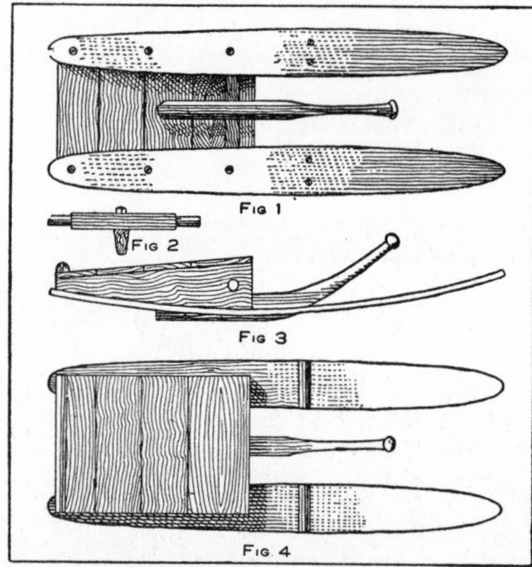

Runners Made of Barrel Staves

2 by 6-in. pine, a piece of hardwood for the rudder and a few pieces of boards. The 2 by 6-in. pieces should be a little longer than one-third the length of the staves, and each piece cut tapering from the widest part, 6 in., down to 2 in., and then fastened to the staves with large wood screws as shown in Fig. 1. Boards 1 in. thick are nailed on top of the pieces for a seat and to hold the runners together. The boards should be of such a length as to make the runners about 18 in. apart.

A 2-in. shaft of wood, Fig. 2, is turned down to 1 in. on the ends and put through holes that must be bored in the front ends of the 2 by 6-in. pieces. A small pin is put through each end of the shaft to keep it in place. The rudder is a 1½-in. hardwood piece which should be tapered to ½ in. at the bottom and shod with a thin piece of iron. A ½-in. hole is bored through the center of the shaft and a lag screw put through and turned in the rudder piece, making it so the rudder will turn right and left and, also, up and down. Two cleats are nailed to the upper sides of the runners and in the middle lengthways for the person's heels to rest against.

Any child can guide this bob, as all he has to do is to guide the rudder right and left to go in the direction named. If he wants to stop, he pulls up on the handle and the heel of the rudder will dig into the snow, causing too much friction for the sled to go any further.—Contributed by Wm. Algie, Jr., Little Falls, N. Y.

How to Make a Small Microscope

Theoretically a simple microscope can be made as powerful as a compound microscope, but in practice the minute size required by the simple lens to give the highest power makes it almost impossible to be used. However, a lens having a reasonable magnifying power can be made in a few minutes for almost nothing. Take a piece of glass tubing, heat one place in a hot flame, hold one end and pull on the other and draw the heated place down to a fine string as shown in Fig. 1. Take about 3 in. of this fine tube and heat one end which will form a glass bead as shown in Fig. 2. This bead is the lens. When in this form it can be used only in an artificial light coming from one direction, but if you take a piece of card-

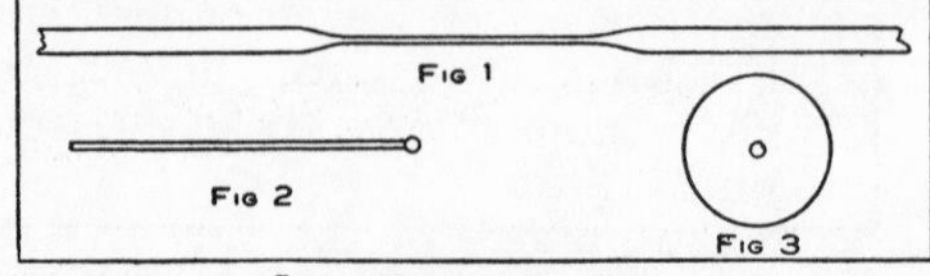

Lens Formed by Heat

board and bore a hole in it a little smaller than the bead on the glass tube which is forced into the hole, Fig. 3, you can use this mounted lens in ordinary daylight. In this case a mirror must be used to reflect the light up through the lens. It is difficult to see anything at first, as the lens must be held very close to the eye, but in practice you will soon learn to see the object as it appears enlarged.

If you soak a little dried grass or hay in water for a few days and look at a drop of this water, germs in various life forms can be seen. The water must be put on the lens. One thing to remember is that the smaller the lens, the greater the magnifying power.—Contributed by Daniel Gray, Decatur, Illinois.

The water in hot water supply pipes will freeze quicker than water that has not been heated. This is because the air, which is a poor conductor of heat, has been driven out by the heat.

How to Carry Books

Almost all school children carry their books with a strap put around and buckled very tight. This will make dents in the cover where the board overlaps the body of the book. If the strap is left loose, the books are liable to slip out. Place the cover of one book between the cover and fly leaf of its neighbor and the difficulty will be remedied. This will place the books in alternate directions. Books stacked in this manner do not require the strap buckled tight, or, they can be carried without any strap just as well.—Contributed by Thos. De Loof, Grand Rapids, Mich.

BOTTLE PUSHERS.—This is a game in which the competitors push bottles on the ice with hockey sticks. All the bottles must be the same size and make. The persons participating must keep their bottles upright at all times. The bottles are lined up for the start and at the word "go," each person pushes a bottle across the field for a distance that is agreed upon.

How to Make a Hammock

Any one can make a hammock as good as can be bought and that at a cost so small that every member of the family can possess one providing there are places enough for hanging them.

The materials required are a needle about 7 in. long, and with a big eye, an iron ring for each end of the hammock, two long smooth sticks on which to knit the hammock and two pounds of strong hemp cord or twine. The twine may be colored in any color or combination of colors desired. A Roman stripe at each end of the hammock makes a pretty effect.

A hammock 45 in. wide will not be too large for solid comfort. To knit it first thread the big needle and holding it in the left hand, hold the cord in place with the thumb until you have looped the cord over the tongue, then pass the cord under the needle to the opposite side and catch it over the tongue. Repeat this operation until the needle is full. Cut a 2-yd. length of cord and make a loop and fasten to the door knob or to some other convenient place. Tie the cord on the needle to this loop 3 in. from the end of the loop. Place the small mesh stick under the cord with the beveled edge close to the loop, and, with a thumb on the cord to hold it in place, pass the needle around the stick and then, point downward, pass it through the loop from the top, and then bring it over the stick so forming the first half of the knot.

Pull this tight and hold in place with a thumb while throwing the cord over your hand, which forms the loop. Pass the needle from under through the loops and draw fast to fasten the knot. Hold this in place and repeat the operation.

Make 30 of these knots and then push them off the stick and proceed in the same way with the next row, passing the needle first through each of the 30 knots made for the first row. Make 30 rows and then tie the last loops to the other iron ring. Stretchers may be made and put in place and the hammock, strong and durable, is finished. The work must be carefully and evenly done. One is apt to have a little trouble getting the first row right, but after that the work proceeds quite rapidly.

How to Obtain Cheap Dry Batteries

Not very many people realize that good, serviceable dry cells can be obtained from an automobile garage very cheap. These cells having been "run out" beyond the required number of amperes for automobile use, will give excellent service, considering their cost. Many of them will give two-thirds of their original amperage. Six of such cells have been in use on my door-bell circuit for nearly a year. They can be used for other purposes just as well.—Contributed by H. H. Cutter.

How to Make a Water Telescope

Before you decide on a place to cast your hook it is best to look into the water to see whether any fish are there. Yes, certainly, you can look into the water and see the fish that are there swimming about, if you have the proper equipment. What you need is a water telescope. This is a device made of wood or metal with one end of glass. When the glass end is submerged, by looking in at the open end, objects in the water are made plainly visible to a considerable depth. In Norway, the fishermen use the water telescope regularly in searching for herring shoals or cod.

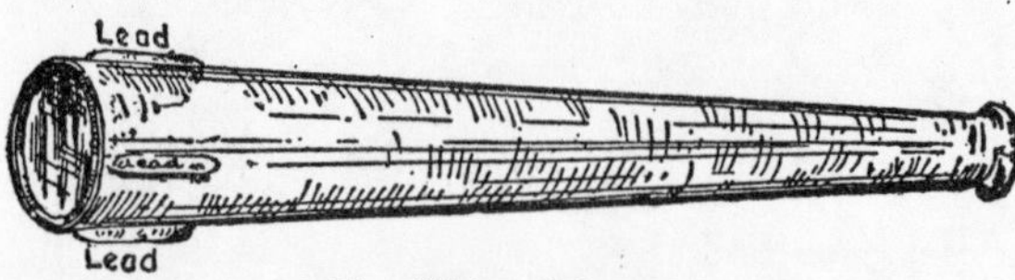

The Water Telescope

All that is necessary to make a wooden water telescope is a long wooden box, a piece of glass for one end and some paint and putty for making the seams watertight. Fix the glass in one end of the box, and leave the other open to look through.

A tin water telescope is more convenient than the wooden one, but more difficult to make. The principal essential for this is a circular piece of glass for the large end. A funnel shaped tin horn will do for the rest. Solder in the glass at the large end and the telescope is made. Sinkers consisting of strips of lead should be soldered on near the bottom to counteract the buoyancy of the air contained in the watertight funnel and also helps to submerge the big end. The inside of the funnel should be painted black to prevent the light from being reflected on the bright surface of the tin. If difficulty is found in obtaining a circular piece of glass, the dottom may be made square and square glass used. Use plain, clear glass; not magnifying glass. To picnic parties the water telescope is of great amusement, revealing numerous odd sights in the water which many have never seen before.

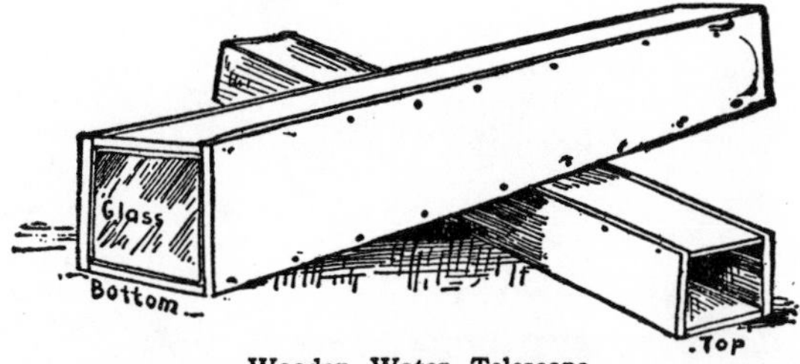

Wooden Water Telescope

How to Rid Your Yard of Cats

The following is a description of a device I built at my home in Brooklyn, which not only gave us relief from the nightly feline concerts, but also furnished much amusement to my friends.

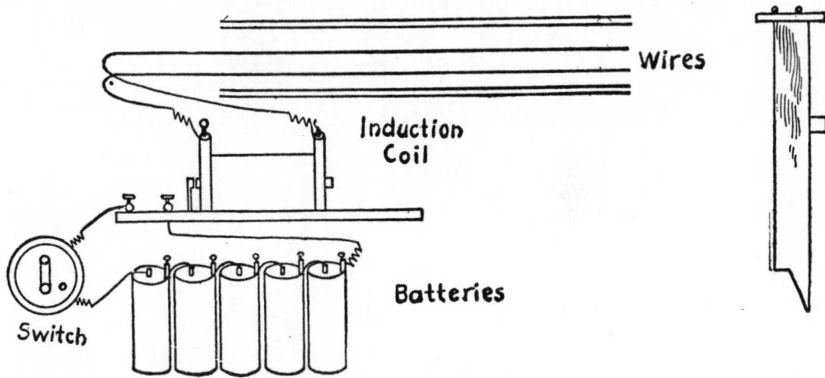

Electric Apparatus for Driving Away Cats

I first ran two bare copper wires along the top of the fence about 1 in. apart, fastening them down with small staples, care being taken that they did not touch. To the ends of these wires I fastened ordinary insulated bell wire, running them to the house and connecting them to the upper binding-posts of an induction coil; I then ran a wire from the lower binding-post of my coil through the batteries back to the other lower binding-post of coil, breaking the circuit by putting in an ordinary switch. The more batteries used, the stronger the current. The switch should always be left open, as it uses up the current very rapidly.

When "tabby" is well on the wires I close the switch and she goes the length of the fence in bounds, often coming back to see what the trouble is, thus receiving another shock.—Contributed by Charles L. Pultz.

A gouge may be used as a substitute bit if a proper sized bit is not at hand. The gouge can be placed in the brace the same as a bit.

Drying Films

The drying of photographic film in full lengths without scratching or curling is quite difficult. Various devices are used to keep the film straight, and push pins or thumb tacks are supplied with almost all of them. The illustration shows a simple and inexpensive device constructed of common wood clothespins without any metal pins to come in contact with the film and cause rust streaks. A pair of pins are fastened at each end of the film by pushing one pin over the other which in turn is clamped on the film. A string tied to the heads of one pair of pins provides a way to hang the whole on a nail. The lower pair of pins makes a weight to keep the film straight.—Contributed by J. Mac Gregor, Montreal, Canada.

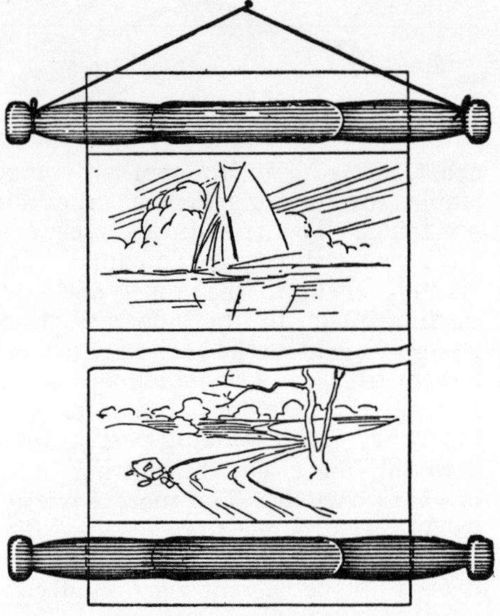

Pins Keep the Film Straight

Grooved Pulley Made from Sheet Tin

A grooved pulley which will run true and carry a round belt may be made without the use of other tools than a compass and pair of shears, with a drill or punch for making two rivet holes.

Lay off a circle on the tin, of the diameter desired for the bottom of the groove. Then lay off a concentric circle of 1/4 in. greater radius. Cut out along the lines of the large circle. On the line of the small circle mark with a prick punch or nail a series of slight dents, about 1/4 in. apart, all the way around. Now make cuts from the line of the large circle to these dents, stopping when the shears give the little "click" on entering the dent. Bend the little tongues thus formed alternately to the right and left, then by shaping them with some care you will have a good running surface for the belt. It will not make any difference if there are more tongues on one side than the other, or if they are not equally spaced, within reason.

For the hub, solder or rivet a "handle" across the center hole and drill a hole through it of the same size as the center hole. With the help of solder a grooved pulley which will answer almost every experimental purpose may be made, and it is remarkable with how slight care a perfectly true wheel may be made in this manner.

The same principle might in some way be applied to gear-wheels, for light and temporary use.—Contributed by C. W. Nieman, New York City.

An Emergency Glass Funnel

Secure a glass bottle having a small neck and tie a string saturated in kerosene around the outside at A and B as shown in the sketch. Light the string and allow it to burn until the glass is heated, then plunge the bottle quickly into water. The top or neck will then come off easily. The sharp edges are ground or filed off smooth. This will make a good emergency funnel which serves the purpose well for filling wide necked bottles.—Contributed by Jos. W. Sorenson, Everett, Wash.

An Electrical Walking Stick

A cane that will produce an electric shock when shaking hands is one supplied with the electrical apparatus shown in the sketch. An ordinary cane, 1 in. in diameter at the top and having a metal band A, is bored about 8 in. deep, to receive the battery B and induction coil C. One of the electrical connections is through the metal tip D to the earth, the other is through the metal band A when the push button E is pressed.

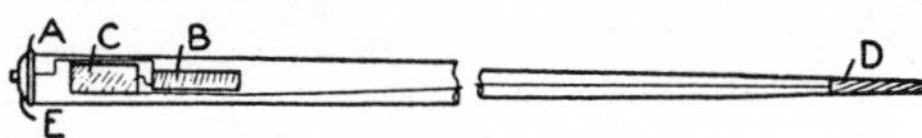

Battery and Coil in Cane

The one using the cane merely holds the metal end D in contact with the earth and while shaking hands with a friend he pushes the button and starts the coil in operation.—Contributed by Stanley Radcliffe, Laurel, Md.

Convenient Shelf Arrangement

A convenient device for crowded shelves and cupboards is shown in the accompanying sketch. Halfway between shelves A and B is installed a second shelf C which is only half as wide as the other shelves. This provides a convenient place for small articles and utensils, while in a china closet it furnishes a splendid space for cups, sauce dishes or other small pieces. It also adds a neat and pleasing appearance.—Contributed by E. M. Williams, Oberlin, Ohio.

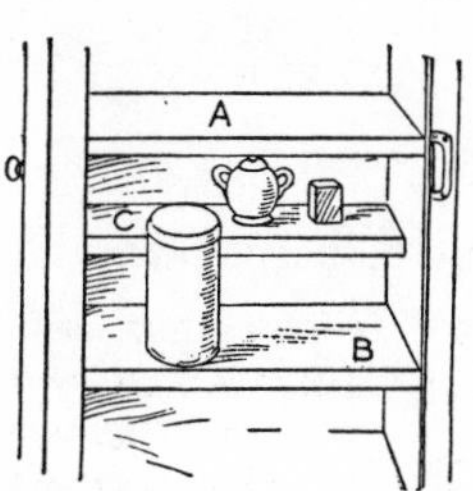

A Shoe Scraper

On steps of public buildings, shops and dwellings is usually found some sort of a mud scraper for the shoes. These remove the mud from the sole of the shoe and leave it on the edge and sides. The scraper shown in the sketch is of simple construction, and removes the mud from the soles and sides of any size shoe in one operation. The scrapers spread and bring pressure to bear on all sizes. The side scrapers must be made of metal that will spring. The standard is of heavy sheet metal with the thinner strips riveted to the projecting uprights at the ends.

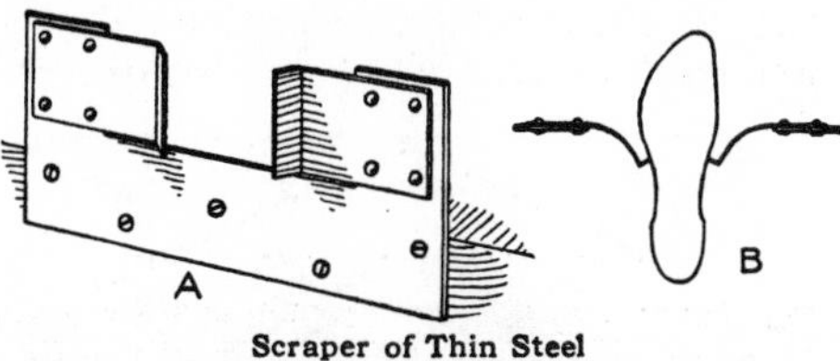

Scraper of Thin Steel

Fastening a Shade to a Roller

Tack the shade A in the usual manner and roll it as far back as possible and while in this position apply an ample quantity of glue near the tacks, as shown at B. A shade attached in this manner will not come loose from the roller.

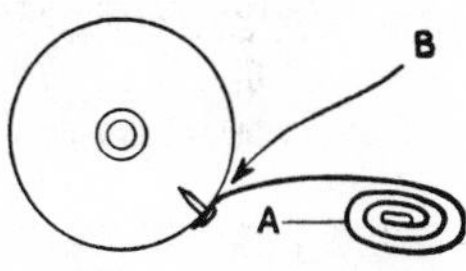

Vegetable Slicer

The slicer is made of a knife blade, screw and pin handle. The screw is soldered into the end of the knife blade. As the screw feeds into the vegetable or fruit, the blade will slice it in a curl of even thickness.—Contributed by H. C. Roufeldt, Toledo, O.

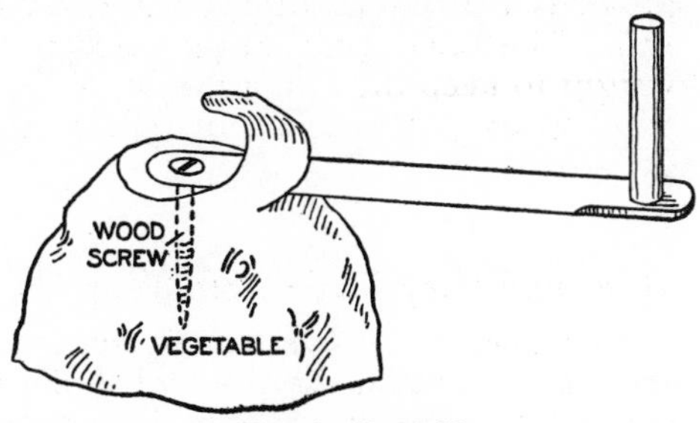

Slicer in Vegetable

How to Make an Etched Copper Picture Frame

Secure a heavy piece of copper about 8 or 10 gauge, cut to 7 by 7¾ in. Make a design on a piece of paper. The accompanying sketch offers a suggestion.

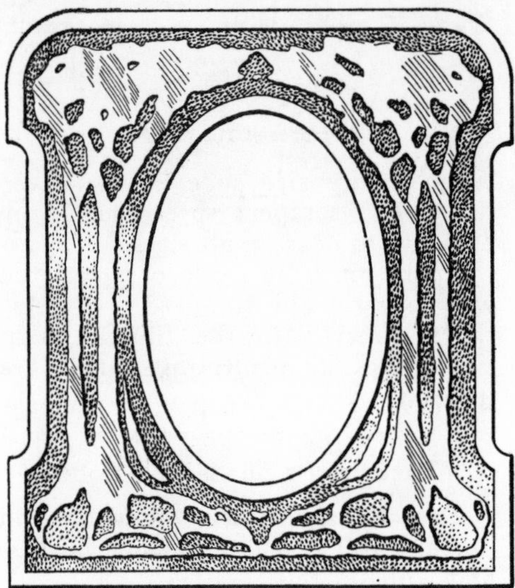

Etched Copper Picture Frame

If the design is to be symmetrical, draw a line down the middle of the paper, make one-half the fold and trace the remaining half by placing a piece of double-surfaced carbon paper between the halves. Fasten this design with a little paste on the copper at two of its corners and trace it on the copper by means of the carbon paper.

Remove the paper, and, with a small brush and black varnish or asphaltum paint, cover the part not to be eaten by the acid of the bath into which the metal is to be immersed. Two or three coats will be necessary to withstand the acid. The conventional trees, the border as shown in the illustration, and the back are covered with the varnish or asphaltum.

The etching solution should be put in a stone vessel of some kind and care should be taken not to allow it to get on the hands or clothes. A stick should be used to handle the metal while it is in the solution. This solution is made by putting in the stone jar the following: Water a little more than one-half, nitric acid a little less than one-half. *Do not add the water to the acid.* Leave the metal in this solution three or four hours. The time will depend upon the strength of the acid and the depth to which you wish the etching to be done. An occasional examination of the object will show when to take it out.

When the etching has been carried as far as desirable, take the copper from the bath and remove the asphaltum by scraping it as clean as possible, using an old case knife. After doing this, put some of the solution, or pickle as it is called, in an old pan and warm it over a flame. Put the metal in this hot liquid and swab it with batting or cloth fastened to the end of a stick. Rinse in clear water to stop the action of the acid. When clean, cut the metal out from the center where the picture is to be placed, using a metal saw.

Solder on the back several small clips with which to hold the picture in place. There must also be a support soldered in place to keep the frame upright. To further clean the metal before soldering, use a solution in the proportion of one-half cup of lye to 3 gal. water. Heat either the solution or the metal just before using.

When soldering, care must be taken to have the parts to be soldered thoroughly clean. Any grease or foreign matter will prevent the solder from running properly. On a piece of slate slab, heavy glass or other hard, nonabsorbent substance that is clean, put a little water and grind a lump of borax around until the resultant is like thin cream. Thoroughly clean the parts that are to be soldered by scraping with a knife, and do not touch with the fingers afterward. Place a piece of thin silver solder between the parts after having coated them and the solder with the borax. Use a pair of tweezers to pick up the solder. Hold the parts firmly together and apply heat—slowly at first until all moisture has been expelled and the borax crystallized, after which the flame may be applied more directly and the parts brought to a soldering heat. An alcohol flame will do. Heat applied too quickly will throw off the solder and spoil the attempt.

painted in some pretty tint, or, if preferred, may be enameled.—Contributed by G. J. Tress.

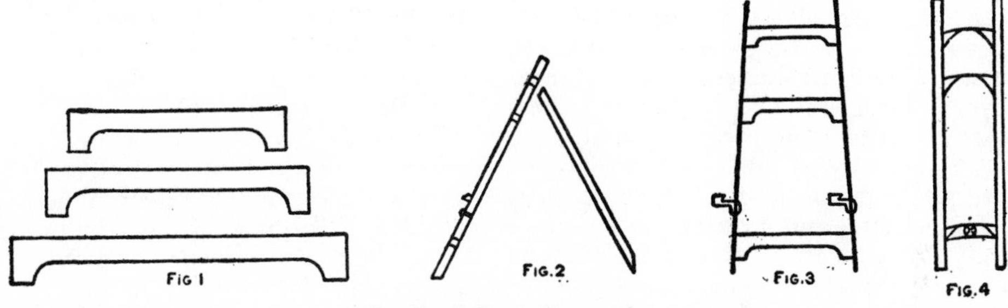

Details of Easel Construction

There are various ways of finishing the metal. It may be polished by means of powdered pumice, chalk or charcoal, and then treated with a coat of French varnish diluted ten times its volume in alcohol. Another popular way is to give the background a bluish-green effect by brushing it over a great many times, after it has been cleaned, with a solution composed of muriate of ammonia, 1 part; carbonate of ammonia, 3 parts; water, 24 parts. The whole may then be treated with French varnish to preserve the colors.

How to Make an Easel

A strong and substantial easel may be made at home with very little expense and no great difficulty.

Smooth down with a plane, four pieces of pine, 1 in. thick, 4 in. wide and 4 ft. long, until suitable for legs. Make three cross-pieces, Fig. 1, and join the legs with them as shown in Fig. 2. With an auger bore a hole in each leg about 3 in. from the bottom, and fit into each a little peg, Fig. 2, for the picture to rest on. The peg should be of hardwood so it will not break.

Cut the handle from an old broom, measure off the right length, and put a hinge on one end. Fasten this leg on the second cross-piece, thus forming a support for the two front legs, Fig. 3. The easel may be finished according to the individual taste. It may be sandpapered and stained and varnished, or

How to Make a Wind Propeller

A wind propeller may be constructed with four old bicycle wheels arranged with shafts pretty much like the shafts of a hand-propelled cart. The platform is flatter, however, and the body one tier so that it is lower. A framework of wood is built at M and this is a support for several purposes. The sail is secured to the mast which is fixed into the body of the cart as shown. The sail is linen fabric. There are two cross-pieces to aid in keeping the sail properly opened. The steering arrangement is through the rear shaft. The shaft is pivoted as in a hand-propelled cart, and the rod I extends from the middle connection of the shaft up to a point where the person seated on the wooden frame can handle it. There is a brake arranged by making a looped piece J and hinging it as shown. This piece is metal, fitted with a leather face. The cord K is pulled to press the brake. I marks the support for the mast underneath the body of the cart. In a steady breeze this cart spins nicely along the roads.

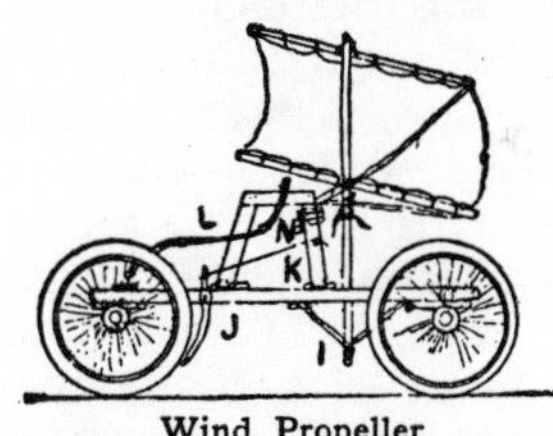

Wind Propeller

Never change a single ball in a bearing. Renew them all.

How to Construct an Annunciator

Oftentimes a single electric bell may be connected in a circuit so that it can be operated from more than one push button. These push buttons are usually located in entirely different parts of the building and it is necessary to have some means of determining the particular push button that was pressed and caused the bell to operate. The electric annunciator is a device that will indicate or record the various calls or signals that may be sent over the circuits to which the annunciator is connected. A very simple and inexpensive annunciator may be made in the following way:

Before taking up the construction of the annunciator it would be best to make a diagrammatic drawing of the circuit in which the annunciator is to operate. The simplest circuit that will require an annunciator is one where the bell may be operated from either of two push buttons. In this case the annunciator must be constructed to give only two indications. Fig. 1 shows how the various elements of such a circuit may be connected. B is an ordinary vibrating electric bell, M1 and M2 are the two electromagnets of the annunciator, A is a battery of several dry cells, and P1 and P2 are the push buttons from either of which the bell may be operated.

When the push button P1 is pressed the circuit is completed through the winding of the magnet M1 and its core becomes magnetized. In a similar manner the core of the magnet M2 becomes magnetized when the push button P2 is pressed and the circuit completed through the winding of the magnet M2.

If an iron armature, that is supported by a shaft through its center and properly balanced, be placed near the ends of the cores of M1 and M2, as shown in Fig. 2, it may assume the position indicated by either the full or dotted lines, depending upon which of the magnets, M1 or M2, was last magnetized. The position of this armature will serve to indicate the push button from which the bell was operated. The magnets should be placed inside a case and the indication may be made by a pointer attached to the shaft, supporting the armature.

If you are able to secure the electromagnets from a discarded electric bell they will work fine for the magnets M1 and M2. They should be disconnected from their iron support and mounted upon some non-magnetic material, such as brass or copper, making the distance between their centers as small as possible. The piece of metal upon which the magnets are mounted should now be fastened, by means of two wood screws, to the back of the board, shown in Fig. 6, that is to form the face of the annunciator. It should be about 1/8 in. thick, 1/2 in. wide and long enough to extend a short distance beyond the cores of the magnets M1 and M2. Drill a 1/16-in. hole through its center, as shown in Fig. 2. Drive a piece of steel rod into this hole, making sure the rod will not turn easily in the opening, and allow about 1/2 in. of the rod to project on one side, and 1 1/2 in. on the other side.

Drill a hole in the board upon which the magnets are mounted so that when the long end of the rod carrying the armature is passed through the hole, the armature will be a little more than 1/16 in. from each magnet core. The short end of the rod should be supported by means of a piece of strip brass bent into the form shown in Fig. 3.

Drill a hole in the center of this piece, so the rod will pass through it. When the armature has been put in its proper place, fasten this strip to the board with two small wood screws. You may experience some difficulty in locating the hole in the board for the rod, and it no doubt would be best to drill this hole first and fasten the magnets in place afterwards.

Two small collars should be fastened to the rod to prevent its moving endwise. Fit the collars tightly on the rod to hold them in place.

Cut the long end of the rod off so it projects through the face of the annunciator about 3/8 in. Take some very thin sheet brass and cut out a needle or indicator as shown in Fig. 4. In a small piece of brass drill a hole so it will fit tight on the other end of the rod. Solder the indicator to this piece and force it in place on the end of the rod.

When the armature is the same distance from each core, the indicator should be parallel to the long dimension of the face of the case. The case of the instrument may be made in the following way:

Secure a piece of 3/8-in. oak, or other hard wood, 3 in. wide and 2½ ft. long. Then cut from this board the following pieces: two whose dimensions correspond to those of Fig. 5 and are to form the sides of the case; two whose dimensions correspond to those of Fig. 6 and are to form the back and the face of the case; three whose dimensions correspond to those of Figs. 7, 8, and 9 and are to form the lower and upper end of the case and the finish for the top.

Secure a piece of window glass, 4½ in. by 3⅛ in. that is to be used as the front. Before assembling the case cut on the inner surface of the pieces forming the sides and the lower end, a groove just wide enough to take the glass and 1/16 in. in depth. The outer edge of this groove should be 3/8 in. from the outer edge of the frame. After the case is fastened together there should be a slot between the piece forming the upper end and the piece that serves as a finish at the top, that will allow the glass to be slipped into place. A small strip of wood should be tacked over this slot, after the glass is put in place, to prevent the dust and dirt from falling down inside of the case.

The piece upon which the works are to be mounted may be fastened in place

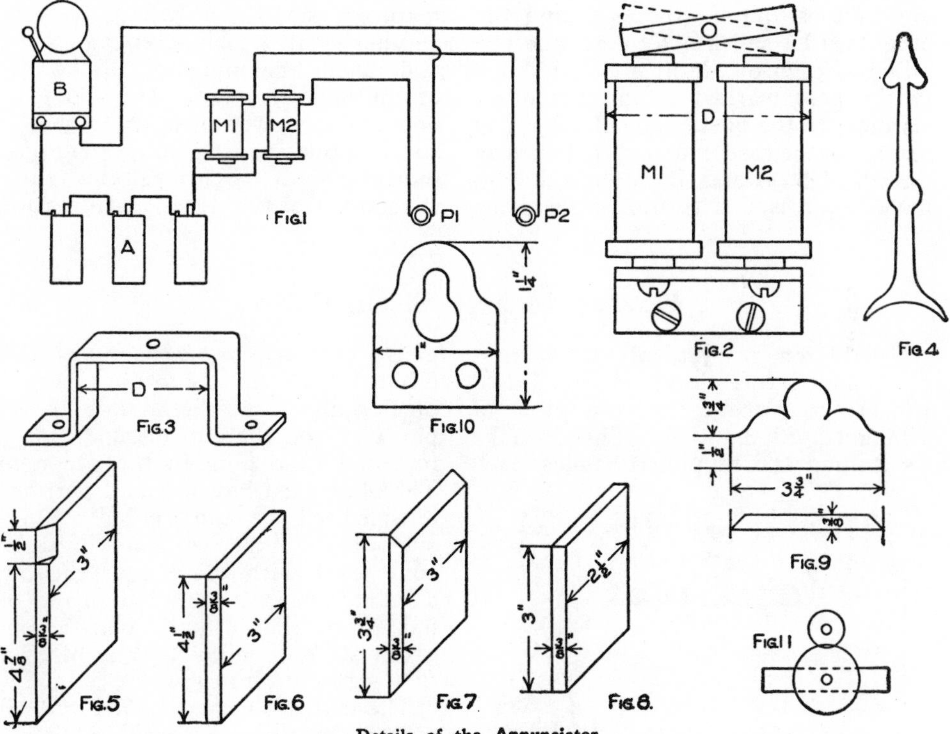

Details of the Annunciator

by means of four round-headed brass screws that pass through the sides of the case. It should be fastened about ½ in. back of the glass front. The back may be fastened inside of the case in a similar manner.

Cut two pieces, from some sheet brass, whose dimensions correspond to those of Fig. 10. These pieces are to be used in supporting the case by means of some small screws. Fasten three binding-posts, that are to form the terminals of the annunciator, on the top of the upper end of the case. Mark one of these binding-posts C and the other two L1 and L2. Connect one terminal of each of the magnet windings to the post marked C and the other terminal to the posts L1 and L2. You can finish the case in any style you may desire. Oftentimes it is desirable to have it correspond to the finish of the woodwork of the room in which it is to be placed. The distance the point of the indicator will move through depends upon the distance between the cores of the magnets and the distance of the armature from these cores. These distances are oftentimes such that the indications of the cell are not very definite. If the armature is moved too far from the cores there is not sufficient pull exerted by them when magnetized, to cause the position of the armature to change.

Mount on the shaft carrying the armature a small gear wheel. Arrange another smaller gear to engage this on and fasten the indicator to the shaft of the smaller gear. Any movement now of the armature shaft will result in a relative large movement of the indicator shaft. Figure 11 shows the arrangement of the gears just described.

How to Make a Steam Calliope

Secure ten gas jet valves, the part of the gas fixture shown in Fig. 1, and prepare to place them in a piece of 1-in. pipe, 12 in. long. This is done by drilling and tapping 10 holes, each

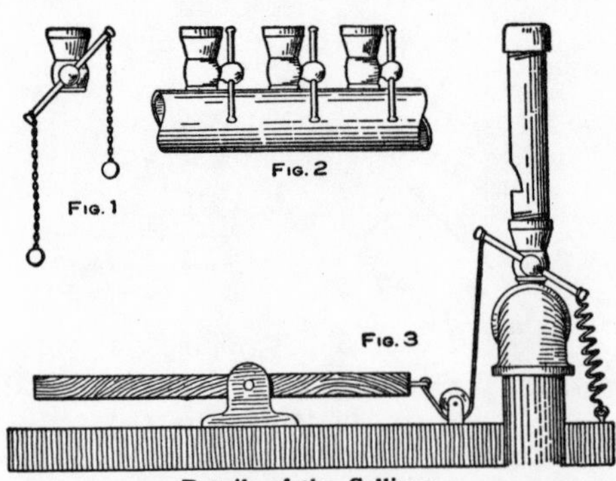

Details of the Calliope

1 in. apart, in a straight line along the pipe. The valves screwed into these holes appear as shown in Fig. 2. The whistles are made from pipe of a diameter that will fit the valves. No dimensions can be given for the exact lengths of these pipes as they must be tried out to get the tone. Cut ten pieces of this pipe, each one of a different length, similar to the pipes on a pipe organ. Cut a thread on both ends, put a cap on the end intended for the top, and fit a plug in the other end. The plug must have a small portion of its side filed out, and a notch cut in the side of the pipe with its horizontal edge level with the top of the plug. This part of each whistle is made similar to making a bark whistle on a green stick of willow. The pipes are then screwed into the valves.

The whistles may be toned by trying out and cutting off pieces of the pipe, or by filling the top end with a little melted lead. The 1-in. pipe must have a cap screwed on one end and the other attached to a steam pipe. The steam may be supplied by using an old range boiler, placed horizontally in a fireplace made of brick or sheet iron. If such a boiler is used, a small safety valve should be attached. The keys and valve operation are shown in Fig. 3. This is so plainly illustrated that it needs no explanation.—Contributed by Herbert Hahn, Chicago.

Sharpening Scissors

When sharpening scissors on a grindstone it is very difficult to procure a straight edge. For those not having the facilities of a grinding arrangement a very handy device that will produce a straight and sharp edge can be easily constructed as follows:

Procure a block of wood, 1½ in. long, 1 in. wide and ½ in. thick, and saw a kerf square with the face of the block, as shown at A. Attach a piece

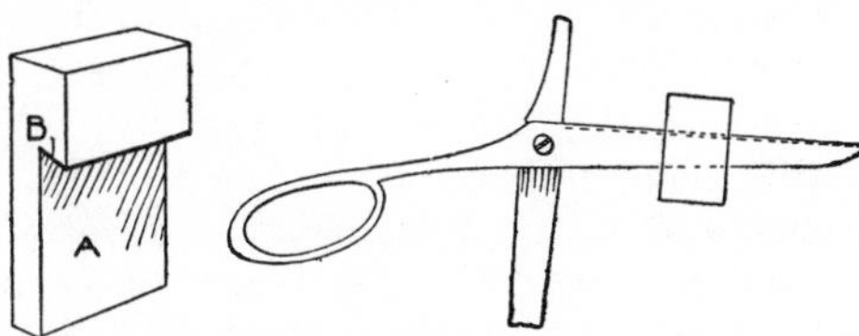

A Block of Wood Fitted with a Piece of Emery Cloth for Sharpening Scissors Correctly

of fine emery cloth in the kerf, at B, with glue, taking care to have it flat on the sloping surface only and allowing no part of the cloth to turn the sharp corner and lie on the back side. Apply the block to the scissor blade as shown and draw it back and forth from one end to the other, being careful to keep the back side of the blade flat against the block. Without being familiar with scissors grinding, anyone can sharpen them correctly with this block. —Contributed by Harriet Kerbaugh, Allentown, Pa.

Counter Brush for a Shop

A very serviceable brush for use around a shop can be made from a discarded or worn-out push broom as shown at A. Pull out the bristles from one-half of the brush and shape the wood of that end with a knife or

A Discarded Push Broom Shaped to Form a Brush for the Bench or Counter

spokeshave to the form of a handle, and the brush will be formed as shown at B.—Contributed by James T. Gaffney, Chicago.

A Curtain Roller

Procure a window-shade roller, an umbrella rib and two strips of oilcloth, each 1 in. wide and 4 in. long. Cut the

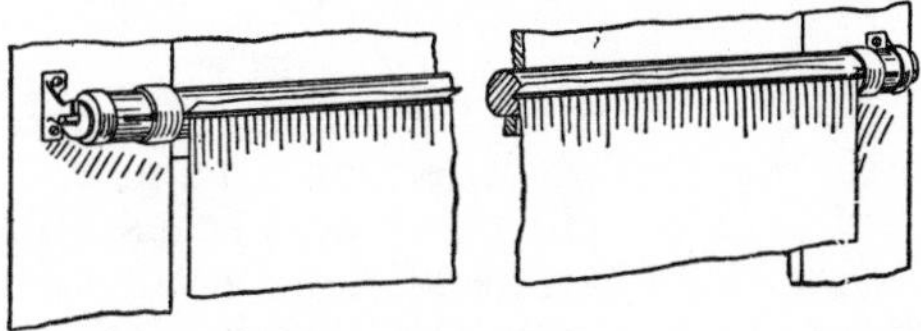

The Curtain is Easily Attached to and Detached from the Roller for Cleaning

roller off so that it will be 6 in. longer than the distance across the window, then cut a groove in it to insert the rib. Sew the pieces of oilcloth so that they will just fit over the ends of the roller. When this is done lay the curtain across the groove, then press the rib and curtain into the groove and push the oilcloth bands over the ends of the rib to keep it in place.—Contributed by E. L. McFarlane, Nashwaakees, N. B.

Shade-Holder Bracket for a Gas Jet

An old umbrella rib makes a very effective shade-holder bracket for a gas jet. The ends of the rib are bent to fit around the pendant upright and the support end is shaped into a hook. It can be quickly applied or removed. The outer end is bent into a hook to

The Bracket for Holding the Shade is Made from an Old Umbrella Rib

hold the shade. The rib can be cut to fit a pendant arm of any length.—Contributed by Edward Keegstra, Paterson, N. J.

To Longer Preserve Cut Flowers

A good way to keep cut flowers fresh is to place a small amount of pure salt of sodium in the water. It is best to procure this salt at a drug store because commercial salt will cause the flowers to wither, due to the impurities in the soda. Call for pure sodium chloride.

Glass Blowing and Forming

Fortunate indeed is the boy who receives a stock of glass tubing, a Bunsen burner, a blowpipe, and some charcoal for a gift, for he has a great deal of fun in store for himself. Glass blowing is a useful art to understand, if the study of either chemistry or physics is to be taken up, because much apparatus can be made at home. And for itself alone, the forming of glass into various shapes has not only a good deal of pleasure in it, but it trains the hands and the eye.

Glass, ordinarily brittle and hard, becomes soft and pliable under heat. When subjected to the action of a flame until dull red, it bends as if made of putty; heated to a bright yellow, it is so soft that it may be blown, pulled, pushed or worked into any shape desired. Hence the necessity for a Bunsen burner, a device preferred to all others for this work, because it gives the hottest flame without soot or dirt. The Bunsen burner, as shown in Fig. 1, is attached to any gas bracket with a rubber tube, but the flame is blue, instead of yellow, as the burner introduces air at its base, which mixes with the gas and so produces an almost perfect combustion, instead of the partial combustion which results in the ordinary yellow flame. All gas stoves have Bunsen burners, and many oil stoves.

If gas is not available, an alcohol lamp with a large wick will do almost as well. The blowpipe, shown in Fig. 2, is merely a tube of brass with the smaller end at right angles to the pipe, and a fine tip to reduce the size of the blast, which is used to direct a small flame. Besides these tools, the glass worker will need some round sticks of charcoal, sharpened like a pencil, as shown in Fig. 3, a file, and several lengths of German glass tubing.

To bend a length of the tubing, let it be assumed for the purpose of making a syphon, it is only necessary to cork one end of the tube and heat it near the top of the Bunsen flame, turning the tubing constantly to make it heat evenly on all sides, until it is a dull red in color. It will then bend of its own weight if held in one hand, but to allow it to do so is to make a flat place in the bend. The heating should be continued until the red color is quite bright, when the open end of the tube is put in the mouth and a little pressure of air made in the tube by blowing. At the same time, the tube is bent, steadily but gently. The compressed air in the tube prevents it from collapsing during the process.

To make a bulb on the end of a tube, one end must be closed. This is easily done by heating as before, and then pulling the tube apart as shown in Fig. 4. The hot glass will draw, just like a piece of taffy, each end tapering to a point. This point on one length is successively heated and pressed toward and into the tube, by means of a piece of charcoal, until the end is not only closed, but as thick as the rest of the tube, as in Fig. 5. An inch or more is now heated white hot, the tube being turned continually to assure even heating and to prevent the hot end from bending down by its own weight. When very hot, a sudden puff into the open end of the tube will expand the hot glass into a bulb, as in Fig. 6. These can be made of considerable size, and, if not too thin, make very good flasks (Fig. 7) for physical experiments. The base of the bulb should be flattened by setting it, still hot, on a flat piece of charcoal, so that it will stand alone.

To weld two lengths of glass tubing together, heat the end of a tube and insert the point of a piece of charcoal in the opening, and twirl it about until the end of the tube has a considerable flare. Do the same to the end of the other tube, which is to be joined to the first, and then, heating both to a dull red, let them touch and press lightly together as in Fig. 8. As soon as they are well in contact, heat the two joined flares together, very hot, and, pulling slightly, the flares will flatten out and the tube be perfectly joined. Tubes joined without previous flaring have a constricted diameter at the joint.

To make a T-joint in two pieces of tubing, it is necessary to make a hole in the side of one piece, as shown at A in Fig. 9. This is accomplished by the aid of the principle of physics that gases expand when heated. Both ends of the tube, which should be cold, are corked tightly. The whole is then gradually warmed by being held near the flame. When warm, a small flame is directed by the blowpipe from the Bunsen flame to a spot on one side of the closed tube. As it heats, the air within the tube expands and becomes compressed, and as soon as the hot spot on the side of the tube is soft enough, the confined air blows out, pushing the hot glass aside as it does so, leaving a small puncture. This is to be enlarged with pointed charcoal until it also flares as shown at B. This flare is then connected to the flared end of a straight tube, C, and the T-joint, D, is complete.

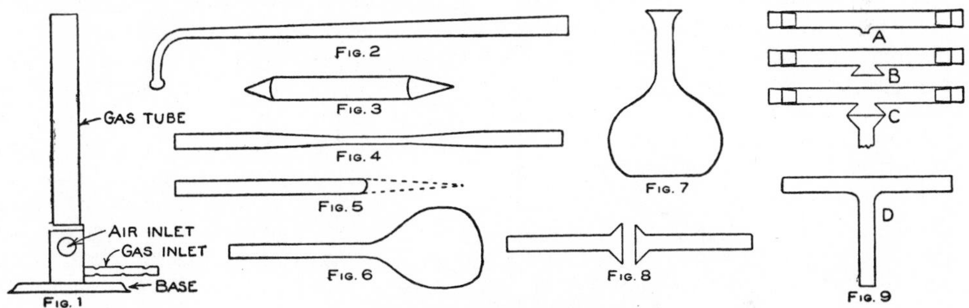

Glass Blowing and Forming

Using the blowpipe is not difficult. The lips and cheeks should be puffed out with a mouthful of air, which is ample to blow a flame while the lungs are being refilled. In this way, it is possible to use the blowpipe steadily, and not intermittently, as is necessary if the lungs alone are the "bellows."

Small glass funnels, such as are used in many chemical operations, are made by first forming a bulb, then puncturing the bulb at the top, when hot, with a piece of charcoal, and smoothing down or flaring the edges. Very small and fine glass tubes, such as are used in experiments to demonstrate capillary attraction, water or other liquid rising in them when they are plunged into it, are made by heating as long a section of tubing as can be handled in the flame—2 in. will be found enough—and, when very hot, giving the ends a sudden vigorous pull apart. The tube pulls out and gets smaller and smaller as it does so, until at last it breaks. But the fine thread of glass so made is really a tube, and not a rod, as might be supposed. This can be demonstrated by blowing through it at a gas flame, or by immersing it in colored liquid. The solution will be seen to rise some distance within the tube, the amount depending on the diameter of the tube.

The file is for cutting the glass tubing into lengths convenient to handle. It should be a three-cornered file, of medium fineness, and is used simply to nick the glass at the place it is desired to cut it. The two thumbs are then placed beneath the tube, one on each side of the nick, and the tube bent, as if it were plastic, at the same time pulling the hands apart. The tube will break off squarely at the nick, without difficulty.

The entire outfit may be purchased from any dealer in chemical or physical apparatus, or any druggist will order it. Enough tubing to last many days, the Bunsen burner, blowpipe, file and charcoal should not exceed $2 in cost.

The addition of cadmium to soft solder composed of tin and lead, lowers its melting point and increases its strength.

TELEGRAPH CODES.

MORSE, USED IN THE UNITED STATES AND CANADA.
CONTINENTAL, USED IN EUROPE AND ELSEWHERE.
PHILLIPS USED IN THE UNITED STATES FOR "PRESS" WORK.

Dash = 2 dots. Long dash = 4 dots.
Space between elements of a letter = 1 dot.
Space between letters of a word = 2 dots.
Interval in spaced letters = 2 dots.
Space between words = 3 dots.

LETTERS

MORSE — CONTINENTAL

A
B
C
D
E
F
G
H
I
J
K
L
M
N
O
P
Q
R
S
T
U
V
W
X
Y
Z
&

NUMERALS

1
2
3
4
5
6
7
8
9
0

PUNCTUATION, ETC.

MORSE — CONTINENTAL

. Period
: Colon
; Semicolon
, Comma
? Interrogation
! Exclamation
Fraction line
- Hyphen
' Apostrophe
£ Pound Sterling
¶ Paragraph
Italics or underline
( ) Parentheses
[ ] Brackets
" " Quotation marks

PHILLIPS

. Period
: Colon
:— Colon dash
; Semicolon
, Comma
? Interrogation
! Exclamation
Fraction line
— Dash
- Hyphen
£ Pound Sterling
/ Shilling mark
$ Dollar mark
d Pence
Capitalized letter
Colon followed by quotation :"
c Cents
. Decimal point
¶ Paragraph
Italics or underline
( ) Parentheses
[ ] Brackets
" " Quotation marks
Quotation within a quotation " ' ' "

ABBREVIATIONS IN COMMON USE

MIN. Minute.	SIG. Signature.	Co. Company.	TW. To-morrow.
MSGR. Messenger.	PD. Paid.	D.H. Deadhead	TGM. Telegram.
MSK. Mistake.	QK. Quick.	EX. Express.	TKT. Ticket.
No. Number.	G.B.A. Give better address.	FRT. Freight.	RC. Receive.
NTG. Nothing.	BN. Been.	FR. From.	ML. Mail.
N.M. No more.	BAT. Battery.	G.A. Go Ahead.	LAT. Latitude.
O.K. All right.	BBL. Barrel.	P.O. Post Office.	DEG. Degree.
OFS. Office.	COL. Collect.	R.P.T. Repeat	AN. Answer
OPR. Operator.	CK. Check.	HQRS. Headquarters.	EXA. Extra.

How to Make a Cruising Catamaran

A launch is much safer than a sailing boat, yet there is not the real sport to be derived from it as in sailing. Herein is given a description of a sailing catamaran especially adapted for those who desire to sail and have a safe craft. The main part of the craft is made from two boats or pontoons with watertight tops, bottoms and sides and fixed at a certain distance apart with a platform on top for the passengers. Such a craft cannot be capsized easily, and, as the pontoons are watertight, it will weather almost any rough water. If the craft is intended for rough waters, care must be taken to make the platform pliable yet stiff and as narrow as convenient to take care of the rocking movements.

This catamaran has been designed to simplify the construction, and, if a larger size than the dimensions shown in Fig. 1 is desired, the pontoons may be made longer by using two boards end to end and putting battens on the inside over the joint. Each pontoon is made of two boards 1 in. thick, 14 in. wide and 16 ft. long, dressed and cut to the shape shown in Fig. 2. Spreaders are cut from 2-in. planks, 10 in. wide and 12 in. long, and placed 6 ft. apart between the board sides and fastened with screws. White lead should be put in the joints before turning in the screws. Cut the ends of the boards so they will fit perfectly and make pointed ends to the pontoons as shown

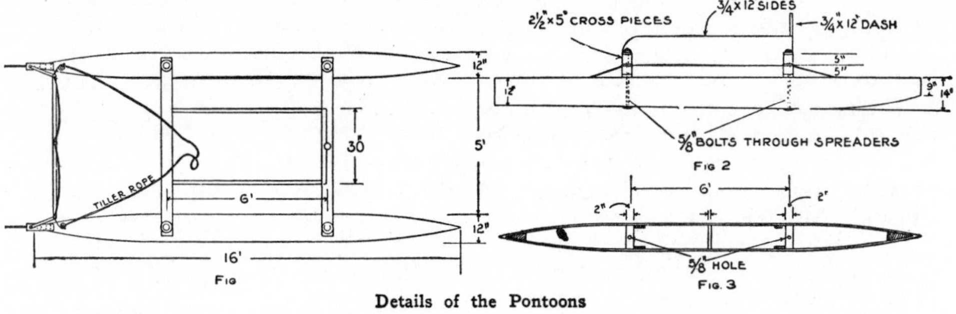

Details of the Pontoons

in Fig. 3, and fit in a wedge shaped piece; white lead the joints and fasten well with screws.

Turn this shell upside down and lay a board ½ in. thick, 12 in. wide and 16 ft. long on the edges of the sides, mark

Completed Boat

on the under side the outside line of the shell and cut to shape roughly. See that the spreaders and sides fit true all over, then put white lead on the joint and nail with 1¾-in. finishing nails as close as possible without weakening the wood. Slightly stagger the nails in the sides, the 1-in. side boards will allow for this, trim off the sides, turn the box over and paint the joints and ends of the spreaders, giving them two or three coats and let them dry.

Try each compartment for leaks by

turning water in them one at a time. Bore a ⅝-in. hole through each spreader in the center and through the

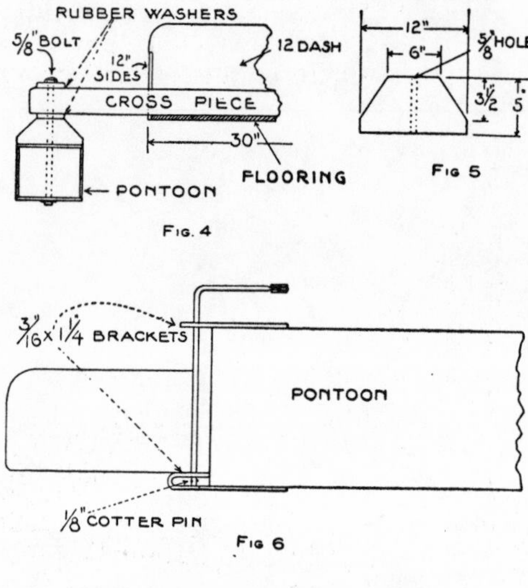

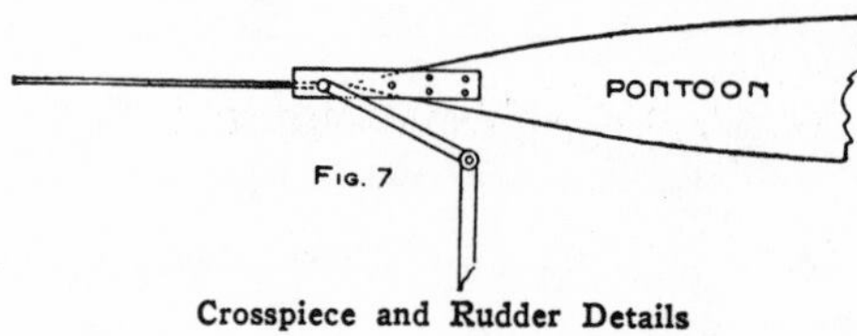

Crosspiece and Rudder Details

bottom board as shown. The top board, which is ¼-in. thick, 12 in. wide and 16 ft. long, is put on the same as the bottom.

After finishing both pontoons in this way place them parallel. A block of wood is fastened on top of each pontoon and exactly over each spreader on which to bolt the crosspieces as shown in Fig. 4. Each block is cut to the shape and with the dimensions shown in Fig. 5.

The crosspieces are made from hickory or ash and each piece is 2½ in. thick, 5 in. wide and 6½ ft. long. Bore a ⅝-in. hole 3 in. from each end through the 5-in. way of the wood. Take maple flooring ¾ in. thick, 6 in. wide, 74½ in. long and fasten with large screws and washers to the crosspieces and put battens across every 18 in. Turn the flooring and crosspieces upside down and fasten to the pontoons with long ⅝-in. bolts put through the spreaders. Put a washer on the head of each bolt and run them through from the under side. Place a thick rubber washer under and on top of each crosspiece at the ends as shown in Fig. 4. This will make a rigid yet flexible joint for rough waters. The flooring being placed on the under side of the crosspieces makes it possible to get the sail boom very low. The sides put on and well fastened will greatly assist in stiffening the platform and help it to stand the racking strains. These sides will also keep the water and spray out and much more so if a 12-in. dash is put on in front on top of the crosspiece.

The rudders are made as shown in Fig. 6, by using an iron rod ⅝ in. in diameter and 2 ft. long for the bearing of each. This rod is split with a hacksaw for 7 in. of its length and a sheet metal plate 3/32 in. thick, 6 in. wide, and 12 in. long inserted and riveted in the split. This will allow ¾ in. of the iron rod to project from the bottom edge of the metal through which a hole is drilled for a cotter pin. The bottom bracket is made from stake iron bent in the shape of a U as shown, the rudder bearing passing through a hole drilled in the upper leg and resting on the lower. Slip the top bracket on and then bend the top end of the bearing rod at an angle as shown in both Figs. 6 and 7. Connect the two bent ends with a crosspiece which has a hole drilled in its center to fasten a rope as shown in Fig. 1.

Attach the mast to the front crosspiece, also bowsprit, bracing them both to the pontoons. A set of sails having about 300 sq. ft. of area will be about right for racing. Two sails, main and fore, of about 175 to 200 sq. ft. will be sufficient for cruising.—Contributed by J. Appleton, Des Moines, Iowa.

Rough alligator finished photograph mounts will not receive a good impression from a die. If a carbon paper is placed on the mounts before making the impression, a good clear imprint will be the result.

How to Attach a Sail to a Bicycle

This attachment was constructed for use on a bicycle to be ridden on the well packed sands of a beach, but it could be used on a smooth, level road as well. The illustration shows the main frame to consist of two boards, each about 16 ft. long, bent in the shape of a boat, to give plenty of room for turning the front wheel. On this main frame is built up a triangular mast, to carry the mainsail and jib, having a combined area of about 40 sq. ft. The frame is fastened to the bicycle by numerous pieces of rope.

Bicycle Sailing on a Beach

Sailing on a bicycle is very much different from sailing in a boat, for the bicycle leans up against the wind, instead of heeling over with it as the boat. It takes some time to learn the supporting power of the wind, and the angle at which one must ride makes it appear that a fall is almost sure to result. A turn must be made by turning out of the wind, instead of, as in ordinary sailing, into it; the boom supporting the bottom of the mainsail is then swung over to the opposite tack, when one is traveling at a good speed.

Removing Iodine Stains

A good way to chemically remove iodine stains from the hands or linen is to wash the stains in a strong solution of hyposulphite of sodium, known as "hypo," which is procurable at any photographic-supply dealer's or drug store.

There is no danger of using too strong a solution, but the best results are obtained with a mixture of 1 oz. of hypo to 2 oz. of water.

Drying Photograph Prints without Curling

Having made some photograph prints at one time that I wanted to dry without the edges curling, I took an ordinary tin can and a strip of clean cotton cloth, as wide as the can was long, and wound it one turn around the can and then placed the prints, one after the other, while they were damp, on the cloth, face downward, and proceeded to roll the cloth and prints quite close on the can. I then pinned the end of the cloth to keep it from unwinding and set the whole in a draft for drying.

The curvature of the can just about

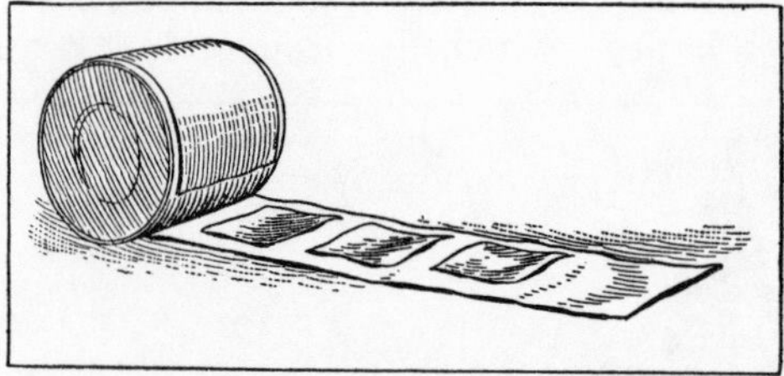

Rolling Up the Prints

counteracted the tendency of the coating on the paper to make the prints curl and when they were thoroughly dried and removed they remained nice and flat.—Contributed by W. H. Eppens, Chicago.

Piercing Glass Plates with a Spark Coil

Anyone possessing a 1-in. induction coil and a 1-qt. Leyden jar can easily perform the interesting experiment of piercing glass plates. Connect the Leyden jar to the induction coil as shown in the diagram. A discharger is now constructed of very dry wood and boiled in paraffine for about 15 minutes. The main part of the discharger, A B, is a piece of wood about 6 in. long and to the middle of it is fastened a wood handle by means of one or two wood screws. A binding-post is fastened to each end of the main piece or at A and B as shown in the diagram.

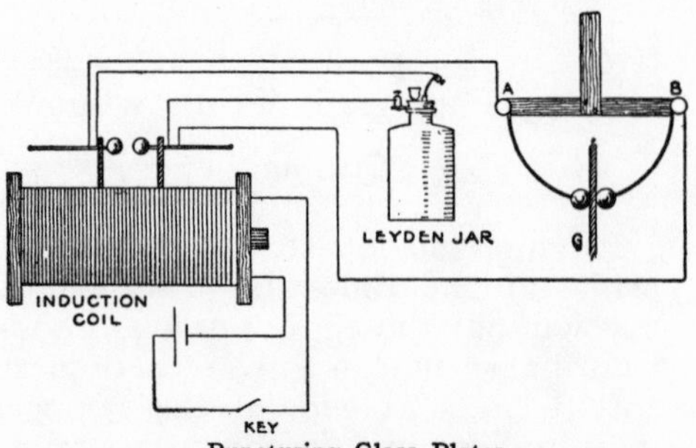

Puncturing Glass Plates

Two stiff brass wires of No. 14 gauge and 6 in. long, with a small brass ball attached to one end of each, are bent in an arc of a circle and attached one to each binding-post.

A plate of glass, G, is now placed between the two brass balls and the coil set in action. The plate will soon be pierced by the spark. Larger coils will pierce heavier glass plates.—Contributed by I. Wolff, Brooklyn, N. Y.

A Home-Made Still

Remove the metal end of an old electric light globe. This can be done by soaking a piece of twine in alcohol and tying it around the globe at the place the break is to be made. Light the string and after it is burned off, turn cold water on the globe. The result will be a smooth break where the string

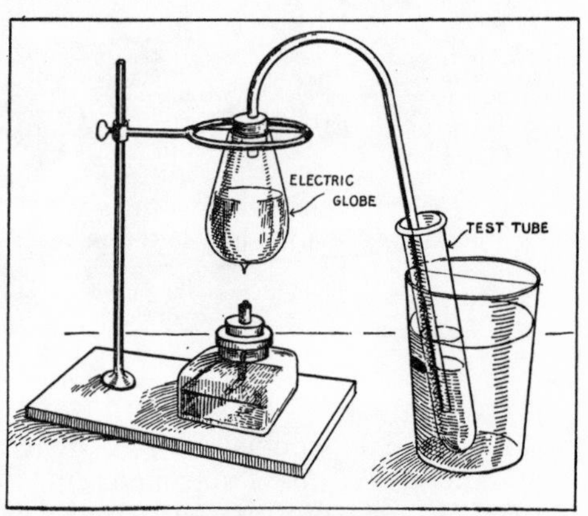

The Complete Still

was placed. Purchase a piece of glass tubing from your druggist and secure a cork that will fit the opening in the glass bulb. Bore a hole in the cork the right size for the glass tube to fit in tightly. If you cannot get a glass tube with a bend in it, you will have to make a bend, as shown in the illustration, by heating the tube at the right place over an alcohol lamp and allowing the weight of the glass to make the bend while it is hot.

Insert the short end of the tube in the cork and place the other end in a test tube that is placed in water as shown. The globe may be fastened in position by a wire passed through the cork and tied to a ring stand. If you do not have a ring stand, suspend the globe by a wire from a hook that is screwed into any convenient place.

A neat alcohol lamp may be made of an old ink or muscilage bottle. Insert a wick in a piece of the glass tubing and put this through a hole bored in a cork and the lamp is ready to burn alcohol or kerosene. Alcohol is cleaner to use as a fuel. Fill the globe about two-thirds full of water or other liquid and apply the heat below as shown. The distilled liquid will collect in the test tube.—Contributed by Clarence D. Luther, Ironwood, Mich.

Old-Time Magic

Balancing Forks on a Pin Head

Two, three and four common table forks can be made to balance on a pin head as follows: Procure an empty bottle and insert a cork in the neck. Stick a pin in the center of this cork so that the end will be about 1½ in. above the top. Procure another cork about 1 in. in diameter by 1¾ in. long. The forks are now stuck into the latter cork at equal distances apart, each having the same angle from the cork. A long needle with a good sharp point is run through the cork with the forks and ½ in. of the needle end allowed to project through the lower end.

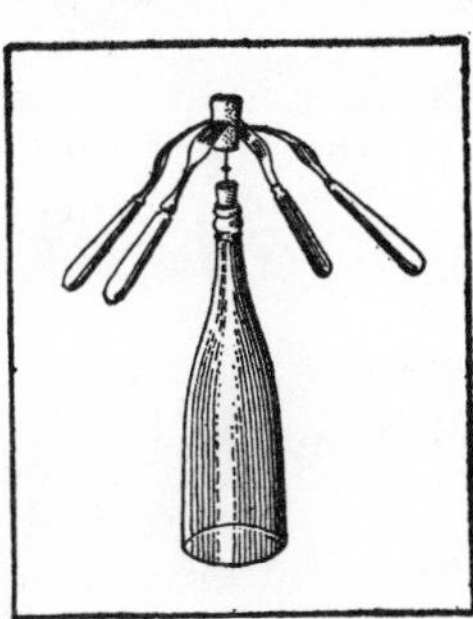

The point of the needle now may be placed on the pin head. The forks will balance and if given a slight push they will appear to dance. Different angles of the forks will produce various feats of balancing.—Contributed by O. E. Tronnes, Wilmette, Ill.

The Buttoned Cord

Cut a piece of heavy paper in the shape shown in Fig. 1 and make two cuts down the center and a slit as long as the two cuts are wide at a point about 1 in. below them. A string is put through the slit, the long cuts and back through the slit and then a button is fastened to each end. The small slit should not be so large as the buttons. The trick is to remove the string. The solution is quite simple. Fold the paper in the middle and the part between the long cuts will form a loop. Bend this loop down and pass it through the small slit. Turn the paper around and it will appear as shown in Fig. 2. One of the buttons may now be drawn through and the paper restored to its original shape.

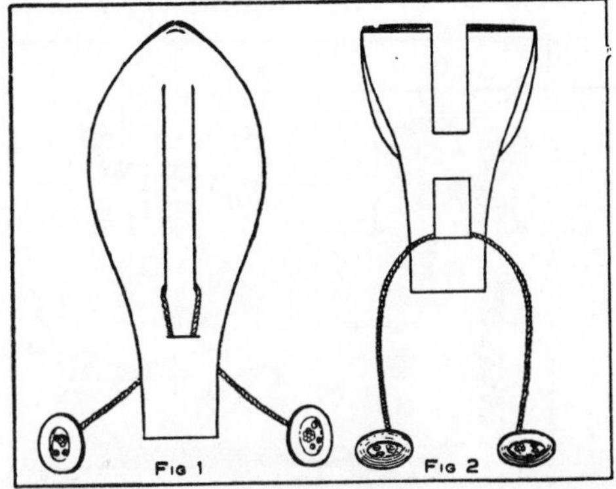

Removing the String

Experiment with an Incandescent Lamp

When rubbing briskly an ordinary incandescent lamp on a piece of cloth and at the same time slightly revolving it, a luminous effect is produced similar to an X-ray tube. The room must be dark and the lamp perfectly dry to obtain good results. It appears that the inner surface of the globe becomes charged, probably by induction, and will sometimes hold the filament as shown in the sketch.—Contributed by E. W. Davis, Chicago.

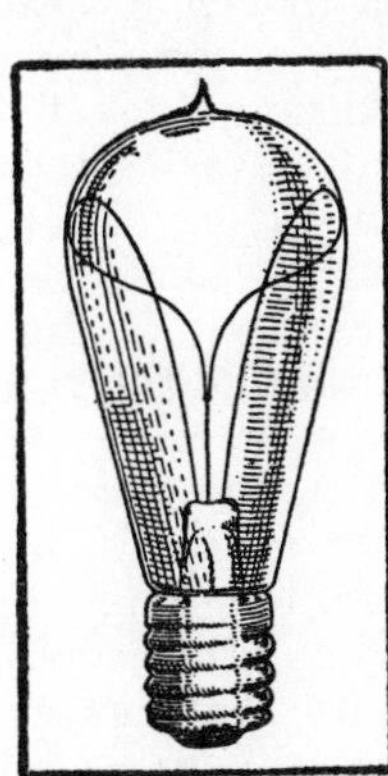

How to Make a Small Motor

The accompanying sketch shows how to make a small motor to run on a battery of three or four dry cells and

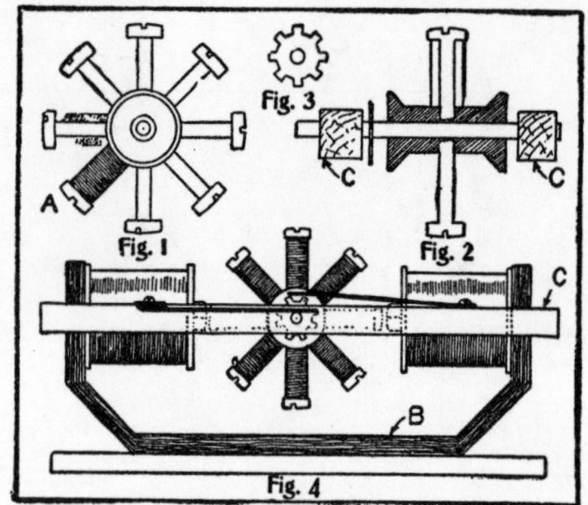

Details of Small Electric Motor

with sufficient power to run mechanical toys. The armature is constructed, as shown in Figs. 1 and 2, by using a common spool with 8 flat-headed screws placed at equal distances apart and in the middle of the spool. Each screw is wound with No. 24 gauge iron wire, as shown at A, Fig. 1. The commutator is made from a thin piece of copper, 1 in. in diameter and cut as shown in Fig. 3, leaving 8 points, 1/8 in. wide and 1/8 in. deep. The field is built up by using 8 strips of tin, 12 in. long and 2 in. wide, riveted together and shaped as shown at B, Fig. 4. Field magnets are constructed by using two 3/8-in. bolts, 1 1/2 in. long. A circular piece of cardboard is placed on each end of the bolt, leaving space enough for the bolt to pass through the field B, and to receive a nut. Wind the remaining space between the cardboards with 30 ft. of No. 22 double-wound cotton-covered copper wire. A light frame of wood is built around the magnets, as shown at C, Fig. 4. Holes are made in this frame to receive the axle of the armature. Two strips of copper, 1/4 in. wide and 3 in. long, are used for the brushes. The armature is placed in position in its bearings and the brushes adjusted as shown in Fig. 4, one brush touching the shaft of the armature outside of the frame, and the other just touching the points of the commutator, which is placed on the shaft inside of the frame. Connect the outside wire of one magnet to the inside wire of the other, and the remaining ends, one to the batteries and back to the brush that touches the shaft, while the other is attached to the brush touching the commutator. In making the frame for the armature bearings, care should be taken to get the holes for the shaft centered, and to see that the screws in the armature pass each bolt in the magnets at equal distances, which should be about 1/8 in.

Aluminum Polish

An emulsion of equal parts of rum and olive oil can be used for cleaning aluminum, says Blacksmith and Wheelwright. Potash lye, not too strong, is also effective in brightening aluminum, and benzol can be used for the same purpose.

A good polish for aluminum consists of a paste formed of emery and tallow, the finish luster being obtained by the use of rouge powder and oil of turpentine.

Homemade Blowpipe

Procure a clay pipe, a cork and a small glass or metal tube drawn to a small opening in one end. Make a hole in the cork just large enough to permit the tube to pass through tightly so no air can pass out except through the hole in the tube. Put the tube in the hole with the small opening at the top

A Pipe Blowpipe

or projecting end. Push the cork into the bowl of the pipe and the blowpipe is ready for use.—Contributed by Wilbur Cryderman, Walkerton, Ont.

Substitute Sink or Bathtub Stopper

Milk-bottle caps make good substitutes for the regular rubber stoppers in sinks and bathtubs. The water soon destroys them, but as a new one usually is had each day, they can be used until a regular stopper is obtained.

A good permanent stopper can be made by cutting a hollow rubber return ball in half, using one part with the concave side up. It will fit the hole of any sink or bathtub. One ball thus makes two stoppers at a cost of about 5 cents.

Safety Tips on Chair Rockers

Some rocking chairs are so constructed that when the person occupying it gives a hard tilt backward, the chair tips over or dangerously near it. A rubber-tipped screw turned into the under side of each rocker, near the rear end, will prevent the chair from tipping too far back.

How to Make a Toy Flier

While a great many people are looking forward to the time when we shall successfully travel through the air, we all may study the problem of aerial navigation by constructing for ourselves a small flying machine as illustrated in this article.

A wing is made in the shape shown in Fig. 1 by cutting it from the large piece of an old tin can, after melting the solder and removing the ends. This wing is then given a twist so that one end will be just opposite the other and appear as shown in Fig. 2. Secure a common spool and drive two nails in one end, leaving at least ½ in. of each nail projecting after the head has been removed. Two holes are made in the wing, exactly central, to fit on these two nails. Another nail is driven part way into the end of a stick, Fig. 4, and the remaining part is cut off so the length will be that of the spool. A string is used around the spool in the same manner as on a top. The wing is placed on the two nails in the spool, and the spool placed on the nail in the stick, Fig. 5, and the flier is ready

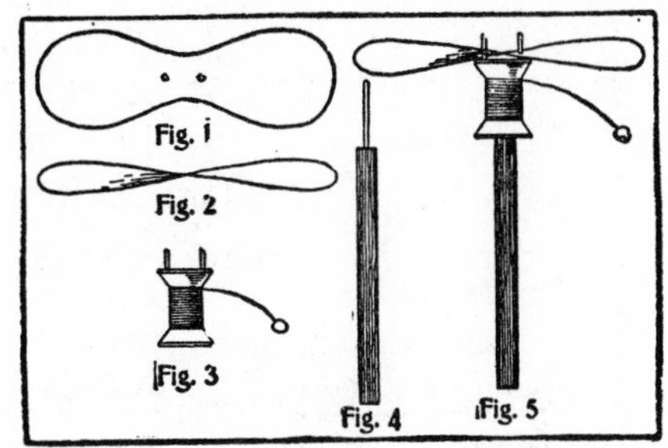

Homemade Flying Machine

for action. A quick pull on the string will cause the wing to leave the nails and soar upward for a hundred feet or more. After a little experience in twisting the wing the operator will learn the proper shape to get the best results.

Be very careful in making the tests before the wings are turned to the proper shape, as the direction of the flier cannot be controlled and some one might be injured by its flight.

How to Make an Ironing-Board Stand

Secure some 1 by 3-in. boards, about 3 ft. long, and plane them smooth. Cut the two pieces A and B 30 in. long and make a notch in each of them, about one-third of the way from one end, 1 in. deep and 3 in. long. These

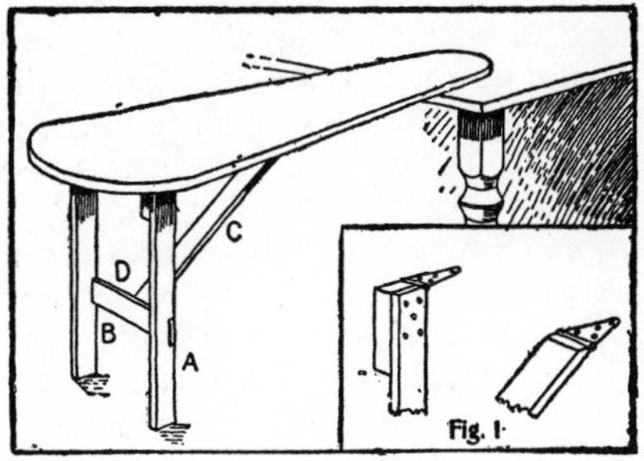

Ironing-Board Stand

notches are to receive the piece D, which has a small block fastened to its side to receive the end of the brace C. The brace C is 36 in. long. The upper ends of the pieces A, B and C are fastened to a common ironing board by using iron hinges as shown in Fig. 1. As the piece D is fitted loosely, it may be removed and the brace, C, with the legs, A and B, folded up against the board.—Contributed by Bert Kottinger, San Jose, Cal.

A Home-Made Electric Plug

A plug suitable for electric light extension or to be used in experimenting may be made from an old electric globe. The glass is removed with all the old composition in the brass receptacle, leaving only the wires. On the ends of the wires, attach two small binding-posts. Fill the brass with plaster of paris, and in doing this keep the wires separate and the binding-posts opposite each other. Allow the plaster to project about $\frac{3}{4}$ in. above the brass, to hold the binding-posts as shown.—Contributed by Albert E. Welch, New York.

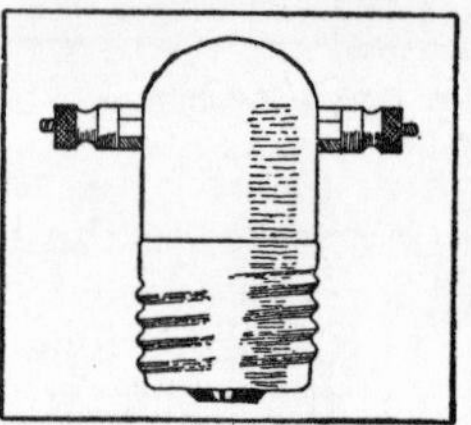

How to Make an Electric Fire Alarm

On each end of a block of wood, 1 in. square and $1\frac{1}{2}$ in. long, fasten a strip of brass $\frac{1}{4}$ by 3 in., bent in the shape as shown in the sketch at A, Fig. 1. These strips should have sufficient bend to allow the points to press tightly together. A piece of beeswax, W, is inserted between the points of the brass strips to keep them apart and to form the insulation. A binding-post, B, is attached to each brass strip on the ends of the block of wood. The device is fastened to the wall or ceiling, and wire connections made to the batteries and bells as shown in the diagram, Fig. 2. When the room becomes a little overheated the wax will melt and cause the brass strips to spring together, which will form the circuit and make the bell ring. Each room in the house may be connected with one of these devices, and all on one circuit with one bell.

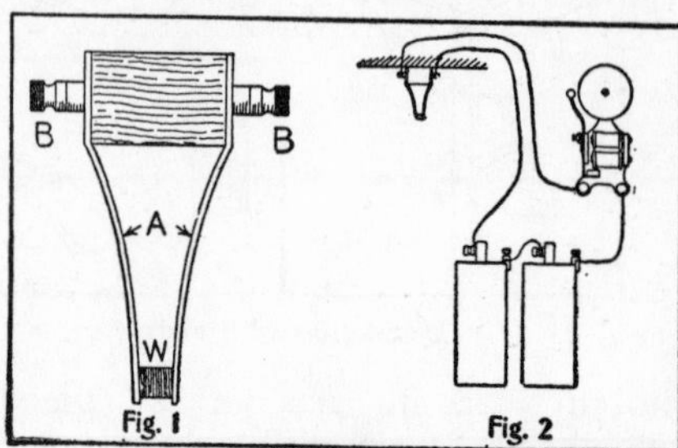

Fire Alarm Device

Home-Made Boy's Car

The accompanying cut shows how a boy may construct his own auto car. The car consists of parts used from a boy's wagon and some old bicycle parts. The propelling device is made by using the hanger, with all its parts, from a bicycle. A part of the bicycle frame is left attached to the hanger and is fastened to the main board of the car by blocks of wood as shown. The chain of a bicycle is used to connect the crank hanger sprocket to a small sprocket fastened in the middle of the rear axle of the car. The front axle is fastened to a square block of wood, which is pivoted to the main board. Ropes are attached to the front axle and to the back part of the main board to be used with the feet in steering the car. To propel the auto, turn the cranks by taking hold of the bicycle pedals.—Contributed by Anders Neilsen, Oakland, Cal.

Boys' Home-Made Auto

Photographs in Relief Easily Made

Relief photographs, although apparently difficult to produce, can be made by any amateur photographer. The negative is made in the usual way and, when ready for printing, a positive or transparency is made from it in the same manner as a lantern slide or window transparency, says the Sketch, London. Use the same size plate as the negative for the transparency. To make the print in relief place the positive in the frame first with the film side out and the negative on top of this with the film side up in the usual manner. Put in the paper and print. This will require a greater length of time than with the ordinary negative on account of printing through double glass and films. In using printing-out papers care should be taken to place the printing frame in the same position and angle after each examination.

Reproduced from a Relief Photograph

ℭPlace the transmitting instruments of a wireless outfit as close together as possible.

with the ordinary negative on account of printing through double glass and films. In using printing out papers care should be taken to place the printing frame in the same position and angle after each examination. The print is treated as any ordinary print.

How to Make a Wireless Telephone

A noted French scientist, Bourbouze, was able to keep up communications with the outside during the siege of Paris by making practical application of the earth-currents. The distance

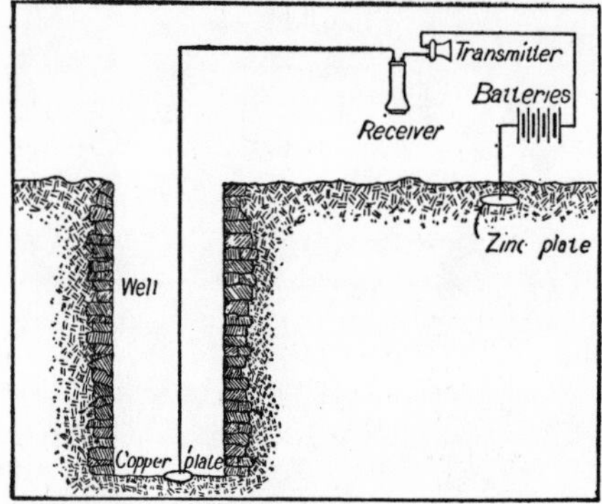

Details of Wireless 'Phone Installation

covered is said to have been about 30 miles. Another scientist was able to telephone through the earth without the aid of wires. Nothing, however, has been made public as to how this was accomplished.

It is my object to unveil the mystery and to render this field accessible to others, at least to a certain degree, for I have by no means completed my researches in this particular work.

In order to establish a wireless communication between two points we need first of all a hole or well in the ground at each point. In my experiments I was unable to get a deep well, but the instruments worked fine for a distance of 200 ft. using wells about 25 ft. deep. As in ordinary telephone lines, we require a transmitter and receiver at each point. These must be of the long-distance type. If a hole is dug or a well is found suitable for the purpose, a copper wire is hung in the opening, allowing the end to touch the bottom. To make the proper contact an oval or round—but not pointed—copper plate is attached to the end of the wire. If a well is used it is necessary to have a waterproof cable for the part running through the water. The top end is attached to the telephone transmitter and receiver, as in the ordinary telephone, to the batteries and to a zinc plate which is to be buried in the earth a few feet away from the well or hole, and should not be more than 1 ft. under the surface. Four cells of dry batteries are used at each station.

Both stations are connected in the same way as shown in the sketch. This makes it possible for neighbors to use their wells as a means of communication with each other.—Contributed by A. E. Joeren.

How to Make a Life Buoy

Any boy may be able to make for himself or friends a life buoy for emergency use in a rowboat or for learning to swim. Purchase 1¾ yd. of 30-in. canvas and cut two circular pieces 30 in. in diameter, also cutting a round hole in the center of them 14 in. in diameter. These two pieces are sewed together on the outer and inner edges, leaving a space about 12 in. in length unsewed on the outer seam. Secure some of the cork used in packing Malaga grapes from a grocery or confectionery store and pack it into the pocket formed between the seams through the hole left in the outer edge. When packed full and tight sew up the remaining space in the seam. Paint the outside surface and the seams well with white paint to make it watertight. —Contributed by Will Hare, Petrolea, Ont.

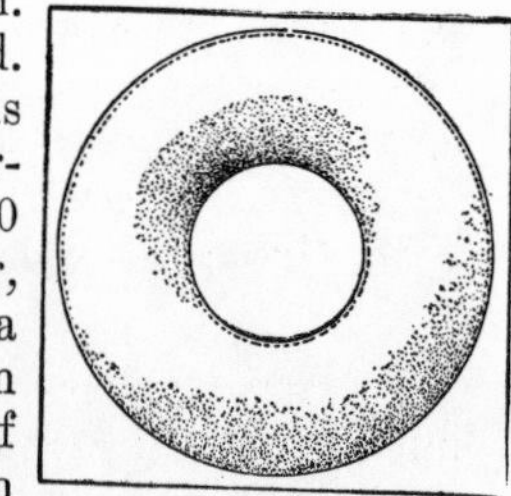

A Home-Made Microscope

A great many times we would like to examine a seed, an insect or the fiber of a piece of wood but have no magnifier handy. A very good microscope may be made out of the bulb of a broken thermometer. Empty out the mercury, which is easily done by holding the bulb with the stem down over a lamp or candle. A spirit lamp is the best, as it makes no smoke and gives a steady heat. Warm the bulb slowly and the mercury will be expelled and may be caught in a tea cup. Do not heat too fast, or the pressure of the mercury vapor may burst the glass bulb, cautions the Woodworkers' Review. To fill the bulb with water warm it and immerse the end of the tube in the water. Then allow it to cool and the pressure of the air will force the water into the bulb. Then boil the water gently, holding the bulb with the stem up; this will drive out all the air, and by turning the stem or tube down and placing the end in water the bulb will be completely filled. It is surprising how much can be seen by means of such a simple apparatus.

A Novel Electric Time Alarm

All time alarms run by clockwork must be wound and set each time. The accompanying diagram shows how to make the connection that will ring a bell by electric current at the time set without winding the alarm. The bell is removed from an ordinary alarm clock and a small metal strip attached, as shown at B. An insulated connection is fastened on the clapper of the bell, as shown at A. The arm holding the clapper must be bent to have the point A remain as close to the strip B as possible without touching it. The connection to the battery is made as shown. When the time set for the alarm comes the clapper will be moved far enough to make the contact. In the course of a minute the catch on the clapper arm will be released and the clapper will return to its former place.

Electric Time Alarm

How to Make a Phonograph Record Cabinet

The core, Fig. 1, consists of six strips of wood beveled so as to form six equal sides. The strips are 3 ft. long and 3 in. wide on the outside bevel and are nailed to three blocks made hexagon, as shown in Fig. 2, from $\frac{7}{8}$-in. material. One block is placed at each end and one in the middle. A $\frac{1}{2}$-in. metal pin is driven in a hole bored in the center of each end block. The bottoms of the pasteboard cases, used to hold the wax records, are either tacked or glued to this hexagon core, as shown in Fig. 3, with their open ends outward.

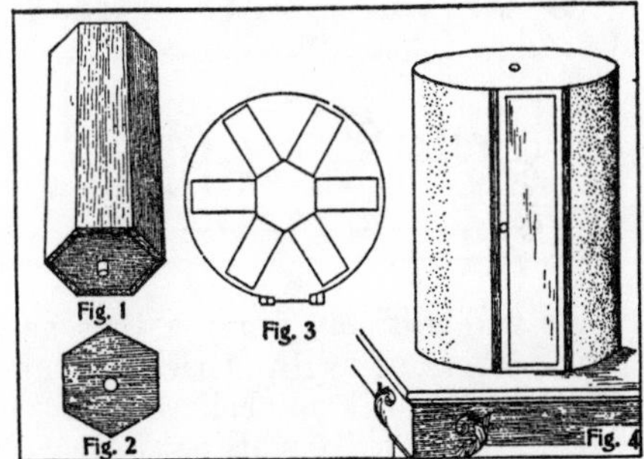

Phonograph Wax Record Case

Two circular pieces are made of such a diameter as will cover the width of the core and the cases attached, and extend about $\frac{1}{2}$ in. each side. A $\frac{1}{2}$-in. hole is bored in the center of these pieces to receive the pins placed in the ends of the core, Fig. 1. These will form the ends of the cabinet, and when placed, one on each end of the core, heavy building paper or sheet metal is tacked around them for a covering, as shown in Fig. 4. A small glass door is made, a little wider than one row of cases, and fitted in one side of the covering. The outside may be painted or decorated in any way to suit the builder.

Experiments with a Mirror

Ask your friend if he can decipher the sign as illustrated in the sketch, Fig. 1, which you pretend to have read over the shop of an Armenian shoemaker.

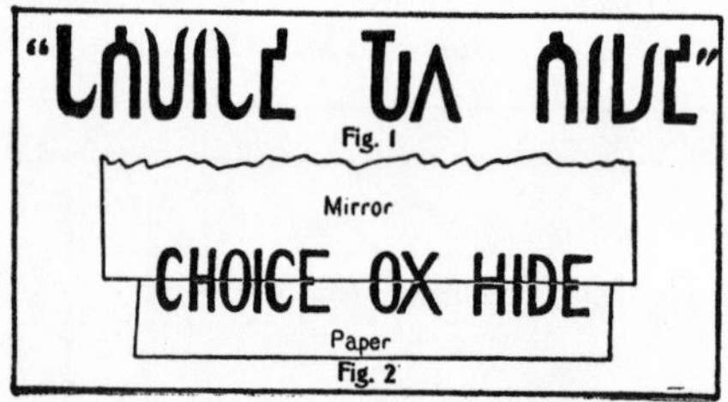

He will probably tell you that he is not conversant with Oriental languages. He will not believe it if you tell him it is written in good English, but place a frameless mirror perpendicularly on the mysterious script, right across the quotation marks, and it will appear as shown in Fig. 2. We understand at once that the reflected image is the faithful copy of the written half.

With the aid of a few books arrange the mirror and the paper as shown in Fig. 3 and ask your friend to write anything he chooses, with the condition that he shall see his hand and read the script in the mirror only. The writer will probably go no farther than the first letter. His hand seems to be struck with paralysis and unable to write anything but zigzags, says Scientific American.

Another experiment may be made by taking an egg shell and trimming it with the scissors so as to reduce it to a half shell. In the hollow bottom roughly draw with your pencil a cross with pointed ends. Bore a hole, about the size of a pea, in the center of the cross. Place yourself so as to face a window, the light falling upon your face, not upon the mirror which you hold in one hand. Close one eye. Place the shell between the other eye and the mirror, at a distance of 2 or 3 in. from either, the concavity facing the mirror as shown in Fig. 4. Through the hole in the shell look at the mirror as if it were some distant object. While you are so doing the concave shell will suddenly assume a strongly convex appearance. To destroy the illusion it becomes necessary either to open both eyes or to withdraw the shell away from the mirror. The nearer the shell to the mirror and the farther the eye from the shell the more readily comes the illusion.

Experimenting with a Mirror

Miniature Electric Lamps

After several years' research there has been produced a miniature electric bulb that is a great improvement and a decided departure from the old kind which used a carbon filament. A metallic filament prepared by a secret chemical process and suspended in the bulb in an S-shape is used instead of the old straight span. The voltage is gauged by the length of the span. The brilliancy of the filament excels anything of its length in any voltage.

Of course, the filament is not made of the precious metal, radium; that simply being the trade name. However, the filament is composed of certain metals from which radium is extracted.

Types of "Radium" Lamps

The advantages of the new bulb are manifold. It gives five times the light on the same voltage and uses one-half of the current consumed by the old carbon filament. One of the disadvantages of the old style bulb was the glass tip, which made a shadow. This has been obviated in the radium bulb by blowing the tip on the side, as shown in the sketch, so as to produce no shadow.

How to Make a Magazine Clamp

This device as shown in the illustration can be used to hold newspapers and magazines while reading. Two pieces of wood are cut as shown, one with a slot to fit over the back of a magazine and the other notched to serve as a clamp. The piece, A, may be slotted wide enough to insert two or three magazines and made long enough to hold several newspapers.

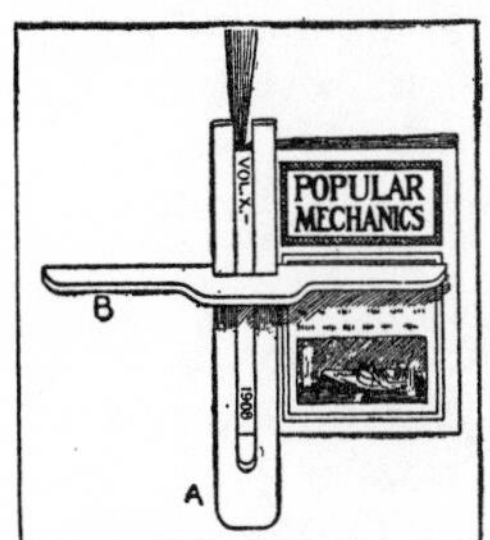

A color resembling pewter may be given to brass by boiling the castings in a cream of tartar solution containing a small amount of chloride of tin.

Drowning a Dog's Bark with Water

The owner of two dogs was very much annoyed by the dogs barking at night. It began to be such a nuisance that the throwing of old shoes and empty bottles did not stop the noise. The only thing that seemed to put a stop to it was water.

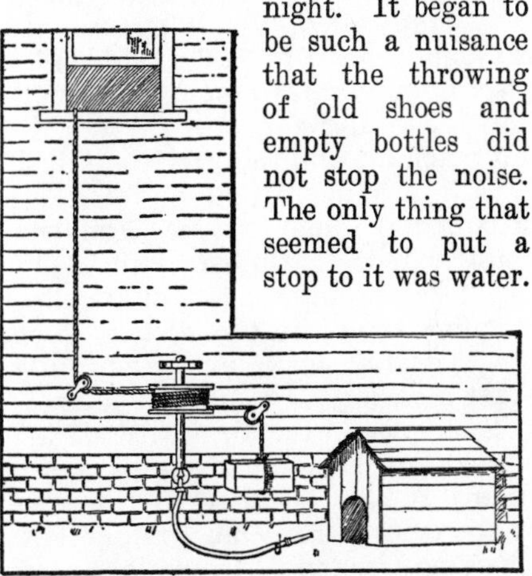

Water Treatment for Dog's Bark

Being on the third floor of the house, and a little too far from the kennel to throw the water effectively, a mechanism was arranged as shown in the sketch.

A faucet for the garden hose was directly below the window. An 8-in. wooden grooved pulley was slipped over an axle which had one end fitted on the handle of the faucet. A rope was extended to the window on the third floor and passed around the pulley several times, thence over an iron pulley fastened to the wall of the house and a weight was attached to its end. By pulling the rope up at the window the large pulley would turn on the water and when released the weight would shut off the flow. The nozzle was fastened so as to direct the stream where it would do the most good.—Contributed by A. S. Pennoyer, Berkeley, Cal.

The average cost of supplying 1,000,000 gal. of water, based on the report of twenty-two cities, is $92. This sum includes operating expenses and interest on bonds.

How to Make a Wondergraph

By F. E. TUCK

An exceedingly interesting machine is the so-called wondergraph. It is easy and cheap to make and will furnish both entertainment and instruction for young and old. It is a drawing machine, and the variety of designs it will produce, all symmetrical and ornamental and some wonderfully c mplicated, is almost without limit. Fig. 1 represents diagrammatically the machine shown in the sketch. This is the easiest to make and gives fully as great a variety of results as any other.

To a piece of wide board or a discarded box bottom, three grooved circular disks are fastened with screws so as to revolve freely about the centers. They may be sawed from pieces of thin board or, better still, three of the plaques so generally used in burnt-wood work may be bought for about 15 cents. Use the largest one for the revolving table T. G is the guide wheel and D the driver with attached handle. Secure a piece of a 36-in. ruler, which can be obtained from any furniture dealer, and nail a small block, about 1 in. thick, to one end and drill a hole through both the ruler and the block, and pivot them by means of a wooden peg to the face of the guide wheel. A fountain pen, or pencil, is placed at P and held securely by rubber bands in a grooved block attached to the ruler. A strip of wood, MN, is fastened to one end of the board. This strip is made just high enough to keep the ruler parallel with the face of the table, and a row of small nails are driven part way into its upper edge. Any one of these nails may be used to hold the other end of the ruler in position, as shown in the sketch. If the wheels are not true, a belt tightener, B, may be attached and held against the belt by a spring or rubber band.

After the apparatus is adjusted so it will run smoothly, fasten a piece of drawing paper to the table with a couple of thumb tacks, adjust the pen so that it rests lightly on the paper and turn the drive wheel. The results will be surprising and delightful. The accompanying designs were made with a very crude combination of pulleys and belts, such as described.

The machine should have a speed that will cause the pen to move over the paper at the same rate as in ordinary writing. The ink should flow freely from the pen as it passes over the paper. A very fine pen may be necessary to prevent the lines from running together.

The dimensions of the wondergraph may vary. The larger designs in the illustration were made on a table, 8 in. in diameter, which was driven by a guide wheel, 6 in. in diameter. The size of the driver has no effect on the form or dimensions of the design, but a change in almost any other part of the machine has a marked effect on the results obtained. If the penholder is made so that it may be fastened at various positions along the ruler, and the guide wheel has holes drilled through it at different distances from the center

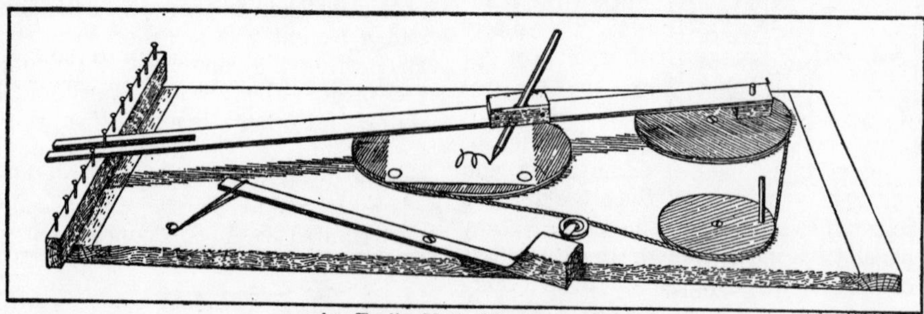

An Easily Made Wondergraph

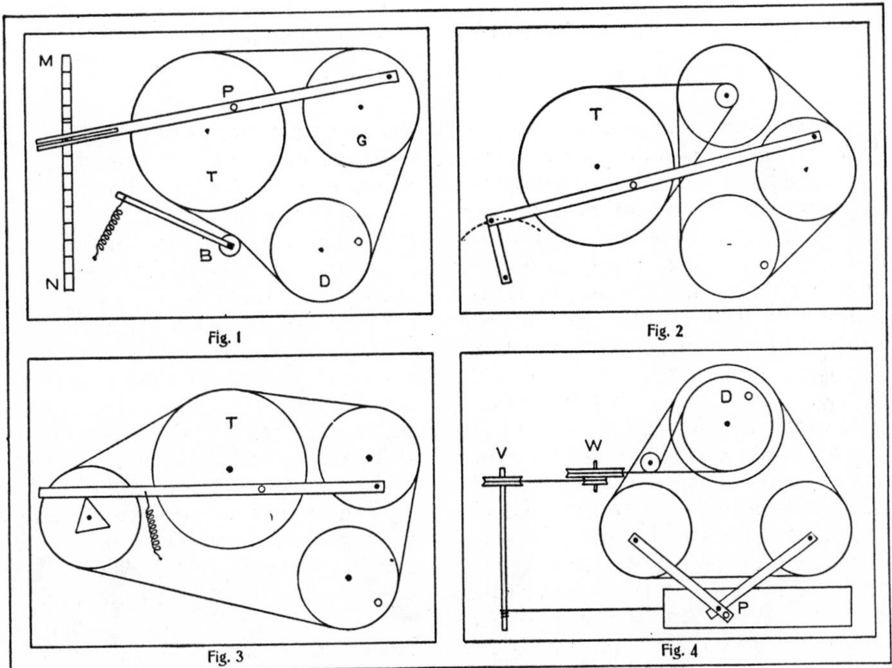

Diagrams Showing Construction of Wondergraphs

to hold the peg attaching the ruler, these two adjustments, together with the one for changing the other end of the ruler by the rows of nails, will make a very great number of combinations possible. Even a slight change will greatly modify a figure or give an entirely new one. Designs may be changed by simply twisting the belt, thus reversing the direction of the table.

If an arm be fastened to the ruler at right angles to it, containing three or four grooves to hold the pen, still different figures will be obtained. A novel effect is made by fastening two pens to this arm at the same time, one filled with red ink and the other with black ink. The designs will be quite dissimilar and may be one traced over the other or one within the other according to the relative position of the pens.

Again change the size of the guide wheel and note the effect. If the diameter of the table is a multiple of that of the guide wheel, a complete figure of few lobes will result as shown by the one design in the lower right-hand corner of the illustration. With a very flexible belt tightener an elliptical guide wheel may be used. The axis may be taken at one of the foci or at the intersection of the axis of the ellipse.

The most complicated adjustment is to mount the table on the face of another disc, table and disc revolving in opposite directions. It will go through a long series of changes without completing any figure and then will repeat itself. The diameters may be made to vary from the fraction of an inch to as large a diameter as the size of the table permits. The designs given here were originally traced on drawing paper 6 in. square.

Remarkable and complex as are the curves produced in this manner, yet they are but the results obtained by combining simultaneously two simple motions as may be shown in the following manner: Hold the table stationary and the pen will trace an oval. But if the guide wheel is secured in a fixed position and the table is revolved a circle will be the result.

So much for the machine shown in

Specimen Scrolls Made on the Wondergraph

Fig. 1. The number of the modifications of this simple contrivance is limited only by the ingenuity of the maker. Fig. 2 speaks for itself. One end of the ruler is fastened in such a way as to have a to-and-fro motion over the arc of a circle and the speed of the table is geared down by the addition of another wheel with a small pulley attached. This will give many new designs. In Fig. 3 the end of the ruler is held by a rubber band against the edge of a thin triangular piece of wood which is attached to the face of the fourth wheel. By substituting other plain figures for the triangle, or outlining them with small finishing nails, many curious modifications such as are shown by the two smallest designs in the illustrations may be obtained. It is necessary, if symmetrical designs are to be made, that the fourth wheel and the guide wheel have the same diameter.

In Fig. 4, V and W are vertical wheels which may be successfully connected with the double horizontal drive wheel if the pulley between the two has a wide flange and is set at the proper angle. A long strip of paper is given a uniform rectilinear motion as the string attached to it is wound around the axle, V. The pen, P, has a motion compounded of two simultaneous motions at right angles to each other given by the two guide wheels. Designs such as shown as a border at the top and bottom of the illustration are obtained in this way. If the vertical wheels are disconnected and the paper fastened in place the well known Lissajou's curves are obtained. These curves may be traced by various methods, but this arrangement is about the simplest of them all. The design in this case will change as the ratio of the diameters of the two guide wheels are changed.

These are only a few of the many adjustments that are possible. Frequently some new device will give a figure which is apparently like one obtained in some other way, yet, if you will watch the way in which the two are commenced and developed into the complete design you will find they are formed quite differently.

The average boy will take delight in making a wondergraph and in inventing the many improvements that are sure to suggest themselves to him. At all events it will not be time thrown away, for, simple as the contrivance is, it will arouse latent energies which may develop along more useful lines in maturer years.

How to Make a 110-Volt Transformer

Secure two magnets from a telephone bell, or a set of magnets wound for 2,000 ohms. Mount them on a bar of brass or steel as shown in Fig. 1. Get an empty cocoa can and clean it good to remove all particles of cocoa and punch five holes in the cover, as shown in Fig. 2. The middle hole is to be used to fasten the cover to the brass bar with a bolt. The other four holes are for the wire terminals. A piece of rubber tubing must be placed over the wire terminals before inserting them in the holes. Fill the can with crude oil, or with any kind of oil except kero-

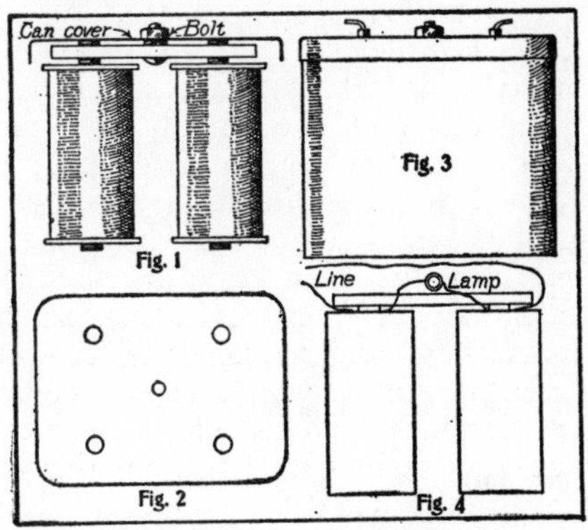

Parts of the Transformer

sene oil, and immerse the magnets in it by fitting the cover on tight (Fig. 3). The connections are made as shown in the diagram, Fig. 5. This device may be used on 110-volt current for electroplating and small battery lamps, provided the magnets are wound with wire no larger than No. 40.—Contributed by C. M. Rubsan, Muskogee, Okla.

Experiment with a Vacuum

Take any kitchen utensil used for frying purposes—an ordinary skillet, or spider, works best—having a smooth

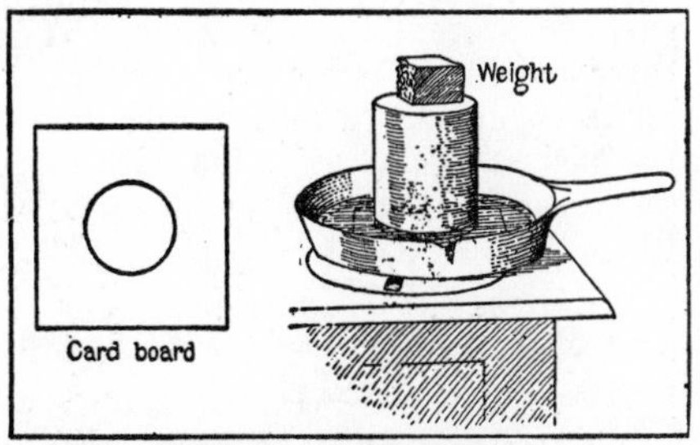

Experimental Apparatus

inner bottom surface, and turn in water to the depth of ½ in. Cut a piece of cardboard circular to fit the bottom of the spider and make a hole in the center 4 in. in diameter. The hole will need to correspond to the size of the can used. It should be 1 in. less in diameter than that of the can. Place this cardboard in the bottom of the spider under the water. A 2-qt. syrup can or pail renders the best demonstration, although good results may be obtained from the use of an ordinary tomato can. The edge of the can must have no indentations, so it will fit perfectly tight all around on the cardboard. Place the can bottom side up and evenly over the hole in the cardboard. Put a sufficient weight on the can to prevent it moving on the cardboard, but not too heavy, say, 1 lb.

Place the spider with its adjusted contents upon a heated stove. Soon the inverted can will begin to agitate. When this agitation finally ceases remove the spider from the stove, being careful not to move the can, and if the quickest results are desired, apply snow, ice or cold water to the surface of the can until the sides begin to flatten.

The spider with its entire contents

may now be lifted by taking hold of the can. When the vacuum is complete the sides of the can will suddenly collapse, and sometimes, with a considerable report, jump from the spider.

The cause of the foregoing phenomenon is that the circular hole in the cardboard admits direct heat from the surface of the spider. This heat causes the air in the can to expand, which is allowed to escape by agitation, the water and the cardboard acting as a valve to prevent its re-entrance. When the enclosed air is expelled by the heat and a vacuum is formed by the cooling, the above results are obtained as described.—Contributed by N. J. McLean.

The Making of Freak Photographs

An experiment that is interesting and one that can be varied at the pleasure of the operator, is the taking of his own picture. The effect secured, as shown in the accompanying sketch, reproduced in pen and ink from a photograph, is that made by the photographer himself. At first it seems impossible to secure such a picture, but when told that a mirror was used the process is then known to be a simple one.

The mirror is set in such a way as to allow the camera and operator, when standing directly in front of it, to be

Photographing the Photographer

in a rather strong light. The camera is focused, shutter set and plate holder made ready. The focusing cloth is thrown over your head, the position taken as shown, and the exposure made by the pressure of the teeth on the bulb while held between them.

Hand Car Made of Pipe and Fittings

Although apparently complicated, the construction of the miniature hand car shown in the accompanying illus-

Boy's Hand Car

tration is very simple. With a few exceptions all the parts are short lengths of pipe and common tees, elbows and nipples.

The wheels were manufactured for use on a baby carriage. The sprocket wheel and chain were taken from a discarded bicycle, which was also drawn upon for the cork handle used on the steering lever. The floor is made of 1-in. white pine, 14 in. wide and 48 in. long, to which are bolted ordinary flanges to hold the framing and the propelling and steering apparatus together. The axles were made from $\frac{3}{8}$-in. shafting. The fifth wheel consists of two small flanges working on the face surfaces. These flanges and the auxiliary steering rod are connected to the axles by means of holes stamped in the piece of sheet iron which encases the axle. The sheet iron was first properly stamped and then bent around the axle. The levers for propelling and steering the car work in fulcrums made for use in lever valves. The turned wooden handles by which these levers are operated were inserted through holes drilled in the connecting tees. The working joint for the steering and hand levers consists of a $\frac{1}{2}$ by $\frac{3}{8}$ by $\frac{3}{8}$-in. tee, a $\frac{1}{2}$ by $\frac{3}{8}$-in. cross and a piece of rod threaded on both ends and screwed into the tee. The cross is reamed and, with the rod, forms a bearing.

The operation of this little hand car is very similar in principle to that of the ordinary tricycle, says Domestic Engineering. The machine can be propelled as fast as a boy can run. It responds readily to the slightest movement of the steering lever.

to the front rail and also connected to the back post by a bearer, 4 in. deep by $1\frac{1}{2}$ in. thick. This bearer is tenoned to the back post.

Fig. 3 shows a sectional view of the bearer joint to front leg, and also the half-round seat battens resting on the bearer, also showing them with their edges planed. It is advisable to have a space between the edges of each batten, say about $\frac{1}{8}$ in., to allow rainwater to drain. The ends of the seat battens are pared away to fit the transverse rails neatly as shown in Fig. 2. The struts for the post range in diameter from $1\frac{1}{2}$ in. to 2 in. The ends of the struts are pared to fit the posts and

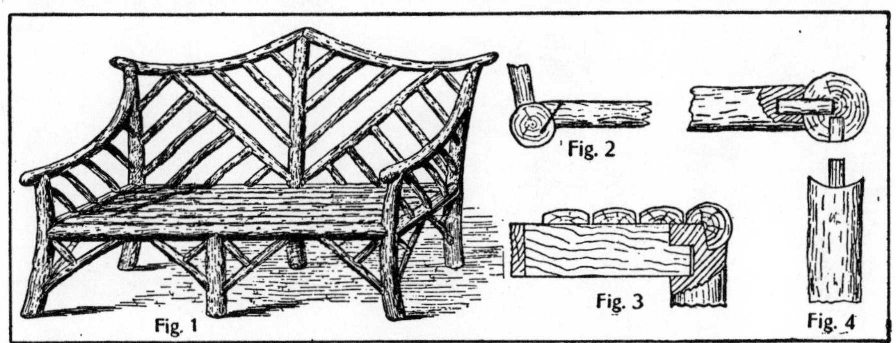

Rustic Seat and Details of Construction

How to Make a Rustic Seat

The rustic settee illustrated in Fig. 1 may be made 6 ft. long, which will accommodate four average-sized persons. It is not advisable to exceed this length, as then it would look out of proportion, says the Wood-Worker. Select the material for the posts, and for preference branches that are slightly curved, as shown in the sketch. The front posts are about $3\frac{1}{2}$ in. in diameter by 2 ft. 4 in. long. The back posts are 3 ft. 4 in. high, while the center post is 3 ft. 8 in. in height. The longitudinal and transverse rails are about 3 in. in diameter and their ends are pared away to fit the post to which they are connected by 1-in. diameter dowels. This method is shown in Fig. 4. The dowel holes are bored at a distance of 1 ft. $2\frac{1}{2}$ in, up from the lower ends of posts. The front center leg is partially halved

rails, and are then secured with two or three brads at each end.

Select curved pieces, about $2\frac{1}{2}$ in. in diameter, for the arm rests and back rails; while the diagonally placed filling may be about 2 in. in diameter. Start with the shortest lengths, cutting them longer than required, as the paring necessary to fit them to the rails and posts shortens them a little. Brad them in position as they are fitted, and try to arrange them at regular intervals.

Motorists that suffer with cold hands while driving their cars may have relief by using a steering wheel that is provided with electric heat. An English invention describes a steering wheel with a core that carries two electrically heated coils insulated one from the other and from the outer rim.

Homemade Workbench

By C. E. McKINNEY, Jr.

The first appliance necessary for the boy's workshop is a workbench. The average boy that desires to construct his own apparatus as much as possible can make the bench as described herein. Four pieces of 2 by 4-in. pine are cut 23 in. long for the legs, and a tenon made on each end of them, ½ in. thick, 3½ in. wide and 1½ in. long, as shown at A and B, Fig. 1. The crosspieces at the top and bottom of the legs are made from the same material and cut 20 in. long. A mortise is made 1¼ in. from each end of these pieces and in the narrow edge of them, as shown at C and D, Fig. 1. The corners are then cut sloping from the edge of the leg out and to the middle of the piece, as shown. When each pair of legs are fitted to a pair of crosspieces they will form the two supports for the bench. These supports are held together and braced with two braces or connecting pieces of 2 by 4-in. pine, 24 in. long. The joints are made between the ends of these pieces and the legs by boring a hole through each leg and into the center of each end of the braces to a depth of 4 in., as shown at J, Fig. 2. On the back side of the braces bore holes, intersecting the other holes, for a place to insert the nut of a bolt, as shown at HH. Four ⅜ by 6-in. bolts are placed in the holes bored, and the joints are drawn together as shown at J. The ends of the two braces must be sawed off perfectly square to make the supports stand up straight.

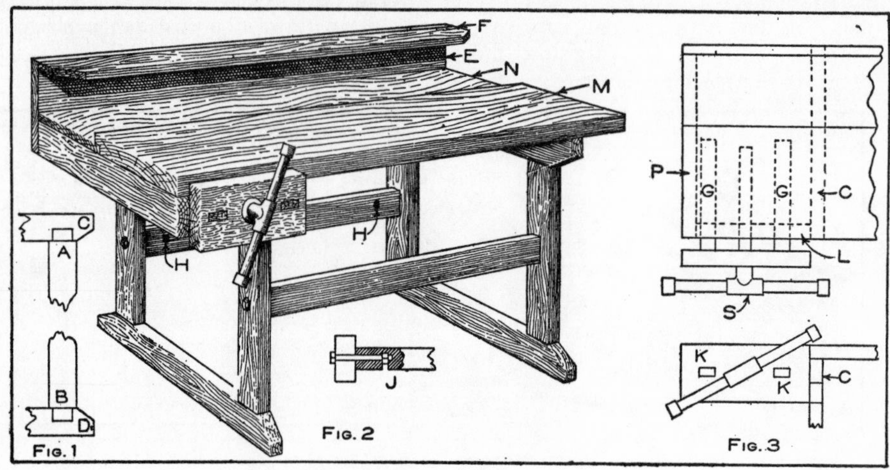

Details of Construction of Homemade Workbench

In making this part of the bench be sure to have the joints fit closely and to draw the bolts up tight on the stretchers. There is nothing quite so annoying as to have the bench support sway while work is being done on its top. It would be well to add a cross brace on the back side to prevent any rocking while planing boards, if the bench is to be used for large work.

The main top board M, Fig. 2, may be either made from one piece of 2 by 12-in. plank, 3½ ft. long, or made up of 14 strips of maple, ⅞ in. thick by 2 in. wide and 3½ ft. long, set on edge, each strip glued and screwed to its neighbor. When building up a top like this be careful to put the strips together with the grain running in the same direction so the top may be planed smooth. The back board N is the same length as the main top board M, 8½ in. wide and only ⅞ in. thick, which is fitted into a ½-in. rabbet in the back of the board M. These boards form the top of the bench, and are fastened to the top pieces of the supports with long screws. The board E is 10 in. wide and nailed to the back of the bench. On top of this board and at right angles with it is fastened a 2½-in. board, F. These two boards are ⅞ in. thick and 3½ ft. long. Holes are bored or notches are cut in the projecting board, F, to hold tools.

Details of the vise are shown in Fig. 3, which is composed of a 2 by 6-in. block 12 in. long, into which is fastened an iron bench screw, S. Two guide rails, GG, ⅞ by 1½ in. and 20 in. long, are fastened into mortises of the block as shown at KK, and they slide in corresponding mortises in a piece of 2 by 4-in. pine bolted to the under side of the main top board as shown at L. The bench screw nut is fastened in the 2 by 4-in. piece, L, between the two mortised holes. This piece, L, is securely nailed to one of the top cross pieces, C, of the supports and to a piece of 2 by 4-in. pine, P, that is bolted to the under sides of the top boards at the end of the bench. The bolts and the bench screw can be purchased from any hardware store for less than one dollar.

Forming Coils to Make Flexible Wire Connections

When connections are made to bells and batteries with small copper wires covered with cotton or silk, it is necessary to have a coil in a short piece of the line to make it flexible. A good way to do this is to provide a short rod about $\frac{3}{16}$ in. in diameter cut with a slit in one end to hold the wire and a loop made on the other end to turn with the fingers. The end of the wire is

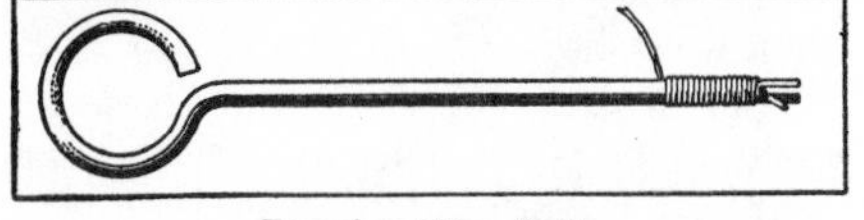

Forming Wire Coils

placed in the slit and the coil made around the rod by turning with the loop end.

Photographing the North Star

The earth revolving as upon an axis is inclined in such a position that it points toward the North star. To an observer in the northern hemisphere the effect is the same as if the heavens

Photograph of the North Star

revolved with the North star as a center. A plate exposed in a camera which is pointed toward that part of the sky on a clear night records that effect in a striking manner. The accompanying illustration is from a photograph taken with an exposure of about three hours, and the trace of the stars shown on the plate by a series of concentric circles are due to the rotation of the earth.

The bright arc of the circle nearest the center is the path of the North star. The other arcs are the impressions left by neighboring stars, and it will be noticed that their brightness varies with their relative brilliancy. Many are so faint as to be scarcely distinguished, and, of course, telescopic power would reveal myriads of heavenly bodies which leave no trace on a plate in an ordinary camera. The North or pole star is commonly considered at a point directly out from the axis of the earth, but the photograph shows that it is not so located. The variation is known astronomically to be 1¼ deg. There is a slight irregularity in the position of the earth's axis, but the changes are so slow as to be noticed only by the lapse of a thousand years. Five thousand years ago the pole star was Draconis, and in eighteen thousand years it will be Lyrae. We have direct evidence of the change of the earth's axis in one of the Egyptian pyramids where an aperture marked the position of the pole star in ancient times, and from this it is now deviated considerable.

This experiment is within the reach of everyone owning a camera. The photograph shown was taken by an ordinary instrument, using a standard plate of common speed. The largest stop was used and the only requirement beyond this is to adjust the camera in a position at the proper inclination and to make the exposure for as long as desired. On long winter nights the exposure may be extended to 12 hours, in which event the curves would be lengthened to full half-circles.

The North star is one of the easiest to locate in the entire heavens. The constellation known as the Great Dipper is near by, and the two stars that mark the corners of the dipper on the extremity farthest from the handle lie in a line that passes across the North star. These two stars in the Great Dipper are called the pointers. The North Star is of considerable brilliancy, though by no means the brightest in that part of the heavens.—Contributed by C. S. B.

How to Relight a Match

A match may be a small thing on which to practice economy and yet a great many times one wishes to relight a match either for economy or necessity. The usual method is to place the burnt portion of the match in the flame to be relighted as shown in Fig. 1. It is very hard to relight the charred end and usually burnt fingers are the result of pushing the match farther in the flame. Hold the burnt end in the fingers and place the other end in the flame as shown in Fig. 2. A light will be secured quickly and the flame will only follow the stick to the old burnt portion.

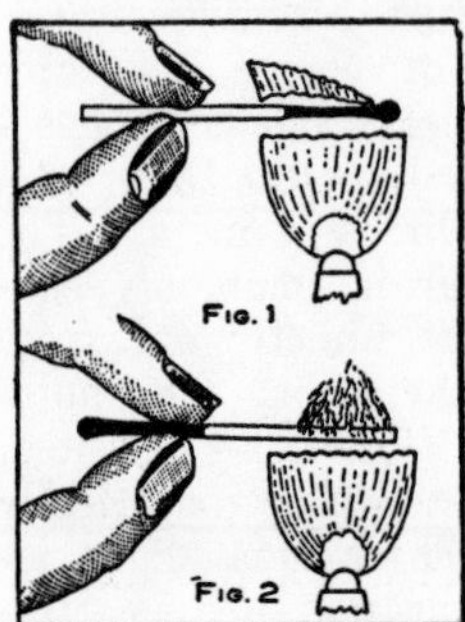

Home-Made Hand Drill

In the old kitchen tool box I found a rusty egg beater of the type shown in Fig. 1. A shoemaker friend donated a pegging awl, Fig. 2, discarded by him due to a broken handle. With these two pieces of apparatus I made a hand drill for light work in wood or metal. By referring to Fig. 3 the chuck, A, with stem, B, were taken from the awl. The long wire beater was taken from the beater frame and a wire nail, C, soldered to the frame, D, in the place of the wire. The flat arms were cut off and shaped as shown by E. The hole in the small gear, G, was drilled out and a tube, F, fitted and soldered to both the gear and the arms E. This tube, with the gear and arms, was slipped over the nail, C, then a washer and, after cutting to the proper length the nail was riveted to make a loose yet neat fit for the small gear. The hand drill was then completed by soldering the stem, B, of the chuck to the ends of the flat arms E. Drills were made by breaking off sewing-machine needles above the eye as

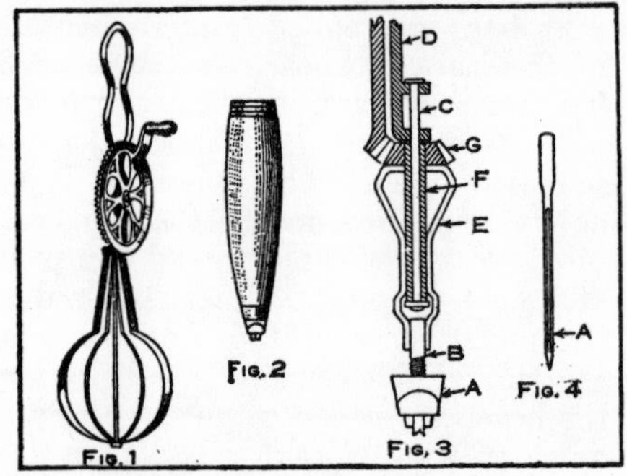

Details of Hand Drill Construction

shown in Fig. 4 at A, and the end ground to a drill point.—Contributed by R. B. J., Shippensburg, Pa.

How to Make a Stationary Windmill

A windmill that can be made stationary and will run regardless of the direction of the wind is here illustrated. Mills of this kind can be built of larger size and in some localities have been used for pumping water.

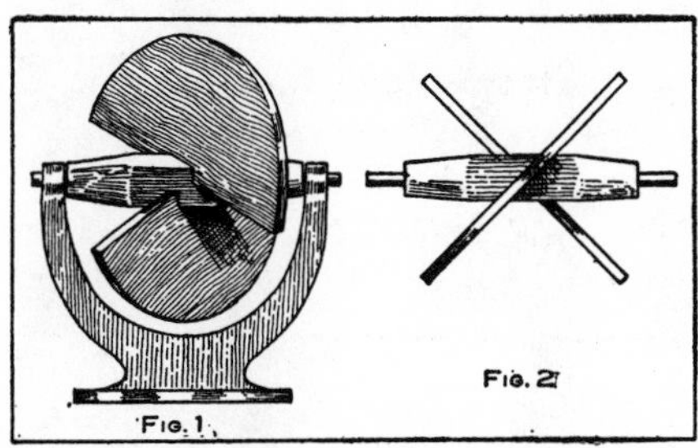

Runs in Any Wind

Two semi-circular surfaces are secured to the axle at right angles to each other and at 45 deg. angle with that of the axle as shown in Fig. 2. This axle and wings are mounted in bearings on a solid or stationary stand or frame. By mounting a pulley on the axle with the wings it can be used to run toy machinery.

Electric Anaesthesia

It is a well known fact that magnetism is used to demagnetize a watch, and that frost is drawn out of a frozen member of the body by the application of snow. Heat is also drawn out of a burned hand by holding it close to the fire, then gradually drawing it away. The following experiment will show how a comparatively feeble electric current can undo the work of a strong one.

I once tried to electrocute a rat which was caught in a wire basket trap and accidentally discovered a painless method. I say painless, because the rodent does not object to a second or third experiment after recovering, and is apparently rigid and without feeling while under its influence.

To those who would like to try the experiment I will say that my outfit consisted of an induction coil with a ⅜-in. iron core about 3 in. long. The primary coil was wound with four layers of No. 20 wire and the secondary contains 4 oz. No. 32 wire, and used on one cell of bichromate of potash plunge battery. The proper amount of current used can be determined by giving the rodent as much as a healthy man would care to take. Fasten one secondary electrode to the trap containing the rat and with a wire nail fastened to the other terminal, hold the vibrator of the coil with your finger and let the rat bite on the nail and while doing so release the vibrator. In three seconds the rat will be as rigid as if dead and the wires can be removed.

Now connect your wires to the primary binding-posts of the coil and wind the end of one of them around the rat's tail and start the vibrator. Touch the other terminal to the rat's ear and nose. In a few minutes he will be as lively as ever.—Contributed by Chas. Haeusser, Albany, N. Y.

A Simple Battery Rheostat

A spring from an old shade roller is mounted on a board 4 in. wide, 9 in. long and ⅜ in. thick. A binding-post is fastened to this board at each end, to which is attached the ends of the spring, as shown in Fig. 1. The temper of a small portion of each end of the

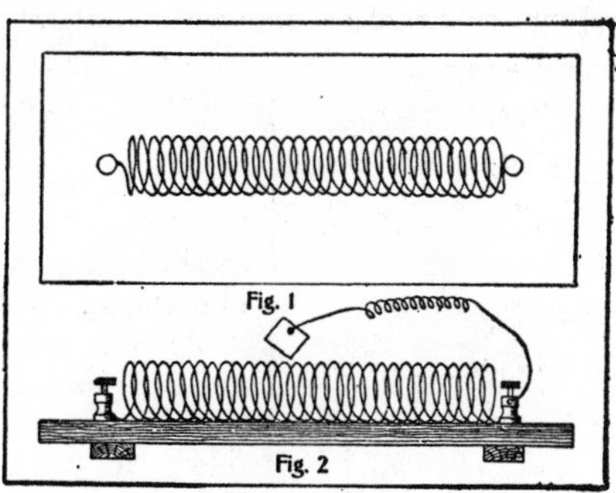

Battery Rheostat

spring will need to be drawn. This can be accomplished by heating over an alcohol lamp or in a fire and allowing it to cool slowly. The ends are then shaped to fit the binding-posts. A wire is connected to one of the binding-posts and a small square piece of copper is attached to the other end of the wire, as shown in Fig. 2. When this device is placed in a circuit the current can be regulated by sliding the small square copper piece along the spring.—Contributed by H. D. Harkins, St. Louis, Mo.

A Frame for Drying Films

No doubt many amateur photographers are troubled about drying films and to keep them from curling. The problem may be solved in the following way: Make a rectangular frame out of pine wood, $\frac{1}{4}$ by $\frac{1}{2}$ in., as shown in the sketch. It is made a little wider and a little shorter than the film to be dried. This will allow the end of the film to be turned over at each end of the frame and fastened with push pins. Do not stretch the film when putting it on the frame as it shrinks in drying. The film will dry quicker and will be flat when dried by using this frame.—Contributed by Elmer H. Flehr, Ironton, Ohio.

A Home-Made Novelty Clock

This clock that is shown in the accompanying engraving is made in scroll work, the cathedral and towers being of white maple, the base is of walnut with mahogany trimmings, all finished in their natural colors. It has 11 bells in the two towers at the sides and 13 miniature electric lamps of different colors on two electric circuits. The clock is operated by a small motor receiving its power from dry cell batteries. This motor turns a brass cylinder over which runs a continuous roll of perforated paper similar to that used on a pianola. A series of metal fingers, connected by wires to the bells, press lightly on this brass roll and are insulated from the roll by the perforated paper passing between. When a perforation is reached a finger will make a contact with the brass roll for an instant which makes a circuit with the magnet of an electric hammer in its respective bell or forms the circuit which lights the electric bulbs as the case may be.

At each hour and half hour as the clock strikes, the motor is started automatically and the chimes sound out the tunes while the colored lights are turned on and off; two small doors in the cathedral open and a small figure comes out while the chimes are playing, then returns and the doors are closed.—Contributed by C. V. Brokenicky, Blue Rapids, Kansas.

Fourth-of-July Catapult

Among the numerous exciting amusements in which boys may participate during the Fourth-of-July celebration is to make a cannon that will shoot life-sized dummies dressed in old clothes. Building the cannon, as described in the following, makes it safe to fire and not dangerous to others, provided care is taken to place it at an angle of 45 deg. and not to fire when anyone is within its range. The powder charge is in the safest form possible, as it is fired with a blow from a hammer instead of lighting a fuse. If the cannon is made according to directions, there cannot possibly be any explosion.

The materials used in the construction of the catapult may be found in almost any junk pile, and the only work required, outside of what can be done at home, is to have a few threads cut on the pieces of pipe. The fittings can be procured ready to attach, except for drilling a hole for the firing pin.

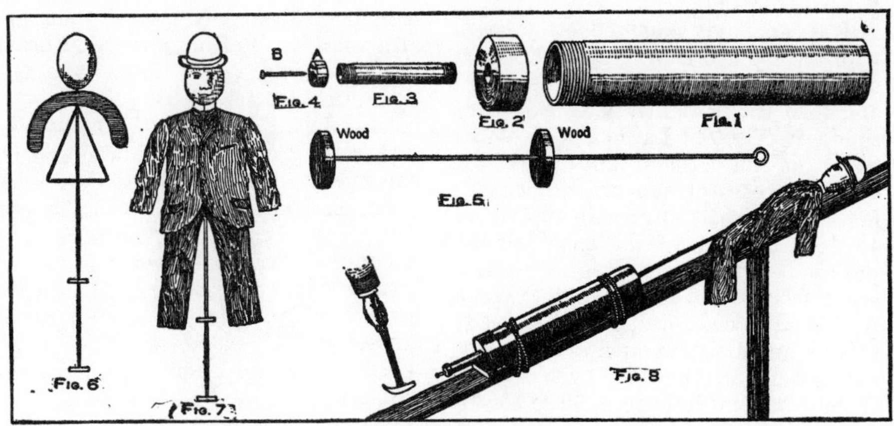

Homemade Cannon Which will Hurl a Life-Size Dummy 100 Ft. through the Air

Secure a piece of common gas pipe, 4 to 6 in. in diameter, the length being from 18 to 24 in. Old pipe may be used if it is straight. Have a machinist cut threads on the outside of one end, as shown in Fig. 1, and fit an iron cap, Fig. 2, tightly on the threaded end of the pipe. The cap is drilled and tapped in the center for a 1-in. pipe. Thread both ends of a 1-in. pipe that is 4 in. long, Fig. 3, and turn one end securely into the threaded hole of the cap. This pipe should project 1/4 in. inside of the cap. Fit a cap, Fig. 4, loosely on the other end of the 1-in. pipe. A hole is drilled into the center of this small cap just large enough to receive a 6-penny wire nail, B, Fig. 4.

This completes the making of the cannon and the next step is to construct a dummy which can be dressed in old clothes. Cut out two round blocks of wood from hard pine or oak that is about 3 in. thick, as shown in Fig. 5. The diameter of these blocks should be about 1/8 in. less than the hole in the cannon, so they will slide easily. In the center of each block bore a 1/4-in. hole. Secure an iron rod, about 4 ft. long, and make a ring at one end and thread 4 in. of the other. Slip one of the circular blocks on the rod and move it up toward the ring about 14 in. Turn a nut on the threads, stopping it about 3½ in. from the end of the rod. Slip the other circular piece of wood on the rod and up against the nut, and turn on another nut to hold the wooden block firmly in its place at the end of the rod. If the rod is flattened at the place where the upper block is located, it will hold tight. These are shown in Fig. 5. Take some iron wire about $\frac{1}{8}$ in. in diameter and make a loop at the top of the rod for the head. Wire this loop to the ring made in the rod and make the head about this loop by using canvas or gunny cloth sewed up forming a bag into which is stuffed either excelsior, paper or hay. The arms are made by lashing with fine wire or strong hemp, a piece of wood 1 in. square and 20 in. long, or one cut in the shape shown in Fig. 6, to the rod. Place the wood arms close to the bottom of the head. Make a triangle of wire and fasten it and the cross arm securely to the top of the rod to keep them from slipping down. A false face, or one painted on white cloth, can be sewed on the stuffed bag. An old coat and trousers are put on the frame to complete the dummy. If the clothing is not too heavy and of white material so much the better. To greatly increase the spectacular flight through the air, a number of different colored streamers, 6 or 8 in. wide and several feet in length made from bunting, can be attached about the waist of the dummy. The complete dummy should not weigh more than 6 lb.

The cannon is mounted on a board with the cap end resting against a cleat which is securely nailed to the board and then bound tightly with a rope as shown in Fig. 8. Lay one end of the board on the ground and place the other on boxes or supports sufficiently high to incline it at an angle of about 45 deg. Enough of the board should project beyond the end of the cannon on which to lay the dummy. When completed as described, it is then ready to load and fire. Clear away everyone in front and on each side of the cannon, as the dummy will fly from 50 to 100 ft. and no one must be in range of its flight. This is important, as the rod of the frame holding the clothes will penetrate a board at short range. An ordinary shot gun cartridge of the paper shell type is used for the charge and it must be loaded with powder only. Coarse black powder is the best, but any size will do. When loading the rod with the wooden blocks, on which the dummy is attached, do not place the end block against the breech end of the cannon, leave about 2 or 3 in. between the end of the cannon and the block. Insert the cartridge in the 1-in. pipe. The cartridge should fit the pipe snug, which it will do if the proper size is secured. Screw on the firing-cap, insert the wire nail firing-pin until it rests against the firing-cap of the cartridge. If the range is clear the firing may be done by giving the nail a sharp rap with a hammer. A loud report will follow with a cloud of smoke and the dummy will be seen flying through the air, the arms, legs and streamers fluttering, which presents a most realistic and life-like apearance. The firing may be repeated any number of times in the same manner.

How to Make a Miniature Volcano

A toy volcano that will send forth flames and ashes with lava streaming down its sides in real volcanic action can be made by any boy without any more danger than firing an ordinary fire-cracker. A mound of sand or earth is built up about 1 ft. high in the shape of a volcano. Roll up a piece of heavy paper, making a tube 5 in. long and $1\frac{1}{2}$ in. in diameter. This tube of paper is placed in the top of the mound by first setting it upon a flat sheet of paper and building up the sand or

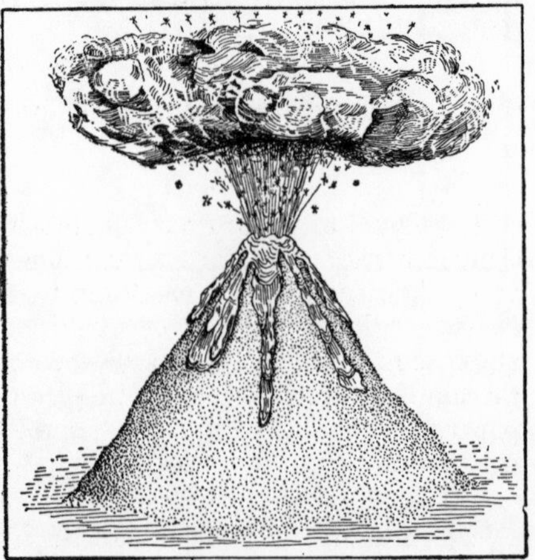

Volcano in Action

earth about the sides until it is all covered excepting the top opening. This is to keep all dampness away from the mixture to be placed within.

A fuse from a fire-cracker, or one made by winding some powder in tissue paper, is placed in the paper tube of the volcano with one end extending over the edge. Get some potash from a drug store and be sure to state the purpose for which it is wanted, as there are numerous kinds of potash that will not be suitable. An equal amount of sugar is mixed with the potash and placed in the paper tube. On top of this put a layer of pure potash and on this pour some gun powder. This completes the volcano and it only remains for the fuse to be lighted and action will begin with an explosion which sends fire, smoke and sparks upward. Flames will follow and the lava pours down the sides of the mound.

Wire Loop Connections for Battery Binding-Posts

The trouble with battery binding-post connections can be avoided by winding the bare end of the connecting wire around the binding-post screw and then back around its extending length as shown in the sketch. Always screw down permanent connections with pliers.

Melting Metal in the Flame of a Match

The flame of an ordinary match has a much higher temperature than is generally known and will melt cast-iron or steel filings. Try it by striking a match and sprinkle the filings through the flame. Sputtering sparks like gunpowder will be the result of the melting metal.

The squirrel slaughter of Russia amounts to 25,000,000 per year.

Landscape Drawing Made Easy

With this device anyone, no matter how little his artistic ability may be, can draw accurately and quickly any little bit of scenery or other subject and get everything in the true perspective and in the correct proportion.

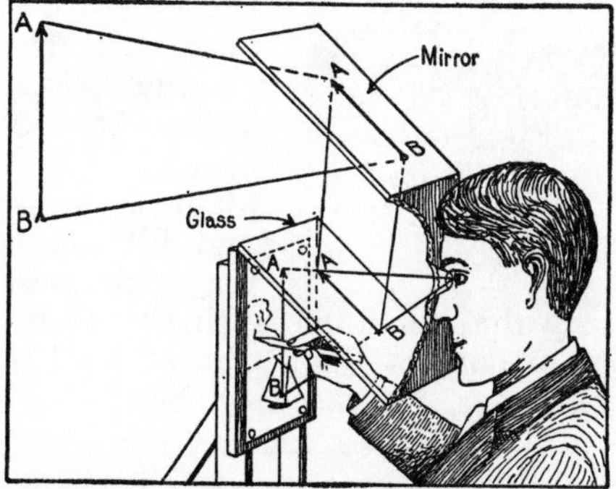

Drawing with the Aid of Reflecting Glasses

No lens is required for making this camera—just a plain mirror set at an angle of 45 deg., with a piece of ordinary glass underneath, a screen with a peek hole and a board for holding the drawing paper. The different parts may be fastened together by means of a box frame, or may be hinged together to allow folding up when carrying and a good tripod of heavy design should be used for supporting it. In order to get the best results the screen should be blackened on the inside and the eyepiece should be blackened on the side next to the eye. A piece of black cardboard placed over the end of the eyepiece and perforated with a pin makes an excellent peek hole.

In operation the rays of light coming from any given object, such as the arrow AB, strike the inclined mirror and are reflected downward. On striking the inclined glass a portion of the light is again reflected and the rays entering the eye of the operator produce the virtual image on the paper as shown. The general outlines may be sketched in quickly, leaving the details to be worked up later. This arrangement may be used for interior work when the illumination is good.

Irrigating with Tomato Cans

The following is an easy and effective way to start plants in dry weather: Sink an ordinary tomato can, with a ⅛-in. hole ½ in. from the bottom, in the ground so that the hole will be near the roots of the plant. Tamp the dirt around both plant and can, and fill the latter with water.

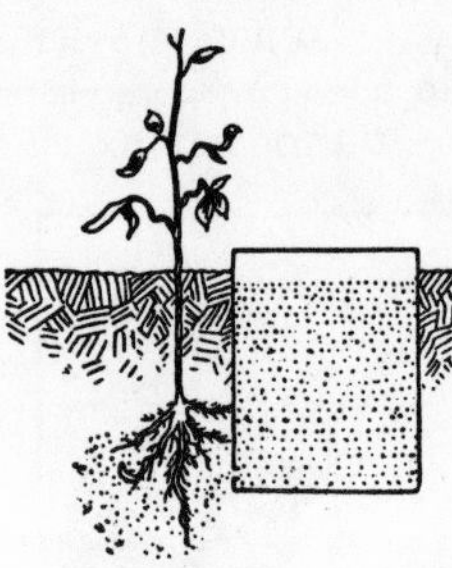

Keep the can filled until the plant is out of danger.—Contributed by L. L. Schweiger, Kansas City, Mo.

Fountain for an Ordinary Pen

Take two steel pens, not the straight kind, and place them together, one above the other, in the penholder.

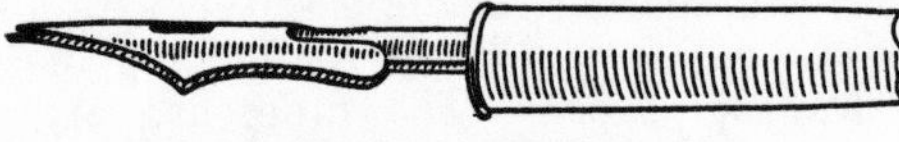

Two Pens in Holder

With one dip of ink 60 or 70 words may be written. This saves time and the arrangement also prevents the ink from dropping off the pen.—Contributed by L. M. Lytle, Kerrmoor, Pa.

Homemade Mousetrap

Bore a 1-in. hole, about 2 in. deep, in a block of wood and drive a small nail with a sharp point at an angle so it will project into the hole about half way between the top and bottom, and in the center of the hole, as shown.

[Hole in Wood Block

File the end very sharp and bend it down so that when the mouse pushes its head past it in trying to get the bait at the bottom of the hole, the sharp point will catch it when it tries to back out. Almost anyone can make this trap in a short time, and it will catch the mice as surely as a more elaborate trap.

Clear Wax Impressions from Seals

A die must be slightly damp to make clear impressions on sealing wax and to keep it from sticking to the wax. A very handy way to moisten the die is to use a pad made by tacking two pieces of blotting paper and one of

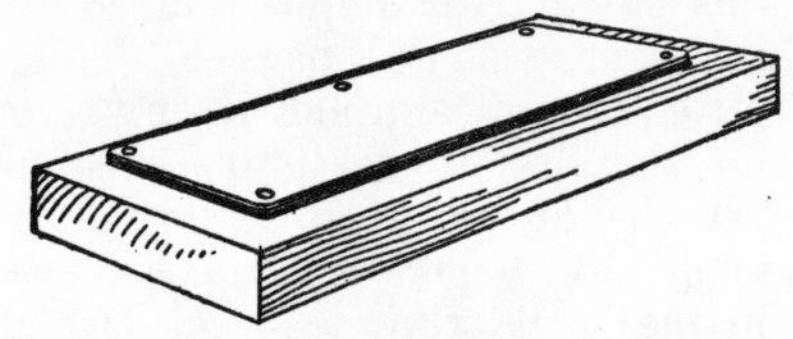

Blotter Pad

cloth to a wooden block of suitable size, and saturate the blotters with water before using. Stamp the die on the pad and then on the hot wax. The result will be a clear, readable impression.—Contributed by Fred Schumacher, Brooklyn, N. Y.

A Window Stick

Although the windows in factories and houses are usually provided with weights, yet the stick shown in the sketch will be found very handy in case all of the windows are not so equipped. It is made of a piece of pine wood long

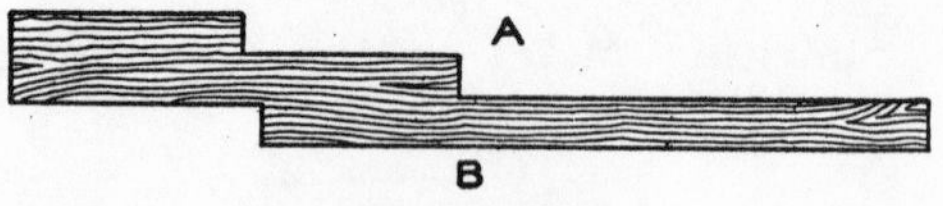

Notches in Stick

enough to hold the lower sash at a height even with the bottom of the upper, and about 1½ or 2 in. wide. Notches may be cut in the stick as shown, each being wide enough to firmly hold the sash. Thus, with the stick illustrated, the sash may be held at three different heights on the side A, and at still another on the side B.—Contributed by Katharine D. Morse, Syracuse, N. Y.

How to Make a Canoe

A practical and serviceable canoe, one that is inexpensive, can be built by any boy, who can wield hammer and saw, by closely following the instructions and drawings, given in this article.

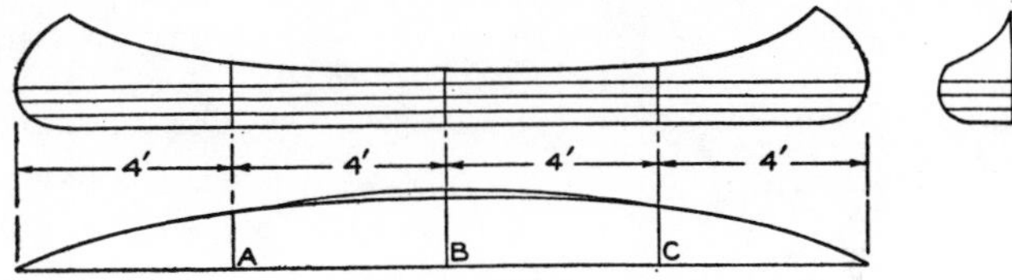

It is well to study these carefully before beginning the actual work. Thus an understanding will be gained of how the parts fit together, and of the way to proceed with the work.

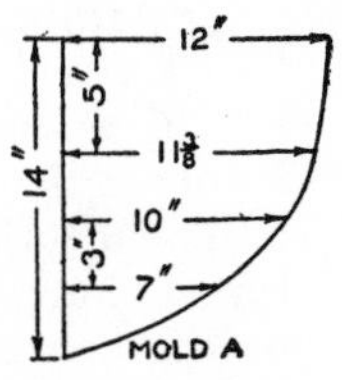

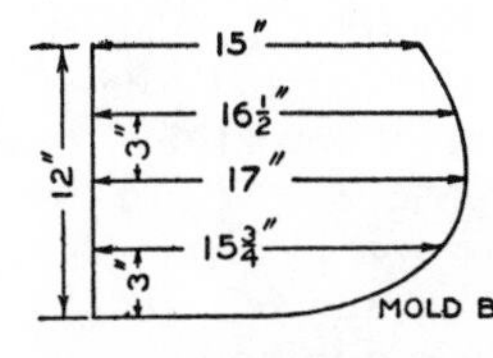

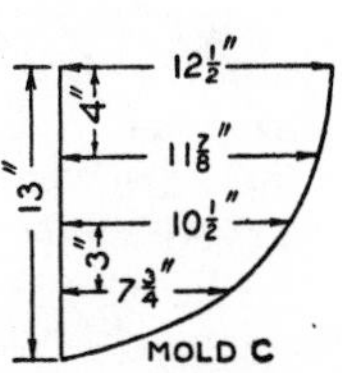

Fig. 1

Canoe and Molds Details

Dimensioned drawings of the canoe and molds are contained in Fig. 1. The boat is built on a temporary base, A, Fig. 2, which is a board, 14 ft. 1 in. long, 3 in. wide and 1½ in. thick. This base is fastened to the trestles and divided into four sections, the sections on each side of the center being 4 ft. long.

The next thing to be considered are the molds (Fig. 3). These are made of 1-in. material. Scrap pieces may be found that can be used for these molds. The dimensions given in Fig. 1 are for one-half of each form as shown in Fig. 3, under their respective letters. The molds are then temporarily attached to the base on the division lines.

Proceed to make the curved ends as shown in Fig. 4. Two pieces of straight-grained green elm, 32 in. long, 1¾ in. wide and 1 in. thick, will be required. The elm can be obtained from a carriage or blacksmith's shop. The pieces are bent by wrapping a piece of wire around the upper end and baseboard. The joint between the curved piece and the base is temporary. Place a stick between the wires and twist them until the required shape is secured. If the wood does not bend readily, soak it in boiling water. The vertical height and the horizontal length of this bend are shown in Fig. 4. The twisted wire will give the right curve and hold the wood in shape until it is dry.

The gunwales are the long pieces B, Fig. 2, at the top of the canoe. These are made of strips of ash, 15 ft. long, 1 in. wide and 1 in. thick. Fasten them temporarily to the molds, taking care to have them snugly fit the notches

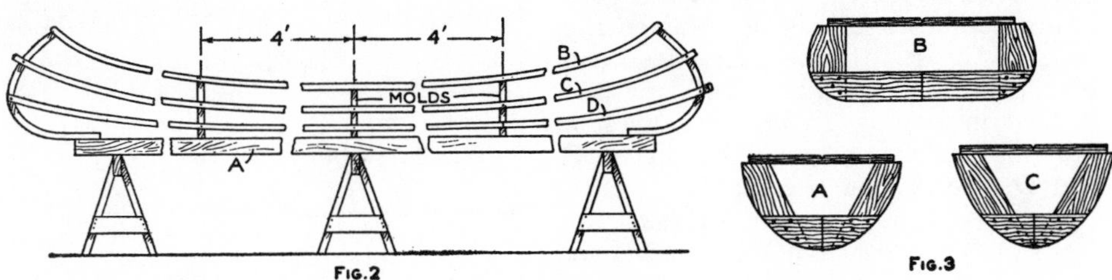

Shaping the Canoe

shown. The ends fit over the outside of the stem and stern pieces and are cut to form a sharp point, as shown in Fig. 5. The ends of the gunwales are fastened permanently to the upper ends of the bent stem and stern pieces with several screws.

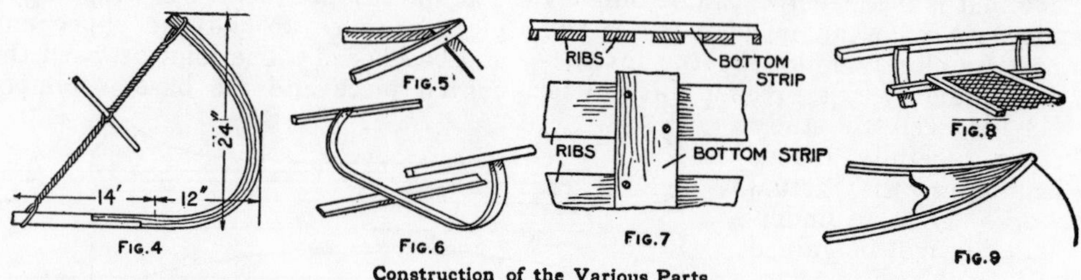

Construction of the Various Parts

Two other light strips, C and D, Fig. 2, are temporarily put in, and evenly spaced between the gunwales and the bottom board. These strips are used to give the form to the ribs, and are removed when they have served their purpose.

The ribs are now put in place. They are formed of strips of well seasoned elm or hickory, soaked in boiling water until they bend without breaking or cracking. Each rib should be 1½ in.

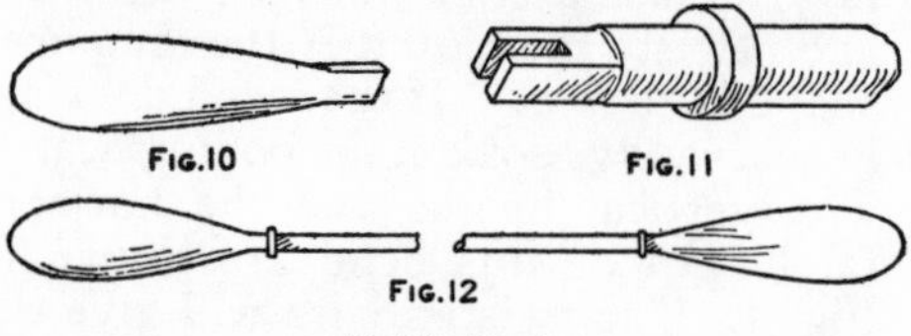

Paddle Parts

wide, ⅜ in. thick and long enough to reach the distance between the gunwales after the bend is made. The ribs are placed 1 in. apart. Begin by placing a rib in the center of the base and on the upper side. Nail it temporarily, yet securely, and then curve the ends and place them inside of the gunwales, as shown in Fig. 6. Fasten the ends of the rib to the gunwales with 1-in. galvanized brads. This method is used in placing all the ribs. When the ribs are set, remove the pieces C and D, Fig. 2, and the molds.

A strip is now put in to take the place of the base. This strip is 1¾ in. wide, ½ in. thick and long enough to reach the entire length of the bottom of the canoe. It is fastened with screws on the inside, as shown in Fig. 7, and the ends are lap-jointed to the stem and stern pieces as shown in Fig. 4. When this piece is fastened in place, the base can be removed. The seats are attached as shown in Fig. 8, and the small pieces for each end are fitted as shown in Fig. 9.

The frame of the canoe is now ready to be covered. This will require 5½ yd. of extra-heavy canvas. Turn the framework of the canoe upside down and place the canvas on it. The center of the canvas is located and tacked to the center strip of the canoe at the points where ribs are attached. Copper tacks should be used. The canvas is then tacked to the ribs, beginning at the center rib and working toward each end, carefully drawing the canvas as tightly as possible and keeping it straight. At the ends the canvas is split in the center and lapped over the bent wood. The surplus canvas is cut off. A thin coat of glue is put on, to shrink the cloth and make it waterproof.

The glue should be powdered and brought into liquid form in a double boiler. A thin coat of this is applied with a paintbrush. A small keel made of a strip of wood is placed on the bottom to protect it when making a landing on sand and stones in shallow

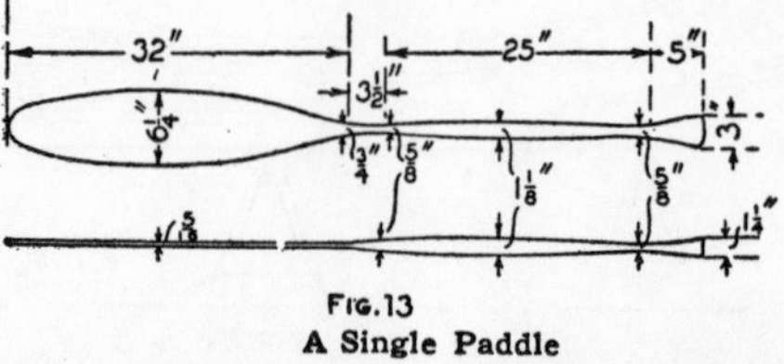

Fig.13
A Single Paddle

water. When the glue is thoroughly dry the canvas is covered with two coats of paint, made up in any color with the best lead and boiled linseed oil. The inside is coated with spar varnish to give it a wood color.

The paddles may be made up in two ways, single or double. The double paddle has a hickory pole, 7 ft. long and 2 in. in diameter, for its center part. The paddle is made as shown in Fig. 10, of ash or cypress. It is 12 in. long, and 8 in. wide at the widest part. The paddle end fits into a notch cut in the end of the pole (Fig. 11). A shield is made of a piece of tin or rubber and placed around the pole near the paddle to prevent the water from running to the center as the pole is tipped from side to side. The complete paddle is shown in Fig. 12. A single paddle is made as shown in Fig. 13. This is made of ash or any other tough wood. The dimensions given in the sketch are sufficient without a description.

Thorns Used as Needles on a Phonograph

Very sharp thorns can be used successfully as phonograph needles. These substitutes will reproduce sound very clearly and with beautiful tone. The harsh scratching of the ordinary needle is reduced to a minimum, and the thorn is not injurious to the record.

Tool Hangers

A tool rack that is serviceable for almost any kind of a tool may be made by placing rows of different-size screw eyes on a wall close to the workbench, so that files, chisels, pliers and other tools, and the handles of hammers can be slipped through the eyes.

A place for every tool saves time, and besides, when the tools are hung up separately, they are less likely to be damaged, than when kept together on the workbench.

Child's Footrest on an Ordinary Chair

Small chairs are enjoyed very much by children for the reason that they can rest their feet on the floor. In many households there are no small chairs for the youngsters, and they have to use larger ones. Two things result, the child's legs become tired from dangling unsupported or by trying to support them on the stretchers, and the finish on the chair is apt to be scratched. The device shown in the sketch forms a footrest or step that can be placed on any chair. It can be put on or taken off in a moment. Two suitable pieces of wood are nailed together at an angle and a small notch cut out, as shown, to fit the chair stretcher.

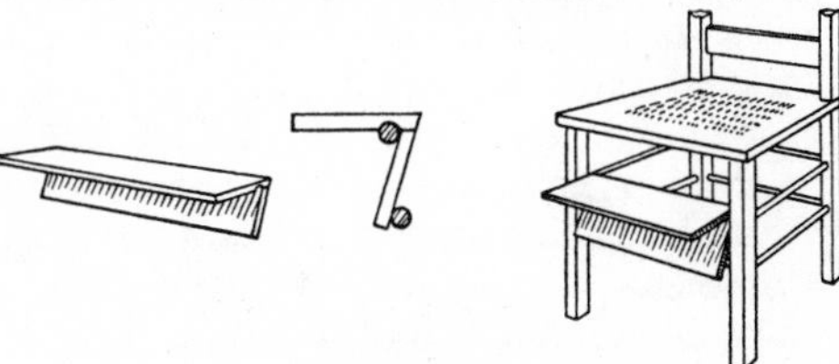

Footrest on Chair

Drying Photo Postal Cards

A novel idea for drying photo postal cards comes from a French magazine. The drying of the cards takes a long time on account of their thickness, but may be hastened by using corrugated paper for packing bottles as a drying stand. Curve the cards, printed side up, and place the ends between two corrugations at a convenient distance apart. They will thus be held firmly while the air can circulate freely all around them.

Card on Dryer

Preserving Key Forms

After losing a key or two and having some difficulty in replacing them, I used the method shown in the sketch

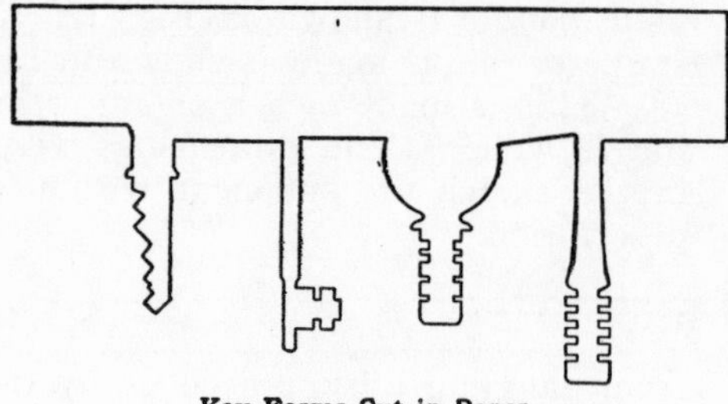

Key Forms Cut in Paper

to preserve the outlines for making new ones. All the keys I had were traced on a piece of paper and their forms cut out with a pair of shears. When a key was lost, another could thus be easily made by using the paper form as a pattern.—Contributed by Ernest Weaver, Santa Anna, Texas.

Renewing Typewriter Ribbons

Roll the ribbon on a spool and meanwhile apply a little glycerine with a fountain-pen filler. Roll up tightly and lay aside for a week or ten days. Do not apply too much glycerine as this will make the ribbon sticky—a very little, well spread, is enough. The same application will also work well on ink pads.—Contributed by Earl R. Hastings, Corinth, Vt.

Drinking Trough for Chickens

A quickly made and sanitary drinking trough for chickens is formed of a piece of ordinary two or three-ply roofing paper. The paper is laid out as shown, and the edges are cemented with asphaltum and then tacked to the side of a fence or shed.

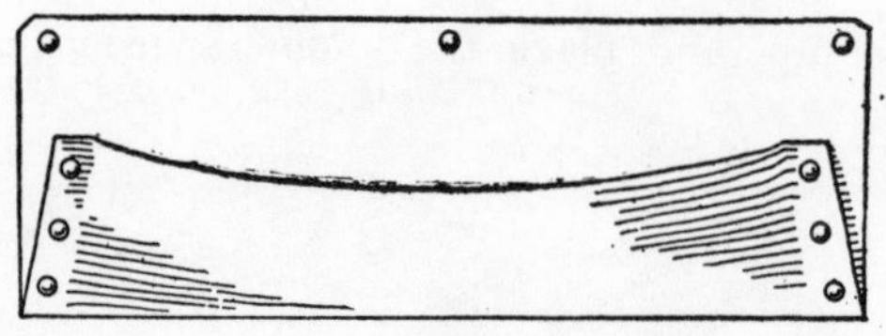

Trough of Roofing Paper

Ordinary Pen Used as a Fountain Pen

It is a very simple matter to make a good fountain pen out of an ordinary pen and holder. The device is in the form of an attachment readily connected to or removed from any ordinary pen and holder, although the chances are that when once used it will not be detached until a new pen is needed.

Take the butt end of a quill, A, from a chicken, goose or turkey feather—the latter preferred as it will hold more ink—and clean out the membrane in it thoroughly with a wire or hatpin. Then make a hole in the tapered end of the quill just large enough to pull through a piece of cotton string. Tie a knot in one end of this string, B, and pull it through the small end of the quill until the knot chokes within, then cut off the string so that only ¼ in. projects. Shave out a small stopper from a bottle cork for the large end of the quill. This completes the ink reservoir.

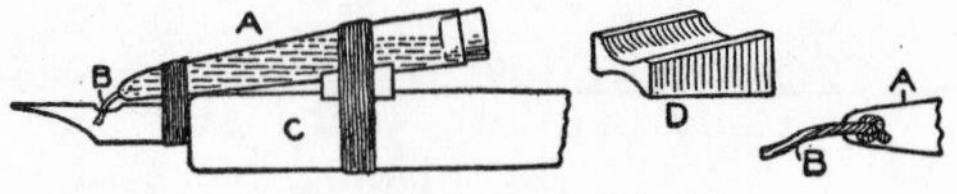

Fountain Attachment

Place the quill on top of the penholder C, so that its small end rests against the pen immediately above its eye. Pull the string through this eye. Securely bind the quill to the pen and holder with a thread, as shown, first placing under it a wedge-shaped support of cork or wood, D, hollowed on both sides to fit the curved surfaces of the quill and holder. The illustration shows the detail clearly.

To fill the reservoir place the pen upright on its point and dip a small camel's-hair brush or cloth-bound toothpick into the ink bottle and "scrape" off the ink it will hold on the inner edge of the quill. Cork tightly, and the device is ready for use. When not in use place the holder at an angle with the pen uppermost.—Contributed by Chelsea C. Fraser, Saginaw, Michigan.

How to Construct a Small Thermostat

By R. A. McCLURE

It is a well known fact, that there is a change in the dimensions of a piece of metal, due to a change in its temperature. This change in dimensions is not the same for all materials; it being much greater in some materials than in others, while in some there is practically no change.

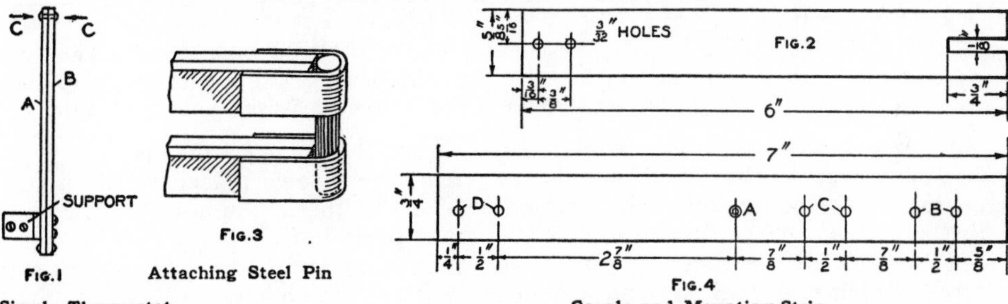

Fig. 1 Simple Thermostat

Attaching Steel Pin

Couple and Mounting Strip

If two thin, narrow strips of different metals, that contract or expand at different ratio due to a variation in temperature, be rigidly fastened together at their ends, and the combination then heated or cooled, the combined piece will have its shape changed. One of the pieces will increase in length more than the other, due to a rise in temperature, and this same piece will decrease in length more than the other when subjected to a decrease in temperature.

If one end of this combined piece be rigidly clamped to a support, as shown in Fig. 1, and the combination then have its temperature changed, the free end will move to the right or left of its original position, depending upon which of the pieces changes in length the more. If there is a rise in temperature and the right-hand piece B increases in length faster than the left-hand piece A, the free end of the combined piece will move to the left of its original position. If, on the other hand, there is a decrease in temperature, the right-hand piece will decrease in length more than the left-hand piece, and the upper or free end will move to the right of its original position.

Such a combination of two metals constitutes a simple thermostat. If the movement of the free end of the combination be made to actuate a needle moving over a properly calibrated scale, we have a simple form of thermometer. If two electrical contacts, CC, be mounted on the right and left-hand sides of the upper end of the combined piece, as shown in Fig. 1, we have a thermostat that may be used in closing an electrical circuit when the temperature of the room in which it is placed rises or falls a certain value. These contacts should be so arranged that they can be moved toward or away from the combined piece independently. By adjusting the position of these contacts, the electrical circuit will be closed when the temperature of the thermostat has reached an experimentally predetermined value.

The following description is that of a thermostat, constructed by the author of this article, which gave very satisfactory results. First obtain a piece of steel, 6 in. long, ⅝ in. wide and 2/100 in. thick, and a piece of brass, 6 in. long, ⅝ in. wide and 3/100 in. thick. Clean one side of each of these pieces and tin them well with solder. Place the two tinned surfaces just treated in contact with each other and heat them until the solder on their surfaces melts and then allow them to cool. A better way would be to clamp the two thin pieces between two heavy metal pieces, and then heat the whole to such a temperature that the solder will melt, and then allow it to cool. This last method will give more satisfactory results than would be obtained if no clamps are used, as the thin metal pieces are liable to bend out of shape when they are heated, and as a result they will not be in contact with each other over their entire surfaces. After these pieces have been soldered together forming one piece, which we shall for convenience speak of as the couple, two small holes should be drilled in one end to be used in mounting it, and a notch cut in the other end, as shown in Fig. 2.

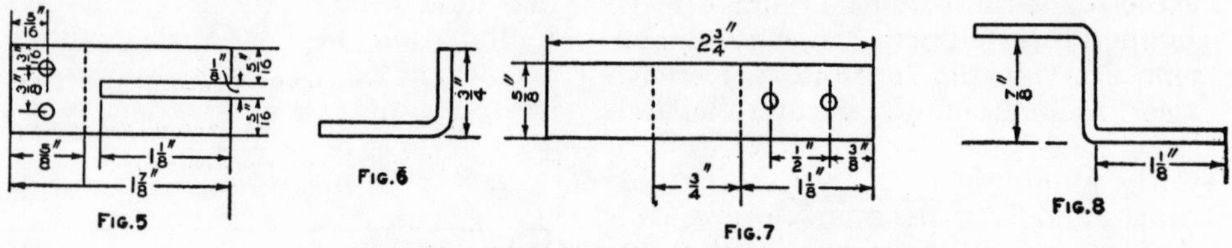

Support for Couple, and Needle-Mounting Strip

Cut from some thin sheet brass, about 2/100 in. in thickness, two pieces, ¼ in. wide and ½ in. long. Bend these pieces of brass over a piece of hatpin wire, thus forming two U-shaped pieces. Cut off a piece of the hatpin, ⅝ in. long, and fasten it across the notched end of the couple by means of the U-shaped piece of brass, which should be soldered in place as shown in Fig. 3. All superfluous solder should then be cleaned from the couple and the steel pin. Now bend the couple so as to form a perfect half circle, the brass being on the inside.

The base upon which this couple is to be mounted should be made as follows: Obtain a piece of brass, 7 in. long, ¾ in. wide, and ⅛ in. thick. In this piece drill holes, as indicated in Fig. 4, except A, which will be drilled later. Tap the holes B, C and D for ⅛-in. machine screws.

Cut from some ⅛-in. sheet brass a piece, 1⅞ in. long and ¾ in. wide, to be used as a support for the couple. In one end of this piece drill two small holes, as indicated in Fig. 5, and tap them for $\frac{3}{16}$-in. machine screws. In the opposite end cut a slot, whose dimensions correspond to those given in Fig. 5. Now bend the piece, at the dotted line in Fig. 5, into the form shown in Fig. 6, making sure that the dimension given is correct. This piece can now be mounted upon the piece shown in Fig. 4, by means of two brass machine screws placed in the holes B. The slot in the support for the couple will permit its being moved along the mounting strip, the purpose of which will be shown later.

Next cut another piece of ⅛-in. brass, 2¾ in. long and ⅝ in. wide. In this piece drill two ⅛-in. holes, as indicated in Fig. 7, and then bend it at the dotted lines into the form shown in Fig. 8. Mount this strip upon the main mounting strip by means of two brass machine screws placed in the holes C, so that the upper part is over the center-punch mark for the hole A in the main mounting strip.

You are now ready to drill the hole A, which should be done as follows: Remove the piece you last mounted and then clamp the main mounting strip in the drill press so that the center-punch mark for the hole A is directly under the point of the drill. Then remount the piece you just removed, without disturbing the piece you clamped in the drill press, and drill a small hole through both pieces. This hole should be about 3/64 in. in diameter. After this small hole has been drilled through both pieces, a countersink should be placed in the drill chuck and the hole in the upper piece countersunk to a depth equal to half the thickness of the metal in which it is drilled. Unclamp the pieces from the drill press, turn them over, and countersink the small hole in what was originally the lower piece. The object of countersinking these holes is to reduce the bearing surface of a small shaft that is to be supported in the holes and must be as free from friction as possible.

We may now construct the needle, or moving portion of the thermostat, which should be done as follows: The shaft that is to carry the moving system must be made from a piece of steel rod, about $\frac{3}{32}$ in. in diameter. Its dimensions should correspond to those given in Fig. 9. Considerable care should be used in turning this shaft down, to make sure that it fits perfectly in the small holes in the supporting pieces. The shaft should turn freely, but it must not be loose in the holes, nor should it have but a very small end play.

Cut from some 1/32-in. sheet brass a piece whose dimensions correspond to those given in Fig. 10. Drill a ⅛-in. hole, A, in this piece, and cut a slot, B, from one side of the piece into this hole, and a second slot, C, along the center of the piece as indicated in the figure. Considerable care should be exercized in cutting the slot C, so that its breadth is exactly equal to the diameter of the piece of steel wire fastened on the end of the couple. Also make sure to get the sides of this slot perfectly smooth. Cut from some ⅛-in. brass a disk having a diameter of ½ in., and solder it to the end of the needle. The dotted line in Fig. 10 indicates the proper position of the disk. Now drill a hole, D, through the disk and needle, of such a diameter that considerable force must be applied to the steel shaft you have already made, in order to force it through the hole. Force the shaft

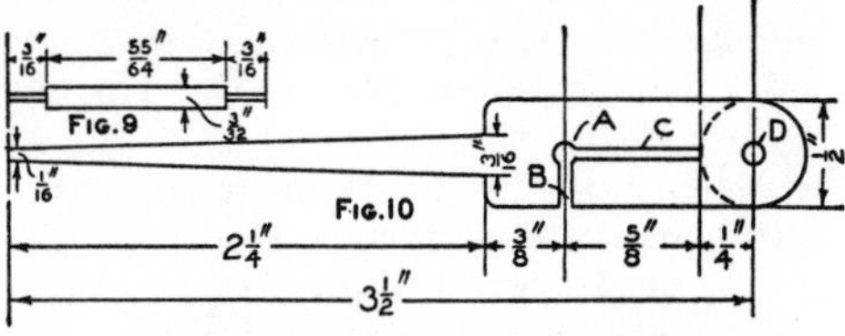

Shaft for Needle and Needle

through this hole until the needle is exactly in the center of the shaft.

The parts of the thermostat thus far made can now be assembled. Place the steel shaft in its bearings and see that it turns perfectly free. Then place the steel pin, on the end of the couple, in the slot C, and fasten the

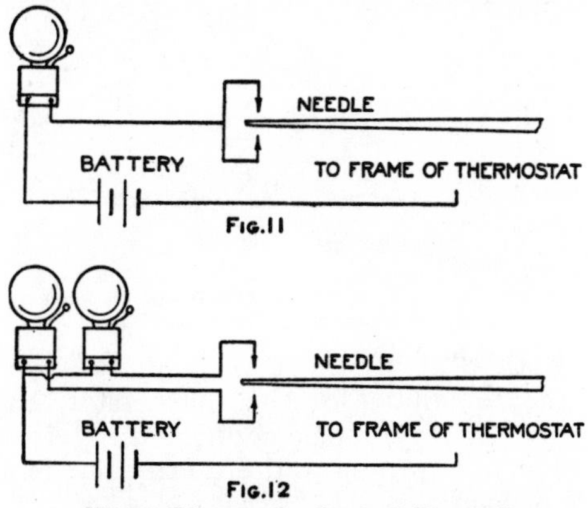

Wiring Diagram for One and Two Bells

other end of the couple, by means of two machine screws, to the support made for the couple. Increase or decrease the temperature of the thermostat and note the results. If everything is working all right, the end of the needle should move when the temperature of the thermostat is changed. The amount the end of the needle moves can be easily changed by moving the support or the couple toward or away from the shaft supporting the needle, which changes the position of the steel pin in the slot C. The nearer the steel pin is to the shaft supporting the needle, the greater the movement of the end of the needle due to a given change in temperature.

A small piece of white cardboard can be mounted directly under the end of the needle by means of small brass strips, that in turn can be attached to the lower ends of the main mounting holes D, Fig. 4. A scale can be marked on this piece of cardboard by noting the position of the needle corresponding to different temperatures as determined by a thermometer. When this scale has been completed, you can use the thermostat as a thermometer.

Two contacts may be mounted, one on each side of the needle, in a manner similar to the method suggested for mounting the cardboard. These contacts should be so constructed that the end of the needle will slide over them with little friction, and so that their position with respect to the end of the needle may be easily changed.

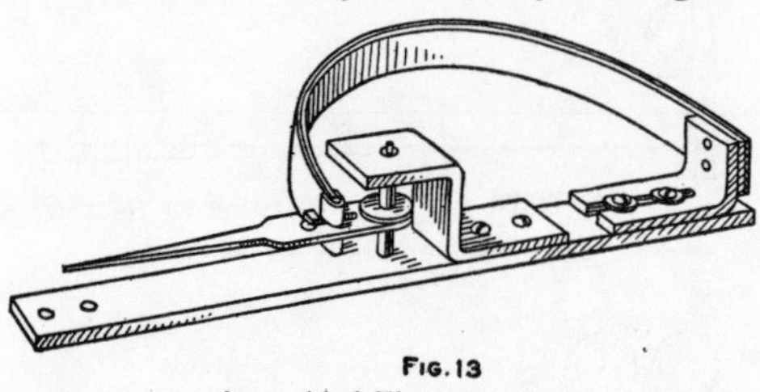
Fig. 13
Assembled Thermostat

Both contacts must be insulated from the remainder of the thermostat, and may or may not be connected together, depending on how the thermostat is to be used.

It would be advisable, if possible, to have the part of the needle that touches the contact points, as well as these points, of platinum, as the arc that is likely to be formed will not destroy the platinum as easily as it will the brass. A small wooden containing case can now be made and the thermostat is complete. There should be a large number of holes drilled in the sides, ends and back of the case so that the air inside may be always of the same temperature as the outside air.

In adjusting, testing, or calibrating your thermostat, make sure that it is in the same position that it will be in when in use.

The connections of the thermostat for ringing one bell when the temperature rises or falls to a certain value, are shown in Fig. 11. The connections of the thermostat for ringing one bell when the temperature rises to a certain value and another bell when the temperature falls to a certain value, are shown in Fig. 12. The complete thermostat is shown in Fig. 13.

A Tailless Kite

The frame of a 3-ft. kite is made of two sticks, each 3 ft. long. These are tied together so that the cross stick will be at a distance of 15 per cent of the full length of the upright stick, from its end, or in this case 5.4 in. The sticks may be made of straight-grained pine, 3/8 in. square, for small kites, and larger hardwood sticks, for larger kites.

The cross stick is bent into a bow

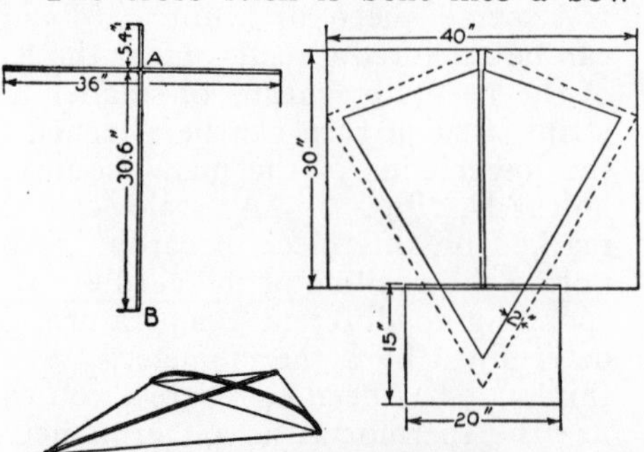

Plan and Dimensions for Kite

by tying a strong cord across from end to end. The center of the bend should be 4½ in. above the ends. The bend is shown in the sketch. Connect all four ends or points with a cord, being careful not to pull the bend of the cross stick down, but seeing that it remains straight across the kite. When this is done the frame is ready for the cover.

The cover will require 2½ sheets of tissue paper, 20 by 30 in., which should be pasted together as the sketch indicates. Cut out the paper, allowing 2 in. margin for lapping over the cord on the frame. Place the frame on the cover with the convex side toward the paper and paste the margin over the cord, allowing the paper to bag a little to form pockets for the air to lift the kite. The corners should be reinforced with circular pieces of paper pasted over the ends of the sticks.

The flying cord is attached to the points A and B of the frame. There is no cross cord. The kite will fly at right angles to the flying cord. It is easily started flying from the ground by laying it with the head toward the operator and pulling it up into the wind.—Contributed by Chas. B. Damik, Cooperstown, N. Y.

The Levitation—A Modern Stage Trick

This illusion has mystified thousands of the theater-going public, in fact, it has been the "piece de resistance" of many illusion acts. The ordinary method of procedure is as follows: The person who is to be suspended in the air, apparently with no support—usually a lady—is first put in a hypnotic (?) sleep. She is placed on a couch in the middle of the stage, and in most cases the spot light is brought into play. The performer then takes a position close to the couch and with dramatic effect makes a few hypnotic passes over the subject. She then slowly rises from the couch until she has attained a height varying from 4 to 5 ft. above the stage, as shown in Fig. 1. The couch is then taken away and a hoop is passed over the floating lady. The performer now causes the lady to float back to the couch or board that she may have been resting on, after which the so-called hypnotic spell is withdrawn.

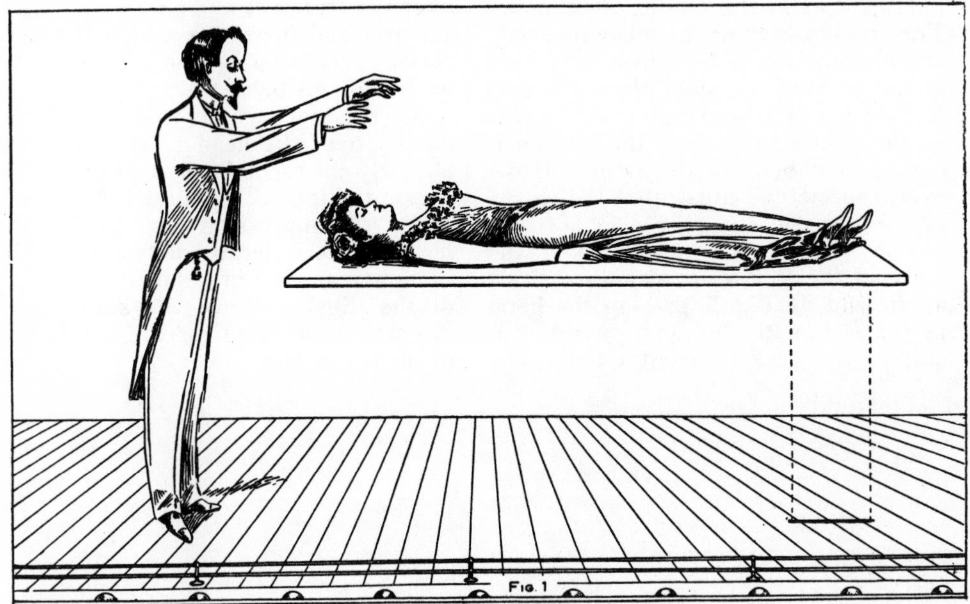

Raising the Subject in Midair

In spite of the claims that the illusion owes its origin to Hindoo magic, it is nothing more nor less than a clever mechanical contrivance, the construction of which will be readily understood by a glance at the accompanying illustrations.

The bottom of the couch, if one is used, contains a cradle-like arrangement which fits the recumbent form of the lady and is connected to a heavy sheet of plate glass by means of a rod, D, Fig. 2, attached to one end, and running parallel to the side of the cradle. When the glass is lifted, the body of the subject is also raised, seemingly at the will of the performer. This is accomplished by the aid of an assistant beneath the stage floor. The plate of glass, E, Fig. 3, passes perpendicularly through the stage down to a double block and tackle. The end of the cable is attached to a drum or windlass and the plate glass held steady with guides at the sides of the slot in the stage floor, through which it passes. The winding up of the cable naturally forces the plate glass and cradle up, causing the lady to rise.

Some illusionists place the lady on a board on two ordinary trestles and cause the board to rise with the lady

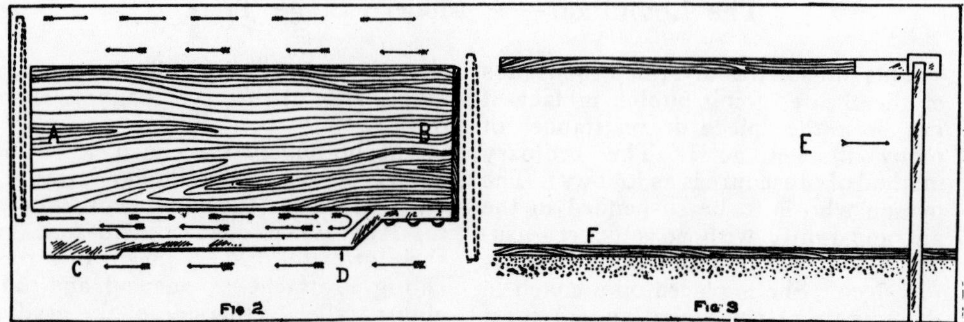

Direction the Hoop Takes in Passing over the Board

on it, as shown in the illustration, thus obviating the use of heavy paraphernalia as in the cradle attachment. The cradle attachment is also generally accompanied by a 2-in. iron bar, used in the place of the plate glass, the performer or operator standing at the rear of the couch to conceal the bar as it comes from beneath the stage. However, the method illustrated is the one generally used.

The solid hoop is passed over the body in the following manner: Start at the end, B, Fig. 2, passing the hoop as far as C with the hoop on the outside of the back horizontal rod. The side of the hoop toward the audience is then turned and swung clear around over the feet at A and entered between the rod and board on which the lady rests. The hoop is then carried as far as it will go back toward the end B. Then the side nearest the operator is passed over the head of the body apparently the second time and passed off free at the feet. Thus to the closest observer the impression is given that the hoop has encircled the lady twice. The illustrations give in detail the working of the illusion above the stage floor. No set rule is used for the tackle and drum below the floor.

INDEX